Lecture Notes in Computer Science   10897

Commenced Publication in 1973
Founding and Former Series Editors:
Gerhard Goos, Juris Hartmanis, and Jan van Leeuwen

T0171906

More information about this series at http://www.springer.com/series/7409

Klaus Miesenberger
Georgios Kouroupetroglou (Eds.)

Computers Helping
People with Special Needs

16th International Conference, ICCHP 2018
Linz, Austria, July 11–13, 2018
Proceedings, Part II

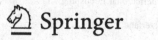 Springer

Editors
Klaus Miesenberger
Johannes Kepler University Linz
Linz
Austria

Georgios Kouroupetroglou
National and Kapodistrian University
   of Athens
Athens
Greece

ISSN 0302-9743   ISSN 1611-3349   (electronic)
Lecture Notes in Computer Science
ISBN 978-3-319-94273-5   ISBN 978-3-319-94274-2   (eBook)
https://doi.org/10.1007/978-3-319-94274-2

Library of Congress Control Number: 2018947426

LNCS Sublibrary: SL3 – Information Systems and Applications, incl. Internet/Web, and HCI

Printed on acid-free paper

This Springer imprint is published by the registered company Springer International Publishing AG
part of Springer Nature
The registered company address is: Gewerbestrasse 11, 6330 Cham, Switzerland

Preface

Welcome to the ICCHP 2018 Proceedings!

ICCHP's mission for inclusion and participation in the information society strives for better Assistive Technology (AT) and
eAccessibility for support, enhancement and restoration of
resources for people with disabilities and compensating limita-
tions of standardized Human–Computer Interaction (HCI). This mission continues to
gain even more importance owing to the ongoing ICT revolution (Internet/Web of
Things/Ubiquitous computing/Cloud-based services).

ICCHP had the honor to accompany and support the revolutionary developments of
AT and eAccessibility over the past three decades. With its roots going back almost 30
years, it provides an outstanding and most comprehensive overview of these revolutionary developments supporting the full inclusion and participation of people with
disabilities in all domains of society. The ICT revolution brings along an increased
potential for inclusion and participation, but also risks for exclusion and thus the
responsibility for implementing eAccessibility.

This provokes a growing number of challenging research questions. Old boundaries
of concepts dissolve, new approaches and fresh thinking are needed: not only in
technical terms, but also in legal, social, economic, pedagogic, and other terms.
The UN Convention on the Rights of People with Disabilities (UNCRPD) is the
globally accepted reference and expression of the societal transformation toward
effective inclusion and participation of all people with disabilities in society.
The UNCRPD refers to AT, eAccessibility, eInclusion, and Design for All as pre-
conditions and means of support.

These are exactly the core topics of ICCHP. Since the first conference in Vienna
(Austria) back in 1989, ICCHP has evolved as a unique and one of the few long-term
references of R&D with evidence on how Information and Communication Technologies (ICT), AT, and eAccessibility have been implemented and have significantly
contributed to the improvement of the life of people with disabilities. By addressing all
these aspects, ICCHP invites and provides a platform for a holistic discussion on
improving the lives of people with disabilities in every corner of our world.

ICCHP is proud to contribute with its scientific excellence to these outstanding
social developments. All 21 volumes of past proceedings, covering more than 2,400
reviewed articles,[1] are a unique source for learning and understanding the theoretical,
methodological, and pragmatic specializations of our field and for reflecting on the
inclusion movement. This collection of work, with its unique user focus, offers a

---

[1] Owing to the increasing interest in ICCHP, the last two conferences published their proceedings in
two volumes.

significant body of evidence for the enormous but often neglected impact on usability for all users regardless of their abilities.

In 2018, the proceedings of the 16th conference are delivered to you as a compendium of the new and exciting scholarly and practical work going on in our field. Again, in a highly competitive process, 136 experts formed the scientific committee compiling at least three reviews for each of the 356 submitted contributions. A panel of 12 conference chairs selected and accepted 101 submissions as full papers and 78 as short papers based on the expert reviews, which you find now in the two volumes of the proceedings. This two-phase selection procedure guarantees the high scientific quality making ICCHP unique in our field. The concept of organizing "Special Thematic Sessions" again helped to structure the proceedings and the program in order to support a deep focus on highly desirable selected topics in the field as well as to bring new and interesting topics to the attention of the research community.

ICCHP hosts a high-quality and fully accessible meeting for scientists, users, practitioners, educators, and policy makers. In addition to the traditional paper sessions, the forum also includes industry representatives showing their new products and looking for new ideas. In particular, ICCHP welcomes young researchers, the next generation of experts in our field, and encourages them to contribute to the Young Researchers Consortium as well as to the Coding for a Cause competition. Additionally, the conference affords spaces and times for less formal discussions – an important factor supporting the transfer of knowledge so needed in our endeavors.

We welcomed the attendees' valuable contribution to ICCHP 2018 and encourage them and their colleagues to become regular participants in its most important mission, which is also recognized through patronage of the United Nations Educational, Scientific and Cultural Organization (UNESCO). It is here that research, innovation, and practical endeavors in important topics of AT and eAccesibility can come together to be shared, explored, and discussed.

July 2018   Klaus Miesenberger
                                              Georgios Kouroupetroglou

Organization

ICCHP Committees

General Chair

Kouroupetroglou, G.   University of Athens, Greece

Steering Board

Bühler, C.   TU Dortmund University, FTB, Germany
Burger, D.   INSERM, France
Murphy, H. J.   California State University Northridge, USA
Suzuki, M.   Kyushu University, Japan
Tjoa, A. M.   Technical University of Vienna, Austria
Wagner, R.   University of Linz, Austria

Publishing Chair

Miesenberger, K.   University of Linz, Austria

Program Chairs

Archambault, D.   Université Paris 8, France
Debevc, M.   University of Maribor, Slovenia
Fels, D   Ryerson University, Canada
Kobayashi, M.   Tsukuba University of Technology, Japan
Manduchi, R.   University of California at Santa Cruz, USA
Penaz, P.   University of Brno, Czech Republic
Weber, G.   Technische Universität Dresden, Germany
Zagler, W.   Vienna University of Technology, Austria

Young Researcher Consortium Chairs

Archambault, D.   Université Paris 8, France
Chen, W.   •   Oslo and Akershus University College of Applied
                            Sciences, Norway
Fels, D.   Ryerson University, Canada
Fitzpatrick, D.   Dublin City University, Ireland
Kobayashi, M.   Tsukuba University of Technology, Japan
Morandell, M.   University of Linz, Austria
Pontelli, E.   New Mexico State University, USA
Prazak-Aram, B.   AIT Austrian Institute of Technology GmbH, Austria
Weber, G.   Technische Universität Dresden, Germany

Workshop Chairs

Petz, A.   University of Linz, Austria
Pühretmair, F.   KI-I, Austria

International Program Committee

Abascal, J   Euskal Herriko Unibertsitatea, Spain
Abbott, C.   King's College London, UK
Abou-Zahra, S.   W3C Web Accessibility Initiative (WAI), Austria
Abu Doush, I.   American university of Kuwait, Kuwait
Andrich, R.   Polo Tecnologico Fondazione Don Carlo Gnocchi
                                    Onlus, Italy
Augstein, M.   University of Applied Sciences Upper Austria, Austria
Azevedo, L.   Instituto Superior Tecnico, Portugal
Batusic, M.   Fabasoft, Austria
Bernareggi, C.   Università degli Studi di Milano, Italy
Bernier, A.   BrailleNet, France
Bosse, I.   Technische Universität Dortmund, Germany
Bu, J.   Zhejiang University, China
Christensen, L. B.   Sensus, Denmark
Chutimaskul, W.   King Mongkut's University of Technology Thonburi,
                                    Thailand
Conway, V.   WebKeyIT, Australia
Coughlan. J.   Smith-Kettlewell Eye Research Institute, USA
Craddock, G.   Centre for Excellence in Universal Design, Ireland
Crombie, D.   Utrecht School of the Arts, The Netherlands
Cudd, P.   University of Sheffield, UK
Darvishy, A.   ZHAW, Switzerland
Darzentas, J.   University of Aegean, Greece
Debeljak, M.   University of Ljubljana, Slovenia
DeRuyter, F.   Duke University Medical Centre, USA
Diaz del Campo, R.   Antarq Tecnosoluciones, Mexico
Draffan, E. A.   University of Southampton, UK
Dupire, J.   CNAM, France
Emiliani, P. L.   Institute of Applied Physics "Nello Carrara", Italy
Engelen, J.   Katholieke Universiteit Leuven, Belgium
Galinski, Ch.   InfoTerm, Austria
Gardner, J.   Oregon State University, USA
Hakkinen, M. T.   Educational Testing Service (ETS), USA
Hanson, V.   University of Dundee, UK
Harper, S.   University of Manchester, UK
Heimgärtner, R.   Intercultural User Interface Consulting (IUIC),
                                    Germany
Höckner, K.   Hilfgemeinschaft der Blinden und Sehschwachen,
                                    Austria

Hoogerwerf, E.-J.	AIAS Bologna, Italy
Huenerfauth, M.	Rochester Institute of Technology, USA
Inoue, T.	National Rehabilitation Center for Persons with Disabilities, Japan
Iversen, C. M.	U.S. Department of State (retired), USA
Kalinnikova, L.	University of Gävle, Sweden
Koumpis, A.	University of Passau, Germany
Kouropetroglou, Ch.	ALTEC, Greece
Kozuh, I.	University of Maribor, Slovenia
Kremser, W.	OCG, HSM, Austria
Küng, J.	Johannes Kepler University Linz, Austria
Lewis, C.	University of Colorado at Boulder, USA
Lhotska, L.	Czech Technical University in Prague, Czech Republic
Magnusson, M.	Moscow State University, Russia
Matausch, K.	KI-I, Austria
Mavrou, K.	European University Cyprus, Cyprus
Mayer, Ch.	AIT Austrian Institute of Technology GmbH, Austria
McSorley, J.	Pearson, USA
Mihailidis, A.	University of Toronto, Canada
Mohamad, Y.	Fraunhofer Institute for Applied Information Technology, Germany
Mrochen, I.	University of Silesia in Katowice, Poland
Müller-Putz, G.	TU Graz, Austria
Muratet, M.	INS HEA, France
Normie, L.	GeronTech-Israeli Center for Assistive Technology and Aging, Israel
Nussbaum, G.	KI-I, Austria
Ono, T.	Tsukuba University of Technology, Japan
Panek, P.	Vienna University of Technology, Austria
Paredes, H.	University of Trás-os-Montes e Alto Douro, Portugal
Parson, S.	University of Southampton, UK
Petrie, H.	University of York, UK
Pissaloux, E.	Université Rouen, France
Pontelli, E.	New Mexico State University, USA
Rassmus-Groehn, K.	Lund University, Sweden
Raynal, M	University of Toulouse, France
Rice, D.	National Disability Authority, Ireland
Seeman, L.	Athena ICT, Israel
Sik Lányi, C.	University of Pannonia, Hungary
Simsik, D.	University of Kosice, Slovakia
Slavik, P.	Czech Technical University in Prague, Czech Republic
Sloan, D.	The Paciello Group, UK
Snaprud, M.	University of Agder, Norway
Sporka, A.	Czech Technical University in Prague, Czech Republic
Stepankova, O.	Czech Technical University in Prague, Czech Republic
Stephanidis, C.	University of Crete, FORTH-ICS, Greece

ICCHP Roland Wagner Award Winners

Award 8, ICCHP 2016 in Linz, Austria

Dominique Burger, BrailleNet, France

Award 7, ICCHP 2014 in Paris, France

- Art Karshmer (✞ 2015), University of San Francisco, USA and
- Masakazu Suzuki, Kyushu University, Japan

Award 6, ICCHP 2012 in Linz, Austria

TRACE Centre of University Wisconsin-Madison, USA

Award 5, ICCHP 2010 in Vienna, Austria

- Harry Murphy, Founder of CSUN's Center on Disabilities, USA and
- Joachim Klaus, Founder of the SZS at KIT, Germany

Award 4, ICCHP 2008 in Linz, Austria

George Kersher and the Daisy Consortium

Award 3, ICCHP 2006 in Linz, Austria

Larry Scadden, National Science Foundation

Award 2, ICCHP 2004 in Paris, France

Paul Blenkhorn, University of Manchester

Award 1, ICCHP 2002 in Linz, Austria

WAI-W3C

Once again we thank all those helping in putting ICCHP 2018 together and thereby supporting the AT field and a better quality of life for people with disabilities. Special thanks go to all our supporter and sponsors, displayed at http://www.icchp.org/sponsors-18.

Contents – Part II

Environmental Sensing Technologies for Visual Impairment

**3D Printing in the Domain of Assistive Technologies (AT)
and Do It Yourselves (DIY) AT**

**Tactile Graphics and Models for Blind People and Recognition
of Shapes by Touch**

Access to Artworks and Its Mediation by and for Visually Impaired People

Digital Navigation for People with Visual Impairments

Low Vision and Blindness: Human Computer Interaction

Future Perspectives for Aging Well: AAL Tools, Products, Services

Mobile Healthcare and mHealth Apps for People with Disabilities

Service and Information Provision

Contents – Part I

Web Accessibility in the Connected World

Accessibility and Usability of Mobile Platforms for People with Disabilities and Elderly Persons: Design, Development and Engineering

Accessible System/Information/Document Design

Accessible eLearning - eLearning for Accessibility/AT

Personalized Access to TV, Film, Theatre, and Music

Accessibility and Usability of Self-Service Terminals, Technologies and Systems

Universal Learning Design

Motor and Mobility Disabilities: AT, HCI, Care

Empowerment of People with Cognitive Disabilities Using Digital Technologies

Augmented and Alternative Communication (AAC), Supported Speech

Environmental Sensing Technologies for Visual Impairment

AcouSTTic: A Training Application of Acoustic Sense on Sound Table Tennis (STT)

Takahiro Miura[1,2](✉), Masaya Fujito[3], Masaki Matsuo[3], Masatsugu Sakajiri[3], Junji Onishi[3], and Tsukasa Ono[3]

[1] Institute of Gerontology (IOG), The University of Tokyo,
7-3-1 Hongo, Bunkyo-ku, Tokyo 113-8656, Japan
miu@iog.u-tokyo.ac.jp
[2] National Institute of Advanced Industrial Science and Technology (AIST),
1-1-1 Umezono, Tsukuba, Ibaraki 305-8560, Japan
[3] Tsukuba University of Technology,
4-12-7 Kasuga, Tsukuba, Ibaraki 305-8521, Japan
fm142309@cc.k.tsukuba-tech.ac.jp, mm163204@g.tsukuba-tech.ac.jp,
{sakajiri,ohnishi,ono}@cs.k.tsukuba-tech.ac.jp

Abstract. Sound table tennis (also known as vision impaired table tennis, and abbreviated as STT) is one of the most internationally popular sports for visually impaired people. Since the players of STT cannot rely on visual information, they must grasp the game situation using their auditory sense. However, it is difficult, especially for STT beginners, to perceive the state of the game, including the positions of the opponents, and the direction and distance of the ball. Therefore, in this paper, we aim to develop an application that enables STT players, especially beginners, to train their acoustic sense to instantaneously recognize the direction and distance of the ball at the service phase hit by opponents without going to the gym. We implemented the application named AcouSTTic (Acoustic + STT), and then evaluated its training effectiveness.

Keywords: Sound table tennis (STT) · Visually impaired people
Acoustical virtual reality

1 Introduction

Sound table tennis (also known as vision impaired table tennis, and abbreviated as STT) is one of the most internationally popular sports for visually impaired people. This sport is similar to table tennis for the sighted, but the players should hit and roll a ball under a net, instead of hitting a ball over a net [1]. They auditorily localize to the direction and distance of a sounding ball with a

---

T. Miura and M. Fujito—Both authors contributed equally to this manuscript.

© Springer International Publishing AG, part of Springer Nature 2018
K. Miesenberger and G. Kouroupetroglou (Eds.): ICCHP 2018, LNCS 10897, pp. 3–11, 2018.
https://doi.org/10.1007/978-3-319-94274-2_1

bell in whose size is the same as a pingpong's ball, and then hit the ball toward the opponent by a special racket.

Since the players of STT cannot rely on visual information, they must grasp the game situation using their auditory sense. However, it is difficult, especially for STT beginners, to perceive the state of the game, including the positions of the opponents, and the direction and distance of the ball. Also, the place to practice is basically limited because the table of STT is specially designed: the table has the net whose lower part is vacant and the low walls along with the table bounds. Moreover, when the players with visual impairments want to play STT, they should set aside the place for STT that is silent enough for them to hear the sound of the ball.

On the other hand, auditory training for visually impaired people have increased and improved. Seki et al. and Wersenyi proposed a training system of orientation and mobility for the blind [5,6,8]. Since their systems employ the technology of acoustic virtual reality (VR), visually impaired trainees can enhance their localization ability without going outside. Also, Hodges et al. reported the effective treatment of virtual environments on the fear of heights [2]. Our group also proposed the GoalBaural enabling goalball players to train their auditory sense to instantaneously recognize the direction and distance of a thrown ball by opponents without going the court and playing [4]. By using these VR techniques and our previous scheme, it can be possible to implement an application to help STT players to enhance their direction and distance localization ability. Watanabe et al. developed a virtual-sound table-tennis system using a 3D-immersive auditory display named the 'Sound Cask' based on the boundary-surface control (BoSC) principle and a depth camera [7]. They reported that sighted participants improved their sound localization ability of direction after playing virtual STT in the sound cask environment. However, though their system can produce 3D-immersive sound with high fidelity and allow a player to move freely, it is difficult to bring their system easily because of the size of the sound cask. In order to have visually impaired STT players train sound localization of the STT easily, it is necessary to develop an accessible training application that people with visual impairments can launch and play with consumer electronics such as personal computers and headphones.

Therefore, in this paper, we aim to develop an application that enables STT players, especially beginners, to train their auditory sense to instantaneously recognize the direction and distance of the ball at the service phase hit by opponents without going to the gym. First, we implemented the training application named *AcouSTTic* (Acoustic + STT), and then evaluated its training effectiveness.

2   Overview of Our Training System

Our application named *AcouSTTic* (Acoustic + STT) enables a user to train the sense of moving sound localization such as the ball hit to various directions. This application firstly presents the binaural sound of a service and, then, asks the user to answer the right direction of the ball to come and then whether they

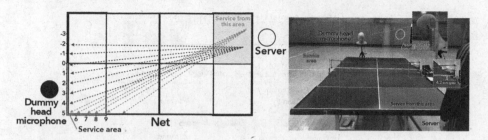

Fig. 1. Recording setup of sound of the serve ball of STT. (Left) This is a schematic bird's-eye view of the recording setup. Dash lines represent the trajectory of the player's service ball. (Right) Photograph of the recording setup. (Color figure online)

should return a ball or not. We developed this application by recording the sound of services binaurally, using a dummy head microphone and, then, implemented the interface to present the sound randomly and to receive a user's reaction. This procedure of the application development was adopted by our previous study [4].

2.1 Binaural Recording of the Services

The schematic setup of the sound recording is shown in the left part of Fig. 1. We used the dummy head to record the moving sounds. The dummy head microphone (Southern Acoustics, SAMREC Type 2500s conforming to the standards IEC 60959 and IEC 60268-7) was set at the right side of the table, with the height of its external ear canals at 52 cm from the surface of the table, in a university gym (background noise level (LAeq): 45.6 dBA, reverberation time: 1.8 s). The 52 cm height simulates the height of a player's head in the actual game.

We used this dummy head for recording the sound of a moving ball that had a bell in it hit by one blind player (early 20s) who experienced in the STT for over three years and regularly play the game. We asked the participant to serve a ball at the diagonal position against the dummy head. At that time, the participant serve the ball to the central and right directions of the service area 30 times each condition (corresponding to blue and green lines in the left part of Fig. 1). Sixty-times services included 48 times of in and 12 times of out.

The recording computer and application were Macbook Pro and Audacity, respectively. The measured sound of the dummy head microphone was captured by them via the audio interface (Roland Edirol UA-4FX) with 44.1 kHz in sampling frequency and 16 bit in quantization bit rate. After the recording, we extracted that the time interval started from participant's hit to the timing just after the ball hitting the bounds of the table from the recorded sounds.

2.2 Application Implementation

We designed the *AcouSTTic* so that individuals with visual impairment can listen to randomized services and learn to judge the ball's direction and whether

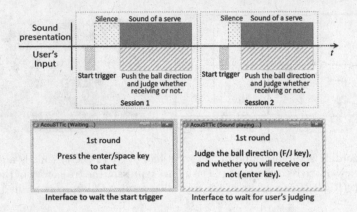

Fig. 2. (Upper) User experience procedure and (lower) Interface of the AcouSTTic.

they should return under training conditions. Similar to our previous application *GoalBaural* [4], the *AcouSTTic* was developed using the HSP (Hot Soup Processor) on Windows 10 and can run on Windows environments with or without screen readers including NVDA, Jaws, and PC Talker. The user should wear headphones to listen to the binaural sound. The inputs of users can also be recorded by the system to enable analysis of whether the player judge the direction and whether they should return correctly or incorrectly.

The upper and lower views of Fig. 2 depict the procedure of the GoalBaural user experience and show its interfaces for the corresponding states. When the user presses the enter or space key, the recorded binaural sound will be emitted via the headphones after a brief silence lasting 1–2 s. This silent time simulates the experience of receivers in the actual game because receivers must wait for sudden serves. Then, the user should judge on which side the virtual ball would come in their first-person view and successively press the F or J key, corresponding to the left or right side, respectively, as soon as possible. Also, soon after the direction judgement, they should decide whether they should press the enter key or not, corresponding to whether they return or not, respectively. If the user does not press a key at the end of the sound at all, the next session will start after a short rest period (of 0.5 times the duration of the presented sound). After the series of the judgement, the application presents an auditory feedback whether the user was correct or not.

3   Evaluation

We carried out an evaluation of the training effects and related effects on STT players and beginners.

3.1   Participants

There were eight individuals in their early 20s (range: 20–22, mean: 21.3, SD: 0.83) with total or partial visual impairments in this experiment. Seven of them were male, and the other was female. Five of them were totally blind, and the others had low vision. Three of the totally blind had experience with STT for over three years, while the others had played for less than a year. All of the participants with visual impairments had been able to manipulate a personal computer with screen reader functions for over a year. All of the participants had hearing within normal limits (20 dB HL) as defined by pure-tone audiometry. The experimenter explained the evaluation procedure to the participants, and all of them agreed to participate.

3.2   Procedure

The experiment was conducted in a silent room at a university. Before the evaluation started, we asked the participants to put on headphones (Logicool, G430) and adjust the sound to a comfortable level. Then, the participants were to press the trigger button, listen to the sound presented binaurally, and decide from which direction a virtual ball would come and, successively, press whether it returned. The order of sound presentations was randomized. The participants did this task 100 times, under 20 sound conditions × 5 repeats, and then answered the semi-structured interviews. The sound conditions included 10 center and 10 right directions corresponding to the blue and green lines towards the service area shown in Fig. 1 that each contained 5 times in and 5 times out status.

The results of reaction time [s], correct responses [%], and other performances in judgement of direction and whether the participant should return were summarized by aggregating participant responses. In the following, we will compare the reaction times, correct rates, and game scores of multiple groups based on the significant differences derived from the four-way repeated measures analysis of variance (ANOVA), Tukey-Kramer test, and Dunnett's test. The factors of four-way ANOVA were participants' visual conditions (total or partial visual impairments), their experience of STT (expert or beginner), repeat counts (1–5), and sound conditions (20 types). However, we mainly focused on participants' visual conditions, their experience, and repeat counts.

Also in this evaluation, because the correct response in a task included two judgements, we decided to rate the points as follows:

- 1.0 point: Correct judgement of both approaching direction and whether they should receive or not.
- 0.5 point: Correct judgement of approaching direction and incorrect decision regarding whether they should receive or not.
- 0 point: Other judgements.

In the section on results and discussion, we used two-point summations employing (i) 1.0 and 0 pts (actual scoring), and (ii) 1.0, 0.5, and 0 pts (our abbreviated scoring). The aggregated scores were tested using Dunnett's test.

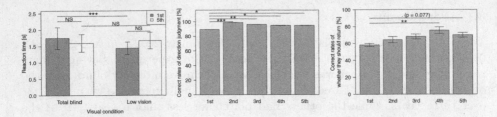

Fig. 3. (Left) Reaction time of participants with total blindness and low vision. (Center/Right) Correct rates of direction judgement and whether the participants should return in the 1st to last 20 times, respectively. Error bars mean standard errors.

4   Results and Discussion

4.1   Reaction Time

The ANOVA of standardized reaction time with the four factors mentioned above revealed the significant main effects or main effects with marginal significance for participants' visual conditions ($p < .001$), participants' experience ($p < .05$), and sound conditions ($p = .066 < .10$). Moreover, there were significant interactions of the participants' visual conditions and repeat counts ($p < .001$). Surprisingly, we could not observe the main effects for repeat counts; our previous study on the goalball trainer application showed this effect [4].

The left graph of Fig. 3 shows the reaction time of totally and partially blind participants in the first and last 20 tasks. We could not observe a significant improvement in reaction time in both participant groups ($p > .10$, Tukey-Kramer test). However, this figure shows that the participants with low vision performed significantly earlier than those with total blindness in the beginning, but there were no significant differences in reaction time. According to the comments by the participants with total blindness, they focused on adjusting the interface using text-to-speech software in the beginning. Thus, this difference might reflect the learning effect of using the interface.

4.2   Correct Rates of Two Successive Judgements

The ANOVA of correct rates of direction judgement with the four factors revealed the significant main effects or main effects with marginal significance for participants' experience ($p = .062 < .10$) and for repeat counts ($p < .001$), but no significant interactions. Also, the ANOVA of correct responses to decide whether they should return yielded the significant main effects of repeat counts ($p < .001$) and sound conditions ($p < .001$). These results indicated that the participants improved the accuracy of these judgements regardless of no training effects in reaction time.

The central graph of Fig. 3 shows correct rates of direction judgement. There were significant differences in the 1st and the other 20 times ($p < .05$, Dunnett's test). The correct response in the first 20 times was 89.4% while trials

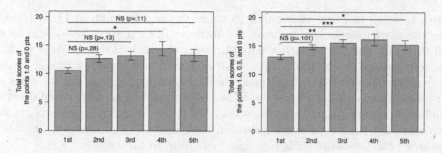

Fig. 4. Total scores of (Left) actual summation of the defined 1.0 and 0 points, and (Right) our abbreviated summation of the defined 1.0, 0.5, and 0 points in the 1st to last 20 times. Error bars mean standard errors.

from second to last 20 times were 96.3% on average. This result indicated that training effects on direction judgement of the approaching STT ball could be immediately taken and also maintained. On the other hand, as shown in the right graph of Fig. 3, the correct rates of deciding whether they return or not shown were significantly difference between the first and the fourth 20 times ($p < .01$, Dunnett's test), but were significant marginally between the first and the last sessions ($p = .077 < .10$, Dunnett's test). Also, the correct rates of this decision were lower than the rates of direction judgement. Based on the results of these two correct rates, the ability to judge the direction of approaching ball was easier and was more likely to improve and maintain than the decision of whether the participant should return or not.

According to the participants' feedbacks, most of them reported that they become accustomed to judge the ball directions, but some of them also indicated that they had difficulty perceiving the distance and direction because of the unique binaural sound reproduction. This subjective unnaturalness could be derived from the difference of head shapes among the participants and dummy head microphone. In the future, we would like to investigate and implement the method of sound recording and reproduction to decrease this compatibility issues. Also, though all of them reported the training effects and the effectiveness of sound localization and decision whether they should return, some of them indicated that the direction to receive and the position and angle of the racket was also important. Watanabe et al. has already implemented the detection of players' movements by using depth camera and reported the training effects to play STT in the special sound cask. Our future work should also include the simple and reasonable measuring method by using consumer electronics.

4.3 Improvement of Game Score

The left and right graphs of Fig. 4 show the total scores of (i) actual summation of the defined 1.0 and 0 points, and (ii) our abbreviated summation of the defined 1.0, 0.5, and 0 points. In the two graphs, there are significant improvements or improvements of nearly marginal significance, in general. The significance of total scores between the first and fourth 20 times in the left graph of Fig. 4 reveals that the participants could improve the accuracy of their successive decisions of ball direction and whether they should return the ball. However, their performance decreased in the last session. This fact may be because of fatigue of the participants: some of them continued the tasks without a rest. On the basis of our abbreviated summation shown in the right graph of Fig. 4, we could observe significant improvements from the second 20 times. The results of two graphs indicated that the participants improved their ability to gain scores, and also, developed the factors of skills that can contribute to their scoring.

Thus, the above results suggested that our application, the *AcouSTTic*, can be effective in improving their ability to decide the direction of a virtual ball and whether they should return it or not. Moreover, according to Honda et al., sound localization training in a virtual auditory environment can significantly decrease the errors of vertical and horizontal localization in the real world [3]. Therefore, our application with consumer electronics would be effective in improving their localization of balls and their judgment skills of whether they should be returned, in the real world.

4.4   Other Feedbacks

According to participant feedback, this application is accessible enough for them to use and may be useful for STT beginners to listen to various types of services. However, some of them pointed out that there is a shortage of service types and servers. Moreover, some of them stated that it was difficult to judge the distance of the ball, compared to its direction. These features will be our future work.

Acknowledgements. This study is supported by JSPS KAKENHI Grant Numbers 15K01015 and 15K04540. Special thanks are due to the members of the STT circle in the Tsukuba University of Technology.

References

1. Japan Association of Sound Table Tennis. http://jatvi.com/
2. Hodges, L.F., Kooper, R., Meyer, T.C., Rothbaum, B.O., Opdyke, D., de Graaff, J.J., Williford, J.S., North, M.M.: Virtual environments for treating the fear of heights. Computer **28**(7), 27–34 (1995)
3. Honda, A., Shibata, H., Gyoba, J., Saitou, K., Iwaya, Y., Suzuki, Y.: Transfer effects on sound localization performances from playing a virtual three-dimensional auditory game. Appl. Acoust. **68**(8), 885–896 (2007)
4. Miura, T., Soga, S., Matsuo, M., Sakajiri, M., Onishi, J., Ono, T.: GoalBaural: a training application for goalball-related aural sense. In: Proceedings of AH 2018, pp. 20:1–20:5 (2018)
5. Seki, Y.: Wide-range auditory orientation training system for blind O&M. In: Antona, M., Stephanidis, C. (eds.) Universal Access in Human-Computer Interaction. LNCS, vol. 9178, pp. 150–159. Springer, Cham (2015). https://doi.org/10.1007/978-3-319-20687-5_15

6. Seki, Y., Sato, T.: A training system of orientation and mobility for blind people using acoustic virtual reality. IEEE Trans. Neural Syst. Rehabil. Eng. **19**(1), 95–104 (2011)
7. Watanabe, Y., Ikeda, Y., Ise, S.: Development of virtual-sound table tennis system using sound cask. Trans. VRSJ **22**(1), 91–101 (2017). (in Japanese)
8. Wersenyi, G.: Virtual localization by blind persons. J. Audio Eng. Soc. **60**(7/8), 568–579 (2012)

Camassia: Monocular Interactive Mobile Way Sonification

Sebastian Ritterbusch[1,2(✉)] and Gerhard Jaworek[3]

[1] iXpoint Informationssysteme GmbH, Ettlingen, Germany
sebastian.ritterbusch@ixpoint.de
[2] VWA-Hochschule, Stuttgart, Germany
[3] Study Centre for the Visually Impaired, Karlsruhe Institute of Technology,
Karlsruhe, Germany
gerhard.jaworek@kit.edu

Abstract. Real-time camera image analysis informs the walking person about the way in front by sonification. For visually impaired people, this opens a new way to experience their surroundings and move more safely outdoors. We extended an image analysis workflow from autonomous robots to human interaction, adaption to alternating way appearance, and various sonification options. The solution is available on off-the-shelf smartphones.

Keywords: Sonification · Navigation · Assistive system · Blind
Free way detection

1 Introduction

Autonomous and self-determined mobility is essential to our life. Visual impairments are a disadvantage with respect to recognition of the way ahead. Systems to detect obstacles like the white cane have been proven to be very effective and helpful. Many technical solutions use various sensors to extend the detected area, or to solve related problems to mobility. This often leads to the use of specialized hardware that can be quite costly, or solutions that do not leave experimental status, and are therefore not generally available.

The presented approach uses the camera and inertial sensors of an off-the-shelf smartphone to enhance the perception of the way in front, by sonification. By a low-latency approach from camera analysis to auditory feedback, the solution gives immediate feedback to the user rotating the camera in order to scan the surroundings.

The adaption of the visual recognition algorithm of a competition winning autonomous robot relies on the user to decide which way to go, instead of let the person being controlled by directions of an expert system.

© Springer International Publishing AG, part of Springer Nature 2018
K. Miesenberger and G. Kouroupetroglou (Eds.): ICCHP 2018, LNCS 10897, pp. 12–18, 2018.
https://doi.org/10.1007/978-3-319-94274-2_2

2 Problem Statement and Related Work

There are several approaches to aid the navigation of visually impaired humans based on smartphones, but they either require detectable markers in the environment [1], or a priori an accurate map [2]. In [3], one of the authors applied sonification methods in combination with a force-feedback device to locate objects in virtual space.

In contrast to many obstacle detecting solutions, the presented approach follows the concept of [4] to identify free space instead. The idea in the vision algorithm [5] of the KAMARO robot car which won the European ROBOTOUR 2015 competition is fundamental to this work. It seems relatively simple compared to the work presented in [6], but instead of detecting the whole road and vanishing point, it aims at robustly and very efficiently computing a one-dimensional angle distribution of free passage probabilities, for interactive real-time and interactive use. A one dimensional density function is very useful for interactive sonification for exploration as in [7], as found with participation of one of the authors. It has to be noted, that the use of the audio channel for wayfinding is generally disadvantageous from the point of cognitive load [8] for the blind, but the choice of the smartphone platform does not offer other appropriate fast updating communication channels, yet.

The aim of the solution is to provide live acoustic feedback of the camera image to aid visually impaired persons in finding passable ways.

3 Methodology

The basic concept is based on the observation of Fürst in [5,9] that pavements generally have low color saturation compared to the surroundings. In contrast to a fixed camera setup on a robot car, first of all, the image of a human controlled camera has to be rectified. Additionally, the method was extended to adapt to general and changing soil appearances.

Due to the perspective mapping of the surroundings onto the camera image, the image analysis yields a one-dimensional angle distribution of free passage probabilities. Figure 1 illustrates the steps of the image analysis workflow: In the first step, an image is taken from the camera. Since we cannot expect the blind user to hold the camera straight, the image then is rectified using the Inertial Measurement Unit (IMU) of the smartphone. Also, image data above the horizon is discarded. In the next step, the remaining image is color adjusted with respect to the last color calibration by the user. The result is then analyzed for way components and finally summarized in the free way probability distribution, which will be shown as a bar on top of the screen.

This result is mapped onto a two octave spanning stereophonic real-time audio synthesizer, giving immediate feedback to the perceived floor image. The distribution is mapped onto 24 half-tones with its intensity representing the assumed probability. Alternative sonification modes allow to replace the synthesizer by stereophonic white noise, or to reduce the sound to local maxima in the density function to reduce the sound, and therefore the cognitive load, even more.

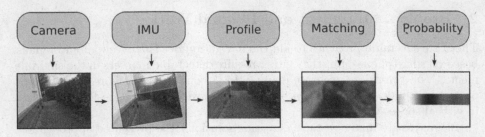

Fig. 1. From the camera the image is rectified and cut, the image is transformed following the color profile, analyzed for its way components and finally transformed to the free way probability distribution. (Color figure online)

The standard sonification method is redundant by purpose, both using sound frequency and panorama to reflect the probability density. This way, the system remains usable with monophonic smartphone speakers. On the other hand, it is offering additional panoramic information when a stereophonic headset is used.

Due to the challenging representation of visual components via polyphonic acoustic representations, the solution is supplemented by an introductory narrated tutorial and a more detailed tutorial introducing and explaining the sound options.

4   Results

While the original algorithm was aimed at pavements, its extension to general soil appearance turned out to be quite robust, see Fig. 2 for two examples. It is quite successful in detecting earth paths as well as colored pavements, as well as colored indoor carpeting. The solution reaches its limits in the case of sidewalks if they are paved in the same way as the street, and is of very limited use when crossing a street.

While the solution should be robust to varying illumination of the path, this has limits due to non-linearity of the camera, and may also lead to false detection of pure white or black areas. Further refinement of the algorithm will take this into account.

On current devices, the algorithm easily analyzes 30 images in a second, leading to a very fast response in the audio output. Due to device based audio buffering and necessity of acoustic fading of sounds, there is short delay from detection to acoustic response lower than a tenth of a second.

Besides the contributions and first hand experience of one of the authors with respect to blindness, twelve candidates being blind or mobility trainers were invited to participate in a test before publication of the software, of which nine persons then participated in the test. They were given an questionnaire covering the information about the test person, usability, application fields, the human computer interface, and the overall impression. Five of the testers gave answers to at least parts of the questionnaire.

Fig. 2. Two screenshots of live path detection show the image of the camera in the lower part, a grayscale bar in the upper part represents the probability density function of assumed free space represented in darker shades. The first screenshot shows how a straight path is detected. The second screenshot shows a branching which two branches were accurately detected. The brush icon as well as the pause or play button on headsets calibrates the color of the way, the three bar icon leads to the configuration. (Color figure online)

Fig. 3. For way detection, the smartphone should be held in front of the person, tilted downwards, slightly. Photo by H. Kucharek.

Fig. 4. The detection algorithm was found to be very effective for paths in parks, as well as pavements enclosed by grass. Photo by H. Kucharek.

As expected from [8], the choice of sonification for representing the free space probabilities understandingly was not enthusiastically received by visually impaired testers. Yet, the applicability for certain situations was both confirmed by blind users and mobility trainers. There was a strong demand for additional training material with sound examples, which was missing in the test version, and was added in the published version.

A useful example was found in identifying side ways that are not easily detectable by the white cane, as illustrated in Fig. 2. Also, the immediate acoustic response in advance to passing cyclists was very well received. The indoor use of the solution was an unexpected response. Another response was the need for more training, especially to take advantage of the immediate response to moving the camera. The use of bone-conduction earphones was preferred to the use of the internal smartphone speaker due to the panoramic response.

In practical use, the solution was efficient both in landscape and portrait mode. While the landscape mode is advised due to a larger field of view, a swinging motion of the camera to the left and right like the white cane, overcame the limitation. Best results where achieved for paved paths enclosed with vegetation and in parks, as illustrated in Figs. 3 and 4. As proposed in the supplied training, additional wide-angle lenses can strongly increase the field of view, but it turned out, that they are not easily attached to the smartphone by a blind person.

The use of a narrated tutorial was well received, stating that it would hardly possible to understand what the solution does without such a short introduction. Following the feedback from the testers, this tutorial was extended by giving more examples on where the App can be used.

5   Conclusion

The adaption and extension from an image analysis workflow from robotics in combination with various sonification modes led to an applicable solution for experienced blind users, as an addition to the concurrent use of the well-established white cane or guide dogs. To the knowledge of the authors, it is the first publicly obtainable solution dedicated to general and interactive path detection on the smartphone.

It is expected to be a starting point for real-time mobile camera-based path detection immediately communicated to the user, and will be followed by more sophisticated concepts based on Artificial Intelligence or more intensive pattern recognition due to the availability of computing power on the smartphone. Also, the future support of external haptic devices, such as vibration bands for arm, foot or waist as an alternative to sonification should improve the cognitive load.

The solution is available for general use on iTunes Store.

References

1. Coughlan, J., Manduchi, R.: A mobile phone wayfinding system for visually impaired users. Assist. Technol. Res. Ser. **25**(2009), 849 (2009)
2. Chen, D., Feng, W., Zhao, Q., Hu, M., Wang, T.: An infrastructure-free indoor navigation system for blind people. In: Su, C.-Y., Rakheja, S., Liu, H. (eds.) ICIRA 2012. LNCS (LNAI), vol. 7508, pp. 552–561. Springer, Heidelberg (2012). https://doi.org/10.1007/978-3-642-33503-7_54
3. Ritterbusch, S., Constantinescu, A., Koch, V.: Hapto-acoustic scene representation. In: Miesenberger, K., Karshmer, A., Penaz, P., Zagler, W. (eds.) ICCHP 2012. LNCS, vol. 7383, pp. 644–650. Springer, Heidelberg (2012). https://doi.org/10.1007/978-3-642-31534-3_94
4. Schauerte, B., Koester, D., Martinez, M., Stiefelhagen, R.: Way to go! Detecting open areas ahead of a walking person. In: Agapito, L., Bronstein, M.M., Rother, C. (eds.) ECCV 2014. LNCS, vol. 8927, pp. 349–360. Springer, Cham (2015). https://doi.org/10.1007/978-3-319-16199-0_25
5. Fürst, M.: Detecting drivable regions in monocular images. Robotour 2015: Autonomous Robot in Parks and Urban Regions (2015)
6. Kong, H., Audibert, J.Y., Ponce, J.: General road detection from a single image. IEEE Trans. Image Process. **19**(8), 2211–2220 (2010)
7. Wörtwein, T., Schauerte, B., Müller, K., Stiefelhagen, R.: Mobile interactive image sonification for the blind. In: Miesenberger, K., Bühler, C., Penaz, P. (eds.) ICCHP 2016. LNCS, vol. 9758, pp. 212–219. Springer, Cham (2016). https://doi.org/10.1007/978-3-319-41264-1_28

8. Martinez, M., Constantinescu, A., Schauerte, B., Koester, D., Stiefelhagen, R.: Cognitive evaluation of haptic and audio feedback in short range navigation tasks. In: Miesenberger, K., Fels, D., Archambault, D., Peňáz, P., Zagler, W. (eds.) ICCHP 2014. LNCS, vol. 8548, pp. 128–135. Springer, Cham (2014). https://doi.org/10.1007/978-3-319-08599-9_20

9. Fürst, M.: Probabilistische Robotik, conversation with S. Ritterbusch in the Modellansatz Podcast, Episode 95, Department of Mathematics, Karlsruhe Institute of Technology (KIT) (2016). http://modellansatz.de/probabilistische-robotik

A Unimodal Interface Device Coupling Distance with Intensities in Luminance and Temperature

Masaki Nishino[1], Junichi Akita[1(✉)], Kiyohide Ito[2], Makoto Okamoto[2], and Testuo Ono[3]

[1] Kanazawa University, Kanazawa, Ishikawa 920-1192, Japan
akita@is.t.kanazawa-u.ac.jp
[2] Future University Hakodate, Hakodate, Hokkaido 041-8655, Japan
[3] Hokkaido University, Sapporo, Hokkaido 060-0808, Japan

Abstract. In this paper, we report the unimodal interface device coupling with intensities in luminance and temperature. It enables the user to recognize two or three types of information through the finger's angle motion and vibration independently and simultaneously. We describe the developed device, as well as its experimental results.

Keywords: ETA · Haptic · Distance · Intensities

1 Introduction

We focus on the nonvisual modalities to provide the information on the surroundings to the users, and we've previously reported "Future Body-Finger (FB-Finger) [2]" that enable visual impaired people to perceive their surroundings, which converts the distance information to the angle of the user's finger. In these works, we assume that a novel subjective experience of the environment (e.g., that of an "extended mind" [1]) could be realized by means of devices that function as parts of our body and endow us with "embodied cognition".

In this paper, we will report the outline of our new improved device, "FB-Finger Unimul (unimodality-multi-information interface)" and demonstration of psychological experiments. The purpose of "FB-Finger Unimul" is to handle more than one kinds of information using single or unimodality, somatic sense, particularly controlling finger joints and vibratory sensation on skin surface. Three types of sensor are used to capture the environment information, the distance, the luminance, and the temperature of the target object. The device has two degree of freedom in information representation; one is the finger's angle motion that is similar to our previous FB-Finger, and the other is the vibrator on the finger skin to represent the intensity of the luminance or the temperature of the target object. We developed this kind of device, and carried out to investigate the capability for recognizing distance and properties of the target object. Finally, we also tried to represent three types of sensors-obtained information simultaneously at a time, for the users to recognize each sensor-specific information separately.

© Springer International Publishing AG, part of Springer Nature 2018
K. Miesenberger and G. Kouroupetroglou (Eds.): ICCHP 2018, LNCS 10897, pp. 19–22, 2018.
https://doi.org/10.1007/978-3-319-94274-2_3

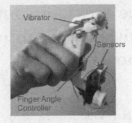 

Fig. 1. The developed "FB-Finger Unimul" device (left) and its third version (right).

2 Mechanism of the Developed FB-Finger Unimul

We've developed the extended "Future Body" device, "FB-Finger Unimal," as shown in Fig. 1 (left). It equips three types of sensors to acquire the target object's physical aspects; the distance sensor (ST Microelectronics, VL6180X, range of 0–100 mm), the luminance sensor (Macron, CdS Cell, range of 1–1000 cd/m^2), and the temperature sensor (OMRON, D6T-44L-06, range of 5–50 °C). It also has two mechanisms to representing the information to the user. One is the finger's angle control mechanism to represent the distance information to the user; the finger is pressed by the lever for near object, and released for far object. Temperature sensor or luminance sensor is connected to the vibrator attached at the side of the finger to represent the vibration stimulation on the user's finger. We can operate this device in two different modes, the distance-luminance device, and the distance-temperature device, where the intensity of the vibration corresponds to the luminance and the temperature magnitude, respectively; the stronger vibration becomes, either the higher luminance or the higher temperature gets. In these devices, two different kinds of information, finger's angle and the vibration, are used to represent the different types of properties of the target object independently and simultaneously using one modality, somatic sense.

We also developed the third device with one finger's angle control mechanism and two vibrator mechanisms on the top of the index finger and the middle of the center finger as shown in Fig. 1 (right). In this device, the luminance and the temperature magnitudes correspond to the vibrators on the top of index finger and the middle of the center finger, respectively. This device can represent three types of properties of the target object.

3 Evaluation Experiment Results

3.1 Experiment 1: Two Types of Information

We have carried out the evaluation experiments to find out how accurate the user can perceive the target object's information represented by the developed devices. Two types of the target objects were used as follows were used for each type of the developed device, the distance-luminance and the distance-temperature device, respectively.

- 8 cm paper cube with LED light, whose luminance is high ($180\,\mathrm{cd/m^2}$), middle ($50\,\mathrm{cd/m^2}$), or low ($1\,\mathrm{cd/m^2}$)
- paper cup (8 cm tall) containing water, whose temperature is high ($50\,^{\circ}\mathrm{C}$), middle ($25\,^{\circ}\mathrm{C}$), or low ($5\,^{\circ}\mathrm{C}$.)

The object was placed in front of the user at the randomly chosen distance from 10 to 50 cm in the step of 10 cm. Participants were asked to use the developed device to find the object, and to report the distance to the object, as well as its luminance or its temperature. Seven sighted participants with blindfolds participated this experiment.

Table 1 shows the percentages of the accurate judgments for the distance and the luminance or the temperature, respectively, for various combinations of the distance and the luminance or the temperature. For example, in case of the presented distance of 20 cm and middle luminance, the percentages of the accurate judgments for the distance and luminance were 85.7% and 42.9%, respectively. These results have shown that the developed device has the ability of representing both the distance in step of 10 cm, and three steps of the luminance or the temperature simultaneously and independently at average percentages of accurate judgments of around 70%.

Table 1. Percentages of the accurate judgments for the distance-luminance and the distance-temperature device experiment

Dis. [cm]	Percentages of accurate judgments for distance-luminance device [%]						Percentages of accurate judgments for distance-temperature device [%]					
	Lumi. = L		Lumi. = M		Lumi. = H		Temp. = L		Temp. = M		Temp. = H	
	Dis.	Lumi.	Dis.	Lumi.	Dis.	Lumi.	Dis.	Temp.	Dis.	Temp.	Dis.	Temp.
10	100.0	100.0	85.7	57.1	85.7	71.4	100.0	100.0	85.7	100.0	42.9	85.7
20	57.1	71.4	85.7	42.9	71.4	71.4	85.7	100.0	42.9	85.7	57.1	85.7
30	57.1	100.0	57.1	85.7	85.7	85.7	57.1	85.7	100.0	100.0	100.0	100.0
40	57.1	71.4	71.4	28.6	71.4	71.4	42.9	57.1	57.1	85.7	42.9	85.7
50	71.4	71.4	71.4	57.1	85.7	28.6	57.1	71.4	57.1	85.7	71.4	71.4
Avg. (SD)	68.6 (4.1)	82.9 (3.7)	74.3 (3.3)	54.3 (4.4)	80.0 (2.6)	65.7 (4.4)	68.6 (4.6)	82.9 (4.1)	68.6 (4.6)	91.4 (2.6)	62.9 (4.6)	85.7 (3.0)

3.2 Experiment 2: Three Types of Information

We have also carried out the evaluation experiments for the "third" developed device that represents three types of object's properties, distance, luminance, and temperature. The target object with LED light source and the iced or the hot water was used to represent both the luminance and temperature information. The luminance was set in two steps; high ($180\,\mathrm{cd/m^2}$) and low ($1\,\mathrm{cd/m^2}$), and the temperature was set in two steps; high ($50\,^{\circ}\mathrm{C}$) and low ($5\,^{\circ}\mathrm{C}$). The object is located in front of the user at the randomly chosen distance from 10, 30, or 50 cm. Participants were asked to use the developed device to find the object, and to report the distance to the object, as well as its luminance and its temperature. Eight sighted participants with blindfolds have participated this experiment.

Table 2 shows the percentages of the accurate judgments for the distance, the luminance, and the temperature, respectively, for various combinations of the distance, the luminance, and the temperature. These results have shown that the developed device has the ability of representing the distance in step of 20 cm, and two steps of both the luminance of 180 and $1\,cd/m^2$, and the temperature of 50 and 5 °C, simultaneously and separately at average percentages of accurate judgments of 94%, 82%, and 76%, respectively.

Table 2. Percentages of the accurate judgments for the distance-luminance-temperature device experiment

Dis. [cm]	Percentages of accurate judgments [%]											
	Lumi. = H						Lumi. = L					
	Temp. = H			Temp. = L			Temp. = H			Temp. = L		
	Dist.	Lumi.	Temp.	Dist.	Lumi.	Temp.	Dist.	Lumi.	Temp.	Dist.	Lumi.	Temp.
10	100.0	50.0	100.0	100.0	75.0	75.0	87.5	62.5	100.0	100.0	100.0	75.0
30	100.0	87.5	75.0	87.5	87.5	75.0	87.5	75.0	62.5	100.0	100.0	100.0
50	100.0	100.0	37.5	100.0	75.0	62.5	75.0	75.0	62.5	87.5	100.0	87.5
Avg. (SD)	100.0 (0.0)	79.2 (4.6)	70.8 (5.1)	95.8 (2.4)	79.2 (2.4)	70.8 (2.4)	83.3 (2.4)	70.8 (2.4)	75.0 (4.2)	95.8 (2.4)	100.0 (0.0)	87.5 (3.2)

4   Conclusion

In this paper, we described the concept of the improvement of our FB-Finger device to represent two or three types of different target object properties simultaneously and separately to the user by using the user's finger angle control and vibration. The experimental results showed that these devices have the capability of representing two or three types of different object properties, distance, luminance, and temperature, simultaneously and separately at average percentages of accurate judgments of around 70%. This study indicates the possibility that the improved FB-Finger enables visual impaired users to detect whether or not hot object with brightening lies present near here, like fire.

References

1. Clark, A., Chalmers, D.: The extended mind. Analysis **58**, 7–19 (1998)
2. Ito, K., et al.: FB-finger: development of a novel electric travel aid with a unique haptic interface. In: Miesenberger, K., Fels, D., Archambault, D., Peňáz, P., Zagler, W. (eds.) ICCHP 2014. LNCS, vol. 8548, pp. 65–72. Springer, Cham (2014). https://doi.org/10.1007/978-3-319-08599-9_11

Basic Study of Blind Football Play-by-Play System for Visually Impaired Spectators Using Quasi-Zenith Satellites System

Makoto Kobayashi[1(✉)], Yoshiki Fukunaga[1], and Shigenobu Shimada[2]

[1] Department of Computer Science, Tsukuba University of Technology, Tsukuba, Japan
{koba,fukunaga}@cs.k.tsukuba-tech.ac.jp
[2] R&D Department, Tokyo Metropolitan Industrial Technology Research Institute, Tokyo, Japan
shimada.shigenobu@iri-tokyo.jp

Abstract. A project to develop a blind football play-by-play system was started. The target of the system is visually impaired spectator. To conduct a basic study, we made an experimental system that detects a position of a player using a Quasi-Zenith Satellites System (QZSS) and shows the position via refreshable tactile display. The QZSS allows users to acquire more precise position information than only with GPS around Japan. The study showed that a certain possibility to acquire an arbitrary position data of the player in the field and display it to the tactile display.

Keywords: Blind football · Visually impaired spectator
Quasi-Zenith Satellites System

1 Introduction

In these days, blind football is more and more popular in the field of para sports. Worldwide championship games have been held regularly by the International Blind Sports Federation (IBSA) [1] and these games are reported in web media and TV programs even in Japan. As a natural consequence, the number of the spectators who would like to enjoy the game on-site is also increasing. Here, it is said that spectators at such a para sport game can be categorized into three groups [2]: the first group consists of athletes who are participating in the game, the second one includes related individuals like family members or friends of these athletes, and the third group members are unrelated individuals with disabilities. Therefore, in the case of blind football, quite a few spectators can be visually impaired people. Our department has a blind football club because we accept only students who have visual impairment, and we can see our students as spectators at the field where our team has a match. However, such visually impaired spectators have some difficulties to understand the precise situation during the game although they want to know about it. To give its information, live coverage of play-by-play announcement is the best solution though, it cannot be performed at the field because everybody there except support members do not make a noise to avoid disturbing blind players. To solve this problem, Panasonic developed a support system to provide live

© The Author(s) 2018
K. Miesenberger and G. Kouroupetroglou (Eds.): ICCHP 2018, LNCS 10897, pp. 23–27, 2018.
https://doi.org/10.1007/978-3-319-94274-2_4

announcements and videos to the smartphone or tablet of visually impaired spectators via network [3]. This solution is enjoyable and effective, but the most problematic point is that it needs to prepare a professional sports commentator and it is difficult to realize this in local game matches.

Because of this background, we started a project to develop a support system for visually impaired spectators, which can automatically explain the situation of blind football in real time, even in local game matches.

2   System Requirements

To develop the blind football play-by-play system for the visually impairment spectators mentioned above, we considered the concept of the system and thought about an input method and an output method (see Fig. 1). The input method should correctly detect the position of players and the output method should effectively display the information to the spectator(s). As an output method, a synthesized voice and/or a refreshable tactile display have a possibility to be effective. From the viewpoint of realizing an automatic live coverage, voice explanation is the final goal though, tactile display is easy to utilize in these days. We can use a consumer version device by KGS Corp., which is spread in Japan and it is already shown that the blind can understand many graphical information using it [4].

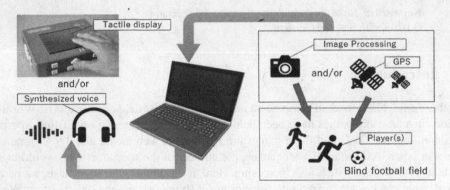

Fig. 1. Concept of blind football play-by-play system.

As an input method, we tried to consider the possibility of using a camera and GPS system to detect the position of the players. If we use cameras with image processing system, these players do not need to wear special devices. However, the position of the camera should be high enough to capture the entire field at once and setting a tall pole to carry the camera might be dangerous and difficult to establish in local game. On the contrary, GPS system forces players to wear some hardware but to prepare the total system will be easier than the camera system.

Of course, the combination of the camera system and the GPS system should be perfect though, we decided to start a basic study to find the possibility to use a GPS system as a first step, since we can use the Quasi-Zenith Satellites System (QZSS) around

Japan with low cost. The QZSS is a national project to make GPS information more precise. It is composed of four satellites and their trajectories are always and almost on the top of the field around Japan. The fourth satellite launched in October 2017 and full-service will start from fiscal year 2018 [5].

3 Experimental System and Result

After consideration of input/output method and devices, we made a set of an experimental system shown in Fig. 2 to conduct basic study. The system composed of a refreshable tactile display, a computer, a mobile wireless LAN access point, and a pair of GPS units. One of the GPS units has an ESP8266 board that can communicate to the wireless LAN access point. Another GPS unit consists of an Arduino Nano board and it directly connects to the computer. A software on the computer communicates to the GPS unit with ESP8266 via the wireless LAN, and the GPS unit sends the computer the precise time, the latitude data, and the longitude data all together. These data will be compared with the coordinate data on the same timing from another GPS unit that is connected to the computer. The compared coordinate data is expected to be more correct than stand-alone data. The calculated position of the moving GPS unit will be displayed on the refreshable tactile display.

Fig. 2. Overview of an experimental system.

Figure 3 shows an example of acquired trajectory data on the soccer field in our university. A person held the GPS unit and walked around the field. This example showed a walking case which started from the corner of the field to the South direction and went back to the North direction. In this figure, the horizontal axis means latitude difference and the vertical axis means longitude difference. The left plot shows data by comparing with static point in the same timing, which is mentioned above. The right one shows simple subtracted data of acquired position and an initial position. Other trajectories had same tendency and we can say that the resolution of comparing with the static point is more precise than the subtraction data. Although sometimes it has errors, it is enough to display on the tactile display because the resolution of the display is only 48 dots by 32 dots.

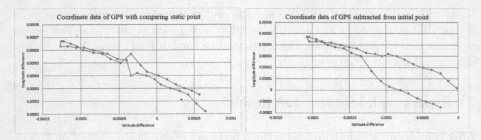

Fig. 3. Example of trajectory data

4   Summary

To develop a blind football play-by-play system for visually impaired spectators, a basic study of combination with QZSS and a tactile display was conducted. The results gave us a certain possibility to display an arbitrary position of the player on the tactile display. In the future, we plan to add image processing to the input method and synthesized voice to the output method.

References

1. Football - general information (IBSA web site). http://www.ibsasport.org/sports/football. Accessed 19 Mar 2018
2. Donna, D.H.: Blind football: spectators' experience of the forgotten. In: Proceeding of 19th Conference of the European Association for Sport Management, pp. 185–186 (2011)
3. Panasonic Demonstrated Spectator Solutions with VOGO Sport for Disabled Sports at Japan-Brazil Blind Football Match. Panasonic newsroom, 4 April 2017. http://news.panasonic.com/global/topics/2017/46362.html. Accessed 19 Mar 2018
4. Kobayashi, M., Watanabe, T.: Multimedia communication system for the blind. In: Ichalkaranje, N., Ichalkaranje, A., Jain, L. (eds.) Intelligent Paradigms for Assistive and Preventive Healthcare. Studies in Computational Intelligence, vol. 19, pp. 165–181. Springer, Heidelberg (2006). https://doi.org/10.1007/11418337_6
5. Murai, Y.: Project overview: quasi-zenith satellite system. In: Proceedings of the 27th International Technical Meeting of the Satellite Division of the Institute of Navigation, vol. 27, pp. 2974–3008 (2014)

An Augmented Reality Audio Device Helping Blind People Navigation

Sylvain Ferrand$^{(\boxtimes)}$, Francois Alouges, and Matthieu Aussal

CMAP, Ecole polytechnique, CNRS, Université Paris-Saclay,
91128 Palaiseau, France
sylvain.ferrand@polytechnique.edu
http://www.cmap.polytechnique.edu/xaudio

Abstract. This paper describes a device conceived to guide blind people. In this device, we use both localization informations provided by a precise and low latency real-time positioning system and head orientation data measured with an Inertial Measurement Unit, coupled with a real-time binaural engine. In this paper we made a special focus on the localization techniques that we have studied. First experiments show that the approach is viable and the system can be used in practice ...

Keywords: Assistive technology · Binaural sound
Real-time localization · Embedded systems

1 Introduction

The visually impaired are able to localize and follow sound sources with a remarkable accuracy. They often use this ability in everyday activities, for example, to follow someone by hearing his/her voice or footsteps.

In principle, we can use this ability to guide blind people with spatialized sound generated in real-time and listened with simple headphones. Indeed, if we can localize the person precisely in real-time, we can give him/her the illusion that the sound is leading him/her at a certain distance ahead, and guide him/her to follow a pre-defined path.

In this project, we are mainly interested in precision and performances for indoor or sports applications. Our goal, in the first instance, is to guide people in predictable areas with known geometries. Typically, we want to permit a subject to run and stay on his lane in a running track, or to guide him/her to follow a precise path in a gym.

Guiding methods have been experimented in various research project, for example GpsTunes and Ontrack [5–7] mostly based on GPS positioning systems. Unfortunately, GPS based systems are not able to give an immediate feedback to the user due to their high latency and imprecision. It is the reason why we developed a Real-Time Localization System (RTLS) especially adapted for our application. This precise localization allows us to position the virtual sound very close in front of the user to guide him/her with a very good accuracy.

K. Miesenberger and G. Kouroupetroglou (Eds.): ICCHP 2018, LNCS 10897, pp. 28–35, 2018.
https://doi.org/10.1007/978-3-319-94274-2_5

This article describes the device that we designed, with a focus on the algorithms implemented for real time localization and control. We also briefly describe the audio renderer and show the results that we obtained during our experiments.

2   Device Overview

Our device couples an accurate 2D positioning system, a head tracker, and a sound renderier in order to simulate a virtual sound source regardless of user's motion. It takes into account both head rotation and user's displacement in real-time. We use sensors for the localization and head tracking connected to an embedded computer running the algorithm which implements the path tracking software and the audio engine. The sound is finally reproduced by a headphone.

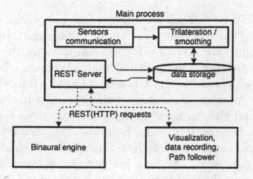

Fig. 1. Software architecture of the device.

The software to be highly modular with a minimal latency operations. This is accomplished through a multi-tier architecture and each component exchange data via a REST API (cf. Fig. 1). The main program, the REST server, manages the communications with multiple clients processes: communication interface with sensors (head-tracker and positioning system), filtering system, control system and audio rendering. This software, mostly written in python, has been successfully tested on architectures as various as: Mac and embedded computers (ARM 8 (Raspberry Pi 3), ARM *Heterogeneous Multi-Processing - Big-Little* (Odroid XU4 et Jetson TX1) and Intel Edison).

3   Accurate and Fast Environment Sensing

In the literature [5–7], several applications use Global Navigation Satellite Systems (GNSS) to provide localization data. The accuracy of such localization systems is typically in the range of 2–5 m horizontal with an update rate in the order of 1–10 Hz (see Table 1). Moreover, they are not usable indoor.

Table 1. Comparison of positioning systems

Technology	Positioning accuracy	Refresh rate	Usable place	Cost
GNSS (GPS)	2–5 m	1–10 Hz	Outdoor	Low
GPS + IMU	2–5 m	100 Hz	Outdoor	Low
UWB	10 cm	10–15 Hz	In/Out	Medium
Differential RTK GNSS	10 cm	1–10 Hz	Outdoor	High

In our application, this is not suffisent, an giving an immediate feedback to the moving user is absolutely crucial. Therefore we propose two different systems which turn out to be faster, more accurate and better suited for our application.

3.1   A Real-Time Locating System (RTLS) with Ultra Wide Band

Ultra Wide Band (UWB) technology allows a fast and precise distance measurement by using the Time of Flight (ToF) of a radio signal. In association with the Two Way Ranging protocol (TWR), we can measure the distance between a master UWB transceiver (the Tag) and multiple slaves (the Anchors). With this protocol, we measure the round-trip time of a data frame sent from the Tag and replied by the Anchors. This elapsed time permits to deduce the distance between the Tag and the Anchors. Compared to systems based on the signal strength (e.g. Wifi, Bluetooth or radio beacons), this technology is very robust in multi-path environments and relatively insensitive to shading of the sensors and RF interference. It is also low-cost, low power and gives high precision measures. The UWB transceivers that we use are based on the DW1000 UWB chip from DecaWave.

In an area with several fixed UWB Anchors with fixed locations, a trilateration algorithm must be used to determine the absolute position of the mobile Tag. A minimum of 3 Anchors is required for 2D localization and 4 Anchors in 3D. The master runs a loop and measures successively the distances to each Anchor. With four Anchors, our electronic device can achieve up to 12 measure cycles per second.

In a system with n Anchors at coordinates $a_i = (a_{x,i}, a_{y,i})$, the distance between Anchor i and the Tag is given by:

$$d_i^2 = (x - a_{x,i})^2 + (y - a_{y,i})^2.$$

(1)

Basically, with known Anchor positions, the Tag coordinates can be estimated by minimizing Least Square Error (LSE):

$$\sum_{i=1}^{n} | d_i^2 - ((x - a_{x,i})^2 + (y - a_{y,i}))^2 |.$$

(2)

It turns that, it is possible to localize automatically the Anchors. In an initialization step, we accumulate some distance measurements to each Anchor while moving around them with the device. Once enough data have been collected, we solve the system (1) for each position and each Anchor. The approximation of this overdetermined system of quadratic equations gives an estimation of the position of Anchors and the Tag along the realized path.

Next, for the real-time localization, we use the Anchor positions estimated as before and estimate the Tag position with a Kalman Filter with the measurement function

$$
h(x_k) = \begin{pmatrix} \sqrt{(x - a_{x,1})^2 + (y - a_{y,1})^2} \\ \sqrt{(x - a_{x,2})^2 + (y - a_{y,2})^2} \\ \vdots \\ \sqrt{(x - a_{x,n})^2 + (y - a_{y,n})^2} \end{pmatrix}.
\tag{3}
$$

We use an Unscented Kalman Filter (UKF), adapted to deal with the Gaussian noise produced by UWB sensors and the nonlinear function given by (3) and a Position-Velocity (PV) model [8].

We find that, with 4 Anchors positioned at the corners of a 3 m side square, the precision of the localization of a fixed Tag with this system is about 1 cm RMSE and 3 cm max in line of sight conditions.

3.2   Data Fusion for Accurate Long-Range Localization

If the previous setup is well suited for indoor localization, the limited range of UWB transceiver (about 50 m) limits its use for larger areas, moreover it needs several Anchors.

To remedy these limitations we have considered an other strategy. We propose to use only one UWB Anchor and others sensors: a low-cost Inertial Movement Units (IMU) and a velocity sensor. The data measured by those three systems are fused together.

– **The IMU.** It consists of a low-cost Microelectromechanical sensor (MEMS) that measures simultaneously, in the three orthogonal axes, the acceleration, the rotational velocity and the earth's magnetic field. Additionally, a microcontroller can combine all of them to compute a drift-free 3D orientation vector (i.e. the Euler angles). A modern all-in-one chip like the Bosch BNO-055 can perform data fusion to provide orientation informations at 100 Hz with 0-drift and very low noise. Notice that we attach the orientation sensor to the body of the user, assuming that he/she moves straight ahead in the direction measured by IMU without any side steps.
– **The velocity sensor.** Unfortunately, it's rather difficult to measure the velocity of a walking person, and most sensors typically used in robotics (e.g. encoding wheels) are unsuitable. We have therefore considered using optical flow sensors (see [1,2] for instance).We use a very low cost optical flow sensor model DNS-3080 from Avago Technologies which is conventionally used in optical mouse. It can capture 30×30 pixels images at up to 6400 frames per second. In our setup, the optical flow sensor is pointing to the ground estimate the displacement, a 2D vector, by the comparison of successive images. This

sensor is positioned next to an IMU and we estimate the magnitude of the velocity, removing also the rotational component of the optical flow as in [2].

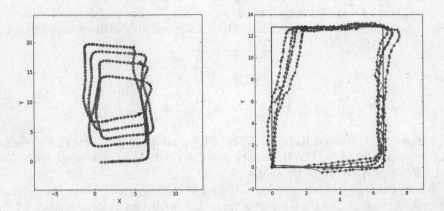

Fig. 2. Position of a user moving along a fixed rectangle estimated with IMU + Optical flow (left) and IMU + Optical Flow + UWB (right). Data fusion with three sensors give a more stable and accurate estimation.

Finally we fuse the measures issued by those sensors with the measure of the distance to a single UWB Anchor, using the measurement vector of the Kalman filter:

$$h(x_k) = \begin{pmatrix} \sqrt{\dot{x}^2/\dot{y}^2} \\ \arctan \frac{\dot{y}}{\dot{x}} \\ \sqrt{(x - a_{x,1})^2 + (y - a_{y,1})^2} \end{pmatrix}. \tag{4}$$

Experiments show that UWB permits to mitigate the accumulation of errors produced using the optical flow sensors only. In the experiments shown in Fig. 2 a user is moving along a 6.5 m × 12.5 m rectangle. Without UWB measures, errors accumulate over time. The Root Mean Square Error of the full system stays below one meter along time. Precision could probably be increased by adding more UWB Anchors.

4   Audio Renderer and Control

Our ability to localize a sound source comes from the deformation and difference of signal received by each ear and interpreted by the brain. These differences are encoded in the so-called Head-Related Transfer Functions (HRTF) [9], that characterize how ears perceive a sound that comes from a specific direction in space. HRTF can be either measured or simulated, and then used to synthesize a binaural sound that, when listened with headphone, seems to come from this specific direction. In this project, we use the localization described before to create a virtual sound source placed in front of the user, a few meters ahead, in the direction he needs to follow. We render this source with the binaural engine that we implemented [3, 4] using a convolution with the HRTF. This software can spatialize a sound and allows real-time filter selection depending on the position of the user. Furthermore, we use a head tracker to keep the scene stable regardless of user's head movement. This is another IMU fixed on the user's head which measures its orientation. The software has been designed to be low latency and adapts the rendering in real-time to take into account all the positional and orientational parameters.

As mentioned before, the virtual sound source is moving along a predefined path. Nevertheless, we can consider to implement a closed loop Proportional Integral (PI) feedback to enhance the guiding precision. Namely, the sound source can be moved by a correction $F_t = K_p e_t + K_i \sum_j e_j$ proportional of the error e and its accumulation over a sliding window (see Fig. 3).

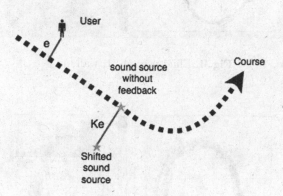

Fig. 3. Proportional feedback illustration

The experiments show that Proportional feedback improves the guiding precision. The Integral feedback is useful to compensate the inaccuracy of localization of the sound source by the user through the binaural rendering.

The whole software, including the audio renderer, has been implemented in Python and Cython for computing intensive tasks.

5   Results

We experimented the device in a 25 m × 35 m gym and we parametrized the system to guide the users along an elliptic shape course, as large as possible. The sound stimulus has been chosen to be appropriate for audio localisation, with rich spectral content and rather continuous level. We tested the system with various users, including two blind peoples. These experiments have been made with UWB localization for optimal precision.

Figures 4 and 5 show the localization of two blind users along the elliptic course performing several laps. With roller skates, the blind user nb. 2 has reached the speed of 12 km/h. After a 500 m long course, at an average speed of 8.7 km/h, he stayed closed to the ideal track with a mean error about 0.5 m (max 1.99 m).

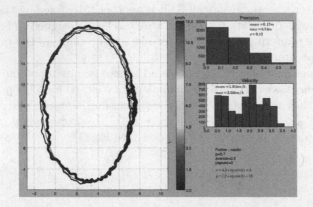

Fig. 4. Blind user nb. 1, walking

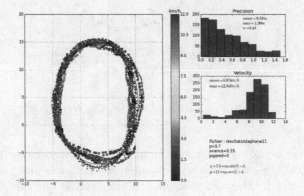

Fig. 5. Blind user nb. 2, roller skating

6   Conclusion

With this device we have been able to guide different peoples, including blind people, running or roller skating, using spatialized sound. Giving the user an immediate feedback is a key factor in the success of these experiments, therefore designing an efficient positioning system associated with a low latency software is decisive. The user reception of the device is very positive, with a very short training, the user follows the sound naturally and quite comfortably.

This device opens lots of possibilities in the domain of the visually impaired guiding, notably for practicing sports. Currently, we are exploring the effect of reverberations cues, because the perception of the lateral walls reverberation is an important facet of blind people displacement. To go faster, we will also try to improve the operating range of the RTLS system and consider other localization systems, for example, computer vision.

Since the beginning of this project, we involved blind people to test and help us to design this device. We are now committed with two associations to a true partnership for development and device improvement. This partnership have been decisive in the success of this project and continues today.

References

1. Gageik, N., Strohmeier, M., Montenegro, S.: An autonomous UAV with an optical flow sensor for positioning and navigation. Int. J. Adv. Rob. Syst. **10**(10), 341 (2013)
2. Lim, H., Lee, H., Kim, H.J.: Onboard flight control of a micro quadrotor using single strapdown optical flow sensor. In: 2012 IEEE/RSJ International Conference on Intelligent Robots and Systems (IROS), pp. 495–500. IEEE, October 2012
3. Aussal, M.: Méthodes numériques pour la spatialisation sonore, de la simulation à la synthèse binaurale (Doctoral dissertation, Palaiseau, Ecole polytechnique) (2014)
4. MyBino Binaural Engine. http://www.cmap.polytechnique.fr/xaudio/mybino. Accessed 19 Mar 18
5. Strachan, S., Eslambolchilar, P., Murray-Smith, R., Hughes, S., O'Modhrain, S.: GpsTunes: controlling navigation via audio feedback. In: Proceedings of the 7th International Conference on Human Computer Interaction with Mobile Devices & Services, pp. 275–278. ACM, September 2005
6. Jones, M., Jones, S., Bradley, G., Warren, N., Bainbridge, D., Holmes, G.: ONTRACK: dynamically adapting music playback to support navigation. Pers. Ubiquit. Comput. **12**(7), 513–525 (2008)
7. Carrasco, E., Loyo, E., Otaegui, O., Fösleitner, C., Dubielzig, M., Olmedo, R., Wasserburger, W., Spiller, J.: ARGUS autonomous navigation system for people with visual impairments. In: Miesenberger, K., Fels, D., Archambault, D., Peňáz, P., Zagler, W. (eds.) ICCHP 2014. LNCS, vol. 8548, pp. 100–107. Springer, Cham (2014). https://doi.org/10.1007/978-3-319-08599-9_16
8. Zhu, Y., Shareef, A.: Comparisons of three Kalman filter tracking algorithms in sensor network. In: International Workshop on Networking, Architecture, and Storages, IWNAS 2006, pp. 2–pp. IEEE, August 2006
9. Blauert, J.: Spatial Hearing (1983)

BluKane: An Obstacle Avoidance Navigation App to Assist the Visually Impaired

Adrian Als[⊠], Adrian King, Kevin Johnson, and Ramon Sargeant

University of the West Indies (Cave Hill Campus),
University Drive, Bridgetown 11000, Barbados
adrian.als@cavehill.uwi.edu

Abstract. In the Caribbean, the cost of technological aids to assist visually impaired persons with navigation is extravagant. Moreover, a recent effort by a student at the University of the West Indies (Cave Hill Campus) to develop a low-cost SmartCane solution for this vulnerable group has been met with limited success. The SmartCane system which uses an ultra-sonic device mounted on a traditional white cane communicates the proximity of objects to the user via vibrations on a Bluetooth connected mobile device. However, the lack of a user-friendly interface, for the mobile application hinders the overall user experience. This research is aimed at developing a new mobile application that will improve the user experience. Application requirements will be gathered through the administration of surveys to visually impaired members of the Barbados Association for the Deaf and Blind. The mobile application is expected to provide visually impaired individuals with assistance in navigating to their desired destinations. Moreover when the mobile device is paired with the SmartCane system users will also have the benefit of obstacle avoidance. This student-led effort to integrate this vulnerable group into society is poised to move beyond the classroom and bring greater awareness of the need for low-cost assistive technological solutions in the Caribbean region.

Keywords: Visually impaired · Obstacle avoidance · Mobile application

1 Introduction

Article 25 (1) of the United Nation's (UN) Universal Declaration of Human Rights states that "everyone has the right to a standard of living adequate for the health and well-being of himself and of his family, including food, clothing, housing and medical care and necessary social services, and the right to security in the event of unemployment, sickness, disability, widowhood, old age or other lack of livelihood in circumstances beyond his control [1]". In facilitating this right the government of Barbados has implemented several measures that aid persons with disabilities, such as providing ramps allowing for wheelchair access, having handicap spots in parking lots installed in many government and private locations and audible cues linked to pedestrian crossings at select locations. Moreover, educators have been trained to assist students with auditory and visual impairments. While this is a good start, there is still

© Springer International Publishing AG, part of Springer Nature 2018
K. Miesenberger and G. Kouroupetroglou (Eds.): ICCHP 2018, LNCS 10897, pp. 36–43, 2018.
https://doi.org/10.1007/978-3-319-94274-2_6

much that can be done. Specifically, initiatives and policies that support the use of assistive technologies (ATs) are missing from the landscape of solutions.

The Barbados Association for the Blind and Deaf (BABD) is the most active organization for the blind and deaf in Barbados. It is a non-profit organization formed through an Act of Parliament in 1957 and has a mandate to protect the welfare of the blind, visually impaired and the hearing impaired in the society. Members of the association earn monies from chair caning and mop making activities. They can also benefit from courses in English Language and Social Studies. These courses prepare the members for examinations governed by the Caribbean Examinations Council. The qualifications gained from passing these examinations can be used for matriculation purposes at tertiary level institutions. Association members may also benefit from information technology training and are taught to use the Job Access With Speech (JAWS) application and document preparation using a word processor. The ATs available to the members are primarily geared towards making electronic or print information more accessible (e.g. screen readers, large print keyboards and video magnification machines). The other class of AT includes braille watches and alerting indicators. While both classes of AT are aimed at promoting independent living there is still a void for a solution that helps with location orientation, object avoidance and independent travel.

2 Literature Review

The use of ultrasonic signals to assist the visually impaired with navigation dates back to the 1970s when Kay [2] employed sonar to aid spatial perception. This work was followed by other pioneering robotics-based obstacle avoidance systems such as the ultrasonic cane [3], NavBelt [4] and the GuideCane [5]. Within the last 5–7 years efforts were made to evolve such systems for both indoor [6] and outdoor usage [7, 8]. Many of the of these systems have are classified as either: electronic travel aids (ETAs) which aid in obstacle avoidance; electronic orientation aids (EOAs) which aid by providing orientation information; or position locator devices (PLDs) which use global positioning data to latitude and longitude data. Nieto et al. [9] provided a solution that potentially captures all three classifications however their work is focused on design and implementation and there is no mention of user-based testing. This work, though similar, focuses more on the user experience.

3 Background

Students pursuing a double major in Computer Science at the University of the West Indies (Cave Hill Campus) are required to complete a research project course. They may elect to register for one of three project courses currently offered be the discipline: Computer Science Project (4 credits); Computer Science Major Research Project (8 credits) or Computer Science Group Project (4 credits). In the first two courses, students are assigned to projects on an individual basis. Between two to four students can be assigned to a group project. The project duration for the four- and eight-credit versions of the project courses is one and two semesters (i.e. 1 academic year), respectively. All students are assessed based on their project proposals, final project report and a project presentation.

Two students taking the year-long project course elected to develop a navigation AT system for the blind and visually impaired community in Barbados. The BABD was selected as the focal point because of its mandate and its respected position in the community. The first student focused on the implementation of a low-cost ultrasonic SmartCane device which communicated with a Bluetooth enabled smartphone. The second student focused on making the mobile application user-friendly and feature rich. This work focuses on the mobile application.

4   The Study

In order to determine the Information Communication Technology (ICT) skills, the nature of their visual challenge and the requirements for the mobile application, a study was conducted with members of the BABD in November 2017. The details are outlined in the following subsections.

4.1   Participants

Eight visually challenged agreed to participate in the study. However, this number represents all of the members who were present at the time the study was conducted. Three of them were male and five were female. Twelve percent of the participants were between the ages 16 and 25; thirteen percent between the ages 26 and 35 and the remaining 75% were aged between 36 and 49 years.

4.2   Data Collection Procedures

Data was collected for this study at the National Disabilities Unit headquarters of the BABD. A convenient sample of members was selected based on their availability when two of the researchers visited the site in November 2017 to collect data. All participants were ensured of the anonymity and confidentially of the research. Since the participants of the study were visually challenged the researchers first read the questionnaire items then recorded the results after receiving the answer. These questionnaires took about fifteen minutes to complete for each participant.

4.3   The Instrument

The questionnaire inquired the demographic information of the participants, specifically age range and gender. The nature and duration of their visual challenge was also determined. Questions also queried their experience using a white cane, if they experience difficulty navigating to unfamiliar locations and their experience with using mobile applications.

4.4   Limitations

The limitation of the study was the size and bias of the sample. Although the sample selected represented less than 1% of the overall population of visually challenged people in Barbados, it represented approximately 32% of the current membership of the BABD. This sample may therefore be deemed as adequate. Bias resulted from the fact that most of the participants were members of the Barbados Association of the Blind and Deaf. This however is acceptable since the BABD is the most active association for the visually challenged in Barbados.

4.5   Survey Results

Approximately sixty-three percent of the participants were visually impaired and thirty-seven percent were totally blind. Five of the participants were visually impaired or totally blind for over twenty years. There was only one participant who recently (<4 years) became impaired. This individual is the only person who never uses a white cane for navigation and it was noted that they are partially sighted.

There was unanimous agreement that the current technologies available to assist the blind were too expensive. Seventy-five percent further reported that these technologies were easy to use. Although sixty-three percent of the participants indicated that they have trouble navigating to destinations they all agreed that navigation would be much easier if there was a software tool to assist.

All of the participants supported the idea of using a mobile app to assist in navigation/obstacle avoidance. One person preferred for navigation information to be related to the user via specific vibration patterns only whereas a second person preferred speech, the remaining seventy-five percent preferred to have both options available.

Although each participant had access to a mobile phone only fifty percent currently used smartphones. The feature phone users indicated that their aim was to eventually acquire a smartphone. The most popular applications used on the phones were Social Media (37%) and Audiobooks (25%). Navigating the applications was accomplished primarily using voice assistance (50%), accessibility mode ($\sim$%13) or special images ($\sim$13%).

4.6   Survey Discussion

Over 60% of the participants indicated that navigation was an issue. The others relied on having someone available to chauffeur them their desired destination. Whilst this support mechanism is commendable it is not ideal as they were still dependent and didn't want to become an inconvenience to their supporter. Thus, there was unanimous support for a mobile application to assist with navigation. Moreover, all of the participants had experience with mobile technology. The survey also allowed for requirements elicitation by providing insight into the necessary usability features. Based on the results of the study and the subsequent discussion it can be inferred that such an application would substantially improve the quality of life of many members of the Association. This device could potentially open the doors for a greater independence and increase social interaction. These are all desirable outcomes.

5   BluKane Android App

The Evolutionary Development Model (EDM) was employed for software development as it focuses on producing a functional product to the client in incremental builds, where each build successively adds functionality. Quality was ensured as testing was done after each software build. The iterative nature of this development model ensured that it was flexible enough to accommodate changes in the project scope. Finally, the client was involved in the software development process since they gave feedback on each increment (build). As the features of the BluKane application needed to be accurate and precise, adequate unit testing was done to ensure that each function of the program operated correctly with valid and invalid data. Moreover, user testing was done to ensure that the user experience was efficient and consistent. The usability metric for the overall application was determined using the System Usability Scale (SUS). Usability testing was done by selected members of the BABD.

5.1   Application Design

Based on the results of the study it was determined that the app would employ a simple fully assistive-enabled user interface. The three main user screens to access the text-to-speech, vibration and location modes are depicted in Fig. 1.

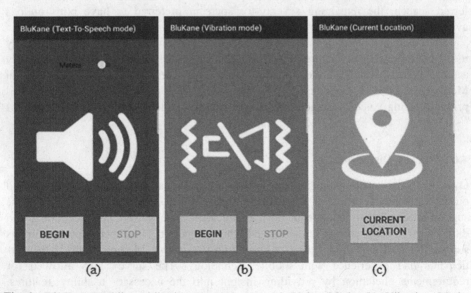

Fig. 1. BluKane mobile application user screens: (a) Voice Mode (b) Vibration Mode (c) Location Mode (Color figure online)

To assist the visually impaired each screen has a unique colour scheme. Red, yellow and green for the voice (i.e. text-to-speech), vibration and location modes, respectively. In addition, a distinct audible tone is produced on selection of each mode to assist those that are completely blind. The first two modes are employed when the application is used in conjunction with the ultrasonic SmartCane navigation device. In these modes the mobile application receives proximity information regarding the distance between the SmartCane device and an impeding object and alerts the user. In voice mode, the distance is provided in either meters or feet depending on the users' preference. In vibration mode, three unique vibration patters are used to indicate if the distance (d) is short ($d < 1.0$ m), medium ($1.0 \leq d \leq 3.0$ m) or 'far' away ($d > 3.0$).

When the current-location button from Fig. 1(c) is pressed a map showing the current location of the user is displayed on the screen as depicted in Fig. 2. The "GET PLACE" feature provides a list of five surrounding places of interest. The Euclidean distance to each location in the list can also be obtained to further assist with orientation.

Fig. 2. BluKane mobile application location screen

5.2   Usability Testing

As usability is subjective, the Systems Usability Scale (SUS) [10] was employed to provide a global view of the user-friendliness of the application. Fifteen visually impaired and totally blind members of the BABD participated in the user testing exercise. These included all of the persons who took part in the initial study and seven additional persons. The total number of testers therefore represents sixty percent of the membership of the BABD. The usability score for the application is 86.5% placing it in the top ten percent and giving it an overall A-grade.

5.3   BluKane Discussion

This work provides access to a low-cost AT navigation tool for visually impaired persons. Moreover, as both the hardware and software components were developed using local expertise there is ample opportunity for growth in this niche market within the Caribbean region. This effort represents a first in this region on many fronts. Chiefly, much of the research found in the literature has not made it to production stage and those that have are well outside of the financial reach of visually impaired persons in the Caribbean. Secondly, when the expensive equipment malfunctions, there are no local service solutions resulting in the product having to be shipped overseas for repair. Most of the literature found during this research caters to the engineering process behind the AT. This work goes further and engages with the users. Additionally, many of the articles that included testing, used sighted persons wearing blindfolds. The users of the application in this work were either visually impaired or totally blind.

All of the testers were impressed and they provided positive feedback regarding the application's purpose and functionality and the work being undertaken to assist the blind and visually impaired. The location mode received the most positive feedback. The testers noted that this mode could be used on public transport buses to provide real-time orientation information. Although this was not an intended feature it can be facilitated as this application mode works independent of the SmartCane device.

6   Conclusion

The results of this work have demonstrated that there is local expertise to create low-cost AT solutions for vulnerable groups within the Caribbean. Future works include leveraging more sensors available on the mobile device to extend the user features of the mobile application. One such example is to use the compass functionality available on the smartphone to provide the bearing information associated with each of the five places of interest identified in location mode. This would prevent totally blind users from having to make assumptions about the travelling direction towards any of the places listed. Ultimately, it is the intention of the authors to provide low-cost access to members of BABD and the wider society.

References

1. United Nations: Universal Declaration of Human Rights, 10 December 1948. http://www.un.org/en/universal-declaration-human-rights/. Accessed 21 Apr 2017
2. Kay, L.: A sonar aid to enhance spatial perception of the blind: engineering design and evaluation. Radio Electron. Eng. **44**(11), 605–627 (1974)
3. Hoydal, T., Zelano, J.: An alternative mobility aid for the blind: the 'ultrasonic cane'. In: Proceedings of the 1991 IEEE Seventeenth Annual Northeast Bioengineering Conference, Hartford, CT (1991)
4. Borenstein, J., Ulrich, I.: The guidecane—applying mobile robot technologies to assist the visually impaired. IEEE Trans. Syst. Man Cybern. Part A Syst. Hum. **31**(2), 131–136 (2001)

5. Ifukube, T., Sasaki, T., Peng, C.: A blind mobility aid modeled after echolocation of bats. IEEE Trans. Biomed. Eng. **38**(5), 461–465 (1991)
6. Fukasawa, J., Magatani, K.: A navigation system for the visually impaired an intelligent white cane. In: 34th Annual International Conference of the IEEE EMBS, Sad Diego, California (2012)
7. van der Bie, J., Visser, B., Matsari, J., Singh, M., van Hasselt, T., Koopman, J., Kröse, B.: Guiding the visually impaired through the environment with beacons. In: The 2016 ACM International Joint Conference on Pervasive and Ubiquitous Computing (UbiComp 2016), Heidelberg, Germany (2016)
8. Nada, A.A., Fakhr, M.A., Seddik, A.F.: Assistive infrared sensor based smart stick for blind people. In: 2015 Science and Information Conference (SAI), London (2015)
9. Nieto, L., Padilla, C., Barrios, M.: Design and implementation of electronic aid to blind's cane. In: 2014 III International Congress of Engineering Mechatronics and Automation (CIIMA), Cartagena (2014)
10. Sauro, J.: Measuring Usability with the System Usability Scale (SUS), 11 February 2011. http://www.measuringusability.com/sus.php. Accessed 17 Mar 2018

Conversation Aid for People with Low Vision Using Head Mounted Display and Computer Vision Emotion Detection

Rafael Zuniga and John Magee[⊠]

Clark University, Worcester, MA 01610, USA
{RZuniga,jmagee}@clarku.edu

Abstract. People with central vision loss may become unable to see facial expressions during face-to-face conversations. Nuances in interpersonal communication conveyed by those expressions can be captured by computer vision systems and conveyed via an alternative input to the user. We present a low-cost system using commodity hardware that serves as a communication aid for people with central vision loss. Our system uses a smartphone in a head-mounted-display to capture images of a conversation partner's face, analyze the face expressions, and display a detected emotion in the corner of the display where the user retains vision senses. In contrast to purpose-built devices that are expensive, this system could be made available to a wider group of potential users, including those in developing countries.

Keywords: Accessibility · Computer vision · Low-vision Head-Mounted-Display

1 Introduction

It is estimated that 285 million people are visually impaired worldwide according to the World Health Organization. Many existing interfaces that aim to help these individuals do not take into consideration that 246 million of them are categorized as having low vision. Macular degeneration is the leading cause of vision loss. This disease is caused by the deterioration of the central portion of the retina resulting in central vision loss but leaving a certain amount of peripheral vision intact. This means that we can take advantage of this little vision they have left to communicate information to them instead of immediately resorting to sound or tactile feedback. One common problem that arises from being visually impaired is not being able to see people's facial expressions as they are having a conversation with someone; leaving out many visual cues that out brain uses to have a more complete interpretation of what a person says. A rough simulation of the challenge posed by macular degeneration is shown in Fig. 1.

Here, we present one approach in which we could take advantage of the little vision a visually impaired person has left to mitigate the common problem described above. Performing Emotion Recognition Analysis with computer

© Springer International Publishing AG, part of Springer Nature 2018
K. Miesenberger and G. Kouroupetroglou (Eds.): ICCHP 2018, LNCS 10897, pp. 44–50, 2018.
https://doi.org/10.1007/978-3-319-94274-2_7

Fig. 1. Two images showing a rough simulation of how macular degeneration could obscure a large portion of the center of a person's vision, while still providing some visual information on the peripheral edges. In the top image, taken from a popular internet meme, a person is showing a strong emotion of joy. In the bottom image, the person's face is entirely obscured. Image credit: memegenerator.net, New Line Cinema

vision, we can computationally analyze the facial expressions of the person the visually impaired user is talking to and categorize them into emotions such as joy, sadness, anger, etc. We use a Head-Mounted-Display (HMD) to display the information right in the part of the eye where the user can still see. Depending on the specific user, we could use preset colors or symbols that map to a specific feeling so that the user knows what expression or emotion the person they are talking to is conveying as they say something.

An example of one of the few ventures that have tried taking advantage of this peripheral view is oxSight (Fig. 2 Left). They created their own customized Head-Mounted-Displays which performs adequately but is too expensive (Approximately $15,000). Another device, the OrCam MyEye 2.0 has a retail cost of approximately $3500 and produces audio output. 90% of the people that are visually impaired live in developing countries where this technology is completely unattainable because of financial reasons. Thanks to the rise of augmented and virtual reality, there now exists cheap Head-Mounted-Display that can have any mobile phone attached to it (Fig. 2 Right). Even in developing countries, android phone devices are widely available at prices that are affordable to the people. The phone then runs an application that uses an Emotion Recognition Analysis API that processes the frames captured from the phone's camera. This allows the phone to become a facial expression recognizer that categorizes them into its appropriate emotion. Once the phone is attached into the Head-Mounted-Display, we have the whole screen available to give information to the user directly into their available vision.

Several wearable and head-mounted technologies have been proposed as assistive devices blind or visually impaired individuals [4]. There are related work with conversation aids for people with autism [2] or aphasia [3]. Adoption of head-mounted assistive technologies nevertheless faces challenges due to the highly intrusive nature and perceived stigma [1]. Nevertheless, we hope that by developing a commodity system that is affordable to people in developing countries, this work has potential to positively impact people's lives.

2   Systems Overview

A flowchart of our system is shown in Fig. 3. A smartphone device is placed within a head-mounted display that contains a head strap and some lenses to hold the phone a short distance in front of the user's eyes. The HMD device does not contain any electronics of its own, so it is relatively inexpensive. The input to the system is the camera built into the back of the smartphone. The camera send a video stream to the computer-vision based face analysis program. Our current system is using Affectiva [5] to detect facial pose and emotion prediction scores. The output from Affectiva is then mapped to output values that the system wants to communicate to the user. These output values are sent to the user-interface generation module which produces video with the emotion and engagement encoded into a user-defined area of the display. This video is displayed on the screen of the smartphone which, as described before, is attached into the head-mounted display device.

Fig. 2. Top: OxSight's smart specs. Image credit: OxSight. Bottom: A $20 Head-Mounted-Display unit for a smartphone.

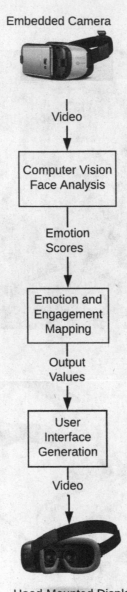

Fig. 3. System Flowchart. The core of the system is a smartphone placed within a head-mounted display. The phone's camera captures live video of the conversation partner. The video is processed by the computer vision system to produce emotion scores, which are then mapped to output values. The user interface generates video to be displayed on the screen in a location that the user still has visual acuity.

The current system recognizes smiles, anger, joy, and sadness. The head pose information is mapped to an attention score. The attention score is highest if the face in the video is looking toward the camera, whereas the score decreases if the face turns away from the camera. This score is intended to convey if the person is looking at their conversation partner. Smiling, Anger, Joy, and Sadness can be mapped to user-defined colors. The intensity of the color reflects the attention score. A screenshot of the prototype display is shown in Fig. 4.

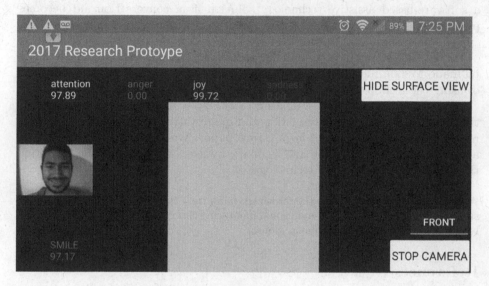

Fig. 4. Prototype system user interface displayed on a smartphone screen. (Color figure online)

3 Preliminary Evaluation

We conducted a preliminary evaluation of the system with two users who do not have visual impairments. The goal of the preliminary evaluation was to determine if the system functioned as intended. The participants took turns wearing the head-mounted display running our system. The display had the live-video feed disabled so that the person could not see the face of their conversation partner. The conversation partner would attempt to convey facial expressions of Smile, Joy, Anger, and Sadness. They would also turn their head away from the conversation at various times. At this stage, we did not yet perform a quantitative evaluation, however, in the opinion of the participants, the system was able to deliver a color-encoded emotion and attention score most of the time.

As a preliminary measure of success, the participants were able to discern the face expression emotion of their conversation partner while using the device.

4   Conclusions and Future Direction

Our proposed system successfully combines together existing techniques in a commodity device that can be deployed inexpensively to a wide range of users, including those in developing countries. Purpose-built devices may be expensive and therefore unattainable to those with economic disadvantages. Even in developing countries, relatively powerful smartphones are obtainable and affordable to the general population. By basing our system on such commodity hardware, a software-based assistive technology solution as a conversation aid becomes practical.

The most significant downside of our approach is the overly intrusive nature of the head-mounted-display with smartphones. The purpose-built devices can be made to look more like glasses, and therefore potentially reduce the stigma of using the technology.

We plan to conduct an evaluation of the system with several participants that will provide empirical evaluation and quantitative results as well as a more robust qualitative evaluation for a future paper. We also hope that we will be able to include an evaluation and feedback by users with macular degeneration that would benefit from the technology.

Acknowledgements. The authors wish to thank the Clark University undergraduate summer research program for funding and mentoring this research project. We also wish to thank the program's anonymous sponsor.

References

1. Profita, H., Albaghli, R., Findlater, L., Jaeger, P., Kane, S.K.: The AT effect: how disability affects the perceived social acceptability of head-mounted display use. In: Proceedings of the 2016 CHI Conference on Human Factors in Computing Systems, pp. 4884–4895. ACM (2016)
2. Boyd, L.E., Rangel, A., Tomimbang, H., Conejo-Toledo, A., Patel, K., Tentori, M., Hayes, G.R.: SayWAT: augmenting face-to-face conversations for adults with autism. In: Proceedings of the 2016 CHI Conference on Human Factors in Computing Systems, pp. 4872–4883. ACM (2016)
3. Williams, K., Moffatt, K., McCall, D., Findlater, L.: Designing conversation cues on a head-worn display to support persons with aphasia. In: Proceedings of the 33rd Annual ACM Conference on Human Factors in Computing Systems, pp. 231–240. ACM (2015)
4. Rector, K., Milne, L., Ladner, R.E., Friedman, B., Kientz, J.A.: Exploring the opportunities and challenges with exercise technologies for people who are blind or low-vision. In: Proceedings of the 17th International ACM SIGACCESS Conference on Computers & Accessibility, pp. 203–214. ACM (2015)
5. Affectiva. https://www.affectiva.com/. Accessed 1 Feb 2018

Indoor Guidance System for the Visual Impaired Using Beacon Sensors

Yao-ming Yeh[1(✉)] and Hung-Ju Chen[2]

[1] Kainan University, Taoyuan, Taiwan
yaomingyeh@gmail.com
[2] National Taiwan Normal University, Taipei, Taiwan

Abstract. This study aims to develop a beacon activated indoor guidance system for visual impaired persons. Based on the "Mobile Accessibility Guidelines" developed by British Broadcasting Corporation, our system provides a vocal feedback mechanism with easy touchscreen gesture design operated with mobile devices which can help instruct the visual impaired people to navigate the indoor spaces area such as department store and office. Our system uses NoSQL database, Firebase, as the backend database which uses JSON (JavaScript Object Notation) as the data exchange and storage format. The design model implemented in the system is MVC (Model-View-Control) which provides the system more maintainable and extendable. In order to provide flexible indoor space configuration in the system, we design a text-based space configuration scheme which can support the users to define a new indoor space very easily.

Keywords: Visually impaired · Beacon · Indoor guide
Mobile barrier detection

1 Research Background

According to the statistics of the international NGO "World Blind Union", there are approximately 285 million visual impaired people who are blind or have partially sighted problems globally. The statistics also shows that the population of visual impaired people is growing in Taiwan lately. The demand for developing the assisting scheme for visual impaired people in their daily life is also growing important.

Visually impaired persons encounter many difficulties and challenges when entering the unfamiliar environment. With the progress of information technologies, mobile devices may be used to provide assisted services such as voice-activated push information, location-awareness using GPS, Beacon (also called Bluetooth Low Energy, BLE), WiFi, etc. Common positioning methods, such as GPS, has the limitation that it must maintain a line of sight with the satellite system. If the user is located inside a building, he or she will not be able to use the GPS signal for any navigation services. Therefore, our objective is to explore the possibilities to use mobile devices incorporated with indoor location sensor technologies which can help visual impaired person to walk or navigate along indoor environment.

© Springer International Publishing AG, part of Springer Nature 2018
K. Miesenberger and G. Kouroupetroglou (Eds.): ICCHP 2018, LNCS 10897, pp. 51–54, 2018.
https://doi.org/10.1007/978-3-319-94274-2_8

2 Indoor Location Sensing Technologies

Sensory guidance devices were developed to help visual impaired persons using various technologies such as GPS (Global Positioning System), RFID (Radio Frequency Identification), NFC (Near Field Communication), and Beacon (also called Bluetooth Low Energy, BLE or iBeacon). According to the objectives of our research, we have listed the functions of our system based on the following important features:

1. Function to assist visually impaired persons in their orientation
2. Understand the current location
3. Information about your destination
4. Use the voice to remind you whether to deviate from the path
5. Create visually impaired mental map

We found that Beacon is much better to be used in in our research. Figure 1 shows the application scenario which can be implemented for indoor application. Beacon sensing technology is developed by Apple in 2013 based on Bluetooth Low Energy (BLE), which can provide Location Based Service (LBS). A beacon sensor will be sent every second a trace of information to any device with Bluetooth 4.0, is a one-to-many broadcast, available in iBeacon access to the following information:

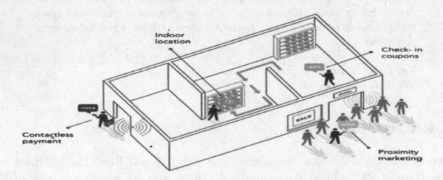

Fig. 1. Beacon indoor application scene ref: business@estimote

UUID: This is a unique ID used to distinguish between deployed areas. For example, deploy multiple iBeacons in a department store. The iBeacon UUIDs will be in the same area for the APP to recognize.

Major: In the previous example, if there was a lot of iBeacon in a department store, it would usually be classified again. There would be many floors in department stores, and in the same floor Major would be the same value.

Minor: There will be more counters on each floor in a department store. The value of Minor is the subdivision area on each floor. Each counter may be from 0 to 5 from left to right. For example, the fifth counter on the second floor, That is, Major = 2, Minor = 5.

Power (TxPower):   Used to determine how close iBeacon is.

Signal strength (Rssi):   Received signal strength indication may be unstable due to obstacles in the middle, such as walls, the human body may affect the value of the signal.

Distance: Information calculated from TxPower and Rssi

3   System Design

To help guide visually impaired persons for indoor activities, this study developed a beacon sensor based guidance services which can sense the interior space and launched a voice guidance information indoor guidance system. Provides complete gestures and voice feedback to help people with visual impairments reach their destinations on their own in an unfamiliar indoor environment. The system block diagram is shown in Fig. 2.

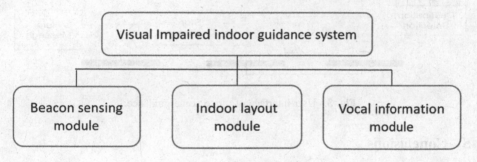

Fig. 2. System block diagram.

We develop three modules in the visual impaired indoor guidance system:

1. Beacon sensing module: This module includes the beacon sensors installed at the predetermined location along indoor scene, and the client sensing module implemented in the mobile devices.
2. Indoor layout module: This module provides the indoor layout data in each indoor scene. The data include beacon sensor's UUID and corresponding location-based information and actions to be taken when the user walks near the sensing area of office and convenient store.
3. Vocal information module: This module uses TTS (text-to-speech) which is embedded in the mobile device to push the information provided from database.

4 Accessible User Interface Design

The system uses the design concept of Model-View-Controller (MVC) to enhance the maintainability and scalability of the program. In order to support the accessible mobile interface for the mobile devices used in this guidance system, we use the "Mobile Accessibility Guidelines" developed by British Broadcasting Corporation to design accessible user interface in the mobile devices. Figure 3 shows the user interface of office scene guidance.

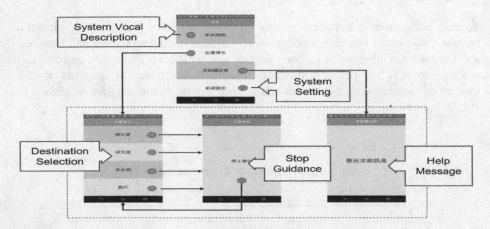

Fig. 3, User interface of office scene guidance.

5 Conclusions

In this study, beacon technology is used for indoor positioning to guide visually impaired persons to walk in an indoor environment, such as an office or a convenient store. This indoor guidance system also incorporated with voice feedback and touch screen gesture plan for visual impaired persons to access the system.

References

1. Google Inc.: Accessibility Testing Checklist (Android). http://developer.android.com
2. Apple Inc.: Verifying App Accessibility on iOS, 23 April 2013. http://developer.apple.com
3. BBC: BBC Mobile Accessibility Guidelines. http://www.bbc.co.uk/guidelines/futuremedia/accessibility/mobile

KrNet: A Kinetic Real-Time Convolutional Neural Network for Navigational Assistance

Shufei Lin [ORCID], Kaiwei Wang[(✉)], Kailun Yang, and Ruiqi Cheng

State Key Laboratory of Modern Optical Instrumentation, Zhejiang University,
Hangzhou, China
wangkaiwei@zju.edu.cn

Abstract. Over the past years, convolutional neural networks (CNN) have not only demonstrated impressive capabilities in computer vision but also created new possibilities of providing navigational assistance for people with visually impairment. In addition to obstacle avoidance and mobile localization, it is helpful for visually impaired people to perceive kinetic information of the surrounding. Road barrier, as a specific obstacle as well as a sign of entrance or exit, is an underlying hazard ubiquitously in daily environments. To address the road barrier recognition, this paper proposes a novel convolutional neural network named KrNet, which is able to execute scene classification on mobile devices in real time. The architecture of KrNet not only features depthwise separable convolution and channel shuffle operation to reduce computational cost and latency, but also takes advantage of Inception modules to maintain accuracy. Experimental results are presented to demonstrate qualified performance for the meaningful and useful applications of navigational assistance within residential and working area.

Keywords: Convolutional neural network · Scene classification
Mobile navigational assistance · Visually impaired

1 Introduction

According to the World Health Organization, 253 million people are estimated to be visually impaired and 36 million people are totally blind all over the world [1]. The most critical navigation task for people with visually impairment is to reach a destination without colliding with obstacles. Towards this end, mobile localization plays an important role beyond obstacle avoidance. In some general mobile navigational applications, the outdoor localization error is around 10 to 20 m, and it is even worse under some severe weather conditions. Visual place recognition provides valuable information to enhance situational awareness. It is important noting that the road barrier, which is designed to limit the passage of vehicles on the road, is usually set at the gate of a residential area or working area, as shown in Fig. 1. The road barrier could be taken as a sign of the entrance or exit. For visually impaired people, the difficulty in these scenarios is that the road barrier can be bypassed instead of being avoided, which is different from ordinary obstacles. Thereby, barrier recognition is clearly desirable to complement general assistance systems featuring obstacle avoidance or mobile localization.

© Springer International Publishing AG, part of Springer Nature 2018
K. Miesenberger and G. Kouroupetroglou (Eds.): ICCHP 2018, LNCS 10897, pp. 55–62, 2018.
https://doi.org/10.1007/978-3-319-94274-2_9

As is known to all, convolutional neural networks have not only achieved remarkable capabilities in both computer vision [2–4] and robotics communities [4] through years of research, but also been applied to visual place recognition [5] to enhance situational awareness. Following this line, we focus on the recognition of road barrier and dedicate to providing assistance based on CNN within specific scenarios where visually impaired people travel in daily environments, such as residential area or working area.

To address the road barrier recognition, this paper proposes a light weight and efficient convolutional neural network named KrNet. The architecture of our network, based on depthwise convolution and channel shuffle operation, has been designed to maximize its performance and keep efficiency that is suitable for real-time inference on a portable CPU. We evaluate the proposed network in navigational assistance within residential community, describing the complete applied process of our multi-sensor system to assist visually impaired people in real-world scenarios.

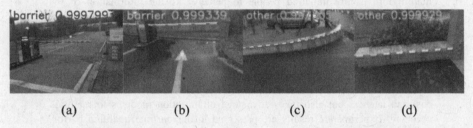

(a)   (b)   (c)   (d)

Fig. 1. Classification results in real-world scenarios. The images are classified as two classes, namely "barrier" and "other" (non-barrier), with the corresponding classification confidence value. (a) Road barrier set at the entrance of a working area. (b) Road barrier set at the entrance of an underground parking lot. (c) (d) Scenarios without road barrier are classified correctly as background even though the texture of curbs is similar to the texture of road barriers.

2 State of the Art

Recent researches on deep convolutional neural networks have concentrated on improving the classification accuracy. Benefit from large datasets (e.g. ImageNet [6]), powerful hardware and improved algorithm, AlexNet [2] eventually achieved its success in 2012. To further promote the accuracy, a straightforward way is to increase the depth and width of networks. VGGNets [7] replaces large filters with 3×3 filters but still simply stacks standard convolutional layers. GoogLeNet [8] proposes Inception module which simultaneously uses four filters with different kernel size to extract feature. ResNet [9] utilizes the bypass connection solving the notorious problem of vanishing gradients to achieve impressive performance. However, all of the networks above have large depth and size, which poses a huge challenge for deploying these deep learning algorithms on the mobile devices with limited computational resources. The compression and acceleration of CNN models have become one of the most important research fields in both academia and industry. Deep compression [10] makes use of pruning, vector quantization and Huffman encoding to compress weights.

Distilling [11] uses a larger pre-trained network and then transfers it to train a smaller network. SqueezeNet [12] is based on the Fire module which is comprised of a squeeze convolution layer and an expand layer. MobileNet [13] uses depthwise separable convolutions to reduce computational cost. A channel shuffle operation is come up with to allow input and output channels to be related with each other [14]. To the best of our knowledge, all these networks have not been used to aid visually impaired individual in navigation.

For the visually impaired, we have already presented preliminary studies related to navigational assistance. Specifically, we expand the detection range of traversable area using RealSense R200 [15], detect water hazards with a polarized RGB-Depth sensor [16], and detect pedestrian crosswalk [17] and crossing lights [18] at intersections. However, the road barrier is taken as a usual obstacle in these researches. In this paper, we include novel contributions and results to extend previous proof-of-concepts.

3 System Overview

Real-time image classification on mobile devices with limited computational resources often requires small memory footprint and rapid response. The critical issue is how to strike a judicious tradeoff between latency and accuracy. For this reason, we need to take the specific application scenario and the hardware platform into consideration. As shown in Fig. 2, our system consists of a pair of wearable smart glasses and a mobile processor (Kangaroo [19]). The pair of wearable smart glasses is integrated with a RGB-Depth sensor (RealSense R200) and a bone-conduction headphone. On one hand, RealSense R200 has high environmental adaptability [15] and delivers real-time RGB-Infrared image streams. The color image contains rich chromatic information while infrared camera provides more stable images than color camera during walking. On the other hand, its small size and light weight make it quite suitable to integrate into a pair of wearable glasses. As far as the feedback is concerned, the bone conduction headphone transfers the recognition results to visually impaired people. This is important as visually impaired people need to continue hearing environmental sound and the bone conducting interface allow them to hear a layer of augmented acoustic reality that is superimposed on the environmental sound.

In the way to destination, the mobile processor continually calculates the distance using GPS signals between the current point of interest (POI) and the destination which we have already marked. To detail this, when the distance is less than 20 m, the processor starts an image classification thread. Firstly, the camera perceives color images as the input images of KrNet. Secondly, KrNet outputs the results of image classification. Lastly, the bone-conduction headphone transfers sound to the visually impaired. Specifically, If the current images are classified as "barrier", the system will remind the visually impaired of reaching the destination. When the distance is larger than 20 m, the processor terminates the image classification thread.

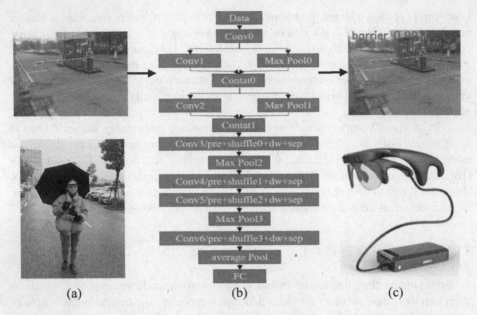

Fig. 2. Overview of the navigation system: (a) The wearable prototype. (b) The outline of the KrNet architecture from the input to the prediction. (c) The navigational assistance system consists of a pair of wearable smart glasses and a mobile processor.

4 Network Architecture

The architecture of KrNet is depicted in Table 1. The data layer takes as input a $160 \times 160 \times 3$ image. The entry module consists of a standard convolutional layer and two Inception blocks proposed by [20], which reduces the grid-size of feature maps while expands the filter banks. The convolutional layer (Conv1) and max pooling layer (Max Pool0) take the output of the first convolutional layer (Conv0) as their input concurrently and filter it with 16 kernels of size 3×3. Afterwards, the output of Conv1 and Max Pool0 are concatenated as input of the next Inception block.

Most networks use standard convolutional layers for convolution operations where every filter operates on all of input channels until Xception [21] assumes that cross-channel correlations and spatial correlations can be mapped completely separately. Xception comes up with depthwise separable convolution which replaces a full convolutional operator with a factorized version that splits convolution into two separate layers. However, it impedes information flow between different channels, which might result in the degradation of an individual convolutional filter and weaken the representation of the network. To avoid this situation, the middle of our model consists of four depthwise separable convolutional blocks whose groups are set at 4, which require less computation than standard convolutions as well as sacrifices only a small reduction in accuracy.

As shown in Fig. 3, a depthwise separable block includes a preparation pointwise convolutional layer, a shuffle layer, a depthwise convolutional layer and a separable pointwise convolutional layer. The preparation pointwise convolutional layer (GConv1) takes as input feature maps from the previous layer, reducing the channel dimension of feature maps as well as dividing the channels into 4 groups. The shuffle layer [14] reshapes, transposes and flattens the output channels to make sure that input and output channels are fully related to each other when the depthwise convolutional layer (GConv2) takes data from different groups after GConv1. Finally, the separable pointwise convolutional layer (GConv3) is used to recover the channel dimension.

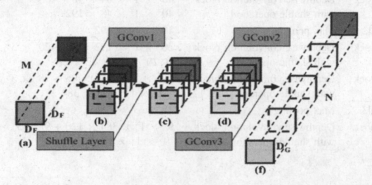

Fig. 3. (a) Input $D_F \times D_F \times M$ feature maps from the previous layer. (b) $D_F \times D_F \times 1/4$ N feature maps from GConv1. (c) $D_F \times D_F \times 1/4$ N feature maps after channel shuffle operation. (d) $D_F \times D_F \times 1/4$ N feature maps from GConv2. (f) Output $D_G \times D_G \times N$ feature maps from GConv3.

If standard convolution takes as input $h_i \times w_i \times d_i$ feature maps and applies convolutional kernel of size $k \times k \times d_j$ to produce $h_j \times w_j \times d_j$ output maps. Standard convolutional layer has the computational cost:

$$h_i \cdot w_i \cdot k \cdot k \cdot d_i \cdot d_j \tag{1}$$

Depthwise separable convolution block with shuffle operation of group 4, while each filter operates only on the corresponding input channels within same group, works almost well as regular convolutions but only cost:

$$h_i \cdot w_i \cdot d_i \cdot d_j \cdot \frac{1}{4} + h_i \cdot w_i \cdot k \cdot k \cdot d_j \cdot \frac{1}{4} + h_i \cdot w_i \cdot d_j \cdot \frac{1}{4} \cdot d_j \tag{2}$$

Our network has a computational cost of 200 million multiply-adds which is much lower than MobileNet [14]. In this regard, the efficiency is guaranteed to enable real-time inference on mobile devices.

All layers are followed by a batch normalization and a ReLU nonlinear activation function. The final average pooling reduces the spatial resolution to 1 before the Softmax loss layer. Our model was trained in Caffe CNN framework with stochastic gradient descent [22]. The dataset is available at [23]. Most of images are manual collected and resized to 320 × 240. To make the model robust against the varied types

Table 1. The outline of the proposed network architecture

Layer name	Type	Computational cost
Conv0	Standard convolution	$160^2 \times 3^2 \times 3 \times 16$
Max Pool0	Max pooling	$160^2 \times 3^2 \times 16$
Conv1	Standard convolution	$160^2 \times 3^2 \times 16 \times 16$
Max Pool1	Max pooling	$80^2 \times 3^2 \times 32$
Conv2	Standard convolution	$80^2 \times 3^2 \times 32 \times 32$
Conv3 block	Depthwise convolution block with shuffle operation	$40^2 \times 1^2 \times 64 \times 48 + 40^2 \times 3^2 \times 48 + 40^2 \times 1^2 \times 48 \times 192$
Max Pool2	Max pooling	$40^2 \times 3^2 \times 192$
Conv4 block	Depthwise convolution block with shuffle operation	$20^2 \times 1^2 \times 192 \times 72 + 20^2 \times 3^2 \times 72 + 20^2 \times 1^2 \times 72 \times 288$
Conv5 block	Depthwise convolution block with shuffle operation	$18^2 \times 1^2 \times 288 \times 96 + 18^2 \times 3^2 \times 96 + 18^2 \times 1^2 \times 96 \times 384$
Max Pool3	Max pooling	$18^2 \times 3^2 \times 384$
Conv6 block	Depthwise convolution block with shuffle operation	$9^2 \times 1^2 \times 384 \times 120 + 9^2 \times 3^2 \times 120 + 9^2 \times 1^2 \times 120 \times 480$

of images from real world, we perform a group of data augmentation including horizontally flipping, adding Gaussian noise and color jittering.

5   Experiments

We perform a set of experiments to validate the accuracy and reliability of KrNet. Table 2 shows the experimental results about the classification performance, which are qualified and satisfactory for the recognition of road barrier. In a binary classification task, true positive (TP) denotes the number of positive samples which were correctly predicted as positive. True negative (TN) denotes the number of negative samples that were correctly predicted as negative. False positive (FP) denotes the number of negative samples which were mislabeled as positive. And false negative (FN) denotes the number of positive samples that were mislabeled as negative. The accuracy for a class is the number of correctly labeled samples divided by the total number of samples as Eq. (3). The precision for a class is the number of true positives divided by the total number of samples labeled as belonging to the positives class (i.e. the sum of true positives and false positives) as Eq. (4).

$$\text{Accuracy} = \frac{TP + TN}{TP + TN + FP + FN} \tag{3}$$

$$\text{Precision} = \frac{TP}{TP + FP} \tag{4}$$

Because it might make the blind confused if misclassification happens frequently. In our work, to provide navigational assistance for people with visually impairment, more attention is paid to the accuracy and precision instead of recall rate. In real-world assistance, we calculate the weighted average classification confidence of multi-frames as the final classification confidence. The current frame has the largest weight and the weight decreases in previous fames. Besides, only if the weighted average confidence is larger than confidence threshold value which is set at 0.98, will the classification result be transferred to the visually impaired. It has been proved that classification performance with weighted average confidence is better than without weighted average confidence both in accuracy and precision. Our method enables a deep-learning-based system to execute at 10–35 fps on CPU and achieves kinetic real-time scene classification.

Table 2. Experimental results.

Model type	Without weighted average confidence		With weighted average confidence		Speed on portable PC	Speed on CPU i5-7400
	Accuracy	Precision	Accuracy	Precision		
KrNet	0.9832	0.8114	0.9949	1.000	10fps	35fps

6 Conclusion and Future Work

According to the demands of people with visually impairment, we come up with a novel CNN named KrNet. The experiments demonstrate the proposed model is effective and efficient. Future works will involve in-depth experiments regarding other scenarios, such as curbs and stairs that people with visually impairment come cross in their daily life. Moreover, the proposed KrNet will serve as whole image descriptor to extract features for visual place recognition to achieve real-time place location on mobile devices.

References

1. Bourne, R.R.A., Flaxman, S.R.: Magnitude, temporal trends, and projections of the global prevalence of blindness and distance and near vision impairment: a systematic review and meta-analysis. Lancet Glob. Health **5**, e888–e897 (2017)
2. Krizhevsky, A., Sutskever, I., Hinton, G.E.: ImageNet classification with deep convolutional neural networks. In: Advances in Neural Information Processing Systems, pp. 1–9 (2012)
3. Shelhamer, E., Long, J., Darrell, T.: Fully convolutional networks for semantic segmentation. IEEE Trans. Pattern Anal. Mach. Intell. **39**, 640–651 (2017)
4. Lin, J., Wang, W.J., Huang, S.K., Chen, H.C.: Learning based semantic segmentation for robot navigation in outdoor environment. In: 2017 Joint 17th World Congress of International Fuzzy Systems Association and 9th International Conference on Soft Computing and Intelligent Systems (IFSA-SCIS), pp. 1–5 (2017)
5. Arroyo, R., Alcantarilla, P.F., Bergasa, L.M., Romera, E.: Fusion and binarization of CNN features for robust topological localization across seasons. In: IEEE International Conference on Intelligent Robots and Systems, pp. 4656–4663 (2016)

6. Russakovsky, O., Deng, J., Su, H., Krause, J., Satheesh, S., Ma, S., Huang, Z., Karpathy, A., Khosla, A., Bernstein, M., Berg, A.C., Fei-Fei, L.: ImageNet large scale visual recognition challenge. Int. J. Comput. Vis. **115**, 211–252 (2015)

7. Simonyan, K., Zisserman, A.: Very Deep Convolutional Networks for Large-Scale Image Recognition. ImageNet Challenge, pp. 1–10 (2014)

8. Szegedy, C., Liu, W., Jia, Y., Sermanet, P., Reed, S., Anguelov, D., Erhan, D., Vanhoucke, V., Rabinovich, A.: Going deeper with convolutions. In: Proceedings of the IEEE Computer Society Conference on Computer Vision and Pattern Recognition, 7-12-NaN-2015, pp. 1–9 (2015)

9. He, K., Zhang, X., Ren, S., Sun, J.: Deep residual learning for image recognition. In: 2016 IEEE Conference on Computer Vision and Pattern Recognition (CVPR), pp. 770–778 (2016)

10. Han, S., Mao, H., Dally, W.J.: A Deep Neural Network Compression Pipeline: Pruning, Quantization, Huffman Encoding. arXiv:1510.00149 [cs], p. 13 (2015)

11. Hinton, G., Vinyals, O., Dean, J.: Distilling the knowledge in a neural network. Comput. Sci. 1–9 (2015). https://arxiv.org/abs/1503.02531

12. Iandola, F.N., Moskewicz, M.W., Ashraf, K., Han, S., Dally, W.J., Keutzer, K.: SqueezeNet. arXiv, pp. 1–5 (2016)

13. Howard, A.G., Zhu, M., Chen, B., Kalenichenko, D., Wang, W., Weyand, T., Andreetto, M., Adam, H.: MobileNets: Efficient Convolutional Neural Networks for Mobile Vision Applications. arXiv, p. 9 (2017)

14. Zhang, X., Zhou, X., Lin, M., Sun, J.: ShuffleNet: An Extremely Efficient Convolutional Neural Network for Mobile Devices. arXiv, pp. 1–10 (2017)

15. Yang, K., Wang, K., Hu, W., Bai, J.: Expanding the detection of traversable area with RealSense for the visually impaired. Sensors **16**, 1954 (2016)

16. Yang, K., Wang, K., Cheng, R., Hu, W., Huang, X., Bai, J.: Detecting traversable area and water hazards for the visually impaired with a pRGB-D sensor. Sensors **17**, 1890 (2017)

17. Cheng, R., Wang, K., Yang, K., Long, N., Hu, W.: Crosswalk navigation for people with visual impairments on a wearable device. J. Electron. Imaging **26**, 1 (2017)

18. Cheng, R., Wang, K., Yang, K., Long, N., Bai, J., Liu, D.: Real-time pedestrian crossing lights detection algorithm for the visually impaired. Multimedia Tools Appl. 1–21 (2017). https://link.springer.com/article/10.1007%2Fs11042-017-5472-5

19. Kangaroo. http://www.kangaroo.cc/kangaroo-mobile-desktop-pro

20. Szegedy, C., Vanhoucke, V., Ioffe, S., Shlens, J., Wojna, Z.: Rethinking the Inception Architecture for Computer Vision (2015)

21. Chollet, F.: Xception: Deep Learning with Separable Convolutions. arXiv Preprint arXiv: 1610.02357, pp. 1–14 (2016)

22. Kingma, D.P., Ba, J.L.: Adam: a method for stochastic optimization. In: International Conference for Learning Representations, pp. 1–15 (2015)

23. Road barrier dataset. http://www.wangkaiwei.org

Prototype Development of a Low-Cost Vibro-Tactile Navigation Aid for the Visually Impaired

Vanessa Petrausch[(✉)], Thorsten Schwarz, and Rainer Stiefelhagen

Study Centre for the Visually Impaired, Karlsruhe Institute of Technology,
Engesserstr. 4, 76131 Karlsruhe, Germany
{vanessa.petrausch,thorsten.schwarz}@kit.edu

Abstract. Vibro-tactile support for navigation tasks is helpful, not only for visually impaired people. However many different prototypes exist which are not available for experimental usage or commercial ones are expensive. We developed a low-cost prototype of a wristlet and anklet that can easily be rebuild. We evaluated them in a two step procedure with 11 and 10 participants. Both prototypes are easy to use and comfortable to wear. However, the wristlet had a high error rate so that it was not used in the second test. Comparisons between the anklet and voice guidance during navigation in the second test showed the potential of vibration for navigation tasks, but implied a refinement of the design, which will be tested in further studies.

Keywords: Vibro-tactile wristlet/anklet · Blind · Visual impaired
User study · Prototype · Navigation

1 Introduction

Navigation generally involves providing directional and environmental information to people. This includes visual markers, which play a major role in orientation. People with visual impairment do not have these navigation options, so they need to help themselves with other means, e.g. a guide dog or the classic white cane. In recent years, electronic navigation aids have been increasingly developed to assist visually impaired people. While these were initially independent systems, today the development of new assistive technologies is often focused on extending or supplementing smartphones, as they are now widely used. These systems are often based on acoustic feedback, such as spoken language or sonification. However, the problem of these issues in noisy environments is obvious, which is why haptic systems are increasingly being researched.

We developed a low-cost prototype of a wristlet and anklet to help visual impaired people during navigation tasks in their daily living. We opted for a wristlet because previous studies have shown that perception on the arm is simple and intuitive [1-3]. With directional instructions, however, there is always the

© Springer International Publishing AG, part of Springer Nature 2018
K. Miesenberger and G. Kouroupetroglou (Eds.): ICCHP 2018, LNCS 10897, pp. 63–69, 2018.
https://doi.org/10.1007/978-3-319-94274-2_10

problem of the arm position, so that right/left instructions can be misinterpreted depending on the position of the arm, e g. when carrying a handbag or the relaxed arm. For this reason, we have developed an additional ankle strap that can be worn around the ankle under the trousers. Both prototypes have been tested in a proof-of-concept study with visually impaired and sighted people for their perception of vibrations.

2   Related Work

In recent years, much research and development has been done in the area of vibro-tactile navigation support. Although many of these developments have taken place in the field of assistive technologies, the benefits of support for almost all people cannot be denied.

A wristlet called GentleGuide [1] was developed at the Dutch University of Technology. It was not only designed to navigate visually impaired people, but to navigate in unknown buildings such as a room in a hospital. The prototype is worn on both the left and right wrist and has one vibration motor per device. The detection of a certain direction therefore only depends which of the two devices vibrates. This easy recognition of the direction offers great advantages in navigation, which could be demonstrated in a practical test by the authors.

VibroTac [3] is another wristlet developed with a focus on ergonomics. It can be flexibly adapted to different arm sizes and consists of six motors, which are mounted in a plastic housing. Although the device can be attached flexibly, a problem arises with thin arm circumference, because the motors are very close to each other and the vibrations cannot be clearly distinguished. This could lead to incorrect behavior during applications. A further disadvantage is the operation via a computer, which leads to problems with a navigation application in particular, if an alternative route has to be calculated due to construction sites or non-passable roads.

With the proliferation of smartphones, some research has also been done to use built-in features, such as vibration, of the devices [4–7]. In the approach of Azenkot et al. either the navigation direction is displayed by actively moving the smartphone or the corner points indicate the direction. Peng et al. use vibration to detect obstacles. If there is an obstacle on the way, the phone vibrates. If you swing the device to the right or left, the vibration stops if the path is clear. In comparison the Cricket system from Spiers and Dollar is an external cubic device that, like the smartphone apps, uses vibrations to indicate direction. The disadvantage of most approaches is the use of the device in the hand, so that the smartphone/system has to be used actively in addition to a white cane or guide dog, which makes it difficult to handle in a real scenario. Especially in bad weather conditions such as rain or extreme cold in winter the permanent holding of a device in the hand makes it uncomfortable to use und therefore not suitable for our use cases.

In addition, there are several studies on vibration belts [8–10] or different haptic devices in combination with additional output variations or camera systems to avoid obstacles [11–13], which shows that the use of vibro-tactile feedback has potential in many areas. However, although many prototypes and studies were carried out on vibration bands, most of them did not lead to a commercially available product or the product is very expensive, so we could not use it in our studies.

3   Vibro-Tactile Wristlet and Anklet

The wireless design of both prototypes is based on a microcontroller with a Bluetooth Low Energy module (BLE) and battery. The main part consists of an Adafruit Feather, which has an integrated Bluetooth and charger module and thus bundles all components in a compact package, resulting in a design that is currently smaller than putting all components together individually. We used three Pololu shaftless vibration motors in each prototype, but integrated ones with more mass for the anklet, which results in a slightly greater vibrational force [14]. The decision to choose two different motors was made deliberately because the threshold of the two-point discrimination at the foot is greater and thus impulses are better recognized by a greater vibration force [15]. In addition, it is known that the perception at the foot decreases due to movement, which is why the higher vibration force is also advantageous here [2].

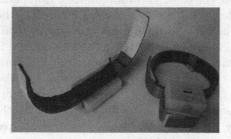

Fig. 1. Final version of both prototypes

In order to protect the components from external influences and to avoid contact with the user's skin, a 3D printer was used to develop a case that firmly encloses the electronics. The electronics were then attached to a tape, which was also produced by 3D printing. The strap is made of an elastic synthetic material and can be individually adjusted to fit different arm (14–20 cm) and leg (19–30 cm) sizes. In order to ensure an even distribution of the three vibration motors, two pockets have been installed on the sides, in which the motors can be reinserted. This ensures that the vibrations are always perceived on the right and left side, the middle one serves as a calibration point. The final design of the prototypes can be seen in Fig. 1.

Table 1. Correct assignments of vibration motors for wristlet and anklet

Prototype	Correct assignments				∅
	100%	86.67%	80%	66.67%	
Wristlet	5	3	2	1	88.67%
Anklet	11	0	0	0	100%

4   Evaluation of Vibro-Tactile Recognition and Patterns for Navigation

Several studies were conducted to evaluate the usability and usefulness of our prototypes. The focus of the first user study was a proof-of-concept test to ensure that the chosen components work together and that the vibration motors are recognized and can be distinguished. Thus, the perception, pleasing strength and duration of different vibration motors for both prototypes were evaluated. The study was taken by 11 volunteers aged 20 to 65 (7 male, 4 female), two of whom were visually impaired (age 23 and 48, both male). The entire test took an average of 30 min to complete.

The tests for wristlet and anklet were similarly structured. Initially, the participants could get used to the prototypes and adjust the intensity and duration individually for each of the three vibration motors. Comparing the intensity and duration of both prototypes it was found that intensity of the middle motor was always higher than the left and right one, which were equal in both cases. The middle duration of all motors was 0.76 s for the wristlet and 0.96 s for the anklet. The value of the anklet is due to the reduction of the duration of one participant to 0.7 s whereas all other participants chose 1 s as the optimal duration. After the adjustments, the participants had to run a straight track during which they received 15 different vibration signals one after the other. All participants walked independently, e.g. in the case of the visually impaired participants, only the white cane was used as an aid. Only one motor was switched on at once and the participants were asked to tell which motor had vibrated. These statements were later compared with the actual motors being controlled. The summary of the correct assignments of all participants for both prototypes is given in Table 1. A more detailed analysis shows that the major problem with the wristlet was the confusion of either the left or the right motor with the middle one. If the wristlet was worn on the right arm, the participants confused the left and the middle motor, while participants wearing it on the left arm confused the right and middle motor. Such problems could not be found with the anklet. For all tasks and adjustments, no differences between visually impaired and sighted persons could be detected [16]. A second study investigated the use of the anklet during navigation and object detection. The wristlet was not used for the test because of the bad recognizability and confusion of the motors. For the navigation task, 10 participants were asked to run a route of about 300 m with junctions and natural occurring objects like bicycle. During the route, there were two types of signals: Prewarnings that an instruction or object was coming and the concrete instruction at the turn-off point. The prewarning consisted of two short impulses (each 1 s with 0.5 s distance) on the side to which the bend should be made, e.g. if the next instruction was "turn left", the signal was sent to the left vibration motor. For the prewarning of an object, all three motors were activated with the before mentioned pattern. The concrete turning instruction consisted of a long signal of two seconds on the side of the instruction, in the above example on the left. The same signal was used to indicate the location of an object.

This study was carried out in the context of the TERRAIN project[1]. The aim of Terrain is to develop a portable assistance system to support the mobility of blind and visually impaired people in the inner city environment. The system combines navigation based on digital map data with camera-based image processing for object detection like obstacles, traffic lights, road crossings as well as interesting landmarks, buildings. For this purpose, a barrier-free, acoustic and haptic user interface is being developed, which can be adapted to the needs and preferences of the users. At the time of the study, navigation instructions were integrated into the self-developed app using natural language and vibration patterns. However, in order to send the signals to each user at the same time, a wizard-of-oz experiment was carried out, so that the user did not have to operate the app himself, but could concentrate entirely on the recognition of instructions. The leader of the experiment used markings on the ground (chalk marks) to trigger the prewarnings or turn directions manually using the app. As the camera-based image processing for object detection is not yet integrated, the obstacles were also triggered by the instructor.

We measured the time needed to complete the navigation task and how often participants missed a signal, did a false turn or had a collision with an obstacle, see Table 2. Comparing the results to a speech navigation on four different routes it can be seen, that there was no significant difference for the time needed. For two routes, the speech was faster, for one the anklet and for the fourth the mean time was equal for all participants. Analysing the misinterpretation, collisions or hesitations, the anklet had worse results compared to speech output. Post-experiment questions indicate, that the participants find it hard to distinguish between the prewarning of a routing instruction and obstacle warning. On the other hand, they liked the intuitive navigation instructions, since they exactly felt in which direction they need to turn, in comparison to the speech approach which troubled three participants, because two have hearing aids and one a right-left weakness. These findings can also be seen in a NASA-TLX rating for both modi which was performed afterwards. For the anklet, the values for *Mental Demand, Performance and Effort* were higher, but not significantly higher, whereas the other three were very similar.

---

[1] https://www.terrain-projekt.de/.

Table 2. Comparing performance of speech and anklet during navigation and obstacle avoidance

Parameters/modus	Speech	Anklet
Mean time [min]	04:14	04:36
Missing prewarning	1	0
Missinterpr. routing	0	5
Collision obstacle	2	4
Hesitation on signal	0	4

5   Conclusion and Future Work

The design and development of both prototypes is based on ergonomic parameters and is easy to rebuild with low-cost materials. Due to the wireless and minimalist design, both devices can be worn underneath the garment without any problems, which prevents stigmatisation on the one hand and on the other hand allows comfortable wearing. The prototypes were tested with regard to software functionality, usability and accessibility of the app and detection rate of the vibration motors. The app and prototypes were easy to use and operable by visual impaired persons. The user study of the detection rate of vibration motors showed that three motors are not suitable for the wristlet, since the middle one was often confused with either the right or left motor, depending on which arm it was worn. We consider a redesign of the wristlet with either only two motors or only one single motor, but with two wristlet for both arms. The vibrations on the anklet on the other hand were easier and no participant confused any of the motors. Nevertheless, the main problem was the difference between the prewarnings for routing instructions and object detection, so a clearer classification could lead to better performance.

In the future, we assume that user will not use the same mode for routing instructions and object detection, so that the distinction between them will no longer cause confusion. For example, it is more likely that natural language will be used for routing instructions and object recognition is indicated by vibration or vice versa. Nevertheless, it will still be possible for the user to use the same mode for both instructions in the final version of the app, if desired. Further studies, carried out this year, will still address this problem, so we expect better results for the anklet, if it is only used for one instruction mode. In addition, we will compare sonification and vibration on the abdomen with the current modes.

Acknowledgments. We would like to thank Patryk Dzierzawski for the design, development and implementation of the first study of the two prototypes.

References

1. Bosman, S., Groenendaal, B., Findlater, J.W., Visser, T., de Graaf, M., Markopoulos, P.: GentleGuide: an exploration of haptic output for indoors pedestrian guidance. In: Chittaro, L. (ed.) Mobile HCI 2003. LNCS, vol. 2795, pp. 358–362. Springer, Heidelberg (2003). https://doi.org/10.1007/978-3-540-45233-1_28
2. Dim, N.K., Ren, X.: Investigation of suitable body parts for wearable vibration feedback in walking navigation. Int. J. Hum-Comput. Stud. **97**, 34–44 (2017)
3. Schätzle, S., Ende, T., Wüsthoff, T., Preusche, C.: Vibrotac: an ergonomic and versatile usable vibrotactile feedback device. In: RO-MAN, 2010 IEEE, pp. 670–675. IEEE (2010)
4. Azenkot, S., Ladner, R.E., Wobbrock, J.O.: Smartphone haptic feedback for nonvisual wayfinding. In: The Proceedings of the 13th International ACM SIGACCESS Conference on Computers and Accessibility, pp. 281–282. ACM (2011)
5. Peng, E., Peursum, P., Li, L., Venkatesh, S.: A smartphone-based obstacle sensor for the visually impaired. In: Yu, Z., Liscano, R., Chen, G., Zhang, D., Zhou, X. (eds.) UIC 2010. LNCS, vol. 6406, pp. 590–604. Springer, Heidelberg (2010). https://doi.org/10.1007/978-3-642-16355-5_45
6. Jacob, R., Winstanley, A., Togher, N., Roche, R., Mooney, P.: Pedestrian navigation using the sense of touch. Comput. Environ. Urban Syst. **36**(6), 513–525 (2012)
7. Spiers, A.J., Dollar, A.M.: Outdoor pedestrian navigation assistance with a shape-changing haptic interface and comparison with a vibrotactile device. In: Haptics Symposium (HAPTICS), 2016 IEEE, pp. 34–40. IEEE (2016)
8. Erp, J.B.F.V., Veen, H.A.H.C.V., Jansen, C., Dobbins, T.: Waypoint navigation with a vibrotactile waist belt. ACM Trans. Appl. Percept. **2**(2), 106–117 (2005)
9. Ross, D.A., Blasch, B.B.: Wearable interfaces for orientation and wayfinding. In: Proceedings of the Fourth International ACM Conference on Assistive Technologies, pp. 193–200. ACM (2000)
10. Tsukada, K., Yasumura, M.: ActiveBelt: belt-type wearable tactile display for directional navigation. In: Davies, N., Mynatt, E.D., Siio, I. (eds.) UbiComp 2004. LNCS, vol. 3205, pp. 384–399. Springer, Heidelberg (2004). https://doi.org/10.1007/978-3-540-30119-6_23
11. Flores, G., Kurniawan, S., Manduchi, R., Martinson, E., Morales, L.M., Sisbot, E.A.: Vibrotactile guidance for wayfinding of blind walkers. IEEE Trans. Haptics **8**(3), 306–317 (2015)
12. Kammoun, S., Jourais, C., Guerreiro, T., Nicolau, H., Jorge, J.: Guiding blind people with haptic feedback. In: Frontiers in Accessibility for Pervasive Computing (Pervasive 2012) (2012)
13. Scheggi, S., Talarico, A., Prattichizzo, D.: A remote guidance system for blind and visually impaired people via vibrotactile haptic feedback. In: 2014 22nd Mediterranean Conference of Control and Automation (MED), pp. 20–23. IEEE (2014)
14. Pololu Robotics and Electronics. https://www.pololu.com/product/1636. Accessed 01 2018
15. Alzheimer, C., Deetjen, P.: Physiologie: mit ... 88 Tabellen plus CD-ROM mit Prüfungsfragen und allen Abbildungen. Elsevier, Urban & Fischer (2007)
16. Dzierzawski, P.: Prototypische Entwicklung einer vibro-taktilen Navigationsunterstützung für Sehgeschädigte (2017)

Stereo Vision Based Distance Estimation and Logo Recognition for the Visually Impaired

Mehmet Biberci[✉] and Ulug Bayazit

Department of Computer Engineering,
Istanbul Technical University, Istanbul, Turkey
{biberci,ulugbayazit}@itu.edu.tr

Abstract. Interpreting images to compute properties of the 3D world is a significant matter of computer vision. Therefore computer vision applications can help people requiring assistance. This paper presents a novel stereo-vision-based perception and navigation approach to assist visually impaired people. Frontal view images of stores in a shopping mall are first searched for logo recognition. Distances to the found logos (store signboards) are estimated by stereo matching. Both logo recognition and stereo matching are based on local image features (keypoint descriptors) calculated via Speeded Up Robust Features (SURF) algorithm. Final refined distances are calculated via statistical filtering and averaging of the individual keypoint distances found by matched keypoint pairs. Experimental results on our self generated stereo dataset of 28 storefront images from various distances and viewpoints demonstrate the performance of the proposed approach.

Keywords: Stereo vision · SURF · Logo recognition
Distance estimation · Blind navigation

1 Introduction

Vision is a key factor in perceiving and navigating through the environment. Visual impairment limits the information flow about the surroundings and restricts these activities, causing inconvenience and disadvantage. Computer vision provides the means to substitute eyesight, thus restoring the missing visual information. Stereo vision algorithms are ideally suited for inferring 3D spatial knowledge and compensate for the human binocular visual system.

Featuring symbols and text, signboards are prominent elements of orientation and navigation, especially in unfamiliar environments. Hence, signboard recognition combined with 3D spatial information facilitates access to the destination. Shopping mall is an example of an indoor environment where we need directions. As we desire to access particular stores, we identify them on their logos to set our target and path. Visual impairment causes a major disadvantage in this respect,

© Springer International Publishing AG, part of Springer Nature 2018
K. Miesenberger and G. Kouroupetroglou (Eds.): ICCHP 2018, LNCS 10897, pp. 70–77, 2018.
https://doi.org/10.1007/978-3-319-94274-2_11

yet can be compensated by computer vision methods, and more specifically in our context by logo recognition.

In the past decade, computer vision algorithms and digital cameras have advanced substantially enabling convenient application in assistive technologies, which are now also available on smartphones. Recent research is focused on 3D vision for obstacle avoidance and detection/recognition algorithms for objects, landmarks, signs, and text. However, merging stereo vision with robust object recognition algorithms for blind navigation is at an early stage. Furthermore, store logo/signboard recognition and accessing to stores have not been introduced in any work related to facilitating assistance to the visually impaired.

We propose a stereo vision based approach to estimate distances to stores in a shopping mall alongside logo recognition. The main objective is to detect and give directions to points of interest, which happen to be stores in this case. As the primary contribution, SURF [1] keypoint matching method is employed for both logo recognition and stereo correspondence matching where distance estimations involve geometric calculations and refinements. Towards this end, a stereo dataset of storefront images with ground-truth distances is collected.

Although developed and tested with stationary digital cameras mounted on a tripod, our approach is also intended to be implemented on qualified smartphones. As smartphones are becoming equipped with multiple cameras, they may run our method to assist the visually impaired, eliminating the need for an extra device.

The rest of the paper is organized as follows. Section 2 gives an overview on the previous work. The details of the proposed method and theoretical framework is described in Sect. 3. Experimental setup and results are presented in Sect. 4. Finally, the paper is concluded by proposing extensions to be investigated in future work.

2   Related Work

Computer vision and image processing techniques aiming to provide visual data through auditory and haptic interfaces have been utilized in portable blind assistance systems since early 1990s.

The vOICe [7] is an image-to-sound conversion system introduced by Meijer, which scans images from left to right for sound generation. Frequency is a function of pixel row, where lower pixels have lower frequency while amplitude denotes pixel intensity. Processing all the columns results in a sequential superimposed audio signal.

Molton et al. [8] described a portable stereo vision-based obstacle detection system as a part of their Autonomous System for Mobility, Orientation, Navigation and Communication (ASMONC) project, where the user wears a backpack holding two cameras and other components. The system represents the ground plane with initial stereo disparity values and predicts the disparities for the following images as the user walks. Obstacles contradict the predicted disparities and are thereby detected. Kalman Filter is used when modeling the walking movement.

Zelek et al. [11] developed a prototype system featuring a dual camera setup and a tactile feedback glove. Images from the two cameras are used to calculate a depth map. The depth map is then divided into five vertical regions and each region is encoded as a vibration on the tactile unit, which happens to be a glove with pager motors attached to each finger.

SmartVision [5] navigation assistance system intends to incorporate a geographical information system with a stereo vision system. Its main objective is to help visually impaired people to navigate in unfamiliar environments as well as giving contextual information about obstacles and points-of-interest. The visual system uses Hough Transform to detect circular landmarks, which represent safe paths in the experiments. Trajectory angle is calculated based on the location of the detected circles. Providing distance information from the stereo camera is stated as a future integration work. In the follow-up project Blavigator [4], range image segmentation is utilized to detect obstacles in 1 m or 2 m proximity.

Wang and Tian [10] proposed a method for detecting and recognizing restroom signs. Image regions containing signage are detected by comparing shape information of the connected components. The head part, modelled as a circle, has an approximate perimeter-to-area ratio. The body part is detected based on the relations to the head part. The detected signs are then recognized by SIFT [6] feature matching.

Schauerte et al. [9] presented an assistive vision system to find displaced objects. Specific textured objects are detected using SIFT feature matching, while a color-based approach is used to extend the detection capability towards a broader range. The objective is to guide the user's hand to the object locations through acoustic feedback. A small hand-held camera, which can also be attached to the wrist, facilitates hands-free movement. The object location is encoded as sound, of varying pan and pitch.

The Sound of Vision system [3] introduces a sensory substitution device employing data fusion. The system comprises of a stereo camera, an IR-based depth camera and an inertial measurement unit (IMU) to provide depth information in any environment at any illumination condition. Stereo stream along with IMU sensor enables 3D environment representation. Ground plane detection and object segmentation are also performed. The system further identifies doors, stairs, signs, and text through edge/line detection, support vector machine (SVM) classification, and optical character recognition (OCR).

3   Proposed Method

Our method makes use of calibrated camera parameters and trained logo images. Stereo images are first converted to grayscale and rectified using the camera parameters. The left image is queried against the trained logos using SURF keypoint descriptor matching. Through image homography, the bounding box of the logo is calculated, which defines the search region in the right image for stereo matching, where again SURF keypoint descriptor matching is employed. Disparity values of the keypoints along with camera parameters enable calculation of the 3D coordinates, hence the distances. The mean and standard deviation of the distances are utilized to filter possible outliers, allowing a more accurate distance estimation. Figure 1 shows an overview of the proposed method.

We make the following assumptions for an efficient implementation of the method. Firstly, camera is not tilted and store signboards are situated overhead. Thus only the upper half of the images are searched for logos. Secondly, signboards have a rectangular/planar shape and upright orientation, so there is no need to consider rotation during recognition. Since signboards are usually located above the entrances of the stores, they are used as targets when calculating distance and directions.

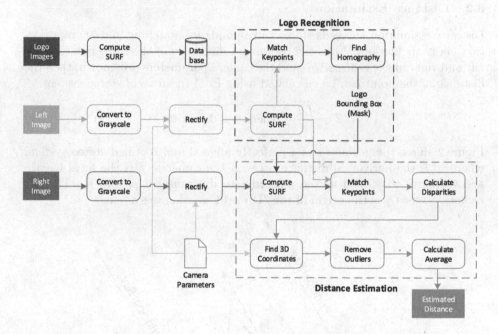

Fig. 1. Flowchart of the proposed method

3.1 Logo Recognition

Logo recognition employs SURF, which is a widespread approach in object recognition due its robustness. First step is the keypoint detection, where the image is searched at different scales of the image pyramid. Blobs and corners are appropriate candidates in this sense, since they are likely to be found in different images of a particular object. SURF uses a blob detector based on Hessian matrix and box filters to speed up keypoint detection. Second step is the calculation of the descriptors. The SURF descriptor of each keypoint is generated using horizontal and vertical Haar Wavelet responses of the region around the keypoint. These wavelet responses indicate significant changes in horizontal and vertical directions. The resulting descriptor is a 128-dimensional vector.

SURF descriptors of the logo images are calculated beforehand and stored in the logo database. When a query image is searched for logos, the same descriptor calculation is performed. Keypoints of the query image are matched with logo keypoints based on the Euclidean distance of the descriptors. In order to avoid false matches, a ratio test is applied as suggested in [6]. The matching process returns two nearest matches for each keypoint. If the ratio of nearest-distance to the second-nearest-distance is above a threshold, the match is rejected. After this filtering, remaining point correspondences are used to estimate the image homography and find the bounding box of the logo.

3.2   Distance Estimation

Distance estimation succeeds stereo correspondence matching and 3D reprojection via triangulation. When the coordinate difference of the same point on the left and right images -*disparity*- and the camera parameters are known, then the distance of the point can be calculated using Eq. 1 in an *ideal* stereo system.

$$Z = \frac{f \cdot T}{d} \quad \text{where } d \text{ is disparity} \tag{1}$$

Figure 2 shows the geometry of a perfectly aligned and rectified stereo system, where T is the horizontal distance between the cameras, f is the focal length, and disparity is defined as the x-coordinate difference of p_l and p_r. The left camera center O_l is the origin of the 3D world coordinate system.

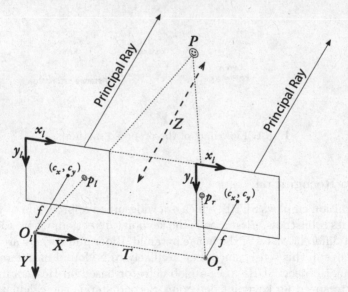

Fig. 2. Stereo geometry [2]

Both left and right images are rectified and aligned to eliminate lens distortions to realize an ideal stereo system before proceeding with SURF. Keypoints and SURF descriptors of the right image are calculated on a restricted area defined by the logo bounding box found in the recognition step. Keypoint matching between the left and right image is accomplished using the same methodology above. The resulting point correspondences enable calculation of disparity values. Using camera parameters and disparities, 3D coordinates of the keypoints are calculated. Since there may be mismatches and miscalculations, the points not satisfying the following condition (outliers) are filtered out:

$$\mu - \sigma \leq P_Z \leq \mu + \sigma$$

where μ is the mean and σ is the standard deviation of the distances P_Z. Averaging over the remaining points yields the estimated distance. The direction angle can be estimated geometrically by dividing the average of P_X values (X coordinates) by the estimated distance, as the 3D world coordinates are relative to the left camera center.

4   Experimental Results

In order to evaluate the performance of the proposed method, we generated a stereo dataset of frontal store images. Two digital compact cameras are mounted on a bracket side by side and attached to a tripod. Making sure that the stereo rig is parallel to the ground, frontal images of 11 stores are captured from various distances and viewpoints, resulting in 28 stereo pairs. For each image pair, ground truth distance is measured with a laser rangefinder while registering the stereo rig location. Figure 3 shows the experimental setup.

Fig. 3. Stereo rig and the laser rangefinder

In the resulting dataset, store distances range from 5.48 to 14.63 m whereas the camera yaw angle varies from −45 to 45°. We evaluated the logo recognition performance and distance estimation accuracy of the proposed method. Our method can recognize logos *en face* and handle camera yaw variations up to 30°. The recognition fails if the logo has an apparent 3D structure and the camera yaw is above 30°, which is the case with one particular store. The average error in estimated distances is 12%, corresponding to 1.2 m as the average ground truth distance is 10 m. Detailed estimation results can be seen in Table 1. Estimation errors in the experiments are likely caused by the focus incoordination of the cameras. Sample stereo matching after a successful logo recognition is shown in Fig. 4.

Table 1. Distance estimation accuracy

Logo	Yaw [°]	Distance [m]	Error	Yaw [°]	Distance [m]	Error	Yaw [°]	Distance [m]	Error
Lacoste	0	12.86	15%	-	−	-	-	−	-
Starbucks	0	9.95	8%	30	14.03	1%	-	−	-
W	0	5.48	12%	45	7.61	12%	-	−	-
Altinyildiz	0	11.20	6%	30	11.67	25%	-	−	-
English home	30	9.10	4%	45	9.10	21%	-	−	-
Derimod	0	8.28	3%	−15	8.70	9%	-	−	-
Inci	0	7.91	8%	−30	10.29	2%	30	9.06	32%
Roman	0	8.32	12%	−45	9.79	8%	−30	9.79	19%
Accesorize	0	8.85	25%	−45	10.16	1%	−15	10.16	1%
Dagi	0	9.02	19%	−30	10.04	20%	−15	10.04	25%
Boyner	0	13.16	16%	−30	14.63	6%	−15	14.63	4%

Fig. 4. Stereo matching on rectified images

5   Conclusion

Logo recognition with stereo vision can assist the visually impaired to navigate more easily in an unfamiliar environment. Robust algorithms can handle variations and recognize logos in most instances. As the experimental results demonstrate, our method achieves a reasonable distance estimation accuracy. A finer calibration and alignment e.g. factory calibrated stereo rig and coordinated focusing of the cameras will improve the accuracy. Further integration with a text-to-speech engine can create a convenient navigation aid.

References

1. Bay, H., Tuytelaars, T., Van Gool, L.: SURF: speeded up robust features. In: Leonardis, A., Bischof, H., Pinz, A. (eds.) ECCV 2006. LNCS, vol. 3951, pp. 404–417. Springer, Heidelberg (2006). https://doi.org/10.1007/11744023_32
2. Bradski, G., Kaehler, A.: Learning OpenCV: Computer Vision with the OpenCV Library. O'Reilly Media, Inc., Sebastopol (2008)
3. Caraiman, S., Morar, A., Owczarek, M., Burlacu, A., Rzeszotarski, D., Botezatu, N., Herghelegiu, P., Moldoveanu, F., Strumillo, P., Moldoveanu, A.: Computer vision for the visually impaired: the sound of vision system. In: Proceedings of the IEEE Conference on Computer Vision and Pattern Recognition, pp. 1480–1489 (2017)
4. Costa, P., Fernandes, H., Martins, P., Barroso, J., Hadjileontiadis, L.J.: Obstacle detection using stereo imaging to assist the navigation of visually impaired people. Procedia Comput. Sci. **14**, 83–93 (2012)
5. Fernandes, H., Costa, P., Filipe, V., Hadjileontiadis, L., Barroso, J.: Stereo vision in blind navigation assistance. In: 2010 World Automation Congress (WAC), pp. 1–6. IEEE (2010)
6. Lowe, D.G.: Distinctive image features from scale-invariant keypoints. Int. J. Comput. Vision **60**(2), 91–110 (2004)
7. Meijer, P.B.: An experimental system for auditory image representations. IEEE Trans. Biomed. Eng. **39**(2), 112–121 (1992)
8. Molton, N., Se, S., Brady, J., Lee, D., Probert, P.: A stereo vision-based aid for the visually impaired. Image Vis. Comput. **16**(4), 251–263 (1998)
9. Schauerte, B., Martinez, M., Constantinescu, A., Stiefelhagen, R.: An assistive vision system for the blind that helps find lost things. In: Miesenberger, K., Karshmer, A., Penaz, P., Zagler, W. (eds.) ICCHP 2012. LNCS, vol. 7383, pp. 566–572. Springer, Heidelberg (2012). https://doi.org/10.1007/978-3-642-31534-3_83
10. Wang, S., Tian, Y.: Camera-based signage detection and recognition for blind persons. In: Miesenberger, K., Karshmer, A., Penaz, P., Zagler, W. (eds.) ICCHP 2012. LNCS, vol. 7383, pp. 17–24. Springer, Heidelberg (2012). https://doi.org/10.1007/978-3-642-31534-3_3
11. Zelek, J.S., Bromley, S., Asmar, D., Thompson, D.: A haptic glove as a tactile-vision sensory substitution for wayfinding. J. Vis. Impair. Blind. **97**(10), 621–632 (2003)

Intersection Navigation for People with Visual Impairment

Ruiqi Cheng⬥, Kaiwei Wang$^{(\boxtimes)}$, and Shufei Lin

State Key Laboratory of Modern Optical Instrumentation, Zhejiang University,
Hangzhou, China
wangkaiwei@zju.edu.cn

Abstract. Utilizing RGB-Depth images acquired by a wearable system, we propose an integrated assistive navigation for visually impaired people at urban intersection, which provides with crosswalk position (where to cross roads), crossing light signal (when to cross roads) and pedestrian state (whether safe to cross roads). Verified by the experiment results on datasets and in field, the proposed approach detects multiple targets at urban intersections robustly and provides visually impaired people with effective assistance.

Keywords: Crosswalk detection · Crossing light detection
Pedestrian detection · Assistive technology

1 Introduction

Lacking the capability to sense ambient environments effectively, visually impaired people always feel inconvenient and encounter various dangers, especially when crossing roads. In urban areas, intersections are ubiquitous, and not all of them are equipped with auxiliary devices. Thereby, perceiving urban intersection scenes is of vital importance for visually impaired people.

On the customized wearable system Intoer [1], we have implemented zebra crosswalk and pedestrian crossing light detection algorithm under challenging scenarios [2, 3]. Nevertheless, the two separate utilities do not provide visually impaired people with comprehensive assistance. In this paper, we propose an integrated assistive navigation for visually impaired people at urban intersection (see Fig. 1), which provides with crosswalk position (where to cross roads), crossing light signal (when to cross roads) and pedestrian state (whether safe to cross roads). The contributions of the novel assistive navigation are three-fold:

- Multiple targets at urban intersections are detected, which verifies mutually the detection results of individual object with each other and provides with comprehensive and accurate assistive navigation.
- RGB-Depth images are utilized for detection, which not only improves detection precision compared with mere RGB images, but also conveys the distance of detected objects to visually impaired people.

© Springer International Publishing AG, part of Springer Nature 2018
K. Miesenberger and G. Kouroupetroglou (Eds.): ICCHP 2018, LNCS 10897, pp. 78–85, 2018.
https://doi.org/10.1007/978-3-319-94274-2_12

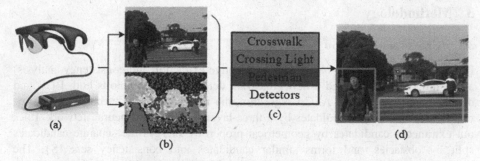

Fig. 1. The overview of intersection navigation. (a) The customized wearable system for assistive navigation: Intoer. (b) An RGB image and a depth image captured by the system. (c) The proposed intersection assistance, which consists of the crosswalk detector, the crossing light detector and the pedestrian detector. (d) The detection results of crosswalk (denoted by green), crossing light (denoted by red) and pedestrian (denoted by blue). (Color figure online)

- The effective interactive approach instructs the visually impaired people to find the exact starting position of crosswalk, to perceive what the state of crossing light is, and to confirm whether other pedestrians are crossing roads.

2   State of the Art

Most of researches were dedicated to detect merely one of landmarks at intersections, such as zebra crosswalks or pedestrian crossing lights. Generally, zebra crosswalks are detected by utilizing the characteristics of crosswalks: linear edge [4, 5], periodical pattern [6, 7] or bright stripe [8]; crossing lights are detected by template matching [9] or image analysis [10, 11].

Several works tried to combine crosswalk with crossing light detection. Shioyama et al. [12] came up with one of earliest intersection assistance algorithms which consists of crosswalk and crossing light detection. Using the conventional analytic image processing, the algorithm detects crossing lights in near-view images, where the light takes a dominant portion and no crosswalk exists, hence crossing lights and crosswalks are not detected simultaneously. Wei et al. [13] proposed a guide-dog robot which assembles template matching-based crossing light detection and Hough transform-based crosswalk detection, but the system is tested simply in one scenario, so the robustness under various situations is not guaranteed. Using similar detection algorithm, Wang et al. [14] proposed intersection assistance based on RGB-Depth images, which is designed specifically for US crossing lights.

To the best of our knowledge, none of the proposed intersection navigation assembles comprehensive utilities, including crosswalk, crossing light and pedestrian detection. Based on our preliminary researches of crosswalk [2] and crossing light [3] detection, we propose a unified intersection assistance that detects crosswalks, crossing lights and pedestrians to help visually impaired people.

3 Methodology

3.1 Crosswalk Detection

Derived from RGB image-based AECA (adaptive extraction and consistency analysis) algorithm [2], we proposed a new crosswalk detector which exploits both RGB and depth images. Same with AECA algorithm, the new crosswalk detector extracts primary crosswalk stripe candidates by a three-layer feed-forward neural network, rules out extraneous candidates by geometrical properties, merges the separate candidates split by obstacles, and forms similar candidates into consistency sets {S}. The improvement of the proposed detector beyond AECA lies in adding depth information into consistency analysis. Apart from the four variances of consistency set (D_1, D_2, D_3 and D_4) [2], depth-wise variance D_5 (as defined in Eq. 1) is also considered, which denotes variance of depth among candidates.

$$D_5 = \frac{1}{N} \sum_{0 < r < N} (Z_r - Z_r')^2 \tag{1}$$

Z_r represents the depth of r-th stripe in the set S. Herein, instead of mean depth of all candidates, Z_r' is utilized to measure the dispersion of set, because the depth values of stripes have intrinsic dispersion. The dispersion relation is expressed by a linear model (see Eq. 2), where the parameters (e and f) are fitted by least square method using the depth and y-axis coordinate of candidates.

$$Z_r' = ey_r + f \tag{2}$$

Finally, the optimal consistency set S*, which is with smallest overall variance, is taken as crosswalk detection result, and the position and orientation of the crosswalk are also obtained.

3.2 Crossing Light and Pedestrian Detection

In order to promote the detection performance of crossing lights, we add sliding window algorithm and renewed SVM classifier to the previous crossing light detection algorithm. The color segmentation-based candidate extraction does not distinguish the cross lights from the background with similar color, and tends to merge them together, which results in the low recall of crossing lights. Therefore, for those candidates that are classified as negative, sliding windows and SVM classifier are applied to detect crossing lights again. Finally, temporal-spatial analysis guarantees stable detection results by comparing recognition results in current frame with those in former frames.

In the same way, the sliding windows and the SVM classifier with pre-trained data [15] are also used to detect pedestrians. The depth images are taken advantage of to further choose pedestrian detections with reasonable three-dimensional size. The similar temporal-spatial analysis is applied to pedestrian detection to achieve pedestrian tracking, and obtain whether the pedestrian is approaching, leaving or static.

3.3   Interactive Paradigm

The intersection navigation with multiple detectors provides comprehensive assistive utilities, which includes finding the starting point of crosswalks, perceiving the state of crossing lights and sensing the pedestrians' walking direction. The system detects the crosswalks at a distance from users (Fig. 2a, b) and instruct users to walk towards the starting point of crosswalks. Then the system detects crosswalks, crossing lights and pedestrians after aligning user with crosswalks (Fig. 2c).

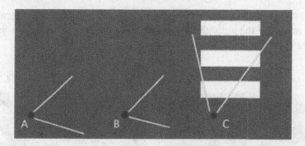

Fig. 2. The schematics of intersection navigation. The green point denotes the position of the user, and the yellow line denotes the horizontal field of view of the camera. (Color figure online)

During instructing visually impaired people to align with crosswalks, the voice prompts are used to inform users of walking forward, turning right or turning left [2]. At the starting point of crosswalks, if the crossing light is green, the beeping sound is conveyed to users, which means the system determines that it is safe to crossroad. At crowding intersections where crosswalks are obscured by pedestrians, the detected approaching or leaving pedestrians are utilized to inform the user that it is safe to cross the roads.

4   Results

In this section, the effective and robust performance of intersection navigation is verified by field tests. At first, we evaluate the detection performance of crosswalk, crossing light and pedestrian detectors separately. Then, the interactive approach is also tested in practical scenarios.

In view that most public datasets concerning urban intersections do not contain depth images, the three detectors are tested through RGB-Depth images captured by ourselves in Hangzhou city, China. The crosswalk detector are compared with our previous detector [2] and bipolarity-based algorithm [6]. As presented in Fig. 3(a), the crosswalks are detected correctly. The newly proposed crossing light detector is compare with the previous detector that proposed in [3]. As shown in Fig. 4(a), the crossing light whose color resembles its background is no longer omitted. As shown in Fig. 5(a) and (c), the distance of pedestrians are obtained, and the false detections of pedestrian are ruled out by the newly-proposed detector, compared with the detector proposed in [15]. Therefore, the proposed detectors are superior to the state of the art and our former detectors.

Fig. 3. The crosswalk detection results of newly-proposed algorithms (see green rectangles in a) and the detection results of the algorithm proposed in [2] (see green rectangles in b) and [6] (see white blocks in c). (Color figure online)

Fig. 4. The crossing light detection results of newly-proposed algorithms (see a) and the detection results of the algorithm proposed in [3] (see b).

Fig. 5. The pedestrian detection results of newly-proposed algorithms (see a and c) and the detection results of the algorithm proposed in [15] (see b and d).

In order to verify the algorithms comprehensively, we test the intersection navigation algorithm in both practical and challenging scenarios. On the customized wearable system Intoer, our algorithm achieves a speed of approximately 200 ms to process one frame. The detection results of the three detectors are shown as Fig. 6.

Fig. 6. The detection results of three detectors of intersection navigation. The pedestrian is labeled with blue rectangles and its distance to the user (in meters). The stripes of crosswalk are labeled with green rectangles. The red or green crossing lights are labeled with red or green tags, respectively. (Color figure online)

Even under severe weather conditions, our algorithms detect crosswalks or crossing lights, as presented in Fig. 7. For verifying the proposed interactive paradigm, a subject with the blindfold is invited to perform field tests at six intersections. At five intersections, the subject manages to reach the starting point of crosswalks. At all intersections, the subject identifies the state of crossing lights correctly.

Fig. 7. The crosswalk and crossing light detection results under conditions of severe weather, such as snow (see a, b and c) and rain (see d and e)

5 Conclusion

In this paper, we put up with a comprehensive intersection navigation approach and implement it on the wearable device - Intoer. The experiments carried out in various scenarios demonstrate the proposed algorithm is robust and effective in practical use. In the future, we will continue to promote the performance of intersection navigation. Deep learning is planned to be utilized to achieve higher detection accuracy for crosswalks, crossing lights and pedestrians. Moreover, the intersection navigation at night is also to be studied.

References

1. KrVision: Intoer: auxiliary glasses for people with visual impairments (in Chinese). http://www.krvision.cn/cpjs/
2. Cheng, R., Wang, K., Yang, K., Long, N., Hu, W., Chen, H., Bai, J., Liu, D.: Crosswalk navigation for people with visual impairments on a wearable device. J. Electron. Imaging **26**, 53025 (2017)
3. Cheng, R., Wang, K., Yang, K., Long, N., Bai, J., Liu, D.: Real-time pedestrian crossing lights detection algorithm for the visually impaired. Multimed. Tools Appl. 1–21 (2017). https://link.springer.com/article/10.1007%2Fs11042-017-5472-5

4. Mascetti, S., Ahmetovic, D., Gerino, A., Bernareggi, C.: ZebraRecognizer: pedestrian crossing recognition for people with visual impairment or blindness. Pattern Recogn. **60**, 405–419 (2016)
5. Shangguan, L., Yang, Z., Zhou, Z., Zheng, X., Wu, C., Liu, Y.: CrossNavi: enabling real-time crossroad navigation for the blind with commodity phones. In: Proceedings of the 2014 ACM International Joint Conference on Pervasive and Ubiquitous Computing, pp. 787–798. ACM Press, New York (2014)
6. Uddin, M.S., Shioyama, T.: Bipolarity and projective invariant-based zebra-crossing detection for the visually impaired. In: 2005 IEEE Computer Society Conference on Computer Vision and Pattern Recognition (CVPR 2005) – Workshops, pp. 22–22. IEEE (2005)
7. Poggi, M., Nanni, L., Mattoccia, S.: Crosswalk recognition through point-cloud processing and deep-learning suited to a wearable mobility aid for the visually impaired. In: Murino, V., Puppo, E., Sona, D., Cristani, M., Sansone, C. (eds.) ICIAP 2015. LNCS, vol. 9281, pp. 282–289. Springer, Cham (2015). https://doi.org/10.1007/978-3-319-23222-5_35
8. Ivanchenko, V., Coughlan, J., Shen, H.: Crosswatch: a camera phone system for orienting visually impaired pedestrians at traffic intersections. In: Miesenberger, K., Klaus, J., Zagler, W., Karshmer, A. (eds.) ICCHP 2008. LNCS, vol. 5105, pp. 1122–1128. Springer, Heidelberg (2008). https://doi.org/10.1007/978-3-540-70540-6_168
9. Ivanchenko, V., Coughlan, J., Shen, H.: Real-time walk light detection with a mobile phone. In: Miesenberger, K., Klaus, J., Zagler, W., Karshmer, A. (eds.) ICCHP 2010. LNCS, vol. 6180, pp. 229–234. Springer, Heidelberg (2010). https://doi.org/10.1007/978-3-642-14100-3_34
10. Roters, J., Jiang, X., Rothaus, K.: Recognition of traffic lights in live video streams on mobile devices. IEEE Trans. Circ. Syst. Video Technol. **21**, 1497–1511 (2011)
11. Mascetti, S., Ahmetovic, D., Gerino, A., Bernareggi, C., Busso, M., Rizzi, A.: Robust traffic lights detection on mobile devices for pedestrians with visual impairment. Comput. Vis. Image Underst. **148**, 123–135 (2016)
12. Shioyama, T., Wu, H., Nakamura, N.: Measurement of the length of pedestrian crossings and detection of traffic lights from image data. Meas. Sci. Technol. **13**, 311 (2002)
13. Wei, Y., Kou, X., Lee, M.C.: A new vision and navigation research for a guide-dog robot system in urban system. In: 2014 IEEE/ASME International Conference on Advanced Intelligent Mechatronics, pp. 1290–1295. IEEE (2014)
14. Wang, S., Pan, H., Zhang, C., Tian, Y.: RGB-D image-based detection of stairs, pedestrian crosswalks and traffic signs. J. Vis. Commun. Image Represent. **25**, 263–272 (2014)
15. Dalal, N., Triggs, B.: Histograms of oriented gradients for human detection. In: 2005 IEEE Computer Society Conference on Computer Vision and Pattern Recognition (CVPR 2005), pp. 886–893. IEEE (2005)

Indoor Localization Using Computer Vision and Visual-Inertial Odometry

Giovanni Fusco and James M. Coughlan[✉]

Smith-Kettlewell Eye Research Institute, San Francisco, CA 94115, USA
{giofusco, coughlan}@ski.org

Abstract. Indoor wayfinding is a major challenge for people with visual impairments, who are often unable to see visual cues such as informational signs, landmarks and structural features that people with normal vision rely on for wayfinding. We describe a novel indoor localization approach to facilitate wayfinding that uses a smartphone to combine computer vision and a dead reckoning technique known as visual-inertial odometry (VIO). The approach uses sign recognition to estimate the user's location on the map whenever a known sign is recognized, and VIO to track the user's movements when no sign is visible. The advantages of our approach are (a) that it runs on a standard smartphone and requires no new physical infrastructure, just a digital 2D map of the indoor environment that includes the locations of signs in it; and (b) it allows the user to walk freely without having to actively search for signs with the smartphone (which is challenging for people with severe visual impairments). We report a formative study with four blind users demonstrating the feasibility of the approach and suggesting areas for future improvement.

Keywords: Wayfinding · Indoor navigation · Localization
Blindness and visual impairment

1 State of the Art and Related Technology

The key to any wayfinding aid is *localization* – a means of estimating and tracking a person's location as they travel in an environment. The most widespread localization approach is GPS, which enables a variety of wayfinding tools such as Google Maps, Seeing Eye GPS[1] and BlindSquare, but it is only accurate outdoors. There are a range of indoor localization approaches, including Bluetooth beacons [1], Wi-Fi triangulation[2], infrared light beacons [2] and RFIDs [3]. However, all of these approaches incur the cost of installing and maintaining physical infrastructure, or of updating the system as the existing infrastructure changes (e.g., whenever Wi-Fi access points change). Dead reckoning approaches such as step counting using inertial navigation [4] can estimate relative movements without any physical infrastructure, but this tracking estimate drifts over time unless it is augmented by absolute location estimates.

---

[1] https://itunes.apple.com/us/app/seeing-eye-gps/id668624446?mt=8.
[2] https://techcrunch.com/2017/12/14/apple-maps-gets-indoor-mapping-for-more-than-30-airports/.

© The Author(s) 2018
K. Miesenberger and G. Kouroupetroglou (Eds.): ICCHP 2018, LNCS 10897, pp. 86–93, 2018.
https://doi.org/10.1007/978-3-319-94274-2_13

Computer vision is a promising localization approach, but most past work in this area has either required special hardware [5] or the use of detailed 3D models of the environment [6] that are time-consuming to generate and make the approach vulnerable to superficial environmental changes (e.g., new carpeting, moved tables and chairs). To overcome this limitation in past work we developed an indoor localization system [7] that combines step counting with computer vision-based sign recognition. However, while the step counting algorithm works well for participants who walk with a regular gait, it is unreliable when the gait becomes irregular and halting – which is not unusual when visually impaired people explore unfamiliar surroundings. Accordingly, in our new approach we replaced step counting with visual-inertial odometry (VIO) [8], which functions well even if the user is walking with an irregular gait.

2 Overall Approach

Our localization approach uses a smartphone, held by the user or worn on the chest, to acquire several video frames per second. A 2D digital map of the indoor environment specifies the location, orientation (i.e., flush against the wall or perpendicular to it) and appearance of each sign in the environment. In each video frame, whenever a sign is recognized, the apparent size and perspective of the sign in the image determine the camera's pose relative to the sign and therefore the user's approximate location on the map (Fig. 1a). Our current prototype recognizes only barcode-like signs [9] printed on paper (Fig. 1b), but in the future we will extend the approach to recognize arbitrary flat signs, such as the standard Exit signs that our previous system [7] recognized.

In our experience with blind users exploring an environment, signs are only visible and recognizable in a small fraction of video frames, so it is crucial that we estimate the user's movements in between sign recognitions. We accomplish this using VIO [8], which combines the tracking of visual features in the environment with data from the smartphone's inertial measurement unit (IMU) to estimate changes in the smartphone's (X, Y, Z) location and 3D orientation (roll, pitch and yaw) over time. These movement estimates are projected to the 2D map domain, so that the user's trajectory on the map is estimated continuously over time.

We have implemented a prototype system on the iPhone 8 smartphone, using OpenCV[3] to perform sign recognition and pose estimation, and Apple's ARKit[4] iOS software to perform VIO. (ARKit is compatible with the iPhone 6s and newer iPhone models; a similar tool, ARCore, is available to perform VIO on newer Android devices.) Currently the system runs as a logging app that captures video in real time, and saves the video and VIO data to the smartphone's memory, which is analyzed on a computer offline. To maximize the chances of capturing images of signs, real-time audio feedback alerts the user whenever the line of sight deviates too far above or below the horizon. In the future we will implement the system as a standalone

---

[3] https://opencv.org/.
[4] https://developer.apple.com/arkit/.

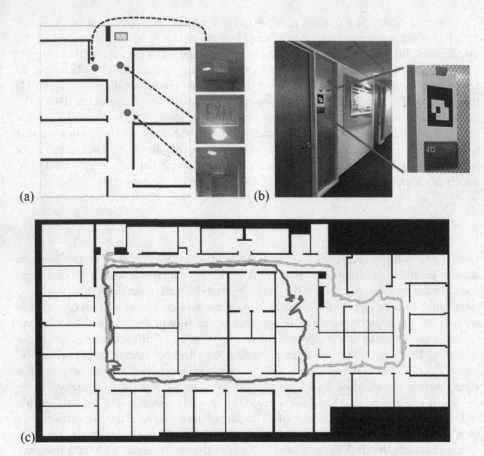

Fig. 1. Overall approach. (a) Signs provide absolute location estimates. Images of an Exit sign (cropped for visibility) taken from three locations are shown on the right, with dashed arrows to corresponding red dots showing approximate location of camera inferred from each image. (b) Prototype system tested in this work uses barcode-like marker patterns, shown here, affixed to the corridor walls instead of Exit signs; we will use Exit signs and other existing signs in place of markers in the future. (c) Map of indoor environment used in our experiments shows sample trajectories estimated along routes R1 (green) and R2 (red). (Color figure online)

wayfinding app that issues directional real-time audio feedback, including turn-by-turn directions and identification of nearby points of interest.

3 Evaluating Localization Accuracy

Both the sign recognition and VIO algorithms contribute significant noise to the location estimates, so we devised a simple procedure to evaluate the localization accuracy. The procedure establishes an approximate ground truth location at selected reference points in the path taken by the user. This is accomplished by having an experimenter follow a few meters behind the traveler and take a video of his/her footsteps. This video is reviewed offline, with the experimenter noting each frame when the traveler passes by a reference point (such as a door) and using visual context (e.g., nearby doors and other features) to determine the corresponding ground truth location on the map. The ground truth location for each reference point is then entered by clicking on the corresponding location on the map. We estimate that the ground truth location is accurate to about 1 m, which implies that errors can be estimated to approximately 1 m accuracy.

In our experiments we used about 15–25 selected reference points to evaluate each route, depending on the length of the route and the visibility of landmarks. The data logged by the traveler's app is time-synched with the video so that any reference point in the video is associated with the corresponding logging data. In this way, the ground truth location of each reference point may be directly compared with the corresponding location estimated from the logging data.

Finally, we estimated the participant's average walking speed in each trial simply by dividing the route length by the time it took to traverse the route. We note that in some trials in which the participant used a guide dog, the dog paused at certain points along the path – thus in these cases the average walking speed estimate is an under-estimate of the typical walking speed.

4 Formative Study

We conducted a formative study that took place on one floor of the main Smith-Kettlewell office building, with dimensions 39 m × 21 m (Fig. 1c). A total of 41 barcode signs (Fig. 1b) were posted on the walls. In all the experimental trials the experimenter followed the participant from a few meters behind, recorded video of the participant's movements, and issued verbal directions (e.g., "turn left in 5 ft") to guide the participant in real time along the desired route; he also acted as a safety monitor, ready to intervene if necessary to avoid a collision or tripping hazard. Each route (Fig. 1c) was a closed circuit, R1 (77 m long) and R2 (58 m long). Participants were instructed to walk with whatever travel aid they wished to use (white cane or guide dog), and in each trial they either held the smartphone in one hand or else attached it to the strap of a satchel (small shoulder bag) that they wore. Before participants used the system, we explained how it worked, including the audio feedback to help them maintain a horizontal line of sight and the need to avoid moving the camera quickly (which causes motion blur and thereby degrades the image quality) or covering the camera lens with the hands.

The study began with a brief evaluation of the system by one blind participant (P0), which allowed us to test the system, our training procedure and experimental protocol and then refine it before testing with three additional participants (P1–P3). In all, the four participants included two females and two males, with ages ranging from 24–40 years; two of them had no form or light perception, and the other two had very limited form and light perception (e.g., allowing them to perceive large objects and shadows).

Participant P0 used a white cane, but was unable to handle the cane while holding the phone, so we only tested him using the satchel. He completed route R1 in both directions (clockwise and counterclockwise), for a total of two trials.

Next, three blind participants participated in the evaluation phase of the study. Each participant completed eight trials: both routes R1 and R2, traversed in both directions, and in the handheld and satchel conditions. Participant P1 used a white cane, while participants P2 and P3 used a guide dog. The performance evaluation for all participants P1–P3 includes the median localization error, maximum localization error and average walking speed for each participant under each combination of route (R1 and R2) and carrying condition (hand and satchel), aggregated over both walking directions (i.e., two consecutive trials). The results are tabulated in Table 1 and shown graphically in Fig. 2. The system's performance was satisfactory for P1 and P2, with median errors around 1 m, but very poor for P3, with errors from a few meters to tens of meters. We note that reference points for which no localization was available were not included in the performance evaluations; such missing points were rare for P1 and P2 but very common for P3.

Table 1. Performance evaluation showing median localization error, maximum localization error and average walking speed for each participant and condition. Errors are in meters, and speeds in meters/second. (Error accuracy is limited to approximately 1 m, the accuracy of the ground truth locations.)

Partic.	R1 satchel	R1 hand	R2 hand	R2 satchel
P1	0.57, 18.34, 0.63	0.49, 1.42, 0.83	0.56, 2.75, 0.86	0.45, 4.01, 0.83
P2	1.22, 3.79, 0.78	0.93, 3.96, 0.91	0.98, 2.86, 0.68	0.87, 3.33, 0.83
P3	24.52, 52.33, 1.05	2.51, 12.11, 1.14	2.63, 4.60, 1.04	1.37, 5.37, 1.16

The poor results for P3 resulted from her very rapid walking speed, which caused motion blur and also severely limited the number of frames in which signs were recognized. Since each sign is visible from only a limited region defined by a certain range of distances and viewing angles, a faster speed implies less time spent traversing this region, and thus fewer chances to glimpse the sign; this resulted in very few sign recognitions in each trial for P3 (in fact, none in one trial). In the future we will explore ways of improving the sign recognition to accommodate faster walking speeds. We also note that we will use signs such as Exit signs in the future, which are visible from a wider range of locations than the signs we used.

All participants expressed interest in an effective indoor wayfinding system, and they commented on possible ways of holding or wearing the smartphone for our approach. P0 suggested many possible ways of wearing the smartphone, including attaching it to a broach or tie clip, or wearing an eyeglass-mounted camera; P1 suggested using a holster to clip the smartphone to the satchel strap, and pointed out the possibility that holding the smartphone while walking might invite theft; P2 felt it should be straightforward to attach the smartphone to the strap of the purse she usually carries with her, but was also pleasantly surprised that it was easy to hold the smartphone while walking; and P3 explained that she would choose to hold the smartphone while walking, since she is already in the habit of doing so (e.g., to text message or use Google Maps). These comments suggest that different users will seek various ways of holding or wearing the smartphone, depending on individual preferences and circumstances. Thus in the future we will explore multiple options to meet diverse needs, including the option of using an external wearable camera, rather than attempting to find a single approach for all users.

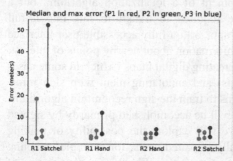 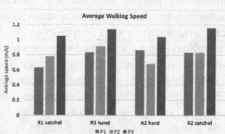

Fig. 2. Graphs of performance evaluation data from Table 1. Data from participants P1, P2 and P3 are shown in red, green and blue, respectively. Left: median and maximum error (meters), indicated by data points connected by vertical lines. Median errors are mostly under 1.5 m, with the exception of P3, whose rapid walking speed led to severe localization errors (see text). Right: average walking speed (meters/second). (Color figure online)

5   Conclusions and Future Work

We have demonstrated the feasibility of a novel indoor localization approach that is usable by visually impaired travelers under a range of normal operating conditions. The approach has the advantage of requiring no added physical infrastructure, and exploits the localization information conveyed by standard informational signs without forcing a visually impaired user to explicitly search for them. We also stress that the approach is applicable to people with normal or impaired vision, who may use a cane or guide dog, and it should also function for people traveling in a wheelchair.

Future work will proceed in several directions. The first will entail enlarging the range of conditions under which our approach functions, such as a rapid walking pace, which may require improved sign recognition and/or a faster frame rate. We will extend the sign recognition algorithms to accommodate arbitrary planar signs, and will focus on maximizing their ability to recognize signs from a wide range of viewing angles and distances.

In addition, we will incorporate more information in the localization algorithm, including (a) sign visibility, enforcing the fact that a sign cannot be seen through an intervening wall or other opaque barrier, and (b) traversability constraints, reflecting the impossibility of walking through walls. A natural way to incorporate this additional information is to maintain and evolve a distribution of multiple location hypotheses over time using a framework such as particle filtering [10], which is standard in robotics applications. The particle filtering framework will be useful for explicitly representing uncertainty about the user's location, which may result from detections of signs at long distances (camera pose estimation is noisy when the sign appears small in the image), ambiguity about which sign has been detected (e.g., multiple Exit signs in a building may have identical appearance), or when no sign has been recognized for some length of time. Another source of absolute localization information that we will incorporate, when available, is the signals from Wi-Fi and from Bluetooth beacons.

This paper has focused on our development of a localization algorithm, but a considerable amount of work will also be required to transform this into a full wayfinding system that runs as a standalone app, with a fully accessible user interface that provides turn-by-turn directions and/or information about nearby points of interest. We will develop a streamlined approach for creating digital maps (which in some cases will have to be scanned in from paper maps) and annotating them with sign information, including photos of non-standard signs to train the sign recognition algorithms. While we envision that the mapping process will be accomplished primarily by sighted assistants (perhaps using crowdsourcing), we will explore the possibility of making some annotation features accessible to visually impaired users, for example, enabling them to add their own points of interest to an existing map. Finally, ongoing testing of the system with both blind and low vision users will guide the entire development process to ensure that the wayfinding system is maximally effective and easy to use.

Acknowledgments. The authors were supported by NIDILRR grant 90RE5024-01-00.

References

1. Ahmetovic, D., Gleason, C., Kitani, K., Takagi, H., Asakawa, C.: NavCog: turn-by-turn smartphone navigation assistant for people with visual impairments or blindness. In: Proceedings of the 13th Web for All Conference (W4A 2016). ACM, New York (2016). Article No. 9, 2 p. https://doi.org/10.1145/2899475.2899509
2. Brabyn, L.A., Brabyn, J.A.: An evaluation of 'Talking Signs' for the blind. Hum. Factors **25** (1), 49–53 (1983). https://doi.org/10.1177/001872088302500105
3. Ganz, A., Gandhi, S.R., Wilson, C., Mullett, G.: INSIGHT: RFID and Bluetooth enabled automated space for the blind and visually impaired. In: 2010 Annual International Conference of the IEEE Engineering in Medicine and Biology, Buenos Aires, pp. 331–334 (2010). https://doi.org/10.1109/iembs.2010.5627670
4. Flores, G., Manduchi, R.: Easy return: an app for indoor backtracking assistance. In: ACM CHI Conference on Human Factors in Computing Systems 2018, Montreal, Canada (2018). https://doi.org/10.1145/3173574.317359
5. Hu, F., Zhu, Z., Zhang, J.: Mobile panoramic vision for assisting the blind via indexing and localization. In: Agapito, L., Bronstein, Michael M., Rother, C. (eds.) ECCV 2014. LNCS, vol. 8927, pp. 600–614. Springer, Cham (2015). https://doi.org/10.1007/978-3-319-16199-0_42
6. Gleason, C., Guo, A., Laput, G., Kitani, K., Bigham, J.P.: VizMap: accessible visual information through crowdsourced map reconstruction. In: Proceedings of the 18th International ACM SIGACCESS Conference on Computers and Accessibility (ASSETS 2016), pp. 273–274. ACM, New York (2016). https://doi.org/10.1145/2982142.2982200

7. Rituerto, A., Fusco, G., Coughlan, J.M.: Towards a sign-based indoor navigation system for people with visual impairments. In: Proceedings of the 18th International ACM SIGACCESS Conference on Computers and Accessibility (ASSETS 2016), pp. 287–288. ACM, New York (2016). https://doi.org/10.1145/2982142.2982202

8. Kelly, J., Sukhatme, G.S.: Visual-inertial sensor fusion: localization, mapping and sensor-to-sensor self-calibration. Int. J. Robot. Res. **30**(1), 56–79 (2011). https://doi.org/10.1177/0278364910382802

9. Garrido-Jurado, S., Muñoz-Salinas, R., Madrid-Cuevas, F.J., Marín-Jiménez, M.J.: Automatic generation and detection of highly reliable fiducial markers under occlusion. Pattern Recogn. **47**(6), 2280–2292 (2014). https://doi.org/10.1016/j.patcog.2014.01.005. ISSN 0031-3203

10. Thrun, S., Burgard, W., Fox, D.: Probabilistic Robotics. MIT Press, Cambridge (2005). ISBN 9780262303804

HapticRein: Design and Development of an Interactive Haptic Rein for a Guidance Robot

Limin Zeng[✉], Björn Einert, Alexander Pitkin, and Gerhard Weber

Technische Universität Dresden, 01187 Dresden, Germany
{limin.zeng,bjorn.einert,alexander.pitkin,
gerhard.weber}@tu-dresden.de

Abstract. In daily life, a guide dog as a companion assists blind and visually impaired people (BVIP) to perform independent and safe journey. However, due to several reasons (e.g., cost and long-term training) only a few BVIP would own their guide dogs. To let much more BVIP would have accessible guidance services in unfamiliar public or private areas, we plan to develop an interactive guide dog robot prototype. In this paper, we present one of the most important components of a guidance robot for BVIP, an interactive haptic rein which consists of force-sensing sensors to control and balance the walking speed between BVIP and robots in a natural way, and vibrated actuators under fingers to acquire haptic information, e.g., turning left/right. The results of preliminary user studies indicated that the proposed haptic rein allow BVIP to control and communicate with a guidance robot via a natural haptic interaction.

Keywords: Haptic interaction · Guidance robot
Blind and visually impaired people

1 Introduction

For blind and visually impaired people (BVIP), a safe and independent indoor and outdoor mobility is an important connection with the society, such as going to office/hospital, shopping, and travelling. White canes and guide dogs have a high acceptance by BVIP, to assist them to detect obstacles and hazards while travelling and exploring the space. In order to overcome the limitations of those traditional travel aids (e.g., limited range, detection of hanging objects, and the expensive cost for owning a guide dog), in the last decades, a large number of electronic travel aids (ETAs) have been developed, like ultrasonic probe [1], vOICe system [2], 3DOD system [3] and Range-IT system [4].

Guidance robots have also been studied to provide guidance services for BVIP, with the help of various sensors [5, 6]. As the development of robotic technologies and service robots in the last decade, an affordable and accessible guidance robot is becoming more and more promising in the near future. Those guidance robots would help BVIP not only detect obstacles and hazards, but also navigate themselves in familiar/unfamiliar areas, that is the traditional travel aids cannot offer. However, it is a

K. Miesenberger and G. Kouroupetroglou (Eds.): ICCHP 2018, LNCS 10897, pp. 94–101, 2018.
https://doi.org/10.1007/978-3-319-94274-2_14

challenge to communicate between BVIP and guided robots in time and in a non-visual way (e.g., auditory, haptic, and audio-haptic). Even auditory feedback (e.g., speech input/output) is a convenient approach, for BVIP it is important to hear environmental sounds. Furthermore, it is also a challenge to balance the walking speed between BVIP and robots.

In this paper, we present a novel haptic rein to support a non-visual commination between BVIP and guided robots. The haptic rein consists of a series of force-sensing sensors and vibrated actuators, where the force-sensing sensors are placed around the four sides of the handle of the haptic rein to detect push/pull movement for speeding up/down, and the vibrated actuators are placed on the bottom of the handle to deliver haptic messages to users' fingers. A preliminary user study indicated the proposed rein was effective to communicate and control a guidance robot to balance the walking speed, and some subjects commented it was a natural way to interact with a guidance robot.

2 Related Work

2.1 Haptic/Tactile Interfaces for BVIP

Haptic/tactile interaction as one of the most important non-visual user interfaces would provide accessible information for BVIP, in addition to auditory interfaces. In the last decades, a large number of accessible systems and devices which adopt haptic interfaces has been developed and evaluated. In general, the haptic interaction can be categorized into several types, such as vibrotactile interfaces [4, 7], pin-matrix display based haptic interfaces [8, 9], force-feedback based interfaces [10, 11] and electrostatic interfaces [12, 13]. BVIP would acquire the direction and distance of the approaching obstacles via an array of actuators in a tactile belt [4], and learn their updated location on a tactile map [8]. However, due to the low resolution it is challenging to encode complex messages via haptic interfaces.

2.2 Accessible Service Robots

With the development of robotic technologies, various service robots have been produced in the last years. Accessible service robots are developed to assist people with speech needs in many different applications, by employing accessible user interfaces. Assistive robots for old people, as one of the primary application domains, would help them observe their health state [14], fetch objects [15], and other daily routines. Smart wheelchair robots enable wheelchair users to navigate intelligently [16], and robot arms allow upper-limb impaired people to interact with physical world flexible and independently [17]. Most of current accessible robots require that users should have considerable vision capability, nevertheless, there are a few accessible robots designed for visually impaired and blind people.

2.3 Haptic Interfaces for Guide Dog Robots

A guide dog robot is a special kind of service robots, which assist BVIP to travel safely and independently, even in unfamiliar environment. Azenkot et al. suggested a guide dog robot should design the three primary accessible features: (1) summon the robot after entering the building, (2) three modes of assistance (Sighted Guide, Escort and Information Kiosk) while travelling, (3) receive information about the building's layout from the robot [18]. For the mode of Sighted Guide which emulates a human sighted guide, haptic interfaces are required to inform BVIP walking instructions (e.g., turning left/right). Table 1 compares some existing guide dog robots. On the one hand, some guide dog robots use canes [6, 19] and soft reins [20] to interact with users who need to perceive the changed direction of the canes or soft reins and follow them. On the other hand, a few systems investigate how to employ haptic sensors to communicate between users and robots. [21] develops an electrocutaneous handheld handle which connects with the robot via a wired cable, however, users have to train hardly to be familiar with the different pulse strength which encode the instructions, e.g., turning left/right and going closed to the robot. There is no study how to balance the walking speed between users and robots via a haptic interface.

Table 1. A comparison of some previous guide dog robots.

Robots	Year	Main Features	(Haptic) Interface for users	Haptic Messages
MELDOG	1985	Obstacle avoidance Map & Route Speech output Haptic output	An electrocutaneous handheld handle Wired rein	**Active** haptic output: Turning Warning
GuideCane	2001	Obstacle avoidance Grid map Control direction	A hard cane with a mini-joystick	**Passive** haptic output: following the steering
eyeDog	2011	Obstacle avoidance Autonomous navigation	A soft rein only	angle of the robot
Co_robotic Cane	2016	Obstacle recognition Speech interface	A hard cane	

3 HapticRein System

3.1 System Overview

The HapticRein system is developed based on a KUKA-Youbot 4-wheel robot platform, and a customized metal rein is attached to the robot platform (see Fig. 1). The length of the rein is 90 cm and the height of its handle to the floor is 88 cm. The total weight of the robot is about 20 kg, and maximal walking speed is about 0.8 m/s. A 2D laser LiDAR sensor is mounted in the front to detect obstacles.

Fig. 1. The overview of the HapticRein system (left: a blind people with his own guide dog; right: a blindfolded people tested with the system).

3.2 System Component of the HapticRein

As illustrated in Fig. 2, there are several hardware components which are attached to the handle:

- Force-sensing sensors: 6 force-sensing sensors are placed around the four sides of the handle, to detect users' pull/push force value and press force.
- Vibrated actuators: 3 actuators are fixed at the bottom of the handle, where users' fingers can acquire haptic messages.
- An embedded board: An ARDUNIO UNO board is used to control the system.
- A thumb joystick: A thumb joystick is place on the top of the handle, and can easily make an input. Note that, the joystick is recognized as a baseline to compare with the force-based interaction.

3.3 Human-Robot Haptic Interaction

To support an interactive haptic interaction when communicating with and controlling the guide robot, the HapticRein system combines force-feedback and vibration feedback:

- **Start walking:** when a user grasp the handle with a considerable force detected by the Force Sensor 2 (on the top of the handle), the robot will start walking and its initial speed is 0.3 m/s;
- **Speed up:** to walk fast a user can push the handle, and the Force Sensor 1 (at the back of the handle) detects the increased force value, and the system speeds up. A user can continuously push the handle to speed up the robot, until a balance between them;
- **Speed down:** to walk slowly a user can pull the handle, and the Force Sensor 5 and Force Sensor 6 detect the reduced force value, when both of the force sensors detect

the reduced force value and the value is bigger than a threshold, the robot will speed down;

- **Soft stop:** a user can continuously pull the handle to speed down the robot, until it stops;
- **Hard stop:** in some situations a user would need a quick or sudden stop, therefore, a hard stop is supported in the HapticRein when a user release the hand from the handle, and at the same time all force sensors can't detect input force value.
- **Turning left/right:** to turn the robot while walking a user can press the Force Sensor 3 and Force Sensor 4, and the press value will decide the turning angles (e.g., 30°, 45°, 60°)
- **Haptic messages:** to deliver navigation messages (e.g., turning left/right and stop) via the 3 vibratos, a simple tactile pattern is designed.

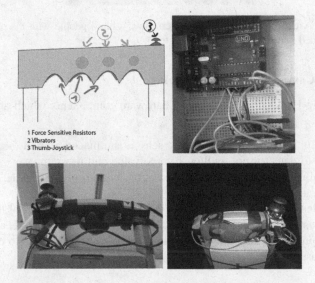

Fig. 2. The hardware components of the HapticRein system (top-left: an overview layout of the main sensors; top-right: the ARDUNIO board; bottom-left: bottom view of the handle; bottom-right: front view of the handle).

4   Pilot Study

A preliminary user study with five blindfolded subjects has been performed, and the subjects were in the average age of 25 years old. In addition to training how to use and control the robot system, the subjects were asked to finish a series of tasks, walking through a straight line and turning with a curve path (see Fig. 3). In the test, two different input tools were evaluated:

- Condition 1: using the mini-joystick
- Condition 2: using the proposed force handle

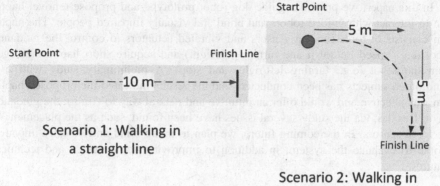

Fig. 3. The two test scenarios

The results indicated that the proposed force handle and the joystick both are effective to interact with the guidance robot, and the joystick was easier to learn. Three of the five subjects feedback that the force handle was intuitive and natural to control the walking speed. In particular, several subjects mentioned within the joystick solution users might make their thumb tried for a long distance walk.

Through the pilot study, several key issues have been found:

- The placement of the force sensors: The position of the force sensors when fixed in the handle is significant to gather precise force value. However, due to the different hand size our placement is not suitable for the subjects with small hands.
- The issue of sudden stop: We observed there were several sudden stops, and after analyzing the log data and evaluation videos we suspected the force value of Force Sensor 2 suddenly became zero that lead to sudden stops. One possible reason is while walking the finger contacted with the Force Sensor 2 was moved and left the sensor.
- The low maximum robot speed: Currently the maximum walking speed of our robot is 0.8 m/s which is lower than the average walking speed with guide dogs (1.05 m/s [22]). In Scenario 1, when the robot quickly reached its maximum speed, the rear wheels were hang over the floor as the subjects walked faster and heavy push the handle.

5 Conclusions and Future Work

For blind and visually impaired people (BVIP), it is important to have a safe and independent indoor/outdoor travel, such as going to school/office, shopping and going to a doctor. Guide dogs would help BVIP avoid obstacles and hazards in their paths, however, it requires a long-term period to train a qualified guide dog and the expensive cost is not affordable for most of BVIP. As the development of service robots in the last decades, a guide dog robot as a promising mobility aid would offer affordable guidance for BVIP.

In this paper, we present a guide dog robot prototype and propose a novel haptic rein to interact with guided robots and blind and visually impaired people. The haptic rein consists of force-sensing sensors and vibrated actuators to control the guidance robot (e.g., speed up/down and turning left/right) and acquire short haptic messages from the robot (e.g., turning left/right, and stop). A preliminary study with five blindfolded subjects has been conducted, and the results indicated the proposed haptic rein was effective and would offer an intuitive and natural way to control the guidance robot. Besides, via the study several issues have been found, such as the placement of the force sensors. In the coming future, we plan to invite blind and visually impaired people to evaluate the system, in addition to improving some design and technical features.

References

1. Kay, L.: An ultrasonic sensing probe as a mobility aid for the blind. Ultrasonics **2**, 53–59 (1964)
2. Meijer, P.B.L.: An experimental system for auditory image representations. IEEE Trans. Biomed. Eng. **39**, 112–121 (1992)
3. Zeng, L., Prescher, D., Weber, G.: Exploration and avoidance of surrounding obstacles for the visually impaired. In: Proceedings of the ACM ASSETS 2012, pp. 111–118 (2012)
4. Zeng, L., Simros, M., Weber, G.: Camera-based mobile electronic travel aids support for cognitive mapping of unknown spaces. In: Proceedings of the ACM MobileHCI 2017 (2017). Article No. 8
5. Tachi, S., Tanie, K., Komoriya, K., Abe, M.: Electrocutaneous communication in a guide dog robot (MELDOG). IEEE Trans. Biomed. Eng. **BME-32**, 461–469 (1985)
6. Ulrich, I., Borenstein, J.: The GuideCane-applying mobile robot technologies to assist the visually impaired. IEEE Trans. SMC **31**, 131–136 (2001)
7. Zöllner, M., Huber, S., Jetter, H.-C., Reiterer, H.: NAVI – a proof-of-concept of a mobile navigational aid for visually impaired based on the microsoft kinect. In: Campos, P., Graham, N., Jorge, J., Nunes, N., Palanque, P., Winckler, M. (eds.) INTERACT 2011. LNCS, vol. 6949, pp. 584–587. Springer, Heidelberg (2011). https://doi.org/10.1007/978-3-642-23768-3_88
8. Zeng, L., Weber, G.: Exploration of location-aware You-Are-Here maps on a pin-matrix display. IEEE Trans. Hum.-Mach. Syst. **46**(1), 88–100 (2016)
9. Zeng, L., Miao, M., Weber, G.: Interactive audio-haptic map explorer on a tactile display. Interact. Comput. **27**(4), 413–429 (2015)
10. Schneider, J., Strothotte, T.: Constructive exploration of spatial information by blind users. In: Proceedings of the 12th International ACM SIGACCESS Conference on Computers and Accessibility, Arlington, TX, USA, pp. 188–192 (2000)
11. Moustakas, K., Nikolakis, G., Kostopoulos, K., Tzovaras, D., Strintzis, M.G.: Haptic rendering of visual data for the visually impaired. IEEE MultiMed. **14**(1), 62–72 (2007)
12. Tang, H., Beebe, D.J.: A microfabricated electrostatic haptic display for persons with visual impairments. IEEE Trans. Rehabil. Eng. **6**(3), 241–248 (1998)
13. Xu, C., Israr, A., Poupyrev, I., Bau, O., Harrison, C.: Tactile display for the visually impaired using TeslaTouch. In: Proceedings of the CHI 2011 Extended Abstracts, pp. 317–322 (2011)

14. Brell, M., Meyer, J., Frenken, J., Hein, J.: A mobile robot for self-selected gait velocity assessments in assistive environments: a robotic driven approach to bring assistive technologies into established homes. In: Proceedings of the 3rd PETRA, pp. 15:1–15:8. ACM (2010)
15. Lee, M.K., Forlizzi, J., Rybski, P.E., Crabbe, F., Chung, W., Finkle, J., Glaser, E., Kiesler, S.: The snackbot: documenting the design of a robot for long-term human-robot interaction. In: Proceedings of the Human-Robot Interaction, pp. 7–14 (2009)
16. Wei, Z., Chen, W., Wang, J.: 3D semantic map-based shared control for smart wheelchair. In: Su, C.-Y., Rakheja, S., Liu, H. (eds.) ICIRA 2012. LNCS (LNAI), vol. 7507, pp. 41–51. Springer, Heidelberg (2012). https://doi.org/10.1007/978-3-642-33515-0_5
17. Graser, A., Heyer, T., Fotoohi, L., et al.: A supportive FRIEND at work: robotic workplace assistance for the disabled. IEEE Robot. Autom. Mag. **20**(4), 148–159 (2013)
18. Azenkot, S., Feng, C., Cakmak, M.: Enabling building service robots to guide blind people a participatory design approach. In: Proceedings of the 11th ACM/IEEE International Conference on Human-Robot Interaction (HRI), Christchurch, pp. 3–10 (2016)
19. Ye, C., Hong, S., Qian, X., Wu, W.: Co-Robotic Cane: a new robotic navigation aid for the visually impaired. IEEE Syst. Man Cybern. Mag. **2**(2), 33–42 (2016)
20. Galatas, G., McMurrough, C., Mariottini, G.L., Makedon, F.: Eyedog: an assistive-guide robot for the visually impaired. In: Proceedings of the 4th PETRA, pp. 58:1–58:8. ACM, New York (2011)
21. Tachi, S., Tanie, K., Komoriya, K., Abe, M.: Electrocutaneous communication in a guide dog robot (MELDOG). IEEE Trans. Biomed. Eng. **BME-32**(7), 461–469 (1985)
22. Clark-Carter, D.D., Heyes, A.D., Howarth, C.I.: The efficiency and walking speed of visually impaired people. Ergonomics **29**(6), 779–789 (1986)

EchoVis: Training Echolocation Using Binaural Recordings – Initial Benchmark Results

Michał Bujacz[1(✉)], Marta Szyrman[1], Grzegorz Górski[2],
Rafał Charłampowicz[2], Sławomir Strugarek[2], Adam Bancarewicz[2],
Anna Trzmiel[3], Agnieszka Nelec[3], Piotr Witek[3],
and Aleksander Waszkielewicz[3]

[1] Lodz University of Technology, Lodz, Poland
bujaczm@p.lodz.pl
[2] Transition Technologies S.A., Warsaw, Poland
[3] Utilitia/Fundacja Instytut Rozwoju Regionalnego, Cracow, Poland

Abstract. In this paper, we describe a recently begun project aimed at teaching of echolocation using a mobile game. The presented research concerns initial echolocation tests with real world obstacles and similar tests performed using binaural recordings. Tests that included detection and recognition of large obstacles in various environments (padded room, non-padded room, outdoors) were performed by three groups 10 persons each: blind children, blind adults and sighted adults. A mixed group of volunteers also tested binaural recordings of the same environments using a mobile application for Android and iOS devices. The presented preliminary research shows a large variance in echolocation ability of the participants. Less than 20% of the 30 volunteers could reliably (with >80% certainty) localize 1 m and 2 m wide walls at distances 1 to 3 m, while about as many showed no echolocation skills and answered at a random level. On average sighted adults performed better in echolocation tests than blind children, but worse than blind adults. Tests in outdoor environments showed much better results than indoors and a padded room was marginally better for echolocation than the non-padded room. Performance with recordings was generally worse than in analogous real tests, but the same trends could be clearly observed, e.g. a proportional drop-off of correctness with distance. The tests with recordings also demonstrated that a repeatable pre-recorded or synthesized clicker originating from a loudspeaker was a better solution than recordings with live clicker sounds.

Keywords: Echolocation · Blindness · Binaural recordings
Obstacle detection

1 Introduction

Although human echolocation is a confirmed and relatively well-documented phenomenon [1, 2, 8, 9], the exact capabilities of average sighted or blind persons, and methods of teaching it to new students are not yet well studied [5, 6, 15]. A number of

K. Miesenberger and G. Kouroupetroglou (Eds.): ICCHP 2018, LNCS 10897, pp. 102–109, 2018.
https://doi.org/10.1007/978-3-319-94274-2_15

nearly "superhuman" echolocators are well known in the blind community [12] and sometimes offer training courses [4], which mainly consist of "tough love" training regimens in real-world environments that force students to utilize their sense of hearing [3]. The authors intended to prepare a less dangerous and demanding training regimen that could be disguised as a mobile phone game. Before development of the actual game the project began with a short study of echolocation itself and the possible binaural recordings that could be utilized in the developed software. The authors plan to repeat the tests in the future to observe improvement (if any) of the real-world echolocation skills after a training regimen with the binaural recordings is developed.

2   Experiments in Real Environments

As initial research on echolocation and as a benchmark for future testing of the skills of project participants, tests were prepared with real obstacles and three groups of participants: 10 blind children, 10 blind adults and 10 normally sighted adults. The tests were performed in three variations: indoors, in a padded and non-padded room, and outdoors.

2.1   Experimental Setup

The indoor tests were divided into 5 stages, each with 3 parts 9 questions each. In the first stage the participants localized a large 2 m × 1.9 m wooden wall, in the first part just its direction (left 45°, center or right 45°) at 1 m distance, in the second its distance (1 m, 2 m or 3 m) when it was in the center, and in the third part both the direction and distance had to be guessed. The second, third and fourth stage were analogous, but different types of obstacles were used: a 1 m × 1 m box, a 1 m wide × 1.9 m tall wall, and a 10 cm wide × 2 m tall cylindrical column. The fifth stage consisted of identifying the type and direction to an obstacle at a 1 m distance. An example task is shown in Fig. 1 along with the researcher's position during the study. The outdoor tests only repeated the first two stages with 1 m and 2 m walls.

Fig. 1. Localization of obstacles by echolocation in a padded room using a mechanical clicker.

The test participants were equipped with a dog-clicker to generate the echoes in a repeatable manner. They were asked to click once then answer, then click N times (up to 10) and answer again. Each time they answered they also judged their certainty in their answer on a scale from 1 ("I'm guessing at random") to 5 ("I feel completely certain"). After providing the answer the second time, the testers were told if they were correct and if not, the correct answer was indicated to them by tapping of the obstacle. While the obstacles were moved, the testers listened to loud music over headphones. All sighted or partially sighted participants were blindfolded.

The results can be analyzed two ways: either to judge the echolocation skills of each individual or a given subgroup, or to judge the general difficulty of the various echolocation tasks. When comparing the tasks, the ones that could be considered "easiest" consisted of determining the direction to an obstacle, especially at the close 1 m distance. The tasks that were most difficult, answered at random or near-random level were the determination of the distance to an obstacle other than the 2 m wide wall, and determination of type of obstacle. Sample results are presented in Table 1.

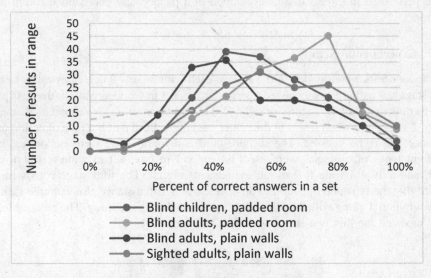

Fig. 2. Comparison of correct results distribution for the different testing groups. The plot shows how many 9-question test set fell into each percent range (0–11%, 12–22% etc.) Each participant went through 6 such series for two sizes of walls. The results are compared to an expected distribution if all answers were random with 33% chance of correctness.

Comparing whole groups of users one can make several observations (Figs. 2 and 3). E.g. on average sighted persons performed worse than blind adults, especially expert echolocators [16], but better than blind children, which is consistent with data in literature [7, 11]. The blind adults fared better in the padded room, although the average difference in the percent of correct answers was minor. Bind adults were also very clearly more certain of their answers and correctly so. For all adults the certainty of an answer was good predictor of its correctness; however, for the blind underage participants, the correlation was not there (often children were very sure of their answers and surprised they were wrong).

The gathered results will serve as a benchmark for the project. The same groups of testers will practice echolocation tasks with various mobile applications and repeat the real scene tests afterwards, hopefully, demonstrating improved echolocation skills.

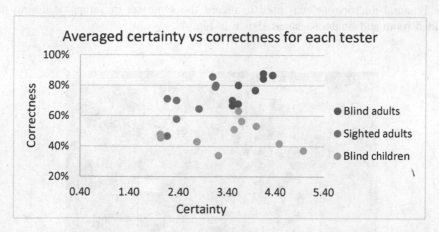

Fig. 3. Averaged certainty vs correctness for all testers (10 blind adults, 10 sighted adults and 10 blind children) in the first two series of indoor echolocation tests (1 m wide and 2 m wide wall).

Table 1. Averaged correctness of distance judgements in indoor trials.

Distance to 2 m-wide obstacle	Blind adults (padded room)	Blind children (padded room)	Sighted adults (normal room)	Blind adults (normal room)
1 m	77%	57%	55%	69%
2 m	65%	40%	52%	71%
3 m	33%	58%	65%	65%

3   Experiments with Binaural Recordings

A Binaural Enthusiast BE-1 dummy head was used in the recordings with a torso constructed from a wooden skeleton and polyethylene foam. The mannequin was placed in the same position as the participants of the previously described experiments, with the head at 150 cm.

3.1   Clicker Sounds

The real-world echolocation trials used a dog-training clicker. The same clicker was initially used in the binaural recordings, but it was difficult to make the clicks consistently repeatable and to not disturb the mannequin's position while clicking next to it. Instead, a recording of the clicker in a small anechoic box was made and played back looped through a UE Roll Bluetooth speaker.

Experiments were also done using variations of the clicker recordings with peak frequencies from 1 to 4 kHz and utilizing synthesized clicker recordings based on mouth-clicks of expert echolocators [13, 14].

3.2 Recorded Scenarios

The binaural microphone was used to record the same set of setups as during the padded room and outdoor tests as shown in Fig. 4.

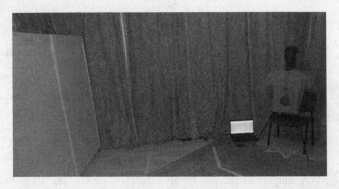

Fig. 4. Binaural recordings were made in the same setups as the live echolocation tests.

Additionally, recordings were made indoors in the school and university buildings, specifically in long hallways and on stairwells, as well as outdoors around university buildings, trees and parking lots.

3.3 Mobile Testing Applications

To perform tests with the binaural recordings a set of mobile applications was prepared that could be ran on Android or iOS devices. There were several goals of the initially prepared applications – to elaborate an efficient user interface (UI), judge plausibility of binaural recording use, develop best recording practices and gather echolocation sounds that were most promising for initial training.

The testing application allowed to manage users, recorded tests and exported data by emailing csv files. All test instructions, questions and answers were read by the OS's default text to speech software (usually Talk Back on Android devices and VoiceOver on iOS). The prototype application was so far tested on a group of 10 persons: 3 sighted and 7 blind (2 with residual color/light perception).

3.4 Results and Discussion

The testing with the binaural recordings was much less formal than the real-world echolocation tests. Our approach was to prepare a set of 10–20 recordings, add them as a testing set to the application, have the 10 volunteers (including the authors) perform each set at least twice, gather and analyze the results. As the number of testing sets grew (currently over 30 tests with a total of 350 recordings), feedback from users and the gathered results were used to modify further recordings and questions, e.g. a single click was replaced by multiple clicks, the real clicker was substituted with a recording of that same clicker, then the recording was downshifted in frequency. Finally, the clicker recoding was replaced with a synthesized click based on an expert echolocator's tongue click [14].

The full results will be published in a later paper are still being processed and too long to present in an abstract, but a number of conclusions can be summarized. The original binaural recordings of the indoor rooms with a mechanical clicker were insufficient to correctly echolocate obstacles (average correctness of locating large obstacles was at 38%). However, recordings made with a synthesized clicker (53%) and those made outdoors (63%) were significantly better. Some sound processing (e.g. amplitude compression or resampling) was shown to improve the perception of the echoes (by about 4–8%), especially when determining direction to an obstacle.

Dynamic recordings made by walking with the binaural dummy or mixing several consecutive static recordings also showed much more potential. Testers showed significantly more adept at identifying an obstacle that was getting closer than one that was static or moving away.

Interesting observations can be made when comparing answers given after first playback of a sound and after repeated playbacks. The repeated listening to a recording seems to have little to no influence on the correctness of answers in static recordings with a 3% average improvement, (when the standard deviation was 12%), but a more significant influence on dynamic recordings with a 12% improvement.

Similarly to the real-world tests, the number of repeated playbacks was actually inversely proportional to correct answers, suggesting that the sounds were listened to more often when the answer was difficult to determine, but the additional playbacks were not helpful in providing the correct answer. A further, more in-depth analysis of correlations between user certainty, types of questions, number of clicks and correctness of answers is currently being performed.

4   Future Work

As this paper is prepared, the echolocation studies continue to expand. Currently, tests with outdoor echolocation were completed. Dynamic tests are also being conducted, with participants tasked with approaching obstacles or localizing them off-path.

The binaural recording tests are also being continued. We are testing the players' ability to imagine and interpret motion (preliminary results show very good understanding of linear motion, especially when approaching obstacles, but very poor understanding of rotation in a virtual environment).

The presented research will be used for the development and evaluation of a mobile game for teaching echolocation, as e.g. [17]. The game will feature binaural recordings in various environments and require the player to determines echoes from buildings, corridors and obstacles to choose travel paths. The initially prepared concept assumes a multistage game starting with simple "quiz-like" episodes based on binaural test sets that have so far shown most correct results. As the user trains, the plot of the game will change to more open tasks, where the user will be able to move by swiping the touch interface and/or select prerecorded paths. The main goal of the game is to deliver different combinations of sound and echo recognition tasks joined by a game plot. Player competition as one of the best mobilizing factors will be taken into account, as plan to have users compare high scores or even compete in tournaments.

5 Summary

We compared echolocation skills in a real world environment for three groups: blind children, blind adults and sighted adults. The test encompassed detection of obstacles at ranges from 1 to 3 meters in a padded and empty room. We also compared the accuracy of recognition of the same scenes using binaural recordings and a mobile application, as well as other tasks such as determination of direction of a corridor or building, or motion around obstacles. The gathered data will be used in the development and evaluation of a training game using binaural recordings.

Acknowledgments. The project is financed by the Polish Ministry of Progress grant for the Sectoral Programme GAMEINN (gaming innovations) no. POIR.01.02.00-00-0137/16.

References

1. Arias, C., Bermejo, F., Hüg, M.X., Venturelli, N., Rabinovich, D., Skarp, A.O.: Echolocation: an action-perception phenomenon. N. Z. Acoust. **25**(2), 20–27 (2012)
2. Arias, C., Ramos, O.A.: Psychoacoustic tests for the study of human echolocation. Appl. Acoust. **51**(4), 399–419 (1997)
3. Bereda, H.: Niech Cię Słuch Prowadzi (Polish, "Let hearing guide you"), Biblioteka Centralna Polskiego Związku Niewidomych (2012)
4. Brogaard, B., Marlow, K.: Sonic vision. Discov. Mag. (2015). http://discovermagazine.com/2015/july-aug/27-sonic-vision
5. Ekkel, M.R., van Lier, R., Steenbergen, B.: Learning to echolocate in sighted people: a correlational study on attention, working memory and spatial abilities. Exp. Brain Res. **235**, 809–818 (2017)
6. Kolarik, A.J., Cirstea, S., Pardhan, S., Moore, B.C.: A summary of research investigating echolocation abilities of blind and sighted humans. Hearing Res. **310**, 60–68 (2014)
7. Nilssona, M.E., Schenkman, B.N.: Blind people are more sensitive than sighted people to binaural sound-location cues, particularly inter-aural level differences. Hearing Res. **332**, 223–232 (2015)
8. Papadopoulos, T., Edwards, D.S., Rowan, D., Allen, R.: Identification of auditory cues utilized in human echolocation. In: Information Technology and Applications in Biomedicine 2009 (2009)
9. Parker, C., Smith, G.: Aspects of cognition and echolocation. Animal Sonar, pp. 683–690 (2012)
10. Smith, G.E., Baker, C.J.: Human echolocation waveform analysis. In: IET International Conference on Radar Systems (2012)

11. Teng, S., Whitney, D.: The acuity of echolocation: spatial resolution in sighted persons compared to the performance of an expert who is blind. J. Vis. Impair. Blind. **105**(1), 20–32 (2011)

12. Thaler, L., Arnott, S.R., Goodale, M.A.: Neural correlates of natural human echolocation in early and late blind echolocation experts. PLoS ONE **6**(5), e20162 (2011)

13. Thaler, L., Castillo-Serrano, J.: People's ability to detect objects using clickbased echolocation: a direct comparison between mouth-clicks and clicks made by a loudspeaker. PLoS ONE **11**(5), e0154868 (2016)

14. Thaler, L., Reich, G.M., Zhang, X., Wang, D., Smith, G.E., et al.: Mouth-clicks used by blind expert human echolocators – signal description and model based signal synthesis. PLoS Comput. Biol. **13**(8), e1005670 (2017)

15. Tonelli, A., Brayda, L., Gori, M.: Depth echolocation learnt by novice sighted people. PLoS ONE **11**(6), e0156654 (2016)

16. Vercillo, T., Milne, J.L., Gori, M., Goodale, M.A.: Enhanced auditory spatial localization in blind echolocators. Neuropsychologia **67**, 35–40 (2014)

17. Wu, W., et al.: EchoExplorer: a game app for understanding echolocation and learning to navigate using echo cues. In: International Conference on Auditory Display (ICAD 2017) (2017)

TactiBelt: Integrating Spatial Cognition and Mobility Theories into the Design of a Novel Orientation and Mobility Assistive Device for the Blind

Marc-Aurèle Riviere[⊠] [iD], Simon Gay [iD], and Edwige Pissaloux [iD]

University of Rouen Normandy, LITIS, Mont-Saint-Aignan, France
marc.aurele.riviere@etu.univ-rouen.fr

Abstract. The aim of this paper is to introduce a novel functional design for an indoor and outdoor mobility assistive device for the visually impaired, based on the theoretical frameworks of mobility and spatial cognition. The originality of the proposed approach comes from the integration of two main aspects of navigation, locomotion and wayfinding. The cognitive theories which underpin the design of the proposed sensory substitution device, called TactiBelt, are identified and discussed in the framework of spatial knowledge acquisition.

The paper is organized as follows: Sect. 1 gives a brief overview of the sensory substitution framework, while Sects. 2 and 3 introduce the importance of navigation and spatial cognition models for the design of mobility aids. Section 4 details the functional design of the Tactibelt.

Keywords: Mobility aid · Sensory substitution · Spatial cognition
Blindness

1 Introduction: Some Remarks on Sensory Substitution

According to the World Health Organization, as of October 2017, 253 million people live with vision impairment worldwide, with 36 million being completely blind.

In the last decades, many devices were developed to compensate for loss of vision, most of them relying on the sensory substitution framework first introduced 50 years ago by Bach-y-Rita [1]. Sensory Substitution, in its most basic definition, consists in conveying information about the environment through "unusual" sensory channels; for example, transmitting information about the distance of remote objects through tactile stimulation. Therefore, Sensory Substitution Devices (SSD) can be seen as a special kind of non-invasive human-machine interface, designed to provide additional (or no longer accessible) information about the environment. SSD devices allow their users to carry out tasks that were previously impossible or troublesome due to a lack of information. SSD are usually comprised of three main elements: sensors, an interface to communicate with the user (usually through touch or sound), and a processing unit to remap the gathered information to the code of the receptive modality.

Sensory substitution mainly relies upon our capacity to actively re-interpret new sensory information and to automate this process through learning, ultimately leading

K. Miesenberger and G. Kouroupetroglou (Eds.): ICCHP 2018, LNCS 10897, pp. 110–113, 2018.
https://doi.org/10.1007/978-3-319-94274-2_16

to an embodied externalized [2] interaction with the environment, interfaced by the SSD. By allowing them to regain access to parts of their *Umwelt*, SSDs improve how well Visually Impaired People (VIP) can interact with the world, restoring their sense of autonomy, control, and safety [3]. However, one of the main constraint of SSD design is the amount of information that can be conveyed to the user without creating an excessive cognitive load [4]. Indeed, the amount of information gathered by our vision is much greater than our tactile or auditory "bandwidth" [5], meaning that SSDs must carefully select what information they convey, and how they encode it.

2 Navigation and Blindness

Autonomous navigation is one of the greatest challenges VIP face, since vision plays a crucial role in gathering the information necessary for many processes involved in this complex task. Recent research supports the idea that VIP can learn the spatial layout of an environment and navigate inside of it as efficiently as the sighted, if given the proper information for this task [6, 7]. Indeed, our spatial representations are amodal [8], meaning they can also be elicited through audition and touch, with functionally equivalent properties. Therefore, with properly designed SSDs, VIP could autonomously perceive, interpret, learn and interact with their spatial environment.

Navigation is traditionally divided into two main categories: wayfinding (also called orientation) and locomotion (or mobility) [9]. Wayfinding refers to the mental processes allowing us to understand the large-scale spatial properties of our environment and localize ourselves amidst it, relatively to salient "visible" or memorized features. Locomotion refers to the mental and physical processes allowing us to move along a chosen path while successfully avoiding obstacles on the way [10].

Many of the current assistive devices for the blind mostly cater to locomotion, but not often to autonomous wayfinding. Indeed, these devices do not provide any large-scale information that would allow users to autonomously plan, navigate and update their path, or to find shortcuts. To accomplish this, we need to develop devices that address both locomotion and wayfinding, thus allowing for the emergence of spatial representations. It is with that aim that the TactiBelt system was developed.

3 The Importance of Spatial Cognition Models in SSD Design

Gaining a better understanding of the underlying mechanisms of space perception and how these mechanisms adapt to blindness would allow researchers to pinpoint precisely what information is crucial to elicit spatial representations and learning.

According to many spatial cognition theories, to properly compensate for the lack of vision, mobility assistive devices should provide information about important environmental cues, such as landmarks. Landmarks, which can be defined as stable, easily remembered and often visible landscape cues, have been shown to improve the ability of VIP to elaborate and organize mental representations of their environment [11, 12], and to navigate thanks to them. Finally, providing information about the surroundings topography, like the disposition of the roads, might prove helpful by allowing VIP to better identify their current location, and to foresee incoming direction changes.

4 The Tactibelt Preliminary Specifications

Based on the aforementioned recommendations, we put forward the following functional design for the TactiBelt system. The device will interface with the user through a belt fitted with vibrators, worn around the waist. We chose this type of interface because it allows the user to intuitively perceive ego-centered spatial information without requiring any complex information recoding. The belt will have 3 layers of vibrators to allow for a better coding of the elevation of obstacles.

The device will also include 2 front-facing cameras, embedded into a pair of glasses, combined with an inertial unit, to provide stable orientation-aware depth information about nearby obstacles. A GPS chip will provide absolute localization and ego-centered distance information about nearby landmarks. Cartographic data will be collected from online services or from buildings' blueprints for indoor navigation.

The TactiBelt will provide 4 types of information: nearby obstacles, landmarks, the surrounding topography (street intersection nodes), and the current destination. Those 4 types will be distinguishable by their tactile representation, i.e. the specific vibration pattern used for each of them. Periodic pulses of varying frequency and intensity will be used for each type of information, in order to introduce discontinuity in the signal in order to avoid habituation [12]. Additionally, the users will be able to manually add new landmarks (e.g. bus stops, their home, ...).

Those 4 information levels will not be presented simultaneously to avoid a cognitive overload [11, 12]. They will be sent sequentially [11], each being displayed for a varying duration depending on their priority: obstacles will have the highest priority, meaning they will be most frequently displayed and will take precedence over the others if a collision is imminent. The second most important one is the street intersection nodes, followed by the landmarks, and lastly, the destination. A maximum of 7 pieces of information of one type will be transmitted simultaneously, based on the specificities of human working memory [13]. However, this number will be adjustable by the users depending on their preferences and their experience with the device.

The distance and relative position of each element the belt "points to" will be given in an abstract and continuous manner: the vibration's intensity will represent the distance to the element, and the direction of the element will be given by activating the vibrator pointing towards the obstacle's direction. The elevation of an obstacle will be given in a symbolic manner, with a movement either pointing down or up, moving through the 3 layers of vibrators. The landmarks' identity will be given through vocal feedback, with bone conduction headphones to keep the users' audition free.

5 Conclusion and Future Work

This paper has addressed the concept of a new non-invasive dynamic navigation aid for the blind, the TactiBelt. Its originality arises from the fact that it assists not only locomotion through obstacle avoidance, but also spatial integration by providing intuitive information that will allow VIP to mentally map and learn their environment.

This will allow them to navigate autonomously and safely indoors and outdoors, enabling them to participate more actively in society.

Moreover, TactiBelt's adaptive design would make it fit for many uses by sighted people, such as providing dynamic, non-distractive and readily interpretable guidance in visually noisy environments (e.g. a smoky building for firefighters), or as a GPS substitute for drivers, allowing them to keep their eyes on the road at all times.

The system prototyping of the device is currently underway. A thorough evaluation with the targeted end users will be done to assert the relevance of our design, its acceptance by the VIP community and its validation against existing similar devices.

References

1. Bach-y-Rita, P., Collins, C.C., Saunders, F.A., White, B., Scadden, L.: Vision substitution by tactile image projection. Nature **221**(5184), 963–964 (1969)
2. Auvray, M., Philipona, D., O'Regan, J.K., Spence, C.: The perception of space and form recognition in a simulated environment: the case of minimalist sensory-substitution devices. Perception **36**(12), 1736–1751 (2007)
3. Kärcher, S.M., Fenzlaff, S., Hartmann, D., Nagel, S.K., König, P.: Sensory augmentation for the blind. Front. Hum. Neurosci. **6**, 37 (2012)
4. Kristjánsson, Á., et al.: Designing sensory-substitution devices: principles, pitfalls and potentials. Restor. Neurol. Neurosci. **34**(5), 769–787 (2016)
5. Spence, C.: The skin as a medium for sensory substitution. Multisensory Res. **27**(5–6), 293–312 (2014)
6. Chebat, D.-R., Harrar, V., Kupers, R., Maidenbaum, S., Amedi, A., Ptito, M.: Sensory substitution and the neural correlates of navigation in blindness. In: Pissaloux, E., Velázquez, R. (eds.) Mobility of Visually Impaired People, pp. 167–200. Springer, Cham (2018). https://doi.org/10.1007/978-3-319-54446-5_6
7. Pissaloux, E.E., Velazquez, R., Maingreaud, F.: A new framework for cognitive mobility of visually impaired users in using tactile device. IEEE Trans. Hum.-Mach. Syst. **47**(6), 1040–1051 (2017)
8. Loomis, J.M., Klatzky, R.L., Giudice, N.A.: Representing 3D space in working memory: spatial images from vision, hearing, touch, and language. In: Lacey, S., Lawson, R. (eds.) Multisensory Imagery, pp. 131–155. Springer, New York (2013). https://doi.org/10.1007/978-1-4614-5879-1_8
9. Montello, D.R.: Navigation. In: Shah, P., Miyake, A. (eds.) The Cambridge Handbook of Visuospatial Thinking Cambridge, pp. 257–294. Cambridge University Press (2005)
10. Waller, D., Nadel, L. (eds.): Handbook of Spatial Cognition. American Psychological Association, Washington, D.C. (2013)
11. Meers, S., Ward, K.: A substitute vision system for providing 3D perception and GPS navigation via electro-tactile stimulation (2005)
12. Srikulwong, M., O'Neill, E.: A comparative study of tactile representation techniques for landmarks on a wearable device, p. 2029 (2011)
13. Miller, G.A.: The magical number seven, plus or minus two: some limits on our capacity for processing information. Psychol. Rev. **63**(2), 81–97 (1956)

Virtual Navigation Environment for Blind and Low Vision People

Andreas Kunz[1]([✉]) [iD], Klaus Miesenberger[2] [iD], Limin Zeng[3] [iD], and Gerhard Weber[3] [iD]

[1] ETH Zurich, Leonhardsrasse 21, 8092 Zurich, Switzerland
kunz@iwf.mavt.ethz.ch
[2] Johannes Kepler University Linz, Altenbergerstraße 69, 4040 Linz, Austria
klaus.miesenberger@jku.at
[3] TU Dresden, Nöthnizer Strasse 46, 01062 Dresden, Germany
{limin.zeng,gerhard.weber}@tu-dresden.de

Abstract. For comprehensively participating in society, independent and safe mobility is an important skill for many daily activities. Spatial cognition is one of the most important human capabilities and addresses the acquisition, processing and utilization of knowledge about the spatial layout of environments. Humans predominantly use the visual sense for this and for blind and low vision people, the lack of spatial perception reduces their quality of life and their ability of independent living. In particular the spatial navigation in unknown environments imposes challenges, since there is no possibility to train navigation tasks in advance. Today, blind and visually impaired people still rely on traditional navigation aids such as a cane for micro-navigation, which - however - does not help for developing orientation at larger scale or for planning of routes. To overcome this problem, this paper introduces the concept of a virtual environment that allows experiencing unknown locations by real walking while still staying in a sage controlled environment. Since this virtual environment can be controlled in its complexity, it can be adjusted from an abstract training scenario to a real-life situation such as train stations or airports.

Keywords: Virtual reality · Real walking · Training environment

1 Introduction

Visually impaired people (VIP) encounter many mobility problems as stated by [1, 2]. To overcome such problems, many mobility aids were developed in the past decades to help VIP acquiring spatial information by avoiding obstacles [3], reading maps [4, 5], and navigating in unfamiliar regions [6, 7] by applying 3 main categories of non-visual interfaces: auditory-only (i.e. non-speech sounds and speech), haptic-tactile only (e.g. vibrotactile, electrotactile), and audio-haptic.

Only little research was done in using Virtual Reality (VR) to train VIP in navigation tasks prior to their exposure to real world. VR was shown to be advantageous for personalized orientation and mobility (O&M) trainings. Research outcomes reach from

K. Miesenberger and G. Kouroupetroglou (Eds.): ICCHP 2018, LNCS 10897, pp. 114–122, 2018.
https://doi.org/10.1007/978-3-319-94274-2_17

a virtual cane (mouse, keyboard, or force-feedback device) to other devices to navigate in an unfamiliar virtual environment [8–10].

The HOMERE system [11] was one of the first VR systems developed for a blind user to navigate a virtual environment (VE) to build a mental model. A real cane was triggered by a force-feedback device depending on the virtual ground. Together with audio and thermal feedback, it provided navigation cues that could help a blind user to orient in a large VE. However, the walking path is predefined, thus prohibiting free navigation by the VIP. A system by [12] offered the possibility of walking, but the range was rather limited due to the tracking that was employed. To answer the question whether a VR system could help to build a cognitive map of the environment, [13] built a VE which could be experienced by a force-feedback joystick together with an audio-output. It turned out that VEs are suitable to train cognitive maps, although there are still differences among users regarding the learned spatial arrangements of objects in the cognitive maps. However, these virtual training environments fail to address the important natural perception of real walking in VEs.

Although [14] reported that real walking in a VE improves sighted users' cognitive maps via visual representation, it is not clear whether such real walking could be applied to VIP, i.e. whether a non-visual representation (i.e. haptic and/or auditory) will improve VIP's spatial cognition as well. In particular, it is challenging for VIP to explore a large VE in a limited physical space while really walking. For an immersive experience for example, a 570 m^2 physical space was built by [15] to implement an early VR system without redirected walking. With redirected walking (RDW) algorithms [16, 17], it is possible to achieve a compression of virtual space into physical space of 10:1. However, RDW has never been applied before to VIP.

In this paper, we introduce the concept of using VR to design a multimodal interface (haptic, acoustic, sensomotoric perception) that will help VIP to build a cognitive map of the surrounding by real walking. The VR is controllable and can be adapted from an abstract obstacle representation like steps, walls, etc. to a complex representation of buildings that exist in real life. VIPs can thus train real world scenarios without leaving a safe and controlled physical space. However, experiencing large VEs in a limited physical space requires a subtle redirection, being achieved by gains. They will be applied to translations, rotations, and curvatures of the user's walking trajectory. This redirection technology will be applied for the first time to VIP.

2 System Description

2.1 Working Principle

VIPs have experiences and capabilities to learn spatial information and thus need personalized mobility training plans. A suitable training system is proposed in Fig. 1. While the VIP is in the training environment, he perceives acoustic and/or haptic feedback when approaching an obstacle. Since time and user position are continuously measured and analyzed in the "Walking Monitor", changes in speed, stops, or sudden turns give hints how familiar the user is with the experienced environment. After a certain amount of trials, the user performance will not exceed upper or lower thresholds anymore, and the next level of complexity can be loaded from the training plan repository. In other cases, it is also possible to reduce the VE's complexity level.

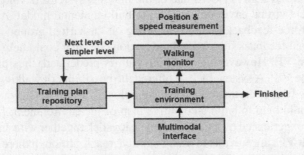

Fig. 1. A personalized training system.

2.2 Technical Setup

The system's hardware consists of an Intersense IS-1200 6 DOF tracking system, which is connected to an Oculus Rift DK 2 head-mounted display (HMD) (although there was no need to display images in the HMD). The tracking system's accuracy is apx. 10 mm in horizontal direction. The HMD is connected to an HP Elitebook 8560w laptop strapped to a backpack that has to be worn by the user. The system also consists of a pair of Sennheiser headphones to provide audio feedback (Fig. 2).

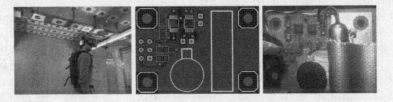

Fig. 2. System hardware (left) with layout of circuit board that drives the two haptic motors (middle) and completed printed circuit board with all components mounted (right).

For providing haptic feedback to a cane, two different vibration motors are mounted to a printed circuit board and driven by an Arduino Uno microcontroller. The board uses the DRV 2605L from Texas Instruments to generate different waveforms for the individual motors. An electronic switch is used to select and address the desired motor. For the communication between the Arduino board and the DRV 2605L, an I2C bus is user. The first motor is a C10-000 from Precision Microdrives, which uses a linear resonant actuator to generate an impulse feedback. The second motor is the 306-117, which is an eccentric rotating mass motor to provide vibrating feedback (Fig. 2). The virtual world was built in Unity and the walkable space comprised a 5 m × 10 m area, which is centered within the walls of a larger physical space. For the first experiments described here, no haptics and redirection are used.

2.3 Obstacle Alert System

A physical cane typically gives binary information whether there is an obstacle in the way or not. The distance to the obstacle is then automatically given by the length of the cane the VIP is familiar with. However, in a VE there is neither a physical cane nor a physical object it could collide with (besides the physical wall boundaries of the tracking space). This imposes the problem that a distance-dependent alert is missing and the VIP's walking speed is not taken into account. Thus, our training system provides a two-phase alert system, which takes into account the user's distance to an obstacle as well as his walking speed [18]. The three phases are shown in Fig. 3.

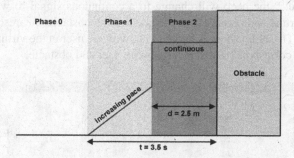

Fig. 3. The magnitude of the alert is determined by the user's time to impact.

Phase 1 is velocity-based and takes into account the time until the user would collide with an obstacle. He is warned if the time is below 3.5 s. In an ideal case, this phase would be sufficient. However, there are certain conditions, e.g. when the user stops moving in phase 1, where the velocity-based alert needs to be supplemented by an additional phase. Thus, phase 2 is distance-based and supplements the velocity-based phase 1. Phase 2 becomes necessary, since there might be the case where the user stands still in a close distance to an obstacle. In this case, phase 1 would not deliver any output, but phase 2 is still active. The two-phase warning system also allows for two different warning outputs. For the VE navigation, we rely on haptic and audio output only. With these two modalities, four different combinations are possible:

- The audio-audio combination consists of a beep with an increasing pace for phase 1, while it provides a continuous tone or phase 2.
- The haptic-haptic combination can make use of a variety of parameters. Since two different motors exist, impulse, continuous vibration, or a combination of both.
- The audio-haptic combination could replay an acoustic sound for phase 1, while a haptic feedback is provided for phase 2.
- The haptic-audio combination will provide a tactile feedback, followed by a sound output for phase 2.

3   Preliminary System Evaluation for Audio/Audio

For the preliminary evaluation described in the remainder of the paper, we focus on the audio-audio combination, while the other combinations will follow in future work. Unlike the mechanical sweep of a cane, which mainly detects obstacles in walking direction, the stereoscopic audio replay using the headphones also allows sonifying obstacles sideward, giving him more information of the objects' spatial distribution.

The audio-audio alert is modelled after the proximity warning system used to aid drivers in parking cars. If a user moves towards an obstacle at a constant speed, he will hear a beep that will increase its pace while the user approaches the obstacle. When the user enters phase 2, the beep will change to a continuous signal to warn him of the collision. The virtual audio sources are located in the obstacles nearest to the user, as shown in Fig. 4. The audio sources move along with the user in the virtual environment and their signals correspond to distance between user and obstacle.

Fig. 4. The audio feedback setup with virtual audio sources placed in the obstacles closest to the user, the fourth audio source behind the user is not shown [19].

To evaluate the acoustic alerts, a series of travel-to-target navigation scenarios was used (Fig. 5). Besides the audio signals, the subjects had no other navigation aids such as a cane. In Fig. 5, the start and end positions are shown, as well as walls and obstacles. Each of these basic layouts could variations as follows:

- Maze level: Each maze consists of 8 90° turns. Each maze also has a box somewhere in its geometry in order to avoid a completely zigzagged path.
- Office level: An open layout with three obstacles on the way. Obstacles include a square obstacle (1 × 1 m), a wall of 2.5 m length, and a wall corner of 2.0 × 1.5 m.
- Door level: A series of four doors on the way from start to finish. The doors can be in one of three positions: adjacent to either the left or right wall, or in the middle.

Fig. 5. The three scenarios for system evaluation (maze, office, door) in a 5 × 10 m [19] area.

Prior to the test, participants get an instruction about the task: *"There is a navigation scenario that you need to get through....Your task is to come from start to finish as quickly as possible. However, there are obstacles in your way from start to finish"*.

For each participant, positional data was recorded, as well as a corresponding time-stamp. From these measures, it is possible to determine the path walked by the participants together with the walking speed, distance travelled, completion time, the ratio of walking to non-walking time, and the proportions they spent in the phases.

All participants also have to complete a simulator sickness questionnaire immediately prior to and after the experiment. None of the participants showed symptoms of experiencing cybersickness. We used the motion sickness questionnaire [20]. For a preliminary technical test, we were not able to recruit VIP. Instead, we had 13 sighted users between 22 to 35 years age. By wearing the HMD, the subjects were blindfolded and could not see the real environment anymore. Seven of the users had prior experience with VR or any other room scale tracking. Four users had experience with low-end VR devices such as Google cardboard, and two users had experience with high-end VR (Rift, HTC Vive).

4   Preliminary Results

The 13 users performed in total 156 trials with the three different geometry types and its 4 variants. Since we wanted to test the alert efficiency only, none of the users experienced the same geometry twice to avoid learning effects. From totally 147 collisions, each of the 12 geometries had an average of $\mu = 3.77$ collisions. Regarding the time users spent in each phase, it is obvious that phase 1 duration was relatively short compared to phase 0 (no alert) and phase 2 (see Fig. 6). Thus, users either were in the safe zone (phase 0), in which no alert was triggered, or they rapidly crossed phase 1 to be in phase 2 and thus more endangered to experience a virtual collision.

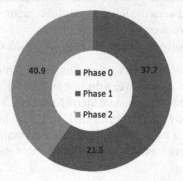

Fig. 6. Proportions of total times spent in each phase.

From the tracking system, the positional information together with the rime stamps was recorded. From this, a path visualization of when the user is walking versus when he has stopped is generated (see Fig. 7). It is clearly visible that users stopped frequently to acoustically detect the position of obstacles, they only walked 53% of the completion time while they used the other time for orientation.

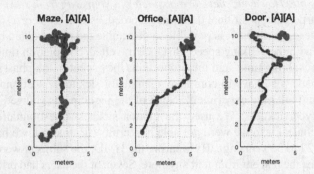

Fig. 7. Visualization of walking versus stopping. The points on the walking path indicate where the subject stopped for orientation.

5   Discussion and Future Work

The results still show a high number of collisions as well as a long time in which users did not walk but stopped for acoustic orientation. This might have several reasons:

- Since the group consisted of sighted users, they might not be trained to use acoustics for navigation as blind users would probably be, e.g. by clicking one's tongue.
- The combination of an increasing beep pace (phase 1) and a jump to a continuous beep (phase 2) might have irritated the users.
- For certain geometries, ambiguities in the audio output signal exist.
- The cognition process is more complex, since not only the existence of an obstacle is alerted, but also its coarse position (distance, orientation). This requires interpreting the beep pace between the left and the right ear, as well as some active movement of the head to overcome possible ambiguities.
- The test environment partly consisted of narrow corridors triggering alerts.

Future work on the acoustic alerts will focus on different syntheses of the sound signals. Since differences in pace between the left and the right ear are difficult to detect, other modalities like frequency or constant alert (for phase 2) will be tested. After these tests, an extensive user study will be performed, verifying how well this VE with real walking will support to train a mental model of the environment. The user studies will also evaluate the other output modalities and their combinations (haptic/haptic, haptic/ audio, audio/haptic).

References

1. Manduchi, R., Kurniawan, S.: Mobility-related accidents experienced by people with visual impairments. Res. Pract. Vis. Impair. Blind. **4**(2), 44–54 (2011)
2. Zeng, L.: A survey: outdoor mobility experiences by the visually impaired. In: Proceedings of Mensch and Computer 2015, pp. 391–397 (2011)
3. Zeng, L., Prescher, D., Weber, G.: Exploration and avoidance of surrounding obstacles for the visually impaired. In: Proceedings of ACM Assets, pp. 111–118 (2012)
4. Wang, Z., Li, N., Li, B.: Fast and independent access to map directions for people who are blind. Interact. Comput. **24**, 91–106 (2012)
5. Zeng, L., Miao, M., Weber, G.: Interactive audio-haptic map explorer on a tactile display. Interact. Comput. **27**(4), 413–429 (2015)
6. Katz, B., Kammoon, S., Parseihian, G., Gutierrez, O., Brilhault, A., Auvray, M., Truilliet, P., Denis, M., Thorpe, S., Jouffrais, C.: NAVIG: augmented reality guidance system for the visually impaired. Virtual Reality **16**(4), 253–269 (2012)
7. Yatani, K., Banovic, N., Truong, K.N.: SpaceSense: representing geographical information to visually impaired people using spatial tactile feedback. In: Proceedings of ACM CHI 2012, pp. 415–424 (2012)
8. Tzovaras, D., Moustakas, K., Nikolakis, G., Strintzis, M.G.: Interactive mixed reality white cane simulation for the training of the blind and the visually impaired. Pers. Ubiquit. Comput. **13**(1), 51–88 (2009)
9. Maidenbaum, S., Levy-Tzedek, S., Chebat, D., Amedi, A.: Increasing accessibility to the blind of virtual environments, using a virtual mobility aid based on the "EyeCane" feasibility study. PLoS ONE **8**(8), e72555 (2013)
10. Brayda, L., Campus, C., Gori, M.: Predicting successful tactile mapping of virtual objects. IEEE Trans. Haptics **6**(4), 473–483 (2013)
11. Lecuyer, A., Mobuchon, P., Meyard, C., Perret, J., Andriot, C., Colinot, J.-P.: HOMERE: a multimodal system for visually impaired people to explore virtual environments. In: Proceedings of the IEEE Virtual Reality Conference, pp. 251–258 (2003)
12. Torres-Gil, M.A., Cadanova-Gonzales, O., Gonzalez-Mora, J.L.: Applications of virtual reality for visually impaired people. WSEAS Trans. Comput. **9**(2), 184–193 (2010)
13. Lahav, O., Mioduser, D.: multisensory virtual environment for supporting blind person's acquisition of spatial cognitive mapping, orientation, and mobility skills. In: Proceedings of the 4th International Conference on Disability, Virtual Reality & Associated Technology, pp. 213–220 (2002)
14. Ruddle, R., Volkova, E., Bülthoff, H.: Walking improves your cognitive map in environments that are large-scale and large in extent. ACM Trans. Comput.-Hum. Interact. **18**(2), 10 (2011)
15. Waller, D., Bachmann, E., Hodgson, E., Beall, A.: The HIVE: a huge immersive virtual environment for research in spatial cognition. J. Behav. Res. Methods **39**(4), 835–843 (2007)
16. Razzaque, S., Kohn, Z., Whitton, M.C.: Redirected walking. In: Proceedings of Eurographics 2001, pp. 289–294 (2001)
17. Nescher, T., Huang, Y., Kunz, A.: Free walking experience using model predictive control. In: Proceedings of the IEEE Symposium on 3D User Interfaces, pp. 111–118 (2014)
18. Zank, M., Yao, C., Kunz, A.: Multi-phase wall warner system for real walking in virtual environments. In: Proceedings of the IEEE Symposium on 3D User Interfaces, pp. 223–224 (2017)

19. Yao, C.: Multi-phase safety system for real walking in virtual environments. Semester project ETH Zurich (2016)
20. Kennedy, R.S., Lane, N.E., Berbaum, K.S., Lilienthal, M.G.: Simulator sickness questionnaire: an enhanced method for quantifying simulator sickness. Int. J. Aviat. Psychol. **3**(3), 203–220 (1993)

Visual Shoreline Detection for Blind and Partially Sighted People

Daniel Koester[✉], Tobias Allgeyer, and Rainer Stiefelhagen

Karlsruhe Institute of Technology, Karlsruhe, Germany
{daniel.koester,tobias.allgeyer,rainer.stiefelhagen}@kit.edu

Abstract. Currently existing navigation and guidance systems do not properly address special guidance aides, such as the widely used white cane. Therefore, we propose a novel shoreline location system that detects and tracks possible shorelines from a user's perspective in an urban scenario. Our approach uses three dimensional scene information acquired from a stereo camera and can potentially inform a user of available shorelines as well as obstacles that are blocking an otherwise clear shoreline path, and thus help in shorelining. We evaluate two different algorithmic approaches on two different datasets, showing promising results. We aim to improve a user's scene understanding by providing relevant scene information and to help in the creation of a mental map of nearby guidance tasks. This can be especially helpful in reaching the next available shoreline in yet unknown locations, *e.g.*, at an intersection or a drive-way. Also, knowledge of available shorelines can be integrated into routing and guidance systems and vice versa.

Keywords: Assistive system · Orientation & mobility · Shorelines

1 Introduction

Today's navigation systems have become ubiquitous, as every smartphone capable of running *Google Maps*[1], it's accompanying *Maps* smartphone application, or other available navigation software, literally puts this capability into everyone's pocket. It was just recently that some of these added specialized pedestrian modes–*Google Maps* did so only in 2015–and provided a huge improvement over the so far road based routing. However, almost none of the existing systems address any special requirements, such as those of people affected by cerebral palsy, people with walking aids, or blind and partially sighted people. Therefore, to this modern day and age, it is common for blind and partially sighted people to mostly rely on other, more traditional means: the traditional skill of white cane usage–a skill that has to be learned through *Orientation and Mobility Training*–as well as guide dogs, or less common, echolocation.

In recent years, mostly through the creation of crowdfunded projects, especially the *Open Street Map*[2] project, innovation in those fields has hugely

---

[1] https://google.com/maps.
[2] https://openstreetmap.org.

© Springer International Publishing AG, part of Springer Nature 2018
K. Miesenberger and G. Kouroupetroglou (Eds.): ICCHP 2018, LNCS 10897, pp. 123–131, 2018.
https://doi.org/10.1007/978-3-319-94274-2_18

improved for researchers and hobbyists alike, as many more data sources are now publicly available [1] and their quality continues to increase over time [2]. Using such available data sources, especially geolocation meta data, *e.g.*, location and availability of accessible pedestrian traffic lights, zebra crossings, ramps, footbridges and many more, the creation of adapted routing algorithms has become feasible. Also, it is now possible to create routes that integrate the usage of assistive systems into low-level routing decisions. Recently, Koester *et al.* [3] have investigated such routing on a shoreline-level detail, in order to provide routes for blind and partially sighted people. They try to adhere to specific requirements and include learned white cane usage patterns by integrating shorelines into the routing process.

In this work, we try to visually detect and track shorelines from a first person view approach, using three dimensional, stereo reconstruction data provided by a body worn camera. A few examples of our shoreline detection can be seen in varying situations in Fig. 1.

(a)   (b)

(c)   (d)

Fig. 1. Four example images, where the yellow dashed line shows the reference label, while the green dotted line is our detection. (a) is the full image of a building's facade, while (b)–(d) are magnified cutouts for improved visibility, where (b) shows a stone-fence, (c) a gap in the shoreline due to a driveway and (d) a stone wall. All four show our algorithm is capable of very accurately detecting shorelines in varying situations. (Color figure online)

First, we calculate and track the main vanishing point in our image and determine a region of interest to search for shorelines, usually below the vanishing point to left and right. Those shorelines are mostly haptic edges of some kind, *e.g.*, between the sidewalk and building walls, walkway side curbs or walkway borders, and are visible as such in a stereo reconstruction. We have developed two slightly different variations to track these, both provide a candidate for each frame. Then we track and average our shoreline candidates over multiple frames and report the most promising one(s).

Our proposed system is able to inform users of available close by shorelines that point towards their current walking direction and can help to locate the next available shoreline from afar. This is especially useful after road crossings or in urban areas, where buildings are separated by driveways and the next shoreline might be hard to find, or navigate to in a straightforward manner. The system proves especially helpful in unknown locations, where a lot of white cane users would most likely not feel comfortable to explore the terrain by themselves. Furthermore, having additional shoreline availability information can greatly improve a user's scene layout understanding in general as well as the personally perceived safety when navigating in busy urban areas.

2 Related Work

While navigation systems have become widespread, they usually don't adapt to special needs, or often require expensive specialized hardware, as stated by Csapó *et al.* [4] in a survey of routing applications for blind and partially sighted people. Except for the recent shoreline level routing proposed by Koester *et al.* [3], existing routing approaches do not acknowledge the special requirements created by shorelining and the specific requirements this technique creates for such systems when it comes to low level decisions.

First person view approaches for navigation and orientation of blind and partially sighted people have so far mostly focused on very specific and limited street crossing modalities, such as zebra crossing detection by Se [5], Ahmetovic *et al.* [6–8], or Ivanchenko *et al.* [9,10], and traffic lights, for example by Ivanchenko *et al.* [11]. A survey by Elmannai and Elleithy [12] provides a comprehensive overview of general wearable assistive navigation and orientation devices, and discusses benefits and limitations in detail.

To the best of our knowledge, no existing work has so far tried to detect and track inner or outer shorelines for white cane related usage of blind and partially sighted people, using a visual approach from a first person viewpoint. The most similar work has been created by Coughlan *et al.* [13,14] and Ivanchenko *et al.* [15], who presented systems for curb and shoreline detection for blind and partially sighted wheelchair users, in order to prevent them from hazards and obstacles. Although their systems were not intended for active white cane usage, their motivation and intention is quite similar to ours.

3   Methodology

Our algorithm consists of two main components: a vanishing point detection and the actual shoreline detection. Furthermore, we use a simple tracking approach for both steps to improve and stabilize their detection over time. Currently, our systems assumes the existence of a vertical segment next to the ground-plane, *i.e.*, a building's wall or a fence adjacent to the pavement and we assume an urban area in a *Manhattan Style World*. Whether such a wall is generally available can also be gleaned from additional information, for example the shoreline-level routing provided by Koester *et al.* [3], although, the required data and accuracy is not guaranteed for in the underlying *Open Street Map*, as the quality might vary greatly between locations.

3.1   Visual Odometry

Visual odometry data is readily provided by the *Stereolabs ZED*[3] camera for our own dataset and we use *LIBVISO2*[4] [16] for the *Flowerbox*[5] dataset (as it does not provide odometry). We estimate the user's current direction of movement from that visual odometry data by averaging the location differences of the last 10 camera positions. This provides us with an estimated direction of possible future shoreline candidates, as those have to be somewhat aligned to the walking direction. Since we assume a *Manhattan Style World*, this direction often also aligns with the vanishing point, which we also try to detect.

3.2   Vanishing Points

Vanishing points are detected similar to Wu *et al.* [17], albeit with some major differences. First, we use a different line detection algorithm, *EDLines* [18], to search for all straight line segments, but discard all almost horizontal and vertical segments, as these usually don't contribute to vanishing points – at least in a *Manhattan Style World* almost all edges are either horizontal/vertical or point straight towards a vanishing point. Similar to Wu *et al.* [17], we then weigh line segments based on their direction, *i.e.*, directions closer to 45° are better, and length, *i.e.*, where longer is better. Finally, we use RANSAC [19] to determine candidates and decide on the point with the highest accumulated score.

These points are tracked over time (one per frame) in world coordinates by converting them into spherical coordinates and using a two-dimensional decaying accumulator array over a sphere's surface, where the maximum of all cells yields the averaged vanishing point coordinates. Those are then projected into the 2D image, which stabilizes the vanishing point in the always moving camera image with respect to the person's own ego-motion.

---

[3] https://www.stereolabs.com/zed/.

[4] http://cvlibs.net/software/libviso/.

[5] https://cvhci.anthropomatik.kit.edu/~dkoester/data/flowerbox.zip.

3.3 Shorelines

Using the vanishing point, we determine a region of interest in the disparity image or the point cloud from the stereo reconstruction. This region is located below the vanishing point, usually to the left or right of it, where one would expect to find inner or outer shorelines, *i.e.*, sidewalk curbs or building walls.

Since the *ZED* depth camera directly provides a point cloud and surface normals, we can use those normals to distinguish between ground (upright surfaces) and walls (vertical surfaces), by comparing them with our movement vector and assuming a somewhat upright held camera (a constraint that is usually satisfied by body worn cameras). We use an implementation [20] of an optimized RANSAC modification by Chum and Matas [21] to generate surfaces from those identified ground and wall pixels. The intersection of ground and wall surface then represents our shoreline candidate for the current frame.

When we do not have point clouds and surface normals (the *Flowerbox* dataset does not provide them), we rely only on the disparity image. We then filter the above mentioned region in the image using a median of a Gaussian to smooth noise and outliers in the depth data. After calculating gradients in X and Y direction of the disparity image, we can separate horizontal surfaces, *e.g.*, ground pixels, from vertical surfaces, *e.g.*, walls or curbs, using fixed thresholds. A morphological *opening* operation closes small holes and discards some more outliers. Finally, we determine shoreline candidate points by combining border regions from horizontal and vertical surfaces in regions where these borders overlap. We then transform these points into 3D space and use RANSAC to calculate our final shoreline candidate.

In both cases, we then merge consecutive shoreline candidates, *i.e.*, from consecutive images in a similar location, by using a confidence based weighted combination of these candidates. We keep a list of candidates and track their confidences over time, updating them each time a candidate is found in the currently evaluated frame. Keeping only valid candidates over time, we return the average of all remaining candidates. This tracking approach also stabilizes the shoreline and improves its distance and orientation with respect to the actually existing shoreline.

4   Experimental Evaluation

We have evaluated our approach on suitable parts of the *Flowerbox* dataset, as this dataset provides us with calibrated stereo images, taken from a first person viewpoint in an urban setting. We only consider videos where shorelines are clearly visible, *i.e.*, building walls or curbs and label the visible shorelines. To calculate an angular error and the minimal distance of our detected shoreline to the label, we convert our 2D labels into a 3D line by projecting the individual pixels of the labeled line in the 2D image into 3D coordinates and then use RANSAC to determine the best fitting line in 3D world coordinates.

This allows us to directly calculate the three dimensional angular error, *i.e.*, the angle between the two lines viewed as vectors from the same origin. The

Table 1. Shoreline detection results for 3 videos of the *FlowerBox* dataset. Angles (median $\tilde{\Theta}$, mean $\bar{\Theta}$, standard deviation δ_Θ) are given in degrees and distances (median $\tilde{d}$, mean $\bar{d}$, standard deviation δ_d) are in cm, calculated using transformed real world points and (shore-)lines.

	$\tilde{\Theta}$	$\bar{\Theta}$	δ_Θ	$\tilde{d}$	$\bar{d}$	δ_d
sidewalk	0.6°	3.8°	9.5°	2.2cm	6.8cm	18.2cm
sidewalk-2	1.4°	3.9°	9.5°	1.7cm	3.3cm	5.7cm
sidewalk-leveled	0.4°	1.1°	3.9°	2.4cm	2.4cm	1.3cm

Table 2. Shoreline detection results for 6 videos of our own data for our disparity image based algorithm (same algorithm as used for *Flowerbox*). Angles and distances are given as in Table 1. Some digits had to be omitted for space reasons.

	frame-wise detection						averaged detection					
	$\tilde{\Theta}$	$\bar{\Theta}$	δ_Θ	$\tilde{d}$	$\bar{d}$	δ_d	$\tilde{\Theta}$	$\bar{\Theta}$	δ_Θ	$\tilde{d}$	$\bar{d}$	δ_d
I	5.8	8.0	11.1	0.28	0.40	0.43	7.2	8.3	5.6	0.40	0.55	0.43
II	13	14	9.9	0.10	0.10	0.06	13	14	8.9	0.12	0.21	0.36
III	2.3	4.4	5.2	0.19	0.21	0.14	1.8	2.8	3.0	0.22	0.26	0.20
IV	2.1	8.2	12	0.12	0.16	0.19	3.2	7.2	10.9	0.13	0.19	0.23
V	2.6	3.0	1.9	0.12	0.12	0.07	3.0	8.4	18.3	0.13	0.43	0.86
VI	2.2	2.5	1.4	0.16	0.16	0.06	2.5	4.2	3.5	0.19	0.46	0.53

Table 3. Shoreline detection results for 6 videos of our own data for our point cloud based algorithm, using surface normales. Angles and distances are given as in Table 1.

	frame-wise detection						averaged detection					
	$\tilde{\Theta}$	$\bar{\Theta}$	δ_Θ	$\tilde{d}$	$\bar{d}$	δ_d	$\tilde{\Theta}$	$\bar{\Theta}$	δ_Θ	$\tilde{d}$	$\bar{d}$	δ_d
I	2.0	6.2	14.2	0.07	0.15	0.26	1.5	2.9	3.4	0.12	0.20	0.24
II	3.0	5.4	7.7	0.05	0.09	0.20	1.6	2.0	1.8	0.06	0.07	0.08
III	1.5	4.6	9.2	0.04	0.06	0.13	1.1	2.0	2.8	0.03	0.03	0.02
III	1.5	4.6	9.2	0.04	0.06	0.13	1.1	2.0	2.8	0.03	0.03	0.02
IV	4.2	7.7	14.1	0.03	0.04	0.06	2.4	3.0	1.8	0.02	0.06	0.14
V	1.2	1.7	2.4	0.03	0.04	0.07	1.1	1.3	0.8	0.02	0.03	0.11
VI	1.4	4.1	8.4	0.04	0.06	0.17	1.3	1.6	1.0	0.02	0.05	0.04

Table 4. Average values over all videos of Tables 2 and 3, comparing the disparity image based algorithm (DI) with the point cloud based algorithm (PCL). Angles and distances are given as in Table 1.

	frame-wise detection						averaged detection					
	$\tilde{\Theta}$	$\bar{\Theta}$	δ_Θ	$\tilde{d}$	$\bar{d}$	δ_d	$\tilde{\Theta}$	$\bar{\Theta}$	δ_Θ	$\tilde{d}$	$\bar{d}$	δ_d
DI	4.6	6.7	7.0	0.16	0.19	0.16	5.1	7.4	8.4	0.20	0.35	0.43
PCL	2.2	4.9	9.3	0.04	0.08	0.15	1.5	2.1	1.9	0.04	0.07	0.10

minimal distance is calculated by determining the three dimensional distance of our detected shoreline candidate to each point on the labeled line, as detection and label are almost always a set of skewed lines that do not intersect.

Evaluation results for the most viable three of the *FlowerBox* videos are given in Table 1. Furthermore, we evaluate our approach on our own data recorded with a *Stereolabs ZED* camera and compare both versions of our algorithm, the disparity image based algorithm in Table 2 as well as the point cloud and surface normal based algorithm in Table 3. We show that, especially for the point cloud based version, the averaging and tracking over multiple frames helps a lot to reduce errors. Finally, we compare both algorithms in Table 4, where the point cloud based method greatly outperforms the disparity image based algorithm.

5   Conclusion

We demonstrate an algorithm to detect shorelines from a first person view. To the best of our knowledge, no such system exists so far for blind and partially sighted people for use with the white cane. Our proposed shoreline detection algorithm, which relies on vanishing points and edges it can detect and track, achieves very promising results and works very accurate for the tested scenarios. This approach could potentially be used to aide in shorelining, *i.e.*, locating and navigating along shorelines, a technique commonly used by blind and partially sighted people. However, some adaption to less strong visible shorelines, such as walkway borders, is required to increase its usefulness and further evaluation is needed. Finally, we plan to test our approach in a user study to determine it's usefulness and integrate it as a part of a guidance system for blind and partially sighted people that is capable of providing fine grained orientation and guidance information to the user.

Acknowledgements. This work has been partially funded by the *Bundesministerium für Bildung und Forschung (BMBF)* under grant no. 16SV7609.

References

1. Goodchild, M.F.: Citizens as sensors: the world of volunteered geography. GeoJ. **69**(4), 211–221 (2007). https://doi.org/10.1007/s10708-007-9111-y
2. Zielstra, D., Zipf, A.: Quantitative studies on the data quality of OpenStreetMap in Germany. In: Proceedings of GIScience (2010). https://www.researchgate.net/publication/267989860_Quantitative_Studies_on_the_Data_Quality_of_OpenStreetMap_in_Germany
3. Koester, D., Awiszus, M., Stiefelhagen, R.: Mind the gap: virtual shorelines for blind and partially sighted people. In: IEEE International Conference on Computer Vision Workshops (ICCVW), pp. 1443–1451 (2017). https://doi.org/10.1109/ICCVW.2017.171
4. Csapó, Á., Wersényi, G., Nagy, H., Stockman, T.: A survey of assistive technologies and applications for blind users on mobile platforms: a review and foundation for research. J. Multimodal User Interfaces **9**(4), 275–286 (2015). https://doi.org/10.1007/s12193-015-0182-7

5. Se, S.: Zebra-crossing detection for the partially sighted. In: IEEE Conference on Computer Vision and Pattern Recognition, pp. 211–217 (2000). https://doi.org/10.1109/CVPR.2000.854787

6. Ahmetovic, D., Bernareggi, C., Mascetti, S.: Zebralocalizer: identification and localization of pedestrian crossings. In: Proceedings of the International Conference on Human Computer Interaction with Mobile Devices and Services, pp. 275–286 (2011). https://doi.org/10.1145/2037373.2037415

7. Ahmetovic, D., Bernareggi, C., Gerino, A., Mascetti, S.: ZebraRecognizer: efficient and precise localization of pedestrian crossings. In: 22nd International Conference on Pattern Recognition (ICPR), pp. 2566–2571 (2014). https://doi.org/10.1109/ICPR.2014.443

8. Ahmetovic, D., Manduchi, R., Coughlan, J., Mascetti, S.: Mind your crossings: mining GIS imagery for crosswalk localization. ACM Trans. Access. Comput. 9(4), 11:1–11:25 (2017). https://doi.org/10.1145/3046790

9. Ivanchenko, V., Coughlan, J., Shen, H.: Detecting and locating crosswalks using a camera phone. In: IEEE Conference on Computer Vision and Pattern Recognition Workshops (2008). https://doi.org/10.1109/CVPRW.2008.4563143

10. Ivanchenko, V., Coughlan, J., Shen, H.: Crosswatch: a camera phone system for orienting visually impaired pedestrians at traffic intersections. In: Miesenberger, K., Klaus, J., Zagler, W., Karshmer, A. (eds.) ICCHP 2008. LNCS, vol. 5105, pp. 1122–1128. Springer, Heidelberg (2008). https://doi.org/10.1007/978-3-540-70540-6_168

11. Ivanchenko, V., Coughlan, J., Shen, H.: Real-time walk light detection with a mobile phone. In: Miesenberger, K., Klaus, J., Zagler, W., Karshmer, A. (eds.) ICCHP 2010. LNCS, vol. 6180, pp. 229–234. Springer, Heidelberg (2010). https://doi.org/10.1007/978-3-642-14100-3_34

12. Elmannai, W., Elleithy, K.: Sensor-based assistive devices for visually-impaired people: current status, challenges, and future directions. Sensors 17(3), 565 (2017). https://doi.org/10.3390/s17030565

13. Coughlan, J., Manduchi, R., Shen, H.: Computer vision-based terrain sensors for blind wheelchair users. In: Miesenberger, K., Klaus, J., Zagler, W.L., Karshmer, A.I. (eds.) ICCHP 2006. LNCS, vol. 4061, pp. 1294–1297. Springer, Heidelberg (2006). https://doi.org/10.1007/11788713_186

14. Coughlan, J., Shen, H.: Terrain analysis for blind wheelchair users: computer vision algorithms for finding curbs and other negative obstacles. In: CVHI (2007). https://www.ski.org/terrain-analysis-blind-wheelchair-users-computer-vision-algorithms-finding-curbs-and-other-negative

15. Ivanchenko, V., Coughlan, J., Gerrey, W., Shen, H.: Computer vision-based clear path guidance for blind wheelchair users. In: Proceedings of the 10th International ACM SIGACCESS Conference on Computers and Accessibility, pp. 291–292 (2008). https://doi.org/10.1145/1414471.1414543

16. Geiger, A., Ziegler, J., Stiller, C.: StereoScan: dense 3D reconstruction in real-time. In: Intelligent Vehicles Symposium (IV), pp. 963–968 (2011). https://doi.org/10.1109/IVS.2011.5940405

17. Wu, Z., Fu, W., Xue, R., Wang, W.: A novel line space voting method for vanishing-point detection of general road images. Sensors 16(7), 948 (2016). https://doi.org/10.3390/s16070948

18. Akinlar, C., Topal, C.: EDLines: real-time segment detection by edge drawing. In: 18th IEEE International Conference on Image Processing (ICIP), pp. 2837–2840 (2011). https://doi.org/10.1109/ICIP.2011.6116138

19. Fischler, M., Bolles, R.: Random sample consensus: a paradigm for model fitting with applications to image analysis and automated cartography. Commun. ACM **24**(6), 381–395 (1981). https://doi.org/10.1145/358669.358692
20. Raguram, R., Chum, O., Pollefeys, M., Matas, J., Frahm, J.: USAC: a universal framework for random sample consensus. IEEE Trans. Pattern Anal. Mach. Intell. **35**(8), 2022–2038 (2013). https://doi.org/10.1109/TPAMI.2012.257
21. Chum, O., Matas, J.: Optimal randomized RANSAC. IEEE Trans. Pattern Anal. Mach. Intell. **30**(8), 1472–1482 (2008). https://doi.org/10.1109/TPAMI.2007.70787

3D Printing in the Domain of Assistive Technologies (AT) and Do It Yourselves (DIY) AT

3D-Printing of Personalized Assistive Technology

Veronika Maria Berger[1]([✉]), Gerhard Nussbaum[2], Carina Emminger[1],
and Zoltan Major[1]

[1] Institute of Polymer Product Engineering, Johannes Kepler University, Linz, Austria
veronika.berger@jku.at
[2] Competence Network Information Technology to Support the Integration of People
with Disabilities, Linz, Austria
gerhard.nussbaum@ki-i.at

Abstract. Mouth sticks were invented to increase the independence of people
with reduced or no hand/arm functionality. To enhance the usability and acceptance of these assistive devices, a process to create fully personalized mouth sticks
has been developed. In order to enable the users to use the mouth stick for diverse
applications like signing, drawing, using smart phones, tablets and computers, or
even doing handcraft, the tips are chosen accordingly. The users can design their
own mouth stick in an online web tool, then the fully personalized geometry of
the mouth piece is 3D-printed with medical grade polymer, and the stick and tip
are customized. As the use of regular computer accessories can be challenging
for mouth stick users, this paper also elaborates on the example of a computer
mouse, how these can be adapted to be more accessible for mouth stick users and
how 3D-printers can help to quickly create, adapt and distribute assistive technology. Several mouse case designs for mouth stick users were developed, 3D-
printed and tested using a participatory design approach and comparing it to a
morphological analysis approach.

Keywords: 3D-printing · Mouth stick · Assistive technology
Computer mouse

1 Introduction

People with reduced or no hand/arm functionality need assistive technology (AT) to
improve their independence. One of the most versatile ATs is the mouth stick. It allows
to perform tasks like signing, turning pages in books or magazines, typing on computer
keyboards, using computer mice, smart phones or tablets, and even do creative tasks
like drawing or macramé [1–7]. At the same time, mouth sticks are relatively cheap low-
tech devices, and easily transportable to be used also in environments, not specifically
adapted for people with special needs (e.g. standard keyboards, elevator buttons…).

A mouth stick consists of three main parts: a mouth piece, a stick and a tip. As the
mouth piece is in direct contact with teeth and mucous membranes, the personalization
of this part is most crucial for health reasons. A medically certified material for long
term use in contact with mucous membranes is highly recommended and the geometry
has to be fit to the mouth of the user. The cut out for the tongue, the height and the width

© Springer International Publishing AG, part of Springer Nature 2018
K. Miesenberger and G. Kouroupetroglou (Eds.): ICCHP 2018, LNCS 10897, pp. 135–142, 2018.
https://doi.org/10.1007/978-3-319-94274-2_19

of the mouth piece should be selected accordingly. Dental imprints help to distribute the biting force equally over all teeth, thus preventing tooth displacement [2, 8]. The stick's length is chosen depending on the type of use. If the object of interest is positioned in front of the user at eye level, a shorter lightweight straight stick can be chosen. If the object is positioned on a table, the stick is recommended to be longer and to be bent in two positions, to be able to sit comfortably, see around the stick, and have gravity pull in the direction the user has to push. For writing, drawing, and painting, pen holders are installed at the tip. Electrically conductive rubbers are needed for touch screen applications; wear resistant rubbers can be used for typing on keyboards, turning pages and a lot of other applications. For board games, pulling things, and most of handcraft, tips like pliers, hooks or even pneumatic grippers can be used [6, 9].

For trained mouth stick users, the use of regular computers, keyboards and mice is feasible. There are keyboards for mouth or head stick users, like the specially designed Maltron Head/Mouth Stick Keyboard or extra compact keyboards like the KeySonic ACK-3400U, but no specially designed mice for the use with mouse sticks could be found [10–14]. Numerous alternative mouse solutions like special trackball mice [12], Touchpads, mouth operated mice like The Lipstick and head-trackers such as SmartNav®, HeadMouseExtreme® and Head Pilot® are commercially available. However, using alternative mouse solutions like head-trackers or mouth operated mice in the combination with mouth sticks is not really practical. Thus, the idea arose to design a 3D-printable mouse case suitable for mouth stick users that can be distributed over the platform "Thingiverse". Like this, globally people will have access to a low-cost solution for the adaption of regular computer mice. An inductive study was conducted involving an experienced mouth stick user directly in the design process in order to find a suitable mouse case solution for mouth stick users that can be downloaded and 3D-printed all over the world.

2   Methods

Mouth Stick. For the development of the personalized mouth stick a participatory design approach was used. By questionnaires, workshops and focus groups throughout the development phases occupational therapists and end users were integrated as experts in the selection of the materials, the development of a web tool (enables the users to design their own personalized mouth sticks by the use of parametric design) up until the testing of the personalized mouth sticks with the 3D-printed mouth pieces designed and 'ordered' via the web tool.

Mouse Case Design. The first approach to design a mouse case especially for the use with a mouth stick was based on morphological analysis, a method for non-quantified modelling. At the start of the design phase, a morphological box showing the needed functions on the vertical axis and several solutions for each function on the horizontal axis was set up, thus creating a table where possible combinations of solutions could be marked. These concepts were then evaluated by giving points to different selected properties like weight, costs, usability, maintenance, functionality, assembly effort and sustainability. The concept with most points, then was selected for prototyping and tested by a user [15].

The second design approach for mouse cases was based on the participatory design principle. Being a quick inductive study, only one experienced mouth stick user could be involved during the whole design process so far. He also tested the prototypes 32 h long for office work and programming.

3   Design and Prototyping of Mouse Cases

For this study, two different types of mouse cases were distinguished. For the first approach a regular mouse was dismantled and a new full mouse case was designed ("full-case"). The second type ("plug-case") aimed to keep the assembly effort as low as possible. Plug-case versions are to be plugged on top of a regular mouse. The diverse prototypes were 3D-printed using Fused-Filament-Fabrication with a Stratasys Dimension Elite, an Evo-tech Evolizer and a low-cost 3D-Printer using ABS for the mouse cases.

3.1   Full-Case

Version 1 was designed using morphological analysis. The circuit board, feet and the optical lens were taken from a standard Microsoft USB mouse. The concept consists of a top, a bottom, a dividing plate, two buttons and six screws (see Fig. 1 left). The click buttons are set up one behind the other, considering that clicking on sides might move the mouse around, and have indentations for the tip of the mouth stick. No wheel function was implemented. The case has to be assembled with six screws and is fully closed.

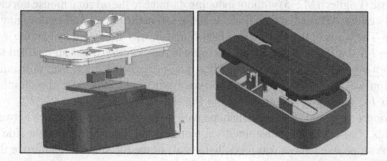

Fig. 1. Exploitation views of full mouse cases for mouth stick users. Left: Version 1 - design following the morphological analysis, Right: Version 2 - design following the participatory design approach.

Taking the user feedback from the user test of *Version 1* into account wireless mice were selected for the further prototypes. *Version 2* (see Fig. 1 right) was built, taking the complete circuit board and the mouse wheel of the wireless mouse Microsoft 1850. This mouse was chosen, because it was easy to dismantle, and the mouse wheel holders sit directly on the circuit board. This is useful to create a design as flat as possible.

Version 2 consists of a case for the circuit board and a lid, which lets the original mouse wheel stick out. The top surface is covered fully with a grid like structure for better grip of the mouth stick tip.

3.2 Plug-Case

The easiest version to adapt a mouse case for the use with a mouse stick is to glue a non-slip foil onto the top surface. Another version would be to glue small parts of plastic with an even surface on top of each of the click surfaces. However, both adaptions do not meet the user requirements of having a flat surface on top. The adaption with the non-slip foil was also not satisfying for the user because after three weeks of usage the foil got discoloured and the non-slip surface was abraded which added to the non-appealing look of this version. Additionally, the round shape of the original mouse was not changed, which still made it hard for the user to perform mouse clicks and drag & drop without slipping along the surface. For the adaption with small cubes either thick double sided tape has to be used in order to balance out the curvature difference between the contact surfaces, or the exact surface of the original mouse has to be scanned and converted into a CAD-surface to create a part that fits perfectly to the mouse surface. Either way, the mouse ends up with two pieces glued on top of the clicking surfaces, which might look botched. This was against the user's wish, so we did not manufacture this version.

The plug-cases were co-designed from the user to also have a solution available for people who do not want to dismantle a mouse and just want to have a non-destructive adaption of a regular mouse (full manufacturer warranty is remaining). Here the main user requirements were the same as for *Version 2* of the full mouse case.

The first plug-case was designed to be 3D-printed and simply plugged over the original mouse (Logitech M235) without inducing damage to the original mouse nor creating assembly effort. All versions facilitate clicking left and right as well as dragging while clicking. The realisation of a mouse wheel function was attempted in *Version 4* and *5*. *Versions 1* to *4* all have a flat surface on top whereas *Version 5* has an inclined surface between a big flat surface and two smaller flat surfaces at the clicking positions. The inclination was designed to make the original wheel accessible for the mouth stick. *Versions 1–5* of plug-cases can be seen in Fig. 2 from left to right.

Version 1 has a quite rectangular shape with broad click pads and space between the click pads. The clicks are transmitted via teeth on the outer left and right side of the design. A stripe like pattern was modelled at half of the top surface to improve the grip during mouse movements.

Version 2 is an adaption of *Version 1* but has a triangular shape for the click pads for higher flexibility and therefore softer clicking. The space between the click teeth is narrower. At the grip surface from *Version 1* an additional stripe perpendicular to the others was added in the middle of the design in order to stabilize the mouth stick during left and right movements.

Version 3 is again a more rectangular shape with extra broad click pads, click teeth in the middle of the original click pads and a border around the click pads for immediate haptic feedback for the user. The whole top surface including the click pads are covered with a grid pattern.

Version 4 was designed to combine a flat surface on the top with a mouse wheel function. Between thin click pads a new mouse wheel is fixed on the side wall of the case, touching the original mouse wheel and thus allowing to turn the mouse wheel with the new wheel in the opposite direction. Because all other version do not need the wheel holder, this is the only version closed on all sides of the original mouse. The stripe like pattern was taken from *Version 2*.

Version 5 is the only plug-case which is not flat on the top. In order to facilitate the usage of the original mouse wheel, the click pads were divided into two parts: an inclined surface over the length of the original click pads and small horizontal click pads sticking out over the length of the mouse. The original mouse wheel peeks out between the inclined surfaces allowing access for mouth sticks. The horizontal faces are necessary not to slip downwards while clicking. For grip, also in this version grid like structure was modelled on the horizontal surfaces.

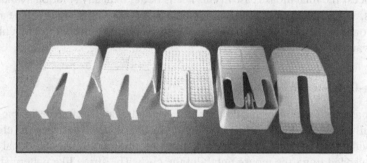

Fig. 2. Prototypes of plug-cases to be used in combination with a regular computer mouse for better accessability for mouth stick users. From left to right: Versions 1 to 5.

4   Results and Discussion

With the development of the personalized mouth stick, it could be shown, that a design tool like the web tool, is a suitable tool, to create personalized devices. The user test of the final personalized prototypes with subsequent focus group showed that the users were able to use their self-designed personalized mouth sticks. Moreover, they showed great satisfaction that they could design their AT fitting exactly to their body and their everyday life. Occupational therapists expressed motivation to use their experience from this development process to recommend mouth stick usage for eligible future clients.

4.1   Full-Case - User Feedback

Version 1, designed with the morphological analysis approach, was the first design tested by the user. The user liked that the case is closed, therefore protects the circuit board from dust and is stable enough against breaking in case of falling from a table. Strong criticism was voiced that the mouse cable orients the mouse, which makes usage for mouth stick users frustrating to impossible. The position of the buttons behind each other was seen as not necessary for the experienced user, on the contrary he commented, that mouth stick movement in front and back is more exhausting than from left to right. The indentations at the buttons were experienced as too deep, making it harder to move the mouth stick quickly in and out of that position.

Version 2 was constructed with the participatory design approach. The user expressed the following requirements: clicking left and right and dragging while clicking are mandatory functions; the mouse wheel function is 'nice to have'. It should be wireless, as low as possible (ideally the same height as his keyboard), good grip on the top surface and easy to move around (low friction coefficient at the bottom), easy to click and steerable also at the click pads. The design was iterated several times with minor adjustments for better fixation of the lid onto the case and lowering the stiffness of the click pads by thinning for softer click resistance. Ideally the case is closed against dust, only with a cut for the original mouse wheel. By involving the user directly into the design process the final mouse case fits his needs better than any solution available until now. Thus, a very high user satisfaction could be achieved. The designs will be available for download on the platform 'Thingiverse' and can be 3D-printed in any colour and material wanted.

4.2   Plug-Case – User Feedback

The plug-case designs considered the user requirements stated before designing *Version 2* of the full cases. For *Version 1* of the plug-cases the distance between the click teeth was too wide, thus pushing the case away from the mouse so that additional fixation would be needed to fix the mouse tightly in the case. The stripe like pattern should be adjusted with a long perpendicular stripe, to hinder sideways slipping of the tip.

Version 2 with the narrower teeth distance fitted very tightly on the mouse but the user did not like that the click pads were smaller than in *Version 1*. He stated that larger click pads need less precision thus making the clicking easier with the mouth stick. The stripe like pattern should be changed to a grid like pattern and should be spread over the whole top surface including the click pads. Additionally a small border should be added around the click pads for direct haptic feedback.

Version 3 was quite satisfying for the user. The grid like pattern gave enough grip on the whole top surface. The haptic feedback at the click pads was experienced as nice to have so the user stated that it would be even better, if the border reaches around the whole top surface. Like this he would not have to look at the mouse to see, where the mouth stick is positioned and where the mouse case ends. Finer grid structure or extra design elements were suggested.

Version 4 with the extra mouse wheel was criticized by the user. Because the mouse wheel turns in the opposite direction more confusion than assistance was created. Adding a third wheel in between would probably create too much friction to allow easy steering with the mouth stick. Therefore, this design version was discarded and instead the user had the idea for *Version 5*.

Version 5 intended to enable the usage of the original mouse wheel by inclining a part of the click surfaces. So, the click surfaces were positioned on the front end of the mouse. During tests it turned out, that they are out of the user's reach. Therefore, also this design was discarded.

To sum up, the plug-case Version 3 achieved best user satisfaction and will be distributed over the platform 'Thingiverse'. As examples for optional extra design features the user showed pictures of 'Steampunk-Mouses' and suggested surface patterns like a cobra, hearts or flowers or adding other materials like leather or plush for extra grip. For people who use 3D-printers that can print also thermoplastic elastomers the upload of a 2-component design, consisting of a stiff and an elastic material was wished for. Like this also two coloured designs are made possible.

5   Conclusion

In the future a high consumer demand for more and more personalized or at least customized products is expected. For such products a design interface that allows the user to transmit his or her ideas directly to a designer will be necessary. With the participatory design approach such a design interface could be developed for mouth sticks and the usability and user satisfaction with the output could be analyzed. Further distribution of the achieved project outcomes and translation of the web tool to English is planned.

For the development of a special mouse case for the use with mouth sticks it could be shown that the cases following the participatory design approach led to higher user satisfaction and better usability than the cases following the morphological analysis approach. By involving the user throughout the whole design process with few design iterations a mouse case fulfilling the user's wishes could be created.

The advantages of these special mouse cases for mouth stick users are that they are quite cheap and quickly manufactured. By uploading the designs to the *Thingiverse account "AssistiveTechnology_JKU"* they are made globally available for 3D-printing so off-the-shelf mice can be adapted easily. Materials and colours can be freely chosen by the users. Additionally, the size of the case can be adapted by scaling in x-, y- and z-direction, thus it can fit also to other regular mice. To make the designs even more adaptable for more experienced 3D-printer or CAD users, a design with adjustable parameters and the upload of the STEP-file is planned. All in all, this process could show, that AT with high user satisfaction can be quickly designed with the participatory design approach and that by using online platforms to upload the 3D-printable files, AT can truly be made globally available at low cost.

Acknowledgement. This work was partly funded by the Austrian Research Promotion Agency (FFG) and the land of Upper Austria in the program "Innovatives Oberösterreich 2020 – Ausschreibung 2015: Medizintechnik" under the grant number 851456.

References

1. Nussbaum, G., Veigl, C., Miesenberger, K.: EMG signal controlled pneumatic gripper for mouthsticks. In: Emiliani, P.L., Burzagli, L., Como, A., Gabbanini, F., Salminen, A.-L. (eds.) Assistive Technology from Adapted Equipment to Inclusive Environments, AAATE 2009, vol. 25, pp. 36–40. IOS Press (2009)
2. Blaine, H.L., Nelson, E.P.: A mouthstick for quadriplegic patients. J. Prosthet. Dent. **29**, 317–322 (1973)
3. Ruff, J.C., Emmanouil, E., Pendzick, M.J.: Mouthstick prosthesis placement in a 19-month-old arthrogryposis multiplex congenita patient: case report. Am. Acad. Pediatr. Dent. **10**(4), 320 (1988)
4. Smith, R.: Mouth stick design for the client with spinal cord injury. Am. J. Occup. Ther. **43**(4), 251–255 (1989)
5. Toor, I.K., Tabiat-Pour, S., Critchlow, S.B.: Mouth sticks: their past, present and future. Br. Dent. J. **219**, 209–215 (2015)
6. Berger, V.M., Pölzer, S., Nussbaum, G., Ernst, W., Major, Z.: Process development for the design and manufacturing of personalizable mouth sticks. In: Cudd, P., De Witte, L. (eds.) Harnessing the Power of Technology to Improve Lives, AAATE 2017, pp. 437–444. IOS Press (2017)
7. Ernst, W., Nussbaum, G., Berger, V., Major, Z.: Mouthsticks – a participatory approach, in harnessing the power of technology to improve lives. In: Cudd, P., De Witte, L. (eds.) Harnessing the Power of Technology to Improve Lives, AAATE 2017, pp. 413–420. IOS Press (2017)
8. Puckett, A.D., Sauer, B.W., Zardiackas, L.D., Entrekin, D.S.: Development of a custom-fit mouthstick appliance. J. Rehabil. Res. Dev. **26**(4), 17–22 (1989)
9. Berger, V.M., Nussbaum, G., Ernst, W., Major, Z.: A new approach to mouth sticks – material selection for additive manufacturing of personalizable mouth pieces. In: Drstvensek, I., Drummer, D., Schmidt, M. (eds.) Paper presented at International Conference on Additive Technologies, 29–30 November 2016, pp. 447–442, Nürnberg, Germany (2016)
10. PCD Maltron Ltd.: Maltron Head/Mouth Stick Keyboard. https://www.maltron.com/head-mouth-stick-keyboard-info.html. Accessed 21 Mar 2018
11. Catea – Center for Assistive Technology and Environmental Access – Georgia Tech: Keyboard Alternative. http://atwiki.assistivetech.net/index.php/Keyboard_Alternative. Accessed 21 Mar 2018
12. Ingenieurbüro Dr. Elisabeth Seveke: Mausersatz. http://www.computer-fuer-behinderte.de/produkte/0-mausersatz.htm. Accessed 21 Mar 2018
13. SPD Ability Centre: Technology for Computer Access. http://www.spd.org.sg/inclusivetech/detail/technology-for-computer-access-9.html. Accessed 21 Mar 2018
14. WebAIM – Web Accessibility In Mind: Motor Disabilities – Assistive Technologies. https://webaim.org/articles/motor/assistive. Accessed 21 Mar 2018
15. Hammer, A., Holzer, C., Ott, T., Pölz, S., Wenninger, M.: New computer mouse design for mouth stick users, protocol in Polymer Process and Product Development PR, supervisor: Martin Reiter (2017)

A Proposed Method for Producing Embossed Dots Graphics with a 3D Printer

Kazunori Minatani(✉)

National Center for University Entrance Examinations, Komaba 2-19-23,
Meguro-ku, Tokyo 153-8501, Japan
minatani@rd.dnc.ac.jp

Abstract. This study examines embossed dots graphics produced with a 3D printer for the purpose of providing practical information to visually impaired people. Using 3D printing to produce tactile graphics has a benefit to make use of our cumulative assets in tactile graphics production: techniques and production tools. The author designed this study to specifically take up the following challenge: develop a system that would convert data created using embossed dots graphics drawing software for a braille embosser into data that could be used with 3D CAD software. The conversion would allow for completely customization of the size and shape of every dot, freeing us from the limitations in dot type associated with the braille embosser. Results are confirmed via physical measurements and tactile observation assessments.

Keywords: Visually impaired people · 3D printer · Tactile graphics Embossed dots graphics

1 State of the Art and Research Aims

This study examines embossed dots graphics produced with a 3D printer for the purpose of providing practical information and educational materials to visually impaired people. The interest in providing visually impaired people with tactile observation materials has led to more active interest in attempting to make use of digital fabrication technologies. Along with these developments have been attempts to produce models of things like astronomical bodies or minute plankton [1], which cannot be tactilely observed directly. Researchers have also been working to produce topographical maps in sharp relief. [2] Unfortunately, the 3D solid model products of such researches and development have yet to be widely used in real-world situations. For the most part, graphical information is provided to visually impaired people in these practical settings via the raised paper methods collectively referred to as tactile graphics.

The significant benefit of using 3D printing to produce tactile graphics is the ability to make use of our cumulative assets in tactile graphics production.

© The Author(s) 2018
K. Miesenberger and G. Kouroupetroglou (Eds.): ICCHP 2018, LNCS 10897, pp. 143–148, 2018.
https://doi.org/10.1007/978-3-319-94274-2_20

These assets can be roughly classified as either know-how in expressive technique which is regularized [4] or production tools. In terms of production tools, we can create tactile graphics with a 3D printer more efficiently if we use production tools specifically designed to create tactile graphics-particularly drawing software. There are three key benefits to tactile graphics produced with computer software: firstly it is easy to edit the designs, secondly the results can theoretically be replicated endlessly, and thirdly the data can be modified and reused. We can enjoy these benefits of using computer software even if we make tactile graphics with a 3D printer.

Now I'll take a closer look at the advantages that tactile graphics made with a 3D printer have over conventional tactile graphics, particularly over embossed dots graphics made using a braille embosser. I'll use the term "3D embossed dots graphics" to refer to the embossed dots tactile graphics that we produced with a 3D printer. These are the main focus of this study. Conventional embossed dots graphics made using a braille embosser will be referred to as "paper embossed dots graphics". The biggest advantage that 3D embossed dots graphics have over paper embossed dots graphics is the ability to freely customize their arrangement namely dots' shapes. Braille embossers primarily use a hammer solenoid to create raised dots on paper, punching out braille as text. The same mechanical process is used when producing embossed dots graphics. Creating embossed dots graphics with a 3D printer does not have the same limitations as using a braille embosser when it comes to the types of dots that can be created.

There is a research to apply modeling with a 3D printer to production of thermoform tactile materials. [3] This study is similarly interested in the use of 3D printing in comparison with tactile graphics, but takes the idea a step further by introducing three-dimensional molding as a method of producing and enhancing the expressive power of the embossed dots graphics, an established form of tactile graphics. To summarize, the benefits of this project is that they make it possible to achieve the expressive power of thermoform plus the ease of design that comes with computer-powered embossed dots graphics. My practical aim with this study is to create a system that makes it possible to take the expertise developed among embossed dots graphics designers and apply it directly to the creation of tactile observation materials using 3D printing technology.

2 Developed Software and Evaluation of Dot Size on a Sample Embossed Dot Graphic

Upon considering these benefits and circumstances surrounding 3D-printed embossed dots graphics, the author designed this study to specifically take up the following challenge: develop a system that would convert data created using paper embossed dots graphics drawing software for a braille embosser into data that could be used with 3D CAD software. The conversion would allow for completely customization of the size and shape of every dot, freeing us from the limitations in dot type associated with the braille embosser. The author then sent the 3D CAD data that the system generated during the conversion to a consumer 3D printer and studied its replicability for molded objects and its effectiveness for use with tactile observation educational materials.

Software: For this study, the author developed software that would take data generated by the embossed dots graphics drawing program Edel and convert it into 3D CAD data. The called the conversion software `Edl2scad`. Edel is a piece of drawing software for designing embossed dots graphics for the ESA 721 [6] embosser. It can punch out three dot sizes. ESA 721 is able to emboss dots without typical cracks which are often caused by a mechanical embosser. By converting data so that it can be edited on OpenSCAD, users can take the drawings they've made on Edel and revise them in SCAD data format on OpenSCAD as solid objects. The small, medium, and large dots included in the Edel data are converted into solid hemispheres on the surface of circular truncated cones in accordance with their respective sizes. Figure 1 (leftside) shows an enlarged photo of the dots from an embossed dots graphics design that were produced using an ESA 721 embosser.

About the Evaluation Sample: The author used Edel to create a map, which he then studied to identify the qualities and characteristics of tactile graphics produced with the 3D embossed dots graphics process. More specifically, the author found a map showing the power relationships on the Italian peninsula during the 15th century, and used small, medium, and large dots to recreate it as an embossed dots graphic. Figure 1 (rightside) is given as an example of how the map he made was displayed on Edel.

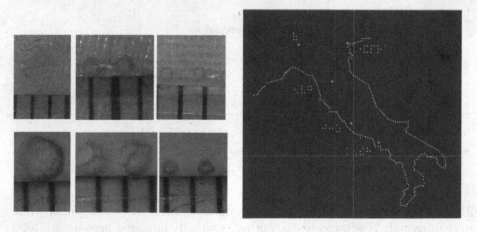

Fig. 1. Three dots embossed by ESA721 (up-left), generated by 3D printer (down-left) and the evaluated embossed dots map (right)

3   Physical Measurements and Tactile Observation Assessments

Measuring and Evaluating Dot Size: The author used the same numbers to create a model in order to get a 3D embossed dots graphic that conformed to ESA 721 output standards. The measured values were then used to form dot modeling solids, and the author attempted to replicate the shape. The model that he actually produced ended up being smaller than the designated values. In response to these results, the author intentionally enlarged the sizes beyond those of the corresponding dots in the embossed model. He repeated this process until he ended up with dots of the same size on the 3D embossed dots graphic.

The author then made further adjustments to the size of the large dots until he was able to use a 3D printer to produce the embossed dots graphic originally intended for the ESA 721. The mechanical components in the ESA 721 are designed to produce a large dot size with a radius of one millimeter. Due to the performance of the hammer solenoid and characteristics of the printing paper, however, the radius of the large dots was actually limited to about 0.75 mm. Because the 3D printer is not limited by these mechanical restrictions, it was able to create the originally intended one-millimeter large dots in the 3D embossed dot graphic. Table 1 shows the settings used in order to get an output that corresponded to the ESA 721 object.

Table 1. The settings and results of test printings

Dot type	Radius (mm)				
	ESA 721 (reference)	Generated 3D embossed dots			
		Using the measured values as settings		Attempting to make dots originally intended for ESA	
		Setting	Result	Setting	Result
Large	0.75	0.75	0.5	1.7	1
Medium	0.5	0.5	0.45	0.55	0.5
Small	0.25	0.25	NA (not observed)	0.3	0.35

Tactile Observation Evaluations: Evaluations made via tactile observation were intensively conducted by the author, a visually impaired person with total blindness. Follow-up assessments were then conducted by other visually impaired people as a group discussion to corroborate these conclusions. The following lists feedback collected in the course of tactile observations. (1) The 3D models were not inferior to the embossed dots graphics produced on paper in terms of their expressive features (2) Changing the three dot sizes made it easier to distinguish them in the 3D model compared to the paper embossed dots graphics. The large dots in particular were greatly improved in terms of palpability. (3) The surface smoothness of the 3D model was inferior to that of the embossed dots graphic produced on paper. (4) The abbreviated city names written on the map in braille were not easy to read.

4   Conclusions

This study created and evaluated a system for using a 3D printer to create solid models corresponding to the embossed dots graphics produced on a braille embosser. The system was able to take embossed dots graphics data generated using embossed dots graphics drawing software and use it as-is to mold a three-dimensional object. The author did discover a problem, however, that he did not give much weight to in the beginning: the dots did not sufficiently protrude when he used the exact size value for the paper embossed dots graphics to create the data for the 3D model.

Acknowledgments. This work was supported by KAKENHI (17H02005).

References

1. Teshima, Y., Matsuoka, A., Fujiyoshi, M., Ikegami, Y., Kaneko, T., Oouchi, S., Watanabe, Y., Yamazawa, K.: Enlarged skeleton models of plankton for tactile teaching. In: Miesenberger, K., Klaus, J., Zagler, W., Karshmer, A. (eds.) ICCHP 2010. LNCS, vol. 6180, pp. 523–526. Springer, Heidelberg (2010). https://doi.org/10.1007/978-3-642-14100-3_78
2. Götzelmann, T.: CapMaps. In: Miesenberger, K., Bühler, C., Penaz, P. (eds.) ICCHP 2016. LNCS, vol. 9759, pp. 146–152. Springer, Cham (2016). https://doi.org/10.1007/978-3-319-41267-2_20
3. Serrano-Mira, J., et al.: Use of additive manufacturing to obtain moulds to thermoform tactile graphics for people with visual impairment. Procedia Manuf. **13**, 810–817 (2017)
4. Braille Authority of North America, Canadian Braille Authority: Guidelines and Standards for Tactile Graphics (2011)
5. Edel and its related software. http://www7a.biglobe.ne.jp/~EDEL-plus/EdelDownLoad.html. (in Japanese, English version of these software are also hosted)
6. ESA721 Ver'95. http://www.jtr-tenji.co.jp/products/ESA721_Ver95/. (in Japanese)

148   K. Minatani

Accessibility as Prerequisite for the Production of Individualized Aids Through Inclusive Maker Spaces

Hanna Linke[✉], Ingo K. Bosse, and Bastian Pelka

Faculty of Rehabilitation Research, University of Dortmund, Dortmund, Germany
Hanna.linke@tu-dortmund.de

Abstract. The article demonstrates by the example of persons with complex needs how to open up 3D-printing and peer production to everybody. It describes the requirements for accessibility and a competence-based scalable approach that empowers persons with complex needs to produce prototypes of products – such as assistive tools. In addition to discussing the systematics of the fields of action, the focus of the presentation will be the developed accessibility checklist and the tested products. Furthermore, first findings and products, such as a methodology for co-constructing products in a design thinking process and up taking results from social innovation, are described. General principles of accessibility for the design of maker spaces are presented, to sensitize the maker scene for this issue. These general principles are complemented by applicable standards, guidelines to be followed and supporting funding.

Keywords: Persons with disabilities · Accessible making · Peer production
Social innovation · 3D-printing

1 Introduction

Within the project SELFMADE, funded by the German Federal Ministry of Education and Research this project, the potentials of maker spaces and "making" for people with disabilities are explored. The project is linked to research and practice of assistive technology with a focus on participation in everyday life/leisure time, work and communication. It is not so much about assistive technology in the narrow sense than about the self-determined production of assistive aids.

For this purpose a maker space – a community space that offers tools and knowledge as well as exchange and learning for simply "making" things [1] – was set up in a Service Center for Augmentative and Alternative Communication (AAC) in Dortmund, Germany, where 12 persons with complex needs, including complex communication needs work daily. This project uses 3D-priniting as technology as well as the processes and platforms of social innovation. Other technologies often found in maker spaces – such as melding, drilling or milling – are not used in this specific maker space in order to focus on the added value 3D-printing is offering for people with special needs. Starting with the group of persons with physical impairments and complex communication

K. Miesenberger and G. Kouroupetroglou (Eds.): ICCHP 2018, LNCS 10897, pp. 149–155, 2018.
https://doi.org/10.1007/978-3-319-94274-2_21

needs, SELFMADE tries to enable all persons with disabilities to design and produce products with a 3D-printer as well as sharing the designs with other people.

Persons with disabilities experience various barriers that prevent them from self-determined participation in social processes. Additional to structural barriers (e.g., accessibility), these include cognitive (e.g. easy language), emotional (e.g. repellent design of places), financial and technical barriers. In order to address these barriers in the research process the theoretical framework "capability approach" [2, 4] is used. This approach focusses the choices, which are necessary to initiate a process of social innovation through network building. Due to the used technology, the planning and producing of 3D-objects are also focused.

2   The Aims of the Project

The aims of the research and development project are:

1. The empowerment of persons with disabilities regarding the definition and production of individualized assistive tools.
2. The production of assistive tools in the areas work, everyday life/leisure time and communication.
3. The development, testing and research of a transferable problem-solving strategy, which is based on the principles of social innovation.
4. The preparation of a checklist for accessible maker spaces: How should maker spaces be designed to meet the minimum accessibility requirements.

Regarding accessibility, the project SELFMADE focuses on the following research questions:

1. How should maker spaces be spatially designed to implement minimum accessibility standards?

This article focuses on a checklist for accessible maker spaces and related tasks concerning the following main topics:

1. the text contents and text representation of information offers
2. architectural barriers, the accessibility of the building and the interior design as well as the availability of sanitary facilities or rest rooms
3. barriers in the product development, the using of CAD software and the production process by 3D-printing.

With this guideline and checklist, managers and planners from the maker scene should receive an instrument for planning and offering maker spaces with as few barriers as possible. In the maker space of the SELFMADE project, we were mainly concerned with 3D printing and describe this production process in this checklist, but it can also be applied to other ways of making.

First of all, this checklist gives an overview of the general notion of accessibility and the benefits of accessibility in maker spaces. General principles of accessibility initially serve as an overview and are substantiated by means of smaller checklists that can be used to check the accessibility.

This step includes the identification of barriers and addressing them, so these barriers will be dismantled. The checklists shows where barriers in a maker space can occur and how a maker space can become more accessible. The identification and addressing of barriers during the design and printing process enables as heterogeneous group as possible to be not excluded from the making process.

While providing the checklist the following questions need to be addressed in the project:

1. How should the connection to public transport be?
2. Which communication channels should be offered?
3. How is it possible to control 3D printers?
4. How modular are the products?
5. How can the "production process" be designed understandable?
6. How can the possible risks be well recognizable?

3   Theoretical Framework

The checklist for accessible maker spaces is an instrument to plan and offer maker spaces without excluding people with disabilities.

The underlying definition of accessibility refers to the German disability equality law:

BGG§4: "…if they (things) are accessible and usable for disabled people in the usual way, without any particular difficulty and in principle without outside help".

The following principles describe the extent of accessibility:

- Foot-Wheel-Principle: Are the building and the offers accessible and usable for wheelchair users as well as pedestrians?
- Two-sense principle (channel rule/multi-sensory principle): Is information perceivable by at least two of the senses (seeing and additionally hearing or touching)?
- KISS Rule: Information is offered using the "Keep It Short and Simple" method.

Additionally, principles of "Universal Design" are considered to enable as many people as possible to take part in a maker space:

1. Principle - Wide usability: The design should be usable and marketable for people with different abilities.
2. Principle - Flexibility in use: The design should support a wide range of individual preferences and possibilities.
3. Principle - Simple and intuitive use: Use of the design should be easy to understand and independent of the user's experience, knowledge, language skills or current concentration.
4. Principle - Sensory information: The design should provide the user with the necessary information effectively, regardless of the user's environment or sensory capabilities.

5. Principle - Fault tolerance - The design minimizes risks and the negative consequences of accidental or unintentional actions.
6. Principle - Low physical effort: The design should be efficient and comfortable to use with a minimum of fatigue.
7. Principle - Size and space for access and use: Provide adequate space and space for access, accessibility, manipulation and use regardless of the user's size, posture or flexibility.

4   Methodology

Regarding the methodology the product development is based on a repetitive research- and development cycle, often used in the context of social innovation, in order to address accessibility in the project SELFMADE.

The products are developed in an iterative cycle, based on the principles of Design Thinking [3].

The Design Thinking is composed of six steps (Fig. 1).

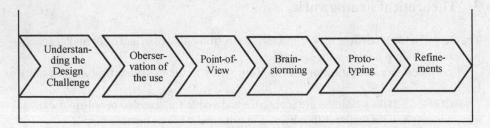

Fig. 1. Design thinking process cf. Schallmo [3], p. 18

In this cycle three product lines are successively tested by persons with disabilities. During this process experiences, gained while developing each "product", are considered in the design of the derived product. Thus, in an early stage of the development a "finished" product is available, the complexity increases across the product generations and a learning process of the participants (e.g. technical procedures, individual cultures, potentials and restrictions) takes place. As a result, the process of identification of needs (which can be addressed with photonic procedures), the implementation competence of the target group as well as the quality of the products, increases with each product generation.

Each of these "products" is identified on the basis of a needs analysis. In the needs analysis the project uses a User Centered Design approach, which is linked with a Design Thinking process and can be seen as both: as a process of creating social innovations and as a social innovation itself. This allows to identify, define, create and test the designed products in a Co-Creation process by persons with disabilities for persons with disabilities.

5   Prerequisite Results

Due to the fact, that the projects still runs until the end of August 2018 it is just possible to present the results at its current intermediate status.

The focus is placed on the accessibility checklist and the tested products.

Every chapter of the accessibility checklist for maker spaces deals with the following topics:

1. The implementation of the general principles: How is it possible to implement general principles of accessibility with small changes?
2. General legal requirements: Further information on the general legal requirements and on support agencies in their area to implement accessibility.
3. Financial support: In the case of extensive conversion measures or changes
4. Quick·check: A short checklist at the end of each chapter can be used to quickly check your maker space for accessibility.

While testing for accessibility it is necessary to examine barriers which might occur during the visit in a maker space and even earlier, from access to the building to barriers which can appear during the making process. This already begins "on the way to the maker space" as soon as one tries to find out something about a maker space on a home-page, in a flyer or on other channels, which are used to present the maker space in public.

In order to make texts comprehensible to as many people as possible, they should be based on specific principles in terms of content, structure and graphic representation. That can be principles of easy-to-read, additional information in capital letters and Braille or touchable logos, which can be printed in 3D.

The next step is the accessibility to public transport or the parking lot situation at the maker space.

Possible barriers include missing elevators at train stations, missing signage on the way to the maker space, or lack of parking lots.

During the project, it turned out to be one of the most crucial barriers that allows only a few people with disabilities to regularly visit a maker space. Reasons for this are the lack of access to public transport, the complex organization of transport services or lack of funds.

Arriving at the maker space, additional areas emerge that need to be checked for accessibility. This includes the accessibility of the building, the respective interior design, sanitary facilities and possibly additional premises.

The financing and design of accessible buildings is clearly defined and differentiated depending on whether it is a private or public building. Organizers of maker spaces often have little influence on that, but if they point out possible barriers, interested people can adjust to it.

Ultimately, the process of making should be checked for accessibility.

That includes the developing of the product, the printing process and the adjusting of hardware like the 3D-printers and the CAD software.

In order to address accessibility in the printing and development process, the following steps of design thinking can be used. This includes the appropriate documentation:

1. Understanding: The first step focuses on the understanding of the problem, this leads to an appropriate question, which defines the needs and challenges of the project. Data sources: photo documentation and written collection, composed from workshops and Open Spaces.
2. Observation: In order to gain important insights and to define the status quo an intensive search and field observation follows. Data sources: field notes and written collection, composed from workshops/Open Space.
3. Point-of-view: the individual needs are clearly defined in one question: Data source: documentation of the brainstorming question.
4. Brainstorming to develop and visualize different concepts. Data source: Different visualized concepts with the program Design Spark Mechanical.
5. Prototyping: In order to test and to demonstrate the ideas, first simple prototypes are developed and tested by the target group. Data source: Prototypes.
6. Refinement: On the basis of the insights gained from the prototype, the concept is further improved and refined until an optimal, user-centered product is developed. This iteration step can be applied on all previous steps.

5.1 Five Levels of Competence

According to the different competences of the target group we distinguish between five competence levels in order to enable everyone to use a 3D-printer and to print their own product.

Communication via Assistants or Assistive Technology, Almost No Movement Abilities, No ICT Skills. A shelf is displaying products that could be printed with a 3D-printer. The selection was made in workshops with persons with similar impairments. Persons with disabilities express which object they like to receive and assistants initiate the printing process.

Communication Only via Assistants or Assistive Technology, Basic Movement Abilities, No Ict Skills. A SIM card is attached to each object and can be inserted in a 3D-printer. We designed the 3D printer in a way that enables most users to initiate the printing process.

Basic ICT Skills. Users with basic ICT skills can click on pre-selected models for printing.

Advanced ICT Skills. For advanced users we offer CAD software that enables the alteration of existing models or design from sketch.

Advanced ICT Skills, Basic Communication Skills. Users become tutors in 3D printing in peer education processes.

To increase the competence level it is necessary to consider if the user needs different keyboards or other peripheral device, changeable font size or contrasts or the possibility of reading function. In addition during the SELFMADE project we developed several adjustments for the 3D-printer like a risk minimizing door or buttons for a better operation.

This approach is particularly attractive for the globally networked maker spaces because it has the potential to reach new target groups by making it as accessible as possible.

References

1. Dougherty, D.: The maker movement. Innov.: Technol. Gov. Glob. **7**(3), 11–14 (2012)
2. Nussbaum, M.: Frontiers of Justice: Disability, Nationality, Species Membership. Harvard University Press, Cambridge (2006)
3. Schallmo, D.R.A.: Design Thinking erfolgreich anwenden. Springer Gabler, Wiesbaden (2017). https://doi.org/10.1007/978-3-658-12523-3
4. Sen, A.: Ökonomie für den Menschen: Wege zu Gerechtigkeit und Solidarität in der Marktwirtschaft, München, Wien (2000)
5. Story, M.: Maximizing usability: the principles of universal design. Assist. Technol. **10**, 4–12 (2010)

Hackability: A Methodology to Encourage the Development of DIY Assistive Devices

Ludovico Orlando Russo[1,2,3], Giuseppe Airò Farulla[2,3(✉)], and
Carlo Boccazzi Varotto[3]

[1] HotBlack Robotics, Via Principe Amedeo 12, 10123 Torino, Italy
[2] Università Ca' Foscari Venezia, Dorsoduro, 3246, 30123 Venezia, Italy
{ludovico.russo,giuseppe.airofarulla}@unive.it
[3] Hackability Association, Via Bezzecca 11, 10131 Torino, Italy
c.boccazzi@gmail.com

Abstract. People with disabilities express specific needs that are not addressable by a mass production approach. We see these people building or hacking custom solutions (e.g., joysticks, handles) for their needs, directly by themselves or with the help of a caregiver. We argue that digital fabrication and modern approaches to rapid prototyping can represent a valid alternative to mass production in assisting these people. In this work we present for the first time Hackability. Hackability is a methodology designed 3 years ago in Turin, Italy, to envisage the cross-contamination of skills among makers, designers, and people with disabilities. This methodology encourages the people with disabilities to express their needs and to actively collaborate in the whole process of design and fabrication of custom solutions. The final aim of Hackability is to produce benefits that are durable in time, as well as outputs that are scalable and economically fruitful. This paper presents the methodology as well as success stories and study cases and encourages researchers from all around Europe to replicate it in their local communities.

Keywords: Digital fabrication · Customized assistive technology
Codesign

1 Introduction

Assistive Technologies (ATs) aims to increase, maintain, or improve the functional capabilities of individuals with disabilities, assisting them in accomplishing

---

This research has been partially supported by the "Smart Cities and Social Innovation Under 30" program of the Italian Ministry of Research and University through the PARLOMA Project (SIN_00132). The authors are extremely grateful to everyone who is or has been involved in Hackability and in Hackability@Barilla.

tasks they might not be able to accomplish otherwise. ATs might represent life-changing solutions for people with disabilities since they help these individuals in breaking social barriers and getting in touch with active society. This goal can be achieved by means of both methodologies and devices.

Assistive devices encompass both home-made and cheap solutions to highly engineered and expensive ones [1,2]: they in fact span from simple low-tech equipment (e.g.,a handle) to cutting-edge high-tech apparatus (e.g., robotic hands and cloud platforms enabling remote communication systems [3]).

In this, we have developed prior experience within the ongoing *PARLOMA*[1] project. PARLOMA aims at developing a pipeline to allow deafblind people to autonomous communicate each other online and remotely (i.e., a *telephone for deafblind individuals*), resorting to the tactile Sign Languages they already know and use.

People with disabilities often require customized solutions and express very specific needs that do not cope well with the rules, costs, mechanisms, and timing of classic mass-production approaches [4]. We often see these people hacking commercial devices or building custom solutions on their own, following a DIY (Do It Yourself) approach to satisfy their needs. Hence, people with disabilities actually may play the role makers have.

Recently, the DIY approach became popular due to the introduction of off-the-shelf low-cost technology for digital fabrication and fast prototyping, such as Desktop 3D printers and affordable programmable devices. This technology is well known by designers and makers [5,6], and in general to people enthusiast of technologies who apply the DIY approach to develop custom technologies to learn, have fun, and solve market's needs. Enthusiastic makers have strong competencies and skills in digital fabrication and fast prototyping, and are continuously looking for projects to learn more and improve themselves.

We have already seen examples of these competencies and skills being applied to the realm of ATs [7–9]. With the support of the Italian network of FabLabs, we have investigated how makers approach ATs, discovering that there is a serious lack of instruments to transform their skills into work opportunities. In addition we have registered the lack of systematic occasions for makers and disabled to get in touch, exchange ideas and knowledge, and collaborate. Moreover, even when it happens, such collaboration is biased: disabled people are often seen by makers like simple end-users of the technology and are not involved during the development process of the ATs; this unfortunately often brings to useless outcomes. An illustrative example is the case of the laser-empowered cane for the active guidance of blind pedestrians: it has been proposed many times in literature since 50 years [10,11], but to date is still not used by any blind individual in the world.

We advocate for the need of a paradigm shift, where end-users are actually turned into begin-users. This work presents Hackability, a methodology to assist makers, designers, and people with disabilities in collaborating to solve specific needs that require custom solutions. The methodology was first applied in Italy

---

[1] https://parloma.github.io.

in February 2015 and has been applied in several occasions in different regions of Italy since that date. The inventors of the methodology have in 2016 funded the Hackability Association[2], that is in charge of encouraging the application of the methodology worldwide.

The remaining of the paper is organized as follows: Sect. 2 presents the paradigm behind Hackability and how we have already implemented it, and plan to implement in the future, to systematically create occasions where people expressing needs can meet makers able to solve them; Sect. 3 presents some preliminary success stories to demonstrate the effectiveness of the Hackability methodology; Sect. 4 briefly presents some best practices and open issues of the methodology; finally Sect. 5 briefly concludes the paper.

2   Hackability: Methodology and Episodes

Hackability is a methodology aimed at identifying, inviting, informing, interesting, and involving makers, designers, technicians, and people with disabilities. The basic idea behind the methodology stems from a simple consideration: *people with disabilities are hackers and makers of some of their own ATs solutions.* We have proven this consideration by interviewing 50 individuals with various disabilities (e.g., motor impairments, blindness) in 2013[3]. We have discovered that these individuals require highly-customized solutions that are not available on the market, or are sold only at a high price.

It took 2 years to design the Hackability methodology to (i) increase the social inclusion of people with disabilities in the very same areas where they live, letting them work with makers on solving their specific needs following a co-design approach; (ii) let the makers focus their efforts considering the real needs expressed by people with disabilities, according to the *User Center Design* [12] paradigm; (iii) develop a repository of ATs where solutions and devices are released Open Source to the community to be later implemented or improved.

The way identified to meet the ambitious goals of Hackability has been the standardization of a format to propose systematic occasions where people with disabilities and makers can meet and work together, creating workgroups that are led by the bearer of the need (i.e., begin-user). This format, that will be freely released in Open Source, coincides with the organization of an *Hackability episode* (also called *hackability*, in lowercase). The management of these episodes has been tested in dozens of occasions since 2015, and the format has been engineered to be easily repeatable. The rules to follow to guarantee the success of a hackability are only a few, but are very detailed.

The format of the hackability has been inspired by hackatons, popular events in the community of makers [13]. The final goal of any hackability is to build strong relationships between the local communities of makers and people with

---

[2] http://www.hackability.it.
[3] http://friendlyhouse.it/la-ricerca/.

disabilities, possibly also fostering business opportunities. This is done by encouraging people of both communities to work together to develop an assistive device solving a specific need expressed by an individual with disabilities.

Each hackability is organized by a team of senior affiliated to the Hackability association, who are also available to tutor junior members when they organize a hackability for the first time. The organizers have mainly three responsibilities within a hackability. They: (i) publish and promote the calls for participants; (ii) organize two public events (in terms of logistics, invitations, catering etc.); (iii) enforce the adherence to the rules expressed in the Hackability manifesto. To start a hackability, a first call (call for needs) is published targeting people with disabilities and their caregivers, who express ideas and needs. A second call (call for skills) is issued in parallel to instead address makers, who are selected by the organizers on the basis of their skills, experience, and motivation. If needed, the organizers themselves might act as makers or may involve paid senior makers.

Both the calls stay open for 30 or 60 days; after, it is time for the first public event. The opening event is the most important in the hackability: all the participants selected through the calls are invited to join. This event always lasts less than 48 h and starts with a brief introduction on the methodology that is given by one of the organizers. After this introduction, each person with disabilities is asked to briefly and informally present him-herself and to propose a specific need.

Makers are later asked to present themselves, their motivations, and skills, and are finally left free to get in touch and to create workgroups together with, and for, each person with disabilities. Makers choice autonomously with whom they want to work with and are not driven in the selection process; nevertheless, it is important to ensure that members of each group live near and can easily work together. This is important to fulfill the logistic needs of people with disabilities (Hackability does not provide with assistance outside the two hackability events). Any workgroup is given time to better understand the real needs expressed by the person with disabilities and to propose concepts for possible solutions, that are prototyped after the opening event.

Workgroups are then given 1 month to come up with their solution. These solutions are developed according to an agile methodology (repeated and continued interaction with the person with disabilities, de-facto product owner and begin-user of the development itself). We want to stress that during this month people with disabilities are actively participating in the developing phase, in a co-design experience that increases their self-esteem and improves their social inclusion.

The solutions prototyped are presented in a public closing event (i.e., the second public event of every hackability). Before ending the hackability, the organizers check that all the projects have been released in Open Source (well documented and published on the website of Hackability and on the GitHub platform, to be repeatable and adaptable to similar needs by everyone). Every solution developed within the hackability is gifted to the disabled person it has been co-designed with.

For both the opening and the final events, the organizers need to cover for the following expenses: (i) Costs for location and refreshments; (ii) Costs for technology and raw material for digital fabrication and prototyping of solutions; (iii) Paid travels and expertise of tutors; (iv) Paid travels to the people with disabilities and for their caregiver and assistants, that are also paid (Hackability does not provide with assistants, caregivers, or with interpreting and signing services).

Finally, each workgroup is given a budget to cover travel and fabrication expenses for their month of work. Organizers are invited to look for sponsors and to reduce the costs of every hackability by creating partnerships with other associations, universities, schools and/or Fablabs that may provide with materials, expertise, and a location.

3   Hackability@Barilla: The Most Recent Hackability

Since 2015, we organized several hackability in Italy. This Section presents the most recent one as case study, which has been organized in the Barilla headquarters settled in Parma, Italy, at the beginning of 2018. This hackability has been envisaged and sponsored by Barilla S.p.A. (world leader in the markets of pasta and ready-to-use sauces); it has been therefore called Hackability@Barilla. The expenses related to this hackability and the fees paid to 6 senior makers hired by Hackability to assist the workgroups and the junior makers (who instead acted on a voluntary basis) were covered by Barilla.

Following the Hackability rules (Sect. 2), two calls (the call for needs and the call for skills) were issued: both stayed open from the 15th of October to the 15th of December 2017. 150+ applicants answered these calls; from these, we selected 9 people with disabilities (bearer of the needs) and 50 makers (bearer of the skills). Participants were selected on the basis of their skills, experience, and availability to reach Parma on the dates of the opening and closing events.

The opening event was held on the 20th of January 2018. During this event, 6 workgroups were created: 3 groups decided to work with, and under the guidance of, 2 individuals with disabilities each who have similar needs. Leitmotiv behind the workgroups has been the accessibility of kitchens and in general of domestic spaces. The findings of 2 of these 6 workgroups are summarized in the remaining of the Section. The closing event was held on the 23rd of February.

3.1   PIC-AP: PIccola Cucina Accessibile Portatile (Small Portable Accessible Kitchen)

Marco, visually impaired, needs an extremely organized workspace to cook in safety and with comfort. His cooking tools must always be stored in the same position and should be easily distinguishable by high contrast and their color. PIC-AP[4] is the solution implemented by his workgroup to provide him with this

---

[4] https://github.com/HackabilityNPO/HackabilityBarilla17-PIC-AP.

comfort zone (Fig. 1). It implements a minimal and personal working environment, where Marco can cook safely, being sure of finding his tools at any time exactly where they are supposed to be. It has been developed resorting to laser cutting on plexiglass and wood.

PIC-AP is customized to store precisely the tools Marco uses and has been designed to be appealing: Marco is using it on the everyday basis and he is not ashamed of bringing it with him when he goes cooking at his friends' houses. We believe that this project represents a valid solution to give (or re-give) the ability to prepare food anywhere and independently, making it a product suitable for many people coping with visual impairments or blindness.

Fig. 1. PIC-AP: small portable accessible kitchen

3.2   La Buona Forchetta (the Good Fork)

Domenico is affected by Parkinson. One of the obvious and disabling symptoms of patients suffering from this disease is the difficulty in handling and

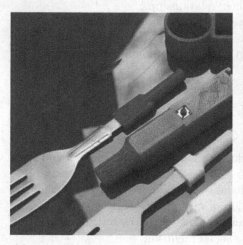

Fig. 2. La Buona Forchetta

moving objects, such as a rotating fork between the fingers while eating a plate of spaghetti pasta, both at home or at the restaurant: this is exactly the problem Domenico reported during the hackability.

The workgroup examined with Domenico off-the-shelf tools that could have helped him but found all of them to be too large and heavy, ugly, or not hygienic due to the presence of a single non-changeable fork tip. La Buona Forchetta[5] is a miniaturized device where a small ergonomic body, supported by a ring to enhance stability even when Domenico's hand trembles and shakes, allows interchangeable fork tips to rotate (Fig. 2).

The workgroup has designed disposable fork tips to be 3D printed or adapted from cheap plastic forks already available in the market; in addition, La Buona Forchetta has been engineered to be compatible with the steel forks Domenico already had in his kitchen.

The device is perfect to be carried out to the restaurant due to its extremely small size (it can easily be hidden in the pocket of the jacket), and we hope it will assist many users other than Domenico himself.

4   Good Practices, Failures, and Lessons Learned

From our experience, we derived a series of good practices that we use to continuously improve the methodology and the participants' experience. Nevertheless, Hackability is still affected by some issues. We learned that:

Stress the co-design approach. Co-design approach is misunderstood by the makers; to avoid workgroups where only technicians work, stress the co-design methodology since from the creation of workgroups.

Projects fails, but this is not a problem. Workgroups may be unable to meet the deadline with a working prototype, but this is not a problem if the co-design approach has been applied: the participants will appreciate anyway the experience and this strengthens their relationship.

Documentation is an issue. Documenting the work done is boring and it is typically left as for last activity by every workgroup. In our experience, only a small fraction of the groups ends up with a good documentation; we tried different platform and approaches for documenting project, but this remains an open issue.

5   Final Remarks

This work presents Hackability, a methodology that encourages makers and people with disabilities to work together on DIY assistive devices, to create relationships, and to seek opportunities for local social business. In Italy in the last 3 years Hackability has enabled the creation of several meeting points for makers and people with disabilities, and has been recognized by several municipalities as an effective methodology to encourage social inclusion.

---

[5]   https://github.com/HackabilityNPO/HackabilityBarilla17-La-Buona-Forchetta.

The methodology of Hackability is guaranteed and promoted by an ONLUS association whom the main goal is to spread the same methodology all over Europe. We are currently at work to organize the first hackability in France. We plan to make the methodology more scalable by preparing guidelines and courses to present our best practices and the common mistakes to avoid. This material will be available free-of-charge and we encourage interested researchers to reach us out, in the hope our efforts will pave the way to a global community of researchers that are interested in creating laboratories for developing ATs solutions well settled in their local territories.

References

1. Nicolson, A., Moir, L., Millsteed, J.: Impact of assistive technology on family care-givers of children with physical disabilities: a systematic review. Disabil. Rehabil.: Assist. Technol. **7**(5), 345–349 (2012)
2. Desch, L.W., Gaebler-Spira, D., et al.: Prescribing assistive-technology systems: focus on children with impaired communication. Pediatrics **121**(6), 1271–1280 (2008)
3. Russo, L.O., Airò Farulla, G., Pianu, D., Salgarella, A.R., Controzzi, M., Cipriani, C., Oddo, C.M., Geraci, C., Rosa, S., Indaco, M.: PARLOMA - a novel human-robot interaction system for deaf-blind remote communication. Int. J. Adv. Rob. Syst. **12**(5), 57 (2015)
4. Harwin, W.S.: Niche product design: a new model for assistive technology. Technology for Inclusive Design and Equality (TIDE), Helsinki (1998)
5. Hatch, M.: The Maker Movement Manifesto: Rules for Innovation in the New World of Crafters, Hackers, and Tinkerers. McGraw Hill Professional, New York City (2013)
6. Dougherty, D.: The maker movement. Innov.: Technol. Gov. Glob. **7**(3), 11–14 (2012)
7. Buehler, E., Branham, S., Ali, A., Chang, J.J., Hofmann, M.K., Hurst, A., Kane, S.K.: Sharing is caring: assistive technology designs on thingiverse. In: Proceedings of the 33rd Annual ACM Conference on Human Factors in Computing Systems, pp. 525–534. ACM (2015)
8. Hamidi, F., Baljko, M., Kunic, T., Feraday, R.: Do-It-Yourself (DIY) assistive technology: a communication board case study. In: Miesenberger, K., Fels, D., Archambault, D., Peňáz, P., Zagler, W. (eds.) ICCHP 2014. LNCS, vol. 8548, pp. 287–294. Springer, Cham (2014). https://doi.org/10.1007/978-3-319-08599-9_44
9. Hurst, A., Tobias, J.: Empowering individuals with do-it-yourself assistive technology. In: The Proceedings of the 13th International ACM SIGACCESS Conference on Computers and Accessibility, pp. 11–18. ACM (2011)
10. Benjamin, J.M., Ali, N.A.: An improved laser cane for the blind. In: Quantitative Imagery in the Biomedical Sciences II, vol. 40, pp. 101–105. International Society for Optics and Photonics (1974)
11. Bolgiano, D., Meeks, E.: A laser cane for the blind. IEEE J. Quantum Electron. **3**(6), 268–268 (1967)
12. Abras, C., Maloney-Krichmar, D., Preece, J.: User-centered design. In: Bainbridge, W. (ed.) Encyclopedia of Human-Computer Interaction. Sage Publications, Thousand Oaks, vol. 37, no. 4, pp. 445–456 (2004)
13. Briscoe, G.: Digital innovation: the hackathon phenomenon (2014)

Tactile Graphics and Models for Blind People and Recognition of Shapes by Touch

Universal Design Tactile Graphics Production System BPLOT4 for Blind Teachers and Blind Staffs to Produce Tactile Graphics and Ink Print Graphics of High Quality

Mamoru Fujiyoshi[1], Akio Fujiyoshi[2](✉), Hiroshi Tanaka[3], and Toru Ishida[4]

[1] National Center for University Entrance Examinations, Meguro, Tokyo, Japan
fujiyosi@rd.dnc.ac.jp
[2] Ibaraki University, Hitachi, Ibaraki, Japan
akio.fujiyoshi.cs@vc.ibaraki.ac.jp
[3] Tsukuba University of Technology, Tsukuba, Ibaraki, Japan
htanaka@k.tsukuba-tech.ac.jp
[4] National Rehabilitation Center For Persons with Disabilities,
Tokorozawa, Saitama, Japan
ishidat@oas.nvrc-unet.ocn.ne.jp

Abstract. In order to extend the usability of BPLOT, a new version BPLOT4 was developed. BPLOT is the first tactile graphics production system for the blind that enables the blind to produce tactile graphics by themselves. BPLOT4 has obtained the following four new features: (1) The usage of variables and mathematical formulas is supported for the description of plotter control commands. (2) The production of ink print graphics is possible at the same time as that of tactile graphics. (3) A new GUI (Graphical User Interface) is developed for sighted users. (4) Everest-D V5 (Index Braille) is added to the list of supported Braille printers.

Keywords: Blind · Tactile graphics · Universal design
Plotter control language · User interface

1 Introduction

This paper introduces the newly updated universal design tactile graphics production system BPLOT4. BPLOT is the first tactile graphics production system for the blind that enables the blind to produce tactile graphics by themselves [1–3]. Existing tactile graphics design applications such as BES [4] and EDEL-plus [5] have sophisticated GUI (Graphical User Interface) and enable the sighted to produce tactile graphics easily. However, because of the necessity for mouse operations, the blind cannot use these applications by themselves. Tiger Software Suite [6] can create tactile graphics by translating graphics on

© The Author(s) 2018
K. Miesenberger and G. Kouroupetroglou (Eds.): ICCHP 2018, LNCS 10897, pp. 167–176, 2018.
https://doi.org/10.1007/978-3-319-94274-2_23

computer screen into tactile graphics automatically. Both the blind and the sighted can use it. However, it is not enough for the blind to produce elaborate tactile graphics for figures in textbooks or questions of entrance examinations. BPLOT produces tactile graphics from a source text file written in our specially designed plotter control language for BPLOT. Because a source file for BPLOT is a text file, it is editable with any text editors by any person who has learned the plotter control language. Therefore, BPLOT enables not only the sighted but also the blind to produce tactile graphics by themselves.

The first version of BPLOT was developed in 2004. It was only with CUI (Character User Interface) and not WYSIWYG (What You See Is What You Get). In 2007, GUI for BPLOT was developed, and BPLOT2 was introduced [1]. With GUI, the usability of BPLOT2 for the sighted was significantly improved because a sighted user does not need a detailed knowledge of the plotter control language. A synchronized mechanism between CUI and GUI was developed, and BPLOT3 was introduced [3]. With the synchronized CUI and GUI, the blind and the sighted can collaboratively produce tactile graphics.

In order to extend the usability of BPLOT, a new version BPLOT4 was developed. BPLOT4 has obtained the following four new features: (1) The usage of variables and mathematical formulas is supported for the description of plotter control commands. (2) The production of ink print graphics is possible at the same time as that of tactile graphics. (3) A new GUI (Graphical User Interface) is developed for sighted users. (4) Everest-D V5 (Index Braille) is added to the list of supported Braille printers.

2   Outline and New Features of BPLOT4

2.1   The System

BPLOT4 runs on Microsoft Windows 7, 8 or 10. The main program of BPLOT4 is written in C++, and the user interface part is written in C#.

It works with the Braille printer ESA721, ESA600G (JTR Corporation) and Everest-D V5 (Index Braille). In order to obtain tactile graphics of high quality, we chose ESA721, ESA600G and Everest-D V5. They can produce tactile graphics with very high resolution: 73 dpi (dot/inch) for ESA721, 100 dpi for ESA600G, and 50 dpi for Everest-D V5. The resolution of ordinary Braille printers is only 10–20 dpi.

2.2   Plotter Control Language

In order to design tactile graphics by text editors, a plotter control language was developed [1]. The plotter control language is like a computer programming language which consists of plotter control commands. Each command consists of a command name and parameters. Basic figures such as a circle, a straight line, a rectangle, a diamond shape and several kinds of arrows can be described by a single command.

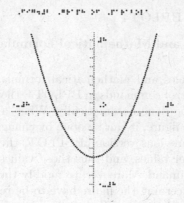

Fig. 1. An example of tactile graphics produced by BPLOT

For figures frequently used, we prepared commands to describe those figures in one line. A parabola, a hyperbola, a trigonometric function, an exponential function and a logarithmic function can be described by a single command. In plotting graphs, the axis of coordinates can also be described by a single command. For example, the horizontal axis, the vertical axis and the parabolic curve in Fig. 1 are described by the following three commands in the plotter control language.

```
xaxis x0 x1 unit pic pitch
yaxis y0 y1 unit pic pitch
vparabola x0 x1 y0 y1 a px py pitch
```

`xaxis` and `yaxis` are command names to draw a horizontal axis and a vertical axis, respectively. The parameters `x0` and `x1` (`y0` and `y1`) specify the range of an axis, `unit` means the intervals of divisions, `pic` indicates the length of divisions, and `pitch` sets the pitch of a dotted line. Likewise, `vparabola` is a command name to draw a vertical parabolic curve. The parameters `x0`, `x1`, `y0` and `y1` specify the range of a curve, `a`, `px` and `py` indicate the parameters of a vertical parabolic curve $y = a(x - px)^2 + py$, and `pitch` sets the pitch of a dotted line.

Graphs including complicated curves can be described by means of spline functions. To import a series of plotter control commands written in another file, we use the "paste" command. To put a Braille caption in a figure, we use the "braille" command. NABCC (North American Braille Computer Code) and Japanese KANA code are supported.

We also have commands to define the virtual coordinate space on a sheet of paper. With them, we can magnify and reduce the output tactile graphics with the same sense of touch because lines are drawn with the same dot pitch.

2.3   New Features of BPLOT4

(1) Usage of Variables and Mathematical Formulas in Plotter Control Commands

Since the usage of variables and mathematical formulas is supported for the description of plotter control commands in BPLOT4, the calculations of parameters of commands can be done automatically. When a user wants to modify the location or shape of a figure, it can be done by changing the assigned values of variables. As for the previous version of BPLOT, the parameters of a command were only numerical values, and thus those values have to be calculated in advance to write a command. Moreover, to modify the location or shape of a figure, all parameters concerning the figure have to be re-calculated by hand.

For mathematical formulas, we can use the four operators (+, |, * and /) and many important functions (sqrt(x), sin(x), cos(x), tan(x), exp(x), log(x) and log10(x)).

Figure 2 is a figure-drawing program describing a star-shaped curve. The produced tactile graphics is shown in Fig. 3. In Fig. 2, l, m, r, pitch, x0,...,x10, and y0,...,y10 are variables. The size of figure can be adjusted with the variables l and m.

```
 1    l = 6                        24    x9 = m*cos(90+9*r)
 2    m = 4                        25    y9 = m*sin(90+9*r)
 3    r = 360/10                   26    x10 = l*cos(90+10*r)
 4    pitch = 2.2                  27    y10 = l*sin(90+10*r)
 5                                 28
 6    x0 = l*cos(90+0*r)           29    define range -10 10 -12 12
 7    y0 = l*sin(90+0*r)           30    define EndofData 9999 0
 8    x1 = m*cos(90+1*r)           31    func = 4
 9    y1 = m*sin(90+1*r)           32
10    x2 = l*cos(90+2*r)           33    dot 1
11    y2 = l*sin(90+2*r)           34    spline range func 0 0 pitch
12    x3 = m*cos(90+3*r)           35       x0 y0
13    y3 = m*sin(90+3*r)           36       x1 y1
14    x4 = l*cos(90+4*r)           37       x2 y2
15    y4 = l*sin(90+4*r)           38       x3 y3
16    x5 = m*cos(90+5*r)           39       x4 y4
17    y5 = m*sin(90+5*r)           40       x5 y5
18    x6 = l*cos(90+6*r)           41       x6 y6
19    y6 = l*sin(90+6*r)           42       x7 y7
20    x7 = m*cos(90+7*r)           43       x8 y8
21    y7 = m*sin(90+7*r)           44       x9 y9
22    x8 = l*cos(90+8*r)           45    EndofData
23    y8 = l*sin(90+8*r)
```

Fig. 2. A figure-drawing program for star-shaped curve

Fig. 3. The tactile graphics described by the program in Fig. 2

(2) Production of Ink Print Graphics

We developed a converter for BPLOT that translates the plotter control language into PostScript. PostScript [7], created by Adobe Systems, is a page description language widely used to describe documents including ink print figures and pictures. Since the plotter control language of BPLOT has many parts in common with PostScript, this conversion is straightforward. With this function, blind teachers and blind staffs can make ink print graphics of high quality for sighted students. Figure 4 shows the ink print graphics obtained from the program in Fig. 2.

Fig. 4. The ink print graphics obtained from the program in Fig. 2

(3) New GUI for Sighted Users

For sighted users, a new GUI (Graphical User Interface) was developed, and the usability improved. Tactile graphics can be edited with simple operations. See Fig. 5.

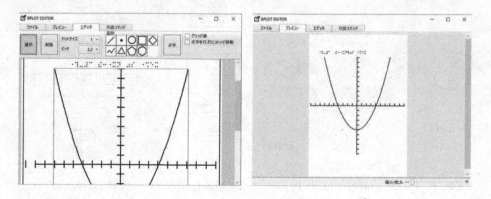

Fig. 5. Edit screen and preview screen of the GUI

(4) Everest-D V5 (Index Braille) Supported

Since it is not difficult for BPLOT to support new Braille printers, the new version can control Everest-D V5. We plans to support other Braille printers if requested.

3   Experimental Evaluation

For the evaluation, two experiments were conducted. The first experiment is to compare time needed to produce tactile graphics for blind persons with BPLOT and sighted persons with a tactile graphics editor. The second experiment is to evaluate the quality of products made by a blind person using BPLOT.

3.1   Comparison of Time Needed to Produce Tactile Graphics

The purpose of this experiment is to compare time needed to produce tactile graphics for blind persons by writing plotter control commands of BPLOT and sighted persons by using the tactile graphics editor EDEL-plus [5].

Method: The blind subjects are two blind men (age 60s and 70s) who are familiar with using BPLOT, and the sighted subjects are two women (age 40s and 60s) who are Braille transcribers. The assignments are to draw the four basic tactile graphics shown in Fig. 6. The blind subjects are given them as a document, while the sighted subjects are given as a set of pictures. The blind subjects are allowed to print out uncompleted products and check them tactually several times before the completions.

Result: The quality of products made by all the four subjects is good enough for teaching materials. Figure 6 shows the products made by one of the blind subjects.

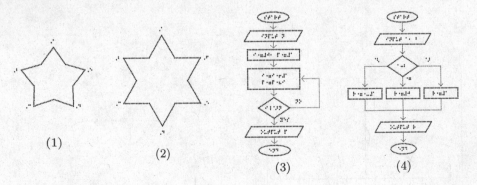

Fig. 6. Tactile graphics made by one of the blind subjects from the assignments

\The time needed to produce tactile graphics for the blind subjects are (1) 46.5 s, (2) 71.0 s, (3) 127.5 s, and (4) 103.0 s on average. The time needed for the sighted subjects are (1) 22.5 s, (2) 9.0 s, (3) 47.0 s, and (4) 36.5 s on average. For (1), (3) and (4), the blind subjects take from 2.1 times to 2.8 times longer than the sighted subjects. However, for (2), the blind subjects take 7.9 times longer than the sighted subjects. This difference may be because the blind subjects had to calculate the coordinates of intersection points, while the sighted subjects can draw two regular triangles and erase dots in the inner part.

3.2   Evaluation of the Quality of Products Made Using BPLOT

The purpose of this experiment is to evaluate the quality of products made by a blind person using BPLOT. Not only tactile graphics but also ink print graphics are evaluated whether they have enough quality for teaching materials.

Method: All the subjects are teachers in a school for the blind. The blind subjects are eight blind teachers, and the sighted subjects are eight sighted teachers. The assignments are to evaluate the quality of tactile graphics and ink print graphics converted from the tactile graphics. There are the four types of tactile graphics and ink print graphics shown in Fig. 7: (A1), (B1) Distribution graph, (A2), (B2) Trigonometric function graph, (A3), (B3) Symbol mark, and (A4), (B4) Box-and-whisker plot.

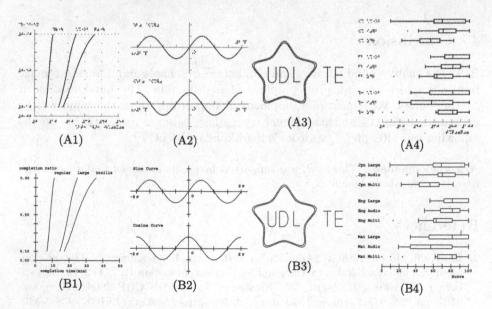

Fig. 7. Tactile graphics and ink print graphics converted from the tactile graphics made by a blind person using BPLOT

The blind subjects are asked to evaluate only tactile graphics, and the sighted subjects are asked to evaluate both tactile graphics and ink print graphics. Ratings for the evaluation are chosen from the following 7 values: Very good (3 points), Good (2 points), Slightly good (1 point), Neutral (0 point), Slightly poor (-1 point), Poor (-2 points), and Very poor (-3 points).

Result: The averages of ratings for the assignments are presented in Table 1. As a result of the evaluation, the quality of tactile graphics made by a blind person using BPLOT is mostly good enough for teaching materials, and ink print graphics converted from the tactile graphics are mostly acceptable for teaching materials for sighted students. However, the ratings by the sighted subjects for box-and-whisker plot are not good. As tactile proofreading by a blind person is necessary for the production of tactile graphics, the production of ink print graphics by the blind might need proofreading by a sighted person.

Table 1. The averages of ratings for the assignments ($n = 16$)

Group	Media	(A1), (B1)	(A2), (B2)	(A3), (B3)	(A4), (B4)	Average
Blind	Tactile	1.69	1.44	0.81	0.50	1.11
Sighted	Tactile	0.63	1.00	1.12	-0.25	0.62
Sighted	Ink print	0.50	1.00	0.75	-0.25	0.50

4   Conclusion

BPLOT4 enables blind teachers and blind staffs in schools and libraries to make tactile graphics and ink print graphics of high quality. The blind can use it by themselves. We expect that employment opportunities for the blind will be expanded. BPLOT4 and its manual with many samples are available on the following web site: http://apricot.cis.ibaraki.ac.jp/BPLOT/.

Acknowledgement. This work was supported by grants for social welfare activities from the Mitsubishi Foundation.

References

1. Fujiyoshi, M., Fujiyoshi, A., Ohtake, N., Yamaguchi, K., Teshima, Y.: The development of a universal design tactile graphics production system BPLOT2. In: Miesenberger, K., Klaus, J., Zagler, W., Karshmer, A. (eds.) ICCHP 2008. LNCS, vol. 5105, pp. 938–945. Springer, Heidelberg (2008). https://doi.org/10.1007/978-3-540-70540-6_141

2. Fujiyoshi, M., Kaneko, T., Fujiyoshi, A., Oouchi, S., Yamazawa, K., Ikegami, Y., Watanabe, Y., Teshima, Y.: Development of tactile graphics production software for three-dimensional projections. In: Miesenberger, K., Klaus, J., Zagler, W., Karshmer, A. (eds.) ICCHP 2010. LNCS, vol. 6180, pp. 541–547. Springer, Heidelberg (2010). https://doi.org/10.1007/978-3-642-14100-3_81

3. Fujiyoshi, M., Fujiyoshi, A., Osawa, A., Kuroda, Y., Sasaki, Y.: Development of synchronized CUI and GUI for Universal design tactile graphics production system BPLOT3. In: Miesenberger, K., Fels, D., Archambault, D., Peňáz, P., Zagler, W. (eds.) ICCHP 2014. LNCS, vol. 8548, pp. 18–25. Springer, Cham (2014). https://doi.org/10.1007/978-3-319-08599-9_4

4. BES. http://www.ttools.co.jp/product/eyes/BES/. (in Japanese)

5. EDEL-plus. http://www7a.biglobe.ne.jp/~EDEL-plus/. (in Japanese)

6. Tiger Software Suite, VIEWPLUS. http://www.viewplus.com/products/software/braille-translator/

7. PostScript, Adobe Systems. https://www.adobe.com/products/postscript.html

A User Study to Evaluate Tactile Charts with Blind and Visually Impaired People

Christin Engel(✉) and Gerhard Weber

Chair of Human-Computer-Interaction, Faculty of Computer Science,
TU Dresden, 01062 Dresden, Germany
{christin.engel,gerhard.weber}@tu-dresden.de

Abstract. Charts, for example bar or line charts, represent data visually. They make use of domain specific skills of the visual sense like fast pattern recognition. Tactile charts enable blind and visually impaired people to access charts by the sense of touch. Their design differ from visual chart design. It is unclear how effective design of tactile charts looks like for different chart types. That is why we conducted a remote user study with 45 blind and visually impaired people to investigate several design criteria for tactile charts. Therefore, we have mailed tactile charts to participants who evaluated the charts on the basis of an online survey. In this paper, we analyze four comparison tasks with two bar charts, line charts, scatter plots, and pie charts, that differ in one specific design criteria - in particular, inner and outer helplines in bar charts, the design of grid lines in line charts, the use of grid lines in scatter plots, and the usage of textures in pie charts. We compare these charts regarding the computed error rate, the number of correct answers as well as a rating given by participants.

Keywords: Tactile charts · Remote user study
Information graphics · Tactile graphics · Accessibility
Effective design · Blind and visually impaired users

1 Introduction

Information graphics enable data analysis in an efficient and effective way. They make use of domain specific skills of the visual sense like fast pattern and outlier detection. Blind and visually impaired people do not have visual access to graphics like charts. Therefore, the BITV (Barrier-free Information Technology Ordinance) state the requirement of text-alternatives that fit the user's needs for non-text content for all websites of public affairs. That may be suitable for simple charts with a few data points. Describing more complex charts verbally, leads to a long description that is hard to understand. Guidelines for chart description recommend to provide the data within a table. However, table data do not give an overview of the data. Especially, analyzing trends is very hard.

Tactile charts are another possibility to provide access to visual charts. They consist of raised lines, symbols and textures that can be perceived by the sense

© Springer International Publishing AG, part of Springer Nature 2018
K. Miesenberger and G. Kouroupetroglou (Eds.): ICCHP 2018, LNCS 10897, pp. 177–184, 2018.
https://doi.org/10.1007/978-3-319-94274-2_24

of touch. Tactile charts can be more efficient for accessing charts than verbal descriptions or data tables [9]. The user can analyze data on their own by exploring the tactile graphic and interpreting spatial relations. The design of tactile charts differs from visual chart design [7]. Guidelines concerning the design of tactile graphics in general also include some recommendations for the design of tactile charts, in particular [2,3]. These guidelines are not sufficient for tactile charts because they only cover few aspects of tactile chart design. Furthermore, they assume that tactile charts are used to get access to a visual chart. Hence, they recommend a design that faithfully reflect a visual chart. A direct translation from a visual to a tactile chart is not suitable [6,8]. The design of tactile charts should support the readability and the analysis of data with the tactile sense.

There is initial research concerning aspects of tactile chart design. In particular, the usage and design of grid lines was much discussed [1,6,8]. On the one hand, grid lines can be helpful and improve the readability of tactile charts [1], on the other hand, they can be confused with chart data such as lines in line charts. It follows that the design of chart elements depends on the specific chart type. Current research focuses on a few chart types like bar charts [7], line charts, and pie charts. It is rarely discussed how the design can support the user in analyzing the underlying data. Goncu et al. [7] compare reading a tactile table with reading a tactile bar chart. Participants preferred the tactile table. In that study, the authors compare bar charts which represent only ten data points. In contrast, another study from Watanabe et al: [9] compare reading a tactile table, a digital text file and tactile scatter plots with 20 data points in respect to identifying the data trend quickly and correctly. Here, the tactile scatter plot outperformed the other representation methods.

In summary, tactile charts are suitable for enabling blind and visually impaired people to access charts and the underlying data. It is still unclear how effective chart design looks like. That is why we investigate studies in tactile chart design. In a first step, we analyzed current tactile charts from online libraries, publications, and guideline sets concerning the design of axes and tick marks, grid lines, fillings, legend, labels, and the size of the represented data set [4]. In a second step, we conducted an online survey among 71 blind, visually impaired, and sighted tactile chart authors and users [5]. The participants were asked about their experiences in creating and exploring tactile charts. As a result, we identified steps as well as challenges in the current creation process of tactile charts. In addition, we summarized general design guidelines for tactile charts. On the basis of these studies and two pilot studies, we developed some design templates for tactile charts. In the following sections, we present a remote user study that aims to evaluate these templates and specific design aspects as well as the effectiveness of tactile charts.

2   User Study on Tactile Chart Design

In this user study, we developed 21 tactile charts: seven bar charts, six line charts and three pie charts as well as five scatter plots that represent different data sets. We asked blind and visually impaired participants to explore and evaluate the tactile charts in an online survey. In addition, participants analyze the underlying data with the help of the given charts.

2.1 Methodology

In the following section, we describe the methods and materials as well as the content of the online survey and present the results.

Methods and Material. We conducted a remote user study in Germany where tactile charts were mailed to the participants. Remote user studies with disabled people have the advantage that the participants can use their own assistive technologies in their personal setup. In addition, they can carry out the study independently which makes them more willing to participate because some blind or visually impaired people have difficulties with traveling.

We asked people for participation by personal e-mails, mailing lists, and social network groups. Every participant got the following materials through the mail: a brief description of the study, an instruction for sending the materials back, a personal access key, and the URL for the online survey as well as the tactile sheets. The tactile graphics were produced with the Braille embosser *TigerPro* by ViewPlus that has a resolution of 20 dpi. The graphics were grouped in line charts, vertical bar charts, pie charts, and scatter plots. To avoid learning effects, we randomized the order of chart types. Pie charts were not randomized, they were always presented at last because they are different from the other chart types. Overall, we used six randomization groups of chart types that were assigned equally often to participants. All participants who completed at minimum the first two chart types got a coupon amounting to 15 € for participation and asked for participation in a short survey to retrieve ratings about the study design.

In addition to the remote setup, we got in personal contact with an institution[1] that produces learning materials for blind and visually impaired students. Therefore, we interviewed four blind people who already carried out the user study and discussed some redesigns that were developed on the basis of the given answers.

Procedure. At the beginning of the online survey, participants receive detailed instructions about the materials and the structure of the study. This is followed by a training phase with a step-by-step manual to explore a given training chart. Participants are asked about their experiences with tactile charts.

Within the main part of the study, participants are guided to explore the tactile charts one after the other. The order of presented chart types depends on the individual randomization. The order of charts within the same chart type as well as the structure of questions for every chart type is similar. Every chart

---

[1] http://www.mediablis-bayern.de/.

type starts with a short definition of the chart type. Afterwards, participants are asked to explore the first chart on their own and to compare the explored information with a given description of this chart. This follows the exploration of all charts from this chart type in a fixed order.

The questions for each chart are structured as follows: First, participants explore the chart initially on their own. If participants have problems in understanding, they get a textual description of the chart. Furthermore, participants answer questions concerning the content of the chart. They have to identify precise data values and interpret the data. Second, participants are requested to rate statements concerning the design of the specific chart and individual preferences on a five-point scale of agreement. At the end of each chart, participants rate the whole chart on a scale from 1 "very good" to 6 "unsatisfying". After completing two chart types, participants can decide to continue with the last two chart types or to finish the study without exploring all charts.

The last part retrieves demographic data - in particular age, profession, level of blindness, braille reading skills, and gender.

Prior to the start of the study, we evaluated the feasibility and accessibility of the online survey with one blind person who works in the field of social education.

Participants. Up until now, 45 participants have completed the study (19 male, 26 female). The mean age is 44 years, whereby the youngest participant is 19 years old and the oldest 77 years.

Overall, 40 blind and five visually impaired people participated. 49% of them are born without vision, while 15.6% went blind/visual impaired before the age of ten - just as much in the age of 11 to 20 years and 21 to 40 years. Just 4.4% are late-blinded. 75% of all participants have experience in exploring tactile charts (19% very high experience, 31% high experience). Four participants are not familiar with charts in general.

The next section presents general results of this study as well as four comparison tasks, each concerning one test criteria.

2.2 Results

34 of 45 participants explored all chart types while 11 participants finished the study after two chart types. In average, participants needed 256 min to complete the study, at least 110 min. However, it is still unclear whether the participants needed the whole time to complete the study and how many breaks are included.

With 3.14 the stacked bar chart received the worst user rating of all chart types. In general, we observed a relation between the familiarity of each chart type and the received user rating. While the minority of participants explored stacked bar charts (33%) and scatter plots (24%) before the study, these chart types were rated worst on average. In contrast, simple bar charts were best rated with 1.92 and are familiar to 88% of the participants.

Due to the large amount of retrieved data, we are restricting our analysis to a few charts that will be discussed in detail. However, we compared design choices and their effect on chart readability by comparison tasks. Overall, we compared four design criteria among - one pair for each chart type. The objective of each comparison task is to answer the following questions: Which design was preferred by the participants? How the design affects the readability of the chart? How effective are tactile charts in reading out values and interpret the presented data?

To answer these research questions, we analyze the results of each chart (see Table 1). *Correct Answers* takes all given answers concerning chart's content into account. There are two kind of questions. First, configurational questions have one correct answer that can be a word or a numerical value, e.g., the number of bars in a bar chart or the line with the highest values in a line chart. Second, we ask to read out precise data values. These numerical values are accepted as correct if their absolute deviation from the correct value is less than 5%. This tolerance is necessary because of embossers' inaccuracy that rasterizes the graphic with low resolution. In addition, we have computed the *Error Rate* as the deviation of the average of given answers from the correct value in percentage. This computation excludes all answers that were incorrect because of misinterpretation of the question. In particular, when participants read out the value of the wrong axis or of a wrong bar. The *Rating* is the average of given ratings overall participants that ranges from 1 ("very good") to 6 ("unsatisfying"). In addition, we evaluated specific design criteria by quantifying the agreement of participants to several statements on a five-point scale. Table 2 shows an extract from the statements for bar charts in comparison 1. The computed values are normalized between 0 ("fully disagree") and 1 ("fully agree").

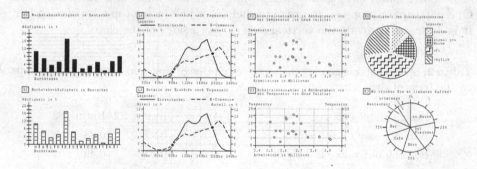

Fig. 1. Comparison tasks used in the study. From left to right: Comparison 1: Bar Charts S2 and S3, Comparison 2: Line Charts L4 and L5, Comparison 3: Scatter Plots P2 and P3, Comparison 4: Pie Charts K2 and K3.

Comparison 1: Bar Charts. We compared the bar charts S4 and S5 concerning the design of bars as well as the design of helplines. While S4 has filled bars and horizontal helplines, S5 uses texture with horizontal lines that represents the helplines inside the bars (see Fig. 1). The results show no significant difference between given correct answers and error rate in both conditions. The error rate is just lower when reading out values in the inner helplines condition. In contrast, participants preferred the use of outer helplines.

Table 1. Results for the four comparison tasks of tactile charts.

Chart type	Test criteria	Correct answers	Error rate	Rating (1–6)
Comparison 1: Bar Charts	S2: outer helplines	77.22%	9.35%	1.57
	S3: inner helplines	74.71%	4.11%	2.66
Comparison 2: Line Charts	L4: dotted helplines	70.79%	2.29%	2.48
	L5: solid helplines	77.98%	0.87%	2
Comparison 3: Scatter Plots	P2: no grid	50.63%	4.38%	3.15
	P3: incised grid	72.71%	5.98%	2.07
Comparison 4: Pie Charts	K2: texture	75.08%	14.60%	2.91
	K3: contour	80.22%	3.61%	1.83

The analysis of design statements (see Table 2) shows that the perception of bars was not much influenced by the design of helplines. Reading out precise values seems to be much easier with outer helplines. In general, they were preferred over the use of inner helplines. Because inner helplines are unfamiliar to the majority of participants, some of them do not understand the functionality of the texture as helplines. In addition, participants reported (in additional comments) that reading out values for a single bar is much easier in inner helpline condition S3 while comparing values among bars caused difficulties. That is why, some participants proposed a design that combines inner and outer helplines. One participant proposed to use outer helplines just at the top edge of each bar. It is desired to provide the vertical axis on both sides of the chart.

Table 2. Statements concerning the tactile chart design that were rated by participants on the basis of their agreement.

Design statement	Rating S2	Rating S3
Bars are easy to distinguish	0.99	0.88
Reading out values is difficult	0.23	0.49
Comparing bars among each other is easy	0.99	0.88
The helplines are helpful for reading out values	0.94	0.78

Comparison 2: Line Charts. The line charts L4 and L5 differ in the style of the grid lines. While L4 uses dotted grid lines, L5 make use of thin, solid lines. Solid grid lines were rated much better than dotted grid lines. In addition, participants gave 13% more correct answers when reading out values in the solid grid condition. Over all questions, they gave 7% more correct answers with the solid grid. While 30 participants fully agree with the statement "The grid lines are highly distinguishable" in the solid grid condition, just 14 participants fully

agreed in dotted grid condition. Some participants stated that the recognition of intersection points are much easier with solid grid lines.

Comparison 3: Scatter Plots. Within the comparison task of P2 and P3 we wanted to find out whether the use of grid lines influences the readability of scatter plots. The evaluation of these scatter plots shows a great tendency toward the use of the incised grid in P3 (embossed on the back side of the paper). The grid condition leads to 22% more correct answers. Furthermore, participants preferred the grid line condition. 97% of participants state that the use of grid lines does not decrease the readability of the chart. In addition, they reported that it took less time to read out values in the grid condition.

Comparison 4: Pie Charts. The pie charts K2 and K3 do not present the same data set, nonetheless they are comparable. K2 uses texture and a legend to reference the presented data. In contrast, K3 just uses contours and labels inside or outside each circle segment. In addition, we added helplines at the outside of the circle. Despite the second design being very unfamiliar to the participants, the results show a high preference for the non-textured pie chart K3. The function of these outer helplines was not explained in the online survey. Nevertheless, just 9% did not recognize and understand this type of helplines. In average, participants rather preferred pie charts with contoured segments instead of the use of textures. In addition, K2 has the highest error rate overall analyzed charts.

3 Discussion and Conclusion

We conducted a remote study to evaluate design criteria for tactile charts. We analyzed four comparisons in detail. We presented a study design that enables the evaluation of tactile graphics with a large number of participants in a remote setup. Within the final evaluation of the study design, 92% of participants rated the study as "very good" or "good". In addition, 70% stated that their personal benefit of participation is "very high" or "high".

The results of the study indicate that tactile charts are suitable to analyze data and their relationship in detail. Overall, 85% of participants recognized the structure and the content of the charts "completely" or "mainly" without getting any additional information about it. This results indicate an intuitive tactile chart design.

These results from four comparisons clarify the influence of specific design criteria on the tactile reading performance. In particular, filled bars with helplines were preferred over textured bars that represent helplines within each bar. Furthermore, results show a strong tendency towards the use of solid grid lines in line charts compared with dotted grid lines. Grid lines leads to 22% more correct answers and a much lower error rate, when reading out precise values from scatter plots. Finally, pie charts with contours and labels are more readable than with the use of texture. Adding a scale on the outer circle leads to lower error rates in pie charts.

In the future, we will analyze the results of the study completely. In addition, we will compare the results for each chart type among each other in order to find out specific design considerations depending on the chart type. In a comparative study we will compare the answers given by blind and visually impaired participants with those from sighted people. Additionally, we consider making a second design iteration to evaluate redesigns based on the results of this study.

Finally, our study demonstrates that blind and visually impaired people are highly interested in tactile charts. We will use the final results to develop a guideline set for tactile charts. In addition, we will develop a software that automates the creation of tactile charts based on these design guidelines. So, our main goal is to improve the design and the creation of tactile charts. Furthermore, the software will enable blind and visually impaired people creating charts independently. That could improve the inclusion of people with visual disabilities.

Acknowledgments. We thank all participants for their contribution. The paper is part of the *Mosaik* project, which is sponsored by the German Federal Ministry of Labour and Social Affairs (BMAS) under the grant number 01KM151112. Only the authors of this paper are responsible for its content.

References

1. Aldrich, F.K., Parkin, A.J.: Tangible line graphs: an experimental investigation of three formats using capsule paper. Hum. Factors **29**(3), 301–309 (1987). https://doi.org/10.1177/001872088702900304
2. Braille Authority of North America, Canadian Braille Authority: Guidelines and Standards for Tactile Graphics (2011)
3. Round Table on Information Access for People with Print Disabilities Inc.: Guidelines on Conveying Visual Information (2005)
4. Engel, C., Weber, G.: Analysis of tactile chart design. In: Proceedings of the 10th International Conference on PErvasive Technologies Related to Assistive Environments, pp. 197–200, PETRA 2017. ACM, New York (2017). https://doi.org/10.1145/3056540.3064955
5. Engel, C., Weber, G.: Improve the accessibility of tactile charts. In: Bernhaupt, R., Dalvi, G., Joshi, A., Balkrishan, D.K., O'Neill, J., Winckler, M. (eds.) INTERACT 2017. LNCS, vol. 10513, pp. 187–195. Springer, Cham (2017). https://doi.org/10.1007/978-3-319-67744-6_12
6. Goncu, C., Marriott, K.: Tactile chart generation tool. In: Proceedings of the 10th International ACM SIGACCESS Conference on Computers and Accessibility - Assets 2008, p. 255 (2008)
7. Goncu, C., Marriott, K., Hurst, J.: Usability of accessible bar charts. In: Goel, A.K., Jamnik, M., Narayanan, N.H. (eds.) Diagrams 2010. LNCS (LNAI), vol. 6170, pp. 167–181. Springer, Heidelberg (2010). https://doi.org/10.1007/978-3-642-14600-8_17
8. Panëels, S., Roberts, J.C.: Review of designs for haptic data visualization. IEEE Trans. Haptics **3**(2), 119–137 (2010)
9. Watanabe, T., Yamaguchi, T., Nakagawa, M.: Development of software for automatic creation of embossed graphs. In: Miesenberger, K., Karshmer, A., Penaz, P., Zagler, W. (eds.) ICCHP 2012. LNCS, vol. 7382, pp. 174–181. Springer, Heidelberg (2012). https://doi.org/10.1007/978-3-642-31522-0_25

Concept-Building in Blind Readers with Thematic Tactile Volumes

Dorine in 't Veld[✉]

Dedicon, Grave, The Netherlands
dorineintveld@dedicon.nl

Abstract. What makes tactile images well understandable and easy to read? What do blind readers need? This should be the starting question for any project developing technology that may help making tactile images common and easily available. This paper shares lessons learnt in a couple of succeeding projects. In the latest project, that is continued this year, thematic tactile volumes are being developed, that explain to blind people subjects that are otherwise very inaccessible for them. The subjects range from trees, letters, mathematical notation to traffic signs and icons. They even contain the two first volumes of a method that is being developed for reading 3D-images; the first volume comes with 3D-printed objects. They were tested with 10 readers who unanimously stated they would have liked to learn this at school. Dedicon had no opportunity for scientific research; this is a practical report, sharing important empirical information for designers of tactile images and developers of software or hardware concerning tablets giving haptic feedback.

Keywords: Tactile images · Concept building · Haptic learning

1 Background: Dedicon and Tactile Images

Dedicon is the national resource-center for reading impaired people. There is a specialist educational department for visually impaired learners. School- and study books for visually impaired students can be ordered here in one or more of the following reading forms: audio-DAISY, photo-pdf, A3-magnification, Braille or Word. The latter two come with tactile images on A4 swell paper.

The production of these tactile images has risen since 2012 from 10,000 to an estimated 17,000 this year. How can this be explained? One reason is a change in the ordering system. Before 2012 educators had to indicate what images should be adapted with a maximum of 50 per book. Since 2012 Dedicon makes the selection. We leave out purely 'decorative' images and images like complex infographics, maps with many details and images with perspective. We select only images that are necessary for proper understanding or doing the exercises. Yet often the selection widely exceeds this number of 50, especially in books with many diagrams and/or (mathematical) graphs. As a consequence, an estimated 80% of the tactile images are diagrams for STEM (Science, Technology, Engineering, Mathematics) subjects. The rest is mainly maps and schemes.

© Springer International Publishing AG, part of Springer Nature 2018
K. Miesenberger and G. Kouroupetroglou (Eds.): ICCHP 2018, LNCS 10897, pp. 185–192, 2018.
https://doi.org/10.1007/978-3-319-94274-2_25

Other reasons for the increasing popularity: (1) nowadays tactile images are better designed and thus quicker to read, (2) we added black writing for sighted peers and teachers who don't read braille, so it is easier to cooperate using tactile images, (3) in a qualitative customer satisfaction survey in 2017 most blind students stated the tactile images are indispensable they would rather have (even) more than less tactile images in the future.

The demand for tactile images is not only rising; it is also changing. There is a growing awareness in education that blind and low vision students often use language or may reproduce a given explanation almost literally, without full and correct understanding. This easily goes unnoticed. One only finds out when the child is asked more specific description in its own words – where it additionally can use its hands – and body – to indicate size, direction, form, attitude, etc.; as in The Netherlands first described by Linders in 1998 [1].

In the last couple of years awareness is growing that blind learners often lack a good mental representation of objects and concepts that are literally out of reach: things too small, large or dangerous to touch or even untouchable. And that there are many things they never come across at all and that are not even described to them. For example, in history lessons at school, many images of buildings and people in a certain time or place are shown in books and video, without ever being described or even mentioned.

Description alone often leaves only a vague impression, especially if there is no solid and correct mental representation as a basis. One needs many words and still the blind person will very probably be left with only a vague or even incorrect mental representation. By combining description and tactile images and sometimes 3D objects – i.e. by using more modalities – it is possible to diminish the length of the description and at the same time enhance the learning effects and the forming of a correct mental representation.

Models, like tactile images, may compensate for this lack of information. But they are often expensive or difficult and/or very time consuming to make or to get. Besides they are not always easy to transport or to store. Tactile images score much better in this respect.

2   Thematic Tactile Volumes: Why and How?

The use of imagery in education and our society grows exponentially and blind learners fall behind. Even though the number of tactile images we produce rises, there are hardly any tactile images explaining what things look like or what are the proportions of parts or their relative position in space. It is hard to make them; pictures in the book often don't display what is needed to get a proper mental representation and a simple copy often is not understandable for a blind reader. E.g. a dolphin: what is the shape of its tail? Looking from the side it is flat. It takes thinking, making choices, sometimes even research to make an effective tactile image. Making tactile images is very instructive! We often joke that sighted students with blind classmates using this type of tactile images would profit from cooperating with them because of the much better explanation. But alas this type of images is scarce.

That is why we started with 'thematic tactile volumes'. Hard-to-access subjects are systematically treated with the help of tactile images. A textual explanation guides the hand and adds the necessary information in order to form a correct and complete mental representation. To our knowledge this approach in education for VI learners is unique and the first in its kind. In some countries we found (audio-)tactile books about specific works of art or important architectural sites, that certainly inspired us, but we found no thematic volumes as in our present project.

2.1 The Basis of Our Know-How

In our approach, we embroidered on outcomes and lessons learned in preceding projects, research and experience. Project Discover your World in 2011 clearly showed that the use of tactile images (1) makes teachers check if the learner has a complete and correct mental representation, (2) stimulates the learner to ask questions and explore further and (3) in combination with a description enhance learning effects [2]. This last finding is coherent with findings in studies about multimodal learning in general. Various projects and experience also showed that practice and training reading tactile images usually lead to quick progress in the skill to read them.

2.2 Requirements for Effective Tactile Images

1. In order to be effective, the images must be well designed (tactilely well readable). We issued internal guidelines, that are in line with those of the Braille Authority of North America [3] and the Project SOCRATE-COMENIUS 3-1 1999/2000 [4].
2. The design must be comprehensible from the perspective of tactile reading. We'll come back to that when discussing the user side.
3. The explanation must be effective. Everything that is drawn must be described and everything described must be drawn. An effective description is as short as possible, clear, vivid, and plastic. This is not easy. It must start with the idea behind the tactile image: what does it reveal, and what is left out and why. By the way: less or even no explanation is needed – after a little practicing – with well-designed and highly standardized tactile images, like our maps, graphs of mathematical functions.
4. This brings us to the user-side. The reader must have learned the necessary skills both to discriminate the lines, dots, shapes and textures, but also to build a mental representation. Reading a tactile image in this perspective is comparable to reading and understanding text, which is much more than just discerning letters. In the case of 3D objects, this is even more complex: in order to be able to give meaning to the drawing the reader needs to know the concept or method that is used to draw them.

2.3 Spatial Awareness and Translating 3D to 2D

Relatively new is the use of tactile images for explaining 3D objects or concepts in The Netherlands. Only this year (2018) a project to set up a curriculum for reading tactile images for primary education was started by Visio and Bartiméus Education for the visually impaired in The Netherlands.

A particular problem with blind born people is, that many have not developed spatial thinking and more specifically: they are not acquainted with the concept of projection. It may be very difficult to understand the relation between a flat and horizontal line drawing and a vertical shape or object with volume. In the education of blind people hardly any attention is paid to vision. How does sight work? What is a drawing? What is projection? What is perspective? What is a profile? And so on. Spatial awareness and more specifically the ability to translate from 3D to 2D v.v. has to be developed and trained, before tactile images giving insight into 3D objects can be used effectively.

3   Description of the Thematic Tactile Volumes

Each volume has between 15 and of 30 images. An accompanying text explains the images. Everything that is described can be found in the images and everything that is drawn can be found in the text. In 2017 10 titles were realized, based on wishes of blind learners and (mainstream and itinerant) teachers.

They cover a wide variety of both subjects and level of readers, which allowed us to experiment with developing a proper 'language' per type of tactile image and accompanying description.

We were bound to use our standard formats for educational materials, which is swell-paper for the images and an accessible digital document or paper Braille document for the text. The volumes are made independent of books or methods of publishers.

Where applicable we chose subjects that meet the requirements for exams. We do not create new methods but assume readers will find further information in their study book, the internet or any other sources.

The explanation in the description helps form a mental representation and hence to understand the information in those sources properly.

Most volumes can be used both by younger and older readers, either at school or at home. Experienced readers 14 and up will mostly be able to use them independently; younger or less experienced readers may need (a little) help.

3.1   3D-2D

This is the first volume in a series where blind people learn to read (and make) tactile images of 3D subjects and to understand about perspective, shadow, projection and other visual concepts. In the images themselves no perspective is used – other than where perspective is explained. Perspective deforms shapes and angles and thus makes tactile images mostly unreadable. Exploring the exact shapes and angles in a drawing on the other hand is much more similar to exploring a 3D object by touch.

The volume 3D-2D is intended as a first step to meet the challenges described in the paragraph 'Spatial awareness and translating 3D to 2D v.v.' above. The method of drawing is 'orthogonal projection', as used for example in industrial design. Its translation for tactile images for blind learners was developed in the Socrates-Comenius project mentioned before [4]. The approach was proved to work well in education, even for children with additional learning difficulties. It was put into practice and promoted by amongst others Corvest [5] and Fabio Levi of TactileVision in Turin, Italy (who at the same moment independently came to the same conclusions).

The volume 3D-2D comes with 3D printed objects, that fit 1-to-1 to the tactile images. It explains the concept of orthogonal projection and then, step by step, trains the reader in working with it. Reactions of the blind testers in our project, aged 16 to 68, definitely showed differences in learning speed. All thought the beginning a bit confusing and difficult, but soon got the hang of it and wanted more. All said it would have been good to learn this at school, since it not only provides a good system for reading 3D images, but also stimulates spatial awareness. The method allows not only to get precise knowledge of the size and proportions of parts, but also of their relative position in space. Some of them presumed it would have helped with developing spatial awareness, learning mathematics, logical thinking and mobility.

3.2   Objects Around Us

This second volume applies this method of drawing and reading to small daily objects like a cup, a fork and next to bigger objects like furniture and a house, a church. It includes exercises like identifying which 'photo' was made on what side of a house. It plays with the drawing-principle of orthogonal projection; sometime it adds or skips the usual three views (from above, from the front and from the side).

For some of the blind testers it took a lot of time (up to 10 to 12 min) to identify the first image – a simple mug with an ear – for an everyday object known to them, when asked to read the image without knowing its subject. Most stated they had expected and thought it would be something else, which subsequently stood in their way of translating the image into a proper mental representation. When the images were explained however, they found it easy to link the images to objects.

When tested the way these tactile images are meant to function, namely accompanied by a description, all found it easy to understand and stated there was real added value in the combination. Descriptions could be shorter, comprehension much more precise. Now and then we ran into discussions like 'But a spatula is flat from the side'! Then, when real spatulas were shown, new discoveries were made. As in 'Discover your world' the images invited to ask questions, discuss and learn.

3.3   Volcanoes and Earthquakes

This subject appears in every schoolbook about 'the earth', often with photos, 3D cross-sections and complex maps with fault lines and hotspots. Since we mostly have to skip these images, we decided to make a thematic tactile volume that can be used next to any school method.

3.4   Topo-NL

This volume was made for the same reason. As a bonus it allowed us to rethink the specifications for maps used in school settings. One of the biggest challenges is how to deal with Braille legends. They cannot be made smaller, since that will rend them illegible. Even when reduced to 1 or 2 characters it is often difficult finding a 'logical' place for the braille labels, or even finding a place at all. In the future we would like to replace all printed Braille with electronical text and/or sound.

Another challenge is to standardize tactile legends in specific types of maps or in one volume as much as possible and avoid that readers have to take their hands off the map to check the legends all the time. We partly found a solution by using less legends and more hand guiding description.

In many school situations an atlas with maps containing too much information at once are not helpful for students We leave out details that are not serving the purpose of the map. Our slogan in this respect is: 'The coast of Norway is straight... unless we explain fjords'. In our TOPO-Holland-volume this means: when a river and a border (almost) coincide, we explain this in the description, but we don't draw the border separately. When necessary, we split maps and build up complexity.

These measures can simplify reading enormously. Textures were overrated in the past and made tactile images unnecessarily difficult to read, as many of our testers stated.

3.5   Trees

What do trees look like? One side of the tree shows what the tree looks like from a distance in summer; the 'winter side' reveals the structure of the branches. A bar at the side shows the size of an adult person. The last page shows their relative shapes and sizes. It was not possible to draw all leaves and fruits on the same scale; the explanation reveals their actual sizes. Of course, it is recommendable that children collect the real leaves and fruits; we chose types that are common in The Netherlands.

3.6   Letters and Digits

Here we explain printed and written black writing notations. Many blind readers never learn how letters, digits, reading signs or symbols are written or printed. Most children want to learn however. It is cool to be able to write as your peers do. And to know things like why a colon followed by a parenthesis to the right makes a smiley. Or what letter-logos are, like the big yellow M of McDonalds. Or what signatures or hand-writing look like. The immediate cause we started letters and digits was the question of a student aged 25: 'I have to make a report in font Arial, size 10. Why is that?' Blind students need to know lay-out can be chosen to style your text and make it more attractive and neatly arranged for sighted readers. Or why they have to use a format when publishing a paper at a congress.

3.7   Mathematical Notation

This volume was made for very much the same reason. We do have a website where we explain to sighted people the mathematical notation we use for blind readers. But we didn't have anything to explain to blind readers how math is notated for sighted students. It is interesting for them to know. Why do you use more parentheses in a linear notation than in the same spatial notation? What is the advantage of putting numbers one under another when adding them? Understanding these things helps in communication.

3.8   Structure Formulae

The volume about structure formulae was made to give access to this part of chemistry. In fact, we solved the problem of how to draw structure formulae, also for the students themselves. In addition to this thematic volume we set up a website, where the same formulas can be accessed through audio. We advise our students and their teachers to start with molecular building kits and the thematic volume. When the concept is understood, they can add using the website. After working through the whole thematic band plus the website, audio-only access will suffice in most cases. We hope to be able to develop a website where students can submit any image out of a book, the will be translated on the fly. Though there are very few blind and partially sighted students, we think it is important to make this discipline accessible. Some 10 years ago we found a solution for math notation; ever since the number of students doing math is rising steadily. The same might happen with chemistry. Many of our students choosing math want to do an academic IT-study. In order to be admitted, they need to pass exams in a set of disciplines, that includes chemistry. In this project we cooperated with Volker Sorge. A report will be published in these proceedings (Volker Sorge, Dorine in 't Veld: The Dutch Best Practice for Teaching Chemistry Diagrams to the Visually Impaired, 2018.

3.9   Titles for the Youngest

For the youngest learners we produced two volumes with images, Braille puzzles and puzzles like 'find the differences' for two Dutch feasts: (1) Sint Nicolaas and (2) Christmas. In this case we added no text. Teachers, parents and children received these books very enthusiastically. As found in former projects, the images invite children to ask questions and hence stimulate conversation and learning. They also promote inclusion. They have been ordered for almost every child and were very well received.

Finally, there is a volume to practice telling time. This one comes with a (very simple) textbook with exercises. This one too is very popular.

4   Conclusion and Planned Activities

In 2018 we will produce another 10 titles and we will experiment with other techniques for the images, e.g. tactile tablets. For the short term (if feasible from a perspective of production costs and available AT on the user-side) we want to add sound directly to the tactile images. We will elaborate on the lessons learned in the 2017 project. The volumes can easily be translated without running into problems like differences in Braille in the different countries. We would like to find international partners to bundle forces to build up a library. And to do research, for though we cannot wait with filling the gaps, it is important to do research and improve (the design of) tactile images further.

References

1. Linders, C.M.: Zweeftaal en andere raadsels in het woordbegrip van blinde kinderen. Visio (1998)
2. in 't Veld, D.: Tactile images for inclusive teaching in primary education nature and science. In: Proceedings of the 2nd ULD Conference, pp. 111–124 (2012). http://www.uld-conference. org/files_of_downloads/2012/ULD2012_Proceedings.pdf
3. BANA Guidelines and Standards for Tactile Graphics. http://www.brailleauthority.org/tg/
4. Project SOCRATE-COMENIUS 3-1 1999/2000, TACTIMAGES & TRAINING, IMAGES TACTILES - ACCES A LA CULTURE – FORMATION. Tactile Images-Access to Culture and Training; annexes techniques
5. Corvest, H.: Tactile images: production, dissemination, pedagogy. Presentation on the International Tactile Reading Conference, Stockholm (2017). https://www.youtube.com/ watch?v=mOsi97bd0QE&feature=youtu.be. More information on Hoëlle Corvest can be found through the conference website. https://www.mtm.se/en/tactilereading2017/

Augmented Reality for People with Visual Impairments: Designing and Creating Audio-Tactile Content from Existing Objects

Lauren Thevin[1](✉) and Anke M. Brock[2](✉)

[1] Inria Bordeaux, Talence, France
lauren.thevin@inria.fr
[2] ENAC - University Toulouse, Toulouse, France
anke.brock@enac.fr

Abstract. Tactile maps and diagrams are widely used as accessible graphical media for people with visual impairments, in particular in the context of education. They can be made interactive by augmenting them with audio feedback. It is however complicated to create audio-tactile graphics that have rich and realistic tactile textures. To overcome these limitations, we propose a new augmented reality approach allowing novices to easily and quickly augment real objects with audio feedback. In our user study, six teachers created their own audio-augmentation of objects, such as a botanical atlas, within 30 min or less. Teachers found the tool easy to use and were confident about re-using it. The resulting augmented objects allow two modes: exploration mode provides feedback on demand about an element, while quiz mode provides questions and answers. We evaluated the resulting audio-tactile material with five visually impaired children. Participants found the resulting interactive graphics exciting to use independently of their mental imagery skills.

1 Introduction

In special education environments, tactile maps and graphics are widely used, for example in O&M (Orientation & Mobility) classes, or for mathematics and biology. There are two design methods for augmenting tactile media with audio feedback. First, tactile graphics can be hand-made, e.g. using paper, tissue or real objects [1] so that they possess a rich tactile dimension (e.g. texture, thermal properties). Yet, it is difficult to make those graphics interactive. Second, the tactile mediums can be digitally designed and edited, then printed and easily made interactive using Text-to-Speech synthesis (TTS) or Braille displays [2]. But such objects are limited, for instance to swellpaper or 3D print. In specialized schools, many objects for visually impaired (VI) people are hand-made, such as small-scale models or students' works made in class. At the same time, people who want to augment tactile objects with audio feedback (e.g. teachers), do not necessarily master 2D and 3D modeling techniques. It is likely that they have knowledge about office software applications, but no specialized computer skills.

© Springer International Publishing AG, part of Springer Nature 2018
K. Miesenberger and G. Kouroupetroglou (Eds.): ICCHP 2018, LNCS 10897, pp. 193–200, 2018.
https://doi.org/10.1007/978-3-319-94274-2_26

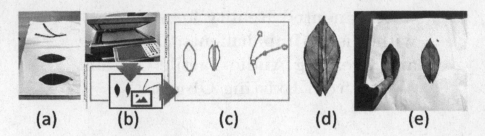

Fig. 1. Augmentation process: (a) designing the tactile content with real objects, (b) scanning it and using the resulting image as basis for (c) creating the SVG file with interactive zones, using PapARt (Fig. 2, left) to project this image on a table, (d) superimposing the projected interactive zones and the real objects, and (e) using the object as an audio-tactile interactive medium.

We propose a first approach of creating augmented content for Augmented Reality (AR) with real objects, thus enabling both rich tactile feedback and interactivity. The audio-content is associated with a SVG file (vector format often used for designing raised-line maps [2]). We present the necessary steps in Fig. 1. We illustrate our work with two use cases: a botanical atlas and a geographic map. This approach allows teachers to design their own pedagogical audio-tactile content from existing objects (leaves, branches, small-scale models, etc.). For the resulting audio-tactile medium, two modes of use are proposed: exploration mode with audio feedback on demand, and quiz mode. The augmented prototype was designed and evaluated in collaboration with IRSA (special education school in Bordeaux). We tested the creation of audio-tactile content with teachers, and the usability of the resulting audio-tactile graphics with VI students.

2   State of the Art

2.1   Tactile and Audio Modalities in Interactive Graphics

Tactile graphics serve the same use cases as pictures for sighted people: they are small-scale representations used e.g. for education. Audio feedback allows to create interactive tactile graphics, using for instance TTS to describe content and events [3]. The tactile modality encodes various types of information, and supports the creation of a rich mental imagery also for VI people [4]. Tactile maps, interactive or not, can be created in relief with a single material (e.g. using laser cutting, swell-paper [5], 3D printing [6]), or composed from objects with various textures [7]. Tactile graphics can support several haptic sensations: graining, softness/stiffness, shapes (circle/square, full/hollow), relief (cavity/bump), thermal behavior (cold/warm), etc. [8]. Using various textures helps to distinguish tactile elements. Using realistic textures can help to recognize elements in real situations. In our use case of a botanical atlas, some plants have a particular texture (such as succulent plants) that makes them easy to recognize by touch.

Braille text normally accompanies tactile graphics [5]. As an alternative, audio feedback allows to augment objects [3]. Unlike with Braille text, there is no need for moving the hands between the object and the associated caption [2]. The exploration and use of audio-tactile maps has proved more effective for complex content [7] than the use of Braille maps, and more efficient and satisfying for simple content [2]. Moreover, interactivity makes it possible to provide adaptive feedback depending on the context for the same tactile support: generic captions for superficial exploration, detailed descriptions for precise exploration, and an interactive answer-question system for testing knowledge [9].

2.2   Augmentation Process

We are interested in augmenting objects and making them interactive using AR. AR is not limited to visual modalities, but is defined as the combination of real objects with virtual objects in real time within a real environment independently of the modalities (vision, audition, touch,...) [10]. In our case, physical objects are combined with virtual audio feedback. We observe two main processes used to augment real objects with digital content. The first approach is to augment the object itself with electrical components [7] or to integrate components directly inside the object material [11]. But this approach offers little flexibility for the augmented content as it is integrated in the hardware. The second approach is to integrate augmented content in the digital representation of the object, e.g. vector images printed later as a raised-line map [9]. This object is then made physical, e.g. with 3D printing. Modeling objects with the associated digital content allows to attach several annotations to the same object (e.g. content with increasing detail). The physical object can then be linked with the digital object and its augmented content. A tracking system can follow the object and the user's action [12]. However in this approach, the augmented object is either artificially created or digitally modeled based on an existing object.

To sum up, creating audio-tactile media is possible with real objects as a starting point or respectively by modeling and annotating digital objects. Yet, these two approaches require advanced skills in computer sciences and for building specific hardware. As far as we know, even for the tools made and tested

Fig. 2. *Left*: PapARt hardware. *Middle*: SVG file with drawing over the scanned image. An audio-description is associated with the drawn elements. *Right*: Overlaying process. The projection displays the interactive zones. Once the tactile medium is aligned with the projection, the audio-tactile content is ready to use (here projection and objects are not aligned for clarity of image).

in participatory design approaches, such as [9], the audio-tactile supports were developed by the researchers and not the target users (e.g. teachers).

3   Proposed System

Our audio-tactile AR system should be compatible with the tactile contents usually used by teachers (swellpaper, 3D printing, scratch, small-scale models), and their design should be possible for people with no specific computer skills.

3.1   Hardware

The technical system is composed of the existing PapARt framework (software and hardware) [13], a PC for the SVG file creation, a scanner, and a sheet of paper with tactile elements placed on it (see Fig. 2). PapARt uses a depth camera to trigger the interactive zones usually on a table surface based on the hand position (the arm is detected, then the hand and fingers position). The contact of the finger with the tactile map is detected using depth analysis.

3.2   Creation of Interactive Content

Defining the Content. To create the tactile content, real objects are glued to an A3/A4 paper sheet which serves as support (see Fig. 1).

Defining the Reference Frame to Superimpose Annotations. One of the main issues in AR is to link an object with its augmented content. We propose to scan a A3/A4 paper with the tactile content. The scanned image becomes a background in a vector graphics software (Inkscape) to draw shapes directly on top of it, respecting *de facto* the scale and alignment with the real graphic. The shapes in SVG format have a textual description rendered by TTS when using the interactive prototype and additional XML fields. The users can add the fields "step" and "question" to any shape to create a quiz (see below).

Usage. When PapARt hardware and software are launched, the user chooses the correct SVG image in the application. The image is then projected, and the projection overlaid on the physical support. Thus, the map or diagram becomes audio-tactile and usable in two modes: (1) in exploration mode an audio-description is provided once the objects are pointed at as in [9], and (2) in quiz mode the system reads questions which the user solves by pointing to the requested element. If the pointed object is not correct, the computer provides directional help to redirect the finger as described in [9]. It is possible to load another SVG file for the same tactile content so the audio-content can evolve in the same session (e.g. quiz getting progressively more difficult).

4   Evaluation

Six O&M Instructors and teachers were asked to evaluate the creation process, and five VI students were asked to evaluate the resulting audio-tactile media. We also evaluated a proof of concept. The user tests were approved by the ethical committee COERLE at Inria.

Fig. 3. *Left*: User Test 1, augmentation of a map and botanical atlas. *Middle*: User Test 2, two botanical atlases visible: one with felt and baize, one with real leaves on the background. *Right*: proof of concept: augmentation of a magnetic board

User Test 1: Can People Without Specific Computer Skills Annotate Existing Tactile Material with Audio Feedback? Three O&M instructors from IRSA were asked to augment an existing tactile map of the school. Three different teachers (2 from IRSA: biology, tutor; 1 teacher in a primary school) were asked to create and augment a tactile biological atlas. We assessed the workload using Nasa-TLX [14] and the usability using UEQ [15]. To be sure that the system is compatible with the available resources and the usual activity of the instructors and teachers, we first asked which material is available at their workplace. We asked the users to spontaneously design a tactile support and to describe the audio feedback which the support should have. This allowed to verify that our audio augmentation process is consistent with the audio interaction which teachers expect. To be sure the users were able to create the audio augmentation autonomously, we provided a manual and asked the participants to follow the instructions.

User Test 2: Are the Created Audio-Tactile Supports Acceptable and Usable by Students with VI? We tested whether the created maps are usable by the end users (i.e. VI children). Five VI children (11 to 13 years old, 2F and 3M, 2 low vision and 3 blind) were asked to use the audio-tactile supports created in User Test 1 by one of the previously participating teachers (map and botanical atlas). The children's teacher was present during the experimentation. We assessed the usability with the UEQ [15].

Proof of Concept: Are Existing Tactile Supports Easy to Annotate? We validated that the proposed design process provides the possibility to augment various existing tactile supports which are not specifically designed to be audio-augmented. Three existing tactile supports were augmented by the research team with audio feedback as requested by instructors of IRSA.

4.1 Results

User Test 1. All users succeeded in creating the audio-tactile content. The content for exploration mode was intuitive and easy for all, while the creation of quiz content was perceived as complicated by some users even if they succeeded. The average time for describing the tactile support was 11 min (min: 2, max: 23), 13 min (min: 8, max: 25) for creating the tactile support, 4 min (min: 1, max: 10) for describing the audio-augmentation and 27 min (min: 15, max: 51) for creating the audio augmentation. All participants needed one more iteration to adjust the audio feedback. The main errors in creating audio feedback were: confusion between questions that can be answered by pointing at an element (e.g. where is the library?) and questions that require verbal replies which is not foreseen in the system (e.g. which building is here?); and adjustment if the answering zone was first too small. Because a scanner was not always available, some of the augmentations were done using a photo, taken as vertical as possible. The results of Nasa-TLX and UEQ (Fig. 4) show that the system is usable without knowledge in programming and vector drawing. A participant noticed that "It is complicated the first time, because I never used it [Bezier curves, inkscape]. But now I feel I can do it again, and it will be ok. I need to manipulate only one software." One user was missing labels indicating which parts of the leaves or map elements were interactive. Such "interactive points" can be made with our system without electronic devices on the tactile maps. Some negative remarks concerned Inkscape (not usable with a picture that has a large filesize as it become slow, no feedback regarding actions).

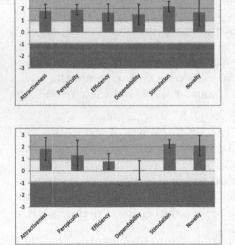

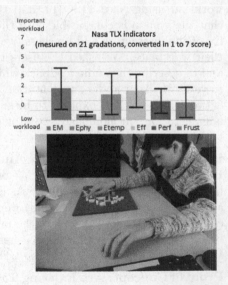

Fig. 4. Top. *Left*: Results of UEQ for User Test 1: all criteria are evaluated as good or very good. *Right*: Results of Nasa-TLX for User Test 1: none of the average indicators is associated with important workload. Bottom. *Left*: Results of UEQ for User Test 2: lower scores for efficiency and dependability can be explained by finger detection. *Right*: A visually impaired child exploring the map.

User Test 2. In this user test we tested the audio-tactile document designed by the professors with VI students. The main result, noticed also by the teachers present during the experiment, was that the technology is interesting for children with good mental representation skills who are already attracted by tactile images (3 of 5 participants), as well as for the children for whom mental imagery tasks are more challenging and who do not necessarily appreciate tactile images (2 of 5 participants). Indeed, 4 children want to participate in future sessions with our prototype; and 3 wanted to continue exploring new tactile supports after the experiment ended. Even though the system is usable by both low vision and blind people, the feedback about the detection of finger positions is entirely visual and thus not accessible to blind people. Moreover, concepts as "no finger should hide other fingers" (to avoid occlusion for the image recognition) are hard to explain. Yet, such feedback can be useful as sometimes the finger detection for the younger participants was not very precise. We think this could be fixed with a better calibration of the system.

Proof of Concept. The instructors from IRSA provided 3 existing tactile supports which we augmented. Students had built a tram station with magnets on a magnet board (Fig. 3). The time to augment was 6 min, and it was fully operational after 1 additional iteration (adapting the text read by the TTS). One usage was identified: by projecting a "photo" of the original magnets' positions, it is possible to re-create the work of the students later on. The Velcro board had similar results. The small-scale model of a house had cardboard as vertical walls and textures on the floor. The time for augmentation of this model was 15 min, the audio-content was fully operational after 1 more iteration (adapting the interactive zones with the finger detection due to the 3D structure). We also built a quiz mode where a question could have multiple solutions.

5 Discussion and Perspectives

In this paper we presented the use of the PapARt AR toolkit [13] and Inkscape to easily and quickly make tactile material interactive. We tested the creation process with teachers. Generally, teachers found the tool easy to use and were confident about re-using it. Then, we evaluated the created material with VI children. They found it exiting and were willing to use it again. However, the finger detection needs to be improved. The annotation of real objects presented in this paper opens new perspectives, such as creating tactile and tangible prototypes in creativity sessions based on manual activities with physical materials (lego, playdough etc.), which can become interactive within 30 min. Some negative feedback concerned the usability of inkscape. Therefore we propose that in the future, the interactive content could be directly created using PapARt only.

Acknowledgment. We thank the participants (teachers and students) especially C. Briant; and J. Laviole (Reality Tech) and J. Albouys for participating in the design of this tool. Done with the support of the EU Erasmus+ Pr. no 2016-1-EL01-KA201-023731.

References

1. Edman, P.: Tactile Graphics. American Foundation for the Blind, New York (1992)
2. Brock, A.M., Truillet, P., Oriola, B., Picard, D., Jouffrais, C.: Interactivity improves usability of geographic maps for visually impaired people. Hum. Comput. Interact. **30**(2), 156–194 (2015)
3. Ducasse, J., Brock, A.M., Jouffrais, C.: Accessible interactive maps for visually impaired users. In: Pissaloux, E., Velázquez, R. (eds.) Mobility of Visually Impaired People: Fundamentals and ICT Assistive Technologies, pp. 537–584. Springer, Cham (2018). https://doi.org/10.1007/978-3-319-54446-5_17
4. Cattaneo, Z., Vecchi, T.: Blind Vision: The Neuroscience of Visual Impairment. MIT Press, Cambridge (2011). https://doi.org/10.7551/mitpress/9780262015035.001.0001
5. Tatham, A.F.: The design of tactile maps: theoretical and practical considerations. In: Rybaczak, K., Blakemore, M. (eds.) Proceedings of International Cartographic Association: Mapping the Nations, ICA, London, UK, pp. 157–166 (1991). https://doi.org/10.1145/2982142.2982163
6. Gotzelmann, T.: LucentMaps 3D printed audiovisual tactile maps for blind and visually impaired people. In: The 18th ACM Conference ASSETS 2016, pp. 81–90 (2016)
7. Giraud, S., Brock, A.M., Macé, M.J.-M., Jouffrais, C.: Map learning with a 3D printed interactive small-scale model: improvement of space and text memorization in visually impaired students. Front. Psychol. **8**, 930 (2017). https://doi.org/10.3389/fpsyg.2017.00930
8. Klatzky, R.L., Lederman, S.J.: Touch. In: Handbook of Psychology (2003)
9. Albouys-Perrois, J., Laviole, J., Briant, C., Brock, A.: Towards a multisensory augmented reality map for blind and low vision people: a participatory design approach. In: International Conference CHI 2018 (2018)
10. Azuma, R., Behringer, R., Feiner, S., Julier, S., Macintyre, B.: Recent advances in augmented reality. In: IEEE CG&A 2011, pp. 1–27, December 2001. https://doi.org/10.1109/38.963459
11. Daudén Roquet, C., Kim, J., Yeh, T.: 3D Folded PrintGami: transforming passive 3D printed objects to interactive by inserted paper origami circuits. In: DIS 2016, pp. 187–191 (2016). https://doi.org/10.1145/2901790.2901891
12. Shi, L., Zhao, Y., Azenkot, S.: Markit and Talkit: a low-barrier toolkit to augment 3D printed models with audio annotations. In: Proceedings of the 30th Annual Symposium UIST 2017, pp. 493–506 (2017). https://doi.org/10.1145/3126594.3126650
13. Laviole, J., Hachet, M.: PapARt: interactive 3D graphics and multi-touch augmented paper for artistic creation. In: Proceedings of the IEEE 3DUI 2012, pp. 3–6 (2012). https://doi.org/10.1109/3DUI.2012.6184167
14. Hart, S.G.: Development of NASA-TLX (Task Load Index): results of empirical and theoretical research. In: Hancock, P.A., Meshkati, N. (eds.) Human Mental Workload. Advances in Psychology, vol. 52, chap. 12, 1st edn, pp. 139–183. Elsevier (1988). https://doi.org/10.1016/S0166-4115(08)62386-9
15. Laugwitz, B., Held, T., Schrepp, M.: Construction and evaluation of a user experience questionnaire. In: Holzinger, A. (ed.) USAB 2008. LNCS, vol. 5298, pp. 63–76. Springer, Heidelberg (2008). https://doi.org/10.1007/978-3-540-89350-9_6

Recording of Fingertip Position on Tactile Picture by the Visually Impaired and Analysis of Tactile Information

Yasuyuki Murai[1]([⊠]), Hisayuki Tatsumi[2], and Masahiro Miyakawa[2]

[1] Nihon Pharmaceutical University,
10281 Komuro, Ina-cho, Saitama 362-0806, Japan
murai@nichiyaku.ac.jp
[2] Tsukuba University of Technology,
4-12-7 Kasuga, Tsukuba, Ibaraki 305-8521, Japan
{tatsumi,mamiyaka}@cs.k.tsukuba-tech.ac.jp

Abstract. It is strenuous to make the visually impaired recognize figures and shapes. It is because there is a lack of understanding about how the visually impaired perceive tactile information. The aim of this research is to elucidate the process by which the visually impaired understand graphics. We video-record touch sensing process. First, the position of the fingertip is detected, and the trajectory of the finger is recorded. Later, using the video-record the locus of the finger is quantified and analyzed. We propose a quantification method for touch sensing. How many times the finger touched and on which part of the figure, finger movement direction, and speed, and the distance between the left and right fingers. The final goal of this research is to visualize cognitive process of figures and shapes by the visually impaired. The result could be used to translate figures, and shapes into languages. This will contribute to information acquisition by the visually impaired.

Keywords: Visual impairment · Tactile diagram/tactile image
Finger position tracking

1 Introduction

It is strenuous to make the visually impaired recognize figures and shapes. The visually impaired understand figures and shapes by touching. However, it has not been clarified how they recognize (tactileize) figures and shapes by touching (by fingers).

The purpose of this research is to clarify cognitive processes of figures and shapes through touch sensing by the visually impaired. In this report, as a preliminary step, we focus on "touch sensing" for searching out contours when tactile information is noticed. We detect the position of the finger during touch sensing, record its trajectory. By this we quantitatively analyze and evaluate movement of the fingers [1, 2]. The quantification is how many times the finger touched and on which part of figure, that is count and data on finger movement, finger moving direction, speed, and the distance between the left and right fingers.

© Springer International Publishing AG, part of Springer Nature 2018
K. Miesenberger and G. Kouroupetroglou (Eds.): ICCHP 2018, LNCS 10897, pp. 201–208, 2018.
https://doi.org/10.1007/978-3-319-94274-2_27

The final goal of this research is to visualize the cognitive process of the figure and shape of the visually impaired. The result could be used to translate figures, and shapes into language. This will contribute to information acquisition by the visually impaired.

2   Recording the Touch Sensing

We video-record how a visually impaired person touches a tactile picture (convex image) and recognizes it. With the cooperation of visually impaired students, using the high-performance camera we have, recorded the detail of the touch sensing in a video (Fig. 1). In the tactile picture used for recording, illustration drawn for the sighted person was subjected to image processing to make it into a line drawing (Fig. 1). Next, it is tactileized with a stereoscopic copying machine.

For video-recording of the touch sensing, a marker is attached to the fingertip for finger position detection. The marker is detected by the image processing programs and its location is set as the finger position. We need to use the stereo camera method to obtain the finger positions in three dimensional space. For this purpose two or more cameras are necessary. In this report two cameras are used. Using three or more cameras will reduce the possibility that the marker will be hidden and the detection will be disturbed [3, 4].

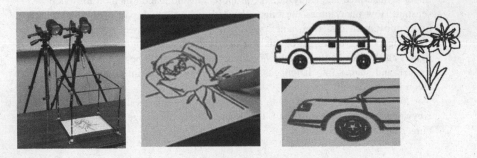

Fig. 1. Experiment environment and tactile pictures

3   Recording of the Experiment Touch Sensing

With the help of two blind people (one blind, one amblyopic), the touch sensing is recorded. The weak-sighted person wears an eye mask. The tactile pictures used for recording are in A4 size 17 sheets: cars (3), flowers (4), fish (5), and rabbits (5). In the experiment the tactile picture is fixed so as not to move out of the position of 30 cm in front of the subject. By the start signal, the examinee moves the hand forward and starts touch sensing. It is not informed to the subject what the figure is. The experiment continues until the subject recognizes the figure. In the case when the participant cannot recognize the object, it stops in about 1 min. We have recorded the scenes with the recording frame size 640 × 480, 90 frames/sec.

As the result of the experiment, Subject 1 (blind) recognized 15 images, and subject 2 (amblyopia) recognized 10 images. In particular, subject 2 could recognize none of the four flowers. In addition, tactile pictures were presented in the kind-wise order (only flowers follow flow) for each kind. Consequently, if the first picture could be recognized, the next picture seems to be recognized easily. In the future experiments, it is necessary to consider the order of presenting the pictures to the subject.

4 Detection and Analysis of Touch Position

To elucidate the cognitive processes of figures and shapes by touch sensing of the visually impaired, we analyze the motion of the fingers. We assume that the position and motion of the fingertip on the tactile picture during the touch sensing are closely related to its recognition. Therefore, we detect the position and motion of the finger from the video, quantify the touch sensing from the trajectory (Fig. 2), and analyze the tactile process.

The quantification of the touch sensing we have used is the number of times of touching the same place on the tactile picture, the direction of movement of the fingertip, its speed, and the distance between the left and right fingertips.

Three-dimensional coordinates of the fingertip are acquired from the video of the touch sensing using motion capture software (Library Co., Ltd. Move-tr/3D (Ver. 8.21)). The motion capture software detects the marker attached to the fingertip from the video calculates its three-dimensional coordinates, and outputs them to the CSV file. Three-dimensional coordinates, time for one frame of video, moving distance of marker, moving speed, and acceleration are also output to the CSV file.

In this report, the x coordinate (width) and the z coordinate (depth) out the three dimensional coordinates are used. The three-dimensional coordinates are real values ranging from 0 to 30 of the working space (width: 30 cm × height: 30 cm × depth: 30 cm) which have set up at the time of calibration of the motion capture software.

Fig. 2. Tactile figure and the fingertip locus for it

4.1 Detection and Analysis of the Contact Counts

The reason for detecting the number of contacts (contact count) for touching the same place of the tactile pictures as follows. As a result of the observation of touch sensing, we have noticed that the line-complicated part and the characteristic part of the tactile picture (convex part) have been repeatedly touched by the subject.

4.2 Visualization of the Contact Counts

The number of contacts is obtained by the following procedure. They should be visualized for easy understanding. The size of the screen for displaying the result of contact counts is set to 600×600 pixels based on the size of the workspace of 30 cm $\times$ 30 cm determined in the calibration of motion capture software. This screen is divided into 60×60 squares with each square having 10×10 pixels. When the fingertip passes through the square, it is counted for one for the square, and it is painted out (Fig. 3).

In Fig. 3 (car: subject 1), the number of contacts is indicated by difference in colors (the number is increased as the brightness is increased). At the end of the drawing, the numbers of contacts for all squares are output to the CSV file.

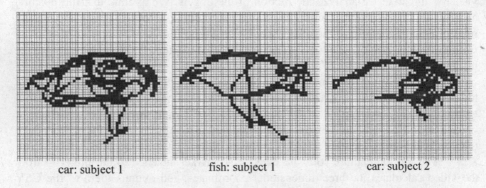

car: subject 1   fish: subject 1   car: subject 2

Fig. 3. Number of contacts on touch sensing locations. (Color figure online)

Figure 3 (car: subject 1) and Fig. 3 (fish: subject 1) are the contact count results of the subject 1 touch sensing the tactile picture of the car and the fish. By Fig. 3 (car: subject 1), it is understood that the number of contacts (contact counts) of the characteristic parts: front portions and rear portions of the car and the complicated portions such as the tires are large. The maximum number of contacts was 8 times for cars and 6 times for fish.

Figure 3 (car: subject 2) shows the result of the subject 2 touch sensing the tactile picture of the car. From this figure, it is also understood that the numbers of contacts for characteristic portions and complicated portion are large. The maximum number of contacts was 6.

Fig. 4. Touch sensing (subject 2)

In the Fig. 3 (car: subject 2), the locus of the front part (left side) of the car is not drawn. This is because the subject 2 moved the left and right fingers separately (Fig. 4), so the trajectory of the left index finger which was without the marker could not be acquired. From this experiment, it became clear that there are individual differences in how to use fingers.

Subject 1 moved the left and right fingers separately first, thus he grasped the whole. Then he held the left and right fingers close to each other, and then touched the contour mainly using the right finger. So the trajectory of the entire tactile figure could be acquired.

4.3 Detection and Analysis of the Movement Directions

We detect the moving directions of the finger during touch sensing. It is to verify whether the direction of movement of fingers affects perception or whether there are individual differences in movement. The direction of movement of the finger is obtained by the following procedure. We draw the result on the screen, the size of which is 600×600 pixels. For the directions of movement of the finger we presume eight directions shown in Fig. 5.

3	2	1
4		0
5	6	7

Fig. 5. The eight directions of movement of the finger

The moving direction is determined from the coordinates of the two points of the moving finger on the tactile diagram. In addition, we obtain the direction for every 10 frames of video. It is too much if we take it for each frame. To detect the direction, the CSV file is read that records the coordinates of the finger and acquire the coordinates (x locus and z coordinate) of fingers for a frame. We obtain the angle from the coordinates of the acquired two points (10 frame intervals), find the direction value (0 to 7) corresponding to the angle, display it along with the line on the screen and write it to the file.

Figure 6 shows an example in which the trajectory and directions of the finger are drawn. Figure 6 (right) is an enlarged view of the start position of Fig. 6 (left). In this example, the touch sensing is started from the lower center. At the start of the touch sensing (recording), since the finger stays still at the start position, there is no movement and the move direction numbers are displayed overlapping. From the numbers "2" and "3" indicating the directions in Fig. 6, it can be seen that the finger is moving upward in Fig. 6.

In addition, the line distance between the numbers represents the speed of the movement. So the longer the distance is, the faster the finger movement is. So in this

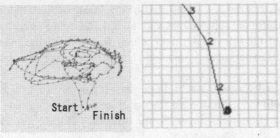

Partial enlargement

Fig. 6. Finger direction and trajectory of sensing (car: subject 1)

case, rather than as observing the feature with the touch sensing, the touch sensing could be considered as to be a movement to the next point or a simple place like a straight line, or a known shape. In the places where the distance of the numbers is short, it could be thought that the figure is complicated around that place or, namely the place could be a characteristic part which deserves carefully touch sensing and observation. Note that the touch sensing has started from the lower center and returned to the lower center in this Figure.

4.4   Difference in Usage of Fingers by Subjects

In this report, the number of subjects was as small as two, but it became clear that there is a big difference in the usage of fingers. Subject 1 first moves left and right fingers separately and confirms the entire figure. After that, he brings the left and right fingers close to each other and use the right fingers mainly for detailed touch sensing. The subject 2 moves the left and right fingers separately and does touch sensing. He does not re-observe with the right finger the portion of the figure that he could recognize earlier by using his left finger.

5   Detecting the Position of the Left and Right Fingers

In this experiment, a marker is attached only to the right index finger of the subject. Therefore, as the Subject 2 did, when one moves left and right fingers separately, the movement of his left finger could not be detected. The position of the camera at the time of recording was set slightly farther. So the marker of the fingertip was recorded small, and even there are cases the marker could not be detected with the motion capture software. So some coordinate data could not be obtained in some cases.

As the markers are attached to the both left and right index fingers and the camera is set closer to the experiment space, (up to the position where it can be calibrated with the motion capture software) the markers of the left and right fingers can be detected in almost all frames, and the trajectories could be acquired (Fig. 7).

However, depending on the movement of the finger, the marker could be hidden and become undetectable, so in future experiments we are planning to increase the

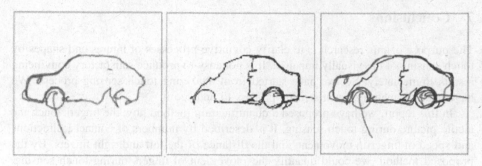

Fig. 7. The loci of the left and right fingers (overlayed)

number of cameras to three or more. Since the positions of the left and right fingers could be detected, it was possible to acquire the distance between the left and right fingers. Figure 8 shows the result. The straight line connecting the points is the distance between the fingers. Since the positions of the left and right fingers could be detected, it was possible to acquire the distance between the left and right fingers.

Figure 8 shows the result. The straight line connecting the points is the distance between the fingers. It is assumed that this operation by the subject will be performed when he measures the distance between the fingers. By acquiring the positions of the left and right fingers, various further analyses of touch sensing could be possible.

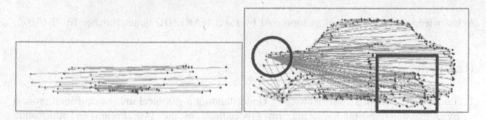

Fig. 8. Distance of the left and right fingers

6 Future Experiment Plan

The experiment in this report is a preliminary one to confirm the possibility of recording and numericalization of touch sensing. The number of subjects was small, and the tactile picture used for the experiment were not very appropriate for analyzing touch sensing. However, it is encouraging that the problem is clarified by the experiment and that the countermeasure also works effectively.

In future, we will increase the number of subjects and gather experimental data. Tactile pictures to be used in the experiment could be simpler. They could be squares and circles and their compositions. We think that the motion of the fingers does not become complicated, and the features become easy to capture. We would like to analyze the data obtained from the experiments and to find general features of touch sensing.

7 Conclusions

The purpose of this research is to clarify cognitive processes of figures and shapes by touch sensing of the visually impaired. It is not easy to produce satisfactory convincing results immediately. So, we have started from analyzing touch sensing process. We have tried to quantify touch sensing process to analyze it.

In this report, we have proposed a quantification method how the fingers touch the tactile picture during touch sensing. It is described by numbers of contacts, directions and speed of fingertip movement, and the distance of the left and right fingers. By the proposed method, we could quantify the movement of fingers during touch sensing. From the obtained results, it has become clear that there is a difference in the numbers of times touched by the fingertip in the parts of the contour of the tactile picture during touch sensing. We could also confirm that there are individual differences in the use of hands and fingers in touch sensing. We also have made a visualization of touch sensing process. In the future, we would like to gather actual touch sensing data among the visually impaired, advance its analysis in order to discover general features of touch sensing.

The results obtained in this paper can be applied not only to analysis and evaluation of palpation but also to information acquisition support of figures and shapes for the visually impaired. For example, we think that it is possible to clarify the reason why it is difficult to acquire the touch sensing goodness evaluation for determining the position and operation of the button for the equipment used by the visually impaired. It will also serve as a judgment index for equipment design.

Acknowledgments. This work is supported by JSPS KAKENHI Grant Number JP17K01092.

References

1. Tatsumi, H., Murai, Y., Miyakawa, M.: Understanding a graphical image acquisition process by finger-touch position tracking. In: Proceedings of the 14th Forum on Information Technology: FIT 2015, Ehime, no. K-032, pp. 543–544 (2015)
2. Tatsumi, H., Murai, Y., Sekita, I., Miyakawa, M.: Forming a fingertip position trace map in graphical image acquisition process by touching: toward understanding graphical image creation by touch-sensing. IEICE Tech. Rep. **114**(512), 67–72 (2015)
3. Tatsumi, H., Murai, Y., Sekita, I., Miyakawa, M.: Detecting and sharing a touch position of fingertip to compensate for visual impairment. Multiple-Valued Logic Technical report, Naha, vol. MVL-15, no. 1, pp. 27–32 (2015)
4. Murai, Y., Tatsumi, H., Tokumasu, S., Miyakawa, M.: Analysis of the graphic image generation process of the visually impaired. In: Proceedings of the 15th Forum on Information Technology: FIT2016, Toyama, no. K-052, pp. 559–560 (2016)

Designing an Interactive Tactile Relief
of the Meissen Table Fountain

Andreas Reichinger[1]([✉]) [iD], Helena Garcia Carrizosa[2],
and Cornelia Travnicek[1]

[1] VRVis Zentrum für Virtual Reality und Visualisierung Forschungs-GmbH,
Vienna, Austria
reichinger@vrvis.at
[2] Open University, Milton Keynes, UK

Abstract. In this paper we highlight the practical experience gained during the
first design iteration of a tactile relief for the Meissen table fountain exhibited at
the Victoria & Albert Museum, London. Based on a 3D scan, we designed a 2.5D
relief that is usable for our gesture-based interactive audio guide. We present a
mixed-perspective view projection technique that combines the advantages of a
top-down view and a frontal view, and developed a detail-preserving depth-
compression technique to flatten less important parts. Finally, we present the
results of a preliminary evaluation with 14 members of our participative research
group, and give an outlook for improvements to be targeted in our ongoing
research.

Keywords: Tactile relief · Blind people · Visually impaired people
Design for all · Accessibility · Museum

1 Introduction

Tactile models are an important aid for blind and visually impaired (BVI) people to
help perceive images and objects that are otherwise difficult for them to comprehend.
However, tactile models need to be carefully designed in order to convey the important
information, without being too complicated to read.

In this work, we report on the practical experience of designing a tactile relief of the
Meissen table fountain "The Triumph of Amphitrite", exhibited at the Victoria and
Albert (V&A) Museum in London. This design is especially challenging, given a
number of restrictions. Although the original is three-dimensional, our goal was to create
a 2.5D relief version, which is suitable for our developed gesture-controlled tactile
audio-guide [9] that detects certain hand gestures during tactile exploration using a
depth camera mounted above the relief, and offers location specific audio descriptions.
For this work, the implementation was extended, and is now based on the HP Sprout 3D
workstation, an all-in-one computer with a built-in depth sensor, touch-screen, desk
lamp and projector, which makes it suitable for the use in museums. Our new software
version includes registered projections onto the tactile relief, as an additional information layer for seeing people, which we currently use to highlight the interaction
regions. However, this setup limits the maximum usable relief size.

© Springer International Publishing AG, part of Springer Nature 2018
K. Miesenberger and G. Kouroupetroglou (Eds.): ICCHP 2018, LNCS 10897, pp. 209–216, 2018.
https://doi.org/10.1007/978-3-319-94274-2_28

Therefore, the challenge was to present all relevant information needed to be conveyed in a single 2.5D tactile relief, with a limited size of maximally 30×40 cm. In addition, reliefs have a limited depth. We typically design tactile reliefs within 25 mm of dynamic depth for the content, plus a fixed base of 10 mm. This ensures that the relief can be machined easily with a three-axis CNC milling machine, and that in the new setup projections may work smoothly. As we currently can't produce undercuts, too high reliefs also tend to become less aesthetic, especially at large depth discontinuities, where a steep vertical wall is created.

For the first relief prototype of this scene we developed a special projection technique to simultaneously show the top-down layout of the fountain, while retaining the frontal view of the different statues. In this way, it is possible to convey the depth ordering and the arch-structure the different pieces describe, and give a plastic rendering of all parts from their most interesting side to show all details. Additionally, we used a custom-built detail-preserving compression technique to flattened less important parts, in order to save the limited depth budget for the more important objects.

The whole process is tightly integrated with the participatory research group of the project ARCHES[1] which consists of a varying number (around 10–40) of people "with differences and difficulties associated with perception, memory, cognition and communication," who bi-weekly meet in the museum and discuss the advances of the tools developed as well as perform their own projects and research. Accordingly, this work targets a wider range of people (not only BVI people) to create a more universally rich museum experience. Preliminary results already indicate that the integration of the tactile sense with tactile reliefs is also helpful for some people with cognitive impairments.

We describe all the steps from the artwork selection process (which included the participatory research group), data acquisition, relief design and results of a first evaluation of the tactile relief by the participatory research group.

2   Related Work

Tactile reliefs of art works is still a relatively new field of research. With the rising popularity of 3D printing, researchers started to adapt it to create 3D replicas and teaching materials for BVI people (e.g. [13, 14, 16]), to create tactile street maps (e.g. [6]), or children books (e.g. [11, 12]). For paintings, raised line drawings have been extensively used and detailed guidelines developed (e.g. [1, 2]). Although Ericsson [3] argued that "high reliefs are difficult to interpret", reliefs have successfully been used to convey paintings, as 3D shapes and surfaces can be rendered in more detail than what is possible with the limited expressiveness of raised line drawings. Formal research was conducted, e.g., at the Instituto Cavazza [5] with hand-made relief interpretations of paintings. Since then, computer scientists started research into reproduction of existing reliefs [7] and to simplify the creation and design process itself (e.g. [4, 10]). Apart from paintings, also three-dimensional objects can be presented in relief form, e.g., demonstrated on replicas of knives [8] that were more robustly presented in high relief

---

[1] See project website at http://www.arches-project.eu/.

but were essentially 1:1 copies of the upper surface. In this work, we practically explore the design process necessary to convert complex 3D scenes into tactile reliefs.

(a)   (b)   (c)

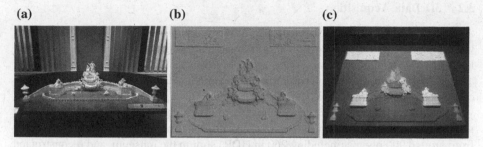

Fig. 1. From left to right: (a) The table fountain as displayed in the museum. (b) Realistic rendering of the final tactile relief design. (c) Produced tactile relief CNC milled from DuPont Corian® used in our interactive audio-guide with projected colors indicating interactive regions. (Color figure online)

3 Design Process

3.1 Participatory Process of Choosing Artwork

During the first phase of our project, a participatory research group in London was introduced with a list of objects, considered by the V&A as a warm up activity. The selection was based on the access within the physical space, but also made according to the popularity and significance of the objects. One of it was the 'Meissen Fountain': A Meissen table fountain named "The Triumph of Amphitrite", created in 1745–47, approximately 3 m wide, 50 cm at the highest point, which was actually used with water. The participants then explored a number of different galleries with a wide range of objects over the course of two sessions. Early in the project, participants were introduced to the technology partner's company profiles. We explained the products our project was aiming to deliver and purpose of the diverse visits. With that information and based on their interactions with the objects participants voted anonymously for one object that they wanted to have reproduced more than any other. The top five answers formed a shortlist, which included the fountain, three other 3D objects (a bed, a harp, a statue "Nature") and one painting. According to the project's plan only 2D objects – specifically paintings – should be processed. After visiting the V&A we realized, that this museum is to a good part dedicated to decorative objects and therefore, although our workflow is targeted at paintings, we decided to make an exception and use a 3D object. On that account, we had to gather data via a 3D scan of the object. The selection of the object was therefore largely dependent on whether or not we could actually scan the object as it is exhibited in the museum. Preliminary tests with a photogrammetric scanning method indicated, that the statue "Nature" and the fountain would be ideal candidates. The final decision was made when we found out that a scan of the fountain was already available. Fortunately, the fountain was also the most voted object in the user survey. The main attraction towards the object was the different elements it had and the rich history of it.

3.2   3D Data Acquisition

As mentioned before, detailed laser scans of the fountain were already available. This was a by-product of the restoration efforts[2], where missing pieces were re-created from laser-scans of remaining pieces found at the Meissen factory. However, only scans of around 35 individual porcelain parts were made, and had to be correctly assembled. We could get an approximate arrangement – completed by copied and mirrored parts – that was made for a short rendered video clip. In order to create it as accurately as possible to the setup in the exhibition, we created an additional photogrammetric scan created from around 900 photos (including 260 in HDR) shot in the museum, and reconstructed using the photogrammetry software Reality Capture[3]. All individual high-quality scans were then exactly scaled and aligned to the respective parts in this scan. Missing pieces were replaced and scan artifacts corrected. For instance, for the front wall only one straight part was scanned, but the actual setup consists of 15 irregularly broken pieces which we manually modeled according to the photogrammetric scan.

3.3   Design Considerations and Viewport Selection

For this particular object we identified three main aspects which should be conveyed:

1. The general setup, i.e. the arrangement of the individual porcelain parts, and the overall shape. For instance, there are 5 main groups of figures arranged in three depths layers: (a) the main group around the smaller basins centered in the back, (b) two river gods in front of the main group slightly shifted to each side, and (c) two vases marking the front and outer-most edge. These are connected by curved stone walls that form a characteristic arch structure, and a contoured lower wall in the front. These define the border of the water pond.
2. The arrangement of the individual figures in the figure groups, especially in the main group, which consists of three platforms, five human and two horse-like creatures and a number of other details.
3. The details of the different figures which were crafted very carefully.

   Unfortunately, there is no single view that conveys all three aspects at once. The general setup (1) is best observed in a top-down view (see Fig. 2a), where the different figure groups can be differentiated, and the arch structure is best observed. However, this view is not suitable to differentiate the individual figures (2), nor their details (3). These details are best explored from a frontal view or from slightly above (see Figs. 1a and 2b), but the depth of the scene would be largely lost, as a relief has limited depth. We wanted to use a large portion of the available depth-budget to convey the 3D shape of the figures, thus as little as possible should be used for the overall depth. And since

---

[2] A video showing the restoration efforts is available at https://youtu.be/9AKtrtqpCag.

[3] Reality Capture's website is available at https://www.capturingreality.com/.

we wanted to have everything in a single relief for our interactive setup, we decided to create a mixed perspective view to convey all three aspects simultaneously.

For this, a skew transform was applied in the yz-plane, so that the distance from the front (y-coordinate) is added to the object height (z-coordinate). The effect is that more distant parts are transformed up in the relief when viewed from the front (see Figs. 3a and b). In this way, the arrangement and the arch structure is apparent in the bottom lines of the objects, while everything is still viewed from the front to convey all details (see Fig. 3d). In addition, the figure groups were tilted individually to view them from their optimal position. For instance, the center group was tilted 30° to the front to allow a better view into the basins and to separate the figures further to distinguish them more easily. In addition, all figure groups were enlarged with respect to the less important walls, in order to convey more detail, without destroying the overall appearance.

Finally, there is a contextually important relief scene on each river god's base, which is, however, too small to be perceivable. To enhance tactile exploration, we added enlarged versions of these reliefs in the free space on the top of our composition.

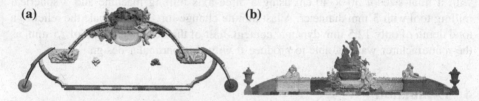

Fig. 2. Original scan data. (a) Top view, with wall approximations in black. (b) Front view.

Fig. 3. Stages of relief design. From left to right: (a) Original scan, left view. (b) Skewed version, left view. (c) Final compressed form, left view. (d) Final form, used in relief, front view.

3.4   Flattening and Production

As mentioned before, a 2.5D bas-relief only has a limited depth budget. Therefore, it was necessary to compress the depth where possible, in order to maximize the available depth for the individual figures to make them as plastic as possible. Although there is a body of research to automate this process (e.g., [15]), we opted for a manual procedure in order to have more control over the process and to optimize the result.

The basic idea was to largely eliminate the depth of the connecting walls, as this information is already present in the skewed version (see Fig. 3c). All figure groups were arranged as far back as possible without destroying the local depth order. In addition, deep parts of individual figures were compressed as well, e.g., the horses' necks. However, a simple scaling technique did not work for the curved walls. Flattening these would also flatten their surface textures. The solution was to construct a smooth shape that approximates the shape of the walls (see black lines in Fig. 2a), render this approximation into a depth map, and subtracting it from the original object's depth using a displacement shader, making it globally flat but preserving the details.

The result was a reduction of scene depth to around 20%, without scaling the depth of the figures. In order to minimize depth discontinuity to the background a background plane was added in the lower portion. A final depth reduction was possible in this particular case, as the scene was gradually coming forward at lower parts. Instead of carving it from a thicker block, we rotated the scene by 5° forward and carved the result out of a thinner block, with the idea to present it later angled the same 5° backward.

The final relief was milled out of a solid block of DuPont Corian®, Glacier White, with a final size of 30 × 40 cm using a three-axis milling machine and a spherical milling tool with 3 mm diameter. A last minute change forced us to scale the relief to a total depth of only 12.5 mm dynamic content, half of the designed height of 25 mm, as the manufacturer was not able to produce it with this particular design.

4   Evaluation

Until now, two test sessions were conducted with a total of 14 users with a diverse range of access, four of them visually impaired. Apart from three participants all had experienced the fountain in the museum environment. The users were presented with the relief, without the projections or interactive audio-guide, and without the planned 5° tilt, but with a large printed photo of the fountain. Prior and during the evaluation participants had one to one support, explaining the purpose of the relief, and rephrasing the questionnaire if necessary.

General questions were answered very positively. People liked exploring the relief (average of 1.4 on a 1–5 Likert scale), found it easy to explore (avg. 1.3), and all but three found to have a generally good impression of the fountain, some mentioning "it is nice to touch" and "I quite like it". However, when asking for details, some design problems came apparent. Four people wanted the relief bigger, one only the top river god reliefs.

Many had troubles identifying all figures in the central group, found them not well separated (avg. 3.6) with the wish to make it simpler and bigger. It was a bit better to find the water basins (avg. 2.2, three people voted 5), and to notice the curved wall (avg. 2.0, four voting 3 or worse). Questions regarding the depth order of the main objects caused a lot of problems, with several people not being sure which are in the front and which in the back, some thinking they are at the same level or even the central group in the front.

5 Conclusion and Future Work

In our work, we used a participatory process that includes people with impairments in the process of making museums and other exhibition spaces more accessible to them. We showed in detail the design process necessary for conversion of a full 3d object into a tactile relief, which may aid as a starting point for similar projects. We developed a mixed perspective method to convey the ground layout and the frontal view simultaneously, and a method for flattening curved parts in order to save the relief depth budget for more important parts.

The preliminary results of the evaluation of the first prototype let us come to the conclusion that the relief on its own is of too complex nature for a wide range of people to enjoy. Though participants liked the texture and material when it came to analyze the conversion of the object from 3D to 2.5D it became noticeable that the size and depth of the figures confused the participant's concept of distance.

We believe that the mixed perspective is a good way to convey all the information, although current evaluation results indicate the opposite. We will conduct further tests, with the planned 5° tilt in place, and combined with projections and the interactive audio-guide, verbally describing the layout and giving detailed texts when touching individual parts. Based on these results, either an improved version of the relief will be produced, or an additional detail will be created as a second relief or a 3d model. Possibly also a separate simplified plan of the fountain may help.

Apart from that, we plan to improve the tactile audio-guide to include multimedia information on the HP Sprout's touch screen and on the tactile relief, and to explore further interaction methods in order to create a single platform that caters the needs of a wide variety of visitors. Possibilities for projections include: original color, high-contrast modes, or highlighting areas that the audio is currently referring to.

Acknowledgements. Special thanks to Reino Liefkes and team who gave permission to reuse the original laser scans, and to Patrick Neubert for providing an already cleaned and approximately arranged version, to all volunteers of the London Exploration Group helping in selection and testing, V&A Museum (esp. Suzana Skrbic and Barry Ginley), the Wallace Collection (esp. Sarah Fairbairn and Anne Fay) and Werk5, Berlin. This work was performed within the framework of the H2020 project ARCHES (http://www.arches-project.eu) which has received funding from the European Union's Horizon 2020 research and innovation program under grant agreement No 693229.

References

1. Art Education for the Blind: Art History through Touch and Sound: A Multisensory Guide for the Blind and Visually Impaired. Optical Touch Systems Publication, New York/American Printing House for the Blind, Louisville (1998)
2. Edman, P.K.: Tactile Graphics. American Foundation for the Blind, New York (1992)
3. Eriksson, Y.: How to make tactile pictures understandable to the blind reader. In: 65th IFLA Council and General Conference, Bangkok, Thailand (1999)
4. Furferi, R., Governi, L., Volpe, Y., Puggelli, L., Vanni, N., Carfagni, M.: From 2D to 2.5D i.e. from painting to tactile model. Graph. Models **76**(6), 706–723 (2014)

5. Gualandi, P., Secchi, L.: Tecniche di rappresentazione plastica della realtà visiva. In: Bellini, A. (ed.) Toccare L'arte: L'educazione Estetica Di Ipovedenti e Non Vedenti, pp. 49–98. Armando Editore (2000)
6. Götzelmann, T.: LucentMaps: 3D printed audiovisual tactile maps for blind and visually impaired people. In: Feng J.H., Huenerfauth, M. (eds.) Proceedings of the 18th International ACM SIGACCESS Conference on Computers and Accessibility, ASSETS 2016, pp. 81–90. ACM, New York (2016)
7. Oouchi, S., Yamazawa, K., Secchi, L.: Reproduction of tactile paintings for visual impairments utilized three-dimensional modeling system and the effect of difference in the painting size on tactile perception. In: Miesenberger, K., Klaus, J., Zagler, W., Karshmer, A. (eds.) ICCHP 2010. LNCS, vol. 6180, pp. 527–533. Springer, Heidelberg (2010). https://doi.org/10.1007/978-3-642-14100-3_79
8. Reichinger, A., Neumüller, M., Rist, F., Maierhofer, S., Purgathofer, W.: Computer-aided design of tactile models. In: Miesenberger, K., Karshmer, A., Penaz, P., Zagler, W. (eds.) ICCHP 2012. LNCS, vol. 7383, pp. 497–504. Springer, Heidelberg (2012). https://doi.org/10.1007/978-3-642-31534-3_73
9. Reichinger, A., Garcia Carrizosa, H., Wood, J., Schröder, S., Löw, C., Luidolt, L.R., Schimkowitsch, M., Fuhrmann, A., Maierhofer, S., Purgathofer, W.: Pictures in your mind: using interactive gesture-controlled reliefs to explore art. ACM Trans. Access. Comput. 11 (1), Article no. 2 (2018)
10. Reichinger, A., Maierhofer, S., Purgathofer, W.: High-quality tactile paintings. ACM J. Comput. Cult. Herit. 4(2), Article no. 5 (2011)
11. Stangl, A., Hsu, C., Yeh, T.: Transcribing across the senses: community efforts to create 3D printable accessible tactile pictures for young children with visual impairments. In: Yesilada, Y., Bigham, J.P. (eds.) Proceedings of the 17th International ACM SIGACCESS Conference on Computers and Accessibility, ASSETS 2015, pp. 127–137. ACM, New York (2015)
12. Stangl, A., Kim, J., Yeh, T.: 3D printed tactile picture books for children with visual impairments: a design probe. In: Proceedings of the 2014 Conference on Interaction Design and Children, IDC 2014, pp. 321–324. ACM, New York (2014)
13. Teshima, Y., Matsuoka, A., Fujiyoshi, M., Ikegami, Y., Kaneko, T., Oouchi, S., Watanabe, Y., Yamazawa, K.: Enlarged skeleton models of plankton for tactile teaching. In: Miesenberger, K., Klaus, J., Zagler, W., Karshmer, A. (eds.) ICCHP 2010. LNCS, vol. 6180, pp. 523–526. Springer, Heidelberg (2010). https://doi.org/10.1007/978-3-642-14100-3_78
14. Teshima, Y., et al.: Three-dimensional models of earth for tactile learning. In: Miesenberger, K., Bühler, C., Penaz, P. (eds.) ICCHP 2016. LNCS, vol. 9759, pp. 116–119. Springer, Cham (2016). https://doi.org/10.1007/978-3-319-41267-2_16
15. Weyrich, T., Deng, J., Barnes, C., Rusinkiewicz, S., Finkelstein, A.: Digital bas-relief from 3D scenes. In: ACM Transactions on Graphics (TOG) - Proceedings of ACM SIGGRAPH 2007, vol. 26, no. 3. ACM, New York (2007)
16. Yamazawa, K., Teshima, Y., Watanabe, Y., Ikegami, Y., Fujiyoshi, M., Oouchi, S., Kaneko, T.: Three-dimensional model fabricated by layered manufacturing for visually handicapped persons to trace heart shape. In: Miesenberger, K., Karshmer, A., Penaz, P., Zagler, W. (eds.) ICCHP 2012. LNCS, vol. 7383, pp. 505–508. Springer, Heidelberg (2012). https://doi.org/10.1007/978-3-642-31534-3_74

Accessibility Guidelines for Tactile Displays in Human-Robot Interaction. A Comparative Study and Proposal

Malak Qbilat(✉) and Ana Iglesias

Computer Science Department, Universidad Carlos III de Madrid,
28911 Madrid, Spain
100344402@alumnos.uc3m.es, aiglesia@inf.uc3m.es

Abstract. Many people face accessibility barriers when interacting with robots, mainly people who do not usually interact with new technologies, elderly people and users with disabilities. Current laws, standards and guidelines protect the right of the users interacting with computers, however, they are not specific for human-robot interaction and they have not considered the special characteristics of robots. This paper is focused on the accessibility requirements of tactile displays integrated into service robots. An extensive study and comparison of the main accessibility guidelines, standards and recommendations is conducted. Moreover, a first draft of guideline for tactile displays in HRI is proposed.

Keywords: Human Robot Interaction · Accessibility · Guidelines

1 Introduction

Human Computer Interaction (HCI) is a field of a study focusing on the design of computer technology and interaction between users and computer [1], while Human Robot Interaction (HRI) is a field of study focused on analyzing, designing, modeling, implementing and evaluating robots that are dedicated to serve humans in several aspects such as domestic tasks, entertainment, elderly and handicap assistance, etc. [2]. Nowadays, there are different accessibility guidelines, standards and recommendations in HCI which help designers and developers to implement accessible products for all users, nevertheless of their capabilities or abilities. However, there are not specific standards, guidelines or recommendations for HRI, considering the special interaction characteristics of the robots. This paper presents an in-depth study of three of the main accessibility guidelines and standards of HCI. Then, based on this study, a specific accessibility recommendation for tactile displays in HRI is proposed. Section 2 summarizes related works, Sect. 3 clarify the methodology, Sect. 4 presents a comparative study of main accessibility guidelines and proposal, while Sect. 5 presents conclusions and further research.

K. Miesenberger and G. Kouroupetroglou (Eds.): ICCHP 2018, LNCS 10897, pp. 217–220, 2018.
https://doi.org/10.1007/978-3-319-94274-2_29

2   Related Works

2.1   Accessibility Laws, Standards and Guidelines for HCI

The necessity to ensure accessibility to all users with different abilities and needs has motivated countries to make laws and decisions. Web Accessibility Initiative (WAI) is continuously updating different guidelines for several web components to improve web accessibility, as the WCAG v2.0 guideline [3], BBC Accessibility Standards and Guidelines, as the BBC guideline [4] and Funka Nu Mobile guidelines [5]. All these laws, standards and guidelines are necessary for designing and developing accessible software products (websites, web applications, mobile applications, etc.). However, none of the available guidelines and standards covers all HRI accessibility aspects.

2.2   Accessibility Barriers in Using Robots

Many researchers study the robots' usability, social acceptance, societal impact or even if the user experience is positive or not. For instance, Yanco et al. research work [6] and USUS evaluation framework [7] provide a basis for research in HRI, addressing multiple research areas like HCI, CSCW (Computer Supported Cooperative Work), and SS (Social Sciences) to offer a holistic picture of research aspects of HRI. However, none of these frameworks considers the interaction accessibility as a central and a necessary feature to be treated in this kind for systems.

3   Methodology

To integrate users' needs and expectations from early robot-system design phases, a User-Centered approach [8] is followed. The process and methods followed in the research study are explained next:

1. A *study of the main accessibility standards, guidelines and recommendations* for web sites, web applications and software applications was conducted. None of them can be completely applied to HRI, due to the differences in physical components and application areas between HRI and HCI. But the similarity in displays components of robots and web sites, web applications and software applications allows to integrate them to form a proposal for accessibility guideline in HRI.
2. A *study of the main interaction characteristics of tactile displays in HRI* was conducted, based on the literature review and the authors' experience.
3. *Selection of the accessibility standards and guidelines to compare*. The authors have chosen three of the main accessibility guidelines in HCI: WCAG v2.0, Funka Nu and BBC, to be studied as the basis for the new proposal.
4. *Analysis of the documentation according to the characteristics of tactile displays in HRI.* The guidelines requirements were carefully studied to check if they apply or not to tactile displays for HRI.
5. *Analysis of guidelines' overlapping.* The intersected requirements were combined.
6. *Requirements Classification*, based on WCAG v2.0 classification: perception, understanding and interaction.

4   Comparative Study of Main Accessibility Guidelines and Proposal

Implementing accessibility guidelines is a complex task and it may require a set of precise processes. In W3C they standardize the web technology accessibility based on the consensus of the membership, team, and public, and the technical report development process [9]. In this study, a first draft of 51 applicable requirements is proposed, as a first step to get a complete guideline. More details and the whole draft is published in *Malakqbilat.com* web page. It is classified into three categories:

– Perception: related to interface component and appearance, interface structure and assistive technology.
– Understanding: related to errors & help, readability, predictability and design.
– Interaction: Interaction: related to keyboard, time, navigation, interface and conformance.

The three guidelines were compared to each other. The main conclusions are:

– Understanding: BBC guideline does not take into account requirements to meet errors & help and predictability issues, where WCAG v2.0 and Funka Nu have no requirements to meet design issue. WCAG v2.0 and Funka overlap in errors & help, readability and predictability issues, while WCAG v2.0 and BBC overlap in readability issue only.
– Perception: Funka Nu guideline does not take into account requirements to meet assistive technology issue. WCAG v2.0 and BBC do not take into account requirements to meet interface structure issue. WCAG v2.0, Funka and BBC guidelines overlap in interface component and appearance issue.
– Interaction: BBC guideline does not take into account requirements to meet time and conformance issues, WCAG v2.0 has no requirements to meet interface issue, while Funka Nu does not have requirements for conformance issue. WCAG v2.0, Funka and BBC guidelines overlap in navigation issue. WCAG v2.0 and Funka overlap in time issue.

5   Conclusions and Further Research

There are many accessibility guidelines, standards and recommendations which are related to HCI. However, there is no specific one for HRI. This paper proposes a first draft proposal of guideline for tactile displays in HRI. A scientific methodology was followed to conduct a comparative study on WCAG v2.0, Funka Nu and BBC guidelines. Currently, the authors are working on evaluating the proposal by involving real users with functional diversity. CLARC robot [10] is a social robot where it's going to be evaluated.

Acknowledgment. This work has been partially funded by the European Union ECHORD++ project (FP7-ICT-601116) and the CSO2017-86747-R Spanish project.

References

1. What is Human-Computer Interaction (HCI)? https://www.interaction-design.org/literature/topics/human-computer-interaction. Accessed 16 Mar 2018
2. Fong, T., Thorpe, C., Baur, C.: Collaboration, dialogue and human-robot interaction. In: Proceedings of the 10th International Symposium of Robotics Research, Lorne, Victoria, Australia (2010)
3. Checklist for Web Content Accessibility Guidelines 2.0. https://www.w3.org/TR/2006/WD-WCAG20-20060427/appendixB.html. Accessed 24 Mar 2018
4. Future Media Standards & Guidelines - Accessibility Guidelines v2.0. http://www.bbc.co.uk/guidelines/futuremedia/accessibility/html/. Accessed 24 Mar 2018
5. Mobile guidelines. https://www.funka.com/en/our-assignments/research-and-innovation/archive—research-projects/mobile-guidelines/. Accessed 16 Mar 2018
6. Yanco, H.A., Drury, J.: Classifying human-robot interaction: an updated taxonomy. In: 2004 IEEE International Conference on Systems, Man and Cybernetics, vol. 3, pp. 2841–2846. IEEE (2004)
7. Weiss, A., Bernhaupt, R., Lankes, M., Tscheligi, M.: The USUS evaluation framework for human-robot interaction. In: AISB2009: Proceedings of the Symposium on New Frontiers in Human-Robot Interaction, vol. 4, pp. 11–26 (2009)
8. Kim, M., Oh, K., Choi, J., Jung, J., Kim, Y.: User-centered HRI: HRI research methodology for designers. In: Wang, X. (ed.) Mixed Reality and Human-Robot Interaction. ISCA, vol. 1010, pp. 13–33. Springer, Dordrecht (2011). https://doi.org/10.1007/978-94-007-0582-1_2
9. How WAI Develops Accessibility Guidelines through the W3C Process: Milestones and Opportunities to Contribute. Web Accessibility Initiative. W3C. https://www.w3.org/WAI/intro/w3c-process.php. Accessed 23 Mar 2018
10. Ting, K.L.H., Voilmy, D., Iglesias, A., Pulido, J.C., García, J., Romero-Garcés, A., Bandera, J.P., Marfil, R., Dueñas, Á.: Integrating the users in the design of a robot for making Comprehensive Geriatric Assessments (CGA) to elderly people in care centers. In: 2017 26th IEEE International Symposium on Robot and Human Interactive Communication (RO-MAN), pp. 483–488. IEEE (2017)

Development of a Graphic and Braille Optimized Plotter for the Blind and Visually Impaired

Denise S. Wußler(✉), Kai Sachsenheimer, Bastian E. Rapp,
and Thorsten Schwarz

Karlsruhe Institute of Technology, Karlsruhe, Germany
denise.wussler@partner.kit.edu,
{kai.sachsenheimer,bastian.rapp,thorsten.schwarz}@kit.edu

Abstract. With the development of this plotter, a cost-effective and easy assembly was created to allow a better accessibility to well-recognizable braille text and tactile graphics on standard DIN-A4 paper for blind and visually impaired users. In comparison to currently employed systems, the developed device consists of a commercially available X/Y-plotter, which enables a movement in two orthogonal directions at once. Thus, not only the embossing of single dots, but also of continuous lines on a flat surface is possible. The plotter was extended by a solenoid that can change the force on a convertible embossing pen in Z-direction. Further parts were constructed and added to enable material feeding, material removal and paper fixation while printing. In a survey with six blind and visually impaired people, the results of the plotter were tested for good readability and recognition and compared to a conventional needle-based-system. Most of the participants would use the results produced by the plotter at hand in their daily life.

Keywords: Graphic and braille optimized printer
Tactile print on paper · Continuous lines

1 Introduction

Since the early beginnings of tactile writing, many different technical solutions were designed to make the written word and tactile graphics more accessible for the blind and visually impaired. But usually, only educational or research institutions have access to a suitable printer due to the large physical dimension and the significant costs involved when purchasing and operating such a system [1]. This paper presents the development of an affordable graphic and braille optimized system that allows convenient set-up with small expenditure. The paper also demonstrates the capability of this system to print braille and tactile graphics highlighting the fact that it can be used to print continuous lines.

© Springer International Publishing AG, part of Springer Nature 2018
K. Miesenberger and G. Kouroupetroglou (Eds.): ICCHP 2018, LNCS 10897, pp. 221–225, 2018.
https://doi.org/10.1007/978-3-319-94274-2_30

2 Related Work

There are several solutions to manufacturing tactile content based on non-paper materials. Some of the most widely used possibilities are microcapsule swell-paper [2] or vacuum forming techniques [3]. Both solutions allow well-defined braille texts, continuous lines and graphics. However, these approaches require cost-intensive instruments and depend on material that users describe as unnatural compared to paper. Many blind and visually impaired people started learning to write with a braille typewriter embossing marks on paper. Also dotted lines are possible with braille embossers [4]. Printers based on the principle of needle-printing on paper are the current state-of-the-art. Observed under a microscope, the printed results show sharp edges, where the needle pierced the paper. Many blind and visually impaired people at the Study Centre for Visually Impaired (SZS) at Karlsruhe Institute of Technology (KIT) have difficulties reading large sections of text produced by this technique. Their fingertips are fatigued more rapidly by the pattern of the pierced paper. A needle-based printer can only produce lines by adding dot after dot. Obviously, for creating a continuous line on standard paper, another technique is needed.

3 Methodology

To generate an affordable and easy to use braille and continuous-lines printer, we had to find low priced components and use as little parts as possible. For this prototype, many components were subsequently designed and 3D-printed. The aim was to utilize standard DIN-A4 paper of $160\,g/m^2$ that is commonly used in the everyday life of a blind or visually impaired person. The main component of the setup is the ready-to-use commercially available X/Y-plotter robot kit from Makeblock (<300€) [5], that uses a pen attached to the plotter head for plotting vector-images. The pen mount was replaced by a solenoid moving in Z-direction. To evaluate the plotting result, different dot sizes and line thicknesses are necessary. Therefore, three writing tips with different diameters were manufactured such that an easy tip-change is possible.

The stepper motors, that move the plotter head across the printing area, are controlled via an Arduino microcontroller board. The Arduino reads the plotting data via USB from the open source software mDraw [6]. This software can be interlinked with a RS-232 based terminal client application that controls the actuation of the solenoid by changing the voltage. The solenoid is then displaced proportionally producing different embossing depths.

To allow the plotting of continuous lines the paper must remain at a secured position. This was achieved by fixing the paper onto a platform using U-shaped clamps in each corner. Among the individual process steps (paper feeding, plotting and paper removal) the most time critical step is the plotting process itself. To reduce energy consumption, the paper is secured by a clamp mechanism using springs and released by solenoid actuators located under the platform in each corner. This also enables nearly unlimited movement of the plotter as the space

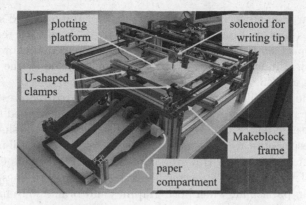

Fig. 1. Makeblock X/Y-robot kit frame with writing tip attached to the solenoid in the middle. The compartment for paper feeding and removal is located on the left. While plotting, the paper is fixed by U-shaped clamps in each corner, which can be released by solenoids beneath the platform.

above the paper remains mostly unoccupied. On top of the platform, a layer of a softer, slightly compressible material is required for obtaining good embossing results in the paper. The so far best suited material was found to be a silicone pad of 2 mm thickness.

The two-level paper compartment consists of a tray for blank paper at the bottom and finished paper at the top. A rubber-roll and a stepper motor from a discarded inkjet printer are the basis for the paper feeding mechanism. With the roll, single sheets of paper are pushed partially on the plotting platform. A small hole in the paper allows the writing tip to move the paper into the correct plotting position. The paper removal works similarly: The writing tip moves the paper from the platform down into the top paper tray (Fig. 1).

4   Evaluation

In order to assess the quality of the plotting results and compare them to conventional needle printers currently used at SZS, a study with six blind or visually impaired students and employees of KIT was conducted.

Participants were asked to rate the best distinguishable dots on a scale of 1 to 5. With an arithmetic mean value of 4.7, the smallest writing tip with a 1 mm diameter was the preferred tip for producing braille text. The tip with a diameter of 2.5 mm was considered unsuitable for braille writing with an average mean value of 1.25, as the dots were perceived to be washy and hard to differentiate. It was assessed at which embossing depth the text became readable, while still producing clear and smooth dots without sharp edges. The best results were achieved for solenoid voltages of 8 V and 10 V (maximum 12 V) for all three writing tips.

Three differently complex graphics were plotted with variations in writing tip diameter and solenoid voltage aiming for the best recognising experience.

Most of the participants were able to identify all of the provided shapes. More complex shapes and multiple angles occurred to be harder to recognise. The participants especially liked the smooth, continuous lines that showed the graph of a mathematical function compared to the graphics made by the conventional needle printers at SZS.

Regarding long braille texts, the participants preferred the presented plotter over the needle printer. For graphics, many participants described the results of the needle printer as easier and faster recognizable because of the sharp edges and noted, that these results are well suited for beginners, who are still in the process of sensitising their fingertips. However, most of the participants embraced the results of the developed tactile plotter because of the smooth lines. The plotter was preferred in particular, when both graphics and braille were mixed.

5 Conclusion and Outlook

In this paper we presented a low cost and easy-to-assemble tactile plotter mainly based on a Makeblock X/Y-robot kit, components from an old inkjet printer and 3D printed parts. The construction is lighter and smaller than commonly used printing systems (e.g. needle-based printers). During a study, participants showed strong interest in the plotted materials and would use these in their daily life. Apparently, the more distinct dots and sharp edges known from needle printers are not necessary or even too rough for most of the experienced braille and tactile material users when employed for a longer period.

At this state, the paper feeding mechanism of the plotter is not just completed yet. The stepper motor can be controlled manually, allows rotating the feeding roll and thus transporting the paper on the platform in most instances. Obviously, this system must also be made more user-friendly by improving the already used software. We believe that low-cost solutions such as the one demonstrated here fill an important niche in everyday life of the visually impaired and will allow the widespread dissemination of tactile printing systems. This should make tactile reproduction equally accessible as regular printing and thus contribute significantly to a more inclusive society.

References

1. Pal, J., Pradhan, M., Shah, M., Babu, R.: Assistive technology for vision-impairments: an agenda for the ICTD community. In: Proceedings of the 20th International Conference on World Wide Web, New York (2011)
2. Hashimoto, T., Watanabe, T.: Expansion characteristic of tactile symbols on swell paper. In: Miesenberger, K., Bühler, C., Penaz, P. (eds.) ICCHP 2016. LNCS, vol. 9759, pp. 69–76. Springer, Cham (2016). https://doi.org/10.1007/978-3-319-41267-2_10
3. Nolan, C., Morris, J.: Improvement of Tactual Symbols for Blind Children: Final Report. American Printing House for the Blind, Louisville (1971)

4. Kouroupetroglou, G., Martos, A., Papandreou, N., Papadopoulos, K., Argyropoulous, V., Sideridis, G.D.: Tactile identification of embossed raised lines and raised squares with variable dot elevation by persons who are blind. In: Miesenberger, K., Bühler, C., Penaz, P. (eds.) ICCHP 2016. LNCS, vol. 9759, pp. 77–84. Springer, Cham (2016). https://doi.org/10.1007/978-3-319-41267-2_11
5. Makeblock: XY Plotter Robot Kit (2018). http://learn.makeblock.com/en/xy-plotter-robot-kit/
6. mDraw Software by Makeblock (2018). http://learn.makeblock.com/en/mdraw/

Prototype Development of a Shape Presentation System Using Linear Actuators

Tatsuo Motoyoshi$^{(\boxtimes)}$, Sota Mizushima, Kei Sawai, Takumi Tamamoto,
Hiroyuki Masuta, Ken'ichi Koyanagi, and Toru Oshima

Department of Intelligent Systems Design Engineering,
Toyama Prefectural University, Toyama 939-0398, Japan
`motoyosh@pu-toyama.ac.jp`

Abstract. We here propose a three-dimensional shape presentation system using linear actuators which can control the displacement of a rod to a precision of 0.1 mm. We assume that this system will be used as a device to present topographical/shape information to people with visual impairments. For this study, we produced a prototype system equipped with precision linear actuators, and conducted experiments to evaluate the capabilities of the system.

1 Introduction

When people with visual impairments access topographical/shape information, the information needs to be expressed tactilely. We previously proposed a computer-aided system enabling people with visual impairments to create and recognize their own figures by using a matrix braille display [1]. However, since a matrix braille display can indicate only the outline of the shape, it is unsuitable for indicating height and inclination information. Using figures created by a three-dimensional (3D) printer is expensive because all the information is needed to create the figures. We are therefore developing a 3D shape presentation system using linear actuators which can control the height of a rod. Since, the proposed system can show information about height and incline of topography precisely, it is useful for understanding a hazard map or a floor map for visual impairments.

2 Shape Presentation System

We previously produced a prototype of a 3D shape presentation system using linear actuators which we call THK:PCS-9RD [2] to indicate height and inclination information. The rod of each actuator can be moved to a maximum height of 50 mm and adjusted in increments of 1.25 μm.

The system consists of two linear actuators equipped with two finger plates, one operation handle, and one pen tablet. An operator holds the operation handle and sets two of his/her fingers on the finger plates, which are joined to the

K. Miesenberger and G. Kouroupetroglou (Eds.): ICCHP 2018, LNCS 10897, pp. 226–230, 2018.
https://doi.org/10.1007/978-3-319-94274-2_31

rods of the actuators, and then adjusts the handle position extensively while detecting the shape information. The coordinate position of the operation handle is detected by the pen tablet installed under the handle. The operation handle can be moved 135 mm vertically and 216 mm laterally. The system can control the height of each rod in increments of 0.1 mm in order to conform to the shape information. Each actuator communicates with a control computer through a CAN communication system (shown The configuration of proposed system is shown in Fig. 1).

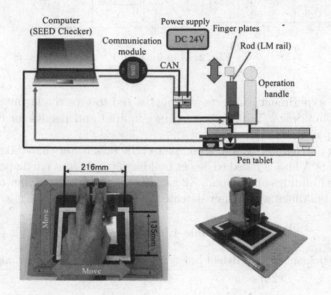

Fig. 1. Prototype of the shape presentation system

3 Evaluation of the Prototype

We conducted two experiments to evaluate the presentation capabilities of the prototype.

Exp. 1: We prepared information of four simple 3D objects representing square buildings. We recorded the time required to report the height differences between the objects, and calculated the accuracies of the recorded height orders.

Exp. 2: We prepared street map information for the proposed system and a tactile map. We recorded the times required to report street map information in each case.

3.1 Exp.1

For exp. 1, we recruited three people with normal sight as participants. Each participant wore a blindfold over his/her face eyes and was presented with a map on which four square buildings of differing heights were represented. We recorded the time required to report the layout and height order of the buildings. In proper order, buildings differed in height by 1 mm. The map is shown in Fig. 2.

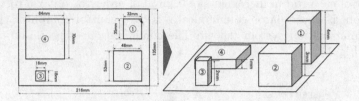

Fig. 2. Map for exp. 1

After the experiment, subjects were instructed to give the layout and height order of the buildings. Table 1 shows time required and results for each of the three participants.

Although participants A and B completed the task faster than did participant C, participants A and B failed to detect building ③, whereas participant C could detect all the buildings on the map. All participants could discriminate the height order of the buildings which they detected.

Table 1. Results

Participant	Time	Height order	Number of recognized buildings
A	191 s	✓	3
B	476 s	✓	3
C	624 s	✓	4

3.2   Exp. 2

For exp. 2, we again recruited three people with normal sight as participants. Each participant wore a blindfold over his/her face eyes and was presented one at a time with the street maps shown in Fig. 3. Map 1 is for the proposed system and map 2 is the tactile map. In the experiment, each participant was told to detect the start and goal positions and structure of the street pattern on the map using either map 1 or 2 in the first session and the other map in the second session. Maps 1 and 2 have the same numbers of buildings and street corners. We recorded the time needed to detect the required information from the map. After the experiment, participants were asked to describe the route to the goal and the overall view of street pattern on the map.

When using the tactile map, all participants could detect the route to the goal faster than when using the proposed system. However, only participant C described the overall street pattern of the map correctly in this case. When

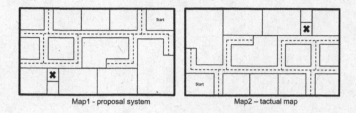

Fig. 3. Map for exp.2

using the proposed system, participants could only describe the route to the goal. All subjects commented that since they use only one hand in operating the proposed system, they found it difficult to understand the reference position. On the other hand, they found it easy to trace their route along the streets by using the proposed system.

Table 2. Results

Participant	Tactile map time	Street pattern	Proposed system time	Street pattern
A	174 s	–	190 s	–
B	590 s	–	660 s	–
C	325 s	–	1008 s	✓

4   Summary

We developed a 3D shape presentation system using linear actuators for people with visual impairments. We then conducted experiments to evaluate the presentation capability of a prototype. From the experimental results, we conclude that the proposed system can communicate height difference information at a 1 mm precision and is advantageous for tracing a streaked or striated pattern, such as a street pattern. In future work, we will add actuators for four fingers and a mechanism for a second hand to allow pointing at a reference position.

References

1. Takagi, N., Morii, S., Motoyoshi, T.: Prototype development of image editing systems available for visually impaired people and consideration of their user interfaces. J. Adv. Comput. Intell. Intell. Inform. (JACIII) **20**(6), 961–967 (2016)
2. THK: Seed Picsel. http://seed-solutions.net/?qeng/node/29

Access to Artworks and Its Mediation by and for Visually Impaired People

Access to Artworks and Its Mediation by and for Visually Impaired Persons

Introduction to the Special Thematic Session

Katerine Romeo[1]([⊠]), Marion Chottin[2], Pierre Ancet[3],
and Edwige Pissaloux[1]

[1] LITIS, Rouen Normandy University, 76800 Saint-Etienne du Rouvray, France
{katerine.romeo, Edwige.Pissaloux}@univ-rouen.fr
[2] CNRS-ENS Lyon, 69007 Lyon, France
[3] Bourgogne University, 21078 Dijon, France

Abstract. Many artworks such as paintings or sculptures are accessible mainly through vision; visually impaired people therefore cannot benefit from the beauty, emotion or information inspired by these objects. Some trials at tactile presentation of artworks exist in research laboratories and some museums. In research laboratories such approaches are related to several synergetic components such as through the design of new multi-touch stimulation devices, the models of percepts' emergence from perceptions (stimulation), object simplification with "conservation of meaning", multimodal data fusion, etc. Museums are not only interested in multimodal (audio-tactile) presentations of artworks, but also in the physical accessibility of exhibition halls and self-guidance through collections. Specific wearable technologies and specific adaptable guides are necessary.

Keywords: Accessibility · Artwork · Painting · Tactile presentation
Multi-modal perception · Blindness · Visually impaired

1 Introduction: Limits of the Sense of Sight…

Access to artworks for a visually impaired person (VIP) who is going to a museum is rarely possible without encountering problems of perception of artworks. Indeed, the sense of sight is predominant in museums; therefore, paintings or sculptures are accessible mainly through vision.

However, we all know that we are easily drown to touch a sculpture or a 3D masterpiece, or to approach too close to the artwork to feel it, risking each time to trigger an alarm signal in the museum. The *vision in those cases seems insufficient* to satiate the aesthetic pleasure. The sense of touch can convey different information both in physical and emotional sense. *The cognitive virtues of touching* are recognized since Aristoteles, and today they are rediscovered and quantified [1, 2]. The touching contact produces aesthetic virtues known since the Antiquity. They are regularly mentioned in the history of art [3, 4]. We have testimonials of famous blind persons such as Helen Keller about tactile and aesthetic experiences [5, 6].

© Springer International Publishing AG, part of Springer Nature 2018
K. Miesenberger and G. Kouroupetroglou (Eds.): ICCHP 2018, LNCS 10897, pp. 233–236, 2018.
https://doi.org/10.1007/978-3-319-94274-2_32

To benefit from the beauty, emotion or information inspired by these objects, *a multimodal representation* could bring the tactile perception and the audio description. But, usually the touching of the artwork is prohibited in museums and the guided visits are organized for the sense of sight.

In France, the prohibition to touch the artworks is applied since the 18th century. The Louvre Museum was opened in 1793. Just two years later, "Please, do not touch" was decreed. This was the consequence of tactile explorations of copyists, some of them having squared with chalk the painting they were copying in order to reproduce its proportions.

This prohibition of touching the artworks was partially lifted in the last decades of the 20th century: in several museums in the world, some new facilities for tactile experiences have been introduced. This means that VIP's can access to certain artworks. However, in most of the cases, these artworks can be deteriorated if they are touched very often. They are generally proposed to public in the form *of replicas or transpositions in some other material*. But it is impossible to duplicate or transpose all the artworks. Actually, there are some technical solutions to this problem such as 3D presentations, virtual museums, haptic devices giving access to many artworks, etc. Some of these ICT (Information and Communication Technologies) based solutions for accessible artworks are presented hereafter.

2   Accessible Artworks in Museums

Tactile presentations of artworks for VIP can be very different using various perceptual aspects and various supports for them. An artwork can be presented *as a static tactile*, full scale or miniaturized, *reproduction* of paintings, sculptures, architectural models (of a city, of a castle etc.) with textual, braille or audio description. The technologies used for these tactile representations are made of embossed paper, thermoformed plastic, 3D printing, resin moulding or carved wood or stone, fabric [7, 8]. This relief painting technique adds volume and texture and helps to create a mental image of a painting by feeling it. Audio guide advises blind visitors how to best explore the paintings through touch.

Artworks could also be presented as an interactive *virtual environment* where objects are individually presented and contextualized. For some of the VIP's who can see some details and some colours, these interactive representations need to have a high resolution and satisfactory chromatic and morphological details that could be *zoomed* easily. *Different viewpoints and perspectives* can be explored through an analytically defined pathway without temporal constraints. Some elements of the artwork could give access to related documents and sources resulting in a rich data set (texts, photos and videos) *using augmented reality* (AR) technique. This data could be used to develop applications for smartphones or tablets providing access to artworks through dynamic AR techniques.

Museums are encouraged to open the exhibitions to a great variety of public including the VIP's. A certain number of museums create *accessible tactile circuits* [9, 10] with pedagogical tactile material and sometimes even a *kind of immersive environment*; e.g. in the grotto of Combarelle (Dordogne, France) the environmental sound, characteristic odour and humidity are simulated. These ersatz should meet the required quality criteria such as tactile and visual readability and comprehensibility (e.g. the presentation of relief images by the angle of 20°), possibility to safely follow the contours and the shapes of objects.

3 Multimodal Analysis of an Artwork

Usually we qualify the sense of vision as synthetic and the sense of touch as analytic. This assertion should be clarified. For the vision, we can observe that after a first quick look taking a global picture of the artwork (a *visual gist* of the artwork), our vision decomposes the painting into elements and discovers the ones that slipped out of the first glance. The sense of touch, for its part, starts also with a first global feeling of the object (*tactile gist*, [11]), before concentrating on its different elements and finally recomposing the whole object, in a unified representation [12].

However, it is true that the sense of touch of our fingertips, unlike the vision, does not access at once but successively to the unified representation: the global feeling of the object does not allow apprehending all the different shapes and their relations; each element should be examined one by one. This feature, induced by the distribution of tactile mechanoreceptors in our hands, is not a weakness by itself and does not mean that the sense of touch is inferior to the sense of vision: the time spent to explore an artwork by touching can allow a better understanding of the latter and gives a more intense aesthetic pleasure than the one provided by a quick and hasty look. As a consequence, a good approach to perception of an artwork is multimodal one: sight, touch, audio, etc. as each perception reinforces other, and leaves a more reliable and lasting aesthetic impression of perceived stimulations.

4 Access to Artworks: A ICCHP 2018 Special Thematic Session

The session "Access to Artworks and its mediation for VIP's" has 5 papers on actual research in this topic. ICT technology induces high expectations on tactile devices, and VIP's are expecting to discover artworks on tablets or on smartphones.

Two papers present new concepts of tactile presentation on haptic surface devices.

The Paper by Karastoyanov et al. presents a new graphical interface and discussed of its use and advantages in the discovery of cultural and historical artworks via touch sensitive contours and decomposition of pictures to salient segments.

The Paper by Gay et al. introduces a new ICT device created by the association of a classic tactile tablet and a specific scalable force feedback structure (F2T) which may be attached to it. Using a kind of joystick, it is possible to explore the image displayed on a tactile tablet. The F2T structure allows perceiving the edges, textures and Braille texts.

Two other papers address the problem of difficulties of transcription of artworks on a tactile surface and analyse the best presentation practices. Indeed, 80% of VIP's prefer to go to museums being accompanied because of the complexity of the presentation of artworks; even in tactile form, it is difficult to apprehend the shapes and induce a meaning form their grouping, without some human or audio-description assistance [13].

The paper by Romeo et al. presents the test results of simplification of the paintings done by Australian Aborigines. The implemented methodology is bottom-up; it starts with tactile representation of basic elements relevant to the whole painting understanding, then their association into more complex concepts and finally into the whole image. The context of associations is explained with audio-description. The results of the tests with visually impaired persons are analysed and explained.

The paper by Cantoni et al. introduces the processing of 3D models of artworks to get tactile objects and haptic presentations with Braille annotations in areas closed by contours. Image segmentation is performed on the image arrays of subsequent segments evaluated and described with the context of individual elements.

Finally the use of virtual and augmented reality techniques are analysed to show the problems of accessibility for VIP's. The obtained results are duly described in the paper of Miura et al.

References

1. Aristote: De l'âme. GF Flammarion, Paris (1999)
2. Hatvelle, Y., Streri, A., Gentaz, E.: Toucher pour connaître. Psychologie cognitive de la perception tactile manuelle. PUF, Paris (2000)
3. Dent, P. (ed.): Sculpture and Touch. Routledge, Abingdon (2014)
4. Marinetti: Le tactillisme. Manifeste futuriste, in Giovanni, L.: Futurisme. Lausanne, Editions l'Âge d'Homme (1973)
5. Keller, H.: Histoire de ma vie. Payot, Paris (2001)
6. Villey, P.: Le Monde des aveugles. Essai de psychologie. Flammarion, Paris (1914)
7. Bris, M.: Recommandations pour la transcription des documents. Service des Documents Adaptés pour Déficients Visuels. CNEFEI Suresnes, 17 November 2003
8. Cantoni, V., Karastoyanov, D., Mosconi, M., Setti, A.: Pavia, the Battle, the Future. Pavia University Press (2016)
9. Culture et Handicap, guide pratique de l'accessibilité. Ministère de la culture et de la communication (2007)
10. Petovari, M.: Culture: Quelle stratégie de développement numérique pour les conseils départementaux? Thèse Université Sorbonne Nouvelle - Paris 3, UFR Arts et Médias, Dépt. De Médiation culturelle, Juillet 2017
11. Pissaloux, E., Velazquez, R., Maingreaud, F.: A new framework for cognitive mobility of visually impaired users and associated tactile device. IEEE Trans. Hum.-Mach. Syst. 47(6), 2168–2291 (2017)
12. Candlin, F.: The dubious inheritance of touch: art history and museum access. J. Vis. Cult. 5 (2), 137–154 (2006)
13. Chauvey, V.: Le texte au musée pour les visiteurs non-voyants : comment aborder les choix de contenus et de formes? La lettre de l'OCIM, N). 132, November–December 2010

Exploiting a Graphical Braille Display for Art Masterpieces

Stanislav Gyoshev[1], Dimitar Karastoyanov[1(✉)], Nikolay Stoimenov[1],
Virginio Cantoni[2], Luca Lombardi[2], and Alessandra Setti[2]

[1] Institute of Information and Communication Technologies,
Bulgarian Academy of Sciences, Sofia, Bulgaria
stanislavgyoshev@mail.bg, dkarast@iinf.bas.bg,
nikistoimenow@gmail.com
[2] Dipartimento di Ingegneria Industriale e dell'Informazione,
Università di Pavia, Pavia, Italy
{virginio.cantoni, luca.lombardi,
alessandra.setti}@unipv.it

Abstract. A new graphical Braille display is presented. Its use, social value and advantages are discussed. In particular is developed an approach allowing objects of cultural and historical heritage to be presented in an intuitive and accessible way to low-sighted or blind people.

Keywords: Graphical braille screen · Tactile image · Visually impaired people
Accessibility · Graphical interface · Dynamic presentation

1 Introduction

Within the European Union, the problem of accessibility to graphical sources for blind people is quite pressing. Studies on European and world scale are carried out in many directions: (i) the attempt for social integration of the visually impaired – mainly creating optimal conditions for assisting and integrating blind students; (ii) development of Braille terminals and printers (mainly with the usage only for symbols and numbers) and adaptation to computer systems; (iii) since the human-computer communication is quite poor (mainly based on text instructions), is searched for suitable techniques for its supporting by voice synthesis or other forms of feedback; (iv) development of haptic interfaces based on electrically addressable and deforming polymer layer.

Practically, the efforts are aimed at the manufacturing of a haptic dynamic input-output device. The IICT department has 3 BG patents, [1–3], and 2 patent applications concerning Graphical Braille Display, [4, 5].

© Springer International Publishing AG, part of Springer Nature 2018
K. Miesenberger and G. Kouroupetroglou (Eds.): ICCHP 2018, LNCS 10897, pp. 237–245, 2018.
https://doi.org/10.1007/978-3-319-94274-2_33

2   State of the Art

During the last decade, a number of touch screen devices for visually impaired users have been announced. In particular, devices for refreshable visualization with pins are still at early development phases, mostly with small displays for just one-finger touch. Three popular examples are:

Graphiti - an Interactive Tactile Graphics Display based on Tactuator technology [6]. It enables the non-visual access to any form of graphical information such as maps, charts, drawings, flowcharts and images, through an array of 60x40 moving pins. Each pin is independently addressable and can be set to "blink" individually at configurable rates. Also, each pin can be set to different heights, which enables multi-level representation, i.e. bas-relief and it is not verified if visually impaired people will find it suited.

BlindPAD - an interactive tactile tablet that can display in real time maps, graphics, and other symbols [7]. The tablet has 12x16 independently controlled pins. It provides graphical information such as geometrical figures, maps or artwork. The tablet has 200 mN holding force. It is based on special and expensive materials, and it is not known the way pins are held in raised position. The force of attraction between the magnet and the tile is small, and is reduced by the resilient resistance of the membranes.

HyperBraille - in the opinion of the authors of the article is the best tactile graphics display at present [8]. It is a graphics-enabled laptop with 9,000 pin-matrix appeared in 2008. The display is touch-sensitive so the user can locate the cursor position. According to [9], in 2015 the model with a pin-matrix of 7,200 dots, arranged in a 120x60 array, costed about $56,000. Using HyperBraille, visually impaired people can manually produce tactile graphics cooperating with sighted people. The construction is complicated as well. It is not evident whether the pins can be controlled individually or by blocks consisting of only 10 pins.

3   The New Graphical Interface

A prototype of a Graphical Braille Display based on the patent application WIPO PCT/BG2014 000038 "Braille Display" is proposed. In the article are described the research on design, optimization and development of magnetic based linear actuator and the human-computer interface.

The Graphical Braille Display represents a matrix (Fig. 1), comprised of a base with fixed electromagnets. They are arranged, including an ȯuter cylindrical magnetic core in which is positioned a winding magnetic core (coil), locking (capping) up the cylindrical magnetic core at the top side. A winding magnetic core locking up the cylindrical magnetic core at the bottom side is placed. The magnetic cores are equipped with axial holes. Into the space between the windings is placed a movable non-magnetic cylindrical body, carrying an axially magnetized permanent cylindrical magnet, as well as a non-magnetic needle. The needle is passing axially through the permanent magnet and the axial holes of the magnetic cores. On the top side of the permanent magnet is arranged a ferromagnetic disc having an axial hole. On its underside is arranged a ferromagnetic disc with an axial hole. The upper disc and the upper magnetic core have cylindrical poles and the lower magnetic core and the lower disc have conical poles. Above the electromagnets is placed a lattice. The needles pass through the openings.

Actuator Construction. The actuator is a linear electromagnetic micro drive (Fig. 2). The mover is a permanent magnet. Its magnetization direction is along the axis of rotational symmetry. The upper and lower coil are connected in series. This connection is constructed so that the flux created by each of them is in opposite directions in the mover zone. By choosing the proper power supply polarity, the motion of the mover will be in desired direction. For example, in order to have motion of the mover in the upper direction, the upper coil has to be supplied in a way leading to the creation of an air gap magnetic flux, which is in the same direction as the one of the flux created by the permanent magnet. The lower coil in this case will create magnetic flux which is in opposite direction to the one of the magnetic flux created by the permanent magnet. In this case motion up will be observed. In order to have motion down, the lower coil should be supplied in a way so that its flux is in the same direction as the flux by the permanent magnet. The upper coil then will create magnetic flux in opposite direction. In order to fix the moving part to the Braille dot, non-magnetic shaft is used. Additional construction variants of the actuator have also been considered, in which two small ferromagnetic discs are placed on both sides - upper and lower - of the moving permanent magnet. This actuator is also energy efficient, as energy is used only for changing the position of the moving part from lower to upper and vice versa. Both at lower and at upper position, no energy is used. At these positions, the mover is kept fixed due the force ensured by the permanent magnet (sticks to the core).

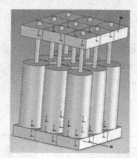

Fig. 1. Braille screen matrix.

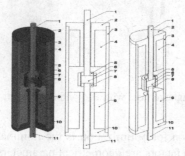

Fig. 2. Principal geometry of the permanent magnet linear actuator: 1, 11 - Needle (shaft); 2 - Upper core; 3 – Outercore; 4 - Upper coil; 5 - Upper ferromagnetic disc; 6 - Non-magnetic bush; 7 - Permanent magnet; 8 - Lower ferro-magnetic disc; 9 - Lower coil; 10 - Lower core.

4 R&D Work and Results

Static Force Characteristics are obtained for different construction parameters of the actuator. The outer diameter of the core is varied. The air gap between the upper and lower core, the length of the permanent magnet and the coils height have been varied too [10]. In Fig. 3 the force-displacement characteristics are given for different values of the permanent magnet height hm, coil height $hw,$ and the air gap between the upper and lower core δ. The magnetomotive force Iw = 180 A, and the apparent current density in the coils J = 20A/mm^2.

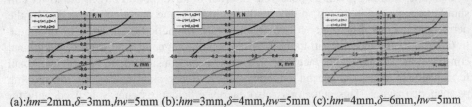

(a):hm=2mm,δ=3mm,hw=5mm (b):hm=3mm,δ=4mm,hw=5mm (c):hm=4mm,δ=6mm,hw=5mm

Fig. 3. Static Force Characteristics

Finite Element Modelling. Magnetic field of the construction variant of the permanent magnet linear actuator with two ferromagnetic discs on both sides of the permanent magnet is analyzed with the help of the finite element method – Fig. 4, [11]. The field is analyzed as an axisymmetric one due to the rotational symmetry of the actuator. The weighted stress tensor approach has been utilized for evaluating the electromagnetic force on the mover.

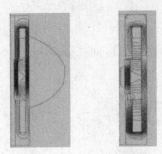

Fig. 4. Magnetic field with and without current in the coil

Optimization. The criterion for optimization is the minimal magnetomotive force of the coils. The optimization factors are geometrical parameters (height of the permanent magnet, height of the ferromagnetic discs and height of the coils). The optimization is subject to the following constraints: minimal electromagnetic force acting on the mover, minimal starting force and overall outer diameter of the actuator have been set – Fig. 5, [12]. Minimization of magnetomotive force is in direct correspondence to the minimization of the energy consumption.

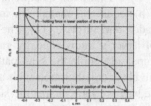 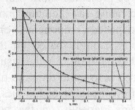

Fig. 5. F/D characteristics of the optimal actuator with and without current in the coils

The proposed development offers the following advantages [13, 14]: (i) the retention of the needles in their final positions does not require an external power supply, it is provided by the permanent magnet; (ii) the lack of additional energy source allows a very precise control of the feed force creating the tactile feedback; (iii) an intermittent power supply voltage allowing an extremely low power consumption (only for moving the needle from one end to the other), as well as more efficient use of materials and reducing of the size of the matrix; (iv) extremely low electric and mechanical time constants, resulting in very good velocity and dynamic characteristics; (v) a considerably broader range of the obtainable tactile feedback due to the fact that all electromagnets can be operated simultaneously and synchronously, which gives the operator a more realistic and closer to reality tactile perception; (vi) extremely high positioning accuracy of the needles and stability of the retaining forces into their final positions; (vii) the chosen propulsion method is distinguished by its exceptional reliability and trouble-free operation and requires no additional settings and service; (viii) the technology as a whole, with its simplicity and easy maintenance, is convenient for the realization of the matrix.

5   Conclusions and Future Developments

We shift from the traditional digitization paradigm (tactile Braille screen for symbols) to other areas such as the accessibility for visual impaired users to cultural and historical heritage: (i) assistive graphical computer interface for using a modern software (icons and similar objects); (ii) presentation of paintings, tapestries, photos, figures etc. via touch-sensitive contours for low-sighted visitors; (iii) fine-tuned decomposition of pictures to salient segments which can be treated as a separate content.

In the emblematic example of artwork "Guernica" by Pablo Picasso, 1937 (Fig. 6) the perspective laws are abandoned for an "extended sensing" suggesting to trigger feelings. Proper interpretation of this painting requires global knowledge about the facts and objects shown there, as illustrated in the few examples. The previous process is followed by a feature analysis and is completed by symbol manipulation, usually on a higher abstraction level referring the intended message.

From a global point of view this may be seen as a feature-to-symbol transform of the "high-level vision approach" in which the data structure is a 2D image array. Here the content can be presented more profitably by a scan-path: a sequence of segments presentation recreating (a) literature motif, (b) icons and metaphors motif, (c) form contrast, (d) juxtaposed components, (e) paradox and surprise [15]. The interpretation of the painting is strongly based on the observer's knowledge by interpreting the information of the painting; for the visual impaired people the scan-path definition is essential. Intended is to build the scan-path in close collaboration with art experts and with the help of eye tracking techniques. The way we look at specific stimuli, such as paintings, strongly depends on the portrayed subject(s), and the analysis of the sequences of fixations, detected on a visual stimulus can suggest analogous "observation" sequences on a tactile artefact. Eye-tracking technologies [16, 17] allow the study and measure of a user's attention, and the investigation of the correlation between suggested interpretations and user's understanding, thus can be adopted to guide visually impaired visitors in their exploration.

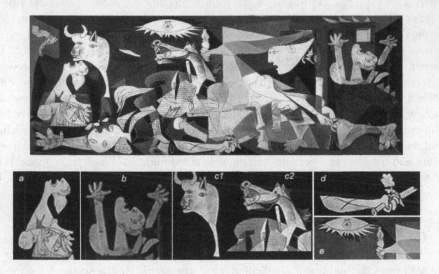

Fig. 6. Top: "Guernica" by Pablo Picasso (1937). Bottom: some selected salient segments

Figure 7(a) and (c) are segments of the painting "Guernica"; (b) and (d) illustrates these segments at the Graphical Braille Display; (e) shows a zoomed detail (x2) of (c). This technique allows to separate and precise salient segments of complex images in a suited optimal "message" delivery. The visual impaired user can "view" dynamically the painting and its details at different levels, accuracy and depth.

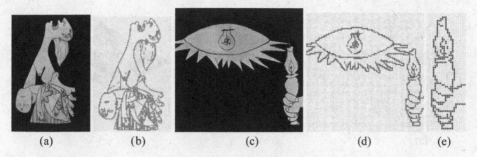

(a) (b) (c) (d) (e)

Fig. 7. Graphical Braille Display of two Guernica salient segments: (a) a woman grieving over a dead child, from the original masterpiece, (b) the corresponding result in the graphical Braille display; (c) a flame-lit lamp close to a bulb, as a symbol of calmness, clashing with the lightbulb, form the original masterpiece, (d) the corresponding result in the graphical Braille display, (e) an enlargement (x2).

5.1 Further Steps

There are three possible variants of the Braille Display for visually impaired people:

- Small, up to 24x16 pins. It will be used by children in schools for exploring simple graphics;
- Average, up to 48x32 pins. It will be used by visually impaired users when working with computers and graphical interface - Windows icons. In this case the display will be able to show schedules with average complexity based on surveys, statistics, and scientific articles.
- Large, up to 128x96 pins and more. These displays will be designed for museums, galleries, training centers etc. They will represent works of cultural and historical heritage - paintings, tapestries, icons, etc. The presentation will be accompanied by explanations of the context, giving possibilities for detailed view, increase or decrease of the image parts, etc.

A further advantage of our approach for construction of Braille Display is that these three options can be implemented with the same technology. Differences between the models will be as follows: the size of the carrier plate, the number of linear electro-magnetic micromotors, and the number of pin addresses in the input file of the software driver. Concerning the software, the size of the device will determine the setting parameters.

The devices will be affordable due to their simple construction and low-priced input materials. Small devices will allow on-line drawings by visually impaired on electronic artboards. A simple Braille Display can visualize the drawings directly – Fig. 8.

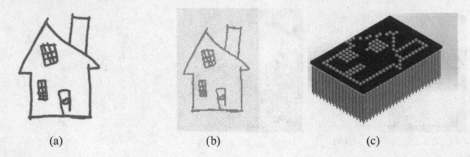

(a)　　　　　　　　　(b)　　　　　　　　　(c)

Fig. 8. Drawing on the Braille screen: (a) User drawings can be shown with lines similar the original ones at a high-resolution Braille Display, (b) Simulated view at a Braille Display with higher resolution, (c) An oversimplified view of user-generated content at a Braille Display with resolution 16x20 pins.

Acknowledgments. The paper is supported by the BG NSF Grant No DN 17/21-2017

References

1. Karastoyanov, D.: Braille screen, Bulgarian Patent No. 66520 (2016)
2. Karastoyanov, D., Simeonov, S.: Braille display, Bulgarian Patent No. 66527 (2016)
3. Karastoyanov, D., Yatchev, I., Hinov, K., Rachev, T.: Braille screen, Bulgarian Patent No. 66562 (2017)
4. Karastoyanov, D., Yatchev, Y., Hinov, K., Balabozov, I.: Braille Screen – Bulgarian Patent Application, No. 111638, 29.11 (2013)
5. Karastoyanov, D., Yatchev, Y., Hinov, K., Balabozov, I.; Braille Display – WIPO Patent Application, No. PCT/BG2014/000038 (2014)
6. Orbit Research: Orbit Reader 20: Revolutionary Technology – A Breakthrough in Affordability Highest Quality Braille at the Lowest Price. http://www.orbitresearch.com/. Accessed 28 Feb 2018
7. Personal Assistive Device for BLIND and visually impaired people (BlindPAD), FP7-ICT-2013-10 Project, Grant No 611621, Final Project Report, vol. 5, October 2017. https://www.blindpad.eu/. Accessed 28 Feb 2018
8. Bornschein, J., Prescher, D., Weber, G.: Inclusive production of tactile graphics. In: Abascal, J., Barbosa, S., Fetter, M., Gross, T., Palanque, P., Winckler, M. (eds.) Human-Computer Interaction – INTERACT 2015. LNCS, vol. 9296, pp. 80–88. Springer, Cham (2015). https://doi.org/10.1007/978-3-319-22701-6_7
9. O'Modhrain, S., Giudice, N.A., Gardner, J.A., Legge, G.E.: Designing media for visually-impaired users of refreshable touch displays: possibilities and pitfalls. IEEE Trans. Haptics 8(3), 248–257 (2015)
10. Yatchev, I., Hinov, K., Gueorgiev, V., Karastoyanov, D., Balabozov, I.: Force characteristics of an electromagnetic actuator for Braille screen. In: Proceedings of the Conference ELMA 2011, 21–22 October, Varna, Bulgaria, pp. 338–341 (2011)
11. Yatchev, I., Hinov, K., Balabozov, I., Gueorgiev, V., Karastoyanov, D.: Finite element modelling of electromagnets for Braille screen. In: Proceedings of the 10th International Conference on Applied Electro-magnetic PES 2011, 25–29 September, Nis, Serbia, pp O8.1–O8.4 (2011)

12. Yatchev, I., Balabozov, I., Hinov, K., Gueorgiev, V., Karastoyanov, D.: Optimization of permanent magnet linear actuator for Braille screen. In: Proceedings of the International Symposium IGTE 2012, 16–18 September, Graz, Austria, pp. 59–63 (2012)

13. Karastoyanov, D.: Energy efficient control of linear micro drives for Braille screen. In: Proceedings of the International Conference on Human and Computer Engineering ICHCE 2013, 14–15 October, Osaka, Japan, pISSN 2010-376x, eISSN 2010-3778, pp 860–864 (2013)

14. Karastoyanov, D., Yatchev, I., Balabozov, I.: Innovative graphical braille screen for visually impaired people. In: Margenov, S., Angelova, G., Agre, G. (eds.) Innovative Approaches and Solutions in Advanced Intelligent Systems. SCI, vol. 648, pp. 219–240. Springer, Cham (2016). https://doi.org/10.1007/978-3-319-32207-0_14

15. Cantoni, V., Levialdi, S., Zavidovique, B.: 3C Vision: Cues, Context and Channels. Elsevier, Amsterdam (2011)

16. Cantoni, V., Merlano, L., Nugrahaningsih, N., Porta, M.: Eye tracking for cultural heritage: a gaze-controlled system for handless interaction with artworks. In: Proceedings of the 17th International Conference on Computer Systems and Technologies (CompSysTech 2016), 23–24 June, Palermo, Italy, pp. 307–314. ACM Press (2016)

17. Cantoni, V., Karastoyanov, D., Mosconi, M., Setti, A.: Pavia The Battle The Future: Nothing was the Same Again. Pavia University Press, Pavia (2016)

Virtual Museum for People with Low Vision: Comparison of the Experience on Flat and Head-Mounted Displays

Takahiro Miura[1,2]([⊠]), Gentaro Ando[3], Junji Onishi[3], Masaki Matsuo[3],
Masatsugu Sakajiri[3], and Tsukasa Ono[3]

[1] Institute of Gerontology (IOG), The University of Tokyo,
7-3-1 Hongo, Bunkyo-ku, Tokyo 113-8656, Japan
miu@iog.u-tokyo.ac.jp
[2] National Institute of Advanced Industrial Science and Technology (AIST),
1-1-1 Umezono, Tsukuba, Ibaraki 305-8560, Japan
[3] Tsukuba University of Technology,
4-12-7 Kasuga, Tsukuba, Ibaraki 305-8521, Japan
ag142302@cc.k.tsukuba-tech.ac.jp,
{ohnishi,sakajiri,ono}@cs.k.tsukuba-tech.ac.jp,
mm163204@g.tsukuba-tech.ac.jp

Abstract. An increasing number of virtual museums (VMs) are used as educational materials because the VM can provide experiencing and learning virtual hands-on exhibitions without being limited in a place and a time for the users. However, most of the VM does not always accessible for people with low vision because of the limited functions including elusive annotations, passive zooming control, and incompatibility of various accessibility functions. In this paper, our objective is to demonstrate the issues and the solutions of VMs for these people. We first developed a prototype of VMs for low vision and then experimentally evaluated the VMs to find the requirements that people with low vision can easily control and have experience learning in VMs. The result shows that those who have immersive tendency would prefer the VM with an HMD.

Keywords: People with low vision · Virtual reality (VR)
Virtual museum (VM) · Head mounted display (HMD)

1 Introduction

As many large commercial complexes opened near from stations, there are increasing interests in and increasing number of interactive exhibitions inside the various types of museums. These interactive exhibitions exceed the limits of conventional museums including the distance between visitors and a showpiece, small letters of explanations about a showpiece, brightness of ambient light, and

---

T. Miura and G. Ando—Both authors contributed equally to this manuscript.

K. Miesenberger and G. Kouroupetroglou (Eds.): ICCHP 2018, LNCS 10897, pp. 246–249, 2018.
https://doi.org/10.1007/978-3-319-94274-2_34

Fig. 1. (Left) external appearance view of the railway vehicle from the outside view-point and (center) inside view of the railway vehicle. (Right) The reference VRM system Odakyu VRM [1].

prohibition to touch and manually run a showpiece. One of the good examples is the digital railway museum reported by Narumi et al. [4]. There contents powered by virtual and augmented reality (VR/AR) enable visitors to see and control the movement of various types of kinematics regarding railway technologies including railroad vehicles, engines, and other machine elements. However, their exhibitions and never meant to support visitors with low vision. Also, in some cases, it is a heavy burden for them to go frequently to actual museums.

On the other hand, there is an increasing number of paradigms that virtual museums (VMs) are used as educational materials. The VM can provide experiencing and learning virtual hands-on exhibitions without being limited in a place and a time for the users. However, most of the VM does not always accessible and usable for people with low vision because of the lack of features such as elusive annotations, passive zooming control, and incompatibility of various accessibility functions. In addition, some VMs provide low quality images that users cannot identify the details when they magnify. For example, the Odakyu Virtual Railway Museum (VRM) enables users to view the appearance of railway vehicles reproduced by 3D computer graphics on the Internet, but they cannot see some parts of the vehicles including the roofs and the bottom faces. Also, as mentioned above, not only the Odakyu VRM but also some VMs on the web are inaccessible or have insufficient accessibility functions for people with low vision.

In this paper, our objective is to demonstrate the issues and the solutions of VMs for people with low vision. In order to compare a conventional VM, we first developed a prototype of VMs of railway vehicles for low vision and then experimentally evaluated the VMs to find the requirements that people with low vision can easily control and have experience learning in VMs.

2 Overview of Our Virtual Museum

Our virtual museum (VM) of a railway vehicle for people with low vision has two views including the external appearance view of the vehicle from the outside (left figure of Fig. 1) and the inside view of the vehicle (central figure of Fig. 1). The appearance view enables users to rotate the vehicle horizontally and vertically and to watch its parts that the users scarcely see precisely including its roof and its bottom. This view also has accessibility functions such as controllable zooming-in/out and flexible viewpoint. Also, the users can adjust the visibility of the parts of the vehicle as visible or invisible.

Our VM was also compatible to not only a conventional flat display but also a head-mounted display (HMD). The user worn the HMD on the head can control the viewpoints of the VM by their head rotation and back-and-forth movement.

We employed the Unity 2017 as an integrated development environment and implemented viewpoint functions by the C# programming language.

3   Evaluation

3.1   Participants

There were 5 individuals aged 20 to 22 years with partial visual impairments in this evaluation. All of the participants with visual impairments had been able to manipulate a personal computer with screen reader functions for over three years. The experimenter explained the evaluation procedure to the participants, and all of them agreed to participation.

3.2   Procedure

We asked the participants to find targets in our VMs (left and center figure of Fig. 1) and the Odakyu VRM (right figure of Fig. 1), and then answer the questionnaires including system usability scale (SUS) [2,3], presence questionnaire (PQ) [5], and immersive tendency questionnaire (ITQ) [6]. In the searching task of targets, the participants were asked to conduct the following three tasks:

1. To find four targets (lost properties) in a cabin of our VM with a 23 in. display. The participants should click the targets when they find the targets.
2. To find four targets (lost properties) in a cabin of our VM with an HMD. The participants should make a declaration orally when they find the targets.
3. To find four targets (annotation icons) in the Odakyu VM with a 23 in. display. The participants were asked to click the white icons when they find the targets.

After finishing each task, we asked the participants to answer the SUS and the PQ. In addition, after finishing all the tasks, the participants answered the ITQ items and then gave us the feedbacks including whether they got motion sickness. We evaluate the effectiveness of the VMs based on the task completion time, the overall SUS score, and the PQ scores of each VM.

4   Results and Discussion

In this paper, we discuss the questionnaire data. The left part of Fig. 2 shows the overall SUS scores of each condition. These scores indicated that the participants tended to score our VM with an HMD the highest (median: 93.0), despite the contents of our VM being scored lower than conventional VM according to the

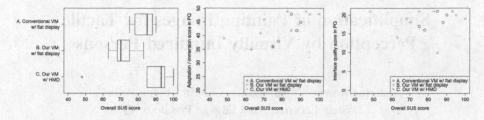

Fig. 2. (Left) overall SUS scores of each VM condition. (Center and right) The relations of overall SUS scores and scores of adaptation/immersion and interface quality in PQ.

overall SUS scores of conditions A and B (median: 85.0 and 70.0). However, one of the participants rated our VM with an HMD the lowest (48 pts). According to the correlation coefficients between overall SUS score in this condition and the FOCUS, INVOL, and GAMES of the ITQ were 0.84, 0.83, and 0.40, respectively. These facts suggest that a VM with HMD is particularly effective to the people with low vision who tend to maintain focus and get involved in the activities on the VM experience. However, low vision people with low immersive tendency preferred to use the VM with a conventional flat display.

On the other hand, our VM with flat display rated lowest in the overall SUS in all conditions. According to the center and right graphs of Fig. 2, in the condition B, there were high correlations between the overall SUS score and the scores of adaptation/immersion and interface quality ($r = 0.63$ and 0.85). These results suggested that our VM with a flat display should improve the operability of the interface: Our VM with a flat display had two view modes to provide multiple perspectives with users but toggling these two sometimes confused the participants.

Acknowledgmentes. This work was partially supported by JSPS KAKENHI Grant Numbers 15K04540 and 15K01015.

References

1. Odakyu virtual railway museum. http://www.odakyu.jp/museum/
2. Bangor, A., Kortum, P.T., Miller, J.T.: An empirical evaluation of the system usability scale. Int. J. Hum.-Comput. Interact. **24**(6), 574–594 (2008)
3. Brooke, J., et al.: Sus-a quick and dirty usability scale. Usability Eval. Ind. **189**(194), 4–7 (1996)
4. Narumi, T., Kasai, T., Honda, T., Aoki, K., Tanikawa, T., Hirose, M.: Digital railway museum: an approach to introduction of digital exhibition systems at the railway museum. In: Yamamoto, S. (ed.) HIMI 2013. LNCS, vol. 8018, pp. 238–247. Springer, Heidelberg (2013). https://doi.org/10.1007/978-3-642-39226-9_27
5. Witmer, B.G., Jerome, C.J., Singer, M.J.: The factor structure of the presence questionnaire. Presence: Teleoper. Virtual Environ. **14**(3), 298–312 (2005)
6. Witmer, B.G., Singer, M.J.: Measuring presence in virtual environments: a presence questionnaire. Presence **7**(3), 225–240 (1998)

Simplification of Painting Images for Tactile Perception by Visually Impaired Persons

Katerine Romeo[1(✉)] ⓘ, Marion Chottin[2], Pierre Ancet[3],
Christele Lecomte[1], and Edwige Pissaloux[1] ⓘ

[1] Rouen Normandy University, 76800 Saint-Etienne du Rouvray, France
katerine.romeo@univ-rouen.fr
[2] ENS Lyon, 69007 Lyon, France
[3] Burgundy University, 21078 Dijon, France

Abstract. The access to artworks by visually impaired people requires a simplified tactile representation of paintings. This paper presents the difficulties of direct transcription of artworks and the test results of simplification of the paintings done by Australian Aborigines which don't have purely visual elements such as shadows or perspective. The implemented methodology is bottom-up: it starts with tactile representation of basic elements relevant to the understanding of the whole painting, then their association into more complex concepts. The context of associations is explained through audio-description. The results of the tests with visually impaired persons are analyzed and explained.

Keywords: Segmentation · Painting · Tactile perception
Multi-modal perception · Blindness · Visually impaired

1 Introduction: Difficulties of a Direct Transcription

When visually impaired people (VIP) go to a museum, they encounter difficulties with the perception of artworks. To benefit from the beauty, emotion or information inspired by these objects, a tactile representation can be one of the solutions for blind persons. The museums for art and science are traditionally organized prominently for the sense of sight, and this organization has been based for a long time on the prohibition of touching the artwork. However, the sense of touch conveys information and aesthetic pleasure as well as the sense of sight. The cognitive virtues of touching have been recognized since Aristotle, and today they are being rediscovered and measured [11, 12]. The aesthetic virtues of contact through touch have been known ever since antiquity and they have been honored regularly in the history of art [13, 14]. Besides, several blind persons such as Marie Heurtin and Helen Keller testify about their tactile and aesthetic experiences [15, 16].

The direct transcription of a painting into a tactile material is possible with different techniques such as embossing, thermoforming, serigraphy, thermo-graphical printing or 3D printing [1]. Examples of realizations with different materials may be touched in the Musée des Beaux Arts of Rouen (France) or the Pinacothcca de Brera of Milan (Italy). Some recommendations for the transcription of documents [2] specify minimum

K. Miesenberger and G. Kouroupetroglou (Eds.): ICCHP 2018, LNCS 10897, pp. 250–257, 2018.
https://doi.org/10.1007/978-3-319-94274-2_35

distances between graphical elements of 2.3 mm in order to respect the tactile acuity. This distance is similar to the gap between the dots in Braille letters. Kinesthetic and proprioceptive perception should be taken into account when geometrical characteristics are used in graphics, such as length of segments or angle: distinction of small contours and very small changes in directions in segments could be ignored and not perceived otherwise. Even when respecting these rules and the original page layout, the result of the transcription of painting images present an overabundance of information which can be discouraging to VIP's.

Another problem in the transcription of paintings is the presence of shadows difficult to recognize when included in the contours of an object. The deformation of objects through perspective, which is usually used for depth perception, may not be as intuitive to VIP's who have to be taught ego-centered and exo-centered views of the body, buildings or objects. Some very interesting work has been done in automatic image transcription of very simple educational graphics [4, 5] that can be applied to tactile transcription of some simple paintings or graphics, but it is necessary to decompose paintings to give access to the meaning of the global picture. Some terms or expressions may mean nothing to congenitally blind persons as mentioned such as "face view" and "profile", or "shadow" and "perspective". However, color names and the semantic field of light should not be banned: these terms are always associated, even with VIP's, to other sensations, (such as the yellow color with heat) and to emotions (such as the red color with anger) and then they can be extremely meaningful [17].

Thus, a direct transcription of the painting on a tactile surface is not relevant for VIP's as it does not allow appropriate understanding of its content and appreciation of the esthetic quality of the artwork. A multi-modal approach is necessary, accompanying the graphical representation with an audio description of the shapes of the objects represented in the painting as well as their location and role [6, 7]. The audio description should use the specific words and definitions from the specific vocabulary used by VIP's [8, 9].

This paper proposes a multi-modal representation of paintings in an interactive way. The paper is organized as follows. Section 2 presents the difficult problem of conservation of meaning after a transcription into a tactile representation. Section 3 discusses the proposed multi-modal representation and the tests with visually impaired persons. Finally we present in Sect. 4 our conclusions and some reflections on future work.

2 Conservation of Meaning

First of all, an artwork is dependent on its visual intensity as explained by De Coster and Loots [3]. It is the degree of vision one can use to understand a painting or a sculpture which can be considered as a visual narrative. Blind people are conscious of this important visual concept on art. The Museums often propose audio-guides or art teachers to explain the artworks in the exhibitions but the explanations are often on the context and not the visual appearance. The cognitive effort produced by visually impaired persons to catch the meaning of an artwork is usually made by the association of the story behind the creation of this artwork and its perceptual features. Of course art is not only about its appearance but also history and philosophy. A meaningful art education would include both explanations and tactile perception. Different details can be presented in an analytical way, including all the eye-catching points of interest. However these details don't have a great significance if the context is not introduced. Only when the global meaning of the painting is understood, can blind persons reach an aesthetic experience [10]. We should also add that aesthetic experiences are not always pleasurable - some are meant to disturb, to perplex or to question – and this can also be described and aroused by the narrative experience, or felt by audio-tactile perception.

The tactile perception is a singular approach to feel a painting: this information is not complete as it is. And it is the same incomplete information when we consider solely the visual appearance of an artwork for seeing people. All of the available information is necessary to explore the artwork in a tactile manner, to understand the shape of its different parts and the relation between them, the context. People, visually impaired or not, generally do not have the experience to explore an artwork tactilely. This is why a multi-modal representation of artworks seems to be quite relevant.

3 Multimodal Representation

To evaluate the relevance of the proposed multi-modal representations of paintings, the bottom-up methodology is implemented. It starts with tactile representation of basic elements relevant to the whole painting understanding, then their associations into more complex concepts and finally into the whole image. The tactile shapes, the context of their associations and the global meaning of the painting are explained with audio-description.

3.1 Experimental Environment

This bottom-up methodology was implemented while testing the aboriginal painting "Dream of the snake" from the Australian painter Warlimpirrnga Tjapaltjarri which is in the Museum of Quai Branly in Paris, France (see Fig. 1 left). It should be noticed that the objects on aboriginal paintings have no edges: they are composed of elementary dots that form different shapes. There are several important reasons for this choice of painting: first of all, this artwork is composed by simple geometric forms, which can be reproduced on a tablet with haptic feedback and that can be recognized through non-expert touch from a user. The second reason is that this painting does not have purely visual elements like shadows, reliefs or perspectives that congenitally blind persons could not understand. Finally, the third reason is that this artwork has a tactile dimension because the original paintings were done on the soil, with fingers digging in the sand [18].

These characteristics of aboriginal paintings guided our selection of a touch stimulation device. The University of Lille's touch-stimulating prototype STIMTAC was selected (Fig. 1 right). This device is designed for displaying tactile textures through scanning the STIMTAC surface with a finger.

Fig. 1. The painting "Dream of the snake" and the touch stimulation device STIMTAC

3.2 Participants

The evaluation of our experiments has been achieved through two series of tests. The first tests were executed to verify the psycho-cognitive perception of stimuli generated by the STIMTAC tactile stimulation device. Three visually impaired persons with one of them congenitally blind, gave us the first results of perception of different textures and forms generated by STIMTACT that supports friction reduction by means of a squeeze film effect.

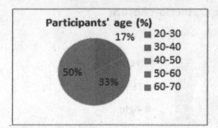
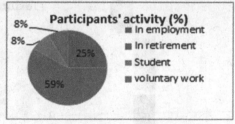

Fig. 2. Participants to the evaluation of the painting on the tactile tablet STIMTAC.

The second set of tests were completed with twelve participants, two of them congenitally blind, six adventitiously blind and four with severe visual impairment. The test was based on the discovery of the aboriginal painting "Dream of the snake". The evaluation was done by VIP's where 58% of the participants were men and 42% women. The majority of the participants were more than fifty years old and some were in their twenties. A great number were retired and 25% were employed (See Fig. 2). All of the participants were expecting a new haptic tool which could help them to discover some artwork through touching.

3.3   Results

The participants to the tests appreciated the idea of discovering a painting in a tactile way. The decomposition of the painting "Dream of the snake" into small elements like dots, lines and composite figures (see Fig. 3) was intended to test the ability to recognize simple forms in the different tactile perception of friction.

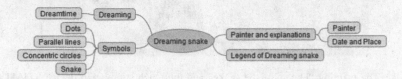

Fig. 3. The decomposition of the aboriginal painting "Dreaming snake" in small elements and the description of the context.

The stimulation of the vibro-tactile device STIMTAC creates the perception of textures and models the interaction between the finger and the surface of the pad. The perception may be the texture of an object or the smoothness/roughness of the explored area comparing to the strength of the finger's contact and the orientation of its movement.

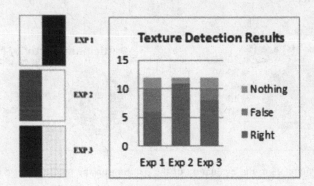

Fig. 4. Results on texture detection tests with visually impaired participants

The experiment was carried out in three phases: First of all, a texture detection test was made. Two different textures were shown side by side and the participant had to feel with a finger on the screen of the STIMTAC tablet, the textures and the limit between them. Then, the participant had to indicate which one of the two textures presented a rough surface. The detection results of this experiment with textures are shown in Fig. 4. The majority of VIP's detected the surface with the rough texture but the novel nature of the signal surprised some of the participants who were expecting to touch some hard material, and they could not name what they felt as "surface with friction" or "rough surface" or anything else. The white textures present a smooth surface and the dark textures create a friction-like perception.

The next experiment had a progressive approach in the detection of figures, from simple to complex shapes. Apart from the explanations on the experiment and the test progress, no help was provided to the participants, no feedback was given. The participants had to describe what they detected. Circular shapes were difficult to recognize, the first figures were dots (See Fig. 5. – pictures 1, 2, 3) and the aim of this experiment was to detect one or several textured patches on the surface. The second set of figures was parallel lines and concentric circles (Fig. 5. – pictures 4, 5, 6). The aim was to feel the transition from one texture to another between the lines and to feel the white areas between them, as well as the center of the circles. The third set was more complex figures as assembled from simple forms (Fig. 5. – pictures 7, 8) where the global perception was asked. Finally the snake (Fig. 5. – picture 9) was scanned with one finger and detected partially or as a global shape. It is a difficult exercise to name the perception of a complicated shape without help. However it can be observed that the detection results are improving with experience as shown in Fig. 6, and the participants have some perception of the global shape on the screen.

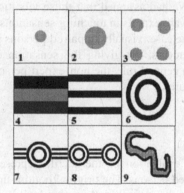

Fig. 5. Simple and complex figures presented for detection by VIP

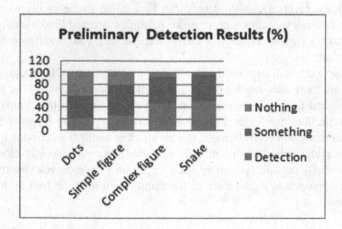

Fig. 6. Preliminary results from the tests with the STIMTAC tablet, on simple and complex figures being part of the painting "The dream of the snake".

The third phase of the experiment continued with the same figures, but this time with an audio signal describing the painting and the meaning of the symbols (Fig. 3) and it finishes with the legend of the snake in aboriginal Australia. The participants were asked if the audio-description helped the detection of the figures. Only fifty percent of them agreed because they found the haptic signal was not sufficiently in relief or in contrast. The alternation of textures and contours was expected. As the second part of the experiment was done without feedback, the figures could not have been learned. An audio-description during the tactile discovery is necessary. The majority of the participants agreed that the figures become meaningful with the context explained and that the tactile perception enhance the meaning given through the audio-description if a real tactile dialogue is provided.

The decomposition of the painting into small elements proved to be too analytic and the integration of these small details in the whole image was not sufficiently clear. We understand that the notion of detail is very well known by visually impaired persons but it appears that contextualizing these details more clearly is necessary.

The nature of the vibratory signal on the tablet did not allow for adequate recognition of defined figures. We had assumed that these vibrations would be more easily recognizable by VIP's who are experts in touching sensations. In fact, the tests showed us that it was not always the case: visually impaired persons perceive the vibrations as small very sensitive movements, not giving the sensation of a shape or the border between two textures. As a general rule, the non-expert persons in touching had better results in perception of figures.

4 Conclusion

This paper addresses the evaluation of the tactile representation of an aboriginal painting by visually impaired persons. The original bottom-up evaluation methodology was defined and implemented. The collected results show that the simplification of the tactile representation linked to the audio contextualization help the tactile exploration of the paintings. Inversely, audio-description is a guide to the tactile recognition of shapes. This is a relevant approach to make paintings accessible to visually impaired people and to all persons curious of tactile experiences who want to enhance their sensibility to art.

Our future work will explore the possibility of a tablet with tactile pins or points (taxels) that are more adequate for perception of the borders of figures. The participants to our tests asked for a greater size of tablet (A4) and they wish to touch with both hands and more than one finger. For the discovery of a painting it seems essential to explore bi-manually and pluri-digitally. For an efficient tactile transcription of paintings and accompanying audio-description, it is really necessary to work in close collaboration with visually impaired people in order to produce the most relevant results. This participative approach is a guarantee of the appropriation of the tool by the visually impaired people.

Acknowledgment. The research on which this work is based is funded by CNRS, TETMOST project, and it is done with the collaboration between University of Rouen Normandy and Department of Seine Maritime and Espace Handicap of the University of Rouen.

References

1. Krivec, T., Muck, T., Fugger Germadnik, R., Majnaric, I., Golob, G.: Adapting artworks for people who are blind or visually impaired using raised printing. J. Vis. Impair. Blind. **108**, 68–76 (2014)
2. Bris, M.: Recommandations pour la transcription des documents. Service des Documents Adaptés pour Déficients Visuels, CNEFEI Suresnes, 17 November 2003
3. De Coster, K., Loots, G.: Somewhere in between touch and vision. In search of a meaningful art education for blind individuals. Int. J. Art Des. Educ. **23**(3), 326–334 (2004)
4. Haddad, Z., Chen, Y., Krahe, J.L.: Image processing and pattern recognition tools for the automatic image transcription. In: Miesenberger, K., Bühler, C., Penaz, P. (eds.) ICCHP 2016. LNCS, vol. 9758, pp. 197–203. Springer, Cham (2016). https://doi.org/10.1007/978-3-319-41264-1_26
5. Chen, Y.: Analyse et Interprétation d'images à l'usage des personnes non-voyantes, Application à la generation automatique d'images en relief à partir d'équipements banalisés. Thesis Paris 8, Ecole Doctorale CLI, 27 November 2015
6. Fryer, L.: An Introduction to Audio Description: A Practical Guide. Routledge, Abingdon (2016)
7. Ginley, B.: Museums: a whole new world for visually impaired people. Disabil. Stud. Q. **33**(2) (2015). http://dsq-sds.org/article/view/4622/3945
8. Kleege, G., Wallin, S.: Audio description as a pedagogical tool. Disabil. Stud. Q. **33**(2) (2015). http://dsq-sds.org/article/view/4622/3945
9. Mills, M.: Listening to images: audio description, the translation overlay, and image retrieval. Cine-Files **8**, (2015). http://www.thecine-files.com/listening-to-images-audio-description-the-translation-overlay-and-image-retrieval/
10. Lorin-Etuy, D., Bauweens, M.: Comment le cerveau réagit-il à l'art? Hors-Série Art, pp. 64–69, October 2016
11. Aristote: De l'âme. GF Flammarion, Paris (1999)
12. Hatvelle, Y., Streri, A., Gentaz, E.: Toucher pour connaître: Psychologie cognitive de la perception tactile manuelle. PUF, Paris (2000)
13. Dent, P. (ed.): Sculpture and Touch. Routledge, Abingdon (2014)
14. Marinetti: Le tactillisme. Manifeste futuriste. In: Giovanni, L. (ed.) Futurisme. Lausanne, Editions l'Âge d'Homme (1973)
15. Keller, H.: Histoire de ma vie. Payot, Paris (2001)
16. Villey, P.: Le Monde des aveugles: Essai de psychologie. Flammarion, Paris (1914)
17. Verine, B. (ed.): Dire le non-visuel: Approches pluridisciplinaires des discours sur les perceptions autres que la vue. Presses universitaires de Liège (2014)
18. Glowczewski, B.: Du rêve à la loi chez les Aborigènes: mythes, rites et organisation sociale en Australie. PUF, Paris (1991)

Towards Haptic Surface Devices with Force Feedback for Visually Impaired People

Simon Gay(✉)⬤, Marc-Aurèle Rivière⬤, and Edwige Pissaloux⬤

LITIS, Université de Rouen Normandie, Mont-Saint-Aignan, France
simon.gay1@univ-rouen.fr

Abstract. This paper presents a new haptic surface tablet that can provide force feedback to the user. Force feedback means that the device can react to the user's movements and apply a force against or in-line with these movements, according to the tactile properties of a displayed image. The device consists of a frame attached to a tactile tablet that generates a force feedback to user's finger when exploring the surface, providing haptic informations about the displayed image. The experimental results suggest the relevance of this tablet as an assistive device for visually impaired people in perceiving and understanding the content of a displayed image. Several potential applications are briefly presented.

Keywords: Haptic accessibility to 2D images
Assistive device for visually impaired · Force feedback · Haptic surface

1 Introduction

Visually Impaired People's (VIP) access to 2D information is still an open question with no fully relevant technology proposed yet. Existing commercially available devices and academia prototypes have several drawbacks which prevent VIP from using them on a daily basis. Indeed, these devices are usually dedicated displaying only one type of data: texture or shape or Braille coded text. For some of these devices, VIP have serious difficulties recognizing simple forms because they cannot feel the edges and their exploration is not assisted [1]. Therefore, a device of new type should be designed and prototyped. This paper proposes such a solution: a Force Feedback Tablet (named F2T), which allows users to feel the edges and textures of 2D objects, and assists the image exploration.

The paper is organized as follows: Sect. 2 gives a review of existing technologies for haptic devices; Sect. 3 addresses the concept of the F2T, its working principles and its functionalities, Sect. 4 explains the F2T simulator's usage and on-going applications. Section 5 encompasses some conclusive remarks and future developments of the F2T project.

K. Miesenberger and G. Kouroupetroglou (Eds.): ICCHP 2018, LNCS 10897, pp. 258–266, 2018.
https://doi.org/10.1007/978-3-319-94274-2_36

2 Status of Haptic Devices

This section reviews existing devices that can display and convey 2D images on a surface (such as a screen) through tactile stimulation. We classified haptic technologies for touch stimulation devices into three groups, based on the method used to convey tactile *stimuli*: haptic tablets that physically modify their surfaces, haptic tablets whose screen stimulates the user's skin, and wearable devices that apply haptic stimuli directly on the skin of the user (e.g. haptic glove and stylus-like devices).

2.1 Haptic Modifiable Surfaces

These devices produce a tactile image using a matrix of movable pins called *taxels* (tactile elements). By moving taxels up and down, it is possible to display the edges and relief of an object. A large variety of actuators are used in academic and commercial devices: piezoelectric benders (*Hyperbraille* [2]), solenoids (flat solenoids in the *BlindPad* [3] and bi-stable solenoids in *Graphical Interface* [4]), electric motors (*InFORM* [5]), and shape memory alloys (SMA) (*TactiPAD* [6]). The advantages of these devices is that they can produce images similar to bas-relief that can be explored with all fingers. However, the size and number of actuators reduces the resolution of displayed images, and makes those devices heavy and expensive.

To reduce these problems, Orbit Research developed the *Graphiti* tablet [7], that uses only one motor per line and per column of pins. However, images cannot be refreshed instantly because all the pins cannot be moved simultaneously. Inventivio GmbH proposes the *Tactonom* [8], that generates images with little steel balls, through a process similar to printing. Although this principle allows high resolution images (the Tactonom device generates images of 10,500 taxels), the image update takes several seconds. A version of the *BlindPad* [9] uses a matrix of cells made of shape memory alloys and an air pump. Electrodes can heat up SMA cells to make them ductile, while the pump blows in or out to push or retract the cells. The refreshment rate is however limited by the heating and dissipation time.

Although these principles reduce the number of actuators, they increase the image update delay. The *Virtual Tactile Display* [10] uses a taxel surface based on the *OPTACON* [11], that the user moves over a large surface, reducing the number of actuators. This principle makes it possible to reduce the number of actuator and to provide real-time image refreshment, but makes it impossible to freely explore the surface with multiple fingers.

Although taxel surfaces allow for easy exploration, they suffer from serious disadvantages: they have a poor resolution, are heavy and expensive. Several solutions allow to reduce these problems, but at the cost of the image refreshment rate or the possibility of free exploration. Moreover, those solutions do not allow the transmission of essential surface properties of the image, such as textures.

2.2 Stimulation Screen Devices

These devices stimulate the user's skin by modifying the screen properties. Unlike taxel tablets, this technology makes it possible to reproduce textures with high resolutions. Another advantage is that the haptic surface can be transparent and placed over a screen, to improve interaction with sighted people. The most common solution is to make the surface vibrate using piezoelectric vibrators. The *StimTAC* [12] tablet uses vibrations (stationary waves) to generate an air cushion between the user's finger and the screen surface, modifying the friction at the contact point. *Hap2U*'s tablet [13] uses several patterns of vibrations to stimulate user's skin receptors and simulate different kinds of textures. The *TeslaTouch* tablet [14] modifies friction through electro-vibrations: by applying high tension between the finger and a conductive layer under an insulated screen, the device generates an attractive electric force that increases friction between the surface and finger.

Haptic stimulation tablets are lighter and less expensive than taxel tablets. As they can be used with a screen, they enable new applications for sighted people, and facilitate the development of viable products for the general public. However, they are limited to a single-touch usage and they do not allow to sense object edges, making it difficult for VIP to identify shapes.

2.3 Wearable Devices

These wearable devices reproduce tactile stimuli directly on the skin of the user, through vibrations and/or taxels, while exploring a surface such as a standard tactile tablet. As stimuli are delivered at specific locations of the skin instead of the whole surface, these stimuli can be generated with only a limited number of actuators and with less energy. Moreover, as stimuli can be provided whether the user is touching a surface or not, more general applications, such as environment exploration, can be considered. The *TactiNET* [15] uses a piezoelectric transducer on each finger to simulate textures, and the *Soft-Actuator-Based Wearable Tactile Display* [16] uses a matrix of dielectric actuators worn under the fingertips, working like a tiny taxel surface that the user can use to explore a large surface. A stylus can be easier to use than gloves, but it is limited to single-touch applications. The *TactiPen* [17] uses a Braille cell which allows to read texts. The *Ubi-pen* [18] provides both edges stimuli, through a matrix of taxels, and textures thanks to a vibration motor. The tip of the *Reflective Haptics Touch Pen* [19] consists of a metal ball, that can be slowed down by a magnetic field, simulating friction changes.

Several devices stimulate mechanoreceptors through stretching skin: Gleeson et al. [20] propose a device where a *tactor* can stretch fingertip skin. Guinan *et al.* [21] integrated this device in thumbsticks of a joypad. The *STReSS* device [22] uses a little matrix of 64 piezoelectric actuators that laterally stretch finger skin when the user laterally explores the surface.

Wearable devices solve several problems met in haptic surfaces: the number of actuators is very limited, and they can be used with regular tactile tablets. However, these devices have to be worn during the whole utilization time, which can make them uncomfortable after long periods, or require to carry and manipulate a stylus in addition to the tactile tablet.

The above short review shows that there is no touch stimulating device that could display both edges and textures of a tactile image, while being light, inexpensive and easy to use. Indeed, these requests seem mutually exclusive when considering the physical phenomena involved in haptic stimulation technologies. Moreover, none of these devices guides the exploration of the displayed information. The F2T offers a new alternative to overcome the limits of the aforementioned categories of systems.

3   Principle of the F2T System

The F2T's aim is to allow VIP to perceive edges and textures without using taxels. A force feedback is used to simulate the edges of a virtual object and guide the finger when following them. Several force feedback 3D pointing devices are available on the market, such as 3D mice (e.g. *Novint Falcon*) and stylus (e.g. *3D System Touch*), but their force feedback systems are based on complex mechanisms, such as robotic arms, which make them expensive and hardly portable. To overcome these disadvantages, we propose a 2D force feedback system based on a very simple actuator system. F2T is based on a mobile support integrating a flat thumbstick on the top. This support is constrained and moved by two actuated orthogonal axis X and Y (Fig. 1). The support position is servo-controlled by the thumbstick to follow the user's finger. Several offsets can be added to this servoing control, according to the support position over the displayed tactile image, to simulate edges and textures through force feedback: a force effect simulating objects' height variations and edges, a fluid friction force and a solid friction force simulating textures of the current object point. The resulting movement $\vec{V}$ of the mobile support is given by (1):

$$\vec{V} = (\vec{V_1} - \delta.F_{s(x,y)}.\frac{\vec{V_1}}{|\vec{V_1}|}) \cdot f_{s(x,y)} \;\; ; \;\; f_{s(x,y)} = \begin{cases} 1 \text{ if } |\vec{V_1}| \geq F_{s(x,y)} \\ 0 \text{ else} \end{cases} \quad (1)$$

$$\vec{V_1} = \alpha.\vec{J} - \beta.\overrightarrow{G_{(x,y)}} - \gamma.F_{f(x,y)}.\vec{J}$$

$\vec{J}$ is the thumbstick input vector, $\vec{V}$ is the speed vector of the mobile support, $\overrightarrow{G_{(x,y)}}$ is the surface gradient (slant) at current position (x, y), and $F_{f(x,y)}$ is the fluid friction at (x, y). f_s and $F_{s(x,y)}$ characterize the solid friction. α, β, γ and δ are coefficients linked to the materials and actuators used for the F2T. α is the servoing coefficient, β, γ and δ weight the different forces applied to the mobile support. Therefore, it is possible to simulate both the edges and textures of objects.

Fig. 1. Left: principle of the F2T. A mobile support, with a thumbstick on its top, is servo-controlled to follow the thumbstick movements. Offsets can be applied to this position control, generating a force feedback. Middle: simulated F2T based on the *Blender Game Engine*. The thumbstick is represented on the orange support. Right: RGB image describing the tactile properties of the surface: red channel indicates fluid friction, green channel indicates elevation and blue channel indicates solid friction. While exploring the surface, we experience fluid friction when moving on red and yellow discs (the mobile support is slowed down), edges of green and yellow circles, allowing to follow them by gently pressing the thumbstick, and solid friction on the blue disc (the support remains stuck if we do not press the thumbstick hard enough). (Color figure online)

An interesting aspect of this force feedback system is that it can also guide the user's finger, which opens new possibilities for VIP assistance, (cf. Sect. 4). The guiding possibilities can be enabled by moving the mobile support without considering the thumbstick values. It is then possible to move the support according to a predefined trajectory (e.g. to draw a figure or a path on a map, or to move toward the location where a relevant information is displayed).

4   Exploring 2D Surface with the F2T

A simulator of the F2T (Fig. 1) was developed using the Blender Game Engine[1]; its control system was developed in Java. The user can interact with the tablet using the thumbstick of a standard USB gamepad. The tactile properties of the picture are defined using the following RGB color code: the red channel indicates fluid friction, green indicates height and blue indicates solid friction. A cyan dot is marked every 100 ms to record the previous positions of the support and observe speed variations. Figure 1 (right picture) gives an example of tactile surface with a surface with high fluid friction (red disc), an elevated smooth surface (green disc), an elevated surface with high fluid friction (yellow disc) and a surface with high solid friction (blue disc). We then move on the surface while observing the reactions of the simulated tablet (Fig. 1 left). When we move on the red circle, the support is significantly slowed down, simulating a fluid friction. When we move on the green (elevated) area, and gently pressing the thumbstick, the support resists to the movement and *slides* along the circle edge. We need to press the

---

[1] https://docs.blender.org/manual/en/dev/game_engine/index.html.

thumbstick harder to make the support move on top of the green area. When the support leaves the green area, we observe a short jump: indeed, the surface gradient is negative, therefore the support moves in the same direction as the thumbstick, simulating the *descent* of the support. We observe similar reactions when moving on top of the yellow area, because it is both an elevated and rough surface. The blue surface simulates solid friction when the support moves over it. While we gently press the thumbstick, the support cannot move. When we press the thumbstick hard enough to overcome the friction, the support moves, but with a constant resistance.

Several applications of the F2T have already been investigated using this simulated tablet. The following applications demonstrate the possibilities of the F2T (texture, relief and edge display and guiding possibilities):

Access to Art Works. The proposed approach [1] allows to discover the content of a painting by providing a tactile representation of the main objects in the scene. The assisted exploration of objects' edges allows faster understanding of the scene, as it is possible to guide VIP while describing the story of a painting/picture through audio feedback. Indeed, F2T assists with the spatialization of all the elements, and helps the user draw complex shapes to better imagine them.

Reading Assistance. For this application, each line of *text* is represented as a trench that guides the finger, and makes it possible to follow lines and to count them. By adding Braille cells or text-to-speech capabilities, the F2T would allow to access text in a spatial way rather than in a sequential way. It is possible to make automatic carriage return and to follow links (such as figure reference or footnote) using the guidance mode. Figure 2 shows an example of tactile image that we tested with the simulated tablet. We observed that while we gently press the thumbstick, the mobile support is maintained in the trench and slides along the line. We need to press the thumbstick strongly to move out of the trench. The support then reacts as it jumps from one trench to another. These jumps can be used to count lines and localize specific information in the text.

Journey Preparation Assistance. In the example given in Fig. 3, buildings are represented as high surfaces, roads as smooth surfaces, and accessible areas as rough surfaces. The path of a journey is represented as a trench, that guides the user through the main path. However, it is still possible, by pressing the thumbstick harder, to move out of the trench and explore surrounding areas. In this map example, we followed the main path, then explored surrounding areas by following a secondary path (smooth surface) before returning to the main path until reaching the destination. The guidance possibilities allows to show the path and locate nearby important places, enabling the user to spatialize important places before freely exploring the environment.

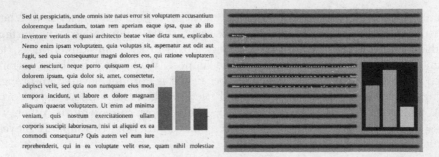

Fig. 2. Reading application. Each line is represented as a trench (dark lines) that guides the finger. Text can be read with a braille cell on the side of the tablet or with a text-to-speech system. These trenches allow to count lines and spatialize information. The guidance possibilities allow to guide the user for an automatic carriage return, to move from a reference link to a specific information (e.g. reference, figure or footnote).

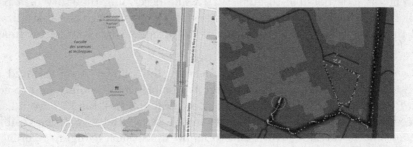

Fig. 3. Left : map from OpenStreetMap. Right: simplified map. The path is a trench (black) that guides user. Building are elevated places, surrounding areas are rough surfaces and other paths are smooth surfaces. The user's finger is guided by the main path. It is however possible to explore surrounding areas too. The guidance possibilities allow to show the main path in order to help user spatialize it, before letting the user freely explore the area.

5 Conclusion and Future Work

We proposed a haptic surface that partially corrects the disadvantages of current haptic devices, as mentionned in Sect. 2. Indeed, the F2T system allows to represent both edges and textures of objects, with a high resolution and no latency, while being light, inexpensive, and easily scalable. Moreover, it brings a new feature: guiding the user's finger, allowing the device to further interact with him, and to help him to spatialize information. We hope that this system will enable new assistive uses for VIP, and help better understand how we construct our spatial perception from touch, thanks to the human-machine interaction possibilities it provides. In our future endeavors, we plan to test the F2T with VIP and develop an improved version of the device, like a multi-touch system (using multiple thumbsticks), a better texture feedback using a piezoelectric vibrator on the thumbstick, and an actuated support to move the thumbstick up and down to improve the experience of relief.

References

1. Ancet, P., Chottin, M., Pissaloux, E., Romeo, K., Rivière, M.-A., Gay, S.L.: Toucher ou être touché: les vertus inclusives du movement et de la sensibilité tactile. Workshop, Défi AUTON, CNRS, Paris (2018)
2. Prescher, D., Borschein, J., Köhlmann, W., Weber, G.: Touching graphical applications: bimanual tactile interaction on the HyperBraille pin-matrix display. Univ. Access Inf. Soc. **17**(2), 391–409 (2018)
3. Zarate, J.J., Gudozhnik, O., Ruch, A.S., Shea, H.: Keep in touch: portable haptic display with 192 high speed taxels. In: Proceedings of the 2017 CHI Conference Extended Abstracts on Human Factors in Computing Systems, pp. 349–352 (2017)
4. Simeonov, S., Simeonova, N.: Graphical interface for visually impaired people based on bi-stable solenoids. Int. J. Soft Comput. Softw. Eng. **3**, 128–131 (2014)
5. Leithinger, D., Follmer, S., Olwal, A., Ishii, H.: Shape displays: spatial interaction with dynamic physical form. IEEE Comput. Graph. Appl. **5**, 5–11 (2015)
6. Velázquez, R., Pissaloux, E., Hafez, M., Szewczyk, J.: Tactile rendering with shape memory alloy pin-matrix. IEEE Trans. Instrum. Meas. **57**(5), 1051–1057 (2008)
7. Aph.org: APH - graphiti graphics display (2016). http://www.aph.org/graphiti/, Accessed 31 Jan 2018
8. Tactonom.com: Tactonom - the tactile graphics display (2017). www.tactonom. com/. Accessed 31 Jan 2018
9. Besse, N., Rosset, S., Zarate, J.J., Shea, H.: Flexible active skin, large reconfigurable arrays of individually addressed shape memory polymer actuators. In: Advanced Material Technologies, vol. 2, no. 10 (2017)
10. Maucher, T., Meier, K., Schemmel, J.: An interactive tactile graphics display. In: Proceedings of the 6th International Symposium on Signal Processing and its Applications, pp. 190–193 (2001)
11. Goldish, L.H., Taylor, H.E.: The optacon: a valuable device for blind persons. New Outlook Blind **68**(2), 49–56 (1974)
12. Biet, M.: Conception et contrôle d'actionneurs électro-actifs dédiés à la stimulation tactile. Ph.D., Université Lille1 (2008)
13. Bernard, F.: Conception, fabrication et caractérisation d'une dalle haptique à base de micro-actionneurs piézoélectriques. Ph.D., Université Grenoble (2016)
14. Bau, O., Poupyrev, I., Israr, A., Harrison, C., TeslaTouch: electrovibration for touch surfaces. In: ACM Symposium on User Interface Software and Technology (2010)
15. Maurel, F.: La TactiNET. 27ème conférence francophone sur l'Interaction Homme-Machine, pp. d09 (2015)
16. Koo, I., Jung, K., Koo, J., Nam, J.-D., Lee, Y., Choi, H.: Development of soft-actuator-based wearable tactile display. IEEE Trans. Rob. **24**, 549–558 (2008)
17. Lecolinet, E., Mouret, G.: TACTIBALL, TACTIPEN, TACTITAB ou comment "toucher du doigt" les données de son ordinateur. In: The Proceedings of IHM 2005. ACM Press (2005)
18. Kyung, K.-U., Lee, J.-Y., Park, J.: Haptic stylus and empirical studies on braille, button, and texture display. J. Biomed. Biotechnol. **2008**, 327–334 (2008)

19. Wintergerst, G., Jagodzinski, R., Hemmert, F., Müller, A., Joost, G.: Reflective haptics: enhancing stylus-based interactions on touch screens. In: Kappers, A.M.L., van Erp, J.B.F., Bergmann Tiest, W.M., van der Helm, F.C.T. (eds.) EuroHaptics 2010. LNCS, vol. 6191, pp. 360–366. Springer, Heidelberg (2010). https://doi.org/10.1007/978-3-642-14064-8_52

20. Gleeson, B.T., Stewart, C.A., Provancher, W.R.: Improved tactile shear feedback: tactor design and an aperture-based restraint. IEEE Trans. Haptics **4**, 253–262 (2011)

21. Guinan, A.L., Montandon, M.N., Caswell, N.A., Provancher, W.R.: Skin stretch feedback for gaming environments. In: IEEE Symposium on Haptic Audio-Visual Environments and Games (2012)

22. Wang, Q., Hayward, V.: Compact, portable, modular, high-performance, distributed tactile transducer device based on lateral skin deformation. In: Proceedings of the 14th Symposium on Haptic Interfaces For Virtual Environment and Teleoperator Systems IEEE VR, 67–72 (2006)

Art Masterpieces Accessibility for Blind and Visually Impaired People

Virginio Cantoni[1], Luca Lombardi[1], Alessandra Setti[1],
Stanislav Gyoshev[2], Dimitar Karastoyanov[2(✉)],
and Nikolay Stoimenov[2]

[1] Dipartimento di Ingegneria Industriale e dell'Informazione,
Università di Pavia, Pavia, Italy
{virginio.cantoni,luca.lombardi,
alessandra.setti}@unipv.it
[2] Institute of Information and Communication Technologies,
Bulgarian Academy of Sciences, Sofia, Bulgaria
stanislavgyoshev@mail.bg, dkarast@iinf.bas.bg,
nikistoimenow@gmail.com

Abstract. A new representation of content for haptic exploration of two-dimensional pictorial art masterpieces is presented. To realize a "tactile image", pictures must be simplified and converted to a bas-relief with distinct and logically homogeneous areas, so that each segment can convey the original content in an intelligible way. Pictures must be digitized, modified, adapted and reconstructed as 3D models that are finally processed by a 3D printer to get an object analyzable through fingertips. We assess the quality and efficiency of the proposed solution through a cooperation with the Italian Union of Blind and Visually Impaired People. The resulting representations were implemented in two different events, gathering visitors' comments. Remarks obtained during the exhibition in Pavia in 2015 led to a version of a tactile image that is now shown in Milan, at the Pinacoteca di Brera, beside the original masterpiece. The collected comments confirm that the approach is appreciated.

Keywords: Accessibility · Tactile image · Haptic exploration
Visually impaired people · Image segmentation · 3D modeling
3D digitization · 3D printing

1 Introduction

Blind or visually impaired people exploit tactile sensing to access information about the outside world; several initiatives to improve the accessibility to public spaces and events, among which museums and cultural exhibitions, offer objects suitable to haptic exploration. For example, the Museum Access Consortium [1] strives to enable people with disabilities to access cultural facilities in the metropolitan area of New York; in Italy, the State Tactile Museum "Homer" [2] is an international reference point in the aesthetic education for visually impaired people who want to approach and learn art by touch. The usage of tactile diagrams is becoming more and more popular, and literature

© Springer International Publishing AG, part of Springer Nature 2018
K. Miesenberger and G. Kouroupetroglou (Eds.): ICCHP 2018, LNCS 10897, pp. 267–274, 2018.
https://doi.org/10.1007/978-3-319-94274-2_37

can be found on the best practices in using them [3–7], but there are no yet easy to use technologies for reliable semantic segmentation of images. The goal is to produce an object as a 3D plate (starting from a 2D original source – pictures, icons, tapestries) with appropriate contours around the salient components and identified by specific Braille annotations [8].

2   State of the Art

Museums have come a long way for the accessibility for visually impaired people. Among the pioneers in this field, Elisabeth Salzhauer Axel in 1987 founded the Art Education for the Blind (AEB) that is still one of the most active organizations in this field [9, 10]. Nevertheless, even today, services for visually impaired visitors are extremely limited in most museums. A few of them adopt Braille descriptive booklets, verbal imaging tours and collections of objects that can be touched. The Museum of Modern Art (MoMA) in New York offers art courses to improve learning through hands-on activities and tactile diagrams [11]. All over the world, exhibitions of masterpiece replicas and specialized tours are provided for the exploration of artwork through touch (e.g. Smithsonian American Art Museum, Metropolitan Museum of Art, Van Gogh Museum Amsterdam [12], etc.). The Kaunas Museum for Blind People [13] offers a completely invisible exhibition; visitors can only feel through the audio, tactile and olfactory senses, with paths realized with hanging objects, elastic bands, sounds, smells, touch finger spaces, including Braille characters and ordinary signs and inscriptions.

Replicas range from 2D+ relief paintings, with added volume and texture, to bas-reliefs, and full 3D. Many kinds of possible representations implemented using computer-based tools are proposed [14] to produce tile diagrams. Recently, a new approach has been introduced: Hybrid - Enhancing the Learning Experience, where Hybrid stands for any combination of Braille, large print, e-text, tactile graphics, accessible-PDF, etc. [15]. In addition, paintings interpretations can be conveyed through proxemic audio for interactive sonic experiences, resulting in an immersive multi-modal experience for both blind and sighted people [16]. Talking Tactile Tablet [17] are produced, simple computer peripheral device acting as viewer for audio/tactile materials. A new approach to painting works, descriVEDENDO [18], states methods and guidelines for the verbal description of the work of art, according to the needs of people with visual disabilities and at the same time facilitating communication between sighted, low-vision and blind people.

3   Methods for 3D Digitization

The new digital model, that can be classified among the Hybrid solutions, is exemplified in the tactile plate represented in Fig. 1 and it consists of salient segments generated by non-trivial image processing methods annotated in Braille.

Over time, painters discovered cues that helped them to develop their works to favor the viewer's interpretation of images. We engaged in solving the "inverse problem": automatic image analysis and interpretation. A "remediation" process that is "the formal logic by which new media refashions prior media forms" throughout a "channel" that lacks the visual bandwidth is exploited [19]. Technologies are coming to the forefront, generating new tools and facilities to improve information broadcasting and optimal strategies to achieve optimal "content media conversion".

Fig. 1. Right side: legend and short explanation in multilingual Braille characters, reading "Christ and the Samaritan woman are standing in front of Jacob's well. Behind them, on the left, is a disciple with loaves in his mantle. Five other disciples are conversing behind the well. In the background a monumental column and a city in the distance are seen." Left side: 2D painting translated for haptic exploration exploiting morphology and Braille Annotation. Note that salient segments are coded by three relief levels.

The first problem is to choose the channels to be used and their primitives: we selected text (Braille characters) and morphology (basic patterns). The four main tasks related to the production of tactile plates are: (i) image segmentation, (ii) assignment of Braille label code to each segment, (iii) label distribution among the internal contours of each detected salient component, and (iv) definition of a suggested scan-path [20]. In all these steps, the explicit author message and the visitors target education must be taken into account. Multiresolution approaches to detect coarse and fine details are used to solve task (i) The approach for artwork segmentation is a hybrid solution based on Hough transform and DoG (Difference of Gaussians) to tackle multiresolution and Canny filter primitives to manage the selection of relevant contours and their propagation until they remain meaningful. During step (ii) a limited set of 5-15 labels per painting is selected, with "smart" mnemonic and likeness characteristics, suited to be combined to a legend constrained in a small tactile border. In step (iii) distribution, density and out- and in-border distance of labels is evaluated to cover effectively the single segments supporting the morphological primitive detection. Task (iv) defines an optimized scan-path to communicate the painting content and the message of the author in a comprehensive and effective way. Art experts' advices are required in all the four phases, even if the goal is a (semi-)automatic process. Interaction with users is mandatory too, particularly in the last phase when a suggested scan-path for the content exploration needs to be defined and audio transmitted or written in the caption, to support visually impaired people in the author message interpretation.

4   Previous Achievements and New Assessment

In the area of application of 3D technologies, in the framework of the European project Advanced Computing for Innovation, the University of Pavia (Italy) and the Bulgarian Academy of Sciences created a new representation of artwork in 2015, for the exhibition "Pavia. The Battle. The Future – 1525-2015, Nothing was the same again" organized as a satellite event of the International Exhibition EXPO 2015 [8]. Seven prestigious large tapestries (7 × 4 m) with scenes from the battle were used as starting 2D data source to extract and create a 3D model of a first version of tactile plates, printed by a color 3D printer (see Fig. 2). This exhibition attracted more than 11,000 visitors. The Italian Union of Blind and Visually Impaired People in Pavia [21] considered it a significant step forward in the digitization of content for visually impaired people.

Fig. 2. Haptic presentation of a tapestry with Braille annotations in areas closed by contours.

A second version of a tactile plate, constituted of seven salient segments, has been produced in 2016 for the masterpiece "Christ and the Samaritan Woman" by Annibale Carracci (1555), at the Pinacoteca di Brera, in Milan (see Fig. 3).

Fig. 3. Left: "Christ and the Samaritan Woman" (2.25 m × 1.75 m) in Brera and its tactile plate 42 × 29 cm placed beside the original masterpiece. Middle: exploration by both hands, for a better comprehension [22, 23]. Right: the 3D morphology and the semantic annotation of image segments.

The heights of the 3D relief lines and the fillings were defined experimentally, and fixed after tests with visually impaired people. The improvements were not limited to analyses and interpretation, but also consistently to fingertip impact (Braille character size, relief and distribution according to internal and external contour). The plate is installed in Brera since November 2016 and positively "tested" by hundreds of visually impaired people.

5   Conclusions and Future Developments

Remarks collected in Pavia, Milan, and during a temporary exhibition, Abilitando 2017 [24], in Bosco Marengo - Italy, devoted to technological solutions to improve life for disabled people, show that the approach is very promising. We did not conduct a formal survey, but we consulted both people with disabilities and their representatives in local and national associations. We interviewed them while, standing in front of the tactile pictures (see Fig. 4), haptically exploring the proposed solution, they were asked to describe the pictures, along with their content perception. Visitors' agreement or disagreement about the employed techniques, were used to refine the presentation method in the following exhibitions. In general, participants were able to navigate through the picture's content and they accessed the proper interpretation.

Fig. 4. Low sighted people exploring the tactile images during the Expo 2015 exhibition.

Different materials have been tested during the 3D printing process, to select the best suitable to haptic processes. In addition, further implementation of the 3D model can be envisaged because a segmented image can be considered as a sequence of components to be visualized as dynamic, personalized and interactive smart content, eventually using a refreshable Braille display with high resolution. We shift from the traditional digitization paradigm (one artefact represented as a single digital object) to a fine-tuned semantic decomposition of pictures to salient segments, which can be treated as separate content objects sequentially scanned.

The development of two protocols is foreseen: the first referring to works of art aimed at faithfully reproducing nature, strictly respecting the laws of optics; the second, instead of passing these laws, to optimize author-user communication in a process that can be called visual reasoning, in which rough representations are employed for fast concept communication.

Fig. 5. Our model superimposed on "The last supper" by Leonardo da Vinci (1495–1498). Central perspective (Jesus Christ head is the vanishing point), four groups of three apostles, full (white) and empty parts alternated.

Two emblematic examples of artworks of the first protocol are here shown, an example of the second one is given in [25]. "The last supper" by Leonardo da Vinci is given in Fig. 5. All the information needed to understand the picture is included in the image, and its interpretation relies just on the knowledge of the elementary laws of physics. Image segmentation is mainly performed on the image arrays, and subsequently each image component (segment) is described by a suitable set of features and evaluated in order to provide the full contextual description of the image segment. This is an image-to-feature transform once called "low level vision" with peculiar computational characteristics.

The second example is in Fig. 6. The author message is so complex that cannot have an easy transposition by a poor coding sequence. The subjective skill of the observer play an important role in which the regular form and the chromatic refinements become negligible towards the expressive modalities treated precociously by the Impressionists and considered in [19].

Future developments are related to two aspects: (i) the tactile image production and (ii) a validation of the quality of the process through a quantitative estimation of the impact on the final users. The automation of the production process refers to the segmentation and labelling phases; the definition of a trade-off between labels and hedges positioning, in order to facilitate the fingertips exploration of the morphological primitives; and, finally, at the semantic level, the selection of the salient segments could be investigated through a more effective content and context interpretation [26]. The validation can be improved from the current interviews to the formal definition of a questionnaire suited for statistical studies on the effective correct interpretation of the painters' message.

Fig. 6. Yan Marquichka's "Rachenitsa" (1894), a painting on Bulgarian lifestyle, customs, images, costumes, dance, food and morals after the Liberation from Turkish slavery. The composition outlines all these aspects, the characters and their roles, the objects and their colors, the clothes, the dance steps, the spices hanging from the beams. The segments with red stripes are in relief.

Acknowledgments. The paper is partly supported by the BG NSF Grant No DN 17/21-2017.

References

1. MAC (Museum Access Consortium). http://www.cityaccessny.org/mac.php. Accessed 28 Feb 2018
2. State Tactile Museum "Homer", Ancona, Italy. https://www.yamgu.com/en/place/6463/state-tactile-museum-homer-ancona/. Accessed 28 Feb 2018
3. Kardoulias, T.: Guidelines for making tactile diagrams and accompanying narratives. http://www.artbeyondsight.org/handbook/acs-tactileguidelines.shtml. Accessed 28 Feb 2018
4. Guidelines and Standards for Tactile Graphics, The Braille Authority of North America (2010). http://www.brailleauthority.org/tg/. Accessed 28 Feb 2018
5. Levi, F., Rolli, R.: Disegnare per le mani. Manual of Tactile Graphics. Silvio Zamorani Editore, Torino (1994)
6. The Prado Museum Creates the First Art Exhibition for the Visually Impaired, Using 3D Printing. In: Art, Life, Museums, Technology, 9 March 2015 (2015). http://www.openculture.com/2015/03/prado-creates-first-art-exhibition-for-visually-impaired.html. Accessed 6 Mar 2018
7. Eriksson, Y.: How to make tactile pictures understandable to the blind reader. In: Proceedings of the 65th IFLA Council and General Conference (1999)
8. Cantoni, V., Karastoyanov, D., Mosconi, M., Setti, A. (eds.): Pavia, la Battaglia, il Futuro. 1525-2015 Niente fu come prima. CVML e SMART Lab alla Mostra / Pavia, the Battle, the Future. 1525-2015 Nothing was the same again. CVML and SmartLab at the exhibition. Pavia University Press, Pavia (2016). http://www.paviauniversitypress.it/catalogo/pavia-la-battaglia-il-futuro/371. Accessed 28 Feb 2018
9. Art Beyond Sight, Bringing Art Culture to All. http://www.artbeyondsight.org/. Accessed 28 Feb 2018

10. Salzhauer, A.E., Levent, N.S.: Art Beyond Sight: A Resource Guide to Art, Creativity, and Visual Impairment. American Foundation for the Blind, New York (2003)
11. Art for the Blind by Kathleen Lang, ART a GoGo, Art Over Easy. http://www.artagogo.com/commentary/artforblind/artforblind.htm. Accessed 28 Feb 2018
12. Feeling Van Gogh, Van Gogh Museum, Amsterdam. Feel, smell and listen to the 'sunflowers'. https://www.vangoghmuseum.nl/en/whats-on/feeling-van-gogh. Accessed 28 Feb 2018
13. Museum for Blind People, Kaunas. http://visit.kaunas.lt/en/to-see/museums-and-galleries/museum/museum-for-blind-people-xx-century-catacombs/. Accessed 28 Feb 2018
14. Carfagni, M., Furferi, R., Governi, L., Volpe, Y., Tennirelli, G.: Tactile representation of paintings: an early assessment of possible computer based strategies. In: Ioannides, M., Fritsch, D., Leissner, J., Davies, R., Remondino, F., Caffo, R. (eds.) EuroMed 2012. LNCS, vol. 7616, pp. 261–270. Springer, Heidelberg (2012). https://doi.org/10.1007/978-3-642-34234-9_26
15. Hybrid, enhancing the learning experience when combining electronic and tactile formats, TBaseEdu. http://accesstext.gatech.edu/wiki/images/0/02/Hybrid_Presentation_Education_Web.pdf. Accessed 28 Feb 2018
16. Rector, K., Salmon, K., Thornton, D., Joshi, N., Morris, M.R.: Eyes-free art: exploring proxemic audio interfaces for blind and low vision art engagement. In: Proceedings of the ACM Interactive Mobile Wearable Ubiquitous Technology, vol. 1, no. 3, September 2017 (2017). Article 93
17. Touch Graphics, Tactile Design for Universal Access. http://touchgraphics.com/. Accessed 13 Mar 2018
18. descriVEDENDO. http://www.subvedenti.it/?event=descrivedendo-2. Accessed 13 Mar 2018
19. Cantoni, V., Levialdi, S., Zavidovique, B.: 3C Vision: Cues, Context and Channels. Elsevier, New York (2011)
20. Duchowski, A.T.: Eye Tracking Methodology - Theory and Practice, 2nd edn. Springer, London (2007)
21. Unione Italiana dei Ciechi e degli Ipovedenti ONLUS Consiglio Regionale Lombardo. http://www.uicilombardia.org/. Accessed 28 Feb 2018
22. Guerreiro, T., Montague, K., Guerreiro, J., Nunes, R., Nicolau, H., Gonçalves, D.J.V.: Blind people interacting with large touch surfaces: strategies for one-handed and two-handed exploration. In: Proceedings of the 2015 International Conference on Interactive Tabletops & Surfaces, pp. 25–34 (2015)
23. Morash, V.S., Pensky, A.E.C., Tseng, S.T., Miele, J.A.: Effects of using multiple hands and fingers on haptic performance in individuals who are blind. Perception **43**(6), 569–588 (2014)
24. Abilitando: Where technology meets disability, series of meetings about the relationship between new technologies, disabilities and integration in school and work. http://www.abilitando.it/download/abilitando-2015-brochure-EN.pdf. Accessed 28 Feb 2018
25. Gyoshev, S., Karastoyanov, D., Stoimenov, N., Cantoni, V., Lombardi, L., Setti, A.: Exploiting a graphical Braille display for art masterpieces. In: Proceedings of ICCHP 2018 - 16th International Conference on Computers Helping People with Special Needs, Special Thematic Session on "Access to Artworks and its Mediation by and for Visually Impaired People", 9–13 July 2018, Linz, Austria (2018)
26. Cantoni, V., Merlano, L., Nugrahaningsih, N., Porta, M.: Eye tracking for cultural heritage: a gaze-controlled system for handless interaction with artworks. In: Proceedings of the 17th International Conference on Computer Systems and Technologies 2016, CompSysTech 2016, 23–24 June, Palermo, Italy, pp. 307–314. ACM, New York (2016)

Digital Navigation for People with Visual Impairments

Public Transit Accessibility: Blind Passengers Speak Out

Fatemeh Mirzaei(✉), Roberto Manduchi, and Sri Kurniawan

University of California, Santa Cruz, USA
{Fmirzaei, skurnia}@ucsc.edu, manduchi@soe.ucsc.edu

Abstract. Riding public transit can be confusing for everyone, especially in an unfamiliar environment. One needs to figure out which transportation lines to take to reach a destination, when and where to catch a bus or a train, when to exit, and how to negotiate transfers. For those with sensorial or cognitive disabilities, these problems become even more daunting. Several technological approaches have been proposed to facilitate use of public transit for everyone. For any assistive technology to be successful, though, it is imperative that it is developed from the ground up with a clear understanding of the intended users' needs and requirements, and possibly with a direct participation of these users throughout the project lifecycle. In this study, we conduct a focus group with blind participants, designed to highlight the main issues, problems, and limitations with the current transit system in our local area as well as the perception of the participants our proposed RouteMe2 technology [1]. We found two core categories of issues faced by blind travelers: (1) spatial/location awareness, and (2) temporal/time awareness. Configurability and accessibility were the most desired features requested for a new transit information app.

Keywords: Assistive technology · Public transit · Focus group

1 Introduction

For many people, especially for those living in suburban or rural areas, driving is the preferred means of transportation. Those who cannot drive (due to a physical, sensorial, or cognitive disability, or to old age) have a number of options. They can use taxi cabs, ride hailing (such as Uber or Lyft), public transit (bus, subways, light or heavy rail), paratransit (a door to door service that is complementary to fixed-route systems), or volunteer ride services. Among these choices, public transit often represents the best compromise between cost and efficiency. Unfortunately, use of public transit is challenging for many potential passengers. In this contribution, we focus on the problems associated with information access. Riding public transit can be confusing for everyone, especially in an unfamiliar environment (e.g. when visiting a new city).

One needs to figure out which transportation lines to take to reach a destination, when and where to catch a bus or a train, when to exit, and how to negotiate transfers. For those with sensorial or cognitive disabilities, these problems become even more daunting. In many cases, some of these potential travelers feel intimidated, and prefer to resort to more expensive or less convenient options.

© Springer International Publishing AG, part of Springer Nature 2018
K. Miesenberger and G. Kouroupetroglou (Eds.): ICCHP 2018, LNCS 10897, pp. 277–282, 2018.
https://doi.org/10.1007/978-3-319-94274-2_38

Several technological approaches have been proposed to facilitate use of public transit for everyone. Some of these systems are designed so as to provide users with location- and event-based information, such as helping with identification of an arriving bus, or notifying the user when it is time to exit the vehicle. For example, RouteMe2 [1], an NSF-funded project at UC Santa Cruz, encompasses location-based services (enabled by an infrastructure of iBeacons) and cloud services, which are in charge of tracking the user's progress in a trip, generating notifications, and coordinating with real-time information provided by the transit agencies. Some of the functionalities of RouteMe2 include: helping with finding the exact location of a desired bus stop or train platform; informing the traveler when the desired bus has arrived at the stop; and notifying an authorized third party if something occurred that requires special attention (i.e., if the traveler has taken a wrong train, and is unresponsive to system-generated notifications).

For any assistive technology to be successful, though, it is imperative that it is developed from the ground up with a clear understanding of the intended users' needs and requirements, and possibly with a direct participation of these users throughout the project lifecycle. For this reason, we decided to conduct a focus group with blind participants, designed to highlight the main issues, problems, and limitations with the current transit system in our local area (the Monterey Bay region in California), as well as the perception of the participants our proposed RouteMe2 technology. We believe that the outcomes of this focus group, as described in this paper, may be of interest to any researcher or practitioner who is looking to build new assistive technology in the field of public transit.

2   Related Work

Previous studies have shown that people with visual impairment experience difficulties at determining the route and schedule information, purchasing fare, finding the correct bus-stop location, getting on the correct bus, and getting off at the right stop [2–6] focused on identifying a correct bus to board when waiting at a bus stop, while the systems described in [7–9] provided alerts for an upcoming stop while riding the bus. [10] proposed gathering spatial and temporal information from different patterns of mobility and travel time using smart card and GSM data. They aimed at building a public transportation system that could adapt to different travel patterns for different situations. [11] proposed a high resolution spatio-temporal, Geographic Information System (GIS) based public transit network model to measure different models of travel time, such as waiting time at bus stop and transfer times between routes. A variety of solutions have been proposed to help people with blindness and with limited vision, including providing non-visual information about the location of bus stops. For example, [4] developed GoBraille, a system that uses crowdsourcing to gather detailed information about the location of stops (a similar system is StopInfo [12]).

This prior work shows that there is a need for people with limited or no vision to be constantly aware of where they are in reference to their travel goal, as well as to obtain the information that is necessary to utilize public transit effectively. However, these prior studies do not offer in-depth knowledge and detail to the level that is necessary to make correct design decisions on the best tool for accessible public transit. Motivated by this observation, we decided to conduct the focus group described in the next section, which allowed us to observe group dynamics of several participants in our target population.

3 Focus Group

3.1 Participants

Our focus group involved seven participants (three females) from the Vista Center for the Blind and the Visually Impaired of Santa Cruz, California. All participants were iPhone users and were familiar with the VoiceOver screen reader. Five participants were totally blind, while two had some residual vision. Three participants stated that they used public transit several times a week; two used it occasionally, while two stopped using public transit, although they had experience with it in the past. Four participants stated that they signed up for paratransit or volunteer driving services. Two participants used dog guides. Participants were compensated $60 for participating in the focus group.

3.2 Methodology

The focus group was organized in two 45 min sessions with a 10 min break between the two sessions. In the first session, participants were asked to discuss their experience with using public transit. Specifically, participants were asked about their opinion of the transit system in the Santa Cruz area; the difficulties experienced using transit; and the factors (impediments and challenges) that discouraged them to use transit. In the second session, a moderator gave an outline of the goals of the RouteMe2 project, then asked participants for feedback about the project, about their preferences, and about what, in their opinion, would make an application such this usable in terms of functionality and user interface.

Audio recording of the focus group was then transcribed for analysis. This data was analyzed using the *grounded theory* method. First introduced by [13], grounded theory is an inductive research methodology used extensively within the social sciences for inspection of qualitative data. Unlike deductive approaches that assume some prior theoretical framework, in grounded theory concepts and theories are built through methodic collection and analysis of data. We used Nvivo, a qualitative data analysis software designed to help researchers organize, analyze, and find insights in unstructured or qualitative data.

3.3 Results

A number of themes emerged from the grounded theory analysis of the first session. Essentially, we found two core categories of issues faced by blind travelers:

1. Spatial/location awareness, and
2. Temporal/time awareness.

Location Awareness. Location awareness deals with being aware of one's geographical position in reference to the public transport throughout the entire trip. Most participants reported situations with loss of location awareness due to multiple reasons, such as knowing whether or not they are in the right vehicle, whether they are waiting for a bus at the right stop, whether the bus vehicle they are waiting for is close or far, and whether they stand next to the entrance door of the bus vehicle or train car. Some of the main themes that emerged during the first session are listed in the following. Some participants complained that routes (including the list of stops) and schedules are not clearly communicated. Finding the exact location of bus stops and train platforms was one of the main challenges for the five participants who were completely blind. This includes understanding which side of the street the bus stop is located at, and whether one needs to cross the street to reach it. Finding the correct train platform is also challenging. In addition, knowledge of the layout of a stop is important when one needs to negotiate a transfer. Participants mentioned that in these situations they often rely on sighted travelers, when available. Locating doors of buses or trains with multiple cars was mentioned as a challenging task, especially for the local subway system (BART). Maintaining awareness of one's surroundings is particularly important. Participants shared experiences of walking in the wrong direction after leaving a train or a bus, as they had no clear idea of the surrounding area. Catching the right bus or train and knowing they are in the right one was an issue mentioned multiple times in the discussion. Excessive ambient noise, and wrong or incomplete announcement from the vehicle's speakers, may causes loss of state awareness in these situations.

Time Awareness. Time awareness is about obtaining exact and detailed temporal information. For example, participants commented that bus schedules are often not as detailed as desired, and that sudden changes of schedule are a source of difficulties. In addition, participants lamented the inability to obtain better estimates of upcoming busses or trains. The need for access to real time bus schedules was a topic that clearly emerged from the discussion. This is particularly important in the case of transfers and connections. Another theme that emerged from the analysis was the lack of awareness of the distance of an upcoming bus. Being able to predict when the bus is about to arrive would give one some time to get prepared to board. Planning ahead of a time for trips to new places often represented a serious challenge. Some participants stated that, to be on the safe side, they double up the estimated total travel time in these cases. Sometimes, due to the very long estimated travel time, they end up using private transportation, or even canceling their trip.

In the second session, participants focused on the desired functionality and user interface of a new transit information app to be developed. Participants concurred in the importance of configurability and accessibility features. The three most requested accessibility features were: VoiceOver control; a simple user interface; and requiring a small number of queries (commands) from the user. An example of desired configurability is the ability to change a route in the middle of the trip. Participants expressed the desire that the app would notify them upon arrival at the correct bus stop; note that this was one of the main issues discussed in Session 1. Another desideratum was the ability of the system to announce all bus stops. This is a functionality that is often (but not always) present in existing busses, but announcements from the speakers are sometimes difficult to hear. Several participants favored implementing alert mechanisms by means of phone vibration in several situations, such as upon arrival at a bus stop, upon bus arrival, and when upcoming stops are announced. On-demand calculation and reporting of all possible routes at any time was another requested desirable feature, with some participants stating that this feature would help them organize their trip more efficiently and save time. Finally, participants were generally in favor of the idea that the same smartphone app could be used to access transit information and for fare payment. Indeed, several participants mentioned situations in which they had difficulties finding where to validate a paper ticket at a transit center.

Acknowledgments. This material is based upon work supported by the National Science Foundation under Grant No. NSF IIP-1632158. Any opinions, findings, and conclusions or recommendations expressed in this material are those of the author(s) and do not necessarily reflect the views of the National Science Foundation.

References

1. Alvarado, A., et al.: RouteMe2: a cloud-based infrastructure for assisted transit. In: Transportation Research Board Annual Meeting (2018)
2. Yoo, D., Zimmerman, J., Steinfeld, A., Tomasic, A.: Understanding the space for co-design in riders' interactions with a transit service. In: Proceedings of the SIGCHI Conference on Human Factors in Computing Systems, pp. 1797–1806. ACM, April 2010
3. Golledge, R.G., Marston, J.R., Costanzo, C.M.: Attitudes of visually impaired persons toward the use of public transportation. J. Vis. Impair. Blind. **91**(5), 446–459 (1997)
4. Azenkot, S., Prasain, S., Borning, A., Fortuna, E., Ladner, R.E., Wobbrock, J.O.: Enhancing independence and safety for blind and deaf-blind public transit riders. In: Proceedings of the SIGCHI Conference on Human Factors in Computing Systems, pp. 3247–3256. ACM (2011). American Foundation for the Blind (AFB). Accessible Mass Transit, May 2013
5. Banâtre, M., Couderc, P., Pauty, J., Becus, M.: Ubibus: ubiquitous computing to help blind people in public transport. In: Brewster, S., Dunlop, M. (eds.) Mobile HCI 2004. LNCS, vol. 3160, pp. 310–314. Springer, Heidelberg (2004). https://doi.org/10.1007/978-3-540-28637-0_28
6. Noor, M.Z.H., Ismail, I., Saaid, M.F.: Bus detection device for the blind using RFID application. In: 5th International Colloquium on Signal Processing and Its Applications, CSPA 2009, pp. 247–249. IEEE, March 2009
7. Jacob, R., Shalaik, B., Winstanley, A.C., Mooney, P.: Haptic feedback for passengers using public transport. In: Cherifi, H., Zain, J.M., El-Qawasmeh, E. (eds.) DICTAP 2011. CCIS, vol. 166, pp. 24–32. Springer, Heidelberg (2011). https://doi.org/10.1007/978-3-642-21984-9_3
8. Kostiainen, J., Erkut, C., Piella, F.B.: Design of an audio-based mobile journey planner application. In: Proceedings of the 15th International Academic MindTrek Conference: Envisioning Future Media Environments, pp. 107–113. ACM, September 2011
9. Flores, G., Manduchi, R.: A Public Transit Assistant for Blind Passengers: Development and Experiments. IEEE Pervasive Comput. (2018, in press)
10. Hara, K., Azenkot, S., Campbell, M., Bennett, C.L., Le, V., Pannella, S., Moore, R., Minckler, K., Ng, R.H., Froehlich, J.E.: Improving public transit accessibility for blind riders by crowdsourcing bus stop landmark locations with google street view: an extended analysis. ACM Trans. Access. Comput. (TACCESS) **6**(2), 5 (2015)

11. Tribby, C.P., Zandbergen, P.A.: High-resolution spatio-temporal modeling of public transit accessibility. Appl. Geogr. **34**, 345–355 (2012)
12. Campbell, M., Bennett, C., Bonnar, C., Borning, A.: Where's my bus stop?: supporting independence of blind transit riders with StopInfo. In: Proceedings of the 16th international ACM SIGACCESS conference on Computers and accessibility, pp. 11–18. ACM, October 2014
13. Glaser, B., Strauss, A.: The Discovery of Grounded Theory. Aldine Publishing Company, Hawthorne (1967)

Indoor Navigation and Audiovisual Aiding Within Public Transport

Clemens Reitbauer[1]([⊠]), Thomas Moder[1], Roman Wilfinger[1], Karin Wisiol[1],
Johannes Weinzerl[2], Werner Bischof[3], and Manfred Wieser[1]

[1] Working Group Navigation of the Institute of Geodesy,
Graz University of Technology, NAWI Graz, Graz, Austria
{clemens.reitbauer,thomas.moder,roman.wilfinger,karin.wisiol,
manfred.wieser}@tugraz.at
[2] c.c.com Moser GmbH, Grambach, Austria
jweinzerl@cccom.at
[3] Energy and Transportation, FH Joanneum, Kapfenberg, Austria
werner.bischof@fh-joanneum.at

Abstract. In this paper, we present a specially designed indoor navigation and audiovisual aiding system for blind or visually impaired people within public transport. The developed system relies on a positioning algorithm, which is based on inertial and radio signal data. With an additional map-matching process, the position solution is restricted to a routing graph, which is designed on the basis of a tactile paving network. In addition, we developed an audiovisual operator help service. With this webRTC based technology, the help seeking user can make an audiovisual call to an acquaintance or professional operator.

Keywords: Visual impairment · Navigation systems
Audiovisual aiding

1 Introduction

Nowadays, 253 million people worldwide are living with a vision impairment [1]. Due to their disability, this population group has a restriction on information when they travel within public transport. A suitable indoor and outdoor navigation system, integrated in an audiovisual aiding and public transport information system, would be of great benefit to compensate their information restriction on their trip. Therefore, a special pedestrian smartphone positioning algorithm based on tactile paving and an Audiovisual Aiding System (AAS) is developed within the INK 2016 project.

2 State-of-the-Art

Unlike outdoor positioning with the availability of Global Navigation Satellite Systems (GNSS), there is no generally accepted equivalent for a ubiquitous

© Springer International Publishing AG, part of Springer Nature 2018
K. Miesenberger and G. Kouroupetroglou (Eds.): ICCHP 2018, LNCS 10897, pp. 283–287, 2018.
https://doi.org/10.1007/978-3-319-94274-2_39

smartphone based indoor positioning method. For an absolute position determination indoors, location fingerprinting with radio signals is widely used. However, the accuracy is limited (up to approx. 4 m, but far worse in average conditions) and the setup cost (in terms of time) is high. On the other side, there is relative positioning with inertial sensors (accelerometers, gyroscopes), which are typically low-cost solutions with poor long-term stability. A combination of both methods can overcome the individual drawbacks, making the positioning more accurate and more reliable. With the incentive of accessibility in our everyday life, the demand for audiovisual aiding systems has emerged. The mobile application Be My Eyes provides a crowd-driven assistance service for visually impaired people by establishing a video call to an anonymous volunteer [2]. Due to privacy protection, no personal data is shared, thus the service focuses more on common daily struggles rather than emergency situations.

3   Methodology

In a navigation and aiding system designed for visually impaired people, a ubiquitously available, reliable and accurate position is needed for a suitable guidance instruction. As shown in Fig. 1, the developed system uses two main sources of positioning information. The Google Play Services Location (GPSL) represents the first part, whereas a Pedestrian Dead Reckoning (PDR) in combination with Bluetooth updates represents the second part. Due to multipath and signal loss, the GPSL solution, which consists of systems like GNSS, WLAN or Cell-Identification, is inaccurate or even fails in indoor areas, see Fig. 3 (left). Therefore, an additional indoor positioning algorithm is developed.

Smartphones with implemented sensors can provide relative positions for pedestrians with a so-called step-based PDR-algorithm [4]. Regarding this, step-events can be detected with the help of acceleration measurements. Furthermore, a specifically developed heading estimator based on data from gyroscope, accelerometer and magnetometer, provides a heading of the pedestrian, independent of the way how the device is carried or fixed to the users body [3]. With this two quantities and a known step length of the user, the change of position due to one step can be estimated consecutively. To increase the accuracy and reliability, a specifically developed PDR map-matching algorithm supports the PDR-trajectory [4]. With this map-matching, the position solution is restricted to a routing graph, which is based on the tactile paving system of the test

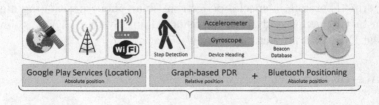

Fig. 1. Position information sources for combined positioning solution

environment, see Fig. 3 (left). In addition, Bluetooth beacons were distributed around the testing environment to support the PDR-Algorithm with an initial starting position and updates the PDR-position along the route if necessary. Finally the positioning algorithm combines the GPSL and the PDR-Bluetooth solution. Regarding this, the algorithm is generally forced to use the PDR combined Bluetooth positions, unless this solution degrades or differs significant from a more accurate GPSL solution.

However, the blind or visually impaired pedestrian can still get lost in an unfamiliar environment during his trip. Hence, the user needs some further assistance, which can be fulfilled by an audiovisual operator help service [5]. With this service, an acquaintance or professional operator can be contacted via an audiovisual call through the help button of the mobile application. The operator then receives an overview about the help seeking person by receiving personal data as well as the current position, the planned route and the video feed, see Fig. 3 (right). The contacted person may access the camera of the smartphone and give dedicated guidance instructions from the perspective of the blind person to lead them to a transport platform or for example a desired shop. The service is based on the open WebRTC framework, which provides real-time communication between web browsers, see Fig. 2. The client, the backend and the server architecture are based on Node.js, which enables the application to run on a server or in the cloud. The initial connection between the client and operator is set up with a web server based on a database, through which clients and operators are matched. The audio and video communication between the client and operator then operates through a TURN server using WebRTC.

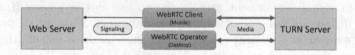

Fig. 2. Server architecture of audiovisual aiding

4   Work and Results

Figure 3 (left) shows a real-time measured test route at the central railway station in Graz from platform 1 along the tactile way to the tramway. The GPSL-based trajectory is visualized as colored dots, whereas their color depends on the position accuracy (3σ). It can be seen, that the GPSL indoor positions do not achieve the accuracy and reliability that is necessary for a visually impaired person to navigate without further assistance in indoor environments. The PDR and Bluetooth based positioning solution (white dots), in contrast, is able to represent the user's position on the tactile way over the entire route. [4] proves in his thesis, that the PDR-Bluetooth algorithm can provide a stable and precise position solution over a 20-min period. Therefore, the GPSL solution is only used when the user leaves the tactile paving system.

Fig. 3. PDR/Bluetooth and GPSL trajectories. Operator interface of the AAS

The operator interface of the AAS is shown in Fig. 3 (right). Once the operator is logged into the system, he can activate his availability. If a help seeking person is activating the audiovisual help, a connection between the client and the operator will be established. In addition to the video feed, the map view with the client's position and the planned trip is shown in the operator view. Based on this information, the operator can help the client by communicating the visual surroundings as well as suggesting alternative paths or trips.

5   Conclusion

People with visual impairment usually try to use tactile paving if available, especially if they are unfamiliar with the surroundings. This tactile paving can easily be mapped as a routing graph and is then used for calculating reliable position solutions as well as guidance information. The scientific impact on the positioning is the concept of a PDR and Bluetooth combination with tactile ways. The practical impact of the presented AAS for visually impaired people lies in the concept of direct pairing between clients and operators. Additionally, the integration of positioning and orientation data as well as the travelled route is of obvious advantage in the presented system. Due to the feature diversity of the developed system, its target audience may further be expanded by elderly people (e.g., dementia patients), locally unfamiliar tourists and even deaf people to grant them safety and confidence when they travel from one place to another.

References

1. World Health Organization: Vision impairment and blindness, 15 March 2018. http://www.who.int/mediacentre/factsheets/fs282/en/
2. Be my Eyes: What is Be My Eyes? 15 March 2018. http://bemyeyes.com/what-is-be-my-eyes/
3. Valenti, R., Dryanovski, I., Xiao, J.: Keeping a good attitude: a quaternion-based orientation filter for IMUs and MARGs. Sensors **15**, 19302–19330 (2015)
4. Reitbauer, C.: Graphen-basiertes Dead Reckoning für Fußgänger. Master thesis, Graz University of Technology, Austria (2017)
5. Bischof, W., Dornhofer, M., Yousefzada, M.: Operator Help Services for Blind Users. Mathematics in Industry Study Group, Adelaide (2017)

A Reproducible Experiment Towards the Accessibility of a Geographical Map

Shirley Alvarado[1(✉)], Nadine Jessel[2(✉)], Philippe Truillet[2(✉)], and Véronique Gaildrat[2(✉)]

[1] ESPE Ecole supérieure du professorat et de l'éducation, Toulouse, France
shirley.alvarado@ac-toulouse.fr
[2] IRIT Toulouse Institute of Computer Science Research, Toulouse University, Toulouse, France
{baptiste, truillet, gaildrat}@irit.fr

Abstract. The "Mappa Mundi d'Albi" is an eighth-century map, registered in the Unesco's World heritage list in 2015. Difficult to understand even visually, it requires explanation and contextualization. In accordance with the legislation regarding the accessibility of cultural works, and to allow its understanding, we have implemented various devices, via digital technology, to make it accessible to as many people as possible. Different criteria of accessibility and perception of sensory modalities have been studied. After an analysis of the already existing accessibility design we have designed and evaluated different prototypes of enhanced digital and tangible maps. These prototypes have been put in place through different partnerships and based on a goal of reproducibility at low cost. The other objective was, taking into account the "diy" culture of fablabs, the work in collaboration for teachers specialized in accessibility or not and non-computer scientists.

Keywords: Accessibility · Sensitive map · Blind people

1 Introduction

The objective of our study is to propose different criteria of design and evaluation of several digital devices that can contribute to the principle of accessibility in the face of a geographical map visually difficult to understand. The chosen map is of the 8th century: the "Mappa Mundi d'Albi" (see Table 1), one of the first representations of the known world, is kept in a public place, the library Pierre Amalric in the city of Albi. Since 2015, it has been inscribed on the UNESCO's world heritage list. It must therefore comply with the law of accessibility of the 11 February 2005 "for equal rights and opportunities, participation and citizenship of people with disabilities" [1]. The interest of the "Mappa Mundi" rests on the fact that it is visually inaccessible to the non-specialist of the ancient world maps, so we looked for ways to adapt it to make it understandable for everyone. In a first section, we will present works and principles which served us to build our adaptation of the map. In a second section, we will detail the different prototype of the map that we propose. Before concluding, we will detail the experiments carried out to test the accessibility of these prototypes.

K. Miesenberger and G. Kouroupetroglou (Eds.): ICCHP 2018, LNCS 10897, pp. 288–291, 2018.
https://doi.org/10.1007/978-3-319-94274-2_40

Table 1. Mappa Mundi

Map	Description
	D : computer screen, swell paper
	A: click or touch on a touchscreen
	R: sighted, visual impaired, deaf
	K: audio and visual feedback on the names of different countries, cities or rivers.
	NeS: touch, hearing, seeing
	S: Inskape, audacity, html and javascript

2 State of the Art

Our accessibility thinking was influenced by the results of research on image adaptation for the visually impaired and by the reproducible principles.

In his thesis [2] shows the importance of the simplification of the tactile image which must represent the essence of the real image, in order to overcome the tactile perception which is of lower resolution compared to the visual perception. The work of [3] showed that blind children had better recognition of images is they are textured. We were also inspired by the principle of audio description, a process born in the United States and which was established in France and Europe by the association Valentin Haüy [4], allowing to describe the images or the video. The audio feedback of tactile images is today privileged thanks to digital. The first interactive map with audio output was introduced by Parkes in 1988. The interactive tactile maps [5] are based on the representation of a relief map with legendary sound output. The work of [6] adds that users better remember information with interactive maps. Our work is therefore based on these observations: inclusion and equal opportunities for all, achievable through adaptations and compensations related to collaboration but also through the plurality of access modes to knowledge. Knowledge of the map can be achieved through different sensory modes and interactive audio return, in order to provide advantages of access and memorization.

The process of building different virtual or real objects to present the information contained in such map has to be reproducible at low cost. The prototype has been made in the Fablab of the University of Toulouse. It uses block programming that does not require syntactic knowledge of a programming language.

3 Prototype Description

We will present various adaptations of the map "Mappa Mundi" and we describe them with the following information: Device, possible Action, useR, feedbacK, seNSe used, Software for realization. (DARKNeSS)

This first prototype principal aims to sighted people to explore and understand this map, the adaptation for visual impaired or deaf people is possible with adaptation (relief drawing, text in black, etc.).

Two representations are designed to visual impaired people based on a sensitive wooden card coupled with an application on a smartphone which provides an audio description (Fig. 1), or with an autonomous system which provides a tactile sound feedback to each element. An adaptation of this prototype has permit to deaf people to manipulate and understand the map (description written on the smartphone, name of country visible on the wood, etc.).

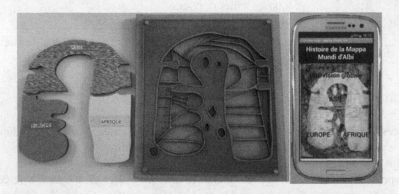

Fig. 1. Sensitive wooden map coupled to an audio description application

Description of this prototype with the previous information DARKNeSS:

- D: wooden card, smartphone, Arduino sound card
- A: Touch the wooden card, click on the mobile phone (4 buttons)
- R: sighted, blind, deaf (the description
- K: audio and visual feedback on the description of the map
- NeS: touch, hearing, seeing
- S: Inskape, audacity, laser cutting, Audacity, Photoscape, AppInventor.

4   End User Tests and Reproducible Process

4.1   First Prototype

Protocol: 19 end users (2 visual impaired) test the first prototype, they answer to 11 geographic location queries: cities, rivers, countries, islands and seas, and 2 queries of presentation and context: map material and orientation during 11 to 25 min.

Result: There is no significant difference between the results of sighted and one visually impaired user.

Overall geographic areas were identified: the number of correct answers ranging from 12 to 19 depending on the question asked.

The clickable area of the contextualization information has not been identified.

4.2   Second Prototype

Protocol: 4 blind users, map exploration with oral feedback during around 1 h.

Result: Continents (form + Braille + texture) were well identified.

The different levels of description, the discovery of the countries and the audio description adaptable to the listening rhythm of the user were positively appreciated.

4.3   Reproducible Process

The reproducibility of our prototype is mainly based on the use of easy to use and free software such as Inkscape for vectorization of images and Audacity for sound processing. The interactive sound card is reproducible as it uses HTML and JavaScript language. The wooden map was made thanks to a FabLab, shared place where digital manufacturing machines are available, such as laser cutting/engraving and 3D printer. The map reproduction is easy and inexpensive. Programming an application with the AppInventor programming uses logic blocks to generate a smartphone application.

5   Conclusion

In this exploratory study, we worked on the accessibility of a map which is very difficult to interpret visually without provided information: the "Mappa Mundi d'Albi". We are now able to reproduce the process for other maps such as the new French regions.

Acknowledgments. We would like to thank Ms. Deschaux Jocelyne, Chief Curator of the Grand Albigeois Libraries and Archivist-Palaeographer and the members of the CTEB for their contributions, and all people who gave their time for testing.

References

1. Handicap law. https://www.legifrance.gouv.fr/eli/loi/2005/2/11/SANX0300217L/jo/texte. Accessed 23 Mar 2018
2. Eriksson, Y.: Images tactiles: représentations pour les aveugles, 1784–1940. Les Doigts Qui Rêvent, p. 379 (2008). Trad. de Ph. Claudet
3. Theurel, A., Claudet, P., Hatwell, Y., Gentaz, E., et al.: Tactile picture recognition by early blind children: the effect of illustration technique. J. Exp. Psychol.: Appl. **19**(3), 233–240 (2013)
4. http://www.avh.asso.fr/fr/lassociation/nos-services/laudiovision. Accessed 23 Mar 2018
5. Brock, A., Oriola, B., Truillet, Ph., Jouffrais, C., Picard, D.: Interactivity improves usability of geographic maps for visually impaired people. Hum. Comput. Interact. **30**, 156–194 (2015)
6. Giraud, S., Brock, A., Macé, J.M., Joffrais, C.: Learning with a 3D printed interactive small-scale model: improvement of space and text memorization in visually impaired students. Front. Psychol. **8**, 930 (2017). https://doi.org/10.3389/fpsyg.2017.0093

Indoor-Outdoor Intermodal Sidewalk-Based Navigation Instructions for Pedestrians with Visual Impairments

Jan Balata[(⊠)], Jakub Berka, and Zdenek Mikovec

Faculty of Electrical Engineering, Czech Technical University in Prague,
Prague, Czech Republic
{balatjan,berkajak,xmikovec}@fel.cvut.cz

Abstract. Visual impairment limits people mainly in their travel related activities. Available navigation systems and aids for people with visual impairment solely focus either on indoor or outdoor environment and thus do not take into account their traveling habits – intermodal transportation. Verified guidelines for creating navigation instructions while transiting between different environments are needed. We present a set of navigation instructions designed for sidewalk-based navigation systems intended for transitions between indoor and outdoor environments and the usage of public transport. In two experiments with people with visual impairment, we evaluated our method on low-fidelity prototypes. We describe how we form the navigation instructions from sentence templates and how we envision the utilization of Bluetooth beacons.

Keywords: Visually impaired · Accessibility · Navigation
Landmarks · Verbal description

1 Introduction

The independent mobility is one of the prerequisites for a high quality of life. Unfortunately, people with visual impairments are limited mostly in traveling related activities [9], which results in low self-esteem, loss of job, friends or hobbies, eventually worsening well-being.

Although many electronic navigation systems for visually impaired people exist nowadays, majority cover only part of daily navigation issues and situations that visually impaired are facing. For instance, navigation between outdoor and indoor navigation is not solved in a satisfactory way. An international study shows [19] that over 64.9% of people with visual impairment struggle to find entrances to buildings, 82.4% lacks audio information about public transport stops and 43.3% have problems crossing complex pedestrian crossings.

In our work, we propose a method which enables seamless connection of indoor and outdoor environment into one navigation system including usage of public transportation – i.e., intermodal navigation – as people with visual impairment tend to optimize their routes via public transport [15].

© Springer International Publishing AG, part of Springer Nature 2018
K. Miesenberger and G. Kouroupetroglou (Eds.): ICCHP 2018, LNCS 10897, pp. 292–301, 2018.
https://doi.org/10.1007/978-3-319-94274-2_41

We analysed existing systems and studies, identified situations in navigation in a city (public transport, indoor, outdoor and transition). We identified and designed a methodology for describing these situations by means of a set of sentence templates, which are in accordance with orientation and mobility strategies and needs of people with visual impairment. We focused mainly on egocentric frames of reference, sequential processing of speech [13,14] and preference of landmarks in route descriptions in general [12] and their prevalence on unknown routes [11]. Prototypes of routes were evaluated in two qualitative user studies resulting in recommendations for future design.

2   Related Work

Many navigation aids for visually impaired have been developed based on traditional sensors such as cameras [5], RFID readers [6] or more exotic ones such as drones in indoor navigation [1]. Other navigation aids are based on geographical information system (GIS) in combination with global navigation satellite systems. However, these systems typically use car-like navigation instructions which are inappropriate for navigation of pedestrians, i.e., Ariadne GPS, BlindSquare, Google Maps or special devices as Trekker Breeze.

Current car navigation systems based on GIS do not support natural human wayfinding behavior. They omit landmarks, which are more appropriate than metric navigation instruction [8], their routing is meant for cars and not humans [17] and lastly the GIS does not contain information about sidewalks/crossings. Moreover, car navigation systems are not suited for storing accessibility information [16], thus for efficient navigation of people with visual impairment sidewalk-based GIS should be used [3].

To support independent traveling using public transport, Azenkot et al. [2] created an aid providing blind and deaf-blind users with information about intersections, address or arrivals together with crowdsourced information about the stops. They also provide useful insights into user requirements mostly the values, which should be supported by the aid – independence and safety.

Finding an entrance the desired destination was also subject of research focused on crowdsourcing. Volunteered information about the entrance such as distances, landmarks, materials or directions support travelers with visual impairments in an unknown environment and let them be independent of the help of passersby [19].

The situation is different in indoor navigation where GIS is from the beginning purposed for use of pedestrians. Navigation instructions for indoor navigation can relate the navigation instructions to landmarks such as doors, elevators, or lockers [7].

Some of the indoor navigation systems do not rely on maps at all [10]. FreeNavi constructs a virtual map from WiFi fingerprints only by landmarks descriptions and their connectivity relations. The generated virtual map does not contain information of turning directions (left or right), i.e. users have to find out by themselves at the junctions in which direction they have to continue to next landmark.

Our work extends work of Balata et al. [3] who use sidewalk-based GIS for automatic generation of landmark-enhanced route itineraries for people with visual impairments and Vystrčil et al. [18] who present design recommendation for landmark-enhanced route itineraries for an indoor environment for people with visual impairment. Our work connects these two approaches to provide seamless navigation instructions from outdoor environment to indoor environment including public transport.

3   Navigation Instructions Templates

We classified environment into outdoor, indoor, semi-indoor (passageways, underground vestibules) and semi-outdoor (courtyards, hospital compounds) categories. Then we identified situations in cities users can encounter with focus on public transportation (tram stations, underground stations, train stations or bus terminals) and environment transitions.

The navigation instructions are composed of individual segments, and each segment contains a description of surrounding environment followed by an action that user should perform.

The part of the route can, for example, look like this:

```
Segment 9 of 11.
You are at the crossing to Cedar & Cathcart station,
across the Cedar street. The station is isle-type.
Cross the Cedar street to the isle via a marked
crossing with traffic lights and one-way traffic from
left. Attention, the crossing has lowered curb.

Segment 10 of 11.
You are at the station Cedar & Cathcart. Turn right
and go about 40 m to station info-table in the
front part of the station. Have tram strip by your
left hand, railing by your right hand.
```

To automatically generate navigation instructions we use the system of sentence templates. For example, the template for the tram station can look like this (description is followed by action in one paragraph):

```
Segment X of Y.
You are at an isle-type station <StationName>.
At isle, there are <StationObjects>.<Crosswalk/Underpass/Overpass>
is at <front/back/middle> part of the isle.
After getting off, turn <Direction>. Have tram
by your <left/right> hand. <Handrail/Roadway> by your
<left/right> hand. Go <Distance> metres straight to
<crosswalk/underpass/overpass> at <left/right>.
```

In total, there are 14 combinations of templates for environment description and action to perform. These templates will enable us to automatically generate navigation instruction from mixed sidewalk-based exterior–interior GIS for an arbitrary route.

The templates are selected based on the priority defined as a constellation of available landmarks and their particular properties. For example, a crossing or a corner can be selected as ending landmark of a segment as follows: if the crossing is on the route it is selected; if not, the corner is selected.

The system of templates enables us to have language-independent algorithms for routing and for navigation instruction generation. Moreover, it makes the translation to other languages more efficient. The context of the templates is, however, limited and for use in completely different environment new templates have to be created, i.e. for a ferry. For the technical details see our Technical Report [4].

4   Evaluation

For the purpose of the evaluation low-fidelity prototypes of routes and their description leading through a city center of Prague were created. The routes and descriptions for outdoor parts of the routes were generated using existing navigation system[1]. The rest of routes leading through stations, entrances and semi-outdoor environment were prototyped manually. Two iterations of experiments were conducted with visually impaired participants.

4.1   First Iteration

Participants. Six visually impaired participants were recruited via email leaflet. They were aged from 25 to 69 years (mean = 37.3, SD = 15.96). Three participants were congenitally blind and three were late blind. Three participants had Category 4 visual impairment (light perception) and three participants had Category 5 (no light perception). Two participants had a guide dog.

Procedure. The first iteration was conducted in a laboratory setting. The purpose of the experiment was to test whether the participants understand route itineraries (in terms of terminology and navigation principles), whether the information in itineraries is sufficient or redundant. First, the purpose of the experiment was explained to the participants. Then the sections of routes itinerary were played individually to the participant using a screen reader on Android cell phone. Both routes were saved as HTML document so that each section of the route was one paragraph. After each section, the participant had time to express his/her opinions about the section.

---

[1] http://www.naviterier.cz.

Routes. The first route led from the metro station to classroom inside the campus building. It consisted of 41 segments and was about 300 m long. It contained the combination of indoor, semi-indoor and semi-outdoor environments. The second route led from tram station to classroom inside the campus building. It consisted of 34 segments and was about 450 m long. It contained the combination of all classified environments.

4.2 Second Iteration

Participants. Six visually impaired participants were recruited via email leaflet. They were aged from 25 to 70 years (mean = 40.17, SD = 16.70). Three participants were congenitally blind and three were late blind. One participant had Category 4 visual impairment (light perception) and five participants had Category 5 (no light perception). Two participants had a guide dog.

Procedure. The second iteration took place in a field. The purpose of the experiment was to test whether the participants understand route itineraries in a real environment and whether they can utilize these instructions for navigation to the destination. First, the purpose of the experiment was explained to the participants. After the experiment, participants were asked about their subjective judgment about comprehension, efficiency, and safety during the route (5 point Likert scales).

Route. The route led from the entrance of campus building A to tram stop and then from other tram stop to entrance of campus building A, through courtyard to classroom inside the campus building E. The route was approximately 1300 m long (850 m walking), contained one-stop ride with tram and combination of all classified environments.

Equipment. Five participants used their own smartphone (iPhone, Nokia) and for one participant we had to read the route itinerary aloud, because of phone failure. The route was prepared as an HTML document enabling the participants to use their phones. They could also use our phone Nokia 6120.

5   Results

Following paragraphs summarize the results of two experiments with participants with visual impairments. At the end of the section we provide key design recommendations for improvement of templates used to describe different situations in the navigation.

5.1   First Iteration

The first experiment was performed in a lab. Following paragraphs summarize key findings reported by participants.

Tram Station. P6 mentioned that the description of ticket machine can be redundant for blind people. For him would be safer, to go towards buildings on the other side of the sidewalk and then turn. He found turning after getting off the tram as very dangerous. In the same situation, P2 would prefer "on the other side of the sidewalk there are buildings" to our description "in front of you are buildings".

Exterior. P5 did not know what "marked crossing" means, he would like to hear "you can find crossing using cane". P3 and P6 would change "You are located at" to "You are at". A shorter version is better for them. P2, P5, P6 commented on entering the building – instruction about the building address (building number) is not useful information to find the entrance. Generally, participants want first find a place where to find an entrance and then obtain next information how to find correct door.

General Comments. P1, P2, P5 would like actions like "go through the door" to be assigned to the previous section when participant for the first time hear information about the door. Similarly, with actions like "go up using escalators", "go upstairs", or "go to floor number 3". All participants mentioned that repeating information about shape and measurements of card reader was distracting, participants want to hear it only once. P3, P5 commented that information about handrail is useful only when there is no handrail or it is dangerous to use the stairs. For P3, P5 number of steps was redundant information. All participant mentioned that summarized description of the building was too long.

5.2 Second Iteration

All participants successfully completed the route in the outdoor environment. The average completion time was 38 min (SD = 6.48 min) excluding waiting time for a tram.

The subjective judgments about efficiency and safety suggest usability of the templates – 5 participants agreed and 1 was neutral about efficiency; 3 strongly agreed, 2 were neutral and 1 disagreed about safety. Regarding comprehension of navigation instructions for different situations on the route 3 participants strongly agreed and 3 were neutral on comprehension of tram station; 3 strongly agreed, 2 agreed and 1 was neutral about comprehension of indoor segments; 3 strongly agreed and 3 agreed on comprehension of outdoor segments; and finally 3 strongly agreed, 1 agreed, 1 was neural and 1 disagree on comprehension of the building entrances.

First Tram Station. P1, P3, P4 missed the isle of tram station and continued farther away on a pedestrian crossing, even if there was information about lowered curb. P6 did not go straight on the crossing and hit the railing of the isle. Either with the guide dog, P6 did not succeed finding the isle. P2 and P5 found the isle without a problem but in the interview, they said they did not feel safe.

Second Tram Station. All participants managed to get off the tram and navigate towards opposite buildings without problems. P1, P2, P3, and P5 used haptic strip on the ground, contrarily P4 and P6 did not because their dog guided them to buildings.

First Entrance. P3, P4 did not recognize the stick-out facade with entrance at all. P4 was guided by the dog so s/he went in the middle of the pavement and sporadically used white-cane to discover the facade. P6 found the facade and entrance but was not sure if it is the correct door, so s/he passed it. P1, P2, and P5 found the facade and door to building without problems.

Courtyard. This section was complicated by heavy noise from ongoing reconstruction and objects (stands for posters and transferable railing) placed in the way. P6 stopped in the middle of the second segment and returned back to the beginning, then continued without major problems. P4 misunderstood the direction instruction in the third segment on the turn of the road and was confused where to go even s/he had a guide dog. All participants had not a good feeling about going through open space in the last segment towards the stairs. P2 appreciated the information about transformer station on the right because s/he was able to hear the noise from it and could assure that s/he is on the right way.

Second Entrance. All participants found the pyramidal stairs to the building and went through the door inside the building. P1 and P3 climbed up the stairs from the side despite there was a danger of falling. Other participants went up in the straight direction. P3 get stuck for a while in front of the second door of the entrance, where s/he was not able to find the correct leaf of this door that can be opened. P2, P5 complained about the distance to the pyramidal stairs, they said that it was less than 30 m and as a consequence of this they thought that there is another stairway, but eventually they recognized the pyramidal shape.

Interior. P5 missed the finish (door to a classroom) of the route because the door was open and he thought that it is a corridor. Other participants found the finish successfully. P2 missed the lift door, P3 missed it as well, but s/he was able to recover from this and return back. All participants apart from P5 had a problem with lift control, because there was no information about the card time limit for controlling the lift.

Building Descriptions. P1 was confused by information about the position of reception, s/he thought that s/he should go there.

5.3   Key Design Recommendations

Based on the findings collected during both experiments, the design recommendations were created. These recommendations can be used for future design.

However, there are still challenging situations in the navigation, e.g., how to find an entrance to the building or how to navigate through semi-outdoor environments e.g., courtyards.

R1: When entering the building, split this section into two. The first section should contain how to recognize the place where the entrance is (e.g., there are steps, different surface, ramp, change in the facade, etc.), the second section should contain detail information about the position and description of the correct door (e.g., second door in the niche).

R2: In segments where users have to find and recognize the entrance to the building, we should inform them in advance that there will be a door to the building. (i.e. "Go ahead and slightly uphill for 150 m to the facade that sticks out to the pavement. There will be an entrance to the building. Have buildings on your right."). Finding entrances is challenging, and this information can be helpful, as they will know what to expect and if they fail to find the entrance, they will be able to ask for help from passerby people.

R3: When navigation leads to the isle of the tram station, prefer using the front entrance if it is available. In an interview, the participants expressed themselves they are used to enter the isle at the front where the info-table is. The guide dogs are trained to find the info-table.

R4: Avoid dangerous turning immediately after getting off tram or bus. Lead the user to the other side of the sidewalk.

R5: When the user gets off the tram or bus inform how they should turn – have the tram behind the back or by the right/left hand. Not all of the participants used the haptic strips on the ground, mainly participants with guide dogs.

R6: Remove redundant information about stairs (handrail, number of steps). Inform users only when the stairs can be dangerous for them. It means that there is no wall or handrail on the sides of the stair, and the user can easily fall off.

R7: Walking through door composes of two segments – find the door – go through it. Merge segments containing identification of door or stairs with next segment containing the action to perform together. Do not merge them if there is an additional action needed, e.g., using a chip card to open.

R8: Navigation in semi-outdoor environments should be considered as navigation in outdoor. If possible use buildings as guiding line, if not use pavement or road borderlines. Avoid navigating through open spaces.

6   Conclusion and Future Work

This work aimed to elaborate on situations in navigation with environment transitions and public transport for people with visual impairment. First, we defined a typology of the environment used for the design of production quality GIS. Second, we prototyped and evaluated templates for automatic generation of landmark-enhanced navigation instruction for the transition between environments and for public transport. Third, we provide insights into the design process, which enables rapid prototyping without costly implementation of routing and templating algorithms.

Future development will focus on the use of Bluetooth beacons that are expected to provide route synchronization points and to help users to find an entrance or identify landmarks more easily.

Acknowledgements. The research has been supported by projects: Navigation of handicapped people funded by grant no. SGS16/236/OHK3/3T/13; Automated mapping of routes and barriers for pedestrians and disabled people funded by grant no. TH02010839 of the Technology Agency of the Czech Republic realized by Central European Data Agency, a.s.

References

1. Avila, M., Funk, M., Henze, N.: Dronenavigator: using drones for navigating visually impaired persons. In: ASSETS 2015, pp. 327–328. ACM (2015)
2. Azenkot, S., Prasain, S., Borning, A., Fortuna, E., Ladner, R.E., Wobbrock, J.O.: Enhancing independence and safety for blind and deaf-blind public transit riders. In: CHI 2011, pp. 3247–3256. ACM (2011)
3. Balata, J., Mikovec, Z., Bures, P., Mulickova, E.: Automatically generated landmark-enhanced navigation instructions for blind pedestrians. In: 2016 Federated Conference on Computer Science and Information Systems (FedCSIS), pp. 1605–1612. IEEE (2016)
4. Berka, J., Balata, J.: Supplementary material: situations classification, evaluation, route examples. Technical report Series of DCGI CS-TR-DCGI-2018-1, DCGI, Czech Technical University, FEE, March 2018
5. Bujacz, M., Baranski, P., Moranski, M., Strumillo, P., Materka, A.: Remote guidance for the blind - a proposed teleassistance system and navigation trials. In: HSI 2008, pp. 888–892. IEEE (2008). https://doi.org/10.1109/hsi.2008.4581561
6. Faria, J., Lopes, S., Fernandes, H., Martins, P., Barroso, J.: Electronic white cane for blind people navigation assistance. In: WAC 2010, pp. 1–7. IEEE (2010)
7. Fellner, I.: Automatic generation of landmark-based indoor routing instructions. In: GI_Forum 2017, vol. 1, pp. 106–113 (2017)
8. Foo, P., Warren, W.H., Duchon, A., Tarr, M.J.: Do humans integrate routes into a cognitive map? Map-versus landmark-based navigation of novel shortcuts. J. Exp. Psychol. Learn. Mem. Cogn. **31**(2), 195 (2005)
9. Golledge, R.G.: Geography and the disabled: a survey with special reference to vision impaired and blind populations. Tran. Inst. Br. Geograph. 63–85 (1993). https://doi.org/10.2307/623069

10. Guo, Y., Wang, W., Chen, X.: FreeNavi: landmark-based mapless indoor navigation based on WiFi fingerprints, pp. 1–5, June 2017
11. Lovelace, K.L., Hegarty, M., Montello, D.R.: Elements of good route directions in familiar and unfamiliar environments. In: Freksa, C., Mark, D.M. (eds.) COSIT 1999. LNCS, vol. 1661, pp. 65–82. Springer, Heidelberg (1999). https://doi.org/10.1007/3-540-48384-5_5
12. May, A.J., Ross, T., Bayer, S.H., Tarkiainen, M.J.: Pedestrian navigation aids: information requirements and design implications. Pers. Ubiquit. Comput. 7(6), 331–338 (2003). https://doi.org/10.1007/s00779-003-0248-5
13. Millar, S.: Understanding and Representing Space: Theory and Evidence from Studies with Blind and Sighted Children. Oxford University/Clarendon Press, Oxford/Wotton-under-Edge (1994)
14. Millar, S.: Space and Sense. Psychology Press, Hove (2008)
15. Sammer, G., Uhlmann, T., Unbehaun, W., Millonig, A., Mandl, B., Dangschat, J., Mayr, R.: Identification of mobility-impaired persons and analysis of their travel behavior and needs. Transp. Res. Rec.: J. Transp. Res. Board 2320, 46–54 (2012)
16. Völkel, T., Kühn, R., Weber, G.: Mobility impaired pedestrians are not cars: requirements for the annotation of geographical data. In: Miesenberger, K., Klaus, J., Zagler, W., Karshmer, A. (eds.) ICCHP 2008. LNCS, vol. 5105, pp. 1085–1092. Springer, Heidelberg (2008). https://doi.org/10.1007/978-3-540-70540-6_163
17. Völkel, T., Weber, G.: RouteCheckr: personalized multicriteria routing for mobility impaired pedestrians. In: ASSETS 2008, pp. 185–192. ACM (2008)
18. Vystrčil, J., Míkovec, Z., Slavík, P.: Naviterier-indoor navigation system for visually impaired. Smart Homes 2012, 25–28 (2012)
19. Zeng, L., Weber, G.: A pilot study of collaborative accessibility: how blind people find an entrance. In: MobileHCI 2015, pp. 347–356. ACM (2015)

Robust and Incremental Pedestrian Path Network Generation on OpenStreetMap for Safe Route Finding

Sebastian Ritterbusch[1,2(✉)] and Harald Kucharek[1]

[1] iXpoint Informationssysteme GmbH, Ettlingen, Germany
{sebastian.ritterbusch,harald.kucharek}@ixpoint.de
[2] VWA-Hochschule, Stuttgart, Germany

Abstract. Automatic route finding is an indispensable service in today's life. As so far, route finding is most used for car navigation, available map data is largely missing information specific to the needs of pedestrians. This is much worse for mobility impaired pedestrians, that need to find safer routes avoiding dangerous crossings. This paper introduces a robust, incremental, and transparent extension of the OpenStreetMap way network to enable the analysis for safe route finding, and its application to safer route finding for pedestrians with visual disabilities.

Keywords: Pedestrian · Route finding · OpenStreetMap
Blind mobility

1 Introduction

Pedestrian route finding is a common feature in route finding systems, and is used very often due to the availability and distribution of smartphones. At time of writing, map data mostly aims at car navigation, leading to inadequate route results, especially for mobility impaired pedestrians [1]. Different approaches have been proposed to mitigate the lack of data: Either to have users annotate paths with respect to their safety, and share this information [2], or encourage the mapping community to include missing information in the future. Like the successful WheelMap initiative making specialized routing feasible for general or electric wheelchairs [3,4], this work aims at closing this gap for safe pedestrian route finding. The development of this method is supported by the German Bundesministerium für Bildung und Forschung (BMBF).

2 Problem Statement and Related Work

In urban areas of developed countries, pedestrians can expect sidewalks to roads. Yet, only rarely they are included in maps such as the OpenStreetMap (OSM).

© Springer International Publishing AG, part of Springer Nature 2018
K. Miesenberger and G. Kouroupetroglou (Eds.): ICCHP 2018, LNCS 10897, pp. 302–309, 2018.
https://doi.org/10.1007/978-3-319-94274-2_42

For safe route finding, the system has to account for the road sides the pedestrian is walking on, as crossing a street can most often be considered to be of significantly higher risk.

As time of writing, only about 1% of roads, counted as ways with a highway-tag, have an information as a tag on existence or absence of a sidewalk attached. Looking at the situation on a well mapped city like Karlsruhe, Germany, with a strong local mapping community, we can easily find all combinations of roads with or without sidewalks with no tags, roads with or without sidewalks with tags, and roads with sidewalks with, with partial, or without informative tag about sidewalks as designated footpath ways.

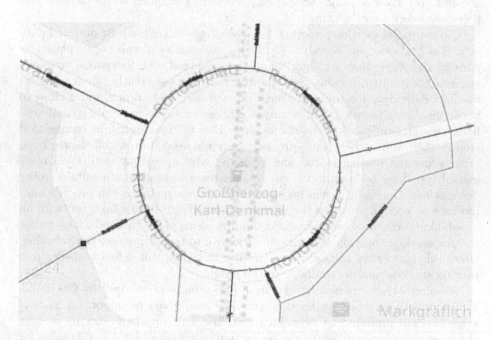

Fig. 1. Example from OSM of a circular road with roads connected to it in north, west, south, and east direction, all in gray. Partially, there are separated sidewalks given, and there are footpaths leading onto the road, all colored in green. OSM data and background image © OpenStreetMap contributors. (Color figure online)

Figure 1 shows a circular road and round open space in Karlsruhe, where side walks are partially given as separated ways, partially they have to be assumed to be at the road, as other footpaths are directly leading onto the road. At time of writing, the roads leading to the circular roads are tagged as having sidewalks on both sides, even when separated designated foot paths are given on the road at the south end of the map, the circular road is tagged having a sidewalk on the outer side. Traditional routing methods can detect crossings when using the separated footpaths on the east side of the given map, but they will route ways directly onto the roads on the west side of the map, generally, without being able to detect any road crossings, at all.

To enable safe route finding, first, the problem is to find a robust transform of the existing map data to a road-side considerate network. Second, it has to transparently include existing detailed sidewalk data, as well as suitably treating incomplete information applicable to life real-world data and application.

Solutions for specialized routing for wheelchairs as in [3,4] are based on the OSM network extended by user contributed information on accessibility and elevation maps. Their routing assume it is the responsibility of the user to choose the appropriate side of the road, and, in general, cannot take road crossings into account. Yet, their solutions should be open to be combined with road-side and therefore safety aware routing.

Closest to the solution presented here, are the works of Schmitz and Ertl [5,6] as well as Naumann and Kovalyov [7], where roads with sidewalks are replaced by parallel sidewalks, that are algorithmically connected with footpaths, crossings and roads without sidewalks. Schmitz and Ertl propose creating map transformations individual for the preferences of each user and adding nodes close to house numbers. Naumann and Kovalyov propose introducing evenly spaced artificial crossings on roads without crossings. Due to the algorithmic connection step in their approaches, a pre-processing step is needed on a sufficiently large area before the routing starts, and have the advantage that traditional routing software may be used, but needs some extensions to generate suitable route descriptions. Generally, it can be assumed that these methods can produce similar safe pedestrian routes as the method proposed within this text, but with an avoidable overhead of individualized pre-processing. Due to the lack of public routing services applying above methods known to the authors, in the following, when this text refers to traditional routing methods, this refers to pedestrian routing services that are available to the public.

An alternative approach is presented by Bolton et al. [8] and the OpenSide-Walks project, in which pedestrian ways are considered as important as road ways and are preferred to sidewalk notations. This approach can be seen as the most elaborate solution to the pedestrian routing problem, as this takes far more data and computing resources into account, and leads to a by far improved mapping. So far, only few cities have adopted this approach, and until the OSM community generally adopts this detail of mapping, there is a need for robust pedestrian routing methods. The method proposed in here, will benefit from such extended pedestrian networks.

Our solution follows the general idea of automatic extension the road network, but in contrast to earlier solutions, it approaches the extension from a node oriented point of view. This is done independent of any tags, simplifies connecting paths, and is leaving all ranking decisions, and therefore all individualization to the route finding algorithm. Furthermore, the network extension is done incrementally as needed by the route finding algorithm, so no global pre-processing step is necessary, even when working on life real-world data. Therefore, the proposed algorithm works on current OSM data without any extension necessary. Yet, we suffer from known logical fallacies, such as the line bundle problem in OpenStreetMap, on which the algorithm will show slightly degraded performance. .

3   OpenStreetMap Network Extension

In OSM, there are three fundamental data types: Nodes, ways, and relations. Nodes are defined by a GPS coordinate and tagged data. Ways are sequences of nodes, again with additionally tagged data, defining a polygonal chain on earth, and that are representing nearly all roads and paths. Relations are sets of all data types, representing more complicated structures, but this is not in the scope of this text.

3.1   Incremental Pedestrian Node Extension

The main concept of the incremental extension is the idea to replace all OSM Nodes by a set of artificial Pedestrian Nodes in the following. For an OSM Node, the set of ways that hit this node, can be split at the node, and can be strictly ordered. This leads to a well defined partition into ordered segments between the sorted way parts. Each segment is assigned a Pedestrian Node, denoting the road-side orientation between way parts with respect to the OSM Node. They also inherit the ways on edges of theirs segments augmented by the road-side orientation. Additional they are given crossing ways between neighbouring Pedestrian Nodes, and starting and terminating ways to OSM Nodes.

The Pedestrian Node extension can be done incrementally, as only the number of ways of OSM Node is needed to do the appropriate naming of Pedestrian Nodes. Therefore, if a route finding algorithm needs information on a Pedestrian Node, at most, the corresponding OSM Node, its neighbouring OSM Nodes, and ways originating from them have to be considered.

3.2   Pedestrian Node Displacement

Using information such as road classification, number of lanes, or very specific information on road width, each way can be assigned an approximate width. For each two ways meeting at a Pedestrian Node, a displacement from the OSM Node coordinate can be computed, to reflect each half-width of the ways. There are special cases, such as very sharp angles, where graceful degradation of the method is applied. While not directly needed for safety classification, this displacement improves visualization, improved guidance and gives more accurate distance estimates for improved route scores.

Figure 2 shows the map of Fig. 1 with Pedestrian Nodes. The original OSM Nodes are still there, to allow routing starting and ending precisely at such points. Preferably, routing should start and end at appropriate road sides, and therefore at the corresponding pedestrian nodes, as the road side of the starting and ending position can have significant impact on the final routing path. Note

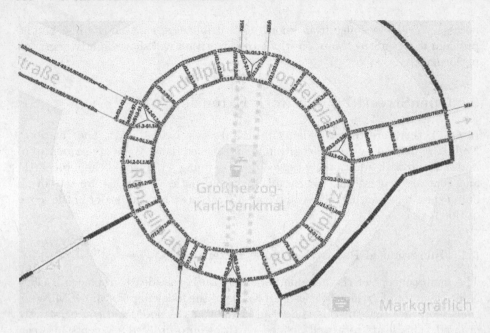

Fig. 2. Example from OSM of a circular road from Fig. 1 extended by Pedestrian Nodes. OSM data and background image © OpenStreetMap contributors.

that, for example, OSM Nodes that had three connected ways, now have three Pedestrian Nodes around them. Clearly, the paths going from and to OSM Nodes are only usable at the start or the end of routing, as else crossing sides was undetectable as with traditional routing methods. Note, that even paths inside the circular road were created, but they will not be used due to a high penalty to paths where explicitly no sidewalk is said to be present. Besides, uncontrolled crossings are also likely to be ruled out compared to the path around the road.

Figure 3 illustrates the known line bundle problem in the OSM. There, tram tracks are given as separate ways on the road with implicit sidewalks further outside. When a footpath crosses the road, the footpath first crosses the tram tracks before it reaches the road. As the sidewalks are topologically identified with the road, the mapping says that the crossing footpath must first cross the tracks before it crosses the sidewalks. A solution for the Pedestrian Node displacement is to locally reduce the road width leading to slight off-path errors, as shown in the figure. Yet, the approach is still better than traditional routing on the center of roads, and there are also more elaborate ways of reducing the impact of the logical error. In the end, this is an example of a common error that has to be corrected within the OSM, and is highlighted by the proposed approach.

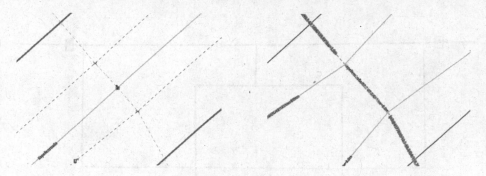

Fig. 3. The OSM map on the left, shows a road in orange with true sidewalks denoted in red. On the road, there are also tram tracks as dashed gray lines. A foot path in green crosses the road. The generated Pedestrian Node map on the right shows the degraded generated pedestrian sidewalk in orange. OSM data © OpenStreetMap contributors. (Color figure online)

4   Safe Route Finding

On a Pedestrian Node graph, safe route finding considering road crossings now is feasible: While all way tags remained the same, but well extended with additional topological information, the route finding algorithm may now apply different and individualized weights for walking along a road, or crossing it. For example, the costs for crossing may be nearly non-existent on footways, but is very costly for ways with no crossing. Also, the more detailed safety scoring allows to consider incomplete mapping data as well as highly accurate map data. Furthermore, the safety scoring may include road widths and classifications for an improved risk analysis for crossings.

In our experiments, we applied an A* route finding, but the general approach can be applied to more efficient hierarchical routing methods, or multi-criteria scoring as proposed in [2].

The generated description texts greatly benefit from the additional topological information in the Pedestrian Node network, and due to the added road-side awareness, directions can express this such as "Cross the road to your left, then turn right and follow the road on the left side." Due to inclusion of the routing into a general Modular Human-Computer Interaction Platform, the routing instructions may be given in a large variety of modes, individualized to the needs of the user, for example using narration, mobile Braille displays, vibration at arm, waist or foot, earcons and spatial sonification.

5   Example

A synthetic example in Fig. 4 illustrates how the method transparently deals with incomplete sidewalk data, as well as road-side dependent crossings. The

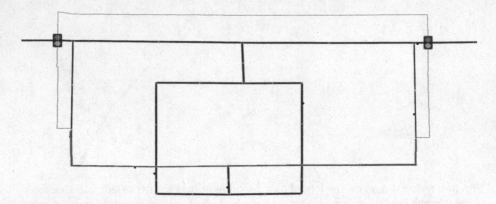

Fig. 4. Safe route in green from a side street without sidewalk tags using traffic lights over a main street with sidewalks. A traditional route finding results in a more direct path in red with uncontrolled crossings. Road widths are exaggerated for clarity. (Color figure online)

proposed routing is safer than a traditional routing based on roads as can take the sidewalks and side roads into account.

In Fig. 5 the proposed method is compared to traditional pedestrian routing on real OSM data of Karlsruhe, Germany, resulting in a slightly longer but safer route with less and mostly traffic light controlled crossings. In contrast to the traditional routing, the proposed method is clearly showing which side of road the user is expected to walk, and will express this in the route descriptions, or GPS path guidance.

Fig. 5. Exemplary routing in the city of Karlsruhe, Germany, comparing the proposed method in green with the path of a traditional router in pedestrian mode in red with several unsafe crossings. By choosing a slightly longer route, the proposed method specifies which sidewalk to use, and prefers a safer path using traffic lights and only one uncontrolled crossing. OSM data and background image © OpenStreetMap contributors. (Color figure online)

6   Conclusion

The proposed method offers a feasible basis for safe route finding based on incomplete real-world OSM map data. It will both help mobility impaired pedestrians finding safer routes, as well as aid the mapping community to understand and gradually improve the available data. Its main advantages to the solutions proposed in [5–7] lie in the robustness to incomplete data, an efficient incremental extension of the map, the independence of map transformation to preferences, the transparent correspondence of Pedestrian Nodes to OSM Nodes, and the additional information available to multi-modal route descriptions.

The safe route finding is currently actively used on daily updated OSM data set for Germany, Austria and Switzerland and improved by evaluating real-world test cases, leading to improved scoring, new scoring methods, or fixes to OSM map data. It is included in the TERRAIN project[1] mobile assistant to aid blind persons for individual mobility in urban environments.

References

1. Völkel, T., Kühn, R., Weber, G.: Mobility impaired pedestrians are not cars: requirements for the annotation of geographical data. In: Miesenberger, K., Klaus, J., Zagler, W., Karshmer, A. (eds.) ICCHP 2008. LNCS, vol. 5105, pp. 1085–1092. Springer, Heidelberg (2008). https://doi.org/10.1007/978-3-540-70540-6_163
2. Völkel, T., Weber, G.: RouteCheckr: personalized multicriteria routing for mobility impaired pedestrians. In: Proceedings of the 10th International ACM SIGACCESS Conference on Computers and Accessibility, pp. 185–192. ACM (2008)
3. Müller, A., Neis, P., Zipf, A.: Ein Routenplaner für Rollstuhlfahrer auf der Basis von OpenStreetMap-Daten. Konzeption, Realisierung und Perspektive n. AGIT (2010)
4. Franke, D., Dzafic, D., Baumeister, D., Kowalewski, S.: Energieeffizientes Routing für Elektrorollstühle. In: 13. Aachener Kolloquium Mobilität und Stadt (AMUS/ACMOTE), Aachen, pp. 65–67 (2012)
5. Schmitz, B., Ertl, T.: Rule-based transformation of map data. In: 2012 IEEE International Conference on Pervasive Computing and Communications Workshops (PERCOM Workshops), pp. 578–583. IEEE (2012)
6. Schmitz, B., Ertl, T.: Individualized route planning and guidance based on map content transformations. In: Miesenberger, K., Fels, D., Archambault, D., Peňáz, P., Zagler, W. (eds.) ICCHP 2014. LNCS, vol. 8548, pp. 120–127. Springer, Cham (2014). https://doi.org/10.1007/978-3-319-08599-9_19
7. Naumann, S., Kovalyov, M.Y.: Pedestrian route search based on OpenStreetMap. In: Sierpiński, G. (ed.) Intelligent Transport Systems and Travel Behaviour. AISC, vol. 505, pp. 87–96. Springer, Cham (2017). https://doi.org/10.1007/978-3-319-43991-4_8
8. Bolten, N., Mukherjee, S., Sipeeva, V., Tanweer, A., Caspi, A.: A pedestrian-centered data approach for equitable access to urban infrastructure environments. IBM J. Res. Dev. **61**(6), 10–1 (2017)

---

[1] http://www.terrain-projekt.de/, federally funded by BMBF, 07/2016–06/2019.

Low Vision and Blindness: Human Computer Interaction

BrailleRing: The Shortest Long Braille-Display in the World – A Review of the State-of-the-Art and a New Approach

Wolfgang L. Zagler[1,2](✉) [iD], Michael Treml[2], Dominik Busse[2],
Mike Busboom[2], and István Deák[2]

[1] Vienna University of Technology (retired), Vienna, Austria
[2] Team TETRAGON, Vienna, Austria
office@tetragon.at

Abstract. After paying tribute to the ground-breaking invention of the tactile alphabet by Louis Braille, the paper describes the technological development of so-called refreshable Braille-Displays in significant steps from the late 1970s up till now. Despite quite many R&D efforts over these 40 years, all Braille-Displays presently available on the market in principle follow the same construction scheme as disclosed by Tetzlaff in 1981: Piezo-electric benders which move small pins up- and down [1]. In order to overcome several drawbacks of the classical solutions, we propose and investigate a radically new approach, where different combinations of rigid tactile points are placed on the surfaces of rotating cuboids which are arranged inside of a rotating cylinder. The lower half of the cylinder resembles the reading area for the finger, whereas a group of a few actuators by rotating said cuboids produces new text-content in the upper half. This can result not only in a complete new way of mobile and reasonably priced Braille reading equipment but also in a revival of Braille worldwide.

Keywords: Braille · Braille-Display · Braille reader

1 Introduction

When the French teacher, Louis Braille, developed a tactile system of dots to enable his blind students to read and write, he probably had little understanding of how his invention would positively impact literacy among blind people worldwide. With just six tactile dots, arranged in a 2×3 matrix, it became possible for blind people to gain literacy, do complicated math and read music notation, among many other things.

Today access to digitally provided text for blind and severely visually impaired people can be achieved in three ways: (i) Printing on thick paper to produce traditional hardcopy Braille, (ii) converting the text into synthetic speech (TTS, speech synthesizer) or (iii) using so called "refreshable Braille-Displays" from which the dot patterns of the Braille characters can be read with the fingertip.

K. Miesenberger and G. Kouroupetroglou (Eds.): ICCHP 2018, LNCS 10897, pp. 313–321, 2018.
https://doi.org/10.1007/978-3-319-94274-2_43

2 Requirements

It has to be mentioned that Braille is not a language but a font consisting of 63 different characters (for 6-dot Braille) or 255 characters (for 8-dot Braille) – not counting the "white space". For this reason Braille can be used for any language on earth as well as for Mathematics, Chemistry, Music and much more. Thus, the requirements for Braille in general and for Braille-Displays in particular have to fulfil the demands of a global market and a "one-size-fits-all" strategy will not necessarily be the best one. Nevertheless, a dot-to-dot spacing of about 2.5 mm and a minimum force of 200 mN (for a single pin pressing against the skin of the fingertip) are readily agreed upon as quasi-standards. What is even more important, above all other mechanical considerations, is the fact that the best and most precise tactile stimulation can only be achieved by sliding the finger across the Braille reading area. Raising and lowering pins beneath a static resting fingertip will not do satisfactorily [2].

3 A Historic Review of Braille-Displays

Despite all R&D efforts of the past decades, up to now only two technologies for building refreshable Braille-Displays have found their way onto the market.

3.1 Electromagnetic Actuators (Solenoids)

Realistic electromagnetic Braille-Displays using solenoid plungers or electromagnetic flappers were first disclosed as early as 1973 e.g. by Lindenmüller and Schönherr [3], but there are still recent publications which try to come up with improvements [4, 5]. Solenoids either need a lot of space and energy to produce sufficient forces or will, when miniaturized to fit beneath the footprint of a single Braille-dot, only provide low forces making latching mechanisms necessary (Fig. 1, left [3]).

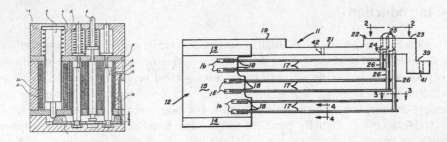

Fig. 1. Left: electromagnetic Braille-Display [3]; Right: piezo-electric benders [1]

3.2 Piezo-Electric Actuators

Piezo-electric actuators (bimorph benders) for Braille-Displays were introduced in 1979 by Tetzlaff [1] and still constitute the operating principle of all present commercially available Braille-Displays (Fig. 1, right).

4 The Search for Alternatives

Presently used technologies have some significant drawbacks such as low forces, relatively big volumes, considerable sensitivity to dirt and moisture and especially high manufacturing and service costs. The search for better alternatives was immediately undertaken. A literature search in 2018 for improvements and alternative technologies revealed about 1,000 patents which match "Braille + Display" and also at least the same number of research papers. The main strands of R&D deal with actuator technology, ways to reduce the number of actuators, or tactile stimulation methods which avoid actuators completely by direct stimulation of the fingertip's skin.

4.1 Alternative Actuators for Forming Single Braille-Dots

- *Shape Memory Alloys* (SMA) are materials which are able to "remember" their shape (length, bending) prior to a deformation and return to this shape after heating. Thus pairs of wires or coils of SMA can be used for moving a Braille-pin up and down. Material fatigue turned out to be the main problem [6].
- *Thermal processes* like in a steam engine e.g. by heating a small volume of paraffin and using the resulting expansion to drive a pin were proposed by [7]. Drawbacks are heat dissipation and low response times especially for the cooling phase.
- *Electro Active Polymers* (EAP) change their shape when exposed to an electric field. Promising research is under way [8] but without significant breakthroughs.
- *Optical/chemical processes* like the expansion of liquid crystal carbon nanotube (LC-CNT) when exposed to light stemming from single LEDs or from an entire display surface (tablet-PCs) are proposed by [9].
- *Micromachines* (MEMS) which can be mass-produced by stereo-lithography are a promising approach to build thermal or ultrasound motors [10] able to move Braille-pins even to different heights, but not yet ready for commercialization.
- *Pneumatic or hydraulic drives*: Here holes or other cavities are sealed with an elastic film. Raising the pressure in the cavity (by air- or fluid-pressure) will cause the film to form a bubble (blister) which will resemble a single Braille-dot [11]. Often so called Electro-Rheological Fluids (ERF) are used which change from low to high viscosity when an electric field is applied. Thus flow and pressure for forming the "bubbles" can be controlled just by electric fields instead of expensive and complicated mechanical valves [12].

4.2 Direct Skin Stimulation – No Moving Parts

To avoid the necessity for any moving parts (pins, actuators) several researchers experimented with direct stimulation of the neural tissue of the fingertip.

- *Electrocutaneous stimulation:* The Braille-Display consists of a flat surface with an electrode (monopolar or better bipolar) for every Braille-dot. When the fingertip moves across this surface, active dots (electrodes) will send a well-defined electric current into the user's skin, causing a feeling comparable to a mechanical stimulus.

Unfortunately, many parameters (impedance, conductance and local sensitivity) are subject to temporal and spatial changes and reliable and comfortable stimulation could not easily be achieved [13].

- *Electromagnetic radiation* by focusing infrared laser light to stimulate deeper skin areas is proposed in [14].
- *Electrostatic forces:* Locally changing the adhesive shear-forces exerted on the sliding fingertip by applying (well isolated) dot-shaped electrostatic charges [15].

4.3   Reducing the Number of Actuators by Using Moving Elements

A major drawback of mechanical solutions is the number of delicate components needed. In piezo-electric Braille-Displays, each pin has its own actuator, adding up to a whopping 320 actuators in a standard 8-dot display with 40 characters. Newer approaches try to solve this issue by moving other parts of the device additionally or instead of the pins.

- *Pins on a disk or drum:* Braille characters are displayed on a rotating disk or drum. The pins are set and reset when passing by a group of (a few) actuators (Fig. 2, left and center [16, 17]).
- *Dots on polygon surfaces:* Instead of pins shifting up and down in a hole, these inventions place rigid Braille-dot patterns on the 3 or 8 lateral surfaces of three- or eight-sided prisms. Using eight-sided prisms turned out to be space consuming and unsuitable for 8-dot Braille (Fig. 2, right [18]). The use of three-sided prisms would allow for displaying dots with two different haptic characteristics – however, the problem of actuating every single dot cannot be avoided this way [19].

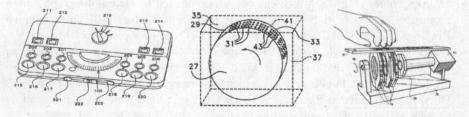

Fig. 2. Braille on a disk [16], on a drum [17] or on the sides of a polygon [18]

5   State-of-the-Art Display Configurations

5.1   Lines Ranging from 10 to 80 Characters – 6 and 8 Dot Braille

The most common configuration for today's Braille-Displays are single lines with 10 to 80 characters. According to a study by Ramstein [20], lines with 40 Braille-cells allow for the most fluent reading. Shorter lines certainly are less expensive and can be used in mobile settings, however, the reader is forced to frequent backward movements which are time consuming and inconvenient (Fig. 3, left). Very long lines ask for extensive arm movements and thus cause unwanted fatigue (Fig. 3, center).

5.2   Multiline and Graphic (Matrix) Displays

Efforts to ease reading by displaying multiple lines or even an entire page of Braille reach back until 1981 with the invention of the "Rose Reader" [21]. Commercialization, however, failed due to enormous complexity and costs. Even more recent developments like the "Hyperbraille" with a 120×60 pin matrix (Fig. 3, right) suffer from a price tag between EUR 45,000 and EUR 50,000 [22].

Fig. 3. Typical Braille-Display configurations: left: Orbit 20 (www.aph.org/orbit-reader-20); centre: Brailliant 80 (www.humanware.com/brailliant); right: Hyperbraille [21]

5.3   Static Single-Cell and Virtual Braille-Displays

To make Braille-Displays more affordable especially for developing countries, several researchers tried to reduce Braille-lines to just one single cell [4]. As pins are raised and lowered below a static resting finger, the missing lateral movements lead to very low reading rates and complete loss of spatial orientation along the line of text.

To overcome the page or line orientation problem, virtual Braille-Displays have been designed, where one [20] or few [23] Braille-cells can be moved along a virtual line or across a virtual page showing the contents of the location thus addressed.

To simulate lateral skin stimulation Fricke [2] proposed "peristaltic" movements of densely spaced pins and Lévesque [24] laterally moving actuators (Fig. 4, right).

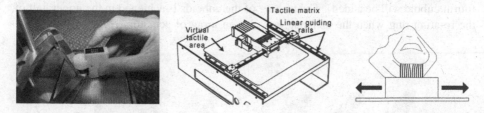

Fig. 4. Left: Pantobraille [20]; centre: Braille on a carriage [23]; Right: lateral stimulation [24]

6   Striving for a New Approach – The *"BrailleRing"*

6.1   The Concept

Starting in 2014 with a basic idea for a robust, pocket-sized and reasonably priced Braille-Display, two students from the TU Wien were successful in proving the concept in their theses [25, 26] and in building an enlarged (2.5:1) prototype. Since then, the concept has been refined and pre-tested by blind users with simple mock-ups. A national patent [27] was granted, international applications are pending.

The *BrailleRing* strives not to replace existing Braille-lines, just as a "Kindle" cannot replace a PC. Moreover, it should become an alternative for those applications where existing technology is too bulky, too heavy, too delicate or too expensive.

The *BrailleRing* will be small and, nevertheless, capable of showing long lines of text. This is achieved by displaying the Braille-characters on the inside of a rotating ring. While the reading finger rests at the bottom of the device, the user will slide the entire device like a computer mouse across a table surface. By friction the ring will rotate proportional to the speed and direction of the hand movement, letting the Braille-characters glide beneath the reading finger (Fig. 5, left).

Fig. 5. Left: Reading with the *BrailleRing*; Right: Braille-cuboids in a ring-shaped assembly

6.2 Realization

Instead of single moving pins, the *BrailleRing* forms the dot-combinations of Braille by turning small cuboids with rigid Braille-dots on their lateral surfaces. Figure 6 (left) shows the transition from "R" to "H" for the conventional approach by lowering pin 3 (bottom-left corner). In the *BrailleRing* the transition is accomplished by a 90° clockwise turn of cuboid 3 (Fig. 6, right). The 64 combinations of Braille-dots are produced by turning one or more cuboids to the desired position (for 8-dot Braille a fourth cuboid will be added). The turning of the cuboids is achieved in the upper half of the rotating ring when the elements pass by an array of actuators [27].

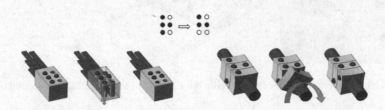

Fig. 6. Transition from "R" to "H": left: conventional display; right: *BrailleRing* method

6.3 Features and Benefits

The *BrailleRing* has a huge potential to significantly increase the mobility of Braille-Displays. The design allows building very compact devices where the line length is completely defined by the user. A later envisaged motor drive could provide even endless lines. The concept will also increase robustness, making the display more suitable for outdoor activities where humidity, sand and dust could be an issue. If built in such a way that the rotating ring can be changed easily, the user would be able to clean the device on his or her own. Different types of rings can be provided according to specific user preferences (e.g. different shaped or sized dots). It should be possible to build a device with much lower production and service costs than conventional piezo-electric Braille-Displays. Therefore, the *BrailleRing* should also be ideally suited for a market in developing countries.

7 Discussion

7.1 Present State of the Development

Presently (March 2018), several mock-ups and simulation devices in real size exist or are under development. These aim to understand the reading experience inside a ring and demonstrate the final size of the device (mobile). As the Braille-dots are not formed by moving pins, the *BrailleRing* will offer much more degrees of freedom in haptic Braille representation. We intend to invest significant efforts to optimize the tactile user experience before the final design.

Another development goal for the second quarter of 2018 will be the search for optimized actuators that are able to turn the cuboids reliably independent of reading speed and direction while at the same time, minimizing the power consumption, which is crucial for a mobile device.

7.2 User Involvement and Trials

While the discovery of the mechanism with disruptive potential was serendipitous, a user-centric approach is what steers further development. Before IP protection, user involvement was on a nondisclosure basis, so only one single (blind) Braille expert was included from the outset. This was changed after the patent was granted and user studies started immediately. They can be described in two major phases:

First, through local news reports about the invention, a call for user-participation triggered 25 curious responses by blind people. Around half of them were invited to semi-structured interviews conducted in-person. Simple mockups were used to explore the new way of reading and the concept of a truly mobile Braille-Display.

In the second phase, the list of candidates for user studies grew to 50 by word-of-mouth. Here the user trials will focus on usability, ergonomics and especially on tests with different Braille pattern sizes and dimensions. This is crucial, as some first trial-users mentioned that the felt character to character distance is smaller when read from a concave surface. Afterwards, user studies with an adapted mockup will follow where reading speed and error rate compared to conventional flat Braille-Displays will be measured quantitatively.

References

1. Tetzlaff, J.F.: Patent US 4283 178 A (1981)

2. Fricke, J., Baehring, H.: Displaying laterally moving tactile information. In: Zagler, W.L., Busby, G., Wagner, R.R. (eds.) ICCHP 1994. LNCS, vol. 860, pp. 461–468. Springer, Heidelberg (1994). https://doi.org/10.1007/3-540-58476-5_169

3. Lindenmüller, H.P., Schönherr, K.P.: Patent US 3987 438 (1975)

4. Anu, U.S., Thomas, A.M., Krishna, C.R., Akhil, A.N.S.K., Potti, S.S.: A low cost refreshable Braille display; a novel approach for the primary education of blind in India. Int. J. Adv. Technol. Eng. Sci. 5(4), 286–292 (2017)

5. Shah, S.: Patent WO 2017 203 536 A1 (2017)

6. Chen, X.: Patent WO 2016 197 928 A1 (2016)

7. Green, S.R., Gregory, B.J., Gupta, N.K.: Dynamic Braille display utilizing phase-change microactuators. In: Proceedings of IEEE Sensors, pp. 307–310 (2006)

8. Bar-Cohen, Y.: Refreshable Braille displays using EAP actuators. In: SPIE Smart Structures and Materials+Nondestructive Evaluation and Health Monitoring, vol. 7642, pp. 764206–764206-5 (2010)

9. Camargo, C.J., et al.: Batch fabrication of optical actuators using nanotube-elastomer composites. J. Micromech. Microeng. 22(7), 75009 (2012)

10. Velázquez, R., Hernández, H., Preza, E.: A portable piezoelectric tactile terminal for Braille readers. Appl. Bionics Biomech. 9(1), 45–60 (2012)

11. Wilhelm, E., Schwarz, T., Jaworek, G., Voigt, A., Rapp, B.E.: Towards displaying graphics on a cheap, large-scale Braille display. In: Miesenberger, K., Fels, D., Archambault, D., Peňáz, P., Zagler, W. (eds.) ICCHP 2014. LNCS, vol. 8547, pp. 662–669. Springer, Cham (2014). https://doi.org/10.1007/978-3-319-08596-8_102

12. Luning, X., Han, L., Yufei, L., Shen, R., Kunquan, L.: Operational durability of a giant ER valve for Braille display. Smart Mater. Struct. 26(5), 54003 (2017)

13. Liu, Z., Luo, Y., Cordero, J., Zhao, N., Shen, Y.: Finger-eye: a wearable text reading assistive system for the blind and visually impaired. In: 2016 IEEE International Conference on Real-Time Computing and Robotics, RCAR 2016, pp. 123–128 (2016)

14. Yu, W.J., Brownell, A.A.: Patent US 2014 0022 162 Al (2014)

15. Bateman, A., et al.: A user-centered design and analysis of an electrostatic haptic touchscreen system for students with visual impairments. Int. J. Hum. Comput. Stud. 109 (May 2016), 102–111 (2018)

16. Shimamura, Y.: Patent EP 1 5222 983 A1 (2004)

17. Roberts, J.W.: Patent US 2002 0045 151 A1 (2002)

18. Al-Qudsi, M.: Patent US 2013 0203 022 A1 (2013)

19. Campos de Leon, G.M.: Patent US 9524 655 B1 (2016)

20. Ramstein, C.: Combining haptic and braille technologies: design issues and pilot study. In: Annual ACM Conference on Assistive technologies, pp. 37–44 (1996)

21. Rose, L., Rose, S.E.: Patent US 4 226 936 (1981)

22. Esteve, J.: Towards smart tactile tablets for the visually impaired persons. In: EPoSS Annual Forum (2011)

23. Chan, J.S., Maucher, T., Schemmel, J., Kilroy, D., Newell, F.N., Meier, K.: The virtual haptic display: a device for exploring 2-D virtual shapes in the tactile modality. Behav. Res. Methods 39(4), 802–810 (2007)

24. Lévesque, V., Pasquero, J., Hayward, V., Legault, M.: Display of virtual braille dots by lateral skin deformation: feasibility study. ACM Trans. Appl. Percept. 2(2), 132–149 (2005)

25. Treml, M.: Grobkonzeption und Steuerung eines Brailledisplays mit gruppierten Punkten. Diplomarbeit TU Wien (2016)

26. Busse, D.: Konstruktion eines Braille-Displays. Diplomarbeit TU Wien (2016)

27. Treml, M., Zagler, W., Busse, D.: Vorrichtung zur Darstellung von tastbaren Zeichen. Patent AT 518 530 A4 (2016)

One-Handed Braille in the Air

Krzysztof Dobosz[✉] and Kornelia Buchczyk

Institute of Informatics, Silesian University of Technology, Gliwice, Poland
krzysztof.dobosz@polsl.pl,
kornbuc255@student.polsl.pl

Abstract. This paper presents a new concept the Braille typing by simple finger movements and swipe gesture in a 3D space. Braille codes are typed row by row. The content of the row is indicated by one or two fingers. At the end, a single swipe gesture must be performed to confirm a character. The best obtained results was 2.12 WPM. Although the value is low, the method has a significant advantage: it can be used for blind people with a paresis of one hand.

Keywords: Braille · Text entry · Leap Motion

1 Introduction

Communication is key to human expression. Information technologies have a significant impact on human relations, from personal to social communication. Information exchange is not only talking, but also text typing. Disability has a significant impact on communication skills and can significantly reduce a human participation in interpersonal, social and professional life. A special case of disability is visual impairment. At the beginning, the blind were used mechanical Braille typewriters. Development of mobile technologies has opened new opportunities. There were introduced virtual Braille keyboards using the surface of touchscreen. Unfortunately, the flat surface of the mobile device also has many inconveniences for the blind.

The goal of the project is to use the benefits of gesture detection in 3D space to a new touchless typing method for blind people with a paresis of one hand.

2 Background

Rapid development of the mobile technology in the 21st century resulted with smartphones and tablets. The interaction started to use touches and gestures on the surface of the touchscreen. In the *BrailleType* [1], the user marked required dots using only one finger by tapping proper buttons one by one. *LeBraille* [2] is the similar project improving the Braille typing by audio and vibration feedback. Two fingers were used in *TypeInBraille* [3], where two dots were type at the same time row-by-row. Another approach called *Perkinput* operated with three fingers, which are used at the same time [4]. First, the left column were entered, then the right one. Next the *BrailleEasy* method combines the comfort of one-handed typing with the speed of two-handed [5]. Another similar method is *OneHandBraille* [6] used three fingers replacing neighboring dots

© Springer International Publishing AG, part of Springer Nature 2018
K. Miesenberger and G. Kouroupetroglou (Eds.): ICCHP 2018, LNCS 10897, pp. 322–325, 2018.
https://doi.org/10.1007/978-3-319-94274-2_44

with swipes. The most efficient solution is BrailleTouch [7]. The application interface includes six virtual buttons corresponding to Braille dots. The smartphone has to be hold horizontally and the touchscreen has to be facing away from the user.

The second aspect of the study is gesture recognition in 3D space realized by the Leap Motion (LM) device generating almost 200 data frames per second (FPS). This controller were analyzed using a high-precision optical tracking system [8]. Provided studies shown high potential of this device in human-computer interfaces. Research [9] has shown that an accuracy is less than 0.5 mm for motions, other study indicated the accuracy of detection for static hands is below the human hand tremor [10]. Although the LM controller is not as precise as more sophisticated optical motion capture systems that is sufficiently reliable for the measurement of motor performance in pointing tasks that do not require high positional accuracy [11]. Some interaction methods focus on the moves in the horizontal axis only [12], due to a way of use common devices: mouse, touch pad, or touch screen. More degrees of freedom require more advanced motor and coordination skills. However, the gesture plane does not have to be parallel to the ground. That was shown in the prototype method of typing Braille in 3D space, where each of six fingers corresponds to proper dot [13].

3 Method

The idea is to enter the text by simple fingers movements and swipe gesture. The idea is to divide each character into three parts where each part corresponds to a particular row of a Braille code. A row is an individual extension of one finger or two fingers (depending on the character). In the case of an empty row in a Braille cell, extension of fingers is replaced by a clenched fist. At the end, a single swipe gesture must be performed to confirm a character. An example of typing Q character is shown in Fig. 1.

Fig. 1. Example of typing U character.

Left and right dot in the current row are indicated by corresponding fingers: index and middle. And here is the great role of the LM controller, which automatically recognized proper finger. For characters from A to J, where only two first rows are used, a third row can be omitted by a swipe gesture.

The proposed method was implemented in the form of a desktop application. When it starting, the user is prompted to show his hand (all fingers) to make a calibration. Then correctness of finger recognition can be verified (Fig. 2).

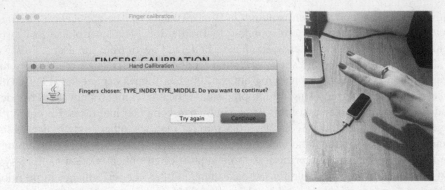

Fig. 2. Verification of right hand index and middle fingers.

4   Evaluation

First we tried to estimate expected speed of typing. The task was not easy due to the variable number of time frames when the controller acquired data from the observed 3D area. This number depends on the overheating of the controller. Considering that number (its lowest value: 50 FPS), time to stabilize the hand position in the area above the controller implemented in the software (80 FPS), and the additional time for a swipe confirming a single code (1 s), the obtained result was 2.07 words per minute (WPM). Assuming that experienced users need less time stabilize the hand (60 FPS) to type, calculated typing speed increases to the value of 2.61 WPM.

The method was evaluated by eight people aged 22–48 with visual impairment on different levels. They were familiar with Braille code. First, during the short pre-phase when they learn to use research environment consisting of desktop application and LM controller. Then their task was typing three times the pangram: *"quick brown fox jumps over the lazy dog"*. The assumption was to ignore errors and keep typing the sentence. Obtained results were: 1.42 WPM and MSD error rate equals 15.25. The experiment was repeated with configuration for more experienced users (shorter time for hand stabilization). Then the typing speed improved (2.12 WPM), but MSD error rate we have got worse (19.75).

5   Conclusions

Previous research shown that the LM controller can be successfully used for typing Braille in the air, where dots of the Braille code can be indicated by corresponding fingers. The independence from the plane of typing is a great advantage, but a big inconvenience is fast tiredness of hands when typing long text. We have shown how to improve that method using only one hand but slowing down the efficiency. The best obtained result was 2.12 WPM. The value is low, but our proposal has the significant advantage: the method can be used for blind people with a paresis of one hand.

Acknowledgements. Publication financed by the Institute of Informatics at Silesian University of Technology, statutory research no. BK/213/Rau2/2018.

References

1. Oliveira, J., Guerreiro, T., Nicolau, H., Jorge, J., Gonçalves, D.: BrailleType: unleashing Braille over touch screen mobile phones. In: Campos, P., Graham, N., Jorge, J., Nunes, N., Palanque, P., Winckler, M. (eds.) INTERACT 2011. LNCS, vol. 6946, pp. 100–107. Springer, Heidelberg (2011). https://doi.org/10.1007/978-3-642-23774-4_10
2. Façanha, A.R., Viana, W., Pequeno, M.C., de Borba Campos, M., Sánchez, J.: Touchscreen mobile phones virtual keyboarding for people with visual disabilities. In: Kurosu, M. (ed.) HCI 2014. LNCS, vol. 8512, pp. 134–145. Springer, Cham (2014). https://doi.org/10.1007/978-3-319-07227-2_14
3. Mascetti, S., Bernareggi, C., Belotti, M.: TypeinBraille: a Braille-based typing application for touchscreen devices. In: The Proceedings of the 13th International ACM SIGACCESS Conference on Computers and Accessibility, pp. 295–296 (2011)
4. Azenkot, S., Wobbrock, J.O., Prasain, S., Ladner, R.E.: Input finger detection for nonvisual touch screen text entry in Perkinput. In: Proceedings of Graphics Interface 2012, pp. 121–129. Canadian Information Processing Society (2012)
5. Šepić, B., Ghanem, A., Vogel, S.: BrailleEasy: one-handed Braille keyboard for smartphones. Stud. Health Technol. Inform. **217**, 1030–1035 (2015)
6. Dobosz, K., Szuścik, M.: OneHandBraille: an alternative virtual keyboard for blind people. In: Gruca, A., Czachórski, T., Harezlak, K., Kozielski, S., Piotrowska, A. (eds.) ICMMI 2017. AISC, vol. 659, pp. 62–71. Springer, Cham (2018). https://doi.org/10.1007/978-3-319-67792-7_7
7. Romero, M., Frey, B., Southern, C., Abowd, G.D.: BrailleTouch: designing a mobile eyes-free soft keyboard. In: Proceedings of the 13th International Conference on Human Computer Interaction with Mobile Devices and Services, pp. 707–709. ACM (2011)
8. Guna, J., Jakus, G., Pogacnik, M., Tomazic, S., Sodnik, J.: An analysis of the precision and reliability of the leap motion sensor and its suitability for static and dynamic tracking. Sensors **14**(2), 3702–3720 (2014)
9. Weichert, F., Bachmann, D., Rudak, B., Fisseler, D.: Analysis of the accuracy and robustness of the leap motion controller. Sensors **13**(5), 6380–6393 (2013)
10. Sturman, M.M., Vaillancourt, D.E., Corcos, D.M.: Effects of aging on the regularity of physiological tremor. J. Neurophysiol. **93**(6), 3064–3074 (2005)
11. Tung, J.Y., Lulic, T., Gonzalez, D.A., Tran, J., Dickerson, C.R., Roy, E.A.: Evaluation of a portable markerless finger position capture device: accuracy of the leap motion controller in healthy adults. Physiol. Meas. **36**(5), 1025 (2015)
12. Bachmann, D., Weichert, F., Rinkenauer, G.: Evaluation of the leap motion controller as a new contact-free pointing device. Sensors **15**(1), 214–233 (2014)
13. Dobosz, K., Mazgaj, M.: Typing Braille code in the air with the leap motion controller. In: Gruca, A., Czachórski, T., Harezlak, K., Kozielski, S., Piotrowska, A. (eds.) ICMMI 2017. AISC, vol. 659, pp. 43–51. Springer, Cham (2018). https://doi.org/10.1007/978-3-319-67792-7_5

Parallel Braille on Smartphones for Deaf-Blind People

Krzysztof Dobosz[(✉)] and Michał Surowiec

Institute of Informatics, Silesian University of Technology, Gliwice, Poland
krzysztof.dobosz@polsl.pl,
michsur195@student.polsl.pl

Abstract. The objective of this work is to develop an interaction method that uses the touch screen of smartphones and embedded vibration mechanisms. During the study, three methods of communication with deaf-blind were analyzed: Morse code, Braille code for one device, parallel Braille code for two devices. The new concept is the third one. The main device send one column of the Braille code to the second device, then both vibrate own columns of the current character. Analysis of methods was carried out by comparing the reading time and correctness of character recognition for different time units of vibration signals. Considering the fact that the efficiency and the correctness of the characters recognition of the parallel Braille are similar to Morse, this approach seems to be quite an interesting alternative for deaf-blind users.

Keywords: Deaf-blind · Braille · Smartphone · Reader

1 Introduction

This work focuses on the issue of facilitating (or even allowing) access to mobile technologies for people with a specific type of disability - both sight and hearing. Due to the particularly difficult communication possibilities, these people may have problems with the development of intellectual, social and emotional skills. This problem is compounded by the need to communicate with these people through the sense of touch that is not used by healthy people for direct communication. Although existing solutions are appreciated [1], we have the need for new approaches to enable deafblind people to participate in the new information and communication systems emerging in today's society.

Most of the existing modern solutions of readers for deafblind require an additional device: dot watch, glove, Braille monitor, etc. The use of these devices involves an additional purchase cost for the deaf-blind person who uses them. The aim of this work is to develop an interaction method that uses the touch screen of common smartphones and embedded vibration mechanisms. This means a much lower cost than other solutions. In the frame of the project, three approaches to reading text were compared: the Morse code, the Braille code and a new one: parallel Braille code.

© Springer International Publishing AG, part of Springer Nature 2018
K. Miesenberger and G. Kouroupetroglou (Eds.): ICCHP 2018, LNCS 10897, pp. 326–332, 2018.
https://doi.org/10.1007/978-3-319-94274-2_45

2 Background

Due to the impairment of both the sense of sight and the sense of hearing, deaf people in communication must use the sense of touch. Different methods of communication are used for deaf-blind persons, based on this sense. The most effective way for a deafblind person to relate to the others is by using the hands to recognize gestures. The set of gestures can be called as an alphabet. The most known implementations of these alphabets use gloves with sensors and vibrators for the communication with deaf-blind persons are:

- Latin alphabet - the characters of the alphabet are drawn in the palm of a hand. It does not require any learning from a non-disabled person to communicate with a deafblind person (although there are additional, optional rules for specifying the characters of the alphabet). It can be particularly helpful for people who have not been deaf since birth and who have lost their sight and hearing is already familiar with the Latin alphabet;
- Lorm alphabet - is based on the touch of fragments of a deafblind person's hand, however single characters of the alphabet are touches of the hand or drawn lines. Thanks to this approach, people familiar with the Lorm alphabet can communicate with each other more quickly [2, 3];
- Malossi alphabet - similar in its assumptions to the Lorm alphabet, but simplified. The single characters of the Latin alphabet correspond only to touching in the right places of the hand (no lines are drawn) [4];
- Braille code - many deaf-blind people know it. The finger fragments correspond to the dots from the six-dot Braille system, with the pressures corresponding to the convex dots of the code. Messages from a mobile device can be received with the glove in the form of vibrations on the fingers corresponding to the Braille code [5, 6];
- Simplified Braille code - a body-Braille systems allows the user to read Braille characters through six micro-vibrators settled on the surface of the body such as the back, head or arms. Unfortunately the dispersed vibration can causes read errors by phantom sensation. The problem can be solved by reducing the number of vibrators to two [7];
- Morse code - a method of transmitting text information as a series of on-off or short-long signals that can be directly listen. The deaf-blind person "hears" Morse code via a vibro-tactile device. Hardware cost to equip a standard personal computer with Morse interface is very low. Vibro-tactile Morse code is particularly easy, because it can be adapted for the individual's particular tactile sensitivities. [8, 9].

In addition to the above mentioned approaches using micro-vibrations, deafblind people can successfully use solutions originally intended for blind people, such as Braille displays. Such solutions are well-suited for systems providing access for deafblind people to the Internet [10].

3 Methods

Three methods of communication with deaf-blind were analyzed during the study:

- Morse code - a short signal of vibration corresponds to a dot, a long signal to a dash,
- Braille code for one device - a six-dot representation of the Braille alphabet is interpreted successively by columns (1-dimensional sequence of 6 dots), where a dot is interpreted as a long vibration signal, no dot - as short,
- Parallel Braille code for two devices – six dots is divided into two parts according to the columns, which are simultaneously interpreted on the two devices by vibrations (as above).

The interpretation of Braille code is analogous to Morse code: the dot corresponds to one time unit, dash - 3 units, space between symbols - 1 unit, space between characters - 3 units, and the space between words - 7 units long.

The realization in the form of the mobile application was easy for methods working on a single mobile device. The method of parallel Braille uses two devices, which had to communicate via Bluetooth. Both have to vibrate own column of the current character code. The total time t allocated to the reading of a current character equals the reading time of the longer (counting time units) column of the code. Two versions of this method were considered:

- unsynchronized – first device sends the right column and immediately vibrates the left one, at the same time waits for timeout equals t, then processes the next character; second device receives the right column and immediately vibrates it;
- synchronized – first device sends the right column and waits for the confirmation of receipt by second device, then both start to vibrate own columns.

4 Evaluation and Discuss

For the purpose of this work, a research tool was prepared in the form of a mobile application for smartphones with the Android operating system. The choice of the reading method is made by the user from the application settings screen (Fig. 1a). For each one it is possible to change the length of the time unit, and in the consequence time of long signal (Fig. 1b). In the case of parallel Braille, the application has to be installed and run on two devices, and the same options ("*Two device Braille reader*" or "*Two device Braille sync reader*") must be selected. Both create a simple Personal Area Network (PAN), where one of them work as a master, second - as a slave.

The study involved nine volunteers aged 22–48 (3 females, 6 males). No one was completely deaf-blind. They partially knew the Morse code and the Braille code. Nevertheless, the limited knowledge of these codes was not a problem, because the research was carried out with the support of an assistant who registered recognized characters spoken by volunteers.

Analysis of methods was carried out by comparing the reading time and correctness of character recognition for different time units of vibration signals. The selected time unit values were: 200, 300, 400 and 500 ms. This range was chosen for practical

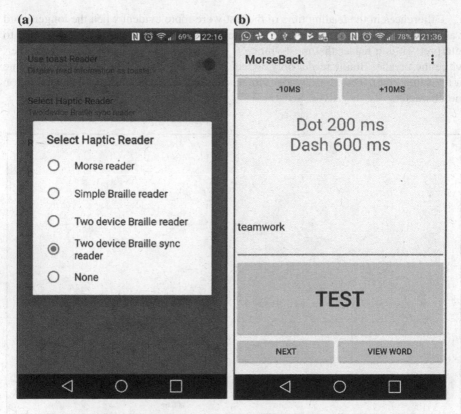

Fig. 1. (a) Menu of the software tool, (b) MorseBack – Morse code reader

reasons. During the preliminary tests, it was noted that below 200 ms the readability of the user decreased very clearly, above 500 ms the average reading rate was very slow. Then it was observed that in the unsynchronized version of the parallel Braille, due to delays of Bluetooth communication, the implementation resulted the desynchronization of read data in cases of long words. Therefore, the evaluation of the unsynchronized version was abandoned.

For each of the previously mentioned three methods, for each unit of time, 15 English words were drawn from a pool of 3700. In terms of reading time, the Morse code reader with the average reading speed (1.8 to 3.75 WPM) was the most advantageous, then the Braille alphabet reader for two devices (1.3 to 2.55 WPM). The slowest is the simple Braille alphabet reader (0.86 to 1.67 WPM). Details of the obtained results (max, min, average values and standard deviation for selected time units) are shown in the Fig. 2 (one by one for the methods: Morse, simple Braille, parallel Braille). As mentioned, the words were random. Their average length ranged from 7 to 9 characters, depending on the experiment. It should be remembered that the results obtained are understated in the comparison to other similar studies, where it is assumed that the average length of the English word is 5 characters.

Differences in the reading time of the test were more evident when the longer word was read. The obtained results for a simple Braille alphabet reader are the easiest to interpret - it is a reader that must vibrate 6 dots (or empty places) for each character, while the parallel Braille reader only 3 (second part vibrates on the second smartphone at the same time). The Morse reader vibrates from 1 to 4 dots or dashes, depending on the character.

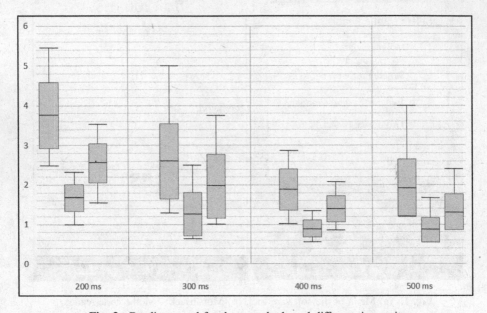

Fig. 2. Reading speed for three methods and different time units

Figure 3 presents obtained results of the correctness of character reading for three methods (Morse, simple Braille, and parallel Braille) one by one, for different time unit values.

It can be observed that for almost all values of the time unit, the highest correctness of character recognition was obtained using a simple Braille alphabet reader, the second one was the Morse reader. An exception is for the unit value of 300 ms, when parallel Braille gave better correctness than the Morse code reader and not much worse than a simple Braille reader. In other hand, the shortest unit time (200 ms) caused a significant difficulty in parallel reading the text using two smartphones.

The best results regarding the correctness of character recognition were obtained for the Morse code and a simple interpretation of the Braille code, for the longest unit values (400 ms and 500 ms), reaching over 90% of correctly read characters. If the speed of reading the words is additionally taken into account, then the Morse code reader is much better with almost two times shorter time.

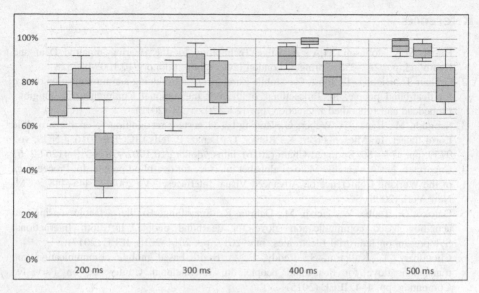

Fig. 3. Correctness of character recognition

5 Conclusions

Summarizing the study, cannot be determined which method of reading information by deaf-blind using smartphones is the best. The Morse code was created to transmit information through modulated signals - sound or light. Therefore, moving it to represent signals by vibration agrees with the intention with which this alphabet was created. However, the Morse code is not as well known by users as the Braille code. Symbols in the Braille alphabet, in basic use, are read as the whole set of dots, when the reader senses them on the fingers. To present the symbols of the Braille code as a sequence of vibration signals in not common. On the other hand, the Braille is the most widespread among people with visual impairments, which may mean a shorter time to adapt the user to use this alphabet than the Morse code.

In the middle between both of these methods is a new proposal of parallel Braille reading. Considering the facts that its efficiency is similar to Morse and the correctness of the characters recognition (additional focus to read some of the data in parallel) can be improved by training, the parallel Braille seems to be quite interesting for deaf-blind users.

Acknowledgements. Publication financed by the Institute of Informatics at Silesian University of Technology, statutory research no. BK/213/Rau2/2018.

References

1. Hersh, M.A., Johnson, M.A.: Assistive Technology for the Hearing-impaired Deaf and Deafblind, pp. 257–273. Springer, London (2003). https://doi.org/10.1007/b97528
2. Gollner, U., Bieling, T., Joost, G.: Mobile Lorm glove: introducing a communication device for deaf-blind people. In: Proceedings of the 6th International Conference on Tangible, Embedded and Embodied Interaction, pp. 127–130. ACM (2012)
3. Schmidt, M., Bank, C., Weber, G.: Zoning-based gesture recognition to enable a mobile Lorm trainer. In: Miesenberger, K., Bühler, C., Penaz, P. (eds.) ICCHP 2016. LNCS, vol. 9759, pp. 479–486. Springer, Cham (2016). https://doi.org/10.1007/978-3-319-41267-2_67
4. Caporusso, N.: A wearable Malossi alphabet interface for deafblind people. In: Proceedings of the Working Conference on Advanced Visual Interfaces, AVI 2008, s. 445–448. ACM, New York (2008)
5. Ozioko, O., Taube, W., Hersh, M., Dahiya, R.: SmartFingerBraille: a tactile sensing and actuation based communication glove for deafblind people. In: 26th International Symposium on Industrial Electronics, June 2017, pp. 2014–2018. IEEE (2017)
6. Choudhary, T., Kulkarni, S., Reddy, P.: A Braille-based mobile communication and translation glove for deaf-blind people. In: International Conference on Pervasive Computing, pp. 1–4. IEEE (2015)
7. Ohtsuka, S., Sasaki, N., Hasegawa, S., Harakawa, T.: Introduction of new body-braille devices and applications. In: Miesenberger, K., Karshmer, A., Penaz, P., Zagler, W. (eds.) ICCHP 2012. LNCS, vol. 7383, pp. 672–675. Springer, Heidelberg (2012). https://doi.org/10.1007/978-3-642-31534-3_98
8. Arato, A., Markus, N., Juhasz, Z.: Teaching Morse language to a deaf-blind person for reading and writing SMS on an ordinary vibrating smartphone. In: Miesenberger, K., Fels, D., Archambault, D., Peňáz, P., Zagler, W. (eds.) ICCHP 2014. LNCS, vol. 8548, pp. 393–396. Springer, Cham (2014). https://doi.org/10.1007/978-3-319-08599-9_59
9. Zuckerman, D.: Use of personal computing technology by deaf-blind individuals. ACM SIGCAPH Comput. Phys. Handicap. 33, 14–17 (1984)
10. Kobayashi, M.: Internet chat system for the deaf-blind using doubled Braille display – DB4DB. In: Miesenberger, K., Klaus, J., Zagler, W.L., Karshmer, A.I. (eds.) ICCHP 2006. LNCS, vol. 4061, pp. 870–873. Springer, Heidelberg (2006). https://doi.org/10.1007/11788713_126

Gaze Based Magnification to Assist Visually Impaired Persons

Stephan Pölzer$^{(\boxtimes)}$, Elias Gander, and Klaus Miesenberger

Institute Integriert Studieren, Johannes Kepler Universität Linz, Linz, Austria
{stephan.poelzer,elias.gander,klaus.miesenberger}@jku.at

Abstract. Screen magnifiers are one of the core tools to assist people with visual impairments in accessing digital content. We introduce an approach to minimize interaction requirements by magnifying at the fixation point/area which is identified using eye tracking. Screen magnifiers mostly use the cursor to define the magnification area and ask for configuring when and how to magnify. This paper presents a modular design of a gaze based magnification tool reducing interaction tasks and thereby also supporting a good overview of the content and thereby showing potential to improve usability. Modularization supports an easy integration of filtering and personalization techniques to support adjustment of gaze based magnification to unusual eye-movements as e.g. nystagmus.

Keywords: Visual impaired persons · Magnification · Eye-tracking
Modular-design

1 Introduction

To do their daily work on computers visually impaired persons use screen magnifiers to access the displayed content. Today's typical screen magnifiers are configured by manually setting the scale level and the mode of the magnifier (lens mode, displaced lens mode or full screen mode). Screen magnifiers are normally adjunct to the actual cursor position. Adjunction of the magnifier to the courser position comes along with the drawback that the mouse has to be used to move the magnified part of the image. Moving the mouse can be a cumbersome task for instance when reading a file on a notebook where only a touchpad is available.

Using a gaze based magnification concept can overcome the above mentioned problem to manually shift around the courser position by a permanent mouse movement. Gaze based magnification concepts work by permanently tracking the users gaze point on the screen via eye-trackers and adapting the displayed information to the tracked gaze-position. Gaze based magnification heavily relies on eye-tracking with all the drawbacks of eye-tracking e.g. expensive devices, calibration issues and tracking problems in the case of abnormal eye-movements. This paper presents a prototype based on the low cost Tobii EyeX eye-tracker. The implemented tool is designed in a modular way, which allows to easily integrate filters to overcome issues of abnormal eye-movements. Further it allows the integration of profiles for specific scenarios and user needs (for instance including a profile for reading).

© Springer International Publishing AG, part of Springer Nature 2018
K. Miesenberger and G. Kouroupetroglou (Eds.): ICCHP 2018, LNCS 10897, pp. 333–337, 2018.
https://doi.org/10.1007/978-3-319-94274-2_46

2 State of the Art

Designing screen magnifiers to support visual impaired persons come along with several challenges. In case of the lens mode one core challenge lies in the field of magnification level together with the magnified part of the screen [1]. A higher magnification level can increase the end users performance, but also requires a larger screen area to present an amount of visual information that can still be put into context by the end-user. In the lens-mode a larger magnification area has the drawback of hiding a larger part of the magnified content's context. Hiding surrounding content come along with the drawback of losing the understanding of the total presented information.

Gaze contingent displays are used in several domains like investigation of spatial vision by high resolution displays and reducing the resolution outside the field of view [2]. In assistive technologies gaze contingent magnification and gaze contingent displays are rarely considered and until now mainly exist as research prototypes.

One approach using gaze based magnification using a fisheye-lens is presented by Duchowski et al. [3]. They try to overcome the problem of hidden content around the magnification lens by two concepts. One strategy is to use the fisheye-lens with the highest magnification level in the center and lower magnification levels at the borders of the fisheye-lens. The second strategy is to present the magnified content only when the user is focusing a point, otherwise the lens is hidden. Another approach of gaze based magnification also developed by Duchowski and Eaddy [4] was especially designed for persons suffering from scotoma, i.e. an area of decreased vision in their field of view. Another gaze based magnification tool was designed by Aguilar and Castet [5]. The focus of this tool is to support reading tasks by using a displaced lens to allow reading without moving the lens. A completely different approach of a magnifier for people suffering under Optic Nerve Hypoplasia is presented by Mousa et al. [6]. The designed device is based on a head mounted camera and eye-tracker. The recorded data is magnified and presented to the user. Therefore this approach is not restricted to screen magnification.

The approaches presented above illustrate the variety of possible application domains of gaze based magnifiers. However the mentioned tools are mainly designed for specific user conditions and are lacking in terms of adaptability. The goal of the following presented prototype and its architecture is to allow an easy adaptation of different parts of the system. The exchangeability and adaptability of the separate modules makes the system customable to different eye-movements and specific user needs.

3 Implementation

As mentioned above the aim of the prototype's architecture is modularity, which should guarantee an easy adaptability/extensibility to different abnormal eye-movements. To achieve the modularity the system architecture is based on a pipe structure. Three independent modules (eye tracking module, processing module and magnifier module) are connected via TCP/IP sockets. Figure 1 represents the architecture. The implementation of the separate modules was done in C++. The choice of C++ was made due to the need for fast data processing and the availability of the Tobii EyeX SDK.

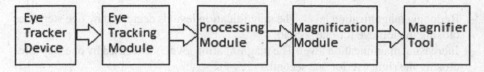

Fig. 1. Pipe architecture

3.1 Eye-Tracking Device and Eye-Tracking Module

The eye-tracking module is mainly responsible for communication with the eye-tracker and recording of the gaze points. It passes the tracked gaze points to the processing module. For the prototype the low cost eye-tracker Tobii EyeX was used, which has a sampling rate of about 60 Hz. The Tobii EyeX needed USB 3.0. In case that the eye-tracker has to be changed only the eye-tracking module, especially the part handling the communication with the hardware device, has to be adapted. A possible replacement in the low cost sector can be the Tobii 4C. In contrast to the Tobii EyeX it only needs a USB 2.0 connection and less computational power but still provides same accuracy as the Tobii EyeX.

3.2 Processing Module

The goal of the processing module is to process, adapt and filter the tracked gaze points to achieve a functional gaze based magnifier for different types of abnormal eye-movements. As an example the actual implemented prototype provides a moving average filter, with configurable window size, to stabilize the gaze based magnifier in the case of a pendula Nystagmus. More complex strategies to separate unintended from intended eye-movements or even to compensate time delays caused by calculation time as presented in [7] can be added to this module. The processed data is passed over a TCP/IP connection to the magnification module.

3.3 Magnification Module and Magnification Tool

The magnification module is responsible for adapting the received data to the used magnification tool. In the prototype the used magnification tool is the Windows magnification lens. Therefore the magnification module sets courser position based on the processed data.

3.4 User Interface

The designed prototype is started via command line. The provided batch file starts the executables in the defined order (eye-tracking module, processing module, magnification module). HCI is based on gaze-based interaction. Eye closure was chosen as activation command for eye-based interaction. As it turns out gaze-based interaction is not very intuitive, however no separate graphical user interface has to be designed. Currently the following commands are integrated:

- Reducing magnification level: The magnification level is decreased by one step after closing the left eye for one second.
- Increasing magnification level: The magnification level is increased by one step after closing the right eye for one second.
- Resizing of the lens: Closing both eyes for one second activates the resizing functionality of the lens. Resizing is done via the provided drag functionality of the windows magnifier, meaning that the user changes the magnifier size via eye-movements.

4 User Evaluation

4.1 Evaluation Scenario and Methodology

User evaluation was done with five participants according to the guidelines for heuristic evaluation by Nielsen and Molich [8]. Two participants suffered from Nystagmus and three participants had normal visual acuity. Whereas the normal sighted participants were mainly evaluating the functionality of the tool the participants with Nystagmus evaluated the usability and the helpfulness of the tool. Based on the low numbers of participants feedback was gained by the operator through observation and collecting users' comments. All participants faced a running setup with an open text editor. The participants were asked to type text and to follow the insert position with the magnification lens. The participants were allowed to type their own text and were not provided with any template text. The lens-size was approximately 200×500 pixels and the zoom level was set according to the user's request. Additionally users were asked to test different commands like changing magnification level by closing one eye for at least one second.

4.2 Results

For all participants the lens was found out to be surprisingly stable. However for the participants with Nystagmus the lens jitter was noticeable. Still with a moving average filter and a maximum scaling size of 200% the jitter was considered acceptable by the evaluation participants. Increasing the scaling size up to 400% increased the jitter substantially.

Evaluation of the commands clearly showed the drawbacks of user interaction via gaze commands. It was hard to change the magnification level by closing one eye and further nearly impossible to resize the lens via the designed interface. Furthermore sometimes commands were triggered unintentionally by the users.

In general using the gaze based magnification tool for a longer period of time showed that users become more aware of their gaze movements while using the system and therefore the stability of the lens increased.

5   Conclusions and Outlook

The prototype showed that an adequate filter can stabilize the lens for patients suffering from Nystagmus and render the enlarged information usable. However to achieve a helpful gaze based magnification system further development has to be done. Special care has to be placed on the design of filters for different pathological eye-movements to guarantee stability for a broad range of target groups. Designing filters for different pathological eye-movements will come along with the challenge task not to risk an increased time delay of when adapting the magnified information on the screen (lens position).

The evaluation of the prototype showed that an interaction via eye-based commands is quite difficult. An alternative Human Computer Interface has to be designed to overcome the existing difficulties, drawbacks and problems of the actual implementation.

Further improvements can be done, by allowing the user to choose different types of magnification modes (for instance a different type of lens in the case of scotoma, or full screen mode to avoid the problem of hidden content). Different profiles can be integrated for different activities like reading, writing or watching movies. Another profile can allow to switch quickly between manual magnification mode and gaze based magnification mode.

Summing up the conducted experiments lead us to the assumption that gaze based magnifiers have the potential to support visual impaired persons in daily work. Still to be usable as a state of the art assistive technology several improvements of the designed prototype have to be made as discussed before. Eye-trackers get cheaper, more accurate and are already used in several different domains like gaming. This gives reason to hope that development of gaze based magnifiers as well as other assistive technology devices based on eye-trackers will get easier in the next years.

References

1. Blenkhorn, P., Evans, G., King, A., Hastuti Kurniawan, S., Sutcliffe, A.: Screenmagnifiers: evolution and evaluation. IEEE Comput. Graph. Appl. **23**(5), 54–61 (2003)
2. Loschky, L.C., McConkie, G.W.: Investigating spatial vision and dynamic attentional selection using a gaze-contingent multiresolutional display. J. Exp. Psychol. Appl. **8**, 99 (2002)
3. Ashmore, M., Duchowski, A.T., Shoemaker, G.: Efficient eye pointing with a fisheye lens. In: GI, pp. 203–210 (2005)
4. Duchowski, A.T., Eaddy, T.D.: A gaze-contingent display compensating for scotomata. In: Eurographics (2009)
5. Aguilar, C., Castet, E.: Evaluation of a gaze-controlled vision enhancement system for reading in visually impaired people. PLoS ONE **12**(4), e0174910 (2017)
6. Mousa, H., Al-saboni, Y., Al-Habash, B., El Din, M.S., Al-Nashash, H.: Visual aid for optic nerve hypoplasia patients. In: MECBME (2014)
7. Pölzer S., Miesenberger K. Assisting people with nystagmus through image stabilization: using an ARX model to overcome processing delays. In: 2017 39th Annual International Conference of the IEEE Engineering in Medicine and Biology Society (EMBC), Series IEEE Xplore, pp. 1222–1225 (2017)
8. Nielsen, J., Molich, R.: Heuristic evaluation of user interfaces. In: CHI, pp. 249–256 (1990)

Blind FLM Web-Based Tools for Keystroke-Level Predictive Assessment of Visually Impaired Smartphone Interaction

Shiroq Al-Megren[✉], Wejdan Altamimi, and Hend S. Al-Khalifa

Information Technology Department, King Saud University,
Riyadh 11451, Saudi Arabia
{salmegren,hendk}@ksu.edu.sa, wejdanaltamimi@gmail.com

Abstract. The keystroke-level model (KLM) is a predictive model used to evaluate motor behaviour in skilled error-free user interaction involving conventional techniques, i.e. mouse and keyboard. A blind fingerstroke-level model (blind FLM) was recently introduced as an extension of KLM to assess visually impaired interaction on smartphones. The model comprises six operators that are used to calculate the time required for a visually impaired expert user to accomplish a task on a smartphone. In this paper, we present two blind FLM tools: calculator and editor. These tools enable designers to create behavioural models of user tasks from which reliable estimates of skilled user task times can be computed. Each tool was used to model a sample task on YouTube to assess its performance against previously recorded values. Both tools accurately predicted user performance with an average error of 1.27%.

Keywords: Keystroke-level model · Blind FLM · Visual impairment
Blind interaction · Smartphone

1 Introduction

Goals, operators, methods, and selection rules (GOMS) is a popular method to compare and evaluate motor behaviour during skilled error-free user performance. The keystroke-level model (KLM) is the simplest implementation of GOMS, in which a task is divided into a set of operations that can numerically predict execution times. The original implementation of KLM only considered desktop environments in which users are assumed not to be disabled and can see and interact with an interface. For that purpose, a blind fingerstroke-level model (blind FLM) was proposed for smartphone interactions by users who are visually impaired [1]. This paper introduces two blind FLM web-based tools implemented to better estimate the task completion times of expert users who are visually impaired. Utilising these tools can substantially reduce the time

© Springer International Publishing AG, part of Springer Nature 2018
K. Miesenberger and G. Kouroupetroglou (Eds.): ICCHP 2018, LNCS 10897, pp. 338–342, 2018.
https://doi.org/10.1007/978-3-319-94274-2_47

required to learn how to use the tools and, more importantly, the time required to model the smartphone interactions of visually impaired users.

Several tools have been developed for the purpose of simplifying and automating KLM modelling. These tools differ in their complexity and modelling capabilities, which consequently affect their learning curves. Cogulator[1] is an open-source performance modelling tool that is used to estimate task times using KLM and other models from the GOMS family. It is also used to assess mental workload. CogTool[2] has been commonly used to construct graphical prototypes from visual mock-ups of web interfaces, which are then used to estimate user performance. Simpler tools can also be found, such as KLM calculators developed by MIT and Sytagm. Although the tools presented in this paper are not intended to replace any of these popular tools, they do consider interaction not previously modelled by other implementations.

2   Blind FLM

Blind FLM is a behavioural model used to predict numerically the time required for a visually impaired expert user to accomplish a task on a smartphone. Unlike other KLM extensions (e.g. [3–5]) that assume users are not disabled and can thus see and interact with an interface, the blind FLM model is based on studies of users who are visually impaired. In blind FLM, tasks are categorised in a list of physical, cognitive, or perceptual operators. These operators are: tap (0.31 s), drag (17 s), flick (12 s), double tap (0.62 s), mental act (1.35 s), and system response (negligible). Moreover, the mental operator is governed by a set of heuristic rules that consider cognitive preparation. Two of these are updated versions of rules from the original KLM [2]. An updated Rule 0 dictates that M is to be inserted in front of all F, T, D and DT operators, and Rule 3 states that M must be removed when it is related to one cognitive unit expect for the first M. A task execution time is calculated from operator unit times as follows: $T_{execute} = T_T + T_D + T_F + T_{DT} + T_M + T_R$. The performance of blind FLM was empirically validated, where predictions resulted in a root mean square (RMSE) of less than 3%, which is within the acceptable KLM RMSE of 21%.

3   Blind FLM Tools

The implemented web-based tools for blind FLM are used to simulate expert users who are visually impaired to numerically predict task performance accurately and early in a interface's development. These tools are intended to reduce the time required to model tasks using blind FLM while requiring minimal training. Two web-based tools were developed: a calculator and an editor[3]. The blind FLM calculator produces task subdivisions that mimic the equation used to compute the execution time. By contrast, the blind FLM editor approaches model

---

[1] http://cogulator.io/.

[2] https://github.com/cogtool/.

[3] https://github.com/blindflm/BlindFLMTools.

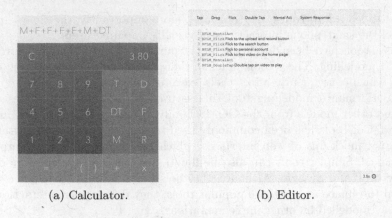

(a) Calculator.   (b) Editor.

Fig. 1. Blind FLM web-based tools.

development using a pseudo-programming approach that allows for more flexibility and expansion. Both tools allow a designer to adjust and reset the original blind FLM operator values. The remainder of this section presents these two tools and assesses their operation against user-measured performances on a sample YouTube task [1]. In this task, the participants were asked to play the first video on their personal homepage by following these steps: flick to upload and record button, flick to search button, flick to personal account, flick to the first video on the home page, and finally double tap on the video to play. In the experiments, execution times were logged for 20 participants and were found to be 4.8 s on average, which is 1.0 s slower than the predicted time (modelled manually) of 3.8 s, with an RMSE of 1.27% [1]. This value considers the manual insertion of two mental act operators following blind FLM heuristic rules: before the first flick and double tap.

3.1   Blind FLM Calculator

The blind FLM Calculator was implemented using HTML and JavaScript. The calculator extends an original calculator with the models' operators (see Fig. 1a). The calculator allows designers to construct divided tasks into an execution time equation. The calculator consists of several functional buttons categorized as: numbers (0–9), math operators (=, +, ×, and parentheses), and blind FLM operators. At the top of the calculator screen is an output window that displays the constructed task execution equation. The results of the modelled task can be exported to a text file along with the predicted execution time. In our experiment, the calculator was used to construct a YouTube task using the following equation: $T_{YouTube} = M + F + F + F + F + M + DT$. The predicted execution time was calculated as 3.8 s, matching the value previously computed manually. This also meant that compared to an observed time of 4.8 s, the RMSE was well below the suggested 21% error [2].

3.2   Blind FLM Editor

Similar to the blind FLM calculator, the editor was implemented using HTML and JavaScript. It embeds CodeMirror[4], an open-source programming API that is implemented with a browser. Using this tool, a designer can model a task using a pseudo-programming approach (see Fig. 1b). Compared to the blind FLM calculator, the editor offers more flexibility, as it allows for comments to be inserted without affecting the computed execution time. In the editor program, a designer can produce a list of predicted interactions. The interactions can then be assigned to a blind FLM operator by either placing the cursor before the listed interaction or by highlighting the listed interaction and then clicking on the appropriate operator. This will place a blind FLM operator (denoted as BFLM_Op) before the listed interaction and assign an execution time. The execution time automatically updates as more operators are assigned. The constructed model and computed values can also be exported to a text file. The YouTube task was modelled using the blind FLM editor and the execution time was predicted to be 3.8 s, a value similar to what was predicted manually and produced by the calculator.

4   Conclusion and Future Work

This paper presented two web-based tools for the modelling of smartphone interaction by users who are visually impaired. The tools adopted two modelling approaches: a calculator constructs equations and an editor adopts a pseudo-programming approach. The performance of both tools was assessed against previously observed user performances and was shown to accurately predict a task execution time. For future work, the tools will be extended to enable model modification, thus allowing for more flexibility. The performance of the tools will also be assessed in real-life design cases and the model's construction examined against users' performances.

References

1. Al-Megren, S., Altamimi, W., Al-Khalifa, H.S.: Blind FLM: an enhanced keystroke-level model for visually impaired smartphone interaction. In: Bernhaupt, R., Dalvi, G., Joshi, A., Balkrishan, D.K., O'Neill, J., Winckler, M. (eds.) INTERACT 2017. LNCS, vol. 10513, pp. 155–172. Springer, Cham (2017). https://doi.org/10.1007/978-3-319-67744-6_10
2. Card, S.K., Moran, T.P., Newel, A.: The keystroke-level model for user performance time with interactive systems. Commun. ACM **23**, 396–410 (1980)
3. El Batran, K., Dunlop, M.D.: Enhancing KLM (keystroke-level model) to fit touch screen mobile devices. In: Proceedings of the 16th International Conference on Human-Computer Interaction with Mobile Devices & Services - MobileHCI 2014, pp. 283–286. ACM (2014)

---

[4] https://codemirror.net/.

4. Lee, A., Song, K., Ryu, H.B., Kim, J., Kwon, G.: Fingerstroke time estimates for touchscreen-based mobile gaming interaction. Hum. Mov. Sci. **44**, 211–224 (2015)
5. Rice, A.D., Lartigue, J.W.: Touch-Level Model (TLM): evolving KLM-GOMS for touchscreen and mobile devices. In: Proceedings of the 2014 ACM Southeast Regional Conference, p. 53. ACM (2014)

Continuous Writing the Braille Code

Krzysztof Dobosz[(✉)] and Tomasz Depta

Institute of Informatics, Silesian University of Technology, Gliwice, Poland
krzysztof.dobosz@polsl.pl,
tomadep124@student.polsl.pl

Abstract. This paper describes a set of new methods of Braille character recognition with the use of mobile devices such as smartphones. In the frame of the studies, a set of four varying solutions was proposed, further called modes. They are: a simple mode, an acute angle mode, a minimum distance mode, and a scaled mode. Using them, the solutions are designed and implemented for the Android OS platform. The solutions were evaluated using a theoretical model called CLC (curve-line-corner). It was designed to deter-mine the speed of pen stroke gesture, although it is proven that there is no significant difference between pen and finger gestures, thus the results of the model appear to be valid. The model de-composes each stroke into simpler elements, allowing to calculate their production time using proper formulae. Once this is done the performance of the proposed solutions is compared with the existing ones. The results are satisfactory, as the average words per minute count was approximately 25. It is quite high result, although still on par with some of similar solutions.

Keywords: Braille · Text entry · Touch screen · Smartphone

1 Introduction

Nowadays, the fundamental element of the mobile devices is a touch screen. The user can give input or control the mobile device touching directly the screen or through simple or multi-touch gestures. However, the change of physical keyboards to touch screens, despite its undeniable advantages, makes mobile devices difficult to use by the special group of users - people with visual impairment. The smartphone has no physical buttons (sometimes excepting a "home" button). The front surface of the smartphone is completely smooth without a tactile border between the touch sensitive area and a frame. This can lead to a situation when a blind person using the phone is not able to determine where his finger is on the screen, but also whether he touches the active area of the display, i.e. screen button of the virtual Braille keyboard.

The aim of this project is to design and develop a new method that has not been introduced before, allowing the user to input Braille characters with a single, contin-uous swipe on the screen of a mobile device. Basing on the path created by the user, the method should, in several different ways, determine what symbol it best corresponds to. Finally, the performance of all methods is to be compared to determine the best one.

© Springer International Publishing AG, part of Springer Nature 2018
K. Miesenberger and G. Kouroupetroglou (Eds.): ICCHP 2018, LNCS 10897, pp. 343–350, 2018.
https://doi.org/10.1007/978-3-319-94274-2_48

2 Related Works

The progress of mobile technologies has resulted in many new methods using touch screens. Looking at the field of new methods of writing Braille, one should first mention two different projects designed mainly for people with mobility impairments, still used in the case of visually impaired people, namely *EdgeWrite* [1] and *GrooveWrite* [2]. Both solutions are non-Braille solutions, and similar in their basic concept. First one utilized a special template with a square hole and a stylus; a user needed to write the symbols with the stylus along the edges and diagonals of the hole. The second one - instead of a square, used a seven-segment layout. This solution determined a character written basing on marked edges rather than corners. This change allowed the encoded symbols to look much more similar to Latin characters and digits as far as shape is concerned.

Next there were proposed approaches directly using Braille dots - user interface consisted of six buttons (*BrailleType* [3]). For each Braille dot positioned similarly to a standard Braille code. To create a Braille character, the user marked required dots by tapping proper buttons. Very similar project called *LeBraille* [4], improved typing the Braille code using audio and vibration feedbacks. Another method: *EdgeBraille* [5] had the interface similar the Braille cell. Each point is activated or disabled by the finger movement. In order to avoid accidental touch, the area of deactivation is less than for activation. Interesting improvements of mentioned methods is used by the *BrailleKey* [6]. The Braille symbols are entered column by column: one touch selects the dot in the first row, two touches - the middle one, and long touch – the point in the last row. In the next one called *BrailleTouch* [7], the authors proposed to hold the device horizontally and with the touch screen facing away from the user, as the intended user does not need to see the screen and only needs to tap on it.

Some approaches do not require six fingers. In the *TypeInBraille* [8] the main idea is to put dots row-by-row, marking two dots of row in the same time. A screen is divided into two rectangles - for the left dots and for the rights. Tapping just one of them makes the appropriate dots, tapping both - makes both dots. Eventually, tapping the screen with three fingers means the row both is without dots. Next interesting solution is *Perkinput* [9] - the method of finger detection in multi-touch mode, operating on reference initial positions. Only three fingers are used at a time, for dots 1–3 or 4–6. First, the left column is entered, then the right one. Similar method is the *OneHandBraille* [10], where neighboring dots (the same row) are replaced by swipes on the touchscreen surface.

Most of mentioned methods are described in the systematic review of the literature [11]. The article provides also a comparison of their performance (speed - measured by words per minutes, and accuracy - measured by the statistical method: Minimum String Distance error rate).

First steps in continuous writing the Braille code, already were done. The solution known as *IPPITSU* (derived from a Japanese word meaning one continuous stroke) uses six regions, which are allocated at the corners and edges of the touch screen [12]. A Braille symbol is inputted by a continuous motion on the touch screen, visiting the corresponding regions. However, the issue of optimization of such gestures have not been addressed.

3 Proposed Approaches of Continuous Typing

In the frame of the studies, a set of four varying solutions was proposed, further called modes. They are:

- simple mode,
- acute angle mode,
- minimum distance mode,
- scaled mode.

The simple mode is the first and, as the name suggests, the simplest of the four, it serves as the basis for the remaining ones. While using this mode, a dot of the cell is marked whenever the user swipes over this particular dot. The layout of the dots is using full screen, dividing it for three rows and two columns to form the dots of equal size.

The acute angle mode is slightly more complex than the previous one, it marks the first and last dot that the user touches, as well as any other dot whenever the stroke produced by the user contains an acute angle over the said dot. It obviously puts some kind of restrictions on how the user inputs characters, but the idea was to restrict the high number of false positives that the simple mode was expected to generate. Nonetheless, this mode requires a small amount of practice to learn how to mark the dots successfully. Figure 1 depicts an example of letter "d". The left stroke in the figure does not contain acute angle over dot 5, therefore it is not marked and the character produced is "c". The right stroke, however, contains obvious acute angle over dot no. 5, hence it is marked and letter "d" is determined correctly. Thus it is important to remember about the restrictions of this mode. It is also worth to mention that in case of the simple mode, both these strokes would be recognized correctly as letter "d".

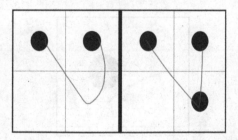

Fig. 1. Incorrect (left) and correct (right) marking of the dot no. 5.

The minimum distance mode is the third mode and it shifts the focus from marking dots on the go while the user is writing to determining marked dots after the stroke is finished and its whole shape is known. To achieve this, each dot is assigned a special numeric coefficient. During the move, the closest dot for each point of the stroke increases the coefficient by a value dependent on the distance between the point and the dot - the closer the touch point is, the bigger the increment. Moreover, it is suspected that the first and the last touch points are most often done on the dots that should be a part of the final symbol, therefore their influence on the coefficient is weighted and the score they yield is increased in comparison to other points. Finally, once the move is finished, a dot is marked if its coefficient is greater than a threshold value, dependent on the total sum of all coefficients. Equations (1) and (2) present exact formulae for calculating the coefficient for a single dot.

$$f_i = \begin{cases} c * \left(1 - \frac{d_i}{d_{max}}\right), for\ i = 0\ or\ i = N \\ 1 - \frac{d_i}{d_{max}}, for\ 0 < i < N \end{cases} \tag{1}$$

$$f = \sum_{i=0}^{N} f_i \tag{2}$$

where: N - total number of touch points closest to a dot, c - increment factor for the first and last point, d_i - distance between the point and the center of the dot, d_{max} -maximal possible distance d_i, f_i - increase of the coefficient from the ith point, f - total value of the coefficient for the dot.

Figure 2 presents an exemplary situation in this mode - a continuous stroke (the curve) was made in the proximity of dot four (top-right). Straight lines mark the borders of the area containing points that are closest to the dot and a red point marks its center. Two points on the stroke, A and B, were randomly chosen and the distances between them and the center of the dot were marked. Following the concept of this mode, both chosen points affect dot four and increase its coefficient, although each by a different value. Point A is much closer to the dot, hence the probability that the user wanted to mark this dot is higher and therefore the coefficient gets increased significantly. Point B, however, is nearly at the border of dot four's zone, so it still increases the coefficient of this dot, but by a relatively small value.

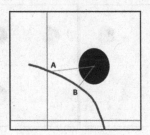

Fig. 2. Concept of minimum distance mode

The scaled mode is the last analyzing mode and it is heavily based on the previous one, the minimum distance mode. The one but crucial change is that the user is not forced to write on the full screen of the device anymore, as the algorithm scales down the whole layout of the dots to the area actually used when performing all calculations. The layout is reshaped as to encompass the whole stroke as well as to maintain proper width to height ratio to ensure it is still shaped similarly to a Braille cell. After the scaling, this mode uses exactly the same algorithm as the minimum distance mode to determine which dots are marked and basing on that, which character was written. The mode is intended to speed up writing, as each user may utilize part of the screen with different size, depending on his preferences. On the other hand, the cost of this may be accuracy, because the user has to keep in mind that the stroke is analyzed in a frame with specific width to height ratio. Thus, when the stroke is relatively small (and fast to make), it is quite easy to make a mistake and create a stroke that will not be interpreted as intended by the user. All in all, this mode is believed to be the most difficult, yet also the best performing one, depending on the skills and experience of the user.

4 Evaluation

4.1 CLC Model

In this study we decide to use a theoretical approach called CLC, where authors developed a quantitative human performance model of making single-stroke gestures in terms of production time [13]. The basic assumption of this model is that any stroke gesture may be decomposed into a number of lower-level elements. These elements are smooth curves, straight lines and corners (hence CLC). The total production time of a gesture is then calculated as follows:

$$T = \sum (curve) + \sum T(line) + \sum T(corner) \qquad (3)$$

Then authors determined set of important factors affecting the final time. Next, they prepared next formulas completely describing their model (3).

However, one could notice that the CLC model was designed for pen stroke gestures. Although some mobile devices use styluses, it is rather uncommon and may even be undesirable for the visually impaired, since it may prove difficult for them to operate a stylus instead of directly touching the screen. Nonetheless, other researchers compared finger and pen stroke gestures in terms of various features [14]. Examining the graphs of stroke time and average speed for different kinds of complexity, they finally observed that the CLC model may be used to analyze strokes produced with a finger, since the time performances of a finger and a pen are almost equal.

4.2 Calculations

The evaluation was performed for three modes: simple, acute angle and minimum distance. The scaled mode was not considered, since all the calculations using the CLC model are dependent on the length of the element and since scaled mode may have lines and curves of arbitrary lengths, it could not be safely evaluated. Nonetheless, the general tendency is that shorter strokes take less time to produce, therefore its results should at least better than those of the minimum distance mode, since they use the same algorithm for character detection. Furthermore, different characters take different amounts of time to produce. On the other hand, dependent on the language, some characters are used more often than the others. Having the frequency of letters in the

English language, it is common to calculate the average production time of a character by weighting the time of writing of each character by its linguistic frequency.

Moreover, since several letters have very low linguistic frequency, they were not considered in the calculations, as their effect on the final result would be minimal. The omitted characters were all with frequency lower than 1%. Finally, the character "a" was treated differently due to the fact that it is composed of a single dot only, thus it can be created by a single tap, which cannot be analyzed with CLC. However, according to Android Operating System documentation, the timeout for a single tap is 125 ms. Therefore it was decided to use a static value of 250 ms (twice the timeout time) for the letter "a" during the calculations.

The calculations were performed basing on the sample strokes. Each evaluated mode has its own set of strokes, although strokes for some letters may be repeated. Each stroke set consists of 27 strokes for the same set of letters. For the sake of calculations, the size of the screen was assumed to be the same as in Samsung Galaxy Ace 4 which was used for testing purposes.

Finally, it should be noted that the times obtained from the CLC model take into account only the pure writing time, without any delays for other actions such as confirming. Therefore, the result reflect the situation when the user is writing the characters without any part of the validation mechanism.

4.3   Results

Having the results from the CLC model, it is finally possible to calculate the word per minute count. However, the values obtained from the CLC model may be slightly adjusted to take into account one of the parts of the validation mechanism. It is impossible to predict how much time a user will spend deleting characters, replaying the saved sequence or exchanging similar characters, but assuming that the user only confirm each character with a double tap, a more realistic values can be obtained. Thus, since a single tap can be estimated as 125 ms, a double tap requires twice as much time for two taps, but also a small amount of time between the taps. The documentations of the Android OS states that this period must not exceed 300 ms for the double tap to be detected, although this is quite a big value. Therefore, after some consideration a decision was made to estimate a double tap as 350 ms in total. Then, this time should be added to the average production time of a character so that WPM count may be calculated.

Table 1 presents the comparison of these solutions and the results. The values obtained using the CLC model seem to be rather high and are comparable only to those of *GroovyWrite*, which also used CLC for its estimations. *BrailleTouch* was tested by several patients and one of them managed to reach similar score, although in general its results were lower. However, the values after considering validation are on par with most of the other solutions. The only exception is *BrailleType*, but its performance is surprisingly low when compared with any other solution.

Table 1. Comparison of different approaches of Braille typing

Solution	WPM
Continuous Braille modes	
Simple mode	24.52
Acute angle mode	25.06
Minimum distance mode	21.19
Continuous Braille modes (validation)	
Simple mode	14.3
Acute angle mode	14.48
Minimum distance mode	13.1
Others	
BrailleTouch	∼10–25
BrailleType	∼1–3.5
EdgeWrite	∼6
GroovyWrite	24.78

5 Conclusions

This paper describes a set of new methods of Braille character recognition with the use of mobile devices such as smartphones. Using them, the solutions are designed and implemented for the Android OS platform. The solutions were evaluated using a theoretical model called CLC. It was designed to determine the speed of pen stroke gesture, although it is proven that there is no significant difference between pen and finger gestures, thus the results of the model appear to be valid. The model decomposes each stroke into simpler elements, allowing to calculate their production time using proper formulae. Once this is done the performance of the proposed solutions is compared with the existing ones. The results were satisfactory, as the average word per minute count was approximately 25. It is quite high result, although still on par with some of similar solutions where WPM was calculated using CLC model.

Acknowledgements. Publication financed by the Institute of Informatics at Silesian University of Technology, statutory research no. BK/213/Rau2/2018.

References

1. Wobbrock, J.O., Myers, B.A., Kembel, J.A.: Edgewrite: a stylus-based text entry method designed for high accuracy and stability of motion. In: Proceedings of the 16th Annual ACM Symposium on User Interface Software and Technology, pp. 61–70. ACM (2003)
2. Al Faraj, K., Mojahid, M., Vigouroux, N.: Groovewrite: a multi-purpose stylus-based text entry method. In: International Conference on Computers Helping People with Special Needs, pp. 1196–1203 (2008)

3. Oliveira, J., Guerreiro, T., Nicolau, H., Jorge, J., Gonçalves, D.: BrailleType: unleashing braille over touch screen mobile phones. In: Campos, P., Graham, N., Jorge, J., Nunes, N., Palanque, P., Winckler, M. (eds.) INTERACT 2011. LNCS, vol. 6946, pp. 100–107. Springer, Heidelberg (2011). https://doi.org/10.1007/978-3-642-23774-4_10

4. Subash, N., Nambiar, S., Kumar, V.: Braillekey: An alternative braille text input system: comparative study of an innovative simplified text input system for the visually impaired. In: 4th International Conference on Intelligent Human Computer Interaction (IHCI), pp. 1–4 (2012)

5. Mattheiss, E., Regal, G., Schrammel, J., Garschall, M., Tscheligi, M.: Dots and letters: Accessible braille-based text input for visually impaired people on mobile touchscreen devices. In: Miesenberger, K., Fels, D., Archambault, D., Peňáz, P., Zagler, W. (eds.) ICCHP 2014. LNCS, vol. 8547, pp. 650–657. Springer, Heidelberg (2014). https://doi.org/10.1007/978-3-319-08596-8_100

6. Facanha, A.R., Viana, W., Pequeno, M.C., de Borba Campos, M., Sanchez, J.: Touchscreen mobile phones virtual keyboarding for people with visual disabilities. Hum.-Comput. Interact.on **3**, 134–145 (2014)

7. Romero, M., Frey, B., Southern, C., Abowd, G.D.: BrailleTouch: designing a mobile eyes-free soft keyboard. In: Proceedings of the 13th International Conference on Human Computer Interaction with Mobile Devices and Services, pp. 707–709. ACM (2011)

8. Mascetti, S., Bcrnarcggi, C., Bclotti, M.: TypeinBraille: a Braille-based typing application for touchscreen devices. In: The proceedings of the 13th International ACM SIGACCESS Conference on Computers and Accessibility, pp. 295–296 (2011)

9. Azenkot, S., Wobbrock, J.O., Prasain, S., Ladner, R.E.: Input finger detection for nonvisual touch screen text entry in Perkinput. In: Proceedings of Graphics Interface 2012, pp. 121–129. Canadian Information Processing Society (2012)

10. Dobosz, K., Szuścik, M.: OneHandBraille: an alternative virtual keyboard for blind people. In: Gruca, A., Czachórski, T., Harezlak, K., Kozielski, S., Piotrowska, A. (eds.) ICMMI 2017. AISC, vol. 659, pp. 62–71. Springer, Cham (2018). https://doi.org/10.1007/978-3-319-67792-7_7

11. Siqueira, J., da Silva Soares, A., de Melo Nunes, F.A.A., Ferreira, D.J., Silva, C.R.G., de Oliveira Berretta, L., Ferreira, C.B.R., Félix, I.M., da Costa, R.M., Luna, M.M.: Braille text entry on smartphones: a systematic review of the literature. In: Proceedings of the 2016 IEEE 40th Annual Computer Software and Applications Conference (COMPSAC), pp. 521–526 (2016)

12. Ushida, K., Sekine, Y., Hasegawa, S.: IPPITSU: a one-stroke text entry method for touch panels using Braille system. In: IEEE 3rd Global Conference on Consumer Electronics, pp. 374–375 (2014)

13. Cao, X., Zhai, S.: Modeling human performance of pen stroke gestures. In: Proceedings of the SIGCHI Conference on Human Factors in Computing Systems, pp. 1495–1504, ACM (2007)

14. Tu, H., Ren, X., Zhai, S.: A comparative evaluation of finger and pen stroke gestures. In: Proceedings of the SIGCHI Conference on Human Factors in Computing Systems, pp. 1287–1296. ACM (2012)

A New Gesture Control for Zooming on Tablets and Smartphones for Visually Impaired People

Nicolas Girard[1](✉), Salma Cherké[1], Hélène Soubaras[2](✉), and Kees Nieuwenhuis[3]

[1] Thales Services, Sophia Antipolis, France
nicolas.girard@inria.fr
[2] Thales Research & Technology, Palaiseau, France
helene.vandenbroek@thalesgroup.com
[3] Thales Nederland, Hengelo, The Netherlands

Abstract. We propose a new interaction model for zooming in and out the screen content of smartphones and tablets for visually impaired people. It consists in gestures that are captured by the front-facing camera to control the zooming factor and to scroll in the zoomed-in image. A first prototype involving video processing has been developed. As it avoids using a hand to touch the screen, this interaction model is interesting for other mobile applications. Human factor study and tests has been performed on visually impaired people and operators using assistance with augmented reality on tablets.

Keywords: Visually impaired · Zooming · Gesture control · Video processing

1 Introduction

Mobile applications are the norm today and they come with the use of small screens on devices such as smartphones and tablets and even watches. These applications are not only targeting the social connectedness of people, but are also rapidly becoming the new standard in the professional work environment. The small screen however poses a serious challenge for people with a visual impairment. To better support the use of these mobile devices by this group of end-users, special functions that enhance the interaction capabilities of the Apps for these devices are needed [1, 2]. In this paper we present a new interaction model for controlling the zoom on devices such as tablets and smartphones with gestures.

The model we propose uses two types of gestures that are intuitive and practical: moving the screen forward and backward to zoom in and out, and panning/tilting the screen to navigate left, right, up, down in the zoomed image. The sensor we use to capture the gestures is the front-facing camera of the device. We developed video processing algorithms to detect the mentioned gestures. As a first step, we developed a prototype on a desktop PC, to help research and testing. The current prototype uses the user's head movements to navigate in the zoomed-in image. Some early tests with end-users were performed.

K. Miesenberger and G. Kouroupetroglou (Eds.): ICCHP 2018, LNCS 10897, pp. 351–358, 2018.
https://doi.org/10.1007/978-3-319-94274-2_49

2   State of the Art

To help visually impaired people to access visual information in classrooms and lecture hall settings for example, there are several tools such as CCTV (Closed Circuit TV) and Electronic Video Magnifiers. Solutions have been proposed for laptop computers [3]. Although modern versions are more portable, these solutions remain heavy and use video input only. For smartphones, telephoto lenses can be used but their field-of-view is very narrow and it is difficult to find one's bearings in the zoomed-in image.

There also exist a variety of keyboard-and-mouse-controlled screen magnifiers for computers (Apple, ZoomText, etc.) and even a joystick-controlled one has also been proposed [4]. But these solutions are not suitable for most mobile devices.

Every smartphone and tablet has of course a zoom function, which is controlled with the fingers on the touchscreen, typically for use with fixed images, and sometimes also for all screen content (in Android accessibility parameters). But this finger-controlled zoom is slow, unsteady, and limited in zoom factor and it is difficult to navigate efficiently in the zoomed-in image.

The finger-controlled zoom on touch screen is not very practical for visually-impaired people:

- It is slow, so the user cannot navigate efficiently if the image has a high zoom factor
- It is not regular and fluid since the user must repeat the same movement several times
- The image often jumps back to its original size unexpectedly
- Visually impaired people are often handling other magnifying objects (lenses, spectacles, etc.) so their hands are not available to touch the screen.

This last argument is true also for many other use cases where mobile operators need to handle other objects in their hands.

Because modern mobile devices have multiple sensors embedded and pack a reasonable amount of real-time signal processing capability, we have investigated an interface solution for a zoom function that can be applied to any content on the screen of a mobile device, which is based on moving the device instead of touching it.

3   Video Processing Algorithms for Gesture Analysis

3.1   Computing an Approximation of the Point of Gaze

As most smartphones have a front-facing camera, we have decided to use that sensor to control the interaction with the device. The front-facing camera films the user's head which allows us to capture head gestures to control the device. More specifically, we aim at computing an approximation of the point of gaze of the user on the device's screen. The core of the program uses the C++ library OpenFace [5], and more specifically the Facial Landmark Detection module [6].

The first step is Face Detection, to localize the face in the image. The system uses the MMOD-HOG classifier [7] from Dlib [8]. It is extremely fast and outputs a crop of the face which reduces the computational load of the next step.

Facial Landmark Detection is then performed on the cropped image. It tracks the same 68 points of the user's face for every frame. OpenFace uses an advanced Constrained Local Neural Field (CLNF) model [6] to detect landmarks. It is "advanced" because it improves the classical CLNF model by adding neural patch experts and multiple initializations based on CNN (Convolutional Neural Network) validation. Some of the detected landmarks are not positioned as accurately as others. For example, a landmark on the jawline moves along the jawline. This is because a change of position in this direction does not visually modify the local neighborhood of the landmark. We filtered out these landmarks so that they are not used for the Head Pose Estimation. Other landmarks that are filtered out are the eyes landmarks because they are generally not rigid: they move when the user changes eye gaze direction. The landmarks that are kept for Head Pose Estimation are the eyebrows, nose and mouth landmarks, see Fig. 1 Facial Landmark Detection.

Fig. 1. Facial Landmark Detection

The next step is Head Pose Estimation, to retrieve the location and rotation of the user's head relative to the camera. It is performed by solving a Perspective-n-Point (PnP) problem: the detected 2D landmarks correspond to 3D landmarks of a known 3D model (typically a model of an average head, although OpenFace computes an adapted 3D model for each set of 2D landmarks). Solving the PnP problem means finding the camera extrinsic parameters (translation and rotation) that correspond to those 3D landmarks being projected by the camera into these 2D landmarks. The camera intrinsic parameters must be known for this to work (such as focal length). See the next sub-section for a method to automatically compute those intrinsic parameters.

We now know the position of the user's head relative to the camera. We can approximate the gaze direction of the user by the forward vector of the face (corresponding to the user looking straight ahead). We define a vector which goes from the head center (given by the head translation) and following the direction of the eye gaze direction approximation: the forward vector of the face (given by the face rotation). As the location of the screen relative to the camera can be known (see the next sub-section for a method computing those parameters automatically), the intersection of this vector with the screen plane is computed. This point of intersection is then converted into the local coordinate system of the screen and then converted into a pixel position.

By projecting the forward vector of the user's head, the computed target on the screen is generally accurate. Because of the noise of the inputs, the target is not fixed in position and moves erratically around the real target due to measurement errors (an accumulation of errors from the camera acquisition, the Face Landmark Detection algorithm and the PnP resolution). For filtering time series such as the translation and rotation, we applied a Kalman Filter [9]. It allows us to smooth the output by correcting each measurement based on our knowledge of the model's dynamic and the model's past behavior. OpenCV [10] implements the main parts of the Kalman Filter. The process matrix which models the dynamics of our system must be specified. Here we modeled the dynamics of the user's head with a constant velocity of translation and rotation. This filtering improved the accuracy when controlling a cursor on the screen with the head during our tests. To evaluate this method, we setup a test where the user follows a computer-controlled cursor on the screen with their head. See Fig. 2 for a plot of the absolute error in space and Fig. 3 for the error in time.

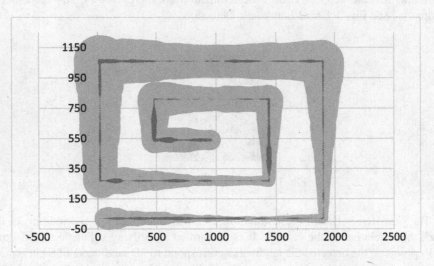

Fig. 2. Absolute error in space represented by circles at each point. In blue: error when following a test cursor using the mouse. In green: error when using the head. Axes are in pixels (on a 1920 × 1080 screen). (Color figure online)

Computing an approximation of the eye gaze position from Head Pose Estimation is accurate enough for zooming in an area. With the Kalman Filter, it would be possible to click on large buttons. On a screen of 50 cm in width, the corners farther away from the camera have too much error to be practical but on a tablet screen the errors in those corners are expected to be less.

3.2   Camera and Screen Calibration

The camera intrinsic parameters (horizontal and vertical focal length in pixels, sensor center x and y coordinates in pixels) must be known quite precisely so that the estimated head pose and eye gaze are closer to reality. Those 4 scalars can be well approximated for webcams just from the image width and height because all webcams have about the same angle of view. This approximation works quite well but for more

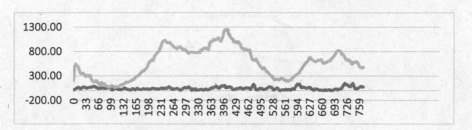

Fig. 3. Absolute error in time. In blue: error of Fig. 2 when using the mouse. In green: error when using the head. X-axis in frames and y-axis in pixels (on a 1920 × 1080 screen). (Color figure online)

precision, OpenCV provides functions to calibrate a camera by taking several pictures of a known image pattern usually printed on a board. OpenCV detects the pattern in all the views and computes the camera internal parameters.

To make use of the fact that we want to calibrate a camera which is on top of a screen, we devised a new calibration technique. It uses the screen of the tablet to display the calibration pattern instead of a piece of paper that must be printed. This makes it even easier to calibrate a camera: no need to own a printer to print the calibration pattern. For the front-facing camera to be able to see the pattern displayed on the screen, a flat mirror is used (an object common enough we can assume the user has one). More precisely, the front-facing camera of the tablet is directed towards the mirror. This way the mirror reflects the pattern displayed on the screen. From the camera's point of view, this setup is like having a physical pattern placed 'inside' the mirror. Absolutely no adaptations to OpenCV's functions need to be made for this to work. They output the correct camera intrinsic parameters as if it was a normal calibration setup.

The real added feature of this new calibration system is the ability to calibrate the screen extrinsic parameters: the x and y position of the top-left corner of the screen (when looking in the direction of the camera) in the camera plane coordinate system and the screen physical dimensions (see Fig. 4).

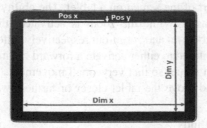

Fig. 4. Screen intrinsic parameters

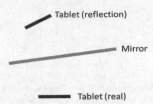

Fig. 5. Mirror setup schema

To retrieve those values, the previous calibration step comes into play because OpenCV's calibration function also outputs for each view the 3D translation and rotation vectors of the detected reflected pattern. The first step is to find the mirror plane for each view. This means finding the plane normal and plane distance to the origin (which is the camera). As the assumption that the screen plane is equal to the camera plane was made, the screen plane is known (direction = (0, 0, 1) and distance = 0). And the reflected pattern plane can be computed from the reflected pattern translation and rotation vectors (the Z component of the rotation matrix gives the screen plane normal and the negative of the scalar product between the translation vector and the reflected pattern normal gives the reflected pattern plane distance to the origin). So now we know the pose of the screen plane and the reflected pattern plane. As the reflected pattern plane is the reflection of the screen plane by the mirror plane, it is possible to compute the mirror plane (which is a plane bisector). See Fig. 5 for better visualization. The final step is to compute the reflection of the reflected pattern for each view i.e. the screen pose. Each view gives a pose for the screen, the final pose outputted by the algorithm is the average of all the poses to minimize the error.

3.3   Gesture Detection

Two kinds of gestures are detected: panning and zooming. The panning is activated by default. The user looks left-right and up-down to pan in the corresponding direction. Internally, an estimation of the point of gaze is used to control a cursor on the screen with the head. The panning gesture is detected when the cursor approaches an edge of the screen. The zooming gesture is activated by continuously pressing a button on a computer or touching part of the screen on a tablet. The ability to zoom is deactivated when the button is released. While the zoom is activated, the user can then move forward or backward to zoom-in and zoom-out respectively. Internally, the z coordinate of the user's head is monitored to either activate a forward zoom or backward zoom if it deviates from a threshold value (so that very small movements are not considered). As such, the user can instead move the tablet closer or farther away to the same effect.

3.4   Optical Flow Methods

Our first idea was to detect the movement of the device by measuring the optical flow of the front-facing camera. We found two methods to compute movement based on measuring the optical flow. [11] uses a histogram of the velocities to detect the main direction of movement and can retrieve panning and zooming gestures. [12] fits a dynamic model to the velocities to retrieve vertical pan, horizontal pan, tilt and zoom. The algorithm described in [12] looks more promising because of its real-time capacity and its very strong robustness towards the varying environment filmed by the camera. An Optical Flow method would give information about the speeds of panning, zooming and tilting. As it only outputs velocities and not absolute positions, the kind of gestures it can detect is restricted. However, the advantage of such a method is its robustness to the varying environment and the fact that it does not require the user's head to be detected.

3.5 Correlation Method

We also explored another method to detect gestures with the front-facing camera. It detects camera movements based an analysis of the correlation between frames and building a kind of map of the environment to handle big movements, the application could detect all three rotations (vertical and horizontal tilting as well as in-plane rotation). Unfortunately, the algorithm was not robust enough to handle varying lightning conditions, varying image texture/amount of details. It also required a lot of parameter tuning.

4 Human Factor Study

Before testing our prototype, some interviews were conducted. This was done to understand the different types of user needs and their context to develop personas. To test the usability of our prototype, we conducted a study in which the user was asked to follow a list of scenarios during two situations:

- the exploration of a map following a precise route
- article reading.

In total the study included 6 participants with an average age of 54 (from 40 to 69), 4 of them were men and 2 women. All users were using their phones/laptops daily with no previous experience with face tracking technology. They were asked to verbally express their feelings or opinions about their actions. The average time for one session was 14 min, and total elapsed time, including the introductory part and the breaks, was approximately and 20 min for each participant.

Most gestures were appreciated by users, but they said that using head movement can be a little tiresome on the long run. They also felt the system was too sensitive which is why they suggested the ability to change some parameters (zoom speed, panning speed, pitch correction) which was implemented later. At the end of the experiment, the user had to complete an AttrakDiff survey [13] and a final survey about the use of such technology. To enhance the relevancy of these results, the tests ought to be conducted among a larger sample of users.

5 Conclusion

We developed a desktop prototype proving the feasibility of the gesture control algorithms for mobile devices such as smartphones and tablets, and performed a first usage study. From the requirement elicitation study, we found that the system must be improved by including fast zooming algorithms for wide images, image processing to improve the image quality, and perform OCR on the texts contained in the zoomed image to display them in augmented reality.

Since our interaction model does not use fingers, it allows the user to keep their hands more available, which is a great advantage in many applications where operators have to work while handling tools: industrial maintenance and operations, pilots, medical imaging in hospitals. This broadens the scope of possible applications beyond the use by visual impaired people using small screens.

References

1. Gajos, K.Z., Wobbrock, J.O, Weld, D.S.: Automatically generating user interfaces adapted to user's motor and vision capabilities (2007)
2. Calvary, G., Coutaz, J., Thevenin, D., Limbourg, Q., Bouillon, L., Vanderdonckt, J.: A unifying reference framework for multi-target user interfaces. Interact. Comput. 15(3), 289–308 (2003)
3. Soubaras, H., Colineau, J.: PortaNum: une nouvelle aide technique comportant du traitement d'images pour les malvoyants. In: Proceedings of HANDICAP 2002, Paris, France (2002)
4. Kurniavan, S., King, A., Evans, D., Blenkom, P.: Design and user evaluation of a joystick-operated full-screen magnifier. In: Proceedings of CHI 2003, pp. 25–32 (2003)
5. Baltrusaitis, T., Robinson, P., Morency, L.-P.: OpenFace: an open source facial behavior analysis toolkit. In: IEEE Winter Conference on Application of Computer Vision (2016)
6. Baltrusaitis, T., Robinson, P., Morency, L.-P.: Constrained local neural fields for robust facial landmark detection in the wild. In: IEEE International Conference on Computer Vision Workshops, 300 Faces in-the-Wild Challenge (2013)
7. King, D.E.: Max-margin object detection. CoRR (2015)
8. King, D.E.: Dlib-ml: a machine learning toolkit. J. Mach. Learn. Res. 10, 1755–1758 (2009)
9. Kalman, R.E., Emil, R.: A new approach to linear filtering and prediction problems. ASME J. Basic Eng. 82(series D), 35–45 (1960)
10. Bradski, G.: The OpenCV library. Dr. Dobb's J. Softw. Tools 25(11), 120–126 (2000)
11. Makkapati, V.V.: Robust Camera Pan and Zoom Change Detection Using Optical Flow (2008)
12. Minetto, R., Leite, N.J.: Reliable detection of camera motion based on weighted optical flow fitting. In: VISAPP, no. 2, pp. 435–440 (2007)
13. Hassenzahl, M., Burmester, M., Koller, F.: AttrakDiff: a questionnaire to measure perceived hedonic and pragmatic quality. In: Mensch & Computer, pp. 187–196 (2003)

Future Perspectives for Aging Well: AAL Tools, Products, Services

Future Perspectives for Aging Well: AAL Tools, Products, Services
Introduction to the Special Thematic Session

Jean D. Hallewell Haslwanter[1]([✉])(iD), Markus Garschall[2], Katja Neureiter[2],
Paul Panek[3], and Özge Subasi[4]

[1] University of Applied Sciences Upper Austria, Wels, Austria
jean.hallewell@fh-wels.at
[2] AIT Austrian Institute of Technology GmbH, Vienna, Austria
{markus.garschall,katja.neureiter}@ait.ac.at
[3] TU Wien, Vienna, Austria
paul.panek@tuwien.ac.at
[4] Koc University, Istanbul, Turkey
ozge.subasi@tuwien.ac.at

Abstract. This Special Thematic Session (STS) was intended to provide a forum to discuss some major issues related to Ambient Assisted
Living (AAL) services and technologies to support aging in place. The
papers in the session are introduced here. These cover a broad range
of topics including the development of new solutions, existing solutions
and their evaluation and also issues and preferences related to specific
systems. The technologies described are very diverse and include communication systems, entertainment platforms, telecare systems, wearable
technologies and assistive robots. Together these contributions can support others developing these types of systems in the future. In the end,
we hope this can benefit the growing number of older people by supporting safety and independence, and thus help people to age with more
dignity and enjoyment.

Keywords: Ambient and Assisted Living · Aging in place
Older people · Accessibility

1 Motivation of Special Thematic Session

Due to the challenges of an aging society in many countries, tools, technologies
and services that allow older adults to grow old in their own homes are increasingly discussed. There are many challenges involved in developing these types of
systems and services. For one thing, older adults are diverse in many ways, and
might differ in their needs, but also with regard to their physical, cognitive and
sensory abilities, making accessibility an important issue. Moreover, they might
interact differently with technologies, due to their knowledge or life experience

© Springer International Publishing AG, part of Springer Nature 2018
K. Miesenberger and G. Kouroupetroglou (Eds.): ICCHP 2018, LNCS 10897, pp. 361–364, 2018.
https://doi.org/10.1007/978-3-319-94274-2_50

[5]. Further, these systems, also termed Ambient Assisted Living (AAL) systems, are very diverse, and include, for example, smart home technologies, i.e., integrated solutions based on ubiquitous computing [2], which support independence and reduce reliance on care [6]. There are also robotic systems available that assist older adults to carry out daily routines [3], or telehealth and telecare monitoring systems that might help avoid institutional care [4]. These systems aim at addressing a variety of needs of older people, support safety and independence, allow people to age with more dignity and enjoyment, and hence increase their quality of life [2].

Although during the past few years, the development of products and services for an ageing society has been promoted via various national and European funding programmes there is still a lot of work to do to intensify the market orientation of the theme across Europe [1].

This Special Thematic Session (STS) thus aimed to provide a forum to discuss the major issues related to Ambient Assisted Living and technologies to support aging in place. We sought to cover a variety of the perspectives, including the theoretical challenges, the development challenges as well as the relationship of the AAL research area to the assistance, accessibility and care topics. This special track therefore covers the following categories:

- Research perspective
- Development perspective
- Business perspective
- Ethical and legal aspects.

2   Papers in the Session

The papers in the session can be grouped into those reporting on projects developing new solutions, those describing existing solutions and their evaluation and those describing issues and preferences that can support others in developing these types of systems in the future.

2.1   Development of New Solutions

This first group of papers in this track illustrates the diversity of the notions that relate to the development of projects and services for older people. The papers show how diverse strategies like co-creation, participatory design, social care and peer-to-peer support can all be beneficial in trying to tackle classical practical issues of AAL, such as accessibility, usability, inclusion or integration of technologies.

A careful selection of an appropriate development methodology is one key success factor for innovative projects in the field of AAL. Incorrect assumptions about the target group and deficit-oriented design approaches are a major pitfall when developing for an older target group. In order to address this, a participatory design approach was chosen by Doppler as a basis for developing a new television and tablet-based communication and entertainment platform. A discussion on aspects that have to be considered in order to optimize the user experience of assistive technologies – such as accessibility, usability and interoperability – is provided by Mohamad et al.

Within their paper, Berker et al. point out the potential of a well-defined co-creation methodology for developing ICT-based systems that really meet the needs of older users in terms of functionality and accessibility. In their project, innovative location-based applications aiming at improving the social inclusion of older adults, such as a digital district guide, have been developed.

In order to address the growing challenge of staff shortage in the care sector, Takahashi et al. explore the potential of assistive robots to act as active link between a senior's household and a local community support center. Within their contribution, design requirements for assistive robots are explored and a concept for integrating assistive robots in a social care ecosystem is proposed.

Addressing the problem of loneliness, Burzagli and Naldini conceptualize a recommender system that is able to generate personalized suggestions for activities not only based on the preferences of one specific user, but also taking account of current activities of other members within a group of people.

2.2   Existing Solutions and Their Evaluation

After almost a decade of the existence and the development of AAL systems, the evaluation of each individual system contributes to the common knowledge of the discipline. The papers in this group include evaluation examples from diverse areas such as telecare, robotics and wearable technologies.

To support new solutions in the rapidly changing area of telecare, important lessons can be learned by carrying out a careful evaluation of existing systems. The paper of Krel et al. describes an in-depth analysis of an existing mobile telecare system in order to elaborate a substantial list of recommendations to be considered when developing telecare solutions.

The work of Isemann et al. investigates state-of-the-art smart watches in order to identify usability issues and interaction problems for older users compared to younger user groups. Interestingly, in many areas very similar problems were found for both age groups.

Hallewell Haslwanter carried out a review of telecare systems on a general level. Based on existing literature, it describes the types of AAL systems available, some examples of systems that have been developed and the benefits brought by them. It outlines also the history of funding schemes supporting the development of technologies for older persons. The paper emphasizes the importance of more research being done on the cost effectiveness of these systems.

Koumpis et al. describe a robotic digital solution to empower older persons to stay actively involved in their work life for longer. This is highly relevant as the aging of the population is also changing the composition of the workforce in many countries. The solution also contributes to the social inclusion of older persons, which is without a doubt an important topic for future research and development.

2.3   Looking Forward: Support for Future Projects

The last group of papers in the session point us to the way ahead, and reflects on some issues related to having older user groups that go beyond single projects, such as biases and preferences with regard to solutions.

The paper by Petrie shows many young developers have biases with regard to older people and their technological abilities. In practice, a large percentage of older people now use laptops, tablet computers and smartphones. If systems are designed for people with little experience, they may in practice not fit the needs or even be stigmatizing.

One way of overcoming these biases is to study the preferences of older people in an effort to support those developing systems. Kyritsis et al. describe preferences with regard to functionality of AAL systems. The study by Iwamoto and Kuwahara investigated appropriate features of photographic images for supporting communication with older people. They aim to provide a quantitative basis for classifying pictures with the goal of increasing the satisfaction of older people. Finally, the study by Schlögl investigated avatars to assess which agent personalities are preferred, but also whether older people recognize the emotions the avatars are trying to express.

In sum, the papers in this session provide developers of future AAL systems with valuable information. We hope these help to overcome some of the challenges in the domain, as these technologies have the potential to support older people living alone and increase their sense of well-being.

Acknowledgements. We thank also the other people involved in organizing this special thematic session: Stephan Schlögl and Beatrix Wais-Zechmann.

References

1. Busquin, P., Aarts, E., Dózsa, C., Mollenkopf, H., Uusikylä, P., Sharpe, M.: Final Evaluation of the Ambient Assisted Living Joint Programme (2013)
2. Demiris, G., Hensel, B.K.: Technologies for an aging society: a systematic review of "smart home" applications. IMIA Yearb. Med. Inform. **3**, 33–40 (2008)
3. Goher, K., Mansouri, N., Fadlallah, S.: Assessment of personal care and medical robots from older adults' perspective. Robot. Biomim. **4**(1), 5 (2017)
4. Greenhalgh, T., Procter, R., Wherton, J., Sugarhood, P., Shaw, S.: The organising vision for telehealth and telecare: discourse analysis. BMJ Open **2**(4), e001574 (2012)
5. Gregor, P., Newell, A.F., Zajicek, M.: Designing for dynamic diversity: interfaces for older people. In: Proceedings of the Fifth International ACM Conference on Assistive Technologies, ASSETS 2002, pp. 151–156. ACM, New York (2002)
6. Liu, L., Stroulia, E., Nikolaidis, I., Miguel-Cruz, A., Rincon, A.R.: Smart homes and home health monitoring technologies for older adults: a systematic review. Int. J. Med. Inform. **91**, 44–59 (2016)

Improving User Engagement and Social Participation of Elderly People Through a TV and Tablet-Based Communication and Entertainment Platform

Jakob Doppler[1]([✉]), Christian Gradl[1], Sabine Sommer[2], and Gernot Rottermanner[1]

[1] Institute for Creative Media Technologies, St. Pölten UAS, St. Pölten, Austria
jakob.doppler@fhstp.ac.at
[2] Ilse Alt Institute on Social Inclusion Research, St. Pölten UAS, St. Pölten, Austria

Abstract. Maintaining healthy relationships and companionship are major challenges to prevent potentially harmful effects of loneliness and social isolation in older age. Therefore, to foster participation and user engagement of elderly people in online communication and entertainment the user experience of devices and services need to be improved substantially. This paper discusses a participatory design approach to design and implement a TV and tablet-based communications and entertainment platform called BRELOMATE. The results of a field study with 30 elderly people over five months shows that each users was online for 37.0 h and played the card game service for 23.3 h on average over the course of 8 weeks.

Keywords: Older user engagement · Social participation
Senior citizens · User centered design · Multi-device · Tablet · TV

1 Introduction

Population ageing is a key societal challenge in western countries. The EU Ageing Report estimates that the demographic old-age dependency ratio (people aged 65 or above relative to those aged 15–64) will increase from 27% to 50% until 2060 because of declining fertility rates and increasing live expectancy [5]. With studies showing that 17% of people aged 80 or over are affected by social isolation, maintaining healthy relationships and participation in communities are major issues [4]. Although mobile devices and online services become the primary means for information access, communication and entertainment the older population is often excluded. To deal with these problems a wide range of assisting technologies are developed and tested in research projects. Despite the intensive research efforts only few systems make it to the market [6]. Common pitfalls are again a lack in user acceptance and wrong assumptions about the target group as well as financial and economic issues, which hinder a successful launch.

K. Miesenberger and G. Kouroupetroglou (Eds.): ICCHP 2018, LNCS 10897, pp. 365–373, 2018.
https://doi.org/10.1007/978-3-319-94274-2_51

A first major step in overcoming design challenges is a user centered design (UCD) approach that involves the older target group early in the idea generation and conceptual phase and evaluates a products or services' success based on user-driven hypotheses and user engagement metrics. While this may seem obvious, technologies for and with the elderly are often developed with a problem-oriented approach towards aging and defined around negative values such as a decline in social and physical activities as well as a higher demand of health and care needs. This leads to wrong assumptions about the actual needs and desires of elderly people [11] for whom information and communication technologies should be as enjoyable as for everyone.

With BRELOMATE we propose a TV and tablet-based communications and entertainment platform that fosters user engagement and promotes social participation among older people. Therefore, this paper discusses a threefold approach to improve and assess user engagement by (1) promoting high-quality interaction and user experience by participatory design (2) developing a robust and fail-safe platform with a multi-device client and a server (3) measuring interaction though an online gaming and communication scenario in a field study with 30 elderly people in 27 households over the course of half a year.

2   Related Work

The positive impact of social media and social interactions over online services for elderly people have been explored in several European countries [7]. Besides training and supporting both older people and care staff in social media these solutions focus mainly on tailoring devices and interfaces to users' needs. To foster older user engagement several research projects developed and examined TV platforms. FoSIBLE is a social TV platform which allows the user to share messages and play games over a SmartTV and tablet [1]. The technology used for user interface and navigating interactive TV content is Hybrid Broadcast Broadband Television (HBBTV) which fails to address requirements for a high-quality user experience. According to analysts[1] especially steaming media player such as Google Chromecast, Amazon Fire TV, Apple TV and Roku share the Smart TV market. GeTVivid is a platform which offers services to elderly to support social and informal care and underlines the potential for gamification on peer-to-peer (P2P) exchange platforms [8]. However, besides proposing a reward system with badges to increase user' motivation to actively participate there is no in-depth analysis of usability and user engagement.

A study of the acceptance of TV-based game platforms and simple games as an remote cognitive evaluation instrument [10] shows a 43% user-friendliness towards TV as a platform compared to smartphones with 29% and PC with 24% (n = 21, 65–90 years old). 91% of all participants stated that the TV is a very easy to use device and 75% would use TV-based gaming services again. Nevertheless, the tested games were mostly puzzles, quizzes and memory games and did not involve P2P communication. Despite the range of research

---

[1] http://www.parksassociates.com/blog/article/pr-08232017.

projects, only a few systems for social participation are available close to or on the market. Media4Care[2] offers a tablet solution to improve the communication between elderly citizen and their relatives as well as their caretakers. Senior Oscar[3] is one of many mobile application that integrates video chat and photo sharing combined with an elaborate interface and remote configuration. However, it lacks sophisticated services. The leading IT companies such as Google, Microsoft and Apple seem to make no effort to design and offer solutions that focus specifically on older peoples' needs. Technical barriers such as complex interaction metaphors (e.g. multi-level menu hierarchies, button with multiple states), high information density and overall poor usability prevent them from participation [9].

3   Participatory Design Methodology

The first pillar in promoting user engagement and social participation in online platforms involves participatory design. BRELOMATE was developed with an iterative user centered design process. Early focus groups in the beginning of the project showed that online communication and entertainment are important to older people [2].

The result of the concept phase was a multi-device platform that consists of a potentially available TV with a set-top box for visualization and a tablet for control. Watching TV is one of the most popular leisure activities for elderly people at home. By facilitating the TV, we integrate the BRELOMATE platform into a familiar environment and extend its functionality with bi-directional communication. The first services implemented on the platform were the turn-based card game Schnapsen, a videochat application called Plaudern, an elaborated contact management and a help section involving FAQ and remote help. All services work with embedded video-conferencing functionality and are only accessible in a direct interaction scenario with a distant companion or co-player.

Multiple focus groups and user tests ensured that not only high-level requirements but also specific characteristics of the interaction design were up for discussion. For instance, the tablet as a control unit was considered as an input device in favor of more natural tangible interfaces such as a NFC-based deck for card games. The older users agreed early that the tablet works as a "remote control for the TV where the menu could be navigated and notifications and events are displayed" [3].

In a focus group, the seven test participants (4 female and 3 male) were presented three clickable HTML-prototypes of menu interaction concepts on both tablet and TV (see Fig. 1). They had to solve tasks such as adding new contacts or starting a Schnapsen game session. Finally they had to choose a winner between concept A "short code selection" that allowed navigating with speed dialing, concept B "thumb navigation" that uses preselecting using ones thumbs and confirming by pressing an OK button or concept C "mirrored screen" that

---

[2] https://www.media4care.de/.
[3] https://www.oscarsenior.com/.

duplicates most menu elements on both tablet and TV screens. In the end concept C was chosen with four votes for further development because of the similar spatial arrangement of menu elements that embodied the least cognitive effort on the test participants.

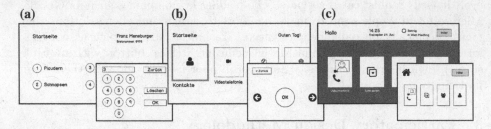

Fig. 1. Three interaction concepts presented at a focus group: (a) A "short code selection", (b) B "thumb navigation" and (c) C "mirrored screen". 4 out of 7 test participants selected concept C.

4   Platform Architecture and Development

As a second pillar user-engagement also sparks from robust and fail-safe design of the platform architecture. BRELOMATE is a distributed entertainment and communication platform. It is based on a central Java EE backend server and multi-device client interacting with the TV in each household. Each client setup consists of a control tablet and a set-top box that connects to the TV for visualization. Each setup requires Internet access with a WIFI network, a TV device with HDMI input and a webcam to connect to the set-top box. Both tablet and the set-top box run on the Android operating system (see Fig. 2). The main application logic is running on the Android set-top box which is responsible for the content on the TV. The tablet acts as the control unit and only handles UI related logic. It only communicates with the set-top box and does not handle any network communication to the server backend. This decision was made to prevent inconsistent application states across the devices.

To guarantee a seamless user experience and high interaction quality of the dual-screen client (tablet and set-top box) required customization of software on three layers: The BRELOMATE Android Applications and BRELOMATE framework run on top of a modified Android system. It is not a custom build of the Android OS but rather a set of system changes of the default Android OS. The configuration includes changes to adapt the UI and disable basic user interactions such as the tablets main menu for accidentally navigating out of the BRELOMATE platform. Additionally the client devices only allows to boot into and operate BRELOMATE applications and services. All rights and privileges to access the system settings or navigate to non-certified applications are permitted. Therefore, most of the preinstalled applications which come with Android such as Google Play Store, Google Play Services and email are disabled or removed.

Fig. 2. The BRELOMATE client system consisting of a set-top box connected to a TV for visualisation and a tablet client mainly for control. The screens show the turn-based card game service Schnapsen with the open game table and integrated video-conferencing on the TV and each players individual hands on their tablets.

These restrictions are necessary to ensure a consistent and unified user experience across all BRELOMATE services. A self-healing mechanism allowed all parts of the system to fully recover in any state in case of Internet breakdown, power outage or battery drain of the tablet. The older users were instructed to turn off the whole setup whenever they felt for it. In the current state the platform is shipped with four preinstalled applications: the videoconferencing service Plaudern, the card game Schnapsen, contact management and the help section with FAQ and remote video support and video tutorials. An additional user interface guidelines and stylesheet were developed to guarantee a consistent look&feel across all screens, menus and interface elements.

5   Field Trial Design and Results

We deployed BRELOMATE in a 5-month field trial with 27 participating households and 33 participants at start. 3 participants had to quit because of technical problems during the installation, the third because of private circumstances. 30 of these finished the field trial (see Table 1 for demographics and characteristics of the trial sample). The main goals were to test the robustness, applicability, and feasibility of the platform in a real world scenario and assess and evaluate the usability of the platform and the deployed online communication and entertainment services. All older users were made aware that data was only collected during their voluntary participation in the field trial and no private data and media was used without their prior consent. The field test was scaled into time slots with 4 to 6 participants with a participation of 6–12 weeks. The test started with 4 participants for 2 weeks and was then increased up to 19 participants by 3 overlapping slots. This design allowed to fix technical issues which occurred at the beginning in the first time slot.

Table 1. Description of field trial sample with 30 older residents in 27 households.

Variables		N = 30 (%)
Gender	Female	15 (50.0%)
	Male	15 (50.0%)
Age Mean 71.8 (SD5.7)	50–64	4 (13.3%)
	65–74	15 (50.0%)
	75–84	11 (36.7%)
Media usage	High TV usage	24 (80.0%)
	First time tablet usage	17 (56.7%)
	Mobile phone available	26 (86.7%)
	Laptop available	27 (90.0%)

In order to quantify the user experience a logging and user tracking framework called Mixpanel[4] was integrated. For quantitative research 270,000 structured data points, defined as single user interaction events, were collected. Figure 3 shows some recorded key performance indicators of the BRELOMATE platform: Overall the 30 participants spent a total of 1108.6 h on the platform and used the main service, the turn-based card game *Schnapsen*, for 699.7 h (63.1%) in 19 weeks. The rest of the sessions sum up to getting used to the system, video-only conversation and looking for players during meeting hours.

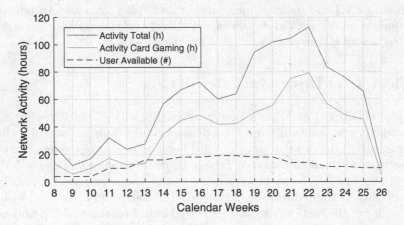

Fig. 3. Brelomate network monitoring with total and gaming activity (hours) and number of users available for entertainment and communication per calendar week.

A single user chart individual gaming result can be assessed. Figure 4 shows that participant #23 initially started with little hours of gameplay and game

---

[4] https://mixpanel.com/.

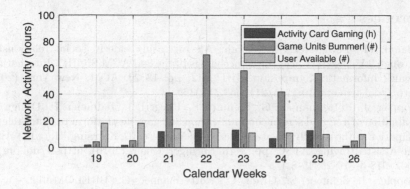

Fig. 4. Single user (#23) game usage statistics.

unit (in *Schnapsen* they are called *Bummerl*). Throughout the weeks the play time increased but the number of games and game units (*Bummerl*) per hours increased from initial 2.45 (week 19) to 4.9 (week 22) to 6.2 (week 24). This indicates a steep learning curve and increased user engagement. As a side effect we also visually perceive changes in usage patterns. When asked, the participant indicated he was ill in week 25 and could not participate as much as he wanted to. For qualitative assessment a set of user experience hypotheses were formulated and examined. Although 56.6% of participants never used a tablet before and had no experience with interactive TV, they thought BRELOMATE was easy to use with 86.7% strongly agreeing and 13.3% agreeing on a 4-point Likert scale. All participants agreed in the final questionnaire that using BRELOMATE was a fun experience and all of them would use a commercial service if it was available yet.

6 Conclusion

We presented a TV and tablet-based communications and entertainment platform that fosters user engagement and promotes social participation among older people. During a 5 month field trial 30 participants were able to use BRELO-MATE on their own after the initial setup. Users spent on average 4.5 h each week during their 8 weeks period on the platform with a mean game time of 2.9 h. During questionnaire all users would have wanted to keep their prototypical client after the trial period. These results show that a participatory design process involving the users at an early concept stage of an online communication and entertainment product or service is crucial for promoting and fostering user engagement in social networks. In the future more services in the areas of tele-health, community care and municipal services will be examined.

Acknowledgement. The authors would like to thank the study participants and our partner Kabelplus GmbH. This work is supported by the Benefit programme of the Austrian Research Promotion Agency (FFG) under grant agreement No. 850849 (BRELOMATE 2) and No. 862054 (UmBrello).

References

1. Alaoui, M., Lewkowicz, M., Seffah, A.: Increasing elderly social relationships through TV-based services. In: Proceedings of the 2nd ACM SIGHIT International Health Informatics Symposium, IHI 2012, pp. 13–20. ACM, New York (2012). http://doi.acm.org/10.1145/2110363.2110369
2. Doppler, J., Rottermanner, G., Sommer, S., Pflegerl, J., Judmaier, P.: Design and evaluation of a second screen communication and gaming platform to foster teleparticipation of the socially isolated elderly. In: Wichert, R., Klausing, H. (eds.) Ambient Assisted Living. ATSC, pp. 3–13. Springer, Cham (2016). https://doi.org/10.1007/978-3-319-26345-8_1
3. Doppler, J., Sommer, S., Gradl, C., Rottermanner, G.: BRELOMATE - a distributed, multi-device platform for online information, communication and gaming services among the elderly. In: Miesenberger, K., Bühler, C., Penaz, P. (eds.) ICCHP 2016. LNCS, vol. 9758, pp. 277–280. Springer, Cham (2016). https://doi.org/10.1007/978-3-319-41264-1_37
4. Eiffe, F.F.: Soziale Lage aelterer Menschen in Oesterreich. Technical report Band 11, Bundesministerium fuer Arbeit, Soziales und Konsumentenschutz, Wien (2012)
5. European Commission, Directorate-General for Economic and Financial Affairs, EC, Economic Policy Committee of the European Communities: The 2015 ageing report: economic and budgetary projections for the 28 EU Member States (2013–2060). Publications Office, Luxembourg (2015). oCLC: 948763579
6. Haslwanter, J.D.H., Fitzpatrick, G.: Why do few assistive technology systems make it to market? The case of the HandyHelper project. Univ. Access Inf. Soc. **16**(3), 755–773 (2017). https://doi.org/10.1007/s10209-016-0499-3
7. Morton, T.A., Wilson, N., Haslam, C., Birney, M., Kingston, R., McCloskey, L.G.: Activating and guiding the engagement of seniors with online social networking. J. Aging Health (2016). https://doi.org/10.1177/0898264316664440
8. Moser, C., Peterhansl, M., Kargl, T., Tscheligi, M.: The potentials of gamification to motivate older adults to participate in a P2P support exchange platform, pp. 655–660. ACM (2015). http://dl.acm.org/citation.cfm?id=2793107.2810326
9. Nef, T., Ganea, R.L., Müri, R.M., Mosimann, U.P.: Social networking sites and older users - a systematic review. Int. Psychogeriatr. IPA **25**(7), 1041–1053 (2013)
10. Rivas Costa, C., Fernández Iglesias, M.J., Anido Rifón, L.E., Gómez Carballa, M., Valladares Rodríguez, S.: The acceptability of TV-based game platforms as an instrument to support the cognitive evaluation of senior adults at home. PeerJ **5** (2017). https://www.ncbi.nlm.nih.gov/pmc/articles/PMC5214704/
11. Vines, J., Pritchard, G., Wright, P., Olivier, P., Brittain, K.: An age-old problem: examining the discourses of ageing in HCI and strategies for future research. ACM Trans. Comput. Hum. Interact. **22**(1), 2:1–2:27 (2015). https://doi.org/10.1145/2696867

Evaluation of an Information System for Elderly with Chronic Diseases and for Their Caregiver

Yehya Mohamad[(⊠)], Henrike Gappa, Gaby Nordbrock,
and Carlos A. Velasco

Fraunhofer Institute for Applied Information Technology (FIT),
Schloss Birlinghoven, 53757 Sankt Augustin, Germany
{yehya.mohamad,henrike.gappa,gaby.nordbrock,
carlos.velasco}@fit.fraunhoder.de

Abstract. This paper presents the accessibility evaluation methodology of an information system (Polycare), which provides an integrated care model, patient-centered, supported by the use of advanced ICT systems and services that allows the monitoring and care of older chronic patients at their home.

Keywords: Accessibility · Evaluation · Usability · Accessibility guidelines

1 Introduction

The Polycare H2020 project[1] mission and biggest challenge is to provide functionality that supports home hospitalization artefacts using IoT (Internet of Things) (See Fig. 1). Polycare consists of adaptable and distributed user interfaces, a knowledge layer and a service layer.

The service layer consists of a smart sensor platform, an FHIR[2] (Fast Health Interoperability Resources) server, a decision support system, a reporting tool and APIs to third party components. In addition, Polycare aims at empowering the caregiving activities as well as providing facilities to integrate the activities of all stakeholders participating in the caregiving process at all stages and minimizing their workload [5]. We have conducted combined usability and accessibility evaluation of the Polycare components as suggested in [3]. Accessibility as indicated by W3C WCAG 2.0 is concerned with aspects[3] of user interface such as: Perceivable, Operable, Understandable, Robust, so that content must be robust enough that it can be interpreted reliably by a wide variety of user agents, including assistive technologies. In this paper we are going to describe the methodology of the accessibility evaluation of the Polycare user interfaces designed as Web app and Android app.

---

[1] http://www.polycare-project.com/.
[2] https://www.hl7.org/fhir/.
[3] https://www.w3.org/TR/UNDERSTANDING-WCAG20/intro.html#introduction-fourprincs-head.

K. Miesenberger and G. Kouroupetroglou (Eds.): ICCHP 2018, LNCS 10897, pp. 374–378, 2018.
https://doi.org/10.1007/978-3-319-94274-2_52

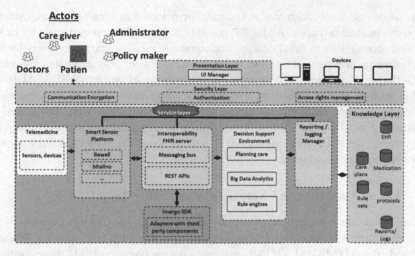

Fig. 1. Overview polycare system

2 Accessibility Evaluation

Two main components of the Polycare system were in focus of the accessibility and usability evaluation in Polycare were the Collaborative Environment (CE) and the Polycare Patient App. The accessibility evaluation was conducted in two ways (1) expert evaluation (2) automated accessibility evaluation.

2.1 Expert Tests

For evaluation of accessibility issues of Polycare web (CE) app and Polycare Patient App (native android) different approaches were chosen in accordance to targeted end users and development environment. The target end users of CE are primarily medical staff such as doctors and nurses where it is to assume that they might be suffering from low vision but not have lost sight such as it is the case in blind people. Therefore, the CE accessibility audit included manual checks with the screen magnifier ZoomText to evaluate presentation of information when enlarged. Also keyboard accessibility as a core requirement of accessibility was tested to ensure that all functionality of the content is operable through a keyboard interface. Keyboard accessibility is not only crucial for users with visual impairments, because it allows them to tab through a web page and reach functionality more readily, but also for users with, e.g., a physical impairment accessing the web with alternative interface technologies such as alternative mice, onscreen keyboards or screen readers. Additionally, manual checks were performed while conducting the expert walkthrough for instance in regard to accessibility issues that cannot be determined by automated accessibility evaluation such as whether text equivalents for non-text content are meaningful or not. This applies also to descriptiveness of link texts and labels. The Polycare Patient App addresses primarily older patients suffering from COPD (Chronic obstructive pulmonary disease), which might well be affected by a serious visual or physical impairment, so this application was evaluated manually with Voice Assistant for Android as standard screen reader for blind users of Android apps. As for CE possible accessibility issues caused by lacking keyboard accessibility to functionality, inadequate or missing text alternatives for non-text content or non-descriptive link texts and labels were also evaluated by manual checks during the expert walkthrough. In accordance to current W3C.WAI recommendations both applications were evaluated for compliance to WCAG 2.0 guidelines, in addition to that requirements from Mobile Accessibility[4] were considered for evaluation of the Polycare Patient App. Violations of guidelines and suggestions for improvement were recorded together with results from the Expert Walkthrough for better handling by developers.

2.2   Markup Validation and Automatic Accessibility Tests

Markup validation is an important step towards ensuring the technical quality of web pages. However, it is not a complete measure of web standards conformance. While the W3C and other HTML and XHTML validators assess pages coded in those formats, a separate validator like the W3C CSS validator can check that there are no errors in the associated Cascading Style Sheet. CSS validators apply current CSS standards to referenced CSS documents. This report focuses on the syntactic markup analysis of the Polycare user interfaces. We have validated the webpages against the HTML5 specification. Validation is an important component of the compatibility WCAG 2.0 guideline 4.1. The validation issue is described in detail under the relevant technique G134. Automatic web accessibility evaluation builds internally a DOM model of every tested page and traverses all elements checking them for any accessibility issues. It can provide an initial assessment much faster, and give a good input for the expert evaluation. There are, however, certain issues which automated testing cannot detect. This depends on the standards or guidelines we are testing for. For example, when we are testing for a specific syntax, such as valid HTML, the existence of programmatic table headers or color contrast automatic testing tools can provide us with 100 percent accurate results. When we are trying to determine if some information is indicated by the use of color only, an automated tool cannot tell with a high certainty and extra expert evaluation is required. Therefore we conducted automatic accessibility tests to complement the manual tests as explained in the previous section.

3   Conclusions and Future Work

This paper presented the methodology of the accessibility evaluation of all components of the Polycare system. The results of our work has shown that only a combined accessibility evaluation consisting of automated and expert evaluation would really unveil the accessibility problem of an application, especially when it provides different and distributed user interfaces in our case a web application and an Android app. Targeting various stakeholder. Additionally we think that a combined accessibility

---

[4] https://www.w3.org/TR/mobile-accessibility-mapping/.

and usability evaluation is required to ensure good user experience of an application, though there certainly some overlap between them, even though there might be different rationales for that, e.g., for visually impaired users who have limited or no access to visual information, it is crucial that adequate text alternatives are provided for non-text content like images and that link texts clearly describe the target otherwise they will not be able to navigate in an application. However, same issues will also pose a usability issue because self-descriptiveness and conformity to user expectations are understood in usability as important features to support users in achieving their tasks and facilitate learnability of an application. In CE as well as the Polycare Patient App there were shortcomings in regard to these aspects, in that text alternatives were missing or not meaningful and link texts were misleading. Sometimes they did not describe clearly the target or links with the same link text were leading to a different target or link texts of a menu link with the same target were worded differently.

Acknowledgments. This work was partially funded by the European Commission H2020 programme; Contract number 690367; POLYCARE Poly-stakeholders integrated care for chronic patients in acute phases. The authors would like to acknowledge the support of the POLYCARE consortium.

References

1. Benyon, D.R., Murray, D.M.: Applying user modelling to human-computer interaction design. AI Rev. (6) 43–69 (1993). http://www.soc.napier.ac.uk/~dbenyon/AIReview.pdf
2. Braunstein, M.L.: Patient—physician collaboration on FHIR (Fast Healthcare Interoperability Resources). In: International Conference on Collaboration Technologies and Systems (CTS), pp. 501–503. IEEE (2015)
3. Mohamad, Y., Nordbrock, G., Gappa, H., Velasco, C.: Study on elicitation and detection of emotional states with disabled users. In: Miesenberger, K., Bühler, C., Penaz, P. (eds.) ICCHP 2016. LNCS, vol. 9758, pp. 563–570. Springer, Cham (2016). https://doi.org/10.1007/978-3-319-41264-1_76
4. Kaklanis, N., Biswas, P., Mohamad, Y., et al.: Towards standardisation of user models for simulation and adaptation purposes. Univ. Access Inf. Soc. 15(1), S.21–S.48 (2016). https://doi.org/10.1007/s10209-014-0371-2. ISSN 1615-5289
5. Velasco, C.A., Mohamad, Y., Ackermann, P.: Architecture of a web of things eHealth framework for the support of users with chronic diseases. In: Proceedings of the 7th International Conference on Software Development and Technologies for Enhancing Accessibility and Fighting Info-exclusion (DSAI 2016), pp. 47–53. ACM, New York (2016). https://doi.org/10.1145/3019943.3019951

378   Y. Mohamad et al.

Co-creation of a Mobile City District Guide with and for Older Adults

Frank Berker, Frank Reins, and Helmut Heck[✉]

Forschungsinstitut Technologie und Behinderung (FTB) of Evangelische
Stiftung Volmarstein, 58300 Wetter (Ruhr), Germany
mobile-age@ftb-esv.de

Abstract. In the European project Mobile-Age co-creation processes of digital
mobile services with older adults have been studied. In order to experience such
co-creation, several mobile apps applying open data have been developed in a
structured co-creation process with senior citizens. Scientific work comprises the
evaluation of the co-creation process itself, methods of co-creation, the exploration of representations of city maps for older adults, and the technical
development and service provision. As an example, the paper describes the co-
creation of a demonstrator application of a city district guide for the district of
Bremen-Hemelingen.

Keywords: Co-creation · Senior citizens · Mobile application
City district guide

1 Background

The portion of older adults in Europe's population is growing steadily. However, senior
citizens do not normally share the same level of connectivity to the Internet or mobile
services as younger generations do. Moreover, government agencies are increasingly
providing their services through digital platforms. As a consequence, a growing percentage of the population, especially senior citizens, faces the risk of being excluded
from the use of digital public services. To overcome this, seniors should be trained in
the usage of such digital services and get involved in their design.

1.1 Co-creation of City District Guides as Mobile Apps

One of the goals of the European project Mobile-Age is to realize a substantive participation of senior citizens in the development of mobile applications by applying and
investigating different co-creation methodologies. The 3 years project, which started in
February 2016, has been implemented at four European pilot sites: Bremen (Germany),
South Lakeland (UK), Zaragoza (Spain) and Central Macedonia (Greece).

In order to practice (and to investigate) co-creation processes at the pilot site
Bremen, two mobile apps have been co-created with senior citizens for two districts of
the city. The initial focus was on connecting older adults and supporting their social
networking by providing open information in a map based mobile application.

© Springer International Publishing AG, part of Springer Nature 2018
K. Miesenberger and G. Kouroupetroglou (Eds.): ICCHP 2018, LNCS 10897, pp. 379–382, 2018.
https://doi.org/10.1007/978-3-319-94274-2_53

1.2   State of the Art

Usually, city guides are commissioned by city councils or tourist information offices; then they are implemented by internal or external agencies. Sometimes target groups may also be involved in the requirements analysis. In contrast, the Mobile-Age project consistently pursued a co-creation approach with much more active user participation. Older adults were part of most conceptual and development decisions, according to their abilities. This included structure, layout and design decisions, data creation, editing content, writing texts and descriptions, and producing photos and videos.

2   Methodology of Co-creation

During the co-creation process there were 23 workshops conducted with older adults, besides workshops with other stakeholders. On average, 5 older adults participated, with one workshop reaching a maximum of 16 participants. During these workshops different activities like conception of the service, data definition and the design of the user interface were conducted.

2.1   Service Concept

Before the beginning of the project it had not been decided what kind of "mobile service" had to be developed. Therefore it was the first co-creation task for the elder users and the technical developers to create a concept for the mobile service based on the needs and wishes of the users, the available open data, the principle technical possibilities of mobile services, and the available resources of the project.

2.2   Data Acquisition and Creation of Data Sets

The second task was the examination of the existing and available data. It turned out that the so-called open data to be used for the mobile service were not as "open" as expected. Therefore it was decided to collect data from a few open sources and to combine them with new created data produced by the older adults themselves. A user friendly and easy to use data backend to create and maintain the data was required in order to collect and provide well-structured sets of data.

2.3   User Interface

The third task was the co-creation and implementation of the user interface. While some specifications already arose from the definition of the data, a first design concept for the prototype was co-created during paper mockup workshops by the older adults. Based on this concept a first functional version was implemented. In the following workshops the development status of the prototype was regularly presented and put up for evaluation and discussion among the co-creators in order to iteratively refine it.

3   The City District Guide for Bremen-Hemelingen

The app aims at improving the social inclusion of older adults. It addresses the domain of social networking and social life of older adults. This includes connecting older adults through joint activities like meetings for walks by providing information about thematically elaborated walks. The application (online at https://mobileage.ftb-esv.de/hemelingen) is a digital district guide which suggests routes for walks and presents insider knowledge about locations on the route and further information (Fig. 1).

Fig. 1.   Various views of the city district guide app on a smartphone

An important finding during the development process was that the presentation of existing map services caused problems for seniors with regard to legibility and information volume. A further investigation showed that commonly used map services do not take into account any accessibility guidelines such as WCAG2.0 or age-related issues such as deterioration of contrast sensitivity and colour perception and lowered speed of information processing. But even sighted users may face problems with various items on a map. E.g., areas, streets and buildings are distinguished by their colours and even if they have borders, the contrasts used in most maps are not sufficient to be perceived by users with low vision [1]. Usually the colours are not chosen to be easily differentiated by people with colour vision deficiencies [2]. Another problem may be the level of details shown on the maps, which "can easily overwhelm the map user's capacity to process and interpret the information presented" [3].

Therefore, the City District Guide app offers a map presentation specially designed to meet the needs of older adults with higher contrast, reduced complexity and larger text fonts [4]. Additional pieces of information can be displayed interactively. Photo galleries give impressions of places and walks. The photos and short videos were produced by the seniors who participated in the co-creation workshops.

4   Conclusion and Planned Activities

Within the project Mobile-Age the methods and possibilities of co-creation with seniors were tested within the framework of a mobile service development. From a technical point of view, the requirements changed rapidly during the process and needed an agile develop methodology in order to iteratively develop a personalized service meeting the needs of the co-creating user group. The rapid prototyping approach proved to be appropriate, as the participants' motivation was maintained during the whole process due to the directly perceptible progress.

One of the main outcomes of the activities was the improved map design adapted to the needs of elder people, which will be published on GitHub in the near future.

The City information portal of Bremen will uptake the service; furthermore it is also planned to extend the service to other cities.

It has been shown that, both, the co-creation process and the app have positive impacts on the co-creators and the city district. Social service providers and neighbourhood managers schedule walking groups with seniors, which enable them to get to know each other and exchange information about other possible activities and offers.

During the co-creation activities most of the participants improved their digital literacy and established a regular tablet group independently from the project, where they learn from each other and share their experiences.

Acknowledgements. The Mobile-Age project has received funding from the European Union's Horizon 2020 research and innovation programme under grant agreement No 693319.

References

1. Understanding SC 1.4.3 - Contrast (Minimum) in Understanding WCAG 2.0 – a guide to understanding and implementing Web Content Accessibility Guidelines 2.0. W3C Working Group Note, 7 October 2016. https://www.w3.org/TR/UNDERSTANDING-WCAG20/visual-audio-contrast-contrast.html
2. Kovanen, J., Oksanen, J., Sarjakoski, L.T., Sarjakoski, T.: Simple maps – a concept of plain cartography within a mobile context for elderly users. In: Proceedings of the GIS Research UK 20th Annual Conference (2012)
3. van Elzakker, C., Griffin, A.L.: Focus on geoinformation users – cognitive and use/user issues in contemporary cartography. GIM Int. **27**, 20–23 (2013). https://www.gim-international.com/content/article/focus-on-geoinformation-users
4. Reins, F., Berker, F., Heck, H.: Customised city maps in mobile applications for senior citizens. In: Cudd, P., de Witte, L. (eds.) Harnessing the Power of Technology to Improve Lives, Proceedings of the AAATE Conference 2017 at Sheffield, pp. 622–629 (2017)

Development of Robot System for Elderly Who Live Alone

Yoshiyuki Takahashi[1](✉), Motoki Takagi[2], and Kaoru Inoue[3]

[1] Toyo University, 48-1 Oka, Asaka-shi, Saitama 351-8510, Japan
y-takahashi@toyo.jp
[2] Teikyo University, 1-1 Toyosatodai, Utsunomiya-shi, Tochigi 320-8551, Japan
[3] Tokyo Metropolitan University,
7-2-10 Higashiogu, Arakawa-ku, Tokyo 116-8551, Japan

Abstract. In this research, new concept elderly people watching system that aims to reduce the burden of the staff of community general support center is introduced. The experiment using robotic dolls to determine the system requirement. As a result, importance of appearance and communication function of the robot was confirmed. The robot which supports watching elderly people has been developed. It can give daily life related information to the elderly user by aural communication.

Keywords: Communication robot · Watching elderly person
Elderly person who live alone

1 Introduction

In Japan, aging, declining birthrate and trend of nuclear family has come to increasing the number of elderly people living alone. In the past, neighborhood community in the local area was actively carried out. However, recently such relationship is getting weak and the number of solitary deaths is increasing. Therefore, importance of watching elderly people living alone is acknowledged today.

Ministry of Economy, Trade and Industry and Ministry of Health, Labor and Welfare promote "Priority Areas to Which Robot Technology is to be Introduced in Nursing Care". It aims to realize self-reliance support by making use of robot technology [1]. In this activity, "Monitoring and communication systems" is listed on. Various monitoring systems for elderly people living alone are already in the market. Almost system consists of combination of a camera, a microphone, an accelerometer, an infrared sensor and so on. The system is connected to the computer network and cloud to share the status of the people who need to observe. Several monitoring systems with communication robot are also in commercial [2]. The robots can communicate with people by audio and physical action. Communication robots are being utilized as care for the elderly, and they are attracting attention.

K. Miesenberger and G. Kouroupetroglou (Eds.): ICCHP 2018, LNCS 10897, pp. 383–386, 2018.
https://doi.org/10.1007/978-3-319-94274-2_54

2 Experiments for System Requirements

Various communication robots already exist and some robot is designed for elderly people. To develop a new communication robot to assist the staff of a community general support center, what functions and appearance are suitable for elderly people especially with cognitive impairment will be required. Then, it was observed that elderly people with dementia who used robotic dolls.

The experiments were carried out with elderly people who are living in nursing home. They are from 70 to 90 years old and with or without dementia. At first, participant selection was done. Elderly people with dementia try to use robotic dolls for one week. A caregiver responds to a questionnaire to evaluate the degree of interest based on the observation, and select participants who are interested in robotic doll. Five different type robotic dolls were used. Table 1 shows characteristics of robotic dolls in the experiment. They have a talking function. However, they cannot listen someone's talk and answer it. They can only speak something.

Table 1. Characteristics of robotic dolls.

Name of Doll	Appearance	Functions
Yumeru	Little boy	Talking, singing, blinking
Kabochan	Little boy	Talking, singing, nodding (designed for elderly)
Primopuel	Little boy	Talking
Dacky	Dog	Talking, singing, blinking
Staffed Animal	Bear	None

In the experiments, selected participants use the robotic doll about 60 to 120 min a day for two weeks. They make a group of three to five participants and play with robotic dolls on one table. During the experiments, caregiver observes participant's response and action with intervention if it needed. After that, caregiver responds questionnaire and evaluates experiment.

In case of 84 years old male participant, he is gentle and a tendency to do things at his own pace. He was difficult to keep short-term memory and sometime wandering around at night. He was asked impression of the robotic dolls at first and he did not have interest about robotic dolls. One of the reason is the robotic dolls have cute appearance. Almost male participants concerned about other people's eye and did not accept them. In case of 94 years old female participant, she likes talking and has a kind personality. She is spot dementia. She used and played with robotic dolls for 90 to 120 min in each day. In the first week, she was talking to the robotic dolls and laughed. However, in the next week, "They talk same thing again", she said. She seemed to be confused by the conversation was not established. According to the observation of the experiments, it is confirmed that appearance preference is individually different and the function that answering question is required.

3 Concepts of New Watching System with Communication Robot for Elderly People

Figure 1 shows the overview of the watching system for assisting community general support center staff. Taking care for elderly people including watching should be done by the people. However, labor population reducing is expected in near future. Then, reducing burdens of staff of community general support center who take care elderly people is strongly required. Developing system is not aimed to replace staff. It will assist and reduce their works e.g. patrol and improve the quality of care. Sensor data and response by the elderly user that inform his/her activity from watching system will send to community general support center via computer cloud. This activity information will send to a caregiver, relatives, neighbors and other related people. The watching system will inform local community related information and personalized information e.g. garbage collection date, local community event, waking up call, time for taking medicine to the user.

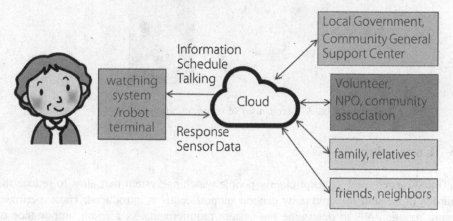

Fig. 1. Overview of the concept of watching system for assisting community general support center staff.

4 Design of the Communication Robot

According to the results of experiment with robotic dolls, communication robot needs changeable appearance. Then, mechanical structure is covered by changeable sheet. And also, the function for answering question is needed. Then, Google Assistant SDK for speech-text conversion and Open JTalk for Japanese language dialogue are implemented to realize aural communication system. Figure 2 shows the structure of the communication robot. RaspberryPi3 is used for robot main computer. Talking log will be used to know the elderly user's activity. Non-verbal actions importance is also mentioned in the experiment. Then, body motion mechanism is equipped. 3 DOF mechanism (pitch, heave and yaw) are controlled by ESP 32. Figure 3 shows mechanism of communication robot.

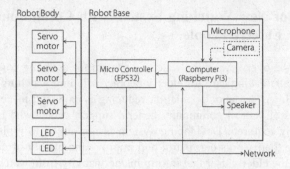

Fig. 2. Structure of the communication robot.

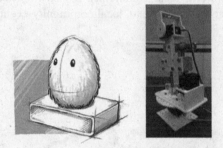

Fig. 3. Mechanism of communication robot.

5 Conclusions

In this research, new concept elderly people watching system that aims to reduce the burden of the staff of community general support center is introduced. The experiment using robotic dolls to determine the system requirement. As a result, importance of appearance and communication function of the robot was confirmed. The robot which supports watching elderly people has been developed. It can give daily life related information to the elderly user by aural communication.

References

1. Ministry of Economy, Trade and Industry (2018). http://www.meti.go.jp/english/press/2017/1012_002.html
2. Inoue, K., Sasaki, C., Nakamura, M.: Communication robots for elderly people and their families to support their daily lives - case study of two families living with the communication robot. Stud. Health Technol. Inform. **217**, 980–983 (2015)

Elderly People and Loneliness: An Innovative Approach

Laura Burzagli[1(✉)] and Simone Naldini[2]

[1] IFAC CNR, Florence, Italy
l.burzagli@ifac.cnr.it
[2] MATHEMA, Florence, Italy

Abstract. The design of a specific service related to loneliness assumes particular relevance for the quality of life of elderly people, because this feeling favorites a large number of pathologies and disabilities status. Since a very dangerous element for this condition is represented by the worsening of and decrease in the network of human relationships, a service able to provide suggestions to the users in a specific context, a condominium, is here presented. The innovative idea is a study of an automatic tool that is able to make a decision as to the best suggestion for a specific user, depending on what both she and other people are doing. The service is not at a personal level, but at the level of a network of people: this implies a different approach also for the adaptation, because different adaptations must necessarily work together. A preliminary interface for tablet is available.

Keywords: Elderly · Loneliness

1 Introduction

The rapid changes that have interested our society at social and technological levels in recent years present new user needs and thus require extending our investigations of user support services, for example those for elderly people [1]. For example support services for cooking activities was studied, implemented and evaluated [2] in the framework of the Italian national project Design for All [3].

Among a large array of new problems, the relevance of loneliness is undeniable. Indeed, this feeling favourites a large number of pathologies [4] and disabilities status, especially in ageing people. Several studies in different sectors, such as psychology, medicine, geriatrics state that a loneliness may lead to heart attacks, depression and/or other pathologies. Therefore, the design of a specific service related to loneliness assumes particular relevance for the quality of life of elderly people, even if the phenomenon is not limited to them.

K. Miesenberger and G. Kouroupetroglou (Eds.): ICCHP 2018, LNCS 10897, pp. 387–390, 2018.
https://doi.org/10.1007/978-3-319-94274-2_55

2   The State of Art

At the European level, we can find research projects that have investigated this aspect. An example of this is the AAL WECARE project (http://www.aal-europe.eu/projects/we-care/). Within this particular project, several technological elements such as video communication, medicine reminder, calendar and others are collected on a platform in order to maintain user autonomy.

For our research, we started from a social approach, with an identification of the critical aspects of such a condition. Undoubtedly, an element, which appear very dangerous, is represented by the worsening of and decrease in the network of human relationships [5, 6].

It is very difficult to consider all the levels of the relationship network of a person, (as is described in Chap. 7 Interpersonal interactions and relationship, of the Activities and Participation Section of the World Health Organization International Classification of Functioning and Disabilities) [7].

3   The Approach

Therefore, in order to set up a first core of the application, we focused on a particular context: a condominium, i.e. a context with a space limitation in which relationship can be mapped. In Italy, there are already initiatives to support people within a specific context. For example, in Genoa there is a service called MANI-MAN [8]. In this initiative, a set of services is offered to a limited group of people: all the people living on a given street. The perspective that is adopted by these services is that the user must require the service and people available for providing it can be found. The structure of the service presents a central unit, which receives all the requests coming from people and tries to find a solution. What is lacking is a direct connection among people, in order to recreate a social network that is able to overcome specific problems of loneliness.

The perspective that we have adopted is a little different, because technology is thought to collect information about a group of people, obviously in accordance with rules regarding privacy and ethics, and in return, to make a suggestion to the user that is closely connected with the condition of people in the group. The innovative idea is a study of an automatic tool that is able to make a decision as to the best suggestion for a specific user, depending on what both she and other people are doing.

Therefore, the different perspective is to consider not one person alone, but a group of users. In other words, this means designing a support service not just for a single user, but also - and at the same time - for all the people involving in the group. This collective approach is used, because the suggestion, which is provided to the user, takes into consideration all possibilities available within the group. In order to create a first group of people, eight different profiles have been identified, including an elderly lady, an elderly couple, a couple with a baby, an elderly couple with a young grandchild, a young girl, a young doctor and an elderly man.

Each of them is characterized by a static profile, in which a starting value for their preferences is set. For example, whether or not they like cooking, whether or not they like football, whether or not they have specific disabilities or limitations of activities.

A set of starting conditions was created. For example if they are working in the kitchen, or watching TV.

At the moment we consider to receive information about the condition of the user from a set of sensors and process such information in order to obtain an appropriate suggestion.

A set of suggestions was created, in order to select, at the moment within a limited but defined set, the best suggestion in each condition.

A starting table, capable of coupling profiles with suggestions was provided and we have begun to work on the Machine Learning algorithms that are able to take in account also the reaction (confirmation or rejection) of the user.

A preliminary interface for tablet is available. This interface allows user to select a person, a situation. A suggestion is so provided by the system, and the user can accept or reject. After three suggestions provided by the system, the user can make his choice among all the suggestions which are stored in the system. In the future it is foreseen a more specific activity on the interface, in order to select the most appropriate device for each user in each context.

4 Technological Characteristics

For the first prototype, the whole system has been developed on a Debian server. The server-side implementation of the operations was carried out using the NodeJS platform, and, specifically, implementing the project via the ExpressJS framework. This choice enables a modular implementation of the system, in order to facilitate the process of integration between all the components, which are identified and built during the design and development cycle.

The data were processed and managed through a MySQL database, while the client-side graphical interface (the user-accessible front end) was created using the HTML, JQuery and CSS languages.

For the execution of any statistical algorithms, it was decided to test the StatisticalR software.

5 Process of Evaluation

For the evaluation, we have also considered both a process with experts and with users. The idea has already been presented to a group of students of Psychology of the Catholic University of Milan (Italy) during a specific lesson about Interactive Systems and new ICT boundaries. The reaction was positive and, as a result, a first collection of notes now is available to improve the service, especially for the aspects related to the list of suggestions. However, we have also planned activities in an actual context for a direct involvement of users, a public structure, which is located close to Florence. This is a structure of cohousing, with up to 80 people living inside, all with a sufficient level of autonomy. We are discussing with caregivers of this structure a list of the most appropriate suggestions and a list of the most appropriate conditions. Together with them, we are also discussing a specific method to involve people. Anyway, people in charge of the centre welcome the idea and the basic application, because is not invasive, does not involve a medical intervention (in absence of pathologies), and can favourites the social life of the guests.

6 Conclusion

The scientific and practical impact of this application are represented by the fact that, in our case, ICT is thought to improve the quality of life of people, not at a general level, but for a specific situation. A condition which is not yet at the level of a disease, but which can cause one is considered. It is not invasive, since for the interaction different interfaces can be selected in different contexts, in order to minimise the disturbance in the user daily life: tablet, laptop, but also TV or other display, which are available to the user, can be selected. Moreover, the service is not at a personal level, but at the level of a network of people: this implies a different approach also for the adaptation, because different adaptations must necessarily work together.

References

1. Burzagli, L., Baronti, P., Billi, M., Emiliani, P.L., Gori, F.: Complete specifications of ICT services in an AAL environment. In: Cavallo, F., Marletta, V., Monteriù, A., Siciliano, P. (eds.) ForItAAL 2016. LNEE, vol. 426, pp. 51–60. Springer, Cham (2017). https://doi.org/10.1007/978-3-319-54283-6_4
2. Burzagli, L., Gori, F., Baronti, P., Billi, M., Emiliani, P.L.: Elements of adaptation in ambient user interfaces. In: Miesenberger, K., Bühler, C., Penaz, P. (eds.) ICCHP 2016. LNCS, vol. 9759, pp. 594–601. Springer, Cham (2016). https://doi.org/10.1007/978-3-319-41267-2_85
3. DESIGN FOR ALL project site. http://www.d4all.eu/en/
4. Niedzwiedz, C.L., Richardson, E.A., Tunstall, H., Shortt, N.K., Mitchell, R.J., Pearce, J.R.: The relationship between wealth and loneliness among older people across Europe: is social participation protective? Prev. Med. **91**, 24–31 (2016). https://doi.org/10.1016/j.ypmed.2016.07.016
5. Cacioppo, J.T., Cacioppo, S.: Social relationships and health: the toxic effects of perceived social isolation. Soc. Pers. Psychol. Compass **8**, 58–72 (2014). https://doi.org/10.1111/spc3.12087
6. Bothorel, C., Lohr, C., Thépaut, A., Bonnaud, F., Cabasse, G.: From individual communication to social networks: evolution of a technical platform for the elderly. In: Abdulrazak, B., Giroux, S., Bouchard, B., Pigot, H., Mokhtari, M. (eds.) ICOST 2011. LNCS, vol. 6719, pp. 145–152. Springer, Heidelberg (2011). https://doi.org/10.1007/978-3-642-21535-3_19
7. WHO: ICF International Classification of Functioning, Disability and Health. World Health Organization, Geneva (2001)
8. Info sul Mani-Man. http://www.consorzioagora.it/it/news/info-sul-mani-man

Heuristic Evaluation of a Mobile Telecare System for Older Adults

Marinka Krel, Ines Kožuh, and Matjaž Debevc[(✉)]

Faculty of Electrical Engineering and Computer Science,
University of Maribor, Koroška cesta 46, 2000 Maribor, Slovenia
marinka.krel@gmail.com,
{ines.kozuh,matjaz.debevc}@um.si

Abstract. Due to the exponential growth of the elderly population, there is an urgent need for development of telecare solutions supporting informal caregiving which allow the elderly to remain independent and age at home. As usability of such solutions is crucial for effective use, we employed heuristic evaluation to assess the user interface of the newly developed mobile application for telecare – TeleStiki. Our aim was to provide guidelines for similar telecare solutions based on both existing research and results of heuristic evaluation. We noticed that, (among other criteria), many applications lack help for the users so it is necessary to include settings or a help button in applications. These guidelines may solve similar solutions in the future on how developers can improve user interfaces of telecare mobile applications and, consequently, improve user experience when supporting aging at home.

Keywords: Heuristic evaluation · Telecare system · eHealth · Older adults
AAL solutions

1 Introduction

According to the World Health Organization (WHO), the aging population will increase globally from 12% to 22% by the year 2050. The threshold for people who are deemed as old is 60 years, while, currently, there are more than 125 million people that are aged 80 years or more (World Health Organization 2017).

The abovementioned aging trend raises questions about the accessibility of user-friendly telecare solutions on the market supporting active aging at home. One of the issues is that these accessibility guidelines are not expressed in an appropriate way. It results in several mobile applications on the market neglecting the needs of informal carers, who are deemed as persons who decide to combine their care and professional obligations as their primary duties.

In the context of related studies, we examined similar researches, studies, reports and conference papers that were relevant for our study. Among others, Kuo et al. (2016), examined the existing literature, through which they developed a home-based management system in order to get nurses to be the first effectively to provide care services.

© Springer International Publishing AG, part of Springer Nature 2018
K. Miesenberger and G. Kouroupetroglou (Eds.): ICCHP 2018, LNCS 10897, pp. 391–398, 2018.
https://doi.org/10.1007/978-3-319-94274-2_56

A similar study was also carried out by Loureiro et al. (2015), which demonstrates the use of an online data storage platform and quality analysis for the care of the elderly.

Our study is aimed at meeting this deficiency, as it provides a comprehensive review of the theory and standards, and, based on heuristic evaluation of a particular telecare mobile application, TeleStiki, it proposes guidelines on how to design the user interface of mobile telecare solutions. In this regard, the following research questions were examined:

– RQ1: What errors and difficulties of errors have the experts found in heuristic evaluation of the mobile application TeleStiki?
– RQ2: What is the relationship between the groups of criteria for heuristic evaluation of the user interface of the mobile application TeleStiki?
– RQ3: How do experts' experiences affect errors they perceived in heuristic evaluation of the mobile application TeleStiki?

It is expected that the experts who assessed the mobile application TeleStiki will detect some errors which may affect how users would understand the solution as it is. We also believe that experts' field of work and experience will affect their error detection, as, perhaps, some experts, who are working more in the areas of Information-Communication Technology (ICT), will focus more on the technical aspect of the application, while visual communications professionals may be more focused on its visual appearance.

2   Mobile Application for Telecare TeleStiki

The mobile application TeleStiki (Fig. 1) is intended to be used by informal carers to provide care to care receivers with whom they do not live. It works by using sensors, that are incorporated primarily in the home of a care receiver, and a mobile application, that is used primarily by the carer.

Fig. 1. TeleStiki *on iOS (own archive) and Android platform (Google Play, 2017)*

The sensors consist of an emergency call key, various contact sensors for doors and windows, motion sensors, and ambient sensors that detect the amount of carbon dioxide in the air, smoke or water spills. Both the well-being and the condition of the patient are informed by the caregiver via text messages and/or calls. They need a GPS connection or a wireless network to access the application itself (Smart Com 2017).

3 Methods

3.1 Instruments and Measures

To determine the usability of the mobile application TeleStiki empirically, we employed heuristic evaluation. We followed the general guidelines suggested by Nielsen and Mack (1994) and included some additional criteria from Sharp et al. (2002) on which we built our criteria on 7 general sections containing several different subsections:

1. User control and freedom: relates to the user's position in the interface itself.
   a. The application has a marked output.
   b. The application has the capability to cancel or enforce (undo - redo).
   c. The user can control the interaction between the user interface and the real world.
   d. The user knows where he is located, where he can go and how to get there.
   e. The user can predict from the current position how many steps he needs to get to the desired destination.
2. Error fixes
   a. If something goes wrong, the application tells the user what happened, why it happened and how to fix it.
   b. Required fields are immediately visually obvious.
   c. The back button or the backward gesture returns you to the previous view, where the data is not lost.
3. Accommodation
   a. The application is in the user's native language, insofar as it appeals to a particular market or target audience.
   b. Relevant metaphors are used where necessary.
   c. The user interface is adapted for the user's capabilities.
4. Linguistic clarity
   a. The application does not contain grammatical errors.
   b. Abbreviations and metaphors are not used, unless they are explained in advance.
5. Simplicity
   a. Viewing is minimalistic and adapted to relevant information.
   b. Different colors are used for different purposes.
   c. The size of the graphics affects the response time.
   d. The use of colors is limited to 3–4 colors.
   e. The purpose of the application is clear at the first glance.

6. Aesthetics
   a. Similarity means that the application adheres to design guidelines.
   b. Consistency means that the same application uses the same elements - from typography, colors and icons.
   c. Closure defines that it must be clearly separated which elements belong together.
   d. Proximity means that the elements are placed correctly in the user interface itself.
   e. The image resolution defines that all icons or other possible graphic elements are in the correct size.
7. System status visibility
   a. The application shows the operation of the sensors.
   b. The application works without needing to have access to the Internet.

With this method, experts for a particular domain evaluate how the planned elements of the user interface works, while using evaluation criteria. With this, experts searched for errors and problems that can be evaluated with an appropriate category, together with the weight of its complexity. Their expected results were supposed to provide us a very detailed brief which will be help us to create the basis for our guidelines, that will focus not just on the user interface, but also on how to achieve the best possible user experience.

3.2 Procedure

Following the guidelines suggested by Nielsen (1995), where 3–5 experts from various fields are advised to evaluate the user interface, we included six experts in our study. Danino (2001), stressed that it is important that the experts are divided according to their main field of activity. He argued that experts with various experiences would find different errors, since they would find to 81–90% of user interface errors altogether. Therefore, we included experts, and divided them by those who have:

1. Academic experiences,
2. Working in industry experience,
3. Academic and industry working experience.

Out of six experts, there was only one female expert. One expert had academic experience, two had experience in working in industry, and three had academic experience, as well as experience in working in industry. The total average age of experts was 31 years old, and they had different areas of expertise. Three experts were testing on the Android operating system, and three were testing on the iOS system. All of the experts had one week to evaluate the app TeleStiki.

The application was tested in August, 2017. While planning the research and its implementation that provided us with the results, we also addressed ethical questions. We took into account the Helsinki Declaration (World Medical Association 2001) and the Code of the American Psychologists Association APA (APA 2010).

4 Results and Conclusion

4.1 Results

The first research question asked what errors and difficulties of errors have the experts[1] found in heuristic evaluation of the mobile application. As one can see from Table 1, the analysis revealed that 22 errors were found, while the most common mistake (among others) was that the TeleStiki application does not show its main purpose at first glance. The user does not know where he is, where he can go and how to get there. It is also hard to predict how many steps separate you from the desired destination. The function of the sensors is not apparent from the application. In fact, the application does not contain information about which sensors it should use.

Table 1. Results

	Criteria - heuristic	E1	E2	E3	E4	E5	E6	Errors found:
1	*User control and freedom*							
a	The application has a marked output	x	x			x	x	4
b	Capability to cancel or enforce (undo - redo)		x			x	x	3
c	The user can control the interaction							
d	The user knows where he is, where he can go and how to get there				x		x	2
e	User can predict how to get the desired destination					x		1
2	*Error fixes*							
a	Application provides the user a feedback, if something goes wrong	x	x		x			3
b	Required fields are immediately visually obvious	x		x	x	x	x	5
c	The back button or the backward gesture returns you to the previous view – no data is lost		x					1
3	*Accommodation*							
a	The application is in the user's native language,	x		x		x		3
b	Relevant metaphors are used where necessary		x		x			2
c	The user interface is adapted for the user's capabilities				x			1

(continued)

---

[1] In Table 1 we denote the experts by the letter "E" and their reference number.

Table 1. (*continued*)

	Criteria - heuristic	E1	E2	E3	E4	E5	E6	Errors found:
4	*Linguistic clarity*							
a	Viewing is minimalistic and adapted to relevant information			x				1
b	Different colors are used for different purposes		x					1
5	*Simplicity*							
a	Viewing is minimalistic and adapted to relevant information				x	x		2
b	Different colors are used for different purposes			x		x		2
c	The size of the graphics affects the response time				x			1
d	The use of colors is limited to 3–4 colors		x		x			2
e	The purpose of the application is clear on the first glance	x	x	x	x	x	x	6
6	*Aesthetics*							
a	Similarity							
b	Consistency	x	x	x				3
c	Closure							
d	Proximity	x						1
e	Distinctness of images			x	x		x	3
7	*System status visibility*							
a	The application shows the operation of the sensors					x		1
b	The application works without the Internet	x	x	x	x	x	x	6

The second research question asked what the relationship between the groups of criteria for heuristic evaluation of the user interface of the mobile application TeleStiki is. Through the research, we now have a a complete insight into how the application is working, not just visually, but also on how it works functionally. This is based on two facts that were stressed by the experts, since they found the most errors right in the heuristics that touched both areas. All of them noted that the purpose of the application is not visible at first glance, as well as the error or application not working, if it's not connected to the Internet.

The third research question asked how experts' experiences affect errors they perceived in heuristic evaluation of the mobile application TeleStiki. Experience has proven to be particularly evident in the perception of the found errors, as well as in the evaluation the error weight. As an example, the expert who works mainly in graphic design, was the only one who pointed out that the icons of the graphic graphics were placed on the edge of the edges, and noted that as a catastrophic problem that should be fixed urgently.

4.2 Delving into Findings

The above-mentioned findings can be compared with the findings of the previous studies. Athiligiam et al. (2016) have pointed out that healthcare mobile technology is already active in an individual's life and, as Shin (2017) noted, the quality of experience can become the leading paradigm for managing the quality of life.

Although there are many potential benefits of supportive technologies, such as distance services, there are also several ethical issues (Perry et al. 2009), and a clear ethical framework is needed, as was already pointed out by Fisk (1998).

Concerns that are reflected in the studies are becoming the notion of issues, which is shown by concern that remote care services could simply be replaced by informal caregivers. Their controversy is due mainly to the fact that the elderly are too often excluded from the design of the remote supply system, and that the installation is often mistakenly seen as a one-time event (Mort et al. 2015).

To sum up the findings, we can see that our findings are consistent with the findings of the previous studies. However, even though many studies focus on testing the user experience with potential users, several studies overlook the heuristic analysis while testing the platforms in the beginning. For development, it is crucial that the errors are prevented before they even appear, to achieve the best results possible.

4.3 Guidelines for Design of the User Interface and Conclusion

Based on the above-mentioned findings, we propose guidelines for design of the user interface of the telecare mobile applications in order to achieve the best possible user experience:

1. **A short onboarding in the beginning.**
2. **The application should be in the user's mother language.**
3. **Users should always be aware of certain activities on the application.**
4. **By Standards, the application should indicate clearly which fields need to be solved for it to work properly.**
5. **Colors should be used according to their function, not just to sort out the visual appearance**.
6. **Settings or a help button should be included in applications**.
7. **The latest suggestion is that the application should also store data, even when you do not have a data connection.**

The above-mentioned findings are to be followed by developers, designers and researchers, while bearing in mind other Standards and Guidelines, to avoid creating a platform that does not work in a user-friendly way. However, we should be also aware of the fact that, for integrated solutions to work, they must be developed precisely, as well as evaluated with well-established research methods. Also, we should not neglect the fact that older people may face particular difficulties in adapting to constant changes and services, which can serve as a starting point for future research.

Acknowledgments. We would like to thank the experts who were included in the research, since, without their work, the analysis would not have been feasible. This study was a part of the Project ICT Solutions for Active and Healthy Aging: Integrating Informal e-Care Services in Slovenia (Slovenian Research Agency, Project No. L5-7626).

References

Athilingam, P., Osorio, R.E., Kaplan, H., Oliver, D., O'neachtain, T., Rogal, P.J.: Embedding patient education in mobile platform for patients with heart failure: theory-based development and beta testing. CIN Comput. Inform. Nurs. **34**(2), 92–98 (2016)

APA: Publication Manual of the American Psychological Association, 6th Edn. American Psychological Association (2010)

Danino, N.: Heuristic Evaluation – a Step by Step Guide Article (2001). https://www.sitepoint.com/heuristic-evaluation-guide. Accessed 20 Oct 2017

Fisk, M.J.: Telecare at home: factors influencing technology choices and user acceptance. J. Telemed. Telecare **4**(2), 80–83 (1998)

Kuo, M.H., Wang, S.L., Chen, W.T.: Using information and mobile technology improved elderly home care services (2016). https://www.ncbi.nlm.nih.gov/pmc/articles/PMC3649237/. Accessed 27 Oct 2017

Google Store: SmartCom – TeleStiki. https://play.google.com/store/apps/details?id=si.smart_com.caresignal.telestiki&hl=en. Accessed 27 Oct 2017

Loureiro, N., Fernandes, M., Alvarelhão, J., Ferreira, A., Caravau, H., Martins, A.I., Cerqueira, M., Queiró, A.: A web-based platform for quality management of elderly care usability evaluation of Ankira (2015). http://www.sciencedirect.com/science/article/pii/S1877050915027167. Accessed 27 Oct 2017

Mort, M., Roberts, C., Pols, J., Domenech, M., Moser, I.: Ethical implications of home telecare for older people: a framework derived from a multisided participative study. Health Expect. **18**(3), 438–449 (2015)

Nielsen, J., Mack, R.L. (eds.) Usability Inspection Methods, pp. 25–62. Wiley, New York (1994)

Nilsen, J.: How to conduct a heuristic evaluation (1995). https://www.nngroup.com/articles/how-to-conduct-a-heuristic-evaluation/. Accessed 20 Oct 2017

Sharp, H., Rogers, Y., Preece, J.: Interaction Design: Beyond Human-Computer Interaction. Wiley, New York (2002)

Shin, D.H.: A user-based model for the quality of experience of the internet of things (2017). https://www.researchgate.net/publication/313593506_A_User-based_Model_for_the_Quality_of_Experience_of_the_Internet_of_Things. Accessed 27 Oct 2017

Smart Com. Rešitve lastnega razvoja (2017). http://www.smart-com.si/resitve/resitve-lastnega-razvoja/telestiki. Accessed 27 Oct 2017

Perry, J., Beyer, S., Holm, S.: Assistive technology, tele care and people with intellectual disabilities: ethical considerations. J. Med. Ethics **35**(2), 81–86 (2009). 65

WHO: Ageing and Life Course - World Health Organization (2017). http://www.who.int/ageing/en/. Accessed 30 Aug 2017 (2009)

World Medical Association: World Medical Association Declaration of Helsinki: ethical principles for medical research involving human subjects. Bull. World Health Organ. **79**(4), 373 (2001)

Identification of Age-Specific Usability Problems of Smartwatches

Nathalie Zotz, Simone Saft, Johannes Rosenlöhner, Patricia Böhm,
and Daniel Isemann(✉)

University of Regensburg, Universitätsstr. 31, 93053 Regensburg, Germany
daniel.isemann@ur.de

Abstract. Since new technology is, in principle, accessible to users of all ages, it needs to be suitable for all generations. The purpose of this study is to identify usability issues of smartwatches and contrast the problems and issues that elderly encountered to those experienced by a younger age group. In total 16 test subjects, eight of each age group (under-30s and over-60s), were observed quantitatively and qualitatively while performing basic tasks on a common smartwatch. The results indicate that the voice command evoked issues for all ages, whereas the older participants were facing more difficulties concerning the menu structure, the user interface and performing gestures on the touchscreen. While the task completion rate did not significantly differ between the age groups and the ease of use was mostly perceived equally, the elderly needed significantly more time and more personal assistance to perform the tasks. Understanding the likely age-specific differences in smartwatch interaction points to a need for further support for the elderly.

Keywords: Usability issues · Small touch screen device · Speech commands
Older citizens · Elderly · Comparative user study · Older vs younger users

1 Introduction

It has been shown that elderly users have some difficulty handling touchscreens [15]. Our study focuses on interaction problems that older as well as younger adults experience on small touchscreen sizes of smartwatches and examines whether these issues pertain to both groups or are only experienced by one age group. Its aim is to inform developers and researchers about special needs and issues elderly users may have and provide recommendations to design user friendly smartwatch applications for all ages.

For this a user study including performance measurements and user observation was conducted with 16 participants, of whom eight were between the ages of 20 and 30 and eight between 65 and 75. The tasks included principal use cases of the smartwatch such as setting the timer, creating a list or receiving and sending a message by using basic touch gestures and the voice command. Some of our results are relevant in other contexts such as basic interaction problems using smartphones or other touchscreen devices. Furthermore, our subjective measures provide a good understanding of the attitudes towards smartwatches of the two age groups.

© Springer International Publishing AG, part of Springer Nature 2018
K. Miesenberger and G. Kouroupetroglou (Eds.): ICCHP 2018, LNCS 10897, pp. 399–406, 2018.
https://doi.org/10.1007/978-3-319-94274-2_57

2   Related Work

Mobile applications can have a positive effect on the quality of life [11]. Particularly smartwatches are becoming an important device as they offer many opportunities with their build-in sensors, especially in the field of healthcare informatics [4]. Many studies focus on developing new applications to monitor health-related issues such as fall detection [2, 9], dementia [1] or diabetes [3]. Kalantarian et al. [7] for example proposed a new system to detect the intake of medication and tested its efficacy in an experimental procedure. This study will not implement a new application, but will examine the standard functions and basic interaction gestures of smartwatches.

Furthermore, it compares the acceptance of young and older adults towards using smartwatches. Research shows that important acceptance criteria are cost and battery life [13] as well as the perceived usefulness and attractiveness [5]. Older people are more likely to use a smartwatch if it helps them to monitor their health [6].

Usability issues of elderly users using touchscreen interfaces have been explored in many other studies. Kobayashi et al. [8], for instance, shows that elderly users experience trouble using basic interaction gestures such as tapping on touchscreen devices and suggested to increase screen size. Another study indicates that buttons of mobile phones are too small or are not pressed when older users try to click it [10]. Using speech commands also causes problems especially for the elderly [17]. Vacher et al. [16] prove the need for adapted speech recognizers. Therefore we assume the elderly are facing more issues when interacting with smartwatches due to the small screen sizes and issues with speech recognition in comparison to younger age groups.

Prior comparisons of younger and older age groups revealed that there are significant age-specific differences using software interfaces. Older users need considerably more time to complete a task than younger participants [15, 18], even though Murata and Iwase [12] found no significant differences in pointing time on touch panels between an older and a younger group.

3   Methods

To identify age specific usability problems of smartwatches a user study evaluating the usability of a specific device with younger and elderly participants was conducted.

3.1   Participants and Test Device

Two age groups participated in the user study: Eight younger adults (23–28 years old) and eight elderly adults (66–72 years old). All but two had previous experience with smartphones, but no one had prior experience with a smartwatch (see Table 1).

The device chosen for this study is the Sony Smartwatch 3 paired with a Google Nexus 5 smartphone. All participants wore the smartwatch on their non-dominant hand to perform seven tasks listed in Table 2. The tasks were not ordered by difficulty to build up coherent narrative. Test sessions, conducted over a period of four weeks, took approximately one hour for older and half an hour for younger adults.

Table 1. Participant demographics.

Young age group						Older age group					
ID	Gender	Age	ID	Gender	Age	ID	Gender	Age	ID	Gender	Age
P1	male	28	P5	female	24	P9	male	66	P13	male	69
P2	male	26	P6	male	23	P10	male	72	P14	female	66
P3	female	23	P7	male	23	P11	female	68	P15	female	69
P4	female	23	P8	female	24	P12	male	68	P16	female	68

Table 2. Seven tasks utilized in this study.

Task ID	Description
Task 1	*General activities:* read actual time
Task 2	*Setting activities:* change font size especially suitable for you
Task 3	*App & voice activities*: add list by voice input with the google notes application
Task 4	*Voice activities:* use voice input to search for lasagne recipes
Task 5	*App activities:* set timer to 40 min
Task 6	*App & voice activities:* receive and reply to a message
Task 7	*App activities:* open and archive list used in task 3

3.2   User Study

In the beginning of each test session, the subject had to read an instruction with a basic explanation of the Smartwatch which includes activating the screen, performing swipe gestures, opening the menu, returning back to the homescreen and using the voice command. The subject could consult the instruction during the whole test. Afterwards the execution of tasks started and the participant was instructed to "think aloud" to gather qualitative data. Besides, several quantitative metrics were assessed including the number of views on the instruction, the number of personal assistances by the test coordinator, the task completion rate, the time on task and the perceived ease of use of each task with the Single Ease Question [14]. For measuring the Single Ease Question (SEQ), every participant was asked to rate each task according to their degree of difficulty on a scale of 1 to 7 in descending order. After the tasks were finished, each subject had to fill out a questionnaire with items assessing demographic data, previous experience regarding smartphone usage, technical affinity, test specific data, general feedback and added value of using a smartwatch.

4   Results

We first performed qualitative analysis with the results of the test protocols using a coding matrix. Furthermore, acceptance criteria were determined for using a smartwatch among young adults and the elderly. The quantitative data was analyzed using the SPSS statistics package regarding five research hypotheses.

4.1   Qualitative Analysis

User comments and behavior were logged by two test coordinators. All observed problems could be clustered in four categories: *voice input, structure of the watch's menu, gestures* and *user interface* to classify them by specific usability problems.

Usability Problems. While performing tasks on the smartwatch, all of the subjects experienced usability problems which were coded and analysed as follows:

Voice Input. All participants were facing problems with the voice input of the smartwatch. The "speak now" notification misled seven of the young and four of the older subjects to click on it, causing unexpected behavior. Three young and two older participants had the feeling that the input took too much time (P2: "Loading takes too long"). Three older participants forgot about the activation sentence "Okay Google" and one older subject was pronouncing it in a way the watch could not interpret. The majority of test participants was not sure about the outcome of their voice input. For example, in task 3 (create a new list) they entered all three terms in a row instead of single parts. This led to a list with only one list entry containing the three terms.

Structure of the Watch's Menu. Participants of the older group encountered problems with the menu of the smartwatch. They could not find the needed apps for task 2, 3 and 7 in the menu (P11: "Google Notes has not appeared so far") because they did not realize that the menu was organized alphabetically. Furthermore, some of the elderly subjects did not know that the menu was scrollable. They only saw the few apps which were displayed at the top of the menu and needed assistance to continue.

Gestures. Particularly the elderly were facing issues performing gestures on the touchscreen because their gestures were not recognized by the smartwatch. In task 6 a usability issue for all age groups was identified: Trying to open the incoming message, 11 subjects were clicking on it before performing the required swipe-gesture. In several cases this led to the loss of messages.

User Interface. The user interface of the smartwatch caused difficulties in terms of readability for the elderly. Four of these were complaining about the poor coloring and contrast (P14: "The font is too small and hard to see"). Especially the small dots at the bottom of the screen - which indicate the possibility of swiping horizontally - were difficult to recognize for the elderly and could have resulted in performing the wrong gestures. The young participants by contrast did not encounter any problems due to the design of the user interface.

Acceptance Criteria. In the end of each test session the test coordinator asked each participant to state his willingness to use a smartwatch in their everyday life and to mention perceived weaknesses of the smartwatch. Two out of eight test subjects of each age group stated they could imagine using a smartwatch in their everyday life. Two elderly mentioned major concerns regarding data security, whereas the younger subjects had a rather negative attitude towards smartwatches due to the poor battery life and the need of a continuous connection to a smartphone. Compared to the elderly, twice as many young subjects (6) perceived the voice command as a useful function. The timer application was mentioned by three older subjects to be the most valuable feature for them, but additionally they wished to measure their blood pressure or blood sugar with the smartwatch.

4.2   Quantitative Analysis

Quantitative metrics of the younger and older groups were analysed with regard to the following five null hypotheses. To test hypotheses 1, 3, 4 and 5 two sample t-tests were conducted with a significance level of $\alpha = 0.05$. To compare the task completion rate (hypothesis 2) the Fisher Exact Test was applied [14].

1. There is no difference between the efficiency (time on task) of younger adults and the efficiency (time on task) of older adults while using a smartwatch.
2. There is no difference between the effectiveness (task completion rate) of younger adults and the effectiveness (task completion rate) of older adults while using a smartwatch.
3. There is no difference between the amount of assistance needed by younger adults and the amount of assistance needed by older adults while using a smartwatch.
4. There is no difference in how often the user instructions were consulted by younger adults and how often the user instructions were consulted by older adults while performing the tasks.
5. There is no difference between the SEQ rating of younger adults and the SEQ rating of older adults while using a smartwatch.

Time on Task. Significant differences were detected when comparing the mean task times of the two age groups. Especially the completion of task 5 and 7 took the elderly significantly longer (T5: $t(14) = -7.539$; $p = 0.000$; two-tailed test; T7: $t(14) = -3.675$; $p = 0.003$; two-tailed test). Also the needed times for task 2 and 4 differed significantly (T2: $t(7.936) = -2.344$; $p = 0.047$; two-tailed test; T4: $t(14) = -2.260$; $p = 0.040$; two-tailed test), meaning the null hypothesis could not get accepted for the tasks 2, 4, 5 and 7.

As shown in Table 3, the younger age group managed also the completion for task 1 and 6 faster than the elderly where no significant difference was found. Only for task 3 the younger age group needed slightly more time ($M = 135.88$; $SD = 57.947$) than the older group ($M = 131.75$, $SD = 84.417$) noting a high standard deviation.

Table 3. Descriptive statistics: time on task in seconds

		Task1	Task2	Task3	Task4	Task5	Task6	Task7
Mean	Young	4.5	27.63	135.88	44.13	39.75	56.75	39.50
	Elderly	7.8	64.75	131.75	87.25	135.25	96.75	79.88
Standard Deviation	Young	1.852	11.237	57.947	30.503	17.450	49.018	64.176
	Elderly	6.792	43.358	84.417	44.516	31.290	64.176	23.775
p-value			.197	.047	.911	.040	.000	.183	.003

Task Completion Rate. Due to the assistance that was provided to participants during the test, only few tasks were not completed by some subjects as shown in Table 4.

Table 4. Descriptive statistics: task completion rate

		Task1	Task2	Task3	Task4	Task5	Task6	Task7	Total
Successes	Young	8	8	3	8	8	8	8	8
	Elderly	8	8	0	8	8	7	8	8
p-value		1	1	0.2	1	1	1	1	

Task 6 was completed by 15 out of all 16 participants. Only one participant of the older group was not able to complete the task. Task 3 was completed by only three out of all 16 participants, all three being part of the younger group. Meaning that for task 3 the younger adults were more effective with a two-tailed p-value of 0.2 when comparing the task completion rates by applying the Fisher Exact Test [14].

Number of Needed Assistance. Comparing the absolute amount of the assistance required shows that the mean number of requests needed by the elderly was significantly higher for all but task 1, where the test coordinator had to help only one participant of the elderly (Table 5). So the null hypothesis regarding the needed assistance could only be accepted for task 1, signifying a great difference between the two age groups.

Table 5. Absolute values: number of needed assistance

	Task1	Task2	Task3	Task4	Task5	Task6	Task7	Total
Young	0	0	10	4	4	8	2	28
Elderly	1	10	21	16	17	23	12	100

Number of Looks at the Instructions. Examining the absolute values, a slightly higher number of looks at the instructions of the younger age group ($\Delta = 3$) was determined (Table 6). For task 1 and 7 none of the participants of both groups consulted the instructions. While the number of looks in task 4 and 5 was slightly higher for the elderly, the younger group needed instructions in tasks 2, 3 and 6 more frequently. Since no significant difference could be shown in any of the tasks, the null hypothesis regarding the looks at the instructions was accepted for all tasks.

Table 6. Absolute values: number of looks at the instructions

	Task1	Task2	Task3	Task4	Task5	Task6	Task7	Total
Young	0	1	1	8	1	3	0	14
Elderly	0	0	0	9	2	0	0	11

SEQ Ratings. We observed only one significant difference between the two groups concerning the SEQ ratings (Table 7). The ease of use of task 2 was perceived significantly more difficult by the older age group ($T(14) = 2.463$; $p = 0.027$; two-tailed test). We assume this is due to the fact that the elderly were facing more issues concerning the structure of the watch's menu (see Sect. 4.1 Qualitative Analysis).

Table 7. Descriptive statistics: SEQ ratings

		Task1	Task2	Task3	Task4	Task5	Task6	Task7
Mean	Young	6.63	5.88	3.50	5.38	4.88	3.75	4.88
	Elderly	6.88	4.25	2.88	3.88	3.88	3.13	3.63
Standard deviation	Young	.744	1.126	1.309	1.598	1.727	1.909	1.808
	Elderly	.345	1.488	.835	2.232	1.727	1.553	1.996

5 Discussion and Conclusion

In this paper, we investigated the usability of a smartwatch among young adults and the elderly. Our qualitative and quantitative results suggest that using a smartwatch can be hampered by serious usability problems for both age groups. For instance, younger and the older users had difficulties using voice commands. Despite experiencing more problems due to the menu structure, the design of the user interface and performing touch gestures, the task completion rate, the number of looks at the user instructions and the perceived ease of use by the older participants barely showed any significant differences when contrasting it to the younger group. However, the elderly needed considerably more time to complete the tasks and required personal assistance to a significantly higher amount. Regarding the acceptance, both age groups are concerned about data security and the need of a constant connection to a smartphone.

Based on our findings we propose some basic design recommendations for smartwatch interaction: Features to set contrast and saturation for the smartwatch display should be implemented. Especially the small dots at the bottom of the screen - which indicate the possibility of swiping horizontally - could have been more visible to the older age group when correctly adjusted to their specific needs. This could help avoid wrong swiping gestures. Since some participants thought the menu was static, we suggest displaying only half of the bottom item when opening the menu and therefore indicate a scrollable list of items. Our investigation also indicated that performing a swipe-gesture to open a recently received message is rather counterintuitive. In this case a click-gesture would appear to better meet user expectations. Lastly, we conclude that in an ideal scenario smartwatches (like other touch devices perhaps) needed to be more sensitive to touch gestures by elderly users. Naturally, the robustness of our findings and recommendations needs to be further scrutinized by, among other things, testing additional smartwatch types with larger sample sizes.

References

1. Boletsis, C., McCallum, S., Landmark, B.F.: The use of smartwatches for health monitoring in home-based dementia care. In: Zhou, J., Salvendy, G. (eds.) DUXU 2015. LNCS, vol. 9194, pp. 15–26. Springer, Cham (2015). https://doi.org/10.1007/978-3-319-20913-5_2
2. Casilari, E., Oviedo-Jiménez, M.A.: Automatic fall detection system based on the combined use of a smartphone and a smartwatch. PLoS ONE 10(11), 1–11 (2015)
3. Costik, J.: Monitor diabetes from your smart watch. http://spectrum.ieee.org/geek-life/hands-on/monitor-diabetes-from-your-smart-watch. Accessed 23 Mar 2018
4. Ehrler, F., Lovis, C.: Supporting elderly homecare with smartwatches: advantages and drawbacks. Stud. Health Technol. Inform. 205, 667–671 (2014)
5. Enér, R., Knutsbo, L.: Factors Influencing Consumer Acceptance of New Technology: A Case Study of Smartwatches. Luleå University of Technology (2015)
6. Glowacki, E.M., Zhu, Y., Hunt, E., Magsamen-Conrad, K., Bernhardt, J.M.: Facilitators and Barriers to Smartwatch Use Among Individuals with Chronic Diseases: A Qualitative Study. (2015)
7. Kalantarian, H., Alshurafa, N., Nemati, E., Le, T., Sarrafzadeh, M.: A smartwatch-based medication adherence system. In: 2015 IEEE 12th International Conference on Wearable and Implantable Body Sensor Networks (BSN), pp. 1–6 (2015)
8. Kobayashi, M., Hiyama, A., Miura, T., Asakawa, C., Hirose, M., Ifukube, T.: Elderly user evaluation of mobile touchscreen interactions. In: Campos, P., Graham, N., Jorge, J., Nunes, N., Palanque, P., Winckler, M. (eds.) INTERACT 2011. LNCS, vol. 6946, pp. 83–99. Springer, Heidelberg (2011). https://doi.org/10.1007/978-3-642-23774-4_9
9. Kostopoulos, P., Kyritsis, A.I., Deriaz, M., Konstantas, D.: F2D: a location aware fall detection system tested with real data from daily life of elderly people. Procedia Comput. Sci. 98, 212–219 (2016)
10. Kurniawan, S.: Mobile phone design for older persons. Interact. Des. Sr. Innov. Graying Times 14(4), 24–25 (2007)
11. Lee, P.S.N., Leung, L., Lo, V., Xiong, Ch.: The perceived role of ICTs in quality of life in three Chinese cities. Soc. Indic. Res. 88, 457–476 (2008)
12. Murata, A., Iwase, H.: Usability of touch-panel interfaces for older adults. Hum. Factors J. Hum. Factors Ergon. Soc. 47(4), 767–776 (2005)
13. Rawassizadeh, R., Price, B.A., Petre, M.: Wearables: has the age of smartwatches finally arrived? Commun. ACM 58(1), 45–47 (2014)
14. Sauro, J., Lewis, J.R.: Quantifying the user experience: Practical statistics for user research. Morgan Kaufman, Amsterdam, Boston (2016)
15. Sonderegger, A., Schmutz, S., Sauer, J.: The influence of age in usability testing. Appl. Ergon. 52, 291–300 (2015)
16. Vacher, M., Aman, F., Rossato, S., Portet, F.: Development of automatic speech recognition techniques for elderly home support: applications and challenges. In: Zhou, J., Salvendy, G. (eds.) ITAP 2015. LNCS, vol. 9194, pp. 341–353. Springer, Cham (2015). https://doi.org/10.1007/978-3-319-20913-5_32
17. Vipperla, R.C., Renals, S., Frankel, J.: Longitudinal study of ASR performance on ageing voices. Interspeech 2008, 2550–2553 (2008)
18. Wirtz, S., Jakobs, E., Ziefle, M.: Age-specific usability issues of software interfaces. In: Proceedings of the 9th International Conference on Work With Computer Systems, pp. 2–10 (2009)

Review of Telecare Technologies
for Older People

Jean D. Hallewell Haslwanter(✉)(iD)

University of Applied Sciences Upper Austria, Wels and TU Wien, Vienna, Austria
jean.hallewell@fh-ooe.at

Abstract. This paper reviews technology to support aging in place. Although the populations in many countries are aging and various funding programmes have supported their development, these technologies are not yet widespread. To support people developing these systems in having more success in the future, here types of systems available and a number of systems that have been developed are described. Furthermore, some of the benefits, both potential and realized, are described.

Keywords: AAL · Aging in place · Older people · Telecare

1 Introduction

Supporting older people is an important issue, since societies are getting older in Europe. By 2030, the absolute number of people 80 and above is expected to increase by more than 10 million [15].

Although many older people are healthy, some require support. Technology can assist people to overcome limitations on their own, whether these limitations are physical or cognitive. The possibilities are as diverse as the breadth of disabilities and human activities, e.g., screen readers and home automation. By assisting people in doing what they want and need to do, these technologies can support independence. Thus, they may increase quality of life and reduce the cost of care.

Special tools may be necessary for older people, as the features of age-related disabilities may differ from the forms experienced by younger people even with disabilities that affect the same faculty. For example, presbyopia, age-related vision problems, affects the ability to focus on things that are close, but does not exclude also having problems seeing in the distance, thus requiring multifocal lenses not usually needed by younger people with vision problems.

Designing technology for older people is also challenging as the extent and number of limitations are likely to worsen as people age [18], sometime suddenly. It is also challenging for older people if they are used to being able to do things independently or have a solution that "works" for them.

© Springer International Publishing AG, part of Springer Nature 2018
K. Miesenberger and G. Kouroupetroglou (Eds.): ICCHP 2018, LNCS 10897, pp. 407–415, 2018.
https://doi.org/10.1007/978-3-319-94274-2_58

In Europe the term AAL is used for assistive information and communication technology (ICT) aimed at supporting older people in their own living environment. AAL initially stood for *"Ambient* Assisted Living", but this was later changed to *"Active* and Assisted Living", as the initial focus on technology shifted to self-empowerment [3]. Another expression used is *aging in place.* A recent study found the areas that have been targeted in practice are: dependency on others in everyday life, risk of falling, chronic illness, dementia, social isolation, depression, personal welfare and medication management [26].

Although funding programmes have supported the development of these technologies, e.g., the Austrian programme *benefit*, the German programme *Altersgerechte Assistenzsysteme* (age-appropriate assistance systems) and the *AAL (Joint) Programme* of European Union (EU), in 2013 the systems were still restricted to a few niches [8]. Perhaps due to this, new funding schemes have been initiated, e.g., the *AAL Programme* was extended with the specific aim to get more systems to market. This indicates the perceived value of these systems.

This paper will review the existing literature to describe the types of AAL systems available, some specific examples of systems that have been developed and some benefits of these types of systems. It updates previous reviews (e.g. [40,42]) and provides more examples of systems. Since people involved in the development feel the lack of overview of which systems have been developed and their benefits impact success with relation to commercialization [20], a review is of value. Note parts of this paper were included in [19].

2   Types of AAL Systems

Based on the overview of telecare in Turner [40], in the following the systems described are grouped as follows: *systems that support well-being and health, telehealth systems, telecare monitoring systems* to increase security and *other systems for older people.*

The systems described cut across a number of the categories in the taxonomy suggested for AAL systems (T*AAL*XONOMY) [28], including the categories: Health & Care, Living & Buildings, Safety & Security, Mobility & Transport, Vitality & Abilities, Leisure & Culture and Information & Communication.

3   Methods

Systems to support older people were searched for in the proceedings of the *AAL Forum*, the digital library of the American computing society ACM and using Google. The search was then expanded to articles referenced by others, further articles by the same authors, portals where articles were found, and searching again with terms found in other articles. A focus was put on peer-reviewed sources. In all over 75 articles were examined, including review articles and reports on specific projects from Europe, the United States, Japan and Australia.

Since the goal is to show the breadth of what has been attempted, for this article systems were chosen (a) to illustrate the different categories and (b) different versions of related systems. In part due to length restrictions, it does not include all systems developed.

4   Some Examples of Telecare Systems

4.1   Systems that Support Well-Being and Health at Home

There is a broad variety of systems that support activities of daily living (ADL) [28]. Simple examples are home automation to support actions that require physical effort, e.g., turning off lights or seeing who is at the door without having to get up. Even reminders about appointments can support memory.

Robotic systems are more complex and can assist people with physical limitations; e.g., to fetch things or to pick things up from the floor. Toyota announced their Human Support Robot (HSR) in 2015, which can fetch objects [25]. Because these solutions promise to be very expensive, there have been initiatives to design cheaper alternatives, e.g., the care robot called the Hobbit [16].

Another area of interest is supporting mobility. In this category there is the iWalkActive: an "off-road" walker that is combined with a tablet to support people in finding and going on walks appropriate to their level of mobility [30].

Communication systems can also support living independently, as these can reduce the sense of isolation and provide a way for people to get assistance [5].

4.2   Telehealth Systems

For people with health conditions, important physiological values may be monitored using telehealth solutions, e.g., measuring blood pressure for people with heart problems. These readings can be used to generate an alarm, or just be recorded. Furthermore, the results may be reserved for private use or may be sent directly to health care professionals. In fact, current European care delivery models center on these types of solutions for people with diabetes, Chronic Obstructive Pulmonary Disease (COPD) and congestive heart failure [41].

There are solutions available on the general market that can be used for telehealth, also for those without known health problems. As an example, many modern scales include Bluetooth wireless technology, which enables them to be connected to a personal computer (PC), tablet computer or even a smartphone. The data about weight is an important indicator for older people, as sudden weight loss may be a sign of emerging dementia [2], and not eating enough can lead to a deterioration of other medical conditions [6].

Even video calls with doctors is a type of telehealth which can be used for remote consultation or diagnosis [40]. Even though there are limitations, these systems can save time, effort and money required for travel, especially for people living in remote locations [40].

Some systems are on the border between telehealth and supporting people living independently. For example, different types of pill boxes: ones to remind people to take their medication at the right time [39], or ones with embedded sensors to detect whether the pills have been removed [27]. Systems like this support health, even though they are used at home, rather than at a distance as implied by the term *tele*health.

4.3   Telecare Monitoring Systems

Whereas *Telehealth* looks more at medical monitoring or treatment, *telecare* is related to alarms [17]. Telecare monitoring systems are also quite broad and can be divided into three generations [40]. The devices from the first generation include sensors with little logic, e.g., to detect whether someone has left the gas or water on, and automatically turn these off [40]. The second generation uses sensor data to generate alarms, e.g., using RFID (Radio Frequency IDentification) or a mobile phone to detect when people with dementia leave their flat [29]. More complex are fall monitors, which can be based on various technologies, e.g., cameras to detect movement typical of falls [44], sensors detecting vibrations from someone hitting the floor or worn devices with accelerometers [40]. The third and latest generation is more focused on quality of life [40], e.g., integrating services that allow older people to get advice or linking to virtual communities.

Activity monitoring can detect whether someone has not moved for a longer time and may need help, but also to detect specific activities, such as whether a person has gone to bed. This requires complex algorithms and errors can lead to missed alarms and/or false alarms [42, p. 33], e.g., a false alarm if someone leaves to go shopping or sits very still while watching a film, or real emergencies may missed, because the person is normally gone at that time of day or the dog is detected instead. Reliability is important, as people come to rely on these systems [17, p. 93].

Different technologies can be used to determine whether there has been any activity, e.g., motion detectors, temperature sensors and sensors installed in beds or on kitchen appliances [42]. These sensors are typically wireless, using either radio waves or infrared [40]. Since the technology being integrated is so diverse, there has also been an attempt to develop open platforms for AAL, e.g. universAAL [21].

One example of a monitoring system for use in private homes is the one from Dutch Domotics [1]. Other systems provide fewer details, but allow for reciprocal data exchange between older people and family carers, e.g., optical fibers in a planter used to display presence to distant family members in an unobtrusive way [24], or a clock that combines activity data and active communication, e.g., "I'm up" [35].

4.4   Other Systems for Older People

Many systems combine monitoring with other features, e.g., Tunstall Assisted Living and Independent Living solutions include both the remote control of devices and safety monitoring. These types of systems may be referred to as domotics or Smarthome systems and may also be targeted at younger people.

An early example of this type of system is PAUL from the German company CIBEK, which was piloted in 2007 [37].

There is also a host of ICT aimed at older people that is not assistive or related to *care*, e.g., systems that support communication or civic involvement and memory games. There are also interactive games that can be played with people who are not close by [14], that aim to reduce the sense of isolation.

5 Benefits of AAL Systems

There have been pilots of comprehensive telecare solutions both in Austria and elsewhere in Europe. One of the largest being the Whole System Demonstrator (WSD) done in the UK. However, the reports regarding their benefits are mixed.

There are potential benefits for older people. These relate to broader goals, such as independence [36] and the wish to continue living at home [34]. However, no significant difference has been found in the quality of life and the psychological well-being of individuals with long-term health problems between having telehealth and normal care [9]. Even with communication technologies, there is some indication that the initial increase in feeling connected socially may decrease with time [11].

There may be more benefits for social systems. Systems that allow people to stay in their own homes have the potential to increase the quality of care [31]. Monitoring systems may also reduce the amount of care needed, number of emergencies, etc. [23]. In fact, they may pay off for social services in just a few months [7].

There is also evidence of financial benefits for health care systems. Studies indicate that the most effective interventions with respect to reducing health service use are automated vital sign monitoring and systems providing information/support. First results of the WSD Trial showed a striking reduction in the mortality rate from telehealth, as well as significant reductions in hospital visits [13,38]. However, some researchers question whether the randomized-control model used to prove the effectiveness of medication is appropriate for comparing the situation with and without a clinical intervention [32]. This is particularly a concern with telehealth, as it is hard to find measures that include the breadth of benefits, but also ones that generate generalizable results, due to the great diversity of contexts and technology [4, pp. 9–10].

Despite indications of concrete benefits, more research is needed with regard to cost effectiveness [26]. For example, there is little agreement whether savings or effectiveness should be considered [10, p. 73]. There is also the question of who saves, i.e. the individual or health systems. With respect to long-term health problems, such as heart problems, there are indications that the costs are actually higher if the costs of the systems are included in calculations [22].

Furthermore, there have not been comprehensive studies on the effects of monitoring systems for people *without* health problems. Thus, it is not known whether people can actually stay at home longer due to detecting problems and enabling faster interventions [42]. More importantly, *"older adults do not look exclusively at technology as a means to enable aging in place; they also consider alternatives such as help by others"* [34, p. 246]. Although there are models for comparing different solutions (e.g. [12,23]), these do not allow for the comparison of technical and non-technical alternatives that older people consider.

This shows that the benefits of AAL are a complex issue. Given the rate of change of technology, by the time the benefits have been proven reliably, new technologies will hopefully be available, which then also need to be proven.

6   Limited Success with AAL Technologies

In conclusion, a variety of systems have been attempted. Perhaps due to the mixed benefits, the uptake of such technologies has been slow [36] even with systems that make it to market. There are a number of factors that could have an influence on this slow uptake: older users are not adopting the technology, a lack of proof of the benefits, technical incompatibilities between vendors and lack of sustainable business cases [33]. Negative attitudes may also relate to systems being targeted at older people and hence being stigmatizing [43]. Due to these factors, it can be difficult to find people willing to use the technology even in trials [36]. And those who do use these systems may then perform some sort pragmatic customization to make them better fit their needs [17]. Given the potential benefits, we can hope more success can be made in the future.

Acknowledgements. Thank you to Geraldine Fitzpatrick & Carolyn Mayr for their assistance with early drafts.

References

1. AAL Programme: AAL project success stories: 10 AAL innovations creating real impact (2015). http://www.aal-europe.eu/success-stories/
2. American Academy of Neurology: Weight loss in old age may signal dementia. ScienceDaily (2009). www.sciencedaily.com/releases/2009/05/090518161110.htm
3. Aumayr, G.: From ambient assisted living to active and assisted living. In: Pietka, E., Badura, P., Kawa, J., Wieclawek, W. (eds.) Information Technologies in Medicine, vol. 472. AISC (2016)
4. Bergmo, T.S.: Using QALYs in telehealth evaluations: a systematic review of methodology and transparency. BMC Health Serv. Res. **14**, 332 (2014)
5. Blythe, M.A., Monk, A.F., Doughty, K.: Socially dependable design: the challenge of ageing populations for HCI. Interact. Comput. **17**(6), 672–689 (2005)
6. Boyce, J., Shone, G.: Effects of ageing on smell and taste. Postgrad. Med. J. **82**(966), 239–241 (2006)
7. Bundesministerium für Gesundheit: Abschlussbericht zur Studie "Unterstützung Pflegebedürftiger durch technische Assistenzsysteme". Technical report, 11 2013. https://iegus.eu/publikationen/unterstuetzung-pflegebeduerftiger-durch-technische-assistenzsysteme
8. Busquin, P., Aarts, E., Dózsa, C., et al.: Final evaluation of the Ambient Assisted Living Joint Programme. Technical report, European Commission, Brussels (2013)

9. Cartwright, M., Hirani, S.P., Rixon, L., et al.: Effect of Telehealth on quality of life and psychological outcomes over 12 months. BMJ 346 (2013)
10. Chan, M., Estève, D., Escriba, C., Campo, E.: A review of smart homes - present state and future challenges. Comput. Methods Prog. Biomed. **91**(1), 55–81 (2008)
11. Chen, R.Y.R., Schulz, J.P.: The effect of information communication technology interventions on reducing social isolation in the elderly: a systematic review. J. Med. Internet Res. **18**(1), e18 (2016)
12. Chessa, S., Furfari, F., Potorti, F., et al.: The evAAL project: evaluating AAL systems through competitive benchmarking. AAL Forum **2010**, 183–192 (2010)
13. Department of Health (UK): Whole System Demonstrator programme: Headline findings. Technical report (12 2011). https://www.gov.uk/government/publications/whole-system-demonstrator-programme-headline-findings-december-2011
14. Doppler, J., Sommer, S., Gradl, C., Rottermanner, G.: BRELOMATE - A distributed, multi-device platform for online information, communication and gaming services among the elderly. In: Miesenberger, K., Bühler, C., Penaz, P. (eds.) ICCHP 2016. LNCS, vol. 9758, pp. 277–280. Springer, Cham (2016). https://doi.org/10.1007/978-3-319-41264-1_37
15. European Commission: The demographic future of Europe - from challenge to opportunity. Luxembourg (2006)
16. Fischinger, D., Einramhof, P., Papoutsakis, K., et al.: Hobbit, a care robot supporting independent living at home: First Prototype and Lessons Learned. Robotics Auton. Syst, 75, Part A, 60–78 (2016)
17. Greenhalgh, T., Wherton, J., Sugarhood, P., Hinder, S., Procter, R., Stones, R.: What matters to older people with assisted living needs? a phenomenological analysis of the use and non-use of telehealth and telecare. Soc. Sci. Med. **93**, 86–94 (2013)
18. Gregor, P., Newell, A.F., Zajicek, M.: Designing for dynamic diversity: interfaces for older people. In: Proceedings of the Fifth International ACM Conference on Assistive Technologies. pp. 151–156. ASSETS 2002, ACM, New York (2002)
19. Hallewell Haslwanter, J.D.: User-Centered Development of sensor-based Systems for Older People. Ph.D. thesis, TU Wien (2017)
20. Hallewell Haslwanter, J.D., Fitzpatrick, G.: Issues in the development of AAL systems: what experts think. In: Proceedings of the 10th International Conference on PErvasive Technologies Related to Assistive Environments. pp. 201–208. PETRA 2017, ACM, New York (2017)
21. Hanke, S., Mayer, C., Hoeftberger, O., et al.: universAAL - an open and consolidated AAL platform. In: Wichert, R., Eberhardt, B. (eds.) Ambient Assisted Living: 4. AAL-Kongress 2011, pp. 127–140. Springer, Heidelberg (2011)
22. Henderson, C., Knapp, M., Fernández, J.L., et al.: Cost effectiveness of telehealth for patients with long term conditions. BMJ 346 (2013)
23. Himmelsbach, J., Bobeth, J., Garschall, M., et al.: EvAALuation: Indikatorenhandbuch für die Messung von Wirkungen und Effizienzsteigerungen (draft), May 2017. http://evaaluation.tech-experience.at/media/EvAALuationHandbuch.pdf
24. Itoh, Y., Miyajima, A., Watanabe, T.: 'Tsunagari' communication: fostering a feeling of connection between family members. In: CHI 2002 Extended Abstracts on Human Factors in Computing Systems, pp. 810–811. CHI EA 2002. ACM, New York (2002)
25. Kalogianni, A.: Toyota jumpstarts robotic elderly care with the HSR robot prototype, July 2015. https://www.digitaltrends.com/cars/toyota-develops-human-support-robot-for-elder-care/

26. Khosravi, P., Ghapanchi, A.H.: Investigating the effectiveness of technologies applied to assist seniors: a systematic literature review. Int. J. Med. Inform. **85**, 17–26 (2016)
27. Lee, M.L., Dey, A.K.: Reflecting on pills and phone use: supporting awareness of functional abilities for older adults. In: Proceedings of the SIGCHI Conference on Human Factors in Computing Systems, pp. 2095–2104. CHI 2011. ACM, New York (2011)
28. Leitner, P., Neuschmid, J., Ruscher, S.: TAALXONOMY - Entwicklung einer praktikablen Taxonomie zur effektiven Klassifizierung von AAL-Produkten und Dienstleistungen - Guidebook. Austria, June 2015
29. Ly, N.T., Serna, A., Aknine, S., Hurtienne, J.: Towards supporting caregivers to monitor the whereabouts of people with dementia. In: Proceedings of the 9th Nordic Conference on Human-Computer Interaction. pp. 57:1–57:4. NordiCHI 2016. ACM, New York (2016)
30. Morandell, M., Rumsch, A., Biallas, M., et al.: iWalkActive: an active walker for active people. In: Encarnação, P., Azevedo, L., Gelderblom, G.J., Newell, A., Mathiassen, N.E. (eds.) Assistive Technology: From Research to Practice. Assist. Technol. Res. Ser., vol. 33, pp. 216–221 (2013)
31. Mynatt, E.D., Essa, I., Rogers, W.: Increasing the opportunities for aging in place. In: Proceedings on the 2000 conference on Universal Usability, pp. 65–71. ACM (2000)
32. Pearce, W., Raman, S., Turner, A.: Randomised trials in context: practical problems and social aspects of evidence-based medicine and policy. Trials **16**, 394 (2015)
33. Peek, S.T.M., Wouters, J.E., Luijkx, G.K., Vrijhoef, J.H.: What it takes to successfully implement technology for aging in place. J. Med. Internet Res. **18**(5), e98 (2016)
34. Peek, S.T.M., Wouters, E.J.M., vanHoof, J., Luijkx, K.G., Boeije, H.R., Vrijhoef, H.J.M.: Factors influencing acceptance of technology for aging in place: a systematic review. Int. J. Med. Inform. **83**(4), 235–248 (2014)
35. Riche, Y., Mackay, W.: MarkerClock: a communicating augmented clock for elderly. In: Baranauskas, C., Palanque, P., Abascal, J., Barbosa, S.D.J. (eds.) INTERACT 2007. LNCS, vol. 4663, pp. 408–411. Springer, Heidelberg (2007). https://doi.org/10.1007/978-3-540-74800-7_36
36. Sanders, C., Rogers, A., Bowen, R., et al.: Exploring barriers to participation and adoption of telehealth and telecare within the Whole System Demonstrator trial: a qualitative study. BMC Health Serv. Res. **12**, 220 (2012)
37. Spellerberg, A., Schelisch, L.: Ein dreiviertel Jahr mit PAUL: Assisted Living in Kaiserslautern. In: Ambient Assisted Living 2009. pp. 393–397. VDE Verlag GmbH, Berlin (2009)
38. Steventon, A., Bardsley, M., Billings, J., et al.: Effect of telehealth on use of secondary care and mortality. BMJ 344 (2012)
39. Svagård, I.S., Boysen, E.S.: Electronic medication dispensers finding the right users – a pilot study in a norwegian municipality home care service. In: Miesenberger, K., Bühler, C., Penaz, P. (eds.) ICCHP 2016. LNCS, vol. 9758, pp. 281–284. Springer, Cham (2016). https://doi.org/10.1007/978-3-319-41264-1_38
40. Turner, K.J., McGee-Lennon, M.R.: Advances in telecare over the past 10 years. Smart Homecare Technol. Telehealth **1**, 21–34 (2013)
41. United4Health: Telehealth in practice - care delivery models from 14 regions in Europe, April 2016. http://united4health.eu/wp-content/uploads/2016/01/U4H-Brochurev1.0.pdf

42. Wagner, F., Basran, J., Bello-Haas, V.D.: A review of monitoring technology for use with older adults. J. Geriatr. Phys. Ther. **35**(1), 28–34 (2012)
43. Yusif, S., Soar, J., Hafeez-Baig, A.: Older people, assistive technologies, and the barriers to adoption: A systematic review. Int. J. Med. Inform. **94**, 112–116 (2016)
44. Zhang, C., Tian, Y., Capezuti, E.: Privacy preserving automatic fall detection for elderly using RGBD cameras. In: Miesenberger, K., Karshmer, A., Penaz, P., Zagler, W. (eds.) ICCHP 2012. LNCS, vol. 7382, pp. 625–633. Springer, Heidelberg (2012). https://doi.org/10.1007/978-3-642-31522-0_95

Longinos/Longinas: Towards Smart, Unified Working and Living Environments for the 70 to 90+

Amina Amara[1], Hiba Sebei[1], Mohamed Ali Hadj Taieb[1(✉)],
Mohamed Ben Aouicha[1], Keith Cortis[2], Adamantios Koumpis[2],
and Siegfried Handschuh[2]

[1] University of Sfax, Sfax, Tunisia
amara.amina@hotmail.com, hiba.sbeii@gmail.com,
mohamedali.hadjtaieb@gmail.com,
mohamed.benaouicha@fss.usf.tn
[2] Universität Passau, Innstraße 41, 94032 Passau, Germany
{keith.cortis,adamantios.koumpis,
siegfried.handschuh}@uni-passau.de

Abstract. The ageing of the human population is a threat to many countries in the world and this fact creates new challenges for age-friendly living, recreational and working environments. Therefore, solutions that can support senior citizens (Longinos for the men and Longinas for the women) will be necessary, in order to help them stay actively involved in their professional life for longer. This is possible by designing fit for purpose working environments and by enabling flexible management of job-, leisure- and health-related activities, considering their needs at the workplace, at home and on the move, with a particular focus on fighting social isolation. This project presents a robotic digital solution that makes provision for Longinos/Longinas persons, that are above 70 years old, a single view of integrated health, business and social data spread respectively in online health communities, online project management websites and social networks, as well as the provision of a set of services, that will allow them to manage huge amounts of data.

Keywords: Independent living · Social media · Life-style
Age-friendly work environments · Big data

1 Introduction

In the future, we shall stay at work for more years than we were expecting ourselves to be; some of us (the lucky ones) because work shall still be fun and we see this as a normal continuation of our social activities, while for some others (the unlucky ones) because we shall not afford to give it up. For this second category, personal financial difficulties either related to a low pension or to increased costs for health and care services that may not be covered by public or private health insurance policies, will make the workplace populated by people of an advanced age. Peter Hartz's innovations in the social system in Germany has left a lasting effect as part of his recommendations

© The Author(s) 2018
K. Miesenberger and G. Kouroupetroglou (Eds.): ICCHP 2018, LNCS 10897, pp. 416–420, 2018.
https://doi.org/10.1007/978-3-319-94274-2_59

that became part of the German government's Agenda 2010 series of reforms, known as Hartz I – Hartz IV. These have also changed the profile of the German labour market system. Peter Hartz has also authored several books [1], and has recently come up with a new innovative idea related to work models for the very old persons (Arbeitsmodelle für Hochaltrige[1]). There he recognises four age categories, namely:

- Longinos/Longinas Junior: people who are between 70 and 75 years old
- Longinos/Longinas Classic: people who are between 75–85 years old
- Longinos/Longinas Senior: people who are between 85–95 years old
- Longinos/Longinas o.e. (open end): people who are above 95 years old

Such an approach might have seemed unrealistic in the past years. However nowadays, the result of demographic change we are experiencing internationally, especially in Europe, makes this case a possible reality. We expect that not only future generations but also people who are currently alive, will live for about 20 or even 30 years longer. This will have a direct impact on the labour market, as longer working hours will be confronted with a serious decline in population statistics. In addition, we have to count on a cost explosion in the healthcare sector and also be ready to face shortages of highly skilled workforce.

2 Motivation and Context

The objective of the Longinos/Longinas project is to contribute to the challenge faced by the growing age group of people between 70 and 90 + years of age and not at the expense of the younger ones. In terms of research, the project will focus on providing such people with a genuinely adaptive and smart working and living environment that can respect them as a category at large, but also at the individual level as persons with highly differentiated psychosomatic needs, capacities and abilities. This would not only manage the big data related to their work requirements, but also prevent them from social and professional isolation by keeping them in touch with their relatives and co-workers or employees by the means of online social networks [2].

It should be clear that this project is not about preparing for an apocalyptic reality or a dystopic future for newly-arrived and long-term senior citizens – nobody needs to be afraid that we want to start now or soon bring the 80- and the 90-year-olds (back) to work. However, the whole idea is based on: (i) what work can mean to the people of this age, (ii) what activity can mean, and (iii) that with the appropriate use of a wide gamut of technological interventions and solutions, we can offer a chance for what might become a potential game changer in the way that newly-arrived and long-term senior citizens people and the society at large consider the aging process as such. Such technological interventions can address the issue of value creation, while considering their health situation, as well as aspects related to their changing lifestyles as a result of the advanced age. Nowadays, there is a variety of products and solutions designed to

---

[1] http://www.shsfoundation.de/fileadmin/contents/longinos/arbeitsmodelle_fuer_hochaltrige_vortrag_Prof_Hartz_20151012.pdf.

support older people affected by e.g. cognitive impairment (CI). However, most of them do not aim or contribute in motivating the user, making him/her feel useful and live with dignity and satisfaction improving their quality of life. Older people are, in general, affected by multiple diseases and they give up on doing many of their daily basal and instrumental activities of living because they and their families do not perceive themselves as safe. Therefore, in order to help older people affected by CI, and work, live and age well, despite any particular impairment, it is important to support rehabilitation and overall the natural process of aging by making it more appealing, socially connected, and changing perceptions to make people feel safe in engaging in various activities or using various technologies. In recent years research has focused on the development and implementation of novel computer-based Information-Communication Technologies (ICT) applications to mitigate cognitive impairment and promote rehabilitation in older people. Emerging ICT applications based on virtual reality environments, including Augmented Reality technology [4]. Studies on small samples show that the introduction of ad-hoc ICT tools could improve the quality of life of older people and increasing the length of time for independent living. Some researchers have investigated new solutions for cognitive assistance in the last three years (serious games and robotic systems) [5–9]. These researches concentrated on exploiting software platforms allowing the support of new assistive tools that are less expensive and more accessible and could be used as a re-education tool helping to slow the decline of people with CI.

3 Solution Against Social Isolation

Same as with younger people, Longinos/Longinas are usually getting involved in a multiplicity of social media platforms, in order to take advantage from their services [3]. Some of these services are related to social life (e.g. Facebook, Twitter, Google Plus), where they allow individuals to keep in touch with friends and relatives as well as exchange a variety of content, such as, online posts, videos and photos. Others are business based services (e.g. LinkedIn, Xing), which aim to build professional networks with co-workers by introducing their jobs and business skills. Moreover, elderly also benefit from other online services, whereby they can easily manage their work-related projects through the use of project management software (e.g., Trello[2], Confluence[3], Basecamp[4]). Furthermore, they make use of healthcare based services, such as the Patient.me website, where people find the required advices about health care. Therefore, an overload of social data is spread over multiple online services, which leaves a negative impact on Longinos/Longinas. In light of this, we propose a digital solution for working and living environments. This includes a wide spectrum of personal and professional activities.

---

[2] https://trello.com/.
[3] https://www.atlassian.com/software/confluence.
[4] https://basecamp.com/.

The digital solution being proposed in the Longinos/Longinas project comprises of a unified user and content model that will act a single point of access to heterogeneous big data sourced from multiple online services. This aims to overcome the above gaps and offer to senior citizens an environment which takes into consideration the entirety of their social, professional and health aspects. Moreover, it shall help them to concurrently connect to all their social relationships, team groups, and online health-related communities. In terms of technology, this will be developed in the form of robotic applications, whereby a robot will accompany senior citizens to assist them in carrying out their daily tasks, being social-, professional- or health-related and thus improve their quality of life. From a Human-Computer Interaction (HCI) point of view, the robot will concentrate on the senior citizen's tasks and characteristics. Our core architecture is based on two main modules: user modelling and content modelling. The user modelling module integrates different user profiles (user metadata) across social, business and health networks as well as their relationships in one single identity. The content modelling module is divided into three main blocks: social (publications, activities), business (project management, meetings) and health (health networks, blogs, forums) content. This content is modelled in a unified view across social networks services. Such services take into account the physical challenges of the elderly, whereby seniors can choose the type of the message to receive i.e. audio, textual and/or visual.

References

1. Hartz, P., Petzold, H.G.: Wege aus der Arbeitslosigkeit: Minipreneure. Chancen um das Leben neu zu gestalten–Zur Bewältigung von Langzeitarbeitslosigkeit. Springer, Wiesbaden (2014). https://doi.org/10.1007/978-3-658-03708-6
2. Jung, E.H., Walden, J., Johnson, A.C., Sundar, S.S.: Social networking in the aging context: why older adults use or avoid Facebook. Telematics Inform. **34**(7), 1071–1080 (2017)
3. Ji, X., Chun, S.A., Cappellari, P., Geller, J.: Linking and using social media data for enhancing public health analytics. J. Inf. Sci. **43**(2), 221–245 (2017)
4. Caroppo, A., et al.: Cognitive home rehabilitation in Alzheimer's disease patients by a virtual personal trainer. In: Longhi, S., Siciliano, P., Germani, M., Monteriù, A. (eds.) Ambient Assisted Living, pp. 147–155. Springer, Cham (2014). https://doi.org/10.1007/978-3-319-01119-6_15
5. Manera, V., Petit, P.D., Derreumaux, A., Orvieto, I., Romagnoli, M., Lyttle, G., et al.: 'Kitchen and cooking', a serious game for mild cognitive impairment and Alzheimer's disease: a pilot study. Front. Aging Neurosci. **7**, 24 (2015)
6. Tarnanas, I., Papagiannopoulos, S., Kazis, D., Wiederhold, M., Widerhold, B., Tsolaki, M.: Reliability of a novel serious game using dual-task gait profiles to early characterize aMCI. Front. Aging Neurosci. **7**, 50 (2015)
7. Lancioni, G.E., Singh, N.N., O'Reilly, M.F., Sigafoos, J., D'Amico, F., Ferlisi, G., et al.: Patients with moderate Alzheimer's disease engage in verbal reminiscence with the support of a computer-aided program: a pilot study. Front. Aging Neurosci. **7**, 109 (2015)

8. Span, M., Smits, C., Jukema, J., Groen-van de Ven, L., Janssen, R., Vernooij-Dassen, M., et al.: An interactive web tool for facilitating shared decision-making in dementia-care networks: a field study. Front. Aging Neurosci. **7**, 128 (2015)
9. Pino, M., Boulay, M., Jouen, F., Rigaud, A.S.: "Are we ready for robots that care for us?" Attitudes and opinions of older adults toward socially assistive robots. Front. Aging Neurosci. **7**, 141 (2015)

Ageism and Sexism Amongst Young Computer Scientists

Helen Petrie[⊠]

Human Computer Interaction Research Group, Department of Computer Science,
University of York, York YO10 5GH, UK
helen.petrie@york.ac.uk

Abstract. A study was undertaken with 189 young computer science students to assess whether as future developers of technologies for older people, they have ageist and sexist attitudes about people as users of technology. They were shown a picture of either a young or old woman or man and asked to assess the likelihood that this person would use a desktop computer, laptop computer and a smartphone, and their level of expertise in each of these technologies. The results showed that the students did have negative perceptions of the older people in comparison to young people. They also thought that women were less expert with the technologies than men, although there was no difference in the likelihood of them using the technology. However, there was no evidence of a "double standard" of older women being perceived particularly negatively.

Keywords: Perceptions of older people · Ageism
Perceptions of older women · Sexism · Perceptions of technology use
Perceptions of technology expertise

1 Introduction

To create technologies that are useful, usable and acceptable to older users, developers need to be able to understand and empathise with the needs and wishes of those users. Yet it is well-known that young people tend to have negative attitudes and beliefs about older people. There has been a considerable amount of research exploring different parameters of these attitudes [e.g. 3] and attitudes by different types of young people [6, 7, 12, 13], particularly those who will interact with older people in their professional lives such as doctors, nurses, and social workers (e.g. [2, 5]). Given that there is an increasing imbalance towards women in cohorts of older people, it is also relevant that there appears to be a "double standard" in attitudes and beliefs about older people, with older women being more negatively viewed than older men [8, 11]. In response to these issues, there has been interesting research on how to overcome such negative attitudes and beliefs (e.g. [1, 4]).

Very little work on the attitudes and beliefs about older people amongst those creating technologies for older people has been conducted. This work explores the attitudes of ageism and sexism, and the potential double standard of these two parameters in a group of young professionals who in the future might be asked to develop technologies for older people – young computer scientists at the beginning of

© The Author(s) 2018
K. Miesenberger and G. Kouroupetroglou (Eds.): ICCHP 2018, LNCS 10897, pp. 421–425, 2018.
https://doi.org/10.1007/978-3-319-94274-2_60

their professional education. It builds on preliminary work [10] by expanding on the sample of young people participating, which allows for more detailed and robust analyses of both ageism and sexism.

2   Method

This study investigated the perceptions of young university students studying computer science of younger and older men and women as users and experts of smartphones and related technologies.

Two classes of first year computer science students at the University of York in the United Kingdom completed a very short survey for the study as part of one of their courses. Students who completed the survey were entered into a prize draw for five Amazon gift vouchers worth £5 (approximately USD 7.50) each.

The survey comprised a photograph of either an old or young man or woman (see Fig. 1). Eight different versions of the survey were created, each with a different photograph. Four of the photographs were of older people, four were of younger people. Photographs were chosen carefully so that the person looked to be in their 70s for the older people, and in their late 20s/early 30s for the younger people (so a little older than the target respondents for the survey, but people they would still consider young). Within each group two images were of women and two were of men. All the photographs were chosen to be close up shots of a person reading a book. All the photographs were copyright free images from the Internet.

Fig. 1. Images of older and younger people used in the survey.

The survey asked the following nine questions about the person in the photograph:

1. Firstly, three questions about the age of the person and old age in genera:
   a. How old do you think the person is?
   b. Would you call this person old?
   c. What is the minimum age you would think of someone as old?
2. Three questions about the person's use of technology:

    a. How likely do you think it is that this person uses a desktop computer regularly (rated on a scale from 1 = not at all likely to 7 = very likely)?

    b. How likely do you think it is that this person uses a laptop computer regularly (same rating as above)?

    c. How likely do you think it is that this person uses a smartphone regularly (same rating as above)?

3. Three questions about the person's expertise with technology:

    a. How expert do you think this person would be with a desktop computer/(rated on a scale from 1 = not at all expert to 7 = very expert)?

    b. How expert do you think this person would be with a laptop computer (same rating as above)?

    c. How expert do you think this person would be with a smartphone (same rating as above)?

Finally, respondents were asked their age and gender.

189 students completed the survey, 162 (85.7%) were men, 24 (12.7%) were women and 3 (1.6%) preferred not to identify their gender. The imbalance between women and men respondents unfortunately reflects the strong male bias in our undergraduate computer science community. Because of the small number of women, no analyses could be attempted on differences due to the gender of the respondents, which would have been interesting to investigate. Respondents ages ranged from 18 to 28 years, with a median age of 18 years.

3 Results

In response to the question on when old age begins, on average respondents estimated that old age begins at 53.2 years (SD: 11.95), with a very wide range of answers, from 18 to 78 years. However, somewhat less than half the respondents (40.9%) felt that old age begins between 60 and 65 years, which are the typical ages for retirement and also those used in demographics and aging research [14].

In response to the likelihood that the people in the photos would use a desktop computer/laptop computer/smartphone regularly, a three way multivariate analysis of variance was conducted: Device (desktop/laptop/smartphone) $\times$ Age of person in the photograph (Young or Old) $\times$ Gender of person in the photograph (woman or man) This showed a significant main effect for device (F $(2, 360) = 48.95$, p $< .000$) with smartphone being rated as the most likely to be used, followed by laptop, with desktop the least likely to be used. There was also a main effect for Age (F $(1, 185) = 427.98$, p $< .000$) with young people rated more likely to use all the devices than older people (mean young people: 5.47; mean older people: 2.74). There was no main effect for Gender (F $(1, 57) = 3.02$, n.s.). There was no significant interaction between Age and Gender (which might suggest the double standard in ageism) (F $(1, 185) = 0.64$, n.s.).

The results for the expertise questions were similar to those for the likelihood of use question, with one interesting difference in relation to gender. The three way multi-variate analysis of variance showed a significant main effect for device (F $(2, 370) = 28.12$, p $< .000$) with smartphone being rated as the device with which people with have the most expertise, followed by laptop, and desktop the device with which people would have the least expertise. There was also a significant main effect for Age (F (1, 185) = 266.88, p < .000) with young people rated more likely to use all the devices than older people (mean young people: 4.75; mean older people: 2.44). In this instance, there was a significant main effect for Gender (F (1, 185) = 6.81, p < 0.01), with women seen as less expert than men. There was no significant interaction between Age and Gender (which might suggest the double standard in ageism) (F (1, 185) = 1.31, n.s.).

4   Discussion and Conclusions

This paper reported on the results of an investigation into the perceptions of older people as users of technology, particularly desktop computers, laptop computers and smartphones by young, predominantly male, British computer science students. The results showed that the students perceived older people as both less likely to use these technologies and less expert in using them. However, there was less evidence of sexism, with no significant differences in the likelihood of women and men as users of technology, although there were significant differences in the perception of expertise, with women being seen as less expert in the technologies than men. However, there was no evidence of a double standard in ageism, in which older women are perceived less positively than older men. It was interesting that for younger people, they were seen as most likely to use and be more expert in smartphones in comparison to laptop computers and least likely to use and be expert in desktop computers. This reflects the move away from desktop machines to mobile devices and computing.

These results agree with numerous previous studies which have shown that young people hold negative attitudes and beliefs about older people (see Introduction). While the uptake of computing technologies by older people is still a lower that of younger people, older people in the UK are currently the fastest group adopting mobile technologies, especially smartphones and tablet computers [9]. Indeed the usage of portable devices such as laptop or tablet computers amongst older people has grown, in 2016 43% of 65 to 74 year olds now use a laptop or netbook (20% of those 75 and older), 31% use a tablet computer (15% of those 75 and older) and 83% use a mobile or smartphone (50% of those 75 and older) [9]. Undoubtedly these figures will continue to grow as the "baby boomer" generation of those born after the World War II ages. And with the decreasing number of younger people to care for them in old age, they will rely much more on technology than previous generations of older people. Thus, it is particularly important that the younger generations of computer scientists appreciate that older people are users of computing technologies. Clearly awareness of the issues around older computer users is needed.

Acknowledgements. I would like to thank all the students who participated in the research for their time and effort.

References

1. Chase, C.: An intergenerational e-mail pal project of attitudes of college students toward older adults. Educ. Gerontol. **37**(1), 27–37 (2011)
2. Ehlman, K., Ligon, M., Moriello, G., Welleford, E.A., Schuster, K.: Oral history in the classroom: a comparison of traditional and on-line gerontology classes. Educ. Gerontol. **37** (9), 772–790 (2011)
3. Flood, M.T., Clark, R.B.: Exploring knowledge and attitudes toward aging among nursing and non-nursing students. Educ. Gerontol. **35**(7), 587–595 (2009)
4. Helmes, E.: Attitudes toward older workers among undergraduates: does status make a difference? Educ. Gerontol. **38**(6), 391–399 (2012)
5. Henry, B.W., Ozier, A.D., Johnson, A.: Empathetic responses and attitudes about older adults: how experience with the aging game measures up. Educ. Gerontol. **37**(10), 924–941 (2011)
6. Kane, M.N.: Ageism and gender among social work and criminal justice students. Educ. Gerontol. **32**(10), 859–880 (2006)
7. Lee, Y.-S.: Measures of student attitudes on aging. Educ. Gerontol. **35**(2), 121–134 (2009)
8. Lin, X., Bryant, C., Boldero, J.: Measures for assessing student attitudes towards older people. Educ. Gerontol. **37**(1), 12–26 (2011)
9. Narayan, C.: Is there a double standard of aging?: Older men and women and ageism. Educ. Gerontol. **34**(9), 782–787 (2008)
10. Office of Communication (Ofcom): Adults' media user and attitudes report 2016 (2016). https://www.ofcom.org.uk/__data/assets/pdf_file/0026/80828/2016-adults-media-use-and-attitudes.pdf
11. Petrie, H.: Young computer scientists' perceptions of older users of smartphones and related technologies. In: Antona, M., Stephanidis, C. (eds.) UAHCI 2017. LNCS, vol. 10277, pp. 209–216. Springer, Cham (2017). https://doi.org/10.1007/978-3-319-58706-6_17
12. Sontag, S.: The double standard of aging. Saturday Rev. Lit. **39**, 29–38 (1972)
13. van Dussen, D.J., Weaver, R.R.: Undergraduate students' perceptions and behaviours related to the aged and to aging processes. Educ. Gerontol. **35**(4), 342–357 (2009)
14. Wurtele, S.K.: "Activities of Older Adults" survey: tapping into student views of the elderly. Educ. Gerontol. **35**(11), 1026–1031 (2009)
15. World Health Organization: Definition of an older or elderly person (2012). http://www.who.int/healthinfo/survey/ageingdefnolder/en/

User Requirement Analysis for the Design of a Gamified Ambient Assisted Living Application

Athanasios I. Kyritsis[1]([⊠]), Julia Nuss[2], Lynnette Holding[3], Peter Rogers[3], Michael O'Connor[3], Panagiotis Kostopoulos[1], Mervyn Suffield[3], Michel Deriaz[1], and Dimitri Konstantas[1]

[1] Information Science Institute, GSEM/CUI,
University of Geneva, Geneva, Switzerland
{athanasios.kyritsis,panagiotis.kostopoulos,michel.deriaz,
dimitri.konstantas}@unige.ch
[2] terzStiftung, Berlingen, Switzerland
julia.nuss@terzstiftung.ch
[3] Karisgroup, Winchester, UK
{lholding,progers,moconnor,mervyn}@karisgroup.com

Abstract. Most countries of the world are heading towards an ageing society. At the same time, newer technologies are constantly created, while the advances in networks and wireless communications allow other technologies like mobile and cloud computing to become ubiquitous. This leads to a problem that we are identifying and confronting, to make the use of modern technology easier for older adults, since it is in principle more easily perceivable by younger people. This paper presents a questionnaire study that took place during the design of a gamified mobile application that targets older people. In total 133 older adults answered the questionnaire consisting of 41 questions, providing an insightful view of their attitude towards modern technology, their health, physical activity tracking, playing games and social interaction using technology. The results provide useful insights to researchers and developers who target this age group for their human-centric applications and services.

Keywords: Ambient Assisted Living · Mobile applications
Senior citizens · Survey · User requirements

1 Introduction

We are heading towards an ageing society and the median age of the population has been rising during the last decades, due to declining fertility rates and/or

This work was co-funded by the State Secretariat for Education, Research and Innovation of the Swiss federal government and the European Union, in the frame of the EU AAL project EDLAH2 (aal-2015-022).

K. Miesenberger and G. Kouroupetroglou (Eds.): ICCHP 2018, LNCS 10897, pp. 426–433, 2018.
https://doi.org/10.1007/978-3-319-94274-2_61

rising of life expectancy [1]. Although the European population is currently the most aged around the world and is projected to remain so, every other continent has been experiencing the same demographic transition [2]. This shift is likely to be of major significance during the coming decades, transforming the age pyramid and leading to a much older population structure.

There is, however, an age technology gap and the ageing population shift is expected to deteriorate it. Older adults often lack awareness of many technologies and are less likely to use them [3]. Elderlies are also less confident with new technologies in general [4], have different concerns and needs than younger technology users and may not be attracted by the latest technological advances [5].

EDLAH2 (Enhanced Daily Living and Health 2) is a European Ambient Assisted Living (AAL) project that plans to make the usage of smart technology easy and to promote wellbeing and health among older people. The goal of the project is to create an easy to use gamified tablet application that includes games, social and health tracking features. The content and the features of the app can be remotely managed via a web interface.

The functionality of the app includes an easy to manage photo library with photos sent by family members, integrated video/audio communication with Skype, an e-mail system, a web browser with an easy way to set bookmarks, calendar functionality with reminders and a number of tablet games. Moreover, the platform includes a way to record health data, such as weight, blood pressure, blood sugar, etc., a plan for health improvement including exercise and weight, and finally a wearable device that will monitor health parameters, such as the number of steps and the amount of sleep. This set of features is manageable and the extracted data are visible to family members and others that have permission via the aforementioned web interface.

The rest of the paper is organised as follows. In Sect. 2 we describe related works, both surveys and applications, that have targeted older populations. The experimental setup and the motivation for carrying out this user requirements study are described in Sect. 3. In Sect. 4 we present and discuss the results that we have obtained and make the relevant recommendations. Finally, we conclude our work with Sect. 5.

2   Related Work

Due to the ageing society, there has been a rapid surge in the developed AAL tools and applications. These promote independent and safe living and aim to reduce the cost of healthcare as well as the caregiver burden [6]. AAL has emerged into a multi-disciplinary field that promotes the advancements of communication and information technologies to be used by older adults. Over the last years, there has been a plethora of AAL systems, platforms, frameworks, standards, and technologies [7]. Each one of those aims to fulfil different needs of the end users [8], but all technologies undeniably target to contribute to the overall wellbeing of older adults [9].

There have been many studies about the perception of technology by people and in our case, by older ones. In principle, the acceptance of a technology depends on its perceived usefulness, its ease of use, the attitude and the intention of the users to actually use it, as well as the actual usage of the system [10]. There has been an implicit assumption that information technologies are of great use throughout all sectors of society, but older adults prove to be more ambivalent towards using such technologies in their day-to-day lives [11].

The use of gamification, that is the application of game-design elements in non-game contexts, proves to be a way to promote the use of technology, encourage a specific behaviour, improve the user experience and reduce the getting used time. In our case, the whole use of the tablet application will be gamified. There have been works that apply gamification techniques to improve older peoples' aspects of wellbeing, either by engaging elderly in telemedicine [12], or by supporting their efforts to maintain good physical activity routines [13].

Designing an application for older adults is a demanding task. In principle, they encounter several constraints when dealing with computer-based technologies [14]. Their attitude towards technology and their learning rate differ when compared to younger adults, but with proper encouragement and explanations, elders prove to be equally effective [15] and may form and participate in online communities [16]. Specific design methodologies should be followed when developing applications that target older adults [17]. With our work, we are pursuing to comprehend how older people think about several aspects of technology, what are their needs and how their wellbeing can be enhanced when developing a platform that satisfies their requirements.

Although there is a lot of research on AAL tools, each work usually targets a relatively narrow aspect of older adults perceptions and needs. With our work, we are pursuing to comprehend how older people think about several aspects of technology and we are examining ways gamification techniques may result in different engagement levels. This survey was conducted in order to understand the users' needs and how their wellbeing can be enhanced when developing a platform that satisfies their requirements.

3   Methodology

The goal of the project is to develop a platform and a set of tablet applications that are easy to use by older adults. In order to do so, one should first understand the needs and requirements of the users of the platform, the elderly. This is the reason why this questionnaire took place, in order to understand the expectations, the needs and the attitude of the users towards physical activity tracking, playing games, gamification and social interaction using a tablet. By understanding how older people feel about technology, their health and social inclusion, then we can apply all the results in the design of the tablet application and gamify the whole experience. Therefore, the goal of the presented work is to understand our target group, in order to design the platform and further orient the development of our project that could motivate people to improve their wellbeing by using a tablet app.

All the consortium partners of the project participated in the creation and the grouping of the questionnaire. The questions were developed in English so that all consortium partners could contribute with suggestions and thoughts. Each partner proposed questions trying to understand how the contribution for every aspect and feature of the project should be done. In total 41 questions were developed and categorised into thematic areas about games in general, computer games, competition, social background, health and technology acceptance. All questions were closed-ended ones with predefined responses.

The survey was carried out in Switzerland and in the United Kingdom (UK). The originally developed questionnaire was used in the UK, while a translated version of it in German was used in the German-speaking part of Switzerland. The survey was created and completed using the Drupal Webform module. The participants were recruited from the partners' existing user base and contacts, from end users of other projects and activities and from newsletters, e-mails and phone calls in order to diversify the sample with previously unknown participants.

In total 133 people completed the questionnaire ($N = 133$). Among them, 59% were Swiss and 39% were British. There were also 2 Germans and 1 Italian. There was an almost equal amount of women and men that participated, with 68 women and 65 men, while the majority of the participants, that is 66%, were from 65 up to 79 years old. 16% were less than 65 and 17% were more than 79 years old.

Half of the interviewees (52%) have obtained higher education qualifications and a quarter of them (24%) have a work based background. The majority of the participants (84%) live in their own home. In fact, all of the participants from Switzerland live in their own home, while all users living in a care village come from the United Kingdom. Most interviewees have no mobility impairments. At least three quarters of the participants walk unaided, drive a vehicle, be it a car, motorbike or bicycle and more than half of them (55%) use public transportation.

Most of the participants (71%) can still live on their own, without the need of any domestic support. Although memory failure problems increase with age, the majority of our sample claims either to not have any memory problems (20%) or to have some, but not frequently (66%). Most participants (59%) do not suffer from either anxiety or depression, while 32% of them rarely do so. A quarter takes no medication, while the rest ought to take at least one type of drug.

4   Results and Recommendations

4.1   Games in General and Computer Games

It is very crucial for our project to understand the attitude of the users towards games, both physical and computer ones. Considering that the goal of the project is to motivate people to use the tablet application and to improve their wellbeing by using gamification techniques, understanding their perception is important before promoting healthier lifestyles with games.

Most of the participants (80%) play games regularly. Only 11% of them do not play at all, while 16% of them are playing daily. Classic board games like dominoes, card games, crosswords, scrabble and bingo, do not seem to be very popular among our target group since the distribution is skewed (towards the "several times a year" and "never" responses). 17% of the participants never play such board games.

The main reasons behind not playing games more frequently are lack of inspiration (30%), lack of time (27%) and lack of partners to play with (21%). On the other hand, for the people playing games, the main reasons for doing so are for fun (60%), for practising the brain (56%) and for social inclusion (40%). Since our platform will include multiplayer features like a leaderboard, we have also asked about the users' experience with multiplayer games and about the type of such games they like. 32% are playing games in pairs, 28% in a team and 27% with lots of others individuals. A lot (38%) would prefer playing on their own and 12% do not like playing multiplayer games.

It seems that just over half (54%) of the users would play video games either on a computer or a tablet. Comparing this result to the previous one of 80% of people playing games in general, we can already highlight the gap that exists between older people and technology. 27% would prefer to play a single player game, while those that would happily play multiplayer games would prefer to do so with people they already know, either with friends (56%), or relatives (39%), or acquaintances (23%).

More than two thirds (69%) are not interested in competing against others and only a quarter of them (26%) would be interested in getting a prize from the game they play on the tablet. Regarding the prize, most (43%) seem to be indifferent to it, while the ones that would happily earn one would rather prefer something physical, either cash and discount vouchers (26%), or a free cup of tea (13%), to some kind of digital reward, since every such reward was ranging between 2% and 8%.

There is a correlation between the frequency of playing games and the interest of a person to play video games on a tablet. So given this, a developer should properly design video games and give enough motivation to the users in order to expect high engagement.

4.2   Social Background

Another goal of the application is to enhance the social life of its users. They will be able to receive e-mails, photos and phone/video calls within our platform. Hence the importance of understanding their social background first.

The majority of the participants (82%) think that social contact is important, three quarters of them (77%) have regular contact with their family through phone calls and visits at most on a weekly basis, but only 40% can imagine engaging with more people using technology. So it seems that older people are not fully aware of the capabilities of technology and how it can be used for communication. Although people willing to socialise want to use technology as a means of socialising, they do not feel able to do so. Only a minority of them do not go out that often (7%) and do not see people often (11%). All the rest do so at most on a weekly basis.

Providing that we are creating a platform that monitors and collects data about different aspects of behaviour and wellbeing, it is of crucial importance for the end users to know how their data are being treated and who is able to view them. Regarding privacy concerns, given that the users know exactly who and which data are shared, permission would have been granted by more than half of the interviewees to certain members of the family (56%), as well as to certain healthcare professionals (59%). Around 24% would not share their data with others. There was, however, a respectable number of participants that were not entirely sure what data sharing means, so attention and careful clarifications should be given by app developers.

4.3   Technology Acceptance

The target application runs on a tablet and addresses many aspects, some even new-found for our target group. As previously discussed, there is a technology-age gap and thus, it is important to understand the older adults' view on several aspects of technology, understand their previous experience and evaluate their technology acceptance.

More than three quarters (76%) have an internet connection, either at home or a data plan on their phone and often use a computer, tablet or smartphone. 18% of them do not have an internet connection and 15% do not own any afore-mentioned device. Most of the people not using a tablet yet would be interested to learn to do so, either by exploring and learning it themselves (35%) or with some practical help (18%) or by written instructions (15%). People that do not use technology, either do not understand it (6%), or do not see the need (3%), or do not trust technological devices (2%). This target group is an undoubtedly challenging one to convince to use our platform.

The most prevalent reasons for using technology is staying in touch with people (75%), staying up-to-date with the world (72%) by reading news or checking the weather forecast, learning new things (50%) and maintaining a hobby (37%). Regarding data security, some people are not worried at all (30%) since they show trust in the platform they use, while more are worried, but would happily use the platform (40%) or would first ask family advice before (16%).

It seems that among older people, there are different age subgroups in terms of familiarity and interest towards technology. We noticed that as the age goes up, the frequency as well as the interest in learning to use modern portable devices decreases. This is why it is important to motivate users of all ages to overcome the initial fear of using technology and then to properly communicate all possibilities that open.

4.4   Health

A big part of the project is about proposing ways to improve one's health through gamification. Several health-related metrics will be monitored and shared with predefined members of the family or healthcare professionals. Health tracking devices are also planned to be utilised by the platform.

It is clear that most older adults would like to improve their fitness level (83%) and would enjoy mental exercise (84%). It is not clear though, whether they would like some encouragement from others in order to do so, with 53% of them liking this idea and 42% not.

Regarding wearing a measuring device, the results are again split, with 54% interested to try to use one and 43% not. The blood pressure monitor (45%), the clip-on pedometer (41%), the panic alarm (35%) and the steps measuring bracelet (32%) seem to be the most popular options.

Our target group would not freely share health-related information with certain family members, with 52% of them voting for this. 38% would like to be able to see a health report on the tablet and 35% would not. It is noteworthy that 20% do not really know if they would be interested in this feature, fact that we can most probably attribute to the technology-generation gap.

Regarding the most appealing aspects of health improvement training, getting a clear goal on what should be done (36%) and training with other people (29%), i.e. enhancing their social life, seem to be the most popular ones. Notably, only one participant would be interested in being able to compete with others and only 9% of them would be interested in receiving some sort of achievement for every successful exercise.

People already familiar with computer, tablets or smartphones are naturally more willing to try new types of devices and applications. But the big number of people not replying to such questions possibly demonstrate once more that the older adults are not up-to-date with the current trends in technology.

5   Conclusion

Our work provides an insight into how older adults perceive technologies, health monitoring and tracking, games and social interaction, in support of researchers and developers who design applications for this target group. Designers should create human-computer interactions that allow seniors to remain active members of their family and the society while pursuing their interests. In general older adults seem to be interested in exploring technology, although sometimes they are unaware of its capabilities. This is why it is crucial to approach older people with proper encouragement and clear explanations when presenting new applications to them.

References

1. Eurostat: Population structure and ageing, June 2017. http://ec.europa. eu/eurostat/statistics-explained/index.php/Population_structure_and_ageing. Accessed 13 Nov 2017
2. United Nations, Department of Economic and Social Affairs, Population Division: Population ageing and sustainable development no. 2017/1, June 2017. http://www.un.org/en/development/desa/population/publications/ pdf/popfacts/PopFacts_2017-1.pdf. Accessed 13 Nov 2017

3. Charness, N., Boot, W.R.: Aging and information technology use: potential and barriers. Curr. Dir. Psychol. Sci. **18**(5), 253–258 (2009)
4. Wu, Y.h., Damnée, S., Kerhervé, H., Ware, C., Rigaud, A.S.: Bridging the digital divide in older adults: a study from an initiative to inform older adults about new technologies. Clin. Interv. Aging 10, 193 (2015)
5. Wagner, N., Hassanein, K., Head, M.: Computer use by older adults: a multi-disciplinary review. Comput. Hum. Behav. **26**(5), 870–882 (2010)
6. Rashidi, P., Mihailidis, A.: A survey on ambient-assisted living tools for older adults. IEEE J. Biomed. Health Inf. **17**(3), 579–590 (2013)
7. Memon, M., Wagner, S.R., Pedersen, C.F., Beevi, F.H.A., Hansen, F.O.: Ambient assisted living healthcare frameworks, platforms, standards, and quality attributes. Sensors **14**(3), 4312–4341 (2014)
8. Baecker, R.M., Moffatt, K., Massimi, M.: Technologies for aging gracefully. Interactions **19**(3), 32–36 (2012)
9. Shapira, N., Barak, A., Gal, I.: Promoting older adults' well-being through internet training and use (2007)
10. Marangunić, N., Granić, A.: Technology acceptance model: a literature review from 1986 to 2013. Univ. Access Inf. Soc. **14**(1), 81–95 (2015)
11. Selwyn, N.: The information aged: a qualitative study of older adults' use of information and communications technology. J. Aging Stud. **18**(4), 369–384 (2004)
12. de Vette, F., Tabak, M., Dekker-van Weering, M., Vollenbroek-Hutten, M.: Engaging elderly people in telemedicine through gamification. JMIR Serious Games **3**(2) (2015)
13. Kappen, D.L., Nacke, L.E,, Gerling, K.M., Tsotsos, L.E.: Design strategies for gamified physical activity applications for older adults. In: 2016 49th Hawaii International Conference on System Sciences (HICSS), pp. 1309–1318. IEEE (2016)
14. Lee, B., Chen, Y., Hewitt, L.: Age differences in constraints encountered by seniors in their use of computers and the internet. Comput. Hum. Behav. **27**(3), 1231–1237 (2011)
15. Broady, T., Chan, A., Caputi, P.: Comparison of older and younger adults' attitudes towards and abilities with computers: implications for training and learning. Br. J. Educ. Technol. **41**(3), 473–485 (2010)
16. Nimrod, G.: Seniors' online communities: a quantitative content analysis. Gerontologist **50**(3), 382–392 (2009)
17. Gonçalves, V.P., de Almeida Neris, V.P., Seraphini, S., Dias, T.C., Pessin, G., Johnson, T., Ueyama, J.: Providing adaptive smartphone interfaces targeted at elderly people: an approach that takes into account diversity among the elderly. Univ. Access Inf. Soc. **16**(1), 129–149 (2017)

Investigation of Quantification of Suitable Photo for Conversation Support with Elderly People by Emotion of Youth

Miyuki Iwamoto[✉] and Noriaki Kuwahara

Kyoto Institute of Technology, Hshigami Matugasaki, Sakyoku, Kyotoshi, Japan
cabotine.six.stars@gmail.com

Abstract. Japanese society is recently facing the problem of having a "super-aging" population. The proportion of aged people is growing. The rate of families consisting of old couples and old singles is increasing. In some cases s/he may pass an entire day without speaking a word, which can lead to a disuse of cognitive functions and a heightened risk of dementia and/or depression. Thus, the younger generations are expected to be talking partners for aged people, but there is a problem in that they are unfamiliar with how to communicate with the elderly. In order to reduce the mental burdens of these partner young adults, they focused on the "reminiscence technique", which is effective in counteracting dementia. To support communication with elderly people using photographs, we aim to study quantification of photographic images suitable for conversation with elderly people by emotion of young people in order to reduce the burden of young people.

Keywords: Senior citizens · Factor analysis · Communication · Photos

1 Background and Purpose

Japanese society is recently facing the problem of having a "super-aging" population. The proportion of aged people is growing. The rate of families consisting of old couples and old singles is increasing. In some cases s/he may pass an entire day without speaking a word, which can lead to a disuse of cognitive functions and a heightened risk of dementia and/or depression. Thus, the younger generations are expected to be talking partners for aged people, but there is a problem in that they are unfamiliar with how to communicate with the elderly. In order to reduce the mental burdens of these partner young adults, they focused on the "reminiscence technique", which is effective in counteracting dementia.

We examined the differences in the mental burden and the quality of communication between patients and caregivers/volunteers when they used photos as communication support content in order to find the best medium for communication.

We revealed that what category is the more ideal as the contents but we did not mention the photos in the category. Such system usually uses contents like photographs, videos and music. It is expected that the volunteers feel less stress when using videos

© Springer International Publishing AG, part of Springer Nature 2018
K. Miesenberger and G. Kouroupetroglou (Eds.): ICCHP 2018, LNCS 10897, pp. 434–437, 2018.
https://doi.org/10.1007/978-3-319-94274-2_62

for the conversation support than when using photographs because videos provide both the volunteers and patients with richer information than photographs did. On the other hand, the photographs give the patients more chances to talk with volunteers. However, there has been no report on the effect of the type of the contents on the stress and the quality of the conversation [1–3].

To support communication with elderly people using photographs, we aim to study quantification of photographic images suitable for conversation with elderly people by emotion of young people in order to reduce the burden of young people.

2 Method

They talk seeing a photo through the PC. We prepared each of the 10 photos of "Food," "Event," "Play," "Living of Showa Era" and "Home Appliance" which was shown along the flow of conversation. We prepared a 10 min photo which was displayed on the TV monitor for 10 min conversation. Young adults answered questionnaires on sensibility evaluation of photographs in 5 stages after the end of conversation. A video camera was used to capture the expressions of the elderly throughout the sessions. The expressions of the elderly were analyzed from the video recordings. Sensibility evaluation of photograph by SD method was carried out. Factor analysis is performed using the average of each image of the sensibility evaluation by the young adults. Figure 1 shows the layout of the experimental environment.

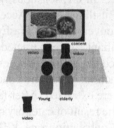

Fig. 1. The layout of the experimental environment

3 Evaluation Method

There are two reasons why the standard deviation of the evaluation value after each sensitivity evaluation increases. One is that the difference in personal experiences is great, and the other is the effect of the emotional character of the photograph. There are individual differences in human sensitivity, so individual differences cannot be avoided in analyzing sensitivity characteristics. The influence of individual differences and the emotional character of the photograph were classified in two orthogonal axes.

Focusing on the average value and the standard deviation of the grading values obtained in the experiment, 30 sensuous words were classified into 4 categories. Let four categories be C1, C2, C3, C4. C1 is a sensitivity word with large individual difference, C2 is influence by emotional character, C3 is a sensitivity word without variation in evaluation, C4 is not conspicuous characteristic. Factor analysis was performed on the obtained evaluation results (Fig. 2).

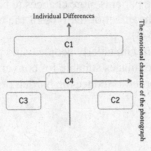

Fig. 2. Factors that increase standard deviation

4 Result

The emotional words with large individual differences are assumed to have large standard deviation in rating values. In this experiment six words were worthy of this.

Furthermore, C2 is not so much of the standard editor, but the standard deviation value of the whole is assumed to be large because the average value of the ratings is scattered.

7 words were extracted for C2. In C1, sensuous words of "Approachable", "traditional", "visual", "Famous", "Bustling" and "Accessible" were extracted. In C2, emotional words such as "Conversable", "Flashy", "Sophisticated", "Simple", "Colorful", "Dynamic" and "Brilliant" were extracted.

Factor analysis was performed on the obtained evaluation results. Primary factor method was used for factor extraction. When the condition that the eigenvalue is 1 or more was performed, 6 factors were extracted. After factor extraction, Promax rotation is performed, and the result and the result of category classification are shown. The first factor is called a bright factor (Contribution rate 17%). The second factor is called a factor of elevation (Contribution rate 16%). The third factor is called a factor of emotion (Contribution rate 11%). The fourth factor is called a natural factor (Contribution rate 9.5%). Fifth factor is called a factor of culture (Contribution rate 7%). The sixth factor is called a factor of movement (Contribution rate 5%). The cumulative contribution rate was 42.4%. Generally, the sensuous words with a factor loading amount of 0.7 or more, which is a value used for scaling was extracted 14 word. By comparing these 14 words with categories, C1 is one. The proportion within the category is 17%. C2 is 6, and the proportion within the category is 85%.

C3 is 2, and the proportion within the category is 67%. C4 is 5, and the proportion within the category is 36%. Since the percentage of sensitivity words belonging to C1 is the smallest, words and phrases that can reflect individual differences are somewhat less, but they are selected from all categories. Therefore, it can be said that these 14 words are important feeling words for selecting photographic images for talking with elderly people without a burden. I will write detailed graphs and tables in camera ready.

5 Conclusion

There are many young people who do not know what to talk about when talking with the elderly, so I thought that conversation might be bounced by providing photographic images as support for conversation, but depending on photographic images, the conversation bounces It turned out that there was an image that felt the conversation burdens, not the image. Therefore, in this experiment, we aimed at quantifying photographic images suitable for conversation support with the elderly by emotion of young people. Experimental results showed that the least number of emotional words for the category of C1 did not depend on individual differences among young people. Also, the category of C2 is the most numerous, and the emotional words categorized into C2 are "Conversable", "Flashy", "Sophisticated", "Simple", "Colorful", "Dynamic" and "Brilliant". It was found that these emotional words strongly depend on the influence by the emotional character of the photographic image.

Acknowledgements. This work is supported by JST CREST Grant Number JPMJCR17A5.

References

1. Astell, A.J., Ellis, M.P., Bernardi, L., Alm, N., Dye, R., Gowans, G., Campbell, J.: Using a touch screen computer to support relationships between people with dementia and caregivers. Interact. Comput. **22**, pp. 267–275 (2010)
2. Kuwahara, N., Kuwahara, K., Abe, S., Susami, K., Yasuda, K.: A method for producing reminiscence videos by using photo annotations: application and evaluation for dementia sufferers. Trans. Jpn. Soc. Artif. Intell. **20**(6), 396–405 (2005)
3. Tuji, A., Kuwahara, N., Morimoto, K.: Implementation of interactive reminiscence photo sharing system for elderly people by using web services. Hum. Interface Soc. SIG-AT **12**, 15–20 (2010)

Seniors' Sensing of Agents' Personality from Facial Expressions

Anna Esposito[1,2], Stephan Schlögl[3(✉)], Terry Amorese[1,2], Antonietta Esposito[4], Maria Inés Torres[5], Francesco Masucci[1], and Gennaro Cordasco[1,2]

[1] Department of Psychology, Università degli Studi della Campania,
Luigi Vanvitelli, Caserta, Italy
anna.esposito@unicampania.it
[2] International Institute for Advanced Scientific Studies (IIASS), Vietri sul Mare, Italy
[3] Department of Management, Communication & IT, MCI Management Center Innsbruck,
Innsbruck, Austria
stephan.schloegl@mci.edu
[4] Ist. Naz. di Geofisica e Vulcanologia, Sez. di Napoli Osservatorio Vesuviano, Naples, Italy
[5] Speech Interactive Research Group, Universidad del País Vasco UPV/EHU, Bilbao, Spain

Abstract. The presented study investigated the preferences of seniors towards artificial avatars showing personality both from a pragmatic and a hedonic point of view. Also, preferences for technological devices were considered. The involved participants were 45 adults (20 female) aged 65+ years in good health. They were asked to watch video clips of 4 agents (two males and two females) showing different personality traits (i.e. angry, depressed, joyful, and practical), and subsequently had to complete a questionnaire. Subjects were not informed about an avatar's personality and not openly interviewed regarding this subject. Rather, the administered questionnaire was devoted to test their perception of agents and whether such complies with the intended characteristics. Results show that subjects prefer female agents with a positive personality (joyful and practical) on both pragmatic and hedonic dimensions of the interactive system.

Keywords: Emotional artificial agents · Facial expressions · Assisted living

1 Introduction

Several research studies have shown that emotions and facial emotional expressions play an important role in everyday life [7, 11, 12]. Indeed, there is a wide field of research dealing with questions concerning emotional facial expressions as a signal that mediates social interaction. Interactional exchanges constitute the main source of emotional appraisals and emotions are indispensable for starting, maintaining, modifying, strengthening or breaking relationships with others [2]. In this context, facial emotional expressions exemplify the visible component of emotions, providing information on the emotional states of the interacting person. To this aim, facial emotional expressions have been subjected to numerous studies and over time they have become the pivotal topic of many researches, some of which focused on the visual appearance of virtual agents

© The Author(s) 2018
K. Miesenberger and G. Kouroupetroglou (Eds.): ICCHP 2018, LNCS 10897, pp. 438–442, 2018.
https://doi.org/10.1007/978-3-319-94274-2_63

in order to investigate the types of reactions such may trigger in individuals. The *Semaine* project[1], for example, aimed at the implementation of artificial conversational agents allowing for *"emotionally colored interactions between a person and a machine"*. To achieve this, the agents had to exploit mostly non-verbal facial expression behaviors in order to elicit similar behavior in human interlocutors [1]. The *Empathic* project[2] attempts to expand this work by *"developing causal models of [agent] coach-user interactional exchanges that engage elders in emotionally believable interactions [...]"*. Doing so, *Empathic* is age contextualized and will account for social and cultural variations in Western Europe, collecting data in Spain, France, Norway, and Italy. It will follow a user-centered design approach so as to establish trusting human-machine relationships, take appropriate actions to provide long-term care, and detect emotional states and negative moods, such as depression. To achieve this, we will build upon previous work [e.g. 4–6], yet aim at developing solutions which are more efficient and more effective (e.g. [3]).

A first pilot study focused on eliciting initial guidelines for designing such user-centered and adaptable interfaces. The study explored user's requirements and expectations with respect to their age and familiarity with technology. The goal was to (1) assess seniors' preferences in initiating conversations with an agent visually expressing emotional behavior; (2) summon elder's emotional responses arising from such non-verbal agent behavior; and (3) measure their interest in these interactions.

2 Material and Methodology

The research sample consisted of 45 healthy seniors (20 females), aged 65+ years (AVG = 70.28 years; SD = ±5.52). They were recruited in Campania, a region in the south of Italy. Participation was voluntary and approved by the ethical committee of the Dept. of Psych. at Univ. della Campania Luigi Vanvitelli (Code No. 25/2017).

Our stimuli were build based upon four conversational agents possessing different personality features able to arise user specific emotional states [10]. For each agent, a video-clip was extracted. Agents' names and videos were assessed by one expert and three naïve, before the following 4 video clips, each 10 s long, showing an agent's half torso while speaking (note: audio was muted), were selected:

- Serena, female, based on *Semaine's* Poppy, committed to expressing optimism
- Gerardo, male, based on *Semaine's* Obadiah, deputed to express pessimism
- Pasquale, male, based on *Semaine's* Spike, deputed to express aggression
- Francesca, female, based on *Semaine's* Prudence, aimed at expressing pragmatism

We used a tripartite questionnaire to collect user feedback. Section 1 focused on participants' socio-demographic information, their degree of technology experience, and their used technological devices with respective ratings on perceived usage difficulty. Section 2 established users' preferences regarding the interaction with each of the proposed agents. This section was clustered in four subsections, each consisting of 7

---

[1] https://cordis.europa.eu/project/rcn/85389_en.html
[2] https://cordis.europa.eu/project/rcn/212371_en.html

items, investigating the practicality (PQ), pleasure feelings (HQI, and HQS), and attractiveness (ATT) experienced while watching the video-clips [8]. Finally, Sect. 3 collected feedback on 10 agent characteristics rated on 5-point Likert scales ranging from 1 = strongly agree to 5 = strongly disagree (note: 3 = I don't know). Section 1 was completed first. Then participants watched the 4 videos, each time followed by a separate Sect. 2, before they eventually completed Sect. 3.

3   Results

Our results show that, 57.8% of the participants regularly use at least one of the proposed technological devices (i.e. smartphone, tablet, laptop), 26.7% use one from time to time, 2.2% had attempted to use one, and 13.3% never used one. The most popular device seems to be the smartphone (68.9% regular usage), followed by the tablet (22.2% regular usage) and laptop (17.8% regular usage). The smartphone appears to be also the device with the highest usability, rated as easy to use by 75.6% of the participants. Asked about their acceptance for the shown avatars, 71.1% liked Francesca, Serena was accepted by 66.7% and Gerardo by 46.7%. Pasquale was the least favored, accepted by only 22.2% of the participants.

Analyzing the Pragmatic Qualities (PQ), Hedonic Qualities of Identification (HQI) and Stimulation (HQS), and the attractiveness (ATT) of the agents, a 2(gender) × 4(PQ, HQS, HQI, ATT) ANOVA was applied (α = .01). No interactions were found between gender and avatars. Significant differences were, however, found among avatars for PQ ($F(1, 43)$ = 40.04, p < .001), HQI ($F(1, 43)$ = 42.32, p < .001), HQS ($F(1, 43)$ = 47.84, p < .001), and ATT ($F(1, 43)$ = 47.51, p < .001). Bonferroni post hoc tests revealed that these significant differences were always between Pasquale and Francesca (with p < .001 for PQ, HQI, HQS, and ATT), between Pasquale and Serena (with p < .001, for PQ, HQI, HQS, and ATT), between Gerardo and Francesca (with p < .001, for PQ, HQI, HQS, and ATT), and between Gerardo and Serena (with p < .001 for PQ, and ATT, and p = .002 for HQI). No significant HQS differences were found between Gerardo and Pasquale, Francesca and Serena, and Gerardo and Serena.

To summarize the preference scores obtained in each cluster of Sect. 2 (PQ, HQI, HQS, ATT), we classified them in *Strong/High* (7–13 points), *Moderate* (14-20 points), *Mild* (21–27 points), and *None* (28–35 points). According to this arrangement, 64.4% of the participants considered Francesca *moderately pragmatic (PQ)* (Serena = 53.3%, Gerardo = 42.2%, Pasquale = 24.5%). They also found her to be *moderately mind-pleasing (HQI)* (66.5%; Serena = 51.1%, Gerardo = 35.6%, Pasquale = 22.2%), *moderately stimulating (HQS)* (75.5%; Serena = 66.6%, Gerardo = 40.0%, Pasquale = 20.0%), and *moderately attractive (ATT)* (64.5%; Serena = 55.6%, Gerardo = 44.4%, Pasquale = 31.1%).

4   Conclusions

Our study showed that a significant number of seniors use at least one technological device, where the smartphone seems to be preferred and perceived as most usable.

Furthermore, it was shown that generally seniors show a positive attitude towards interactions with an artificial avatar, and that they favor avatars which express a positive personality. That is, regarding pragmatic, hedonic, and attractiveness features our avatars Francesca and Serena did consistently score higher than Pasquale and Gerardo. Although participants were not informed about an avatar's personality, they were able to perceive relevant facial expressions, suggesting that they have preferences for positive facial dynamics. Future work requires a deeper investigation of this capability as those avatars showing positive facial dynamics were females, indicating a potential gender influence on the processing of emotional facial expressions [9]. Also, the effect of voice has to be explored, as for now the utilized avatars were moving their lips yet audio output was deliberately muted.

References

1. Bevacqua, E., Pammi, S., Hyniewska, S.J., Schröder, M., Pelachaud, C.: Multimodal backchannels for embodied conversational agents. In: Allbeck, J., Badler, N., Bickmore, T., Pelachaud, C., Safonova, A. (eds.) IVA 2010. LNCS (LNAI), vol. 6356, pp. 194–200. Springer, Heidelberg (2010). https://doi.org/10.1007/978-3-642-15892-6_21

2. Campos, J.J., Barrett, K.C.: Toward a new understanding of emotions and their development. In: Izard, C., Kagan, J., Zajonc, R. (eds.) Emotions, cognition, and behavior, pp. 229–263. Cambridge University Press, New York (1984)

3. Cordasco, G., Esposito, M., Masucci, F., Riviello, M.T., Esposito, A., Chollet, G., Schlögl, S., Milhorat, P., Pelosi, G.: Assessing voice user interfaces: the vAssist system prototype. In Proceedings of the 5th IEEE International Conference on Cognitive InfoCommunications, Vietri sul Mare, Italy (2014)

4. Esposito, A., Esposito, A. M., Vogel. C.: Needs and challenges in human computer interaction for processing social emotional information. Patt. Recog. Lett. **66**, 41–51 (2015)

5. Esposito, A., Fortunati, L., Lugano, G.: Modeling emotion, behaviour and context in socially believable robots and ICT interfaces. Cognit. Comput. **6**(4), 623–627 (2014)

6. Esposito, A.: The situated multimodal facets of human communication. In: Rojc, M., Campbell, N. (eds.) Coverbal Synchrony in Human-Machine Interaction, pp. 173–202. CRC Press, Taylor & Francis Group, Boca Raton (2013)

7. Esposito, A., Esposito, A.M.: On the recognition of emotional vocal expressions: Motivations for an holistic approach. Cognit. Process. J. **13**(2), 541–550 (2012)

8. Hassenzahl, M.: The interplay of beauty, goodness, and usability in interactive products. Hum. Comput. Interact. **19**, 319–349 (2004)

9. Marsh, A.A., Ambady, N., Kleck, R.E.: The effects of fear and anger facial expressions on approach- and avoidance-related behaviors. Emotion **5**(1), 119–124 (2005)

10. Ochs, M., Niewiadomski, R., Pelachaud, C.: How a virtual agent should smile? In: Allbeck, J., Badler, N., Bickmore, T., Pelachaud, C., Safonova, A. (eds.) IVA 2010. LNCS (LNAI), vol. 6356, pp. 427–440. Springer, Heidelberg (2010). https://doi.org/10.1007/978-3-642-15892-6_47

11. Seibt, B., Mühlberger, A., Likowski, K.U., Weyers, P.: Facial mimicry in its social setting. Front. Psychol. **6**, 1122 (2015)

12. Seidela, E.V., Habela, U., Kirschnerc, M., Gurd, R.C., Derntla, B.: The impact of facial emotional expressions on behavioral tendencies in females and males. J. Exp. Psychol. Hum. Percept. Perform **36**(2), 500–507 (2010)

References

Mobile Healthcare and mHealth Apps for People with Disabilities

Mobile Healthcare and mHealth Apps

Introduction to the Special Thematic Session

Frank DeRuyter[1]([⊠]) [iD] and Mike Jones[2] [iD]

[1] Duke University Medical Center, Durham, NC 27514, USA
frank.deruyter@duke.edu
[2] Shepherd Center, Atlanta, GA 30309, USA
mike_jones@shepherd.org

Abstract. Over the past decade, technologies have transformed society, education, entertainment, business and now healthcare. Today, these technologies are reaching a level of maturity needed to support the robust and broad scope of healthcare. It has only been recently that smart phones, tablets, wearable information and communication devices as well as smart home hubs for automation and control, environmental sensors, cloud computing, interfacing with high-speed networks have vastly expanded the technological foundation associated with healthcare. This Special Thematic Session will address mHealth for people with disability from several disease, disorder and technology perspectives.

Keywords: mHealth · Mobile healthcare · Apps · Disability

1 Overview of mHealth

Mobile healthcare or mHealth refers to the use of mobile devices and other wireless technologies such as wearables and sensors in the delivery, facilitation and communication of health-related information [1, 2]. The convergence of these mobile and wireless technologies has enabled the development of a new ecosystem that has provided alternative support to the achievement of health objectives [3]. Not only has mHealth made healthcare more personalized and precise, it is attempting to make it more efficient, thereby improving quality while reducing cost, and improving access.

The broad scope of mHealth has had a significant impact on the monitoring of health as well as the delivery of healthcare especially in highly developed countries with advanced technological infrastructures and economies. Surprisingly, it has also recently emerged as a popular service delivery option within underserved countries that incorporate widespread mobile phone usage by their populations [2]. While the important role that assistive and mainstream technologies play in the lives of people with disabilities has been well recognized, it is unclear what impact mHealth will have on people with disabilities beyond the delivery and monitoring of care and especially on improvements in quality of life and full participation.

Today, using a wide range of mobile telecommunication and multimedia technologies, it is possible to not only provide healthcare information but also deliver direct

© Springer International Publishing AG, part of Springer Nature 2018
K. Miesenberger and G. Kouroupetroglou (Eds.): ICCHP 2018, LNCS 10897, pp. 445–448, 2018.
https://doi.org/10.1007/978-3-319-94274-2_64

care as well as collect clinical health data for real-time monitoring by practitioners and researchers. With the integration of wearables, sensors and the constellation of Internet of Things (IoT) devices into the healthcare domain, a profound shift has occurred in how providers are using mHealth technologies. In addition, App enabled mHealth has also expanded exponentially. However, while providers typically utilize mobile health apps for clinical decision support at the time of a patients visit, patients on the other hand are using mobile health apps for several different purposes.

The expectations for mHealth are high. The advances in consumer facing mHealth technologies (e.g. wearable sensors and interfaces, home control & automation, geo-location, machine learning, artificial intelligence, etc.) has the potential to place people with disabilities at the center of powerful, real-world rehabilitation ecosystems. Despite advances, recent reports indicate significant health disparities continue to exist between the general population and people with disabilities [4]. Concerns have been raised that the proliferation of mHealth apps and technology could increase health disparities if they disproportionately benefit advantaged populations and leave vulnerable populations behind, including people with disabilities.

While little is specifically known about the current state of mHealth for people with disabilities, albeit the early evidence suggests they have not been well represented in the growth of mHealth, and particularly in the proliferation of mHealth apps [5]. Their omission in mHealth has the potential to lead to further significant health disparities which cannot be allowed to occur.

2 Session Papers

This Special Thematic Session consists of 11 papers which range from an overview of mHealth and disability consumer focused survey data to the development of emerging mHealth applications and technologies for children and adults. The papers include assessment as well as care management not only for disability areas but also for specific congenital and acquired disorders. The following highlight the papers to be presented:

- A short overview and background information related to mHealth will be presented by the STS chairs DeRuyter & Jones. Specifically, types of mHealth technologies, the availability of mHealth apps designed for people with disabilities, the known effectiveness of mHealth apps for people with disabilities, and emerging trends will be discussed.
- Little is known about the current state of mobile healthcare for people with disabilities. Jones, Morris & DeRuyter will present data on current use and experience with mHealth apps from surveying their 1,600-member Consumer Advisory Network. Results confirm that people with disabilities are underrepresented in the growth of mHealth.
- Adherence to exercise is a challenging task and Upsahl & Chen will describe the design and evaluation of a mobile app to support physical exercise and adherence among people with Parkinson's disease.
- Walking speed is a critical performance measure that has been shown to be a strong indicator of long-term health and life expectancy and yet the gold standard for

measurement is a tape measure and stopwatch. Caves, Davis & DeRuyter will describe the development and validation testing results of a microprocessor based Gaitbox designed to measure, calculate & display walking speed.

- The co-occurrence of traumatic brain injury (TBI) and post-traumatic stress disorder (PTSD) is common among military service members returning from the battle field. It results in debilitating stress and anxiety which negatively impacts independent living and quality of life. Jones & Wallace will describe development and testing results of BreatheWell Wear, a stress management app for Android Wear smart-watches. While designed for TBI and PTSD this app developed on a wearable platform has the potential to offer support to broad based behavioral and health monitoring within the mHealth space.

- Based on over 5 years of action-based research in improving health goals for children with special needs, Anderson et al. will describe the value of interactive art as a strategy to increase the quality of health and health promotion in this population. Their work goes beyond the traditional biomedical approach and has potential with elderly persons with dementia.

- The potential of virtual reality (VR) presents a unique opportunity for amputee patients who suffer from Phantom Limb Pain (PLP). Kokturk, Rossini, Molteni & Covarrubias will describe VR rehab potential in treating PLP through the fully immersive VR application and system they have developed. The successful implementation of this low cost application has significant implications for clinical management at home and within the medical environment.

- People with complex chronic conditions experience everyday dynamic challenges. Fels and colleagues have designed a system to enable multimedia, person-centered recordings of experiences while living with chronic conditions. Videobooking has the potential to offer patients active engagement rather than passive acceptance of their management care plans.

- Memory problems are a common sequela of brain injury. Wallace and Jones will describe the development and field testing of EyeRemember, their app to serve as an external memory aid designed to run on wearables.

- Dementia Care Mapping (DCM) is an observational method widely used for evaluating the quality of dementia care. However, implementing DCM is complex and time intensive. Yamamoto & Yokokohji will describe their development of an ICT based support system making it easier to practice DCM.

- Asthma is a heterogeneous disease characterized by chronic airway inflammation. Patients have different triggers and experience different symptoms which when managed can control asthma. This requires personalization and Quinde with will describe development and outcomes of an Android mobile app that allows patients to personalize context aware solutions to support their asthma management.

These papers not only illustrate the complexity and diversity of this topic area but more importantly demonstrate that many solutions exist. The key to understanding the possibilities of mHealth is to better understand the technologies and how they can come together to create new opportunities for people. As we create those opportunities, we must continuously ask ourselves what impact these mHealth developments will have on people with disabilities beyond the delivery and monitoring of care and especially on improvements in their quality of life and full participation.

Acknowledgements. The organizing chairs of this Special Thematic Session wish to thank all who contributed papers to this session for presentation, publication and the exemplary work that they have conducted. The response to this session was overwhelming and reinforces the importance of this emerging area of focus. Finally, a special thank you to the ICCHP for providing a platform to address this important topic.

References

1. Frontera, W.R., et al.: Rehabilitation research at the National Institutes of Health moving the field forward. Am. J. Phys. Med. Rehabil. **96**, 211–220 (2017)
2. http://searchhealthit.techtarget.com/definition/mHealth
3. https://www.k4health.org/topics/mhealth
4. National Academies of Sciences, Engineering, and Medicine: Communities in Action: Pathways to Health Equity. The National Academies Press, Washington, DC (2017). https://doi.org/10.17226/24624. https://www.ncbi.nlm.nih.gov/books/NBK425844/
5. WHO: Disability and health (2016). http://www.who.int/mediacentre/factsheets/fs352/en. Accessed 7 Dec 2016

Mobile Healthcare and mHealth Apps
for People with Disabilities

Frank DeRuyter[1](✉) ⓘ and Mike Jones[2]

[1] Duke University Medical Center, Durham, NC 27514, USA
frank.deruyter@duke.edu
[2] Shepherd Center, Atlanta, GA 30309, USA
mike_jones@shepherd.org

Abstract. This paper provides an overview and background information related to the mHealth technology landscape specific for the ICCHP 2018 Special Thematic Session of the same title. Specifically, it contains: (1) an overview of mHealth including a working definition, its broad scope on healthcare, and its current state for people with disabilities; (2) types of mHealth technologies; (3) the availability of mobile health apps designed for people with disabilities; (4) the state of the art of the effectiveness of mHealth apps for people with disabilities; and, (5) a review of emerging trends in mHealth technology development and its adoption.

Keywords: mHealth · Mobile healthcare · Apps · Disability

1 Overview of mHealth

Over the past decade, technologies have transformed society, education, entertainment, business and now healthcare. Today, these technologies are reaching a level of maturity needed to support the robust and broad scope of healthcare. It has only been recently that smart phones, tablets, wearable information and communication devices as well as smart home hubs for automation and control, environmental sensors, cloud computing, interfacing with high-speed networks have vastly expanded the technological foundation associated with healthcare.

Many proposed terminologies describe these digital technologies that support overlapping healthcare services and practices. The most common and all-encompassing term however is digital health. It is the convergence of digital technologies with health and healthcare to enhance the efficiency of its delivery [1]. As Sonnier states, digital health includes the elements of "...*mHealth, Wireless Health, Health 2.0, eHealth, Health IT, Big Data, Health Data, Cloud Computing, ePatients, Quantified Self and Self-tracking, Wearable Computing, Gamification, Telehealth & Telemedicine, Precision Medicine and Personalized Medicine, plus Connected Health*" [1]. It is these elements of digital health that have empowered consumers to better track, manage and improve their health.

Mobile healthcare or mHealth is a more recent element that has emerged and refers to the use of mobile devices and other wireless technologies such as wearables and sensors in the provision of care [2, 3]. More specifically, mHealth refers to the delivery,

© Springer International Publishing AG, part of Springer Nature 2018
K. Miesenberger and G. Kouroupetroglou (Eds.): ICCHP 2018, LNCS 10897, pp. 449–456, 2018.
https://doi.org/10.1007/978-3-319-94274-2_65

facilitation and communication of health-related information via these technologies. It has been through information and communication technologies (ICT) that the convergence of mobile and wireless technologies have enabled the development of a new ecosystem that has provided alternative support to the achievement of health objectives [4]. Not only is mHealth making healthcare more personalized and precise, it is attempting to make it more efficient, improving quality while reducing cost, and improving access.

Over the past few years, the broad scope of mHealth has had a significant impact on the delivery of healthcare and monitoring health in countries with highly developed, advanced technological infrastructures and economies. Surprisingly, it has also recently emerged as a popular service delivery option within underserved countries that incorporate large populations with widespread mobile phone usage [3]. Most notable in this domain has been the work conducted by the mHealth Alliance. This group has been actively and successfully advocating for and building worldwide public-private partnerships to develop new ways for increasing the availability, accessibility and effectiveness of health information and services using mHealth technologies and strategies to countries throughout the developing world [5].

While the important role that assistive and mainstream technologies play in the lives of people with disabilities has long been recognized; it is unclear what impact mHealth has on people with disabilities. Despite advances, recent reports indicate significant health disparities continue to exist between the general population and people with disabilities [6]. Adults with disabilities are four times more likely to report having fair or poor health as compared to adults with no disabilities [7]. Living with a disability presents barriers to accessing healthcare services and navigating the health care system. Alarmingly, even for people with a disability who have health insurance, they are more than twice as likely as those without disabilities to not receive care because of cost [8, 9]. While little is known about the current state of mHealth for people with disabilities, the early evidence suggests they have not been well represented in the growth of mHealth, and particularly in the proliferation of mobile health software applications (mHealth apps) for smartphones [9]. Their omission in mHealth has the potential to lead to further significant health disparities.

2 Types of mHealth Technologies

A key to understanding the possibilities of mHealth is to better understand the technologies and how they can come together to create new opportunities for people. Today, using a wide range of mobile telecommunication and multimedia technologies, it is possible to not only provide healthcare information and deliver direct care to patients but it is also possible to collect clinical health data from patients for real-time monitoring by practitioners and researchers. This increasingly ubiquitous and powerful mobile technology holds the potential to address long-standing issues in health disparities and healthcare provision. Advances in consumer mHealth technology – wearable sensors and interfaces, home control & automation, geo-location, machine learning, artificial intelligence, etc. – literally places people with disabilities at the center of powerful, real-world rehabilitation ecosystems. mHealth has been called "*the biggest technology breakthrough of our time to address our greatest national challenge (managing the rising cost of chronic health conditions)*" [10].

With the advent and integration of wearables, sensors and the constellation of Internet of Things (IoT) devices into the healthcare domain, a profound shift has also occurred in how providers are using mHealth technologies. A recent survey recently revealed that over 80% of providers in the United States were using mHealth technologies in their provision of patient care [11]. Their utilization of these technologies included: (1) access to clinical information through mobile health apps and mobile-enabled EHRs; (2) collaboration with care teams; (3) communication with patients through patient portals; (4) real-time monitoring of patients; and (5) provision of remote health care. Patients on the other hand were most likely to use mobile health technologies to: (1) track their own health data through mHealth apps and devices like the Fitbit® or AppleWatch; (2) access their clinical records through mobile-enabled patient portals; and (3) communicate with their providers through HIPAA compliant e-mail and secure text messaging [11].

App enabled mHealth has also expanded exponentially. Providers typically utilize mobile health apps for clinical decision support at the time of a patients visit. Patients on the other hand are using mobile health apps for several different purposes. Apps in the mHealth patient domain tend to be segmented in the following areas: (1) chronic care management apps for managing blood pressure, diabetes, cancer, mental health, or other illnesses; (2) medical apps that include various diagnostic, alerting, and care apps that generate awareness among patients, create alerts, or serve as medical reference; (3) health and fitness apps associated with nutrition, health-tracking, fitness and weight loss; (4) women's health apps related to pregnancy, fertility, breastfeeding, and child raising; (5) medication management apps to keep track of taking medication in order to improve adherence among patients; and (6) personal health record apps that allow patients to store their medical conditions data, allergies etc. and share it with their providers [12].

Healthcare and social trends for people with disabilities and chronic conditions have intensified the need for these expanding mHealth apps and technological capabilities. However, without a continued targeted effort, the continued proliferation of these mHealth apps and technologies has the potential to increase health disparities and leave vulnerable populations, including people with disabilities behind, if they are not properly available.

3   Availability of mHealth Apps for People with Disabilities

Software applications for smartphones comprise a popular form of mHealth and have become an important new tool for the management of chronic health conditions. The number of health-related mobile apps has been growing at a prodigious rate, from approximately 40,000 in 2012 to over 318,000 in 2017. At the end of 2017, the global mHealth app market reached US $26B in revenue and projected to reach US $102.43B by 2022. Over 70% of mHealth app publishers are choosing multi-platform (both iOS and Android) development [12, 13]. The rapid expansion of the app market, coupled with over 340 commercially available wearable devices on the market worldwide, illustrates the dramatic growing value of mHealth [02]. Initially, the majority of mHealth apps were associated with general wellness. However, over the past couple of years increasing focus has been on health condition management apps, which today represent 40% of all mHealth apps [13].

Capital investments by major tech and healthcare players in digital health (e.g., Verily, Apple/Aetna partnership) also signals the continued growth of this market. In 2017 alone, there were 224 digital health venture capital funding deals constituting over US \$5B in investments [14]. Most recently has been the launching of a new healthcare business that brings together Amazon, Berkshire Hathaway and JP Morgan [15]. Combined these companies have a market valuation of over \$1.6 trillion dollars. Speculation is that the Amazon-Berkshire-JPMorgan healthcare partnership will disrupt healthcare delivery through technological solutions. Much of this growth is sparked by the potential of mHealth to support patient engagement and self-management of chronic health conditions. Indeed, patients' management of their own chronic conditions and active engagement in their healthcare are associated with improved independence and life quality, and reduced healthcare utilization and cost.

In addition, numerous startups as well as other major companies have introduced mHealth solutions and whole platforms (e.g., Apple's HealthKit, Google Fit, Samsung Health) to support the capture, storage and reporting of user health, fitness and activity data. Mobile app development companies (e.g. MobileSmith, Salesforce) are targeting the healthcare vertical marketplace for app development and maintenance. Meanwhile, specialized vendors are offering cloud data collection, storage and visualization tools for patient form-based data (questionnaires, surveys, inventories, etc.) as well as for health and activity data generated by clinicians or by remote sensors (e.g., Evidation, Pt Pal, Datu Health, Salesforce, etc.). As recently stated: *"The use of information and communication technologies eliminates distance barriers and can make rehabilitation and health care services available to people who have limited access to transportation and other access issues"* [16].

The expectations for mHealth are high. About half of patients recently surveyed predict that mHealth will improve the convenience, cost and quality of their healthcare. An overwhelming 96% of current mHealth app users believe the apps help improve their quality of life. Meanwhile, 6 in 10 doctors and payers believe that widespread mHealth app adoption is inevitable, and 7 in 10 believe mHealth apps will encourage their patients to take more responsibility for their health. However, serious consideration must be given to discoverability with respect to the availability and effectiveness of mHealth apps. Over 80% of the apps in the Apple and Android marketplaces are so-called "zombie" apps that never make it to the list of top 300 apps by category [17]. Apps are listed based on popularity, so apps that get the most exposure are the apps that are already popular while the remainder are effectively invisible to consumers. This poses a significant challenge for people with disabilities because the specialty apps they may need are not likely to top the list of popular apps. Nor are the most popular apps necessarily usable by of effective for people with disabilities. Zombie apps can only be discovered by searching for a specific type of app, or by searching for the app's name directly. Rarely is this strategy successful, unless the name of the app is already known. Adding to the challenge of discoverability is the fact that most users spend little effort looking for suitable apps. A recent survey found that 36% of users only look for apps on their smartphone's home screen and just 28% look in the app stores for new apps [17].

Finally, there is limited information about the representation of people with disabilities in the market for mHealth apps although a recent study may provide useful insight into the current landscape of mHealth apps for people with disabilities. The IMS Institute for Healthcare Informatics published a report in 2015 describing use, evidence and remaining barriers to mainstream adoption of mHealth apps by patients and healthcare providers [18]. The report compares findings from a 2013 and 2015 study of mHealth apps available for download from the US Apple iTunes store and Google (Android) Play marketplace. Over 165,000 mHealth apps were identified. Through review and selection criteria, including frequency of downloads, 26,864 apps were selected for further study as representative of the most widely used mHealth apps by consumers. Only 15% of the apps targeted a specific disease or condition, most commonly diabetes, blood pressure and mental health conditions. Disability-focused apps (including mental health) accounted for only about 2% of all mHealth apps examined [18].

4   Effectiveness of mHealth Apps for People with Disabilities

It is difficult to overstate how life changing assistive and mobile technologies have been for people with disabilities. Within the mHealth space, apps operate with a variety of objectives. These include increased access to healthcare and information as well as the increased ability to track information in an effective and timely manner. As one examines the space specific to mHealth apps for people with disabilities, both the accessibility and effectiveness must be considered.

With respect to the accessibility of mobile health apps for users with disabilities, there is ample reason for concern. A recent survey examined app accessibility for blind users of nine iPhone mHealth apps [19]. The apps tested were for either glucose or blood pressure monitoring, and all interfaced with an external sensor to measure blood glucose or blood pressure. Existing accessibility guidelines were used to evaluate the apps. The results revealed that none of the nine apps was deemed to be accessible to blind users [19]. In another study, 137 highly rated or recommended mHealth apps targeting high-need, high-cost populations (i.e., those with chronic conditions) were analyzed [19]. Of concern were findings about the apps' reaction to dangerous information. Only 23% of apps that recorded health-related information responded appropriately with an alert or warning when information was entered that indicated a health danger (e.g., suicidal mood or ideation, dangerously high blood pressure reading) [20]. This is particularly troublesome for people with disabilities, who in general are a higher at-risk population.

Although mHealth technologies that can support and extend the efficacy of healthcare services beyond the clinic and in-person visits are beginning to offer new opportunities to support remote and mobile rehabilitation healthcare, challenges persist. The overall body of clinical evidence on app efficacy has grown substantially and now includes almost 600 published studies, enabling the identification of a list of top apps with increasingly robust clinical evidence [21]. However, mHealth apps and technologies are promising albeit still limited by narrow functionality [22], uncertain measurement accuracy of apps and sensors, concerns over privacy [23], uneven durability and usability, and high rates of user abandonment [17]. Narrow functionality, or the lack of integration into a more comprehensive model of care, is a particularly critical concern for people with disabilities and chronic conditions, who often suffer from multiple conditions, ailments and limitations. Additionally, the vast majority of the solutions are designed, calibrated and tested for people *without* disabilities. This can mean that measurement and thresholds for normal health and activity ranges are misleading at best (e.g., measurement of calorie usage by a person using a manual wheelchair). Lack of testing with people with disabilities may also result in the persistence of basic accessibility barriers that should have been identified in beta testing. Furthermore, the solutions that *are* tested for people with disabilities are often tested in isolation or in a vastly different manner and environment than the way in which rehabilitation care is actually delivered in the real world. This methodology does not yield sufficient information to effectively select and translate solutions, especially in post-acute and chronic care environments. All of this illustrates the need to validate/calibrate instruments with people with disabilities and to employ ecologically valid, pragmatic testing methods that permit deployment of interventions that compares mHealth apps to current practice to determine which practice produces the best outcomes.

5 Emerging Trends

Globally, healthcare organizations and entities have been gradually incorporating mHealth tools into clinical practice. Many of these efforts are still in pilot stages with an increasing number of full-scale rollouts. With a few notable exceptions (autism, mental health, stroke), people with disabilities have not been the primary target for mHealth app and technology development. Despite the progress to date, barriers exist to widespread adoption. As these barriers are addressed, the use of mHealth is likely to become mainstream over the next 10 years throughout the world.

Concerns have been raised that the proliferation of mHealth apps and technology could increase health disparities if they disproportionately benefit advantaged populations and leave vulnerable populations behind, including people with disabilities. This pattern of widening disparities, termed the "inverse care law", has been observed following the introduction of other health interventions, particularly those with a social media component [23]. Our own research provides early evidence to suggest that disparities may already exist between disabled and non-disabled populations in the adoption of mHealth apps. While smartphone ownership is about equal among disabled and non-disabled adults (71% vs. 68%), the rate of adoption of mHealth apps is lower by half – 17% of disabled vs. 34% of non-disabled adults report downloading at least one app that is meant to support their health [24, 25].

References

1. Sonnier, P.: The Fourth Wave: Digital Health (2017). ISBN-13:978-1976791550. https://storyofdigitalhealth.com/definition. Accessed 21 Jan 2018
2. Frontera, W.R., et al.: Rehabilitation research at the National Institutes of Health moving the field forward. Am. J. Phys. Med. Rehabil. **2017**(96), 211–220 (2017)
3. http://searchhealthit.techtarget.com/definition/mHealth
4. https://www.k4health.org/topics/mhealth
5. http://www.unfoundation.org/what-we-do/issues/global-health/mhealth-alliance.html
6. National Academies of Sciences, Engineering, and Medicine: Communities in Action: Pathways to Health Equity. The National Academies Press, Washington, DC (2017). https://doi.org/10.17226/24624. https://www.ncbi.nlm.nih.gov/books/NBK425844/
7. Krahn, G.L., Walker, D.K., Correa-De-Araujo, R.: Persons with disabilities as an unrecognized health disparity population. Am. J. Public Health **105**(Suppl 2), S198–S206 (2015)
8. CDC: QuickStats: delayed or forgone medical care because of cost concerns among adults aged 18–64 years, by disability and health insurance coverage status—National Health Interview Survey, United States, 2009. Morb. Mortal. Wkly Rep. **59**(44) (2010). http://www.cdc.gov/mmwr/preview/mmwrhtml/mm5944a7.htm. Accessed 7 Dec 2018
9. WHO: Disability and health (2016). http://www.who.int/mediacentre/factsheets/fs352/en. Accessed 7 Dec 2018
10. Sebelius, K.: US Health and Human Services Secretary. Keynote address at the 2011 Annual mHealth Summit, Washington, DC
11. Mobile Health Technology Knowledge Hub: AthenaHealth. https://www.athenahealth.com/knowledge-hub/mobile-health-technology/healthcare
12. Healthcare Mobile App Development and mHealth Apps in 2017: Adoriasoft Report, 21 April 2017. https://medium.com/@Adoriasoft_Com/healthcare-mobile-app-development-and-mhealth-apps-in-2017-eb307d4cad36. Accessed 16 Jan 2018
13. The Growing Value of Digital Healthcare: IQVIA Institute Report, 07 November 2017. https://www.iqvia.com/institute/reports/the-growing-value-of-digital-health. Accessed 28 Jan 2018
14. Digital Health Funding Deals in 2017: MobiHealthNews, 29 December 2017. http://www.mobihealthnews.com/content/224-digital-health-funding-deals-2017. Accessed 26 Jan 2018
15. Bloomberg Report: Amazon, Berkshire, JPMorgan Link Up to Form New Health-Care Company, 30 January 2018, https://www.bloomberg.com/news/articles/2018-01-30/amazon-berkshire-jpmorgan-to-set-up-a-health-company-for-staff
16. NIH Medical Rehabilitation Coordinating Committee: National Institutes of Health Research Plan on Rehabilitation. Am. J. Phys. Med. Rehabil. **2017**(96), e64–e67 (2017)
17. Perez, S.: "Zombie" Apps on the Rise – 83% of Apps Not on Top Lists, up From 74% Last Year. Techcrunch.com, 30 January 2015. https://techcrunch.com/2015/01/30/zombie-apps-on-the-rise-83-of-apps-not-on-top-lists-up-from-74-last-year. Accessed 19 Jan 2018
18. IMS Institute for Healthcare Informatics: Patient adoption of mHealth: use, evidence, and remaining barriers to mainstream acceptance. The Institute, Parsippany (2015)
19. Milne, L.R., Bennett, C.L., Ladner, R.E.: The accessibility of mobile health sensors for blind users. J. Technol. Persons Disabil. (2014)
20. Singh, K., Drouin, K., Newmark, L.P., Lee, J., Faxvaag, A., Rozenblum, R., et al.: Many mobile health apps target high-need, high-cost populations, but gaps remain. Health Aff. **35**(12), 2310–2318 (2016)
21. https://www.iqvia.com/institute/reports/the-growing-value-of-digital-health

22. mHealth Intelligence: mHealth wearables market to surge over next 4 years, 6 February 2017. http://mhealthintelligence.com/news/mhealth-werables-market-to-surge-over-next-4-years

23. Jameson, J.E.: Inverse care law. Lancet **1**(7700), 648–649 (1971)

24. Jones, M., Mueller, J., Morris, J.: App factory: a flexible approach to rehabilitation engineering in an era of rapid technology advancement. Assistive Technol. (2016). http://dx.doi.org/10.1080/10400435.2016.1211201

25. Morris, J., Sweatman, M., Jones, M.: Smartphone use and activities by people with disabilities: 2015–2016 survey. J. Technol. Persons Disabil. **5**, 50–66 (2017)

Mobile Healthcare and People with Disabilities: Results from a Preliminary Survey

Michael L. Jones[1]([✉]) [iD], John Morris[1], and Frank DeRuyter[2]

[1] Virginia C. Crawford Research Institute, Shepherd Center, Atlanta, USA
{mike_jones, john_morris}@shepherd.org
[2] Department of Surgery, Duke University Medical Center, Durham, USA
frank.deruyter@duke.edu

Abstract. Significant health disparities exist between the general population and people with disabilities, particularly with respect to chronic health conditions. Mobile healthcare – the delivery of healthcare via mobile communication devices – is witnessing tremendous growth and has been touted as an important new approach for management of chronic health conditions. At present, little is known about the current state of mobile healthcare for people with disabilities. Early evidence suggests they are not well represented in the growth of mobile healthcare, and particularly the proliferation of mobile health software applications (mHealth apps) for smartphones. Their omission in mHealth could lead to further health disparities. This article describes our research investigating the current state of mHealth apps targeting people with disabilities. Based on a survey of disabled smartphone users, we confirm that people with disabilities are under-represented in the growth of mHealth. We identify several areas of future research and development needed to support the inclusion of people with disabilities in the mHealth revolution.

Keywords: People with disabilities · Chronic health conditions
Mobile healthcare · mHealth · Software applications for smart phones
Information and communication technologies

1 Introduction

Over 80% of people with disabilities have one or more chronic conditions that compound the effects of disability on health and function [1]. Moreover, there is growing evidence that people with disabilities, as a group, face significant disparities in accessing healthcare and particularly preventive health and wellness services that may mitigate chronic health conditions [2]. Compared with their non-disabled peers, individuals with disabilities are: (1) less likely to receive recommended preventive health care services (e.g., routine physicals, cancer screenings); (2) at greater risk for poor health outcomes (e.g., obesity, hypertension, fall-related injuries, mood disorders); and (3) more likely to engage in behaviors that put their health at risk (e.g., smoking, inadequate physical activity) [3–5].

© Springer International Publishing AG, part of Springer Nature 2018
K. Miesenberger and G. Kouroupetroglou (Eds.): ICCHP 2018, LNCS 10897, pp. 457–463, 2018.
https://doi.org/10.1007/978-3-319-94274-2_66

The health disparities are alarming. For adults with disabilities, the prevalence of physical inactivity is 120% higher [6], obesity rates are 57% higher [7], smoking rates 47% higher [8], and the prevalence of hypertension is 13% higher [9] than for nondisabled adults. People with disabilities of all ages have more than twice the incidence of diabetes [10, 11]. And rates of cardiovascular disease – the leading cause of death in the US – are 3 times higher among adults with disabilities [12].

Mobile healthcare is being touted as an important new tool for management of chronic health conditions. Mobile healthcare, or mHealth, can be broadly defined as the delivery of healthcare services via mobile communication devices. More specifically, mHealth refers to the delivery, facilitation and communication of health-related information via mobile telecommunication and multimedia technologies – including mobile phones, tablet devices, and wireless infrastructure [13].

Expectations are high for mHealth, and the number of health-related mobile apps is growing at a prodigious rate, from an estimated 40,000 in 2012 to over 165,000 in 2015 [14, 15]. Much of this growth has been sparked by the potential of mobile healthcare to support patient engagement and self-management of chronic health conditions. Indeed, patients' management of their own chronic conditions and active engagement in their healthcare are associated with improved independence and life quality, and reduced healthcare utilization and cost [16, 17].

With a few notable exceptions (autism, mental health, stroke), people with disabilities have not been a primary target for mHealth app development. Concerns have been raised that the proliferation of mHealth could increase health disparities if the apps disproportionately benefit advantaged populations and leave vulnerable populations behind, including people with disabilities. Early evidence suggests that disparities may already exist between disabled and non-disabled populations in adoption of mHealth apps. While smartphone ownership is about equal among disabled and non-disabled adults (71% vs. 68%), the rate of adoption of mHealth apps is lower by half – 17% of disabled vs. 34% of non-disabled adults report downloading at least one app that is meant to support their health [18, 19].

At present, there is limited information about the representation of people with disabilities in the market for mHealth apps, despite the fact that they experience many of the chronic conditions targeted by these apps. This article describes our preliminary efforts to examine the current state of disparities in the growing mHealth market for people with disabilities. We gathered input from people with disabilities about their experiences with mHealth apps and preferences for future app development.

2 Methods

We conducted an on-line survey of members of our Consumer Advisory Network (CAN) to determine current use and experience with mHealth apps. The CAN is a nationwide sample of over 1,500 individuals with disabilities, representing a broad spectrum of vision, hearing, dexterity/mobility, intellectual/cognitive, and communication difficulties. Except for higher education and income levels, CAN members reflect the population of non-institutionalized people with disabilities in the US. This results from the fact that our primary source for recruiting CAN members is through the

Internet. We believe this is an acceptable variance from the general population of people with disabilities in the US because we are primarily interested in their experiences with information and communication technologies (ICT).

Established in 2001 and maintained through ongoing recruitment efforts, CAN members are frequently called upon to provide insights and feedback on emerging issues of use, usability, needs, and wants related to ICT. Insights from CAN members have formed the empirical basis for reports, presentations, and regulatory filings, and have also contributed directly to proposed research and development projects. CAN members participate in regular surveys including our cornerstone Survey of User Needs (SUN), which has been updated and repeated at regular intervals to provide a longitudinal view of changes in access and use of ICT by people with disabilities [19–23].

We reached out to CAN members via email to encourage them to participate in the online survey on mHealth and disability. The survey was active from February to August 2017. We specifically sought out mobile app users for the survey, and respondents were frequent users of mobile apps with (relatively) high adoption rates of mHealth apps. The survey requested demographic and disability information, and included six force-choice questions, with an opportunity to provide additional comments about each question. We also included an open-ended question for respondents to describe their "wish list" of apps for unmet health and wellness needs.

3   Results

A total of 377 respondents completed the mHealth survey. Average age of respondents was 54 (SD = 14.5 years); 53% were female and 74% were white/Caucasian. About half (47%) of respondents reported household income below $50,000. Respondents were asked to identify whether they had difficulties in any of nine general functional categories (Table 1). Most reported, on average, having two functional limitations/difficulties, with the most common being difficulty walking, climbing stairs, and difficulty hearing.

Respondents reported using a wide variety of mHealth apps. Exercise and activity tracking apps were the most commonly reported mHealth app, used by 40% of respondents. Diet and nutrition apps were used by 27% of respondents and lifestyle management (stress management, sleep quality) apps by 17% of respondents.

Two key questions in the mHealth survey focus on: (1) ease of finding usable and effective mHealth apps, and (2) satisfaction with the use of mHealth apps. Respondents were asked to rate ease or difficulty on a 5-point scale from very difficult to very easy. Ratings of "ease of finding a usable and effective mHealth app" were summarized into a single "Ease index" by assigning values of 1 to 5, respectively, to the responses "very difficult" to "very easy." These values were multiplied by the number of respondents who reported each level of ease/difficulty. The product of this operation was then divided by the highest possible value that would result if all respondents rated their ease/difficulty in funding a usable app as "very easy."

Table 1. "Which of the following types of health and wellness apps do you use? (Check all that apply)," by disability type.

	Fitness	Diet	Lifestyle	Other
Difficulty concentrating, remembering, deciding	60%	24%	22%	22%
Frequent worrying, nervousness, or anxiety	50%	24%	24%	29%
Difficulty seeing	44%	23%	23%	29%
Difficulty hearing	45%	30%	17%	18%
Difficulty speaking so people can understand you	47%	41%	29%	29%
Difficulty using your arms	30%	30%	22%	30%
Difficulty using your hands and fingers	44%	31%	26%	21%
Difficulty walking or climbing stairs	37%	28%	17%	22%
Difficulty with fatigue/limited stamina	40%	30%	23%	26%
All respondents	40%	27%	17%	20%

Respondents were asked to rate their satisfaction with usability of mHealth apps on a 5-point scale, from very dissatisfied to very satisfied. A Satisfaction index was calculated using the same methodology as with the Ease index. Table 2 presents the Satisfaction and Ease index for each disability type and overall. Feedback was mixed concerning the ease or difficulty in locating a suitable mHealth app, and overall satisfaction with existing mHealth apps. Only 46% of respondents reported that it was easy/very easy to locate a suitable app and the same proportion indicated they were satisfied or very satisfied with use of the app. There were modest differences by disability group - individuals with impairments related to using their arms and fatigue/stamina reported lower satisfaction, and those with impairments related to seeing, using arms, walking, and fatigue/stamina reported greater difficulty in locating mHealth apps.

This difficulty/dissatisfaction was also reflected in the comments about accessibility and usability issues participants experienced with the use of mHealth apps. Of the comments received concerning accessibility/usability issues with apps: 26% were related to the difficulty in setting up and using apps consistently; 17% commented on problems with the accuracy of apps that involved monitoring or measurement; and 10% of comments related to the lack of apps that adequately account for disability. For example, respondents with activity limitations requested that diet and exercise apps more accurately measure activity levels (e.g., when using a wheelchair or other mobility aid) or allow for adjustments to diet/nutrition goals to suit their more limited caloric intake needs. Many respondents requested compatibility with assistive technology (e.g., screen reader) or alternatives to manual keypad entries (e.g., difficulty using zoom or keypad gestures; using radio buttons; an "undo" function). Blind respondents indicated the need for captioning in apps using video.

When asked about "wish list" items for mHealth app development, a common theme was the need for an app to help manage health information, symptom tracking, and communications with healthcare providers about a person's disability and its effects on health. Many respondents wished for apps that were better integrated—an "all-in-one" app that could be used to track exercise, diet, medications, and biologic

Table 2. Satisfaction with mHealth apps and ease of finding mHealth apps that work for me.

Disability type	Satisfaction index	Ease index
Difficulty concentrating, remembering, making decisions	3.51	3.38
Frequent worrying, nervousness, anxiety	3.68	3.70
Difficulty seeing	3.31	2.98
Difficulty hearing	3.57	3.23
Difficulty speaking so people can understand you	4.00	3.43
Difficulty using your arms	3.19	2.99
Difficulty using your hands and fingers	3.24	3.05
Difficulty walking or climbing stairs	3.29	2.97
Difficulty with fatigue/limited stamina	3.12	2.95
All respondents	3.46	3.25

data (e.g., heart rate, blood glucose level, blood pressure) without the need to interface with other devices. There were also numerous requests for disability-specific apps for exercise, fitness and diet tracking.

Finally, respondents overwhelmingly (89%) supported the idea of a curation website with information about mHealth apps suited for people with disabilities. They particularly supported the value of app reviews by people with similar disabilities as a method to locate a suitable app.

4 Discussion

Our survey of disabled users of mobile apps indicated a high adoption rate (40%) of mHealth apps among these users, but also pointed to difficulties in locating suitable apps for disabled users, problems with accessibility of apps, and concerns about the accuracy or relevance of content in "mainstream" mHealth apps for disabled users. These insights emphasize the need for additional research to: (1) determine the availability, usability, and clinical utility of mHealth apps for people with disabilities, and (2) identify priority needs for mHealth app development, based on the gap between healthcare needs and available/accessible apps to address those needs.

Input from consumers suggests that three types of mHealth apps are needed. First, mainstream health and wellness apps and those for managing chronic health conditions and risk factors (e.g., diabetes, cardiovascular disease, obesity) may need to be "re-calibrated" for use by people with disabilities. For example, diet and exercise apps for people with paralysis need to be tailored to their nutritional needs, physical capabilities, and accessibility requirements for use of exercise equipment (e.g. from a wheelchair).

Second, mHealth apps are needed that target health conditions or risks unique to people with disabilities. While apps exist addressing specific disability conditions such as MS, most of these are informational in nature or provide limited functionality, such as symptom tracking. There are a number of health conditions or risks unique to disabling conditions that would benefit from mHealth apps. For example, apps targeting pressure ulcer prevention behaviors or management of respiratory functioning for people with paralysis could be important to prevention of secondary conditions.

And third, accessibility interfaces or add-ons that work with mHealth apps may be needed for some disabled users. mHealth apps need to be designed to accommodate the accessibility needs of disabled users, including those with limitations in vision, hearing, dexterity and motor control, speech, and cognitive abilities.

In addition to development efforts, work is needed to help people with disabilities in locating apps that are suitable to their needs. As noted in our survey findings, there is strong support for a curation website with information about mHealth apps suited for people with disabilities. Accessibility ratings of apps and reviews by people with similar disabilities were viewed as especially helpful as methods to locate a suitable app.

5 Conclusions

Substantial health disparities support the need for effective healthcare and health maintenance interventions for people with disabilities. Responding to this need requires a sustained, focused, and well-resourced effort, including: (1) research to identify priority needs of people with disabilities for mHealth app development and to keep abreast of evolving mHealth technology; (2) development aimed at designing, deploying, and validating new mHealth solutions that respond to the most pressing needs; (3) a knowledge translation effort to assist consumers and healthcare providers in identifying accessible and effective mHealth apps that address health disparities and improve health outcomes for people with disabilities.

References

1. Kinne, S., Patrick, D.L., Lochner, Doyle D.: Prevalence of secondary conditions among people with disabilities. Am. J. Public Health **94**(3), 443–445 (2004)
2. Iezzoni, L.I.: Eliminating health and health care disparities among the growing population of people with disabilities. Health Aff. **30**(10), 1947–1954 (2011)
3. Centers for Disease Control and Prevention. Disability and health data system [online database], Atlanta, GA (2010). http://dhds.cdc.gov. Accessed Nov 2015
4. Centers for Disease Control and Prevention (CDC), National Center for Health Statistics. DATA2020 [Internet database]. Hyattsville, MD: author; (2010). http://www.healthypeople.gov/2020/data-search/Search-the-Data. Accessed 2 Nov 2015
5. Centers for Disease Control and Prevention (CDC), National Center for Health Statistics. DATA2010 [Internet database]. Hyattsville, MD (2010). http://wonder.cdc.gov/data2010/focus.htm. Accessed 30 Sept 2015
6. Centers for Disease Control and Prevention (CDC). The Prevalence of Physical Inactivity in Adults with and without Disabilities, BRFSS (2009). https://www.cdc.gov/ncbddd/disabilityandhealth/documents/physical-inactivity-tip-sheet-_phpa_1.pdf. Accessed 30 Jan 2017

7. Centers for Disease Control and Prevention (CDC). Overweight and Obesity Among People with Disabilities, BRFSS (2008). https://www.cdc.gov/ncbddd/disabilityandhealth/obesity.html. Accessed 30 Jan 2017
8. Centers for Disease Control and Prevention (CDC). Current Cigarette Smoking Among Adults - United States. Morbidity and Mortality Weekly Report, 9 Nov 2012, 61(44), pp. 889–894 (2011)
9. Centers for Disease Control and Prevention (CDC). People with Disabilities and High Blood Pressure, February 2015. https://www.cdc.gov/ncbddd/disabilityandhealth/features/high-blood-pressure.html. Accessed 30 Jan 2017
10. McDermott, S., Moran, R., Platt, T., Dasari, S.: Prevalence of diabetes in persons with disabilities in primary care. J. Dev. Phys. Disabil. **19**, 263–271 (2007)
11. Stevens, A., Courtney-Long, E., Gillespie, C., Armour, B.S.: Hypertension among US adults by disability status and type, national health and nutrition examination survey, 2001–2010. Prev. Chronic Dis. **11**(E139), 140162 (2014)
12. Herrick, H.W.B., Luken, K.J.: The burden of heart disease among North Carolina adults with disabilities. N. C. Med. J. **73**(6), 499–503 (2012)
13. ResearchNow. mHealth apps supporting a healthier future, April 2015. http://www.researchnow.com/en-gb/PressAndEvents/News/2015/april/ ~ /media/64741EEB37534570B1FCD A62204717E2.ashx
14. Pelletier, S.G.: Explosive growth in health apps raises oversight questions. AAMC reporter, October 2012. www.aamc.org/newsroom/reporter/october2012/308516/health-care-apps.html
15. IMS Institute for Healthcare Informatics. Patient adoption of mHealth: use, evidence, and remaining barriers to mainstream acceptance. The Institute, Parsippany (NJ) (2015)
16. Boult, C., Green, A., Boult, L., Pacala, J., Snyder, C., Leff, B.: Successful models of comprehensive care for older adults with chronic conditions: Evidence for the Institute of Medicine's "Retooling for an aging America" report. J. Am. Geriatr. Soc. **57**(12), 2328–2337 (2009)
17. Berry-Millett, R., Bodenheimer, T.: Care management of patients with complex health care needs. Synth. Proj. Res. Synth. Rep. (19) (2009)
18. Gallup Press Release. How mobile technology can improve employee' well-being. 3 November 2014
19. Morris, J., Jones, M., Sweatman, M.: Wireless technology use by people with disabilities: a national survey. J. Technol. Persons Disabil., pp. 101–113, September 2016
20. Mueller, J., Jones, M., Broderick, L., Haberman, V.: Assessment of user needs in wireless technologies. Assistive Technol. **17**, 57–71 (2005)
21. Mueller, J., Morris, J., Jones, M.: Accessibility of emergency communications to deaf citizens. Int. J. Emerg. Manage. **7**(1), 41–46 (2010)
22. Morris, J., Mueller, J., Jones, M., Lippincott, B.: Wireless technology use and disability: results from a national survey. J. Technol. Persons Disabil. **1**, 67–77 (2014)
23. Morris, J., Mueller, J., Jones, M.: Use of social media during public emergencies by people with disabilities. W. J. Emerg. Med. **15**(5), 567–574 (2014)

A Mobile App Supporting Exercise Adherence for People with Parkinson's Disease

Kristoffer Upsahl, Annette Vistven, Astrid Bergland, and Weiqin Chen[✉]

Oslo Metropolitan University (OsloMet), POB 4, St. Olavs plass, 0130 Oslo, Norway
Weiqin.Chen@oslomet.no

Abstract. Researches have shown that physical exercise in patients with Parkinson's disease (PD) is an effective method reduce or limit the progress of the disease and improve physical and psychological health. However, exercise adherence is a challenge task. Many existing mobile exercise apps did not consider the special conditions of people with PD. This paper aims to design a mobile app to support physical exercise adherence among people with PD. Through the design of the app, we hope to test and contribute to the improvement of the existing guidelines and recommendations for mobile apps for people with PD.

Keywords: Parkinson's disease · Exercise adherence · Mobile app

1 Introduction

Parkinson's disease (PD) is one of the most widespread neurodegenerative conditions in the world [1]. It is an age-related disease and mostly affects people in the later years of life. As the older population continues to grow, the number of people with PD is expected to increase. Symptoms in PD include tremor in limbs, slowness of movement, stiffness in muscles, and impaired balance [1]. These symptoms result in a loss of fine motor skills. The progressive nature of PD and its increasing prevalence have resulted in a substantial economic burden to society, health care providers, individual patients and their family [2].

Researches have shown that physical exercise in patients with PD is an effective method to control PD-related symptoms, reduce or limit the progress of the disease, and improve physical and psychological health [3]. However, due to PD related conditions such as dementia, apathy, excessive daytime sleepiness, and sleeping problems [4] exercise adherence is a challenging task. Adherence can be understood as the extent to which the patient's behavior corresponds with caregivers' recommendations and follows the mutual agreement to achieve established goals [5]. Since adherence to an exercise program often involves a behavioral change, the addition of support for this process might provide a valuable contribution to adherence. Adherence to exercise programs is fundamental for achieving positive outcomes. Barriers for continuing regular exercise is decline in health, time constraints, and lack of motivation [6]. To our knowledge no previous studies have qualitatively explored the use of digital technology to facilitate exercise adherence after rehabilitation in people with PD.

K. Miesenberger and G. Kouroupetroglou (Eds.): ICCHP 2018, LNCS 10897, pp. 464–467, 2018.
https://doi.org/10.1007/978-3-319-94274-2_67

The usage of smartphones and tablets is increasing among elderly. Various mobile apps have been developed for older adults [7]. Existing exercise apps for elderly people in general, such as Senior Fitness - Strength & Flexibility Training and Daily Senior Fitness Exercise, are not suitable for people with PD, as they do not consider their special conditions. Even the exercise apps for people with PD such as 9zest Parkinson's Therapy and Parkinson Home Exercises have usability issues. For example, some have an interface with buttons too close to each other, which causes mistakes for people with declined motor skills.

To support physical exercises among people with PD, we have designed a mobile exercise app that reminds and motivates people with PD to exercise, following guidelines and recommendations for mobile apps for people with PD and taking their special conditions into consideration.

2 Related Work

The variety of symptoms for people with PD can make this user group difficult to design for and a user-centered design approach is important and efficient when designing solutions for people with PD [8]. As basis for creating their own framework for people with PD, McNaney et al. [8] used existing guidelines for participatory design with elderly users. This method was found to inadequately address several specific issues with PD, including speech, general mobility and dexterity, medication, and age difference.

Some mobile apps have been developed for people with PD, for training, self-management, monitoring progression, medication, diagnosis, treatment guides, information (about symptoms and treatment options), analyzing tremor, connecting (with family, experts, and peers), and transportation. Very few have been studied in terms of usability and effect [9]. The Parkinson's tracker app for Android and iOS is a self-management and adherence tool to manage PD [10]. It was used in a study to investigate whether those who used the app showed improved medication adherence compared to those receiving usual treatment. Participants could review and compare their scores with each other, receive alerts and track medicine intake, they had the option to generate a report detailing the trial period, and play games to track physical responsiveness. The study lasted for 16 weeks and the app was found to have significantly improved adherence, compared to those who received usual treatment. According to the authors, this study had a higher level of user retention because of the design of the user interface and user experience, and simplicity of the app.

3 Design and Development

We follow a user-centered approach in the design and development of the mobile app. The initial requirements were gathered based on literature review and focus group interviews with people with PD and health care workers. Based on the requirements we have developed the first prototype.

3.1   Focus Group Interview

The focus group interviews were conducted in a rehabilitation center with 20 people with PD and 7 health care workers. The most pressing challenge is that after their stay in the rehabilitation center where they have learned how to exercise and live with PD, they have difficulties in following the exercise plan. Ideas for how to support the exercise adherence with the mobile app were discussed. These include showing videos of exercises, allowing care workers to add videos or links to online videos and create/customize exercise plan, reminding users to take medication, which is very important for the effect of physical exercises, and providing contact information to doctor, physiotherapist, or other people who can help with exercises. Some people have also responded that they would like to have the app include functions for self-reporting, so that it can replace the use of paper forms for such purpose. Given the conditions of people with PD, the majority prefer to have the app on a tablet, which has a bigger screen size that a mobile phone.

3.2   Initial Prototype

Based on the results from the focus group interviews and conversations with experts in rehabilitation for people with PD, we established the initial requirements for the mobile app. They are: remind the user to exercise and take medication; show the user how to perform exercises; support user to create and customize exercise plan; and confirm that exercise has been performed.

Through literature review, we have also selected an initial set of design guidelines and principles to follow during the design of the interface for the exercise app. They are based on the 12 guidelines for designing for people with PD by Nunes, Silva, Cevada, Barros and Teixeira [9] and the 10 usability heuristics by Nielsen [11]. Figure 1 shows the interface of the prototype where users can see today's exercise, a demonstration of exercises, exercise plan, contact persons' information, help information on how to use the app, and how to configure reminders and other types of settings.

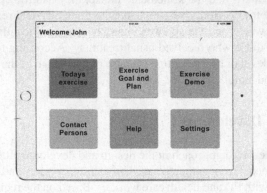

Fig. 1. Main interface of the mobile app

4   Conclusion and Future Work

In this paper we aim to address the challenges of exercise adherence among people with PD with developing a mobile app. This app is mainly intended to remind users to exercise and demonstrate to them how-to with videos. We are currently planning for the first user testing with the initial prototype. The feedback from the user testing will be used to further develop the app.

References

1. http://www.epda.eu.com/about-parkinson-s/what-is-parkinson-s/
2. Whetten-Goldstein, K., Sloan, F., Kulas, E., Cutson, T., Schenkman, M.: The burden of Parkinson's disease on society, family, and the individual. J. Am. Geriatr. Soc. **45**, 844–849 (1997)
3. Eriksson, B.M., Arne, M., Ahlgren, C.: Keep moving to retain the healthy self: the meaning of physical exercise in individuals with Parkinson's disease. Disabil. Rehabil. **35**, 2237–2244 (2013)
4. Sveinbjornsdottir, S.: The clinical symptoms of Parkinson's disease. J. Neurochem. **139**, 318–324 (2016)
5. Gardner, C.L.: Adherence: a concept analysis. Int. J. Nurs. Knowl. **26**, 96–101 (2015)
6. van der Kolk, N.M., King, L.A.: Effects of exercise on mobility in people with Parkinson's disease. Mov. Disord. **28**, 1587–1596 (2013)
7. Baldwin, S., Hsu, Y.-C., Ching, Y.-H.: Mobile apps for older adults: health, learning, and living. In: E-Learn: World Conference on E-Learning in Corporate, Government, Healthcare, and Higher Education 2015, pp. 1402–1407. Association for the Advancement of Computing in Education (AACE), Kona (2015)
8. McNaney, R., Balaam, M., Holden, A., Schofield, G., Jackson, D., Webster, M., Galna, B., Barry, G., Rochester, L., Olivier, P.: Designing for and with people with Parkinson's: a focus on exergaming. In: Proceedings of the 33rd annual ACM conference on Human Factors in Computing Systems, pp. 501–510. ACM
9. Nunes, F., Silva, P.A., Cevada, J., Barros, A.C., Teixeira, L.: User interface design guidelines for smartphone applications for people with Parkinson's disease. Univ. Access Inf. Soc. **15**, 659–679 (2016)
10. Lakshminarayana, R., Wang, D., Burn, D., Chaudhuri, K.R., Galtrey, C., Guzman, N.V., Hellman, B., Ben, J., Pal, S., Stamford, J., Steiger, M., Stott, R.W., Teo, J., Barker, R.A., Wang, E., Bloem, B.R., van der Eijk, M., Rochester, L., Williams, A.: Using a smartphone-based self-management platform to support medication adherence and clinical consultation in Parkinson's disease. NPJ Parkinson's Dis. **3**, 2 (2017)
11. http://www.nngroup.com/articles/ten-usability-heuristics/

Development and Evaluation of a Device to Measure Walking Speed

Kevin Caves$^{(\boxtimes)}$ ⓘ, Leighanne Davisⓘ, and Frank DeRuyterⓘ

Duke University, Durham, NC 27710, USA
kevin.caves@duke.edu

Abstract. This manuscript describes the development and testing of a device to measure walking speed. The Gaitbox is a custom, microprocessor-based device that uses an infrared distance sensor to automatically measure, calculate and display walking speed. Walking speed is a critical performance measure that has been shown to be a strong indicator of long-term health and life expectancy in older people. The Gaitbox was compared to the measures obtained by clinicians administering the timed NIH 4-m walk test and the Sprint System device.

Keywords: NIH walk test · Walking speed

1 Background

Recently coined the 6th vital sign [1], gait speed is one of the strongest predictors of functional status and survival amongst older adult populations [2]. Walking speed is already used for a variety of clinical populations including those with peripheral arterial disease, vertebral fracture and osteoporosis, Parkinson disease, stroke, total hip replacement and fracture, among others [1]. A JAMA publication reiterated this point by predicting life expectancy using age, sex and gait speed, showing that it was as accurate as predictions of life expectancy based on other clinical measures [3]. Another study showed that over an eight-year follow-up period, older adults who had an improvement in gait speed over at least one-year, had a 68% higher survival rate compared to their counterparts with no change or a decrease in gait speed [4]. It has also been shown that a reduction of 0.10 meters per second has been associated with a 12% decrease in life expectancy in older adults [3]. These studies provide opportunity for more accurate monitoring and faster intervention to ensure a higher quality of life and life expectancy for older adults.

1.1 NIH Toolbox 4-m Clinical Walk Test

The NIH toolbox 4-m clinical walk test (NIH-WT) is a clinically validated walking speed test used across the world to evaluate walking speed in a variety of patient populations [5]. Set up of the walking path includes marking the beginning and end of the walking path and beginning and end of timing section of the walking path to allow for acceleration and deceleration. A standard manual stopwatch is used to record time. The examiner demonstrates the task then instructs the participant to "Walk at a

© Springer International Publishing AG, part of Springer Nature 2018
K. Miesenberger and G. Kouroupetroglou (Eds.): ICCHP 2018, LNCS 10897, pp. 468–471, 2018.
https://doi.org/10.1007/978-3-319-94274-2_68

comfortable pace" after a countdown: "3, 2, 1, go." The clinician starts and stops the timing at the marks. Walking speed is calculated by dividing the distance walked by the elapsed time.

Previous development work (unpublished) demonstrated that walking speeds calculated from measurements taken by experienced testers using the NIH-WT procedures can vary significantly with and between testers due to a variety of factors including differences in the reaction time of the person holding the watch and the techniques used to identify the starting and stopping locations. These inaccuracies were the motivation for the development of an automatic walking speed measurement device.

1.2   Device Design and Use

We have developed a compact device, the Gaitbox, which measures walking speed automatically. The device is based on an Arduino Uno microcontroller and uses an infrared (IR) light sensor to acquire accurate measurements over a distance of approximately 5 m. We built devices based on two different IR sensors: a Sharp IR Range Sensor (Model GP2Y0A710K0F) and a Garmin LIDAR-Lite V3 Laser Ranging Module. The Sharp sensor is very inexpensive but requires collection of data to create a custom calibration for the sensor. The Garmin LIDAR sensor can be used out of the box without calibration. The device has a 2-line LCD display and some LEDs for user feedback. The device is encased in a custom 3D printed enclosure (Fig. 1).

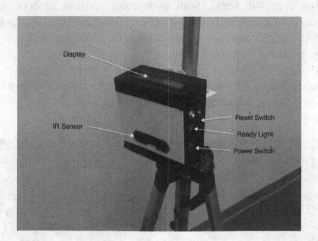

Fig. 1. Gaitbox device

We completed validation testing on only the device with the Garmin sensor. In preliminary comparative testing between the two sensors we determined that the less expensive Sharp sensor was less accurate than the Garmin, especially at the far distances. Also, it would not be practical to calibrate the sensor for each device.

The device is designed to be used with the typical setup of the NIH-WT described above. The device is setup at the end of the walking path at a height of 4 ft from the floor. To make recordings, the clinician turns the device on, presses the reset switch, waits for ready light and tells subject to go. The device continuously monitors distance and when the subject passes an investigator specified "start" distance (currently 4 m) the distance (in mm) and time (in sec) are stored. When the subject reaches the "stop" distance (currently 2 m) the distance and time are recorded and the speed in m/sec is automatically calculated and the result is displayed on the LCD.

2   Validation Study

2.1   Study Design

We have completed a prospective, validation study. Thirty-five healthy community dwelling subjects participated (25 males age 71.9 ± 5.6 years, 9 females age 74.0 ± 11.0 years). The study is being conducted under the review of the Duke IRB. Subjects completed the 4-m walk test, four (4) times, one practice and three tests. Three speed measuring methods were conducted simultaneously: Gaitbox, NIH-WT, and Sprint System [6] a commercially available timing system used to time track running events by breaking two invisible light beams. Timing starts when the subject breaks the first light beam and stops when the second is crossed. The times are displayed on a handheld display.

Both male and female subjects aged 55 or older were recruited. Subjects must be able to complete four 4-m walks, with or without assistive devices such as canes, crutches or walkers. Subjects with a physical, cognitive, or behavioral impairment that would prevent the safe completion of the testing or affect the ability to follow study directions were excluded from participation.

The testing setup is shown in Fig. 2. The track is laid out per the NIH-WT specifications, which include a 4-m walking space with acceleration and deceleration zones. The start and stop timing locations were marked with tape.

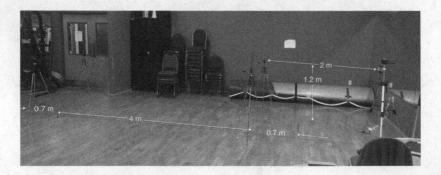

Fig. 2. Measurements for testing path

The Sprint System devices were set up at the start and stop lines. The Gaitbox was positioned at the end of the walking track 2 m past the stop timing mark. Figure 2 shows the layout and location of the testing devices and timing marks. Thirty-five subjects completed 4 walks each. Each trial was simultaneously timed by two experienced clinicians skilled in performing the NIH-WT, the Sprint System and by the Gaitbox.

2.2 Data Analysis

The purpose of the study is to validate the Gaitbox to the clinical measurements taken in accordance with the NIH toolbox 4-m test and against the Sprint System device. At the time of submission of this paper, data analysis was ongoing. Confidence levels for the comparisons between human timer 1 to human timer 2, average human timer to Gaitbox, Gaitbox to Sprint System will be calculated. Bland-Altman (difference) plots will be created to facilitate visualization of the differences.

3 Discussion/Conclusion

At the time of submission, we have completed testing and data collection and are in the process of data analysis. We plan to report results at the meeting.

Gait speed is rapidly becoming recognized as one of the strongest predictors of functional status and survival amongst older adult populations. Being able to easily, accurately and consistently measure walking speed is an important clinical need.

Future testing will evaluate the accuracy of the device over both 4-m and 10-m lengths. The device will next be evaluated in several medical clinics at Duke University Medical Center, including the Perioperative Optimization of Senior Health (POSH) and Geriatric Evaluation and Treatment (GET) clinics. We also see a potential use of the device for collecting passive walking data in home settings. The device could be modified to collect walking speed in a set location, for example a hallway, and look for changes in average walking speed. The device can easily be modified to send data periodically for review or even automatically look for trends in data and automatically notify a care giver or heath care provider.

References

1. Lusardi, M.M.: Is walking speed a vital sign? Absolutely. Top. Geriatr. Rehabil. **28**(2), 67–76 (2012)
2. Guralnik, J.M., Ferrucci, L., et al.: Lower extremity function and subsequent disability: consistency across studies, predictive models, and value of gait speed alone compared with the short physical performance battery. J. Gerontol. MS **55A**(4), M221–M231 (2000)
3. Studenski, S., Perera, S., et al.: Gait speed and survival in older adults. JAMA **305**(1), 50–58 (2011). https://doi.org/10.1001/jama.2010.1923
4. Hardy, S.E., Perera, S., et al.: Improvement in usual gait speed predicts better survival in older adults. J. Am. Geriatr. Soc. **55**(11), 1727–1734 (2007)
5. NIH Toolbox: Assessment of Neurological and Behavioral Function. http://www.nihtoolbox.org. Accessed 14 Sept 2017
6. Sprint system. http://browertiming.com/products/tc-timing-system/. Accessed 14 Sept 2017

BreatheWell Wear: Development and Testing of a Stress Management App for TBI and PTSD on Android Wear Smartwatches

John T. Morris[(⊠)] [iD] and Tracey Wallace [iD]

Shepherd Center, Atlanta, GA 30309, USA
{john.morris,tracey.wallace}@shepherd.org

Abstract. This paper describes the development and testing of BreatheWell Wear, a stress management application (mobile app) developed for Android Wear smartwatches to assist military service members with post-traumatic stress disorder (PTSD) and traumatic brain injury (TBI) to use deep, slow diaphragmatic breathing for managing stress. The paper describes rehabilitation needs and challenges of daily living of the user population, and the limitations of existing solutions for training and using diaphragmatic breathing. Features and functioning of BreatheWell Wear are presented along with a summary of our user-centered design approach to development. Testing for clinical effectiveness was conducted with a small sample. Participants were recruited from the SHARE Military Initiative at Shepherd Center in Atlanta, Georgia, USA where they were receiving comprehensive rehabilitation for TBI and PTSD. The effectiveness of the intervention was evaluated through collection of patient reported outcomes: (1) stress ratings, entered into the app by the user before and after each breathing session; (2) Goal Attainment Scaling (GAS) to measure impact of using BreatheWell Wear after extended use; (3) changes in PTSD symptom severity gathered at study completion using the Posttraumatic Checklist-5 (PCL-5); (4) changes in anxiety, depression and psychological well-being were measured at study completion using the Beck Anxiety Inventory (BAI), the Beck Depression Inventory (BDI) and the Flourishing Scale. Clinical measures of PTSD, anxiety, depression, and psychological well-being, showed moderate or greater clinically meaningful change. Participants also reported positive experiences using BreatheWell Wear.

Keywords: Post-Traumatic stress disorder · Wearable technology
Diaphragmatic breathing

1 Introduction

Hundreds of thousands of military service-members returning from Iraq and Afghanistan have traumatic brain injury (TBI) and/or post-traumatic stress disorder (PTSD), often resulting in debilitating stress and anxiety. The co-occurrence of TBI and PTSD can increase symptomatology and slow recovery, thereby negatively impacting capacity for independent living and quality of life [1]. Some of the more common clinical features of PTSD include excessive anxiety and perception of threats, avoidance of anxiety and

© Springer International Publishing AG, part of Springer Nature 2018
K. Miesenberger and G. Kouroupetroglou (Eds.): ICCHP 2018, LNCS 10897, pp. 472–478, 2018.
https://doi.org/10.1007/978-3-319-94274-2_69

hyper-arousal symptoms, such as anger, startle response and hyper-vigilance [2]. TBI can result in cognitive deficits such as impairments in memory and executive functioning, which can also cause increased stress and anxiety. Further, TBI may contribute to the occurrence of PTSD. The presence of both pathologies may significantly complicate and hinder recovery [1, 3].

Breathing retraining, the practice of using slow, deep breathing to promote relaxation, is a widely used technique in stress reduction therapies [4]. It can be used to manage acute stress and aid processing during cognitive behavioral therapy interventions [5–7]. When stress is triggered, the sympathetic nervous system is activated, initiating the "fight or flight" response [8]. This physiological response causes a person's heart rate and respiration to increase. Deep, slow diaphragmatic breathing activates the body's parasympathetic nervous system which facilitates homeostasis and calming after the fight or flight response is initiated. It increases the supply of oxygen to the brain, initiates a "relaxation response" by decreasing heart rate and blood pressure and changes the sensations in the body that are associated with stress.

People who experience PTSD and executive dysfunction, a common sequela of TBI, may be more vulnerable to intrusive memories and difficulties with emotion regulation, due to reductions in self-awareness, self-monitoring and initiation of emotion regulation strategies. Impairments in executive functioning and memory can interfere with a person's ability to pace their breathing, remember and initiate daily practice (which is important to support effective use) and/or use deep breathing during periods of increased stress, thereby reducing the effectiveness of using breathing as a stress management tool. Technology, mobile apps for coaching diaphragmatic breathing in particular, can be used to help overcome these barriers. Most existing breathing coach apps offer limited utility to people with TBI and PTSD due to restricted customization options and a dependence on the user to remember to practice daily use of the breathing strategy. BreatheWell Wear has several features not typically offered in breathing apps on other platforms that may be beneficial to military service members who experience both PTSD and TBI.

2 BreatheWell Wear: A Stress Management Solution

BreatheWell Wear is a stress management mobile application, or "app" developed for Android Wear smartwatches to assist military service members with PTSD and TBI to use deep, slow diaphragmatic breathing to manage stress. Although it is designed for a specific user population, it is potentially useful to other populations who would benefit from stress management and cognitive aids. Android Wear smartwatches are wearable computers that use a smartphone-like format and allow users to download apps, which are generally designed for brief interactions. Several breathing-based stress management apps have been available for smartphones for several years, yet none existed for wearables at the time development efforts were initiated. Wearable platforms may offer some advantages over smartphones for use of breathing-based stress management apps. Wearables may allow the user to access an app more quickly and discretely. Users are also more likely to have the wearable device with them when it is needed as it is worn on the body. And wearables may also offer additional opportunities to support behavioral and health monitoring more broadly through the incorporation of biosensor technology. Following the initial release of BreatheWell Wear, Apple released a breathing coach app and similar apps began to be available on some wrist-worn fitness trackers. However, BreatheWell Wear is the only breathing coach app available on Android Wear. None of the breathing coach apps for wearables were designed with attention to the specific wants and needs of users with PTSD and TBI, a large and vulnerable population who may benefit considerably from technology-supported breathing coaching.

BreatheWell Wear assists users in performing deep, slow, diaphragmatic breathing by providing visual, tactile and auditory guidance to pace breathing. It also displays the user's heart rate in real time. Users can pace their breathing by matching it to the movement of a blue pace bar that runs along the perimeter of the watch face. The Android Wear device vibrates at the end of each inhalation and exhalation as the visual pace bar reverses the direction of movement for the corresponding segment of the breathing cycle. Rates of inhalation and exhalation and the number of breathing cycles attempted can be changed while in use ("on the fly").

User defined settings can be programmed directly in the app on the wearable device or on the companion app that resides on the smart phone or tablet paired with the Android Wear smartwatch. These settings allow users to program a pause in breathing after inhalation and/or after exhalation, which is sometimes practiced in relaxation breathing. The settings also provide the user with a variety of voice guidance options (choice of male voice, female voice and no voice) and the option of listening to calming sounds and music or selecting a song from their own music library.

BreatheWell Wear allows users to program reminders to practice during periods of low stress to help them perform the breathing technique effectively during periods of high stress. Before and after each breathing practice session, users are asked to rate their stress, a feature they can disable in the settings if desired. Additionally, an instructional video of a military service member with PTSD and TBI demonstrating the breathing technique can be viewed through the companion app residing on the smart phone or tablet paired with the Android Wear smartwatch.

BreatheWell Wear was initially developed for Google Glass (the Glass version is named simply BreatheWell). Development efforts shifted to Android Wear as Google Glass began its exit from the mainstream consumer marketplace and smartwatches began gaining popularity. Both the Google Glass and Android Wear versions have been fully developed. The source code for the Google Glass version is available at https://github.com/ShepherdCenter. The Android Wear version is available for download in the Play Store and has undergone clinical testing with target users.

3   Design and Development Methodology

The development of BreatheWell Wear followed user-centered, participatory design principles by including target users, both military service members with TBI and PTSD and their healthcare providers throughout the development process, resulting in multiple iterations [9, 10]. Enhancements to the initial prototype aimed at addressing the expressed needs, wants and limitations of stakeholders resulted in seven "builds" of the app. The initial design concept was led by a clinician with expertise in TBI cognitive rehabilitation in collaboration with a psychologist with expertise in PTSD treatment. The Google Glass version and several leading smart phone breathing apps were demonstrated in a focus group of five military service members living with PTSD and mild to moderate TBI, aimed at gathering feedback on the features, settings and display.

Feedback shared by the focus group reinforced the development aims and guided the team to maximize the app customizability, particularly for the voice guidance and the calming sounds. Subsequently, 25 songs and ambient noise tracks were collected based on focus group participants' input and then played for six people, four of whom had a diagnosis of PTSD and TBI while the other two were clinicians with expertise in PTSD and TBI rehabilitation. Each were asked to use a 5-point scale to rank how relaxing the music and sounds were, resulting in a set of seven songs and ambient noise tracks (two meditation melodies and sounds of rain, a river, a fan, the ocean and a rainforest).

4   Clinical Testing Research Design

Twenty military service members or veterans living with PTSD and TBI participated in testing of BreatheWell Wear, 6 of whom completed usability testing through "sit-by" demonstrations along with four clinical experts in PTSD and TBI (a speech-language pathologist, 2 clinical psychologists, and one clinical social worker). Refinements incorporating feedback gathered in the sit-by testing informed development of a beta version of the app.

The remaining 14 participants completed full clinical take-home testing to further understand usability in clinical and natural environments, as well as to begin to assess clinical efficacy. Participants were recruited from the SHARE Military Initiative at Shepherd Center in Atlanta, Georgia, where they were receiving comprehensive rehabilitation for TBI and PTSD. The SHARE psychologist identified participants who met the inclusion criteria and then collaborated with each participant's treating SLP by using feature matching, a clinical practice used to guide selection of assistive technology for cognition (ATC), to determine whether the participants' goals, needs, interest in technology and functional abilities were matched to the technology being studied [11–15]. Participants were primarily male (12 of 14) with ages ranging from 29 to 50. Time since onset of TBI or PTSD ranged from 2 years to 24 years. All reported experiencing significant stress, anxiety and/or emotion dysregulation and described symptoms of memory impairment and/or executive dysfunction. Participants were asked to wear the Android Wear smartwatch and use the breathing app daily for 2–4 weeks. Initial training and setup was conducted by each participant's behavioral health provider, either a clinical social worker or psychologist.

The effectiveness of the intervention was evaluated through collection of patient reported outcomes. Stress ratings, entered in the app by the user before and after each breathing session were collected through Google Analytics. Connectivity and other technical barriers – including one participant's choice to turn off Bluetooth pairing between the smartwatch and paired phone due to fears associated with side-effects of using Bluetooth technology – resulted in unreliable ratings for some users and could only be obtained for the last six participants enrolled in the study. Goal Attainment Scaling (GAS), a tool used in rehabilitation for measuring improvement on relevant functional tasks, was used to measure whether use of the BreatheWell Wear app resulted in meaningful change for the user [16, 17]. Changes in PTSD symptom severity were gathered at study completion for all 14 participants via the Posttraumatic Checklist-5, PCL-5 [18]. Changes in anxiety, depression and psychological well-being were measured at study completion for 7 of the participants via the Beck Anxiety Inventory (BAI), the Beck Depression Inventory (BDI) and the Flourishing Scale (the measures were added after initial testing began) [19–21]. And a structured clinical interview about the user's perceived effectiveness of the technology and their overall experience with the technology was completed with each participant upon study completion.

5   Results

Eighty-six percent of participants reported they would very likely continue to use BreatheWell Wear after the study (assuming they owned an Android Wear smartwatch). User comments following study completion included, "It's the single best thing I've gotten from this therapy program" and several participants purchased an Android Wear smartwatch to continue using BreatheWell Wear following study completion. Favorite features identified included: the quick accessibility to the app provided by the wearable format, customizability of music/sounds, the ability to set reminders to practice and the biofeedback provided by the heart rate display. The main concern reported was related to some difficulty operating the small Android Wear screen, particularly for those with fine motor deficits.

All 14 participants performed at 'Expected' or higher levels on their GAS goals for how well they used the technology to achieve an individualized, person-centered goal related to stress management (remember to practice breathing, perform the breathing technique accurately, etc.). This correlates to interview data indicating 100% felt the app was helpful to them. Additionally, all 14 participants performed at 'Expected' or greater for GAS goals for learning to use the app from a technical aspect, which was important to consider given the coexistence of memory impairment experienced by target users. This correlates to interview data indicating 86% found the app "very easy" to use.

The average stress rating collected after breathing sessions declined from 3.75 on a 7-point scale (7 is highest stress) before a breathing session to 2.6, equating to a moderate clinically meaningful reduction in stress rating [22]. Half of the participants also had 5+ points or greater reduction on the PCL-5 measure of PTSD symptoms at study completion. This reduction indicates an effective response to treatment. Further, four of these participants had 10+ points or greater reduction in responses, indicating clinically significant and meaningful change.

Anxiety symptom severity was reduced by over 11 points on average on the BAI, reducing average anxiety severity from Moderate to Low. Depression symptom severity was reduced by over 13 points on average on the BDI, reducing average severity from Moderate Depression to Borderline Clinical Depression. Responses on the Flourishing

Scale, a measure of psychological well-being, improved by 6 points on average at study completion, indicating an average per-item improvement of 0.75 points. This is a meaningful change on item responses for self-reports of psychological well-being that use a 7-point scale, such as the Flourishing Scale [22].

6 Conclusion, Scientific and Practical Impact and Contributions to the Field

The results of this study suggest BreatheWell Wear is a clinically effective means of stress management for some people with PTSD and TBI. Additionally, the qualitative measures used in this study indicate wearables, such as smart watches, may be well received by and useful for this population. Also, the results validate previous research supporting slow, deep breathing as an effective stress management tool. However, the extent to which results and conclusions can be generalized is limited because the study did not control for the participation in other interventions that may relieve PTSD symptoms.

7 Planned Activities

Several new directions based on both participant and researcher experiences during the clinical testing of the app are planned in a version 2.0. The reminder feature will be expanded with increased customizability, and a version will be built for Apple Watch. Periodic user queries about well-being and functioning will be added through ecological momentary assessment to refine collection of impact data. A progress tracking screen will be added within the companion app to provide feedback to the user including changes in heart rate, stress ratings, well-being ratings, and frequency of breathing practice. Integration with external stress detecting biosensor will be made possible and biosensor data captured will be leveraged to aid the user in anticipating onset of episodes of stress. Finally, more extensive clinical testing with a focus on impact and comparative effectiveness will be completed.

References

1. Tschiffely, A.E., Ahlers, S.T., Norris, J.N.: Examining the relationship between blast-induced mild traumatic brain injury and posttraumatic stress-related traits. J. Neurosci. Res. **93**(12), 1769–1777 (2015)
2. American Psychiatric Association: Diagnostic and Statistical Manual of Mental Disorder, 5th edn. American Psychiatric Publishing, Washington, D.C. (2013)
3. Cooper, D.B., Kennedy, J.E., Cullen, M.A., Critchfield, E., Amador, R.R., Bowles, A.O.: Association between combat stress and post-concussive symptom reporting in OEF/OIF service members with mild traumatic brain injuries. Brain Inj. **25**(1), 1–7 (2011)
4. Brown, R.P., Gerbarg, P.L., Muench, F.: Breathing practices for treatment of psychiatric and stress-related medical conditions. Psychiatr. Clin. North Am. **36**(1), 121–140 (2013)

5. O'Donohue, W.T., Fisher, J.E.: General Principles and Empirically Supported Techniques of Cognitive Behavior Therapy. Wiley, Hoboken (2009)
6. Ursano, R.J., Bell, C., Eth, S., et al.: Practice guideline for the treatment of patients with acute stress disorder and posttraumatic stress disorder. Am. J. Psychiatry **161**(11), 3–31 (2004)
7. VA/DoD: VA/DoD clinical practice guideline for management of post-traumatic stress. Department of Veterans Affairs, Department of Defense (2010). www.healthquality.va.gov/PTSD-Full-2010c.pdf. Accessed 30 Jan 2018
8. Jansen, A.S., Nguyen, X.V., Karpitskiy, V., Mettenleiter, T.C., Loewy, A.D.: Central command neurons of the sympathetic nervous system: basis of the fight-or-flight response. Science **270**(5236), 644–646 (1995)
9. Luna, D., Quispe, M., Gonzalez, Z., Alemrares, A., Risk, M., Garcia Aurelio, M., Otero, C.: User-centered design to develop clinical applications. literature review. Stud. Health Technol. Inform. **216**, 967 (2015)
10. International Organization for Standardization: ISO FDIS 9241-210, Ergonomics of human-system interaction–Part 210: Human-centered design for interactive systems. ISO (2010)
11. LoPresti, E.N., Mihailidis, A., Kirsh, N.: Assistive technology for cognitive rehabilitation: state of the art. Neuropsychological Rehabil. **14**(1/2), 5–40 (2004)
12. Wild, M.R., Sohlberg, M.M.: Principles of app selection and training after brain injury. Perspect. Augmentative Altern. Commun. **23**(3), 140–147 (2014)
13. Wild, M.: Assistive technology for cognition following brain injury: guidelines for device and app selection. Perspect. Neurophysiol. Neurogenic Speech Lang. Disord. **23**, 49–58 (2013). SIG 2 Perspectives on Neurophysiology and Neurogenic Speech and Language Disorders
14. Scherer, M., Jutai, J., Fuhrer, M., Demers, L., Deruyter, F.: A framework for modelling the selection of assistive technology devices (ATDs). Disabil. Rehabil. Assistive Technol. **2**(1), 1–8 (2007)
15. Scherer, M.J., Hart, T., Kirsch, N., Schulthesis, M.: Assistive technologies for cognitive disabilities. Crit. Rev. Phys. Rehabil. Med. **17**(3), 195–215 (2005)
16. Malec, J.F., Smigielski, J.S., DePompolo, R.W.: Goal Attainment Scaling and outcome measurement in postacute brain injury rehabilitation. Arch. Phys. Med. Rehabil. **72**, 138–143 (1991)
17. Malec, J.F.: Goal attainment scaling in rehabilitation. Neuropsychological Rehabil. **9**(3/4), 253–275 (1999)
18. Weathers, F.W., Litz, B.T., Keane, T.M., Palmieri, P.A., Marx, B.P., Schnurr, P.P.: The PTSD Checklist for DSM-5 (PCL-5). https://www.ptsd.va.gov/professional/assessment/adult-sr/ptsd-checklist.asp. Accessed 30 Jan 2018
19. Hewitt, P.L., Norton, G.R.: The Beck Anxiety Inventory: a psychometric analysis. Psychol. Assess. **5**(4), 408–412 (1993)
20. Beck, A.T., Ward, C.H., Mendelson, M., Mock, J., Erbaugh, J.: An inventory for measuring depression. Arch. Gen. Psychiatry **4**, 561–571 (1961)
21. Diener, E., Wirtz, D., Tov, W., Kim-Prieto, C., Choi, D., Oishi, S., Biswas-Diener, R.: New measures of well-being: flourishing and positive and negative feelings. Soc. Indic. Res. **39**, 247–266 (2009)
22. Guyatt, G.H., Juniper, E.F., Walter, S.D., Griffith, L.E., Goldstein, R.S.: Interpreting treatment effects in randomised trials. BMJ **316**(7132), 690–693 (1993)

The Health Promoting Potential of Interactive Art

Birgitta Cappelen[1] and Anders-Petter Andersson[2(✉)]

[1] Oslo School of Architecture and Design, Oslo, Norway
birgitta.cappelen@aho.no
[2] Norwegian University of Science and Technology, Gjøvik, Norway
anders.p.andersson@ntnu.no

Abstract. In this paper, we argue for the *value of participatory* and *interactive art*, to *increase the quality* of *health* and *health promoting technology*, for children with special needs. UN states through several conventions that everyone has a *right* to take part in art and cultural experiences, also children and people with disabilities, because art is an important value in our society. With technology, we can make art *accessible* to people with special needs in completely new ways. By building on the *participatory art* tradition, in *combination* with *new technology*, we can develop *new forms of expression* and groundbreaking *experiences*. By incorporating knowledge about *health promotion* and *universal design*, we can create new health promoting technology and *artistic empowering experiences*, by making them more *engaging*, *inspiring* and *participating* for children with special needs. This opportunity has in too little extent, been recognized within Assistive Technology. The paper is based on our research and experience from testing an interactive art installation, with children with special needs at six schools within the Norwegian national school art program.

Keywords: Health promoting technology · Art · Design for diversity

1 Introduction and Framework

Art is a Valuable Right. The UN Declaration of Human Rights (UDHR) states "All human beings have the right to participate in cultural life, enjoy art…", later in the Convention on the Rights of the Child (CRC) including children and persons with special needs in the Convention on the Rights of Persons with Disabilities (CRPD). This shows the importance of art and culture, on an individual and a social level. To meet these UN-demands, several countries, such as Norway, have created cultural programs to offer children art and culture activities at school. As a consequence of the ratification of CRPD in 2013, the Norwegian national art program, the *Cultural Schoolbag* [1], has from 2015 also offered a unique "Accessible Program" for children with disabilities.

The value of art has been formulated in many ways: As a *breathing space* in our society, a *free voice* that *challenges established thinking* and *prejudice* and provide an *alternative understanding* of the world. A source that provides experiences that can be decisive in order to develop the individual's *identity* and *quality of life* [1], a *strong subject* that invites us in and mobilizes our own subjective *will* to *create* and *express* [2], *connects* and challenges our *minds* [3], and helps our *communities* to grow [4].

K. Miesenberger and G. Kouroupetroglou (Eds.): ICCHP 2018, LNCS 10897, pp. 479–483, 2018.
https://doi.org/10.1007/978-3-319-94274-2_70

Health and Health Promotion. WHO states that "Health is a state of complete physical, mental and social well-being and not only the absence of disease or infirmity...". Traditionally within health research, we divide health in two main areas, the *biomedical* and *humanistic* [5]. The biomedical health approach focuses on the patient's diagnoses and disease, where the humanistic on the person's resources, not his weaknesses, and on *strengthening these resources*, i.e. *health promotion* [4, 6].

Designing for Health promotion represents a much more ambitious and complex design challenge than the traditional 7 Principles of Universal Design [7]. Among other things, it represents that design has to offer the user; *many roles to take,* many *positive experiences* to make in every situation, where there are *no wrong* actions or failing possibilities, and *few dependencies* and no closed paths. It has to offer many ways to *express oneself,* act and *build competence* over time. Further, it has to offer many ways to develop and *build relations* to things, people and actions. In other words *many ways* to share, relate, participate and create meaning over time [8].

Participatory and Relational Art is art where the *audience participate* in creating the artwork in various ways, outside traditional art institutions. The artwork becomes a process, a *reflective awareness* act or exercise.

Interactive Art is art where the *audience create* in an intelligent technical *interactive medium*, which can be both digital and physical. It reminds of a computer game, but has an *expressive intent,* instead of a gaming goal as a guiding idea. In doing so, the artist uses *artistic rhetoric*: a strong and *engaging language* and a *seductive tone* of voice to shape a clear character and *consistent, aesthetic qualitative* experience [2].

Art in Therapy.   Art has an important role in therapy forms such as Art Therapy, *Music Therapy* [4] and Psychodrama. Art Therapy has to a very little extent used technology, where Music Therapy traditionally use acoustic music instruments, but also electronic instruments and tailored, *accessible switches* for individual users. The RHYME project, which is the basis for this paper has taken this much further [9, 10].

The State of the Art in this Area.   There are a number of interactive installations, but few have health promoting goals. There are a lot of health technology, but with limited art qualities (see above), such as the therapy seal "Paro" [11]. "Vocal Vibrations" (MIT) is a meditative art installation, which is static and do not adapt to users' ability or musical taste [12]. "Reactable" is a tactile musical social tabletop used to train social abilities of autistic children [13]. It is too complex to use and thereby risks to cause fatigue [14].

2   Methods

4th Generation of PAR.   The ground for this paper is the testing of the interactive installation "Polly World" through the Cultural Schoolbag *Accessible Program* at 6 schools in Norway. Polly World is the *4th generation* of tangible technology developed in the research project RHYME [10], where the goal was to create health promoting musical tangibles for children with severe disabilities, based on *Participatory Action Research* (PAR) and *Research-by Design* methodology [10].

The Polly World installation consists of many parts. The version we tested here have 3 body sized wireless interactive objects with diverse shapes: A soft "ball", a "banana shaped cushion" (Fig. 1-1) and a "hybrid blanket". They have touch, bend (Fig. 1-2), microphone (Fig. 1-3) and RFID-reader (Fig. 1-4) as input sensors and light and sound as output. In addition, there are many RFID-tagged familiar artefacts and music-tunes, that play when the tag is close to the RFID-reader on the interactive object [15]. An interactive dynamic video projection on the whole wall, made the familiar school environment into a wondrous magical world.

Fig. 1. Parts of Polly World: 1. Banana shaped Interactive object, 2. Bend sensor, 3. Microphone, 4. RFID-reader and music-tune RFID-tagged cover (Michael Jackson).

Participatory Observation. We *videotaped* all user sessions when we toured with Polly World as part of the cultural program, in total 6 schools. 78 children with *multi-functional disabilities* (physical, cognitive, social), from the age of 7 to 18 tested the installation. The children tested in diverse *group constellations,* and diverse *object selections,* to change and *improve* the *user experience*, from session to session in an *action-based* manner. We did additional *interviews* with the teachers.

3   Observations and Findings

We observed that children preferred to start by exploring *alone* to get an overview and to know us and the Polly World installation, *before* interacting with *others*. Later, when they could choose freely, they formed groups of 2–3 to co-create together. As the *groups grew* in number, the communication got louder and the children got more passive and *tired*. In the start, they choose a *familiar artefact* (RFID-tag), e.g. a soft toy and a familiar music-tune to play with (Fig. 1-4). The familiar picture of the singer on the *music-tune cover* with a physical RFID-tag, motivated them to change music. Quickly they mastered to *record* their voice, with the lighting microphone (Fig. 1-3), and playback sound through the speakers, by interacting with the *input sensors* (Fig. 1-2). The children showed low interest in interacting with non-familiar artefacts, until they could master the *RFID-reader* and tags. Then they wanted to explore much more.

Children selected familiar music-tunes and was enticed by the seductive process of *repeating* elements and re-playing them. Just as 10 year old John insisted on playing the "Itsy bitsy spider" tune over and over again, while performing rhythmic hand movements to the lyrics where the spider climbs up and the rain falls down. As John laughed and comforted himself with choreographed movements to the rhythm of "Itsy bitsy spider", he *regulated* his *feelings* of stress and comfort through altering the *volume control* (RFID). John also used rhythms in the music and movements in the tune to connect and co-create with other kids, teachers and us. The algorithmic composition rules made the music, video and the whole interactive environment repeat and vary, changing dynamically with the user interaction. The algorithms created a constant push and insisting atmosphere that motivated the children to continue interact. The music and the physical design created a social arena, inviting the children into a new world of experiences. The children experienced being in *control*, when moving the interactive objects without wires. Because the possibilities to *stage*, *include* and *exclude* sensory stimulating objects and experiences, the environment challenged the children's whole register of actions and expressions, based on their sensory profile. It made them take risks they normally did not and provided comfort when needed. The diverse children used many *different ways* to access the sensors. Anna was flipping the motion sensor in the big arm back and forth to change the pitch of her voice recording, while John stepped on the same motion sensor arm to get a short sound feedback on his action. David was lying with his ear on the speaker in the soft interactive object, speaking and singing into the microphone. He collaborated with one of us that played back each of his sayings by interacting with the arm with movement sensor. We observed that input-tag and sensor should have *equal and consistent sensory form* (tactile, sound, visual) to provide users with diverse impairment with consistent interaction form (Fig. 1-4). For instance, Maria that is blind found out how to use her hands to *sense* the triangular *shape* of the RFID-reader and triangular RFDI-tags, which made it possible for her to find and play all sounds, change music-tunes, and thereby master the whole environment, where others related the colour to each other (Fig. 1-4).

4   Conclusion

In this paper, we argue for the *value* of *participatory* and *interactive art*, to increase the *quality of health* and *health promoting technology*, for persons with special needs, based on our comprehensive testing of an interactive installation as part of the national school art program in Norway. Art is not only a UN stated *right*, an environment for ground-breaking experiences, but has also great *health promoting potential* if *shaped* and *staged* in a *suitable way*. Participatory artworks should have a strong *subjective voice*, *consistent aesthetic quality*, *evoke* and *connect* with the audience, *inviting* them into a seductive, mental and physical awareness experience, and *insisting* them to interact and *co-create* along with the artist and the artwork.

We show that participatory art thinking has potential to increase the quality of traditional health technology, for instance by changing the focus from disease, weaknesses and difficulties to an artistic *seductive experience*, built on *artistic rhetoric*; *By creating* interactive installations with a user interface that the children can *manage on their own terms*, regardless of disability, without failing possibilities. *By including familiar elements* the children can *relate* to and use as *guides* into new experiences, first to *master alone* and later *co-create together*, to make the art installation a rich imaginative unique *arena for participation* and new creative mastering experiences.

We observed how the children experienced to engage and *evoke positive* emotions, the *ability to master*, feeling *self-efficacy* and *ability to self-regulate* feelings and their experiences. Further how they *built relations* to each other on equal terms.

The art thinking and its qualities can open up to *innovations* and *collaborations*, within the field of health promoting technology. This requires that the *artists* take the *health promoting-* and *design for diversity-requirements*, into their work. Further, that *technicians* open up to what *qualities art* can offer, to *improve health technology*. Technology that currently has a measurement and tool oriented focus, because of its biomedical roots. We hope this paper is a small contribution to this development.

References

1. Norwegian Min. Culture: Report No. 8 (2007–08), A Cultural Rucksack, pp. 11–12 (2007)
2. Christensen-Scheel, B.: Mobile Homes. Ph.d. thesis. University of Oslo (2009)
3. Sleinis, F.: Art and Freedom. University of Illinois Press, Chapel Hill (2002)
4. Ruud, E.: Music Therapy: A Perspective from the Humanities. Barcelona (2010)
5. Blaxter, M.: Health. Polity (2010)
6. Antonovsky, A.: Unraveling the Mystery of Health. Jossey-Bass, San Francisco (1987)
7. RL Mace Universal Design Inst. http://udinstitute.org/principles.php. Accessed 20 Mar 2018
8. Cappelen, B., Andersson, A.: Towards an empowering tangible interaction design for diversity. In: Proceedings Include conference, Royal College of Art, London, Hong Kong (2013)
9. Stensæth, K.: Musical co-creation? Int. J. Qual. Stud. Health Well-being **8** (2013). https://doi.org/10.3402/qhw.v8i0.20704
10. Research Council of Norway: RHYME. http://www.rhyme.no. Accessed 20 Mar 2018
11. Jøranson, N., et al.: Group activity with Paro in nursing homes. Int. Psychogeriatrics **28**(8), 1345–1354 (2010)
12. Holbrow, C., et al.: Vocal vibrations. In: Proceedings of NIME 2014, pp. 431–434. ACM (2014)
13. Villafuerte, L., et al.: Acquisition of social abilities through musical tangible user interface. In: Proceedings of CHI 2012, pp. 745–760. ACM (2012)
14. Magee, W., et al.: An exploratory study of the use of electronic music technologies in clinical music therapy. Nordic J. Music Ther. **17**(2), 124–141 (2008)
15. Cappelen, B., Andersson, A.: Embodied and distributed parallel DJing. In: Studies in Health Technology and Informatics, vol. 229, pp. 528–539 (2016)

Utilization of Limb Orientations for a Home-Based Immersive Virtual Reality Rehabilitation System to Treat Phantom Limb Pain

Eser Köktürk[1]([⊠]), Franco Molteni[2]([⊠]), Monica Bordegoni[3],
and Mario Covarrubias[3]

[1] Department of Design and Engineering, Politecnico di Milano, Milano, Italy
`eser.kokturk@polimi.it`
[2] Valduce Hospital, Villa Beretta, Rehabilitation Centre, Costa Masnaga, Italy
`fmolteni@valduce.it`
[3] Department of Mechanical Engineering, Politecnico di Milano, Milano, Italy

Abstract. The growing potential of virtual reality (VR) systems presents an immense opportunity for amputee patients who are suffering from the medical condition which causes sensation of pain at the location of the missing limb called Phantom Limb Pain (PLP). The occurrence rate of PLP is reported 60–80% [1] among amputee patients and treatment methods vary between physical therapy, surgery and medication. One of the proven treatment methods is "Mirror Therapy" [3] and it is applied by visually projecting a healthy limb on the amputated part with the help of a mirror to create the perception of presence. Similar approach can also be represented in a virtual environment and immersion of VR can enhance the rehabilitation experience. Therefore, we aimed to improve the mirror therapy treatment by a VR application and to overcome the physical limitations by presenting potentially engaging activities with a way to treat double-limb amputees.

Keywords: Phantom Limb Pain · Mirror therapy · Tele-rehabilitation

1 Introduction

A simple home-based approach for the system was desired to involve the rehabilitation process in the daily routine of the patient to improve the treatment outcome while presenting a cost-efficient solution to PLP. Besides Oculus Rift head mounted display (HMD) which was initially included in our design, we also provided an option for smartphone-based VR display to take advantage of smartphone trend. In this paper, we analyzed the potential of VR rehabilitation to treat PLP by introducing a fully-immersive VR rehabilitation system controlled by an input device through a software designed in Unity. Additionally, we conducted a case study research among healthy subjects to present effects of visual

© Springer International Publishing AG, part of Springer Nature 2018
K. Miesenberger and G. Kouroupetroglou (Eds.): ICCHP 2018, LNCS 10897, pp. 484–488, 2018.
https://doi.org/10.1007/978-3-319-94274-2_71

perception and degree in involvement during VR rehabilitation. The initial concept was to design a practical approach for a home-based VR rehabilitation that is robust, interactive and practicle to use. Patients had to be engaged with the treatment activities rather than getting intimidated or demotivated. Therefore, we created a software application called LIMBrehabVR (Fig. 1) in Unity game engine for Windows OS to acts as a user interface for rehabilitation practices.

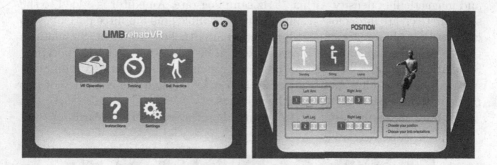

Fig. 1. LIMBrehabVR software user interface.

Both input device and HMD were to be connected to and operated through the software. Presenting patients with options was also a key factor to involve them to select their own exercises and virtual assets that are included in the software. Choice of gender, clothing, skin color and surrounding environment was provided for the user to increase immersion and personalization during the exercise. Additionally, LIMBrehabVR contains user-defined key and speech commands that can help patients to navigate the software easily during the exercises. It was important to include a speech recognition system for the upper limb amputees who might not desire to use key commands during operation.

2   Architecture

Oculus Rift VR headset is set as the default HMD but an option for smartphones is included with the inclusion of TrinusVR application which transmits stereoscopic projection of the virtual scene from the PC to the mobile device. Both wired and wireless communication can be achieved through TrinusVR although it requires a high-speed internet connection to decrease latency for wireless operation. Patients can use their own phones for the rehabilitation activities and they are not obligated to have an additional VR display. Only main downside of smartphone VR projection is the low-resolution problem compared to Oculus. Which can also be overcame with software application directly operated from a smartphone. For a cost-efficient input device which can provide accurate and low disturbance representation of the limb motion, we decided to use orientation tracking with an inertial measurement unit (IMU). Since limb motions are rotations with respect to the human body frame, representation of the limb in VR environment can be achieved by real world orientations. 9-axis MPU-9255 IMU is decided to be used for the system among several sensors in terms of size and cost. IMU is connected to Arduino Nano microprocessor through I2C protocol to extract the sensory information from accelerometer, gyroscope and magnetometer. Three degrees of freedom orientation estimation is computed by Madgwick [2] quaternion sensor fusion filter from angular velocity, acceleration and magnetic flux density with a 75 Hz sampling rate. An editor is added to the software to create limb motion simulations for double limb amputee patients who can passively observe the pre-set limb action in virtual environment. Simulations can be saved as files and up to seven files can be submitted to a VR operation. Simulations can also be used as practice exercises for patients to mimic the motion presented on a model in front of them. We tested the efficiency of this method in our case study on healthy subjects.

Figure 2 shows the input device mounted on the left user's forearm.

Fig. 2. Oculus Rift VR operation with the device attached to the left forearm.

3   Results

Final VR rehabilitation setup was tested to analyze the limitations of the system and how it can be improved. A case study is conducted between 5 healthy subjects aged between 24 and 40 who were required to complete a survey regarding their experience with the system. Survey questions were based on 1–6 (1-totally disagree to 6-totally agree) Likert Scale and divided into four sections (3 for testing, 1 for software). After each test, subjects were required to answer the survey questions. First test was with active limb control using the input device on Oculus Rift HMD, second with the passive motion of a pre-set limb simulation on Oculus Rift and the final test was done with limb simulation on a smartphone display. Tests were mainly designed to compare HMD to smartphone projection and active limb control to limb simulation.

Figure 3 shows the survey results of the case study.

Results of the survey showed that healthy subjects were more pleased with the input device control than with the simulation and they mostly agreed upon it's potential in rehabilitation. They were nearly natural on the experience of mimicking a simulation. Oculus Rift tests were relatively more comfortable for

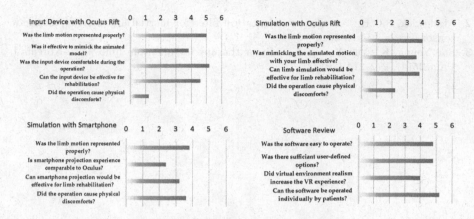

Fig. 3. Survey results of the case study.

the subjects than the smartphone projection test which was initially expected due to low-resolution limitations. Software solution is very well received by the subjects and approved viable for rehabilitation.

4   Conclusion

A method for low-cost rehabilitation application was implemented successfully for PLP patients to be used in their home and in medical facilities. Options for different exercises and games were added to provide a variety of interactions and activities for the patients. More detailed analysis of the system can be done through tests on PLP patients with a controlled case study including more subjects. In addition, a better rehabilitation experience can be achieved by converting our software to a mobile version to overcome the resolution limitations of projecting scene from a PC. Smartphone solution tends to be a viable option to lower the cost of the VR rehabilitation. Potential of our proposal can be very beneficial for regular rehabilitation practices to improve life quality of patients affected by PLP and other medical conditions. A widely applied home-based rehabilitation is an essential solution to treat numerous patients who cannot benefit from medical facility resources due to their condition, location and other various reasons. Overcoming these limitations can be achieved through low-cost applications with a VR system. Therefore, our system can be an efficient way to utilize global usage of VR technology and provide a general treatment method similar to the mirror therapy.

References

1. Nikolajsen, L., Jensen, T.S.: Phantom limb pain. BJA Br. J. Anaesth. **87**(1), 107–116 (2001)

2. Madgwick, S.O.H.: An efficient orientation filter for inertial and inertial/magnetic sensor arrays, March 2018
3. Sae Young, K., Yun Young, K.: Mirror therapy for phantom limb pain. Korean J. Pain **25**(4), 272–274 (2012)

Videobooking: A Person-Centred Record of Living with Chronic Conditions and Associated Disabilities

Deborah I. Fels[1]([✉]), S. Fatima Lakha[1], Carly B. Holtzman[1,2], Alamgir Khandwala[2], Margot Whitfield[1], West Suhanic[3], and Peter Pennefather[1,3]

[1] Ryerson University, 350 Victoria St., Toronto, Canada
dfels@ryerson.ca
[2] York University, Toronto, Canada
[3] gDial Inc., Toronto, Canada

Abstract. People with complex chronic conditions must learn to live with the disabilities and challenges that come with those conditions on a continuous basis. MyHealthMyRecord (MHMR) was designed to allow people to record video vignettes of enabling and/or disabling situations, opinions, musings, and other thoughts regarding their attempts to cope with, manage or work around those situations. One person living with a sudden onset chronic condition used MHMR to document their journey. Main findings were that vignettes were short duration, less than 1 min, and covered a range of topics regarding pain, accessibility and barriers, emotional reactions, systemic issues and recommendations, and MHMR improvements.

Keywords: Video scrapbook · Person-centred qualitative narratives

1 Introduction

People with complex chronic conditions experience everyday but dynamic challenges. These are met through active participation in medical/clinical interventions, informal/ formal cultural practices, and personal choices. Care for chronic conditions is much less dependent on direct cures than for acute diseases. Rather, it involves actively involving people in negotiating episodic and debilitating disabilities [1]. Personal engagement, ownership, and meaningful use of health data have been discussed as an opportunity for achieving person-centred care [2]. It is critical, therefore, that broader acceptability, accessibility, and adaptability of those informatic resources be considered.

Digital scrapbooking uses electronic input to allow users to selectively capture moments in time to remember them later using various media but often images and text are dominant [3]. It is intended to be spontaneous, fun and personalized. It may also offer a more accessible and inclusive method for capturing person-centred data because of its flexibility, lack of an imposed structure and use of multi-media formats. These alternative formats allow users of all ages and abilities to represent situations and experiences, and then communicate using a variety of media as desired [4].

Together with gDial Inc., we have begun to develop a system, called MyHealth-MyRecord(MHMR), that involves short duration, qualitative patient narratives that

© Springer International Publishing AG, part of Springer Nature 2018
K. Miesenberger and G. Kouroupetroglou (Eds.): ICCHP 2018, LNCS 10897, pp. 489–492, 2018.
https://doi.org/10.1007/978-3-319-94274-2_72

could be combined as non-linear collections of concerns, issues, successes and failures. In this paper, we report on a first prototype of MHMR as well as an initial set of data and participant experiences with the prototype. The question we answer in this paper is what types of issues arise from a person with a chronic condition using MHMR?

2   System Description

The MHMR system is designed to enable multimedia expressions of experiences living with a chronic condition. It consists of a tablet-based video application that accepts short duration audio/video user input and a server system for secure transfer, processing and storage of video records. The system was designed to be inclusive of users with different needs (e.g., sign language users) by allowing them to record audio and/or video on various topic at their leisure using a touch screen interface. The main goal of MHMR is to provide users with a safe way to record not only their physical state, but also their emotional state, without sacrificing their independence or privacy. Although data indexing and encryption strategies are not a focus of this paper, the need for privacy influenced our design.

One potential use of the recorded data could be to organize video records along a linear timeline or by other structures such as theme, and then curate who can access various videos or organizing structures. For example, medical personnel could access a set of clips related to pain experiences while a school accessibility specialist could access clips related to difficulties accessing school resources. As such, it can function as a digital video scrapbook which documents and bundles a person's experiences.

3   Case Study

One participant who had experienced a sudden onset chronic illness, PX, was asked to use the MHMR application over a three-month period to assist in developing the system interface and determining the usefulness of it. PX began using the system during a 3-week business/pleasure excursion recording 18 videos with an average duration of 1 min (range from 31 to 70 s). Once returned, PX used the system at school for 11 weeks recording 29 videos with an average length of 40 s (from 17 to 148 s).

In 2015 PX experienced the sudden onset of an arthritis-like inflammatory condition with mysterious origins. This resulted in multiple motoric disabilities including limited use of his/her legs and hands. After a 3-month hospitalization that was unsuccessful in diagnosing a cause and providing a treatment strategy, s/he was discharged home to other formal caregivers (physiologists, rheumatologists, etc.) and PX's family to find ways to cope with this new situation. PX was asked to record as many videos as desired on a tablet version of MHMR documenting physical pain, experiences, difficulties or successes in daily activities, overall frustrations or other events that required attention. The videos were open coded for relevant and recurring themes. Consensus between two researchers and PX was used to assign video content to the various themes.

3.1   Results and Discussion

From the video content, three main themes are identified. A majority of comments fall under the theme *System-Facing* defined as descriptions or comments about physical, communication and attitudinal barriers experienced in various settings. Comments about physical barriers included permanent/temporary structural environmental obstacles. For example, PX describes physical barriers as "potholes", "hills", "curvy roads", or stepped entry ways. Maneuvering these barriers often required inventive solutions such having the wheelchair tied to the back of a rickshaw.

Communication barriers included comments on institutional practices and policies related to emergencies, infrastructure repair, education delivery, and accommodation response time not communicated to individuals. For example, PX's professor did not provide timely notes for a lecture s/he missed "I told the professor, he didn't have any slides for the class. He tried to gather some notes but by the time he gave me the notes it was the day the assignment was due. I should have been accommodated."

Attitude comments included ingrained and/or inaccurate beliefs or perceptions about PX's ability or goals. For example, s/he recounts a teacher unwilling to speak louder even though PX was unable to move to the front of the class. S/he recounts the teacher's response and then his/her reaction: "I tend to tell students to come up to the front if they didn't hear me. I didn't even see the wheelchair to remind me… [in class] we were talking about discrimination. S/he sort of did that. It was a genuine mistake."

Person-Facing is the second main theme and is defined as physical and mental pain experiences related to the individual. Comments relating to PX's physical pain, included intensity, duration, changes and location of pain. For example, PX describes the physical pain during a conference: "I just couldn't take it going the whole day. It's very painful." Comments relating to PX's mental pain included unpleasant feelings and emotions such as stress, pressure, frustration, annoyance and boredom and often coincided with physical barriers. For example, "In the evening I didn't really do much just bored in the room … because obviously if I have to go out, I'm relying on others." PX also commented that a mobile app would have been preferred as it was difficult to store and manage a tablet and a wheelchair simultaneously.

The next theme was the *Accessibility-Experiences* theme, defined as comments and emotions related to accessibility, actions taken by others to make something accessible or systems designed to be accessible. Examples of comments relating to Accessibility Experiences included PX's experience of an accessible train platform ramp communication system: "As soon as I arrive at the station the doors would open, there's a person standing there with a ramp just waiting to connect the platform with the trains. It was mind blowing." In contrast to positive and manageable traveling occasions, PX also strongly criticised accessibility to many hotels, restaurants, public spaces and touristic destinations in several developed and developing nations s/he visited. "The city and neighbourhood were not accessible with the wheelchair and there was false information for getting around the city."

During the video creation process, PX discovered some best practices: "It is imperative for users to make a video immediately after a significant event takes place to express their thoughts while simultaneously capturing the emotions in their purest form."

Initially, the system was designed to be used as an inclusive, personal journal for managing chronic health issues. As our research progressed, the use of the system shifted from a video journal to a video scrapbook. The MHMR interface seemed to support PX's needs for recording a variety of topics including barriers encountered, expressing frustration, deliberating issues, describing pain, and conveying excitement.

Although a video duration cutoff was not imposed, it would seem that short duration videos were preferred. Limiting videos to less than one minute would be a viable interface option for the system. Another interface issue is allowing the retaking or deleting of a video. PX suggested that a single take provides more authentic commentary. However, it may be difficult for others to communicate everything the first time through. There may be a trade-off between the perception of authenticity and the clarity that comes with practice. Further research about limiting or saving the number of takes, and the impact on authenticity and effort is required.

The video and networked nature of the system caused unanticipated issues for PX's family. For example, PX's parents were concerned about the security of the videos. This then stimulated algorithmic and policy attempts to mediate these concerns.

3.2 Future Work

Up to this point, the system has only been used by PX and videos shared with family members. Other members of the circle of care including physicians, therapists, and accessibility staff at school have not been involved. One issue is how to organize the large quantity of information into digestible and informative reports. However, we must determine what type of information the various stakeholders want and can use.

Acknowledgements. Funding was generously provided by the Canadian Institute for Health Research. We thank PX for participating and persisting with this project.

References

1. Richards, N.C., Gouda, H.N., Durham, J., Rampatige, R., Rodney, A., Whittaker, M.: Disability, noncommunicable diseases and health information. Bull. World Health Organ. **94**, 230–232 (2016)
2. Butler, D.S., Moseley, G.L.: Explain Pain, 2nd edn. Noigroup Publications (2013)
3. Nerius, M.G.: Digital Scrapbooking: Using Your Computer to Create Exciting Scrapbook Pages. Lark Books (2004)
4. Crafty Bricolage: Pinterest as Digital Scrapbooking by Maura D'Amore. https://nanocrit.com/issues/issue10/crafty-bricolage-pinterest-digital-scrapbooking. Accessed 31 Jan 2018

Development and Testing of EyeRemember: A Memory Aid App for Wearables for People with Brain Injury

Tracey Wallace(✉) ⓘD and John T. Morris ⓘD

Shepherd Center, Atlanta, GA 30309, USA
{tracey.wallace,john.morris}@shepherd.org

Abstract. EyeRemember is a mobile app designed to run on wearable electronic devices and serve as an external memory aid for people with brain injury (BI). EyeRemember allows users to voice-record information about family, friends and caregivers (referred to as 'contacts' in the app). The technology detects the presence of Bluetooth low energy (BLE) beacons carried by the user's contacts and reminds users of the recorded information when contacts are present. EyeRemember was first developed for Google Glass and later for Android Wear smartwatches. Both versions were developed in accordance with user-centered design principles, by including end-users and identifying their needs, wants and limitations throughout the design process. This paper describes the features and functionality of EyeRemember, its interaction with BLE beacons and the implementation of the user-centered design process used to collect ongoing feedback from people with brain injury, their caregivers and clinicians at Shepherd Center, a rehabilitation hospital in Atlanta, Georgia, USA. The research design and results of clinical testing are also described. Results indicate EyeRemember is a clinically effective tool for memory compensation for some people with BI and suggests combining wearable computers with BLE beacons may be effective assistive technology. These results support previous research summarized in systematic guidelines recommending the use of external memory aids for memory compensation after BI and indicate it is likely these guidelines are applicable to novel and emerging technologies. The results also further validate previous research demonstrating systematic instruction as an effective method for training the use of technology for people with memory problems.

Keywords: Assistive technology · Brain injury · Memory

1 Introduction

Memory problems are a common sequela of brain injury (BI) and can affect a person's ability to store information and recall it when it is needed [1, 2]. Difficulty recalling factual information and past experiences or remembering to perform future tasks can negatively impact a person's well-being and participation in life as well as add stress and burden on their caregivers [1, 3–7].

© Springer International Publishing AG, part of Springer Nature 2018
K. Miesenberger and G. Kouroupetroglou (Eds.): ICCHP 2018, LNCS 10897, pp. 493–500, 2018.
https://doi.org/10.1007/978-3-319-94274-2_73

Cognitive rehabilitation literature supports the use of external aids for treatment of memory impairments following brain injury. Several systematic reviews have generated guidelines for treating people with memory impairments after traumatic brain injury (TBI), each of which recommend the use of external aids [8–12]. Most recently, INCOG, an international team of TBI rehabilitation experts, developed recommendations for best practice in the management of impairments in memory following TBI. Based on based on INCOG's review of the evidence, the use of "environmental support and reminders are recommended for TBI patients who have memory impairment, and most especially for those who have severe memory impairments" [11].

A wide range of forms of external aids have been cited in the literature. Successful low-tech options described include memory notebooks, whiteboards and pill boxes while high tech options include smartphones, computers and voice recorders [9, 13]. Downloadable applications, or 'apps' can be used to further enhance and customize the functionality of some high-tech devices. Now a new breed of electronic devices known as wearables is emerging, offering additional options for external support to people with memory impairment. Wearables include body borne computer technology, such as computer glasses, fitness trackers and smart watches. These mainstream portable electronics are becoming commonplace and may offer advantages for some users over both low tech and other high-tech options. Yet while wearable technology often contains native functions to enhance memory (e.g., note-taking, alarms or reminder functions) no downloadable apps for wearables have previously been developed and researched specifically for people with memory impairment following BI.

2   EyeRemember: An External Memory Aid Solution

EyeRemember is an app designed to run on wearables and serve as an external memory aid for people recovering from and living with BI [14]. EyeRemember allows the user to voice record important information related to individuals in their circle of family, friends and caregivers (referred to as 'contacts' in the app) and then be reminded of the information when they are with those individuals. The technology works by detecting the presence of Bluetooth low energy (BLE) beacons carried by the user's contacts. Users are reminded of the recorded information through cued prompts presented when contacts are present and by scrolling through screens containing the information along with a photo of the contact. EyeRemember can be used in several contexts:

(1) Recall of the name, relationship or other information about a contact (e.g. remind the user that their neighbor's name is Sally and her dog's name is Pete).
(2) Recall of information to share with a contact (e.g. a reminder to tell a spouse that a new medication was prescribed during a medical appointment).
(3) Recall of information previously shared by a contact in order to support social communicative interactions (e.g. a reminder that a friend told the user she got engaged).

User-defined settings in the app include:

- Scan Time – adjusts the duration of scanning for contacts before resting; works with Sleep Time Between Scans setting to ensure detection of paired BLE beacons is successful in the user's local environment (home, clinic, etc.), while simultaneously conserving battery
- Sleep Time Between Scans – adjusts the length of time the app rests between scanning for contacts; works with Scan Time
- Contact Distance – adjusts the distance a contact must be from the app user in order to trigger a notification of a contact's presence; works with Notification Away Time to optimize the app for the user's particular memory deficit and local environment
- Notification Away Time – adjusts the time between notifications of a contact's presence; works with Contact Distance
- Off/on toggle for adding notes for contacts – controls the ability to add notes

EyeRemember was first developed and tested on Google Glass (aka "Glass"), and subsequently for Android Wear devices. Both versions were developed in accordance with user-centered design principles, by including end-users and considering their needs, wants and limitations at every step possible during the design process. While the Glass and Android Wear versions are similar, the main contrast between the two versions is the method in which information is delivered through the technology. In the Glass version, when a user comes within the specified distance of a contact, an auditory tone cues them to look up at the Glass screen and receive the information. In the Android Wear version, a unique tactile vibration cues them to look at the Android Wear screen to receive the information. Development and testing of the Glass version is complete and has directly informed the design of the Android Wear version, which is currently in beta testing.

3   Design and Development Methodology

Initial design concept of the Glass version was led by a clinician with expertise in BI cognitive rehabilitation and was influenced by the clinically relevant experience of team members, the existing evidence base on the use of high-tech assistive devices and apps used to support memory, and the features and functionality of Glass. A working prototype of the Glass version was developed prior to engaging other end users, as the novelty of Glass made it necessary to build first in order to be able to demonstrate how a Glass-based memory aid would function.

The prototype was demonstrated to four Speech-Language Pathologists (SLPs) and four Occupational Therapists (OTs) with expertise in BI rehabilitation. The clinicians provided feedback which further informed the development of the app as well as highlighted barriers to patient use and design considerations for clinical testing. Next three sit-by demonstrations and interviews were conducted with patients with BI and their caregivers. Participants included a 21-year-old female and her mom as caregiver, a 34-year-old male and his fiancée as caregiver, and a 62-year-old male with his wife as caregiver. Glass and EyeRemember were demonstrated and all participants spent time wearing the device and testing the app. Feedback gathered led to additional refinements of the app. Clinician feedback was then gathered again in a large focus group including four SLPs, five OTs, five physical therapists (PTs) and two recreational therapists (RTs). Again, feedback on the design and testing considerations was gathered. Of note, the clinicians strongly recommended first testing in a controlled environment, such as an outpatient therapy clinic, before considering take-home-use. They also recommended testing the most basic features of the design first.

4   Clinical Testing Research Design

Clinical testing of the Glass version of EyeRemember was completed using a baseline and repeated measures design which used a combination of quantitative and qualitative measures. A pilot study format was selected due to the need to investigate the methods and procedures used on a small scale because of the novelty of technology. Adhering to the guidance from clinician target users, the study examined the usability and clinical efficacy of EyeRemember for recall of the name, relationship and other basic functional information about a user's contacts (but not for use of the note-taking feature) and was tested within a controlled clinic environment. Pre- and post-testing evaluated each participant's use of the technology to effectively recall targeted information at targeted times. Additionally, gains participants made in recalling the targeted information without use of the technology were measured. Feedback about each participant's experience was also gathered at study completion for qualitative review.

Six individuals, five males and one female, ranging from 18 to 54 years of age, with memory problems following brain injury participated in the study. Participants were recruited from the outpatient day program at Shepherd Pathways, Shepherd Center's post-acute community-based brain injury rehabilitation SLP. The referring SLPs identified participants who met the inclusion criteria and then collaborated with each participant's treating OT by using feature matching, a clinical practice used to guide selection of assistive technology for cognition (ATC), to determine whether the participants' goals, needs, interest in technology and functional abilities were matched to the technology being studied [13, 15–18].

The treating SLP obtained input from the participant and provided recommendations regarding the type and amount of information targeted to be remembered resulting in collaboratively established participant goals for using the technology. The EyeRemember app on Glass, was programmed to recognize beacons worn by the primary therapists (worn on the ring attached to their employee badge) on the participant's rehabilitation team and provide the associated targeted information when the beacons were detected. All participants established goals related to remembering information about their SLP, OT, PT, RT and counselor, with exception of one client who was not receiving counseling and therefore did not have a goal to remember information about a counselor. Five of the participants targeted recall of their therapists' names, the type of therapy provided by each therapist and the location within the clinic they received the therapy, while one client only targeted recall of his therapists' names and the type of therapy provided by each.

Goal Attainment Scaling (GAS), a well-established tool in cognitive rehabilitation for measuring improvement on relevant functional tasks, was used to collaboratively establish a scale for measuring the participant's successful use of the technology to recall the targeted information [19, 20]. Each participant was also shown pictures of their therapists and was asked to recall the targeted information in order to establish a baseline of recognition and recall of the targeted information without use of the device. GAS ratings measuring functional use of the technology and performance on picture identification of therapists were then collected again at study completion. A questionnaire was also completed by each participant at study completion to gather qualitative feedback about their experience.

Trainings for use of EyeRemember following the initial session were provided by the participant's SLP using systematic instruction and occurred during 45-min Speech Therapy (ST) sessions each participant was scheduled for as part of their participation in the day program. During in-session trainings, the screencast feature of Glass was used to display the Glass screen on a tablet to allow both the participant and SLP to view the information contained on the Glass display at all times, no matter who was wearing the device. Participants wore the Glass throughout the duration of the treatment day within the clinic (approximately six hours, five days per week), permitting additional opportunities for practice and supporting generalization by allowing practice to occur in multiple environments with a variety of people [10, 13, 21]. Other rehabilitation team members, those wearing beacons and programmed as contacts on Glass, were trained by the SLP to support this practice by saying, 'Hi. You've been working on remembering my name. What is my name?' whenever they were approached by a participant in the clinic.

Study duration for each participant was variable, ranging from two weeks to four weeks. Five of the six participants completed the study in less than four weeks based on the SLPs judgment that the participant mastered the technology training. Participants spent an average of 21.3 days (3 weeks) in the study and received a range of 6–12 individual ST sessions (averaging 7.5 individual sessions) prior to sessions measuring end of study results. Measurements taken at study completion occurred over the course of two successive sessions on separate days.

5   Results

All six participants demonstrated the ability to use EyeRemember on Glass to aid recall of the targeted information about their therapists with 100% accuracy across a total of six trials, measured on two separate days. Five of the six participants performed at 'Much More Than Expected' while one participant performed at 'More Than Expected' when their performance was compared against their GAS goals. Five of the six participants also demonstrated marked gains in recall of the targeted information without using the technology when they were shown pictures of their therapists at study completion while one participant showed no change. Prior to the intervention, the participants averaged 29% accuracy for unaided recall of the targeted information when shown the pictures of their therapists. After the intervention, the participants averaged 74% accuracy unaided by the technology. Qualitative interviews completed with both patient participants and the SLPs who trained the participants indicated most felt the app was useful and easy to learn. All patient participants indicated they felt the app helped them and were comfortable wearing the technology all day.

Feedback on user experiences gathered throughout development and testing identified benefits and limitations to the use of Glass as assistive technology for people with memory problems after brain injury. The wearable format of Glass allows it to be quickly accessed when needed and allows the user to stay "in the moment" during use. The ability to provide automated contextual cueing when paired with BLE beacons extends the functionality of the device as a memory aid. The screencast feature is particularly useful for training use of the technology as it allows a trainer to view a live display of the Glass screen the trainee sees. The use of swipe and tap gestures to access functions may make it easy for experienced smartphone users to learn to operate it. However, some users with memory impairments that affect learning could experience a steep learning curve. Glass is designed so the display screen is viewed with the right eye and the control pad is operated with the right hand which may impact accessibility for users without functional right sided vision and upper extremity use. Heavy use of the device may result in inadequate battery life and cause the battery to become warm. Because Google Glass is no longer available for consumer purchase, the option to use the technology is limited to the initial "explorers" of the device or those who purchase it secondhand. Regardless, as computer wearables continue to be developed and released into the marketplace, the value of these initial data findings on app interfaces for wearable displays may increase.

6   Scientific and Practical Impact and Contributions to the Field

The results of this study suggest EyeRemember is a clinically effective means of memory compensation for some people with BI. It also suggests wearable computers, such as Google Glass, as well as BLE beacons may be effective ATC options for people recovering from and living with BI. As such, these results support previous research summarized in systematic guidelines recommending the use of external memory aids for memory compensation after BI and indicate it is likely these guidelines are applicable to novel and emerging technology. The results also further validate previous research demonstrating systematic instruction as an effective method for training the use of technology for people with memory problems. The qualitative measures used in this study indicate the technology may be well received and useful for this population.

The small sample size, although common in investigational pilot studies, limits the extent to which the results can be generalized and limits the weight of the study conclusions. A larger participant number could increase the power of the study and lead to additional conclusions about performance variances relative to etiology or other participant characteristics. The power of the study conclusions was also limited by the study design. A randomized controlled trial would have strengthened conclusions and may have clarified which factors had the greatest contribution. While most participants demonstrated improvement in their ability to recall the targeted information even without the aid of the technology, it is not clear whether their ability to recall the information occurred due to the high rate of 'correct' practice provided while using the technology or whether natural recovery or other therapy interventions they received during day program treatments contributed to this gain. While the training techniques used were successful, it was not possible to determine whether all or only some of the components of systematic instructions contributed to the success. Further, it is not known whether the learning was maintained over time.

7   Conclusion and Planned Activities

While all participants reported the intervention was helpful, how it was helpful was not elaborated upon. Information about the secondary impact of improvements in participants' memory and/or increased independence with memory functions, such as those examined through measures of mood and quality of life, could be of value both clinically and from a service reimbursement standpoint. Also, measuring the impact of these changes on participants' caregivers could also reveal important information. Clinical testing of the Android Wear version (following completion of beta testing), as well as testing additional features of EyeRemember and testing them within a user's home or community would help to more fully evaluate its potential as an external memory aid. Additional ways wearables and BLE beacons can assist people with cognitive limitations following BI should be explored.

References

1. Mateer, C., Sohlberg, M., Crinean, J.: Focus on clinical research: perceptions of memory function in individuals with closed-head injury. J. Head Trauma Rehabil. **2**, 74–84 (1987). https://doi.org/10.1097/00001199-198709000-00009
2. Fish, J., Wilson, B., Manly, T.: The assessment and rehabilitation of prospective memory problems in people with neurological disorders: a review. Neuropsychol. Rehabil. **20**, 161–179 (2010). https://doi.org/10.1080/09602010903126029
3. Kreutzer, J., Rapport, L., Marwitz, J., Harrison-Felix, C., Hart, T., Glenn, M., Hammond, F.: Caregivers' well-being after traumatic brain injury: a multicenter prospective investigation. Arch. Phys. Med. Rehabil. **90**, 939–946 (2009). https://doi.org/10.1016/j.apmr.2009.01.010
4. Ponsford, J.: Dealing with the impact of TBI on psychological adjustment and relationships. In: Ponsford, J., Sloan, S., Snow, P. (eds.) Traumatic Brain Injury: Rehabilitation for Everyday Adaptive Living, pp. 226–263. Lawrence Erlbaum Associates, East Sussex (1995)
5. Bradley, V., Kapur, N.: Neuropsychological assessment of memory disorders. In: Gurd, J., Kischka, U., Marshall, J. (eds.) Handbook of Clinical Neuropsychology, pp. 147–166. Oxford University Press, New York (2004)
6. Kreutzer, J., Marwitz, J., Walker, W., Sander, A., Sherer, M., Bogner, J., Fraser, R., Bushnik, T.: Moderating factors in return to work and job stability after traumatic brain injury. J. Head Trauma Rehabil. **18**, 128–138 (2003). https://doi.org/10.1097/00001199-200303000-00004
7. Baddeley, A., Harris, S.: Closed head injury and memory. In: Levin, H.S., Grafman, J., Eisenberg, H.M. (eds.) Neurobehavioral Recovery from Head Injury, pp. 295–315. Oxford University Press, New York (1987)
8. Haskins, E.C., et al.: Cognitive Rehabilitation Manual: Translating Evidence-Based Recommendations into Practice. Beta Edition, pp. 41–68. ACRM Publishing, Reston (2011)

9. O'Neil-Pirozzi, T., Kennedy, M., Sohlberg, M.: Evidence-based practice for the use of internal strategies as a memory compensation technique after brain injury. J. Head Trauma Rehabil. **31**, E1–E11 (2016). https://doi.org/10.1097/htr.0000000000000181

10. Cicerone, K., Langenbahn, D., Braden, C., Malec, J., Kalmar, K., Fraas, M., Felicetti, T., Laatsch, L., Harley, J., Bergquist, T., Azulay, J., Cantor, J., Ashman, T.: Evidence-based cognitive rehabilitation: updated review of the literature from 2003 through 2008. Arch. Phys. Med. Rehabil. **92**, 519–530 (2011). https://doi.org/10.1016/j.apmr.2010.11.015

11. Velikonja, D., Tate, R., Ponsford, J., McIntyre, A., Janzen, S., Bayley, M.: INCOG recommendations for management of cognition following traumatic brain injury, Part V. J. Head Trauma Rehabil. **29**, 369–386 (2014). https://doi.org/10.1097/htr.0000000000000069

12. Cappa, S., Benke, T., Clarke, S., Rossi, B., Stemmer, B., Heugten, C.: EFNS guidelines on cognitive rehabilitation: report of an EFNS task force. Eur. J. Neurol. **12**, 665–680 (2005). https://doi.org/10.1111/j.1468-1331.2005.01330.x

13. LoPresti, E.N., Mihailidis, A., Kirsh, N.: Assistive technology for cognitive rehabilitation: state of the art. Neuropsychol. Rehabil. **14**(1/2), 5–40 (2004)

14. Wallace, T., Morris, J., Bradshaw, S.: EyeRemember: memory aid app for Google Glass. J. Technol. Persons Disabil. **3**, 116–129 (2015)

15. Wild, M.: Principles of app selection and training after brain injury. Perspect. Augmentative Altern. Commun. **23**, 140 (2014). https://doi.org/10.1044/aac23.3.140

16. Wild, M.: Assistive technology for cognition following brain injury: guidelines for device and app selection. Perspect. Neurophysiol. Neurogenic Speech Lang. Disord. **23**, 49–58 (2013)

17. Scherer, M., Jutai, J., Fuhrer, M., Demers, L., Deruyter, F.: A framework for modelling the selection of assistive technology devices (ATDs). Disabil. Rehabil. Assist. Technol. **2**, 1–8 (2007). https://doi.org/10.1080/17483100600845414

18. Scherer, M., Hart, T., Kirsch, N., Scherer, M., Schulthesis, M.: Assistive technologies for cognitive disabilities. Crit. Rev. Phys. Rehabil. Med. **17**, 195–215 (2005). https://doi.org/10.1615/critrevphysrehabilmed.v17.i3.30

19. Malec, J.F., Smigielski, J.S., DePompolo, R.W.: Goal attainment scaling and outcome measurement in postacute brain injury rehabilitation. Arch. Phys. Med. Rehabil. **72**, 138–143 (1991)

20. Malec, J.: Goal attainment scaling in rehabilitation. Neuropsychol. Rehabil. **9**, 253–275 (1999). https://doi.org/10.1080/096020199389365

21. Parente, R., Twum, M., Zoltan, B.: Transfer and generalization of cognitive skills after traumatic brain injury. Neurorehabilitation **4**(1), 25–35 (1994)

Development of an ICT-Based Dementia Care Mapping (DCM) Support System

Hirotoshi Yamamoto[✉] and Yasuyoshi Yokokohji

Department of Mechanical Engineering, Graduate School of Engineering,
Kobe University, 1-1 Rokkodai-cho, Nada-ku, Kobe 657-8501, Japan
yamamoto.hirotoshi.38v@kyoto-u.jp

Abstract. Dementia Care Mapping (DCM) is an observational evidence-based method for evaluating the quality of dementia care, and is widely used to implement Person-centred Care in dementia care settings. However, it is not easy to practice DCM because the method sets high requirements on the observer (mapper) to ensure it, causing difficulties and/or a burden during mapping.

Authors have developed a new ICT-based DCM support system to solve this issue. We also developed a new evaluation test method using role-play videos, and assessed the reliability and usefulness of the system. The results revealed that (1) the prototype support system has already reached the level of conventional DCM in terms of mapping accuracy, (2) mappers highly appreciated the system for burden reduction and easier operation during mapping, and (3) new functionality of the system looked promising to increase mapping accuracy.

Keywords: Dementia Care Mapping · Person-centered care
ICT-based support system · Evaluation test method using videos
Reliability and usefulness

1 Introduction

Among several methods attempting to look at quality of life of older people with dementia [1, 2], Dementia Care Mapping (DCM) is widely used [3, 4] to implement Person-centred Care [5] in dementia care facilities. DCM promotes an understanding of care practice from the viewpoint and personal experience of the person with dementia [6]. In brief, an observer (mapper) observes five people with dementia (participants) continuously over a representative time period (e.g., 6 h during the waking day) in communal areas of care facilities. The mapper records, after each 5-min period (time-frame), detailed ratings of the participants' well/ill-being and activities they are engaged in, by using two types of codes: the *Behaviour Category Code* (BCC) and the *Mood and Engagement value* (ME value). BCC describes one of 23 different domains of participant behavior. ME value describes the participant's mood state alongside their level of engagement with their environment, being expressed on a 6-point scale ranging from −5 to +5. ME values can be averaged to arrive at a WIB score, indicating the

© Springer International Publishing AG, part of Springer Nature 2018
K. Miesenberger and G. Kouroupetroglou (Eds.): ICCHP 2018, LNCS 10897, pp. 501–509, 2018.
https://doi.org/10.1007/978-3-319-94274-2_74

participant's total well/ill-being during the whole mapping period [7]. The mapper analyses the mapping results to evaluate the quality of care, and provides feedback to the care staff team so that they are motivated to improve care quality.

DCM is a well-developed method, however, practicing DCM is not easy [8]. The reasons behind include high requirements to (1) remember the unique coding systems, (2) observe and record the participant's behavior and mood/engagement in detail on a frequent basis, (3) decide a representative pair of BCC and ME value after each time-frame (Fig. 1) according to rather complex operational rules [9]. These requirements are all quite burdensome, and long hours of mapping might result in detracting relia-bility (IRR) due to observer fatigue [10].

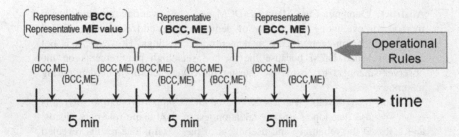

Fig. 1. Decision of representative (BCC & ME) value for each time-frame

Towards the goal of this study to make it easier to practice DCM utilizing ICT, authors first investigated what difficulties and/or burden they feel during mapping from 33 mappers (6 advanced, and 27 basic DCM users) by questionnaires (Table 1). Based

Table 1. Mappers' responses/requirements for questionnaires on DCM operation

		Difficulties and/or burden that mappers feel during mapping
1. Operational rules	BCC	① Choose higher potential BCCs when two or more occur in one time-frame
		② Keep track of time accurately to record the BCC of longest duration
		③ Record the BCC with the most extreme ME value, if ①&② are the same
		④ Record the BCC of latter part of time-frame, if ①–③ are the same
	ME	⑤ Choose from limited ME values properly for [B, C, N, U, W]
		⑥ Allocate ME value properly from M and E values based on the 3 rules
		⑦ Keep track of time accurately to choose the predominating ME value
	Other	⑧ Mark "*" in 6th time-frame when uninterrupted negative ME continues
		⑨ UNME (uninterrupted negative ME) is not interrupted by [N]

(continued)

Table 1. (*continued*)

	Difficulties and/or burden that mappers feel during mapping
2. Observation and recording	⑩ Keep track of time accurately to recognize time-frame every 5-min interval
	⑪ Do not miss observing when recording time-frame results every 5-min
	⑫ Decide representative BCC correctly when various BCCs occur continuously
	⑬ Decide representative ME correctly when M and E change continuously
	⑭ Take notes at the right moment, do not lose the chance to take notes
	⑮ Make easy-to-read notes; time & timing, order of occurrence, duration, etc.
	⑯ Correct and/or add codes or notes during mapping
	⑰ Correct data/info on Raw Data Sheet for report writing after mapping

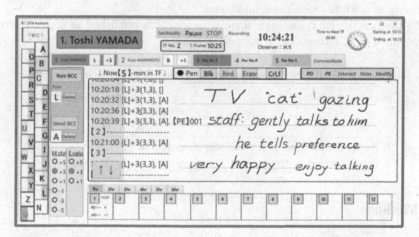

Fig. 2. GUI of the developed DCM support system with handwritten notes

on their responses including requirements for burden reduction we have developed a DCM support system, which we have implemented on a tablet PC (Fig. 2). It works as follows: Once started, the system keeps time. A mapper is to simply record what is observed at a given moment. Then the system processes recorded BCCs and MEs automatically to finalize the representative (BCC, ME) pair for every time-frame according to the operational rules. Thus, a mapper can concentrate on observation, without paying attention to keeping track of time and the operational rules.

We also developed a new evaluation method for the support system using role-play videos (Fig. 3). Role-play video mapping is advantageous for the system evaluation tests over actual mapping in dementia care settings because (1) there is no risk of

Fig. 3. Snapshot of a system evaluation experiment

abusing privacy of people with dementia, (2) it is easier to conduct the experiments, and (3) every subject watches the same videos; i.e. tests can be repeated under the same condition every time.

The results of assessing the reliability and usefulness of the support system were promising as a whole, with some limitations.

To the best of our knowledge, there is no research published to date concerning development of ICT-based DCM support systems.

Table 2. Number of subjects per mapping sequence, and by mapper level

Mapping sequence	Mapper level			Total (head)
	A	B	C	
1. Part 1: conventional >> Part 2: support system	2	3	5	10
2. Part 1: support system >> Part 2: conventional	2	3	7	12

2 Methods

2.1 Video Mapping, Subjects and Experiment Sites

We made two sets of videos, each shows a role-play of different participant (elderly person with dementia) in a dementia care setting, and is composed of two parts: Part 1 (the former half scene) and Part 2 (the latter half scene), one-hour long each.

- At most three subjects at a time were asked to watch videos on two displays.
- Each subject conducts mapping for two hours in total, either by *Mapping Sequence 1* or by *Mapping Sequence 2*, as shown in Table 2.
- Twenty-two mappers volunteered as subjects, whose experiences and skill levels were categorized into A, B, and C, in ascending order (Table 2).
- The experiments were conducted at nine places across the country (Japan).

2.2 Reliability Evaluation of the Support System

Calculate the *Ratio of concordance rates* (RC) using Cs and Cc; the concordance rates of mapping results over the model answers (correctly answered rates; %) with and without using the support system respectively, as follows:

$$(RC) = k \cdot (Cs/Cc), \tag{1}$$

where k is the compensation coefficient for equalizing the difficulty level of the video Part 1 and video Part 2, which is obtained by using total average values of Cc's for videos Part 1 and Part 2 (see Table 3). If mean(RCi) $\geq$ 1, then the reliability of the system is validated, where (RCi) is the *Ratio of concordance rates* of subject i (i = 1 to 22) and mean(RCi) is the average value of (RCi) of all subjects.

Table 3. Mean values of correctly mapped rates Cs and Cc, with and without using the support system, respectively, and the resultant ratio (RC) compensated by k

	Correct answer (%)		Ratio (with/without support system)		
Mapping (Subjects)	Video Part1	Video Part2	Cs/Cc	k	(RC)
without >> with (10)	$Cc_1 = 76.9$	$Cs_2 = 70.6$	0.92	$Cc_1/Cc_2 = 1.18$	1.09
with >> without (12)	$Cs_1 = 82.7$	$Cc_2 = 65.1$	1.27	$Cc_2/Cc_1 = 0.85$	1.08

2.3 Usefulness Evaluation of the Support System

Ask a subject, concerning each item in Table 1, their usual feeling of *Level of difficulty* (D) and *Level of help* (H) that they have felt after using the support system. Then calculate the *Obtained easiness level* (E) by the support system as follows:

(D) = {−3: difficult, −1: somewhat(s.wh.) difficult, +1: s.wh. easy, +3: easy}
(H) = {−3: unnecessary, −1: s.wh. unnecessary, +1: s.wh. helpful, +3: helpful}

$$(E) = (H) - (D), \tag{2}$$

where $-6 \leq (E) \leq 6$, and the more (H) exceeds (D), the larger (E) becomes.

Calculate the *Obtained easiness level* (E(j)i) concerning each item j (j = 1 to 17) for each subject i (i = 1 to 22). If mean(E(j)i) > 0, then item j is considered to have become easier by the support system, where mean(E(j)i) is the average of (E(j)) of all subjects.

For evaluation of usefulness of the support system, consider other positive effect by utilizing the newly implemented functions, such as "Reservation function" and "Alert function", as well.

Reservation function allows a mapper to record the time, without entering a specific BCC, when they cannot decide or recall a proper code that illustrates the participant's specific behavior. They can assign an appropriate BCC retroactively when the code is fixed, thus can avoid entry delay in mapping.

Alert function helps a mapper avoid overlooking changes of participants' activities or mood/engagement during observation, by means of prompting them to update BCCs or ME values. Red Blinking (*Prompting*) emerges after a given length of time (ΔT_1) when certain codes have been kept unchanged, followed by Red Light (*Warning*) after another set of time (ΔT_2), for an alert. Not to be a nuisance, ΔT_1 was set to 95 s for BCC and 85 s for ME value. ΔT_2 was set to 60 s for both BCC and ME value.

3 Results and Discussion

3.1 Reliability Evaluation–Accuracy Rate of Mapping Results

Mean values of *Ratio of concordance rates* (RC)s after the compensation were 1.09 and 1.08 for *Mapping Sequence 1* and *Mapping Sequence 2* respectively, as shown in Table 3. The results show that the correctly answered rate was slightly higher when using the support system than by conventional way, meaning that the prototype support system has already reached the level of conventional DCM in terms of mapping accuracy. Thus, reliability of the system has been confirmed.

3.2 Usefulness Evaluation

Easiness Level of Mapping. *Obtained easiness level* (E) for each item in Table 1, estimated by Eq. (2), was all positive, as shown in Fig. 4. Eight items were ranked quite high (+3.5 or above), five items (②, ⑦, ⑩, ⑫, ⑬) among which were related to burdensome keeping track of time. Whereas, two items, ⑭: easy notes taking and ⑯: easy correction of notes and codes, received a relatively low score of 1.3 and 1.0, respectively. This indicates that the support system is not as flexible as conventional paper-and-pencil method on making and/or correcting notes. Despite some limitations, usefulness of the support system has been achieved substantially as a whole for reducing the mappers' burden and difficulties.

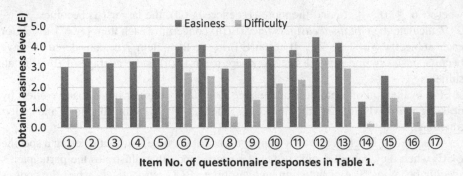

Fig. 4. Obtained easiness level (E), with Difficulty; expressed as "–2(D)" for reference

Making Qualitative Notes. Total average numbers of notes (handwritten items) were slightly smaller with using the support system than with conventional paper-and-pencil method, as shown in Table 4. It is very important to record as much qualitative notes as possible in DCM, therefore, the results showed limitation of the system and there needs some improvement on this point.

Table 4. Numbers of handwritten items, made with and without using the support system

Video Part1		Video Part2	
Support system	Conventional	Support system	Conventional
37.5	41.9	45.7	46.1

On the other hand, descriptions were more accurate with time stamps when using the support system, which is advantageous over the conventional method.

3.3 Additional Value of the Support System

Reservation Function for BCC Entry. 18 subjects out of 22 utilized this function 161 times (around 9 times per subject on average). Number of cases in which complemented time is 10 s or longer, alongside the mean delay-times (durations) for those cases, are shown in Table 5.

Table 5. Complement of BCC entry delay by Reservation function

	Number of cases applied	Mean duration	Max. duration
Video Part1	19	22.3 s	28 s
Video Part2	19	23.6 s	75 s

When the entry time delays by ΔT_{delay} for recording a certain BCC, its duration will count shorter for that amount, and the duration of the previous BCC will count longer instead, which will end up with the duration error of $2\Delta T_{delay}$ in total. Therefore, it is necessary to avoid BCC entry delays to ensure mapping accuracy. The maximum delay-times of 28 s and 75 s (Table 5) were quite significant, in this regard. For the sake of accuracy, 10 s may be a practically non-negligible amount of time, and such delay-times have actually been observed and complemented for most subjects. Thus, it is expected that the *Reservation function* can lead to higher mapping accuracy.

Alert Function to Prompt Updating Codes. *Prompting*s were invoked 1,297 times against all subjects (59 times per subject on average during 1-h mapping), 14 times out of which ended up with *Warning*s. Numbers of cases in which mappers updated (changed) the entered codes or continued them within 10 s after *Prompting*s, alongside the average response time, are shown in Table 6. Number of cases where *Warning*s emerged, alongside the average response time, are also shown in Table 6.

Table 6. Numbers of cases in which mappers updated/continued codes within 10 s after *Prompting* or *Warning* emerged, alongside the average response time

		Video Part1		Video Part2	
		Updated	Continued	Updated	Continued
Prompting	Number of cases	76	340	79	426
	Mean time (s)	5.1	4.1	5.4	4.2
Warning	Number of cases	2	3	3	6
	Mean time (s)	21.5	23.3	38	12.7

It is not easy to keep one's concentration all the time during a long-hour mapping. In fact, the *Alert function* was invoked frequently. And the sooner a mapper respond to *Prompting*, the more effectively the function serves. The results showed that *Promptings* led to updating within around 5 s in many cases; 76 and 79 for video Part1 and video Part2, respectively (Table 6). Therefore, the periodic prompting of obser-vation seems to be effective for increasing mapping accuracy.

4   Conclusions

Dementia Care Mapping (DCM) is a well-developed evidence-based observational method, and is widely used to implement Person-centred Care (PCC) in dementia care settings. However, it is not easy to practice DCM because of its rather complex operational rules and burdensome six-hour consecutive observation normally required for mapping. Aiming to reduce the difficulties and burden during mapping, authors have developed a new ICT-based support system for DCM. We also developed a new test method using role-play videos, and evaluated reliability and usefulness of the support system. As the results, we found out that the prototype support system has already reached the level of conventional DCM in terms of mapping accuracy, and received positive feedback from mappers regarding burden reduction and easier operation of DCM. In addition, the new functionality of the system looked promising for increasing mapping accuracy. Thus, reliability and usefulness of the developed system has been confirmed. In order to put the support system into practical use, however, there is a need for further improvement with resolving remaining issues. Future studies include validation and extension of current DCM method by utilizing the advantages of the ICT-based system over the conventional paper-and-pencil method.

Acknowledgements. The authors would like to thank the following for their contributions to this work: Dr. Yutaka Mizuno, Strategic Lead of PCC/DCM in Japan, for his continuing support and encouragement for us. Dr. Tetsuro Ishihara and all the volunteer mappers across the country for their support and participation in the evaluation tests. Special thanks to Yasuko Murata and Yuko Nakamura for their assistance, as accredited advanced trainers of DCM, to prepare model answers for the role-play videos, and to Satoshi Yoshikawa and his colleagues for providing us with the opportunity to run pilot tests in their facilities to finalize the system evaluation procedure.

References

1. McKee, K.J., Houston, K.M., Barnes, S.: Methods for assessing quality of life and well-being in frail older people. Psychol. Health **17**(6), 737–751 (2002). https://doi.org/10.1080/0887044021000054755
2. Chung, J.C.C.: Activity participation and well-being of people with dementia in long-term-care settings. OTJR Occup. Participation Health **24**(1), 22–31 (2004)
3. Chenoweth, L., King, M.T., Jeon, Y., et al.: Caring for Aged Dementia Care Resident Study (CADRES) of person-centred care, dementia-care mapping, and usual care in dementia: a cluster-randomised trial. Lancet Neurol. **8**(4), 317–325 (2009). https://doi.org/10.1016/S1474-4422(09)70045-6
4. Ervin, K., Koschel, A.: Dementia care mapping as a tool for person centred care. Aust. Nurs. J. **19**(10), 32–35 (2012). PMid:22715608
5. Kitwood, T.: Dementia Reconsidered: The Person Comes First. Open University Press, London (1997)
6. Fossey, J., Lee, L., Ballard, C.: Dementia Care Mapping as a research tool for measuring quality of life in care settings: psychometric properties. Int. J. Geriatr. Psychiatry **17**, 1064–1070 (2002). https://doi.org/10.1002/gps.708
7. Brooker, D.J., Surr, C.: Dementia Care Mapping (DCM): initial validation of DCM 8 in UK field trials. Int. J. Geriatr. Psychiatry **21**, 1018–1025 (2006). https://doi.org/10.1002/gps.1600
8. Thornton, A., Hatton, C., Tatham, A.: Dementia Care Mapping reconsidered: exploring the reliability and validity of the observational tool. Geriatr. Psychiatry **19**, 718–726 (2004). https://doi.org/10.1002/gps.1145
9. DCM 8 User's Manual. Bradford Dementia Group, University of Bradford (2005)
10. Cooke, H., Chaudhury, H.: An examination of the psychometric properties and efficacy of Dementia Care Mapping. Dementia **12**(6), 790–805 (2012). https://doi.org/10.1177/1471301212446111

Personalisation of Context-Aware Solutions Supporting Asthma Management

Mario Quinde[1,2(✉)], Nawaz Khan[1], and Juan Carlos Augusto[1]

[1] Research Group on Development of Intelligent Environments,
Middlesex University, London, UK
MQ093@live.mdx.ac.uk, {N.X.Khan,J.Augusto}@mdx.ac.uk
[2] Universidad de Piura, Piura, Peru
mario.quinde@udep.pe

Abstract. Personalisation of asthma management plans is important because asthma patients experience different triggers and symptoms as a result of the high heterogeneity level of the condition. Although this makes context-awareness suitable to support asthma management, existing context-aware solutions do not allow patients to personalise their management plans. This research proposes an approach to develop context-aware solutions allowing the personalisation of asthma management plans. It is derived on the basis of the literature review and a qualitative research that includes both asthma patients and carers. A prototype to illustrate the application of the approach is demonstrated.

Keywords: Mobile health · Asthma · Personalisation
Context-awareness

1 Introduction

Asthma is a heterogeneous disease characterized by chronic airway inflammation. A patient's asthma is defined by his/her history of airflow limitation and respiratory symptoms (such as wheeze, shortness of breath, chest tightness and cough) that are variable over time and in intensity [1]. Although there is no cure, asthma can be controlled with a treatment based on a management plan to avoid triggers and reduce symptoms [2–4].

Hospitalizations and deaths from asthma have declined in some countries but its prevalence is increasing in many [1]. In 2015 in the US, 24.6 million people had asthma, 11.5 million suffered one or more attacks and 3 thousand died because of it [5]. In 2015 in the UK, 5.4 million people had asthma, every 10 s someone suffered a potentially life-threatening attack and the annual cost to the NHS of treating asthma was more than £1 billion [6].

The heterogeneity of asthma is challenging when defining treatments as triggers and symptoms are different to each patient. This makes personalisation

K. Miesenberger and G. Kouroupetroglou (Eds.): ICCHP 2018, LNCS 10897, pp. 510–519, 2018.
https://doi.org/10.1007/978-3-319-94274-2_75

important because each patient assigns different priorities to the indicators framing his/her condition. E.g. a patient whose asthma is triggered by low temperatures is more concern about the weather than a patient only allergic to pollen.

From this perspective, context-aware solutions can aid the personalisation of the asthma management process. A context-aware solution *"uses context to provide task-relevant information and/or services to a user"*, where context is *"any information that can be used to characterize the situation of an entity, where an entity can be a person, place, or physical or computational object"* [7]. Hence, a context-aware solution supporting asthma management should provide information and/or services considering the indicators defining the patient's condition.

This research proposes an approach to develop context-aware solutions aiding the personalisation of asthma management plans. This research attempts to determine the existing gaps of using context-awareness in asthma management and set out the functionalities of such context-aware system based on a qualitative research. This article is divided as follows: Sect. 2 shows the state of the art, Sect. 3 explains the methodology, Sect. 4 describes the proposal and prototype, and Sect. 5 presents the Discussion and Conclusions.

2   State of the Art

The application fields of context-awareness, as a component of Intelligent Environments, can be linked to Transportation, Education, Production Places, Smart Offices, Intelligent Supermarkets, Energy Conservation, Entertainment and Health [8]. Examples of context-aware solutions supporting health care are Medication Assistant [9], Hefestos [10] and SOSPhone [11]. Context-awareness has also shown potential to improve management of chronic diseases. An example is a system aiding patients' technique when measuring blood pressure [12]. Another is a system collecting blood-glucose values from diabetes patients to determine their health status and perform actions according to this status [13].

Research works about solutions supporting asthma were reviewed. After an extensive review, eight works were selected as they offer or suggest the use of context-aware features. Table 1 shows the wide variety of indicators tracked by these solutions, which is associated to the high heterogeneity level of asthma. The context-aware features of the researches are linked to: recognizing symptoms and/or triggers [15,17,20], notifying asthma patients and carers when health status is abnormal [14,16,17,19,20], showing near hospitals in emergencies [16], reminding patients to take readings [19], providing advice regarding patients' status [20], and predicting asthma attacks based on patients' context [21].

Although personalisation is the key to implement asthma plans, none of these works allows users to choose the indicators to track, nor the features to use for supporting the management of their condition. The researches do not support a comprehensive framing of context including indicators of several indoor and outdoor places of interest (e.g. home, workplace, path to work). This research aims to close this gap by proposing an approach to develop context-aware solutions allowing the personalisation of asthma management plans and providing a more comprehensive way of framing patients' context to aid in decision-making.

Table 1. Indicators tracked by the reviewed solutions

Research	Patient's indicators	Environmental indicators
[14]	Medication, control level	-
[15]	PEF	Overall air quality
[16]	PEF, control level	Sand storms
[17]	Wheezing, motion	-
[18]	PEF, FEV1, FEV6, NO, CO, O2	-
[19]	NO, control level	Temperature, humidity, CO
[20]	PEF, FEV1, FVC,O2 level, wheezing, exercise, medication	Temperature, humidity, CO, O3, NO2, Cl
[21]	PEF, FEV1, FVC, heart rate, respiratory rate, wheezing, motion	Temperature, humidity, O3, VOC

3   Methodology

The User-Centred Intelligent Environments Development Process (U-CIEDP) led the research, focusing on its first primary stage: Initial Scoping. The U-CIEDP suggests to engage stakeholders in the scoping, development and installation of Intelligent Environments. It has been used to co-create smart technology for people with special needs [22].

The qualitative research included 4 asthma patients, 2 carers of asthma patients and 1 physician expert in respiratory diseases. The interview was the research method chosen because context-awareness is complex to explain through a questionnaire. Each interview lasted between 40–60 min. It included an explanation of context-awareness before asking a set of open questions to know the indicators they would like to monitor and the features they desire from a context-aware solution supporting asthma management. The interviews were held in the Smart Spaces Lab of Middlesex University.

A prototype is demonstrated as an example of using the approach to create context-aware solutions supporting the personalisation of asthma management. It is under development and uses sensors from the Smart Spaces Lab to monitor indoor environmental factors. Its functionalities are shown in Sect. 4.1.

4   Personalisation of Context-Aware Solutions for Asthma

The interviews re-confirm the heterogeneity of asthma. Participants stated the variables to track depend on each patient's specific triggers and symptoms. The expected context-aware features are also linked to the patient's contexts. For instance, while a participant said he *"wants to be reminded to open the windows when the indoor air quality is not good"*, another said he *"would like to be reminded to close the windows if the forecast says that temperature will drop."* Most participants said carers should be notified in emergencies and when patient's status is abnormal. They affirmed the notifications should be person-alised depending on the patient's scenario. For example, *"The solution should notify parents if the patient is a child, and the partner if the patient is an adult..."*

The proposal focuses on identifying and classifying the indicators framing the context of a patient to facilitate the personalisation of asthma management plans. It facilitates the description and it provides a more comprehensive support for decision-making. The indicators are classified into Patient's indicators, Indoor Environmental Indicators (IEIs) and Outdoor Environmental Indicators (OEIs) (Fig. 1).

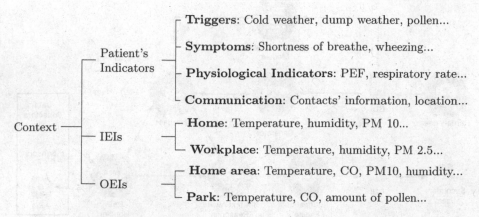

Fig. 1. Classification and examples of indicators framing patient's context

Patient's indicators include triggers and symptoms characterizing the patient's asthma, physiological indicators regarding his/her status and commu-nication information. For instance, a person can choose cold weather and pollen as triggers, shortness of breathe and breathing faster as symptoms, Peak Expira-tory Flow (PEF) and heart rate as physiological indicators, and his/her spouse contact information to define the communication component.

IEIs and OIEs define the status of places the patient is interested on. This status is linked to the external factors triggering patient's asthma. These indi-cators show how exposed the patient would to these factors if s/he is in those places. IEIs are linked to indoor places and OEIs are linked to outdoor places. Following the previous example, the patient would choose to monitor temper-ature and PM 2.5 at home and workplace (IEIs) as s/he is sensitive to cold weather and pollen. S/he would also choose to monitor temperature and pollen level in the area nearby home or at a park s/he frequents (OEIs).

One of the reasons to separate indoor and outdoor places is the sources used to get the data. IEIs data tends to be obtained from sensors. OEIs data is usually gathered through APIs (e.g. Google Awareness). It is important to clarify that it is possible to monitor a set of IEIs that is partially or totally different to the set of OEIs. It is even possible to have IEIs (or OEIs) varying from place to place.

Figure 2 shows the proposed architecture allowing the personalisation of context-aware solutions supporting asthma management. The Personalisation Module alters the Database (DB) according to the personalisation settings chosen by the user. The Report Generator gets these settings and values from the DB to generate the reports for users. The Data Handler gets values from the Data Collectors and inserts it into the DB. The Context-Aware Reasoner (CAR) gets values from the DB to analyse patient's personalised context. Finally the Notification Engine send notifications to users when the context is meaningful.

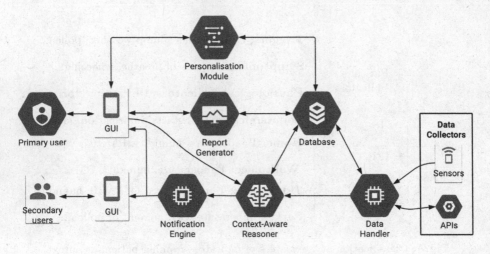

Fig. 2. System architecture

4.1   Prototype

The prototype aims to clarify the use of the approach. It is an under development mobile application allowing users to set the indicators they want to track according to the specific characteristics of their asthma. The option "Personalise your Asthma" from the main screen (Fig. 3a) leads to the screen shown in Fig. 3b, which shows the personalisation set by the user. The settings can be changed through the *options menu* of the screen. An example of how to personalise the indicators to track is shown in Fig. 3c, where user can set the indicators for HOME and establish the control values (MIN,MAX). Users can also choose their triggers, symptoms and the people to contact in case of emergency.

The option "Check your Indicators" (Fig. 3a) allows users to see the values of the indicators they chose. "Deploy Emergency Notifications" automatically sends SMS and emails to the people chosen to be contacted. It also shows a notification on their phones if they have the application installed (Fig. 3d).

The sequence diagram explaining how the fully functional prototype will work is shown in Fig. 4. When the user personalises (1.1), the GUI sends the

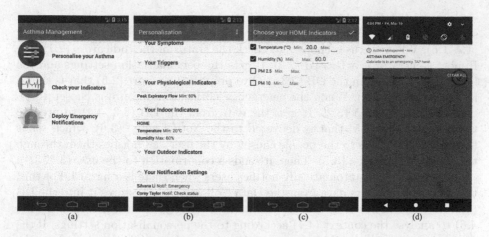

Fig. 3. Screens of the prototype

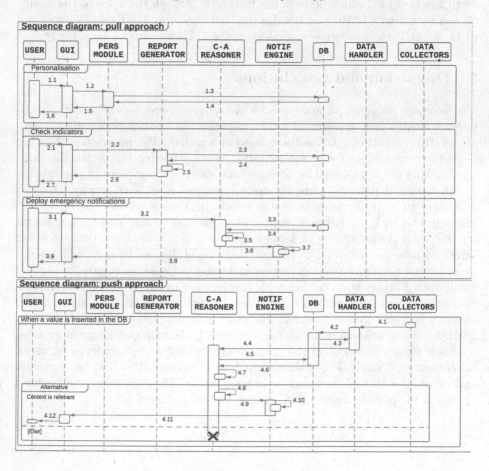

Fig. 4. Sequence diagram

settings to the Pers. Module (1.2), which modify the DB according to these settings (1.3). The DB replies with a confirmation message that goes to the user (1.4–1.6). When the user chooses to check the status of the indicators (2.1), the Report Generator is activated (2.2). It gets the personalisation settings and the indicators values from the DB (2.3, 2.4) to prepare the report (2.5) that is shown to the user (2.6, 2.7). When the emergency notification feature is chosen (3.1), the CAR is activated (3.2). It gets the data from the DB (3.3, 3.4) to prepare the context data (3.5) that is delivered to the Notif Engine (3.6), which sends the emails and SMSs to the people chosen by the user and notifies them through the mobile application (3.7). Then, it sends a confirmation to the user (3.8, 3.9).

The system also automatically notifies users when there is a hazard. For this, the Data Handler gets data from the Data Collectors (4.1), stores it into the DB (4.2, 4.3) and activates the CAR (4.4). The CAR gets data from the DB (4.5, 4.6) to analyse the context (4.7) according to the personalisation settings. If the context is relevant, the CAR prepares the context data (4.8) that is sent to the Notif Engine (4.9), which delivers notifications (through the app) to the people chosen by the user (4.10) and notifies the user regarding the hazard(s) detected (4.11, 4.12). If the context is not relevant, the CAR terminates its activity.

5   Discussion and Conclusions

The research proposes an approach to personalise context-aware solution supporting asthma management. The main contribution is to combine patient's indicators, IEIs and OEIs to frame the context of a patient. The proposal enables the users to accommodate their own scenarios, hence, allowing the personalisation.

Tracking the right variables is important given heterogeneity of patients [2–4]. Moreover, if patients agree to share information with their physicians, it will allow to monitor patients' status regularly. This is relevant as physicians are only able to know patients' status when they go to the medical centres for regular visits (twice a year) or for emergencies [14]. Personalised context-aware solutions have the potential to provide meaningful data to be used as input for more complex decision-making process including technologies related to big and small data. Furthermore, the strategic involvement of carers in the communication process has the potential to enhance preventive and reactive actions. The research provides a more comprehensive way of framing the context of a patient with the aim of enhancing decision-making in the asthma management process.

Some future directions of the research are: assessing the prototype by users, implementing Case-Base Reasoning to detect abnormalities and emergencies, and creating a Virtual Assistant to support tasks. These features will be built on top of the personalisation and context-awareness layers.

References

1. Global Initiative for Asthma: Global Strategy for Asthma Management and Prevention. www.ginasthma.org (2017). Accessed 31 Jan 2018
2. Asthma UK: What is Asthma? www.asthma.org.uk. Accessed 30 Jan 2018
3. Asthma Australia: Understanding asthma. www.asthmaaustralia.org.au. Accessed 30 Jan 2018
4. NHS: Asthma-NHS.UK. www.nhs.uk/Conditions/Asthma. Accessed 30 Jan 2018
5. Center for Disease Control and Prevention: CDC - Asthma Surveillance Data. https://www.cdc.gov/asthma/asthmadata.htm. Accessed 30 Jan 2018
6. Asthma UK: Annual Report & Accounts. www.asthma.org.uk. Accessed 30 Jan 2018
7. Dey, A.K.: Understanding and using context. Pers. Ubiquit. Comput. 5(1), 4–7 (2001). https://doi.org/10.1007/s007790170019
8. Augusto, J.C., et al.: Intelligent environments: a manifesto. Hum. Centric Comput. Inf. Sci. 3, 12 (2013). https://doi.org/10.1186/2192-1962-3-12
9. Teixeira, A., et al.: Design and development of Medication Assistant: older adults centred design to go beyond simple medication reminders. Univ. Access Inf. Soc. 16(3), 545–560 (2017). https://doi.org/10.1007/s10209-016-0487-7
10. Tavares, J., et al.: Hefestos: an intelligent system applied to ubiquitous accessibility. Univ. Access Inf. Soc. 15(4), 589–607 (2016). https://doi.org/10.1007/s10209-015-0423-2
11. Paredes, H., et al.: SOSPhone: a mobile application for emergency calls. Univ. Access Inf. Soc. 13, 277–290 (2014). https://doi.org/10.1007/s10209-013-0318-z
12. Wagner, S., Toftegaard, T.S., Bertelsen, O.W.: Increased data quality in home blood pressure monitoring through context awareness. In: 5th International Conference on Pervasive Computing Technologies for Healthcare PervasiveHealth and Workshops, pp. 234–237 (2011). https://doi.org/10.4108/icst.pervasivehealth.2011.245968
13. Chang, S., Chiang, R., Wu, S.: A Context-Aware, Interactive M-Health System for Diabetics. IT Prof. 18(3), 14–22 (2016). https://doi.org/10.1109/MITP.2016.48
14. Osuntogun, A.A., Arriaga, R.I.: Physician usage of technology and opportunities for continuous care management of pediatric Asthma patients. In: 4th International Conference on Pervasive Computing Technologies for Healthcare, pp. 1–6 (2010). https://doi.org/10.4108/ICST.PERVASIVEHEALTH2010.8868
15. Yun, T.J., et al.: Assessing Asthma management practices through in-home technology probes. In: 2010 4th International Conference on Pervasive Computing Technologies for Healthcare, pp. 1–9 (2010). https://doi.org/10.4108/ICST.PERVASIVEHEALTH2010.8839
16. Al-Dowaihi, D., et al.: MBreath: Asthma monitoring system on the go. In: IEEE ICCMA 2013, pp. 1–4 (2013). https://doi.org/10.1109/ICCMA.2013.6506169
17. Uwaoma, C., Mansingh, G.: Towards real-time monitoring and detection of Asthma symptoms on resource-constraint mobile device. In: Annual IEEE CCNC 2015, pp. 47–52 (2015). https://doi.org/10.1109/CCNC.2015.7157945
18. Kwan, A.M., et al.: Personal lung function monitoring devices for Asthma patients. IEEE Sens. J. 15(4), 2238–2247 (2015). https://doi.org/10.1109/JSEN.2014.2373134
19. Anantharam, P., et al.: Knowledge-driven personalized contextual mHealth service for Asthma management in children. In: 2015 IEEE International Conference on Mobile Services, pp. 284–291 (2015). https://doi.org/10.1109/MobServ.2015.48

20. Ra, H.-K., et al.: AsthmaGuide: an Asthma monitoring and advice ecosystem. In: 2016 IEEE Wireless Health, pp. 128–135 (2016). https://doi.org/10.1109/WH. 2016.7764567
21. Dieffenderfer, J., et al.: Low power wearable systems for continuous monitoring of environment and health for chronic respiratory disease. IEEE J. Biomed. Health Inform. **20**(5), 1251–1264 (2016). https://doi.org/10.1109/JBHI.2016.2573286
22. Augusto, J.C., et al.: The user-centred intelligent environments development process as a guide to co-create smart technology for people with special needs. Univ. Access Inf. Soc. **17**(1), 115–130 (2018). https://doi.org/10.1007/s10209-016-0514-8

Service and Information Provision

Tracking Individual Assistive Technology Interventions and Measuring Their Outcomes

Renzo Andrich[(✉)]

IRCCS Fondazione Don Gnocchi, Milan, Italy
renzo.andrich@siva.it

Abstract. This paper reports the findings of a study that developed a standardized method to track individual assistive technology (AT) interventions for any user, able to generate reports needed in clinical practice, measure the outcome and detect possible critical issues requiring adjustment. Individual AT interventions were carried out with 120 participants, and the process was tracked by means of a purposely-developed template including five sections: (1) contact data, (2) Assessment Report, (3) Verification Report, (4) Follow-up Report, and (5) statistical data. The outcome of the interventions was measured for 34 participants by means of three instruments (KWAZO, IPPA and QUEST). KWAZO proved useful to capture the user's perception about the quality of the process. IPPA proved useful to describe the perceived effectiveness of the assistive solution provided; negative IPPA scores are clear alerts that the user needs to be contacted again to check what happened and - if possible - undertake corrective interventions; near-to-zero (<1) IPPA scores also suggest to check whether the assistive solution has proved ineffective or brought about positive effects in relation to some problems and negative effects in relation to others. Likewise, possible low QUEST scores (<3) alert that the related products had critical problems and corrective actions may be required, in order to increase the assistive solution effectiveness.

Keywords: Outcome measurement · Cost effectiveness
Assistive technology intervention

1 Introduction

The assistive technology (AT) provision process has been extensively studied in recent literature [1]. One of the most quoted models is the seven-step process initially depicted by the EU HEART Study in 1995 and later revised by the 2013 AAATE Position Paper [2].

One of today's key issues in AT provision process is to measure the outcome of the intervention, in order to make sure that the investment carried out led to successful results for the person's life [3]. However, measuring the outcome of an AT intervention is a complex task. Although there is still paucity of literature on this subject, it is clear that an AT solution has a systemic effect [4]. An AT solution brings about a *"perturbation"* in the system composed of the person (involving his/her clinical condition, personality and life goals), his or her environment (architectural, human, organizational) and his or her occupation (activities, life roles, lifestyle) [5]. The system needs

© Springer International Publishing AG, part of Springer Nature 2018
K. Miesenberger and G. Kouroupetroglou (Eds.): ICCHP 2018, LNCS 10897, pp. 523–531, 2018.
https://doi.org/10.1007/978-3-319-94274-2_76

time to absorb the perturbation and evolve towards a new balanced situation; the outcome is positive when this new situation is perceived by the person and by his or her primary network as beneficial to their lives. A variety of actors and factors are involved in this system, some of them being predictable and others unpredictable; thus the actual outcomes can be detected only when the perturbation transient has expired: this involves that outcome measurement should be carried out not "in the clinic" but "in real-life environment"; not "here and now" but "there and tomorrow" [6]. Various methods have been developed for this purpose; however they are mainly focused on specific user groups or categories of assistive products [7].

This paper reports the findings of a study that worked at developing a standardized method to track any individual AT interventions for any user, able to generate all reports needed in clinical practice, measure the outcome and detect possible critical issues requiring adjustment. In this paper, the term *assistive product* will be used to indicate any specific assistive device or environmental adaptation adopted in the intervention, while the term *assistive solution* will be used to indicate the whole set of assistive products that work together to solve the patient's problem.

2 Method

2.1 Participants

The study involved eight rehabilitation Centres of the Fondazione Don Gnocchi (FDG) network, located in various Italian regions. Each Centre has an AT assessment unit (SIVA) staffed with therapists with expertise on AT and supported (on demand, when needed) by a central bioengineering unit specializing in ICT assistive technology (SIVA Lab). Overall, 23 professionals were involved as experimenters in the study, including medical doctors (physiatrists), physiotherapists, occupational therapists, speech therapists and biomedical engineers.

Each Centre was asked to select - among the served population - a number of subjects who needed assistive solutions and carry out the assessment process on the basis of a set of instruments provided by the research team. The inclusion criteria were quite broad. No limitations were established in relation to age, gender or pathology. The only requirement was the need of significant AT interventions addressing heavy restrictions in one or more of the following areas: communication (ICF d3), mobility (ICF d4), self care (ICF d5) and domestic life (ICF d6). Only users who signed informed consent were included. Overall, 120 patients were recruited and the work started after receiving clearance by the FDG Ethical Committee.

2.2 Material

A template for tracking the individual AT intervention was designed, based on the experience of previous projects and consultation with all professionals involved in the study. It was shaped as a fillable-PDF file, developed by means of a commercially available software (Adobe LiveCycle Designer©) in such a way to make data extraction possible for aggregate processing (first in XML and in turn imported to MS Excel © file according to purposely-defined schemas).

The template (see Table 1) is composed of five sections: (1) contact data, (2) Assessment Report, (3) Verification Report, (4) Follow-up Report, and (5) statistical data. In the Verification and Follow-up sections includes three outcome measurement instruments, each to be administered to the user, or to the primary caregiver, or to both:

- **KWAZO** ("Kwaliteit van Zorg" i.e. "Quality in care") [8] measures the user satisfaction with the process (to be administered at Verification); it consists of seven items (accessibility, information, coordination, competence, efficiency, user influence, instructions), each to be rated 1 ("*unsatisfied*") to 5 ("*very satisfied*").
- **IPPA** (Individual Prioritized Problems Assessment) [9] measures the perceived effectiveness based on seven self-defined "problems" which the user expects to solve thanks to the new assistive solution. At Verification, the user is asked to rate 1 to 5 ("*not really important*" to "*very important*") the importance of each problem ("*how much is it important to solve this problem for me, in my life*") and the difficulty experienced (1 to 5 i.e. "*none*" to "*insurmountable*") with that problem ("*how difficult is it me now, before having the new assistive solution*"). At Follow-up, the question about difficulty is administered again ("*how would you score the difficulty you have with that problem now, with the new assistive solution*"). The difference between the first-interview overall score (Ippa1) and the second-interview overall score (Ippa2) returns the IPPA indicator.
- **QUEST** (Quebec User Evaluation of Satisfaction with AT) [10] - to be administered at Follow-up - measures the user satisfaction with each product (8 items) and the related services (4 items); each item is rated 1 to 5 ("*totally unsatisfied*" to "*very satisfied*").

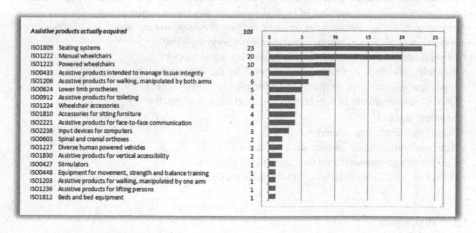

Fig. 1. Assistive products actually acquired by the participants in the study

Table 1. Structure of the SIVA assistive technology intervention report

Contact data
- Client's surname/name, address, phone, email etc.
- Person or agency who asked for referral

Assessment report
- Initial request
- Clinical-functional summary
- Environmental analysis
- Assistive devices or equipment already in use
- Goals of the intervention (as initially agreed)
- Revised goals (as finally agreed - if applicable)
- Recommended solutions
- Proposed NHS (National Health Service) prescription codes (if applicable)
- Additional notes, indications or remarks (if applicable)
- Date or the Report and assessor's signature (original or digital)
- Assessment diary (date, participants, activities carried out in each session)
- Photos (max 3 pictures that clarify details of the recommended solutions)
- References and resources (link to product records or documentation files)

Verification report
- Inventory of assistive products and environmental adaptations actually carried out
for each item: short description, supplier, ISO assistive product code, brand, model, link to the product record in the national assistive products database, price, amount paid by the user in case the funding body could not pay for all the price
- Remarks on the quality of the provision (as observed by the verificator)
- Possible difficulties experienced (as reported by the user and/or the caregiver)
- KWAZO questionnaire on the quality of the provision process
- Ippa1 questionnaire on the expectations with the new assistive solution

Follow-up report
- Inventory of assistive products and environmental adaptations in use
For each item: months of actual use so far, average hours/week of use (either independently or with human assistance, number of critical events (if any), cost incurred for maintenance/management/repairs, amount paid by the user, overall user's and caregiver's satisfaction (1 to 5 i.e. "totally unsatisfied" to "very satisfied")
- Observation of the equipment while in use (by the inspector)
- Possible difficulties experienced (as reported by the user and/or the caregiver)
- Ippa2 questionnaire on the perceived effectiveness (IPPA score)
- QUEST questionnaire of satisfaction with each assistive product

Statistical data
- Functional limitations considered (ICF b)
- Activities/participation restrictions considered (ICF d)
- Environmental barriers/facilitators considered (ICF e)
- Assistive products considered (ISO 9999:2016 classification of assistive products)

2.3   Procedure

Individual assistive technology interventions were carried out with 120 participants (70 males and 50 females), aged 2 to 97 (average 52,7 median 56,5).

While all completed the Assessment, 34 (aged 5 to 83, average 44,9, median 46,5) completed also the Verification and the Follow-up phases within the time window of the project. The results presented in this paper are based on these 34 participants.

For participants having a primary caregiver, the outcome measurement instruments were administered *also* to their caregiver, or *only* to the caregiver in case of inability to understand the questions. In both cases, the caregivers were asked to express their personal view, not to guess the participant's view.

3 Results

The assistive solutions actually acquired were related to mobility (56%), communication (15%), domestic life (10%) and personal care (7%). All participants had assistive solutions composed of more than one assistive product (103 products, for 34 people). The most recurring devices were seating units (n = 23), manual wheelchairs (n = 20) and powered wheelchairs (n = 10); many other products were also included such as pressure-sores prevention aids, walkers, lower limb prostheses, communicators, communication software, computer access peripherals and stair climbers (see Fig. 1).

The overall cost of the solutions acquired ranged from no cost (solutions composed of free software) to very high cost (70.314 €), with 6.041 € as average. In most cases the assistive solution was totally reimbursed by the National Health Service (NHS). However, 11 users had to contribute partly or totally out of their pocket (seven over 5.000 €), as some devices were not yet eligible for NHS provision,

Overall, KWAZO revealed high satisfaction with the quality of the service (average score: 4,63 by users, 4,60 by caregivers); only 3 users and 3 caregivers expressed scores lower than 4, due to a perceived unsatisfactory coordination among all professionals involved.

IPPA indicated that the interventions were in most cases effective (average scores +4,79 by users, +6,64 by caregivers), in other words they brought about a positive change in the person's life in relation to the problems indicated by each respondent. However, in two cases IPPA was negative (−6,14 by a user, −0,83 by a caregiver) and in other two cases it was null, which raised the question as whether the assistive solution had damaged the person's life or any unforeseen external circumstances had made the assistive solution ineffective (in both cases the persons were contacted: it was found that a worsening of the clinical status had occurred, which required reassessment). These results are shown in Table 2, which indicates for each user the assistive solution acquired, its overall cost, the cost incurred by the user, the user's and/or the caregiver's IPPA scores (Ippa1: first interview at Verification; Ippa2: second interview at Follow-up). The table is sorted in descending IPPA score (Ippa1-Ippa2; the average between the user's and the caregiver's scores is considered in case both are available).

QUEST indicated high satisfaction with most devices acquired, by either users (average product score 4,46, average service score 4,49) or caregivers (average product score 4,62, average service score 4,58). Only one product was judged totally unsatisfactory (the user was contacted and it was found that the product quality was insufficient in relation to the usage requirements).

Table 2. IPPA scores (perceived effectiveness)

Age	Sex	Assistive solution	Total cost	User share	User			Caregiver			Aver.
					Ippa1	Ippa2	IPPA	Ippa1	Ippa2	IPPA	
34	M	Highchair, seating system	4.165	0	23,75			25,00	5,00	**20,00**	20,00
45	M	Wheelchair, home adaptations	16.100	16.100				25,00	10,00	**15,00**	15,00
43	M	Pw.wheelchair, home adaptations	70.314	65.493	19,20	7,33	**11,87**				11,87
71	F	Wheelchair, seating system	1.635	0	25,00	14,00	**11,00**				11,00
20	M	Spinal orthosis	636	0				21,67	11,67	**10,00**	10,00
21	M	Symbolic communication device	1.560	0				25,00	15,00	**10,00**	10,00
67	F	Pw wheelchair, seating system	4.694	0	18,67	9,29	**9,38**				9,38
12	F	Highchair, wheelchair, seating unit	5.041	450				19,29	10,00	**9,29**	9,29
5	M	Tilting wheelchair, seating system	4.567	0				20,29	11,43	**8,86**	8,86
8	F	Wheelchair	1.882	0				13,67	5,00	**8,67**	8,67
49	F	Pw.wheelchair, seating system	4.506	200	20,17	11,86	**8,31**				8,31
70	M	Pw.wheelchair (tilting, adj.backrest)	3.000	0	18,86	10,57	**8,29**				8,29
33	F	Symbolic communication device	2.236	0				19,00	11,00	**8,00**	8,00
42	M	Wheelchair, seating system, ramp	2.270	50	8,67	8,57	**0,10**	20,00	4,50	**15,50**	7,80
55	M	Trackball, access interfaces	286	256	20,00	12,67	**7,33**				7,33
74	M	Manual wheelchair, cushion, tripod	1.221	1.221	17,57	11,29	**6,29**				6,29
68	F	Pw.wheelchair, seating system	11.641	4.400				9,71	4,86	**4,86**	4,86
61	F	One side drive wheelchair, cushion	500	0	19,20	15,33	**3,87**	25,00	19,17	**5,83**	4,85
38	M	Wheelchair, seating system	1.601	0	21,25	9,80	**11,45**	23,00	25,00	**-2,00**	4,73
11	M	Wheelchair, seating system	3.452	250	17,00	12,29	**4,71**				4,71
66	F	Electronic knee, walker	13.353	7.143	11,86	8,00	**3,86**				3,86
73	F	Leg prosthesis, wheelchair, walker	6.170	2.900	12,86	9,57	**3,29**				3,29
34	F	Pw.wheelchair, seating system	4.945	580	8,14	4,86	**3,29**				3,29

(continued)

Table 2. (continued)

Age	Sex	Assistive solution	Total cost	User share	User			Caregiver			Aver.
					Ippa1	Ippa2	IPPA	Ippa1	Ippa2	IPPA	
58	M	Leg prosthesis, wheelchair, walker	4.151	0				10,57	7,43	3,14	3,14
83	F	Powered wheelchair, seating system	3.145	0	8,57	5,57	3,00				3,00
60	M	Functional electrical stimulator	400	0	20,00	17,57	2,43				2,43
24	F	Walker	2.028	250				14,40	12,00	2,40	2,40
48	M	Walker, I-phone vocal assistant	74	0	16,00	14,29	1,71	16,67	15,83	0,83	1,27
45	F	Hip dis.prosthesis, wheelchair	9.770	0	10,86	9,71	1,14				1,14
66	M	Wheelchair, seating system, hoist	2.921	0	10,43	9,86	0,57				0,57
12	M	Tablet PC, communication software	1.231	0				20,71	20,71	0,00	0,00
53	F	Highchair, seating system	0	0				25,00	25,00	0,00	0,00
7	F	Folding pushchair, seating system	1.089	0				17,50	18,33	-0,83	-0,83
71	M	Pw.wheelchair, home adaptations	14.804	9.520	12,14	18,29	-6,14				-6,14
Average ≫			6.041	3.200	16,20	11,04	4,79	19,53	12,88	6,64	

4 Discussion

The project led to a standardized method to track individual AT interventions and generated the first set of outcome data ever available in our Institution for actual use in clinical practice. Now the method is being implemented in the daily routine of all rehabilitation centres of the FDG network.

KWAZO proved useful to capture the user's perception about the quality of the process. Possible low scores related to any of the eight indicators help identify and correct possible inconsistencies that may occur when several professionals, departments of agencies are involved in the process.

IPPA proved useful to describe the perceived effectiveness of the assistive solution provided; negative IPPA scores are clear alerts that the user needs to be contacted again to check what happened and - if possible - undertake corrective interventions; near-to-zero (<1) IPPA scores also suggest to check whether the assistive solution has proved ineffective or brought about positive effects in relation to some problems and negative effects in relation to others.

Likewise, possible low QUEST scores (<3) alert that the related products had critical problems and corrective actions may be required, in order to increase the assistive solution effectiveness.

Study Limitations. Due to organizational reasons (the recruitment of participants was possible only among the patients accessing the AT services within a limited time windows), the inclusion criteria had to be necessarily broad, in terms of either clinical conditions or assistive solutions. The data gathered in the study so far are not yet sufficient to infer relations among the person's clinical-functional status, the assistive products, their effectiveness and their costs.

5 Conclusion

Despite the above-mentioned limitations, the Study was able to develop and fine-tune a method that allows tracking the whole AT intervention and measuring its outcome in a standardized manner; this method also prepares the ground for higher-level analyses which will be possible as the intervention database gradually grows thanks to its implementation in the centres' information system.

The method also allows to easily detect possible critical events that may compromise the effectiveness of the assistive solution, and to understand which corrective actions are needed in those cases. As a matter of fact, looking after the client along the whole intervention is of paramount importance, as many unexpected events may happen for which the user needs help.

The method is currently embodied in a tool - the SIVA Template of the AT Intervention Report - that is publicly available and freely downloadable in Italian and English from the Italian national AT Portal [11].

Acknowledgements. This study was partially supported by the Italian Ministry of Health within the Current Research Biomedical Programme - ASSET Project (Individual ASSessment of Environmental facilitators: AT and AAL).

References

1. Cook, A., Polgar, J.M.: Assistive Technology: Principles and Practice (4th edition). Elsevier Mosby, St. Louis (2014)
2. Andrich, R., Mathiassen, N.E., Hoogerwerf, E.J., Gelderblom, G.J.: Service delivery systems for assistive technology in Europe: a Aaate/Eastin position paper. Technol. Disabil. **25**(3), 127–146 (2013)
3. Fuhrer, M.J.: Assessing the efficacy, effectiveness, and cost-effectiveness of assistive technology interventions for enhancing mobility. Disabil. Rehabil. Assistive Technol. **2**(3), 149–158 (2007)
4. Arthanat, S., Bauer, S.M., Lenker, J.A., Nochajski, S.M., Wu, Y.W.B.: Conceptualization and measurement of assistive technology usability. Disabil. Rehabil. Assistive Technol. **2**(4), 235–248 (2007)
5. Federici, S., Scherer, M.J.: Assistive Technology Assessment Handbook. CRC Press, Boca Raton (2012)
6. Andrich, R., Caracciolo, A.: Analysing the cost of individual assistive technology programmes. Disabil. Rehabil. Assistive Technol. **2**(4), 207–234 (2007)
7. Desideri, L., Roentgen, U., Hoogerwerf, E.J., De Witte, L.: Recommending assistive technology (AT) for children with multiple disabilities: a systematic review and qualitative synthesis of models and instruments for AT professionals. Technol. Disabil. **25**, 3–13 (2013)
8. Dijcks, B.P., Wessels, R.D., De Vlieger, S.L., Post, M.W.: KWAZO, a new instrument to assess the quality of service delivery in assistive technology provision. Disabil. Rehabil. **28** (15), 909–914 (2006)
9. Wessels, R., Persson, J., Lorentsen, O., Andrich, R., Ferrario, M., Oortwijn, W., Van Beekum, T., Brodin, H., de Witte, L.: IPPA: individual prioritised problem assessment. Technol. Disabil. **14**, 141–145 (2002)
10. Demers, L., Weiss-Lambrou, R., Ska, B.: The Quebec user evaluation of satisfaction with assistive technology (QUEST 2.0): an overview and recent progress. Technol. Disabil. **14**, 101–105 (2002)
11. SIVA template for the assistive technology intervention report (2017). http://portale.siva.it/ en-GB/databases/libraries/detail/id-306

Assistive Technology Abandonment: Research Realities and Potentials

Helen Petrie[✉], Stefan Carmien, and Andrew Lewis

Human Computer Interaction Research Group, Department of Computer Science,
University of York, York YO10 5GH, UK
{helen.petrie, stefan.carmien, andrew.lewis}@york.ac.uk

Abstract. Abandonment of assistive technologies (ATs) is a serious problem – rates of abandonment can be high, 78% has been reported for hearing aids. The paper argues for the importance of studying the abandonment of ATs by collecting real-time data about the use and non-use of ATs in the lived experience of their users. In the AART-BC Project, we are studying the use and abandonment of mobility ATs including wheelchairs, walkers and prostheses. We present two apps, ESMMobilityAT and ProbMobilityAT to facilitate the collection of real-time data about mobility AT use and problems encountered with these ATs. ESMMobilityAT is based on the experience sampling method (ESM) and asks mobility AT users to answer a short questionnaire about their AT use seven times a day. ProbMobilityAT allows mobility AT users to report problems with their AT when they occur. The apps have been successfully piloted on Android and IOS smartphones, although a number of problems with deployment have been highlighted. They will now be used in a field study with mobility AT uses and can be adapted for other AT domains.

Keywords: Assistive technology abandonment · Mobility assistive technology
Experience Sampling Method (ESM)
Apps for measuring assistive technology use · ESMMobilityAT app ·
ProbMobilityAT app

1 Introduction

Although assistive technology (AT) can have a profound positive impact on the daily life of people with disabilities, many initially adopted devices and systems are unfortunately abandoned. An estimated 13 million AT devices are used in North America alone [7] and there are more than eleven million people with disabilities in the United Kingdom, many of whom depend on AT [22]. Studies have reported abandonment rates of up to 78% for hearing aids [10, 16]. Causes for abandonment have many dimensions [10, 14]. For example, AT abandonment may start with the improper fit of a device to a user and to the tasks the user wishes to undertake [17]. If the AT is something that needs to be worn (e.g. a hearing aid), sat in (e.g. a wheelchair) or held (e.g. a joystick to control a computer) and does not physically fit the user's body or is not comfortable for long-term use, it may well be abandoned even though it meets the particular user's needs. If the AT does not enable the performance of the tasks, or all

© The Author(s) 2018
K. Miesenberger and G. Kouroupetroglou (Eds.): ICCHP 2018, LNCS 10897, pp. 532–540, 2018.
https://doi.org/10.1007/978-3-319-94274-2_77

the tasks, that the user wants to do and cannot (easily) do without an AT, there is also a likelihood of abandonment.

Studies of causes of abandonment have noted that changes in the needs of users are an important predictor for abandonment [11, 13]. Such changes can be permanent (e.g. a progressively worsening sight condition, such as macular degeneration), temporary (e.g. an increased tremor in Parkinson's disease which can be addressed with altered medication) or fluctuating (e.g. increased problems with spelling by people with dyslexia when tired or stressed). Such changes might be accommodated by technology that is easier to adjust to the changing needs of the user or their situation. Difficulties in configuring and modifying the settings of an AT will often lead to abandonment [6]. Compounding the problems of abandonment is the fact that this AT is often needed rather than wanted. AT is not about more easily and effectively doing a task; it is often about doing or not doing the task at all. There is also a positive type of abandonment, which is not using a device or system because the need for it no longer exists or because a better device has become available. For example, blind people have used dedicated devices for detecting the colour of objects for some time (e.g. the Colorino [15], or the Cobolt Talking Colour Detector [1], these were particularly useful for knowing what colour clothes one might wear. But these dedicated devices have now been replaced by apps for a smartphone (e.g. ColorID [5] or aidColors [2] for iPhones, Color Grab for Android phones [9]. This "good" type of abandonment of AT is interesting, but not in the scope of the current paper.

1.1 Scope of Problem and Existing Research

Critical to the successful introduction and adoption of AT is initially choosing the correct device or system [12]. This is a complex and multidimensional process, requiring both knowledge of available systems and knowledge of the wishes, needs and abilities of the intended user. There are numerous frameworks to aid AT professionals in making this selection [17, 19]. However, in many cases, validation of the correct choice consists merely of the absence of abandonment. And, if abandonment does occur, only a narrative record of the process of abandonment is typically documented, sometimes long after the actual event.

A study by Phillips and Zhao reported that a "change in needs of the user" showed the strongest association with abandonment [11]. Thus, those ATs that cannot accommodate the changing requirements of users were most likely to be abandoned. It follows (and is confirmed by interviews with several AT experts: Bodine 2003; Kintsch 2002) that an obstacle to AT retention is difficulty in reconfiguring the device. A survey of abandonment causes by Galvin and Donnell [3] lists "changes in consumer functional abilities or activities" as a critical component of AT abandonment. A study by Scherer and Galvin [18] states that one of the major causes for AT mismatch (and consequently abandonment) is the myth that "a user's assistive technology requirements need to be assessed just once". On-going re-assessment and adjustment to changing needs is the appropriate response. A source for research on the other dimensions of AT abandonment, and the development of outcome metrics to evaluate adoption success is the ATOMS project at the University of Milwaukee in the USA [12].

The mark of success in the selection and use of AT, and in particular AT for mobility, is the long-term adoption of the technology for day-to-day use. To understand the process of successful adoption, it is also necessary to study the process of abandonment [4]. To understand both use and abandonment of ATs, including mobility ATs, requires an approach [23] that goes beyond retrospective data collection such as surveys and interviews. We believe that gathering real-time data about AT use and problems with the use of AT, over reasonably long periods of time (e.g. weeks or months) will allow us to develop a far deeper understanding of people's lived experience with their ATs, and what factors lead to successful adoption or abandonment. This understanding can then lead to the development of guidelines to support the design and selection of ATs.

2 Studying AT Use and Abandonment: The Combined Sensor and Experience Sample Method (ESM) Approach in the AART-BC Project

The Adaptive Assistive Rehabilitative Technology – Beyond the Clinic (AART-BC) Project is investigating how to provide health professionals such as occupational therapists and physiotherapists with better information about their patients' use of mobility ATs such as wheelchairs, walkers, and lower limb prostheses. There is currently little data about what AT users do with their mobility aids in their day-to-day lives ("beyond the clinic" where they can be observed by their therapists). Without this information, it is difficult to understand lived experience with ATs, their use and abandonment. This research involves collecting two types of real-time data from mobility AT users: sensor data which objectively tracks their use of the mobility AT, and data about the perceptions of their mobility AT, their mood, fatigue and any problems they are having with the mobility AT. In this paper we will concentrate on the second type of data and how it can be collected.

In the AART-BC project we are exploring the use of the Experience Sampling Method (ESM) developed by Csikszentmihalyi [8] as a way of gathering immediate information about people's lived experience with their mobility AT. This method sends a very short questionnaire to participants at seven pseudo-random times during the day to collect information about their current mobility AT use. In Csikszentmihalyi's original work he used pagers to alert participants to the need to complete a paper questionnaire, now we use an app (ESMMobilityAT) deployed on smartphones to both alert participants and deliver the questionnaire. Participants can answer the questions very quickly via their phone. Each questionnaire should take no more than two minutes to answer. The questions are always the same, so participants become familiar with them, and include mainly multiple choice and Likert item responses to make answering quick and easy (Fig. 1 shows the smartphone questionnaire screens for these two types of questions).

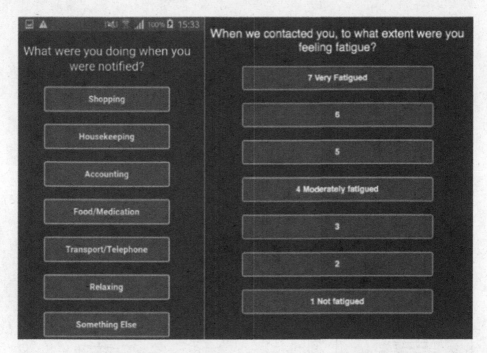

Fig. 1. Questionnaire screens for mobility AT users from the ESMMobilityAT app with "Activity" (left) and "Fatigue" (right).

Participants can select what time in the morning requests to answer the questionnaire start and what time in the evening they should finish, to suit their personal schedules. Requests should be no less than one hour apart, but are sent at random times within those constraints, so that participants cannot predict exactly when they will arrive.

Questions ask about what the participant was doing immediately before the request arrived, whether they were using their mobility AT, whether they were having any problems with it, and if so what they were. In addition, participants are given the PANAS-SF [21], a validated short form of the PANAS scale [24] which measures positive and negative affect, what would commonly be called "mood". Finally, after consultation with occupational therapists and physiotherapists, a question about how fatigued the participant felt was added. The full set of questions and logic of the questionnaire is illustrated in Fig. 2 (apart from the PANAS-SF questions, which are given in Table 1). The questionnaire has been implemented as an app using the framework developed by Thai and Page-Gould [20]. Deployment of the applications is relatively straightforward, via an APK package for Android devices, or an IPA package for iOS devices. It is worth noting that deployment on to iOS devices requires an Enterprise developer licence that involves a paid subscription, but allows the installation of apps without using the Apple store. Apple devices also require "over the air" (OTA) installation from a custom or third party website (e.g. diawi.com) that supports IPA installations. Android deployment requires no special considerations, and the APK package can be downloaded directly or sent to the target device via email for installation.

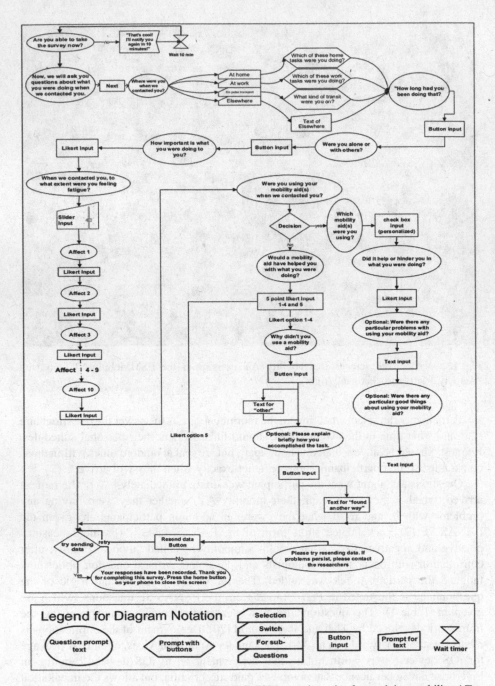

Fig. 2. Questions and logic of the AART-BC ESM questionnaire for studying mobility ATs.

Table 1. PANAS-SF questions to measure positive and negative affect.

Positive affect	Negative affect
Active	Afraid
Alert	Ashamed
Attentive	Hostile
Determined	Nervous
Inspired	Upset

We have also developed a second app, ProbMobilityAT, which allows participants to report any problems them are having with their mobility AT, when it occurs. This will allow for the collection of much more detailed information about problems which occur with mobility ATs. The questions used by the ProbMobilityAT app are very similar to those in ESMMobility to collect the context of the problem, but the main emphasis is on a free text description of the problem that the participant supplied (see Fig. 3).

Fig. 3. Problem reporting screen in the ProbMobilityAT app

We have extensively piloted these two apps, in a range of realistic situations of use, on a range of different IOS and Android smartphones. It emerges that there are numerous problems in deploying such apps, particularly to Android smartphones. For example, if the app is suspended when the phone is in power-saving mode, the pseudo-random notifications will not be received, or will be received later than expected. Similar problems can be found on smartphone that have battery-extending applications installed, as they can aggressively manage the running of background applications.

The process of delivering notifications can become even more problematic when moving between different versions of the Android OS, as there are functional differences in the way that file paths are referenced that can cause an app to crash when it tries to access a resource file such as a custom notification sound. Many of the problems encountered are related to the diverse range of operating system versions now available on smartphone, the number of third-party plugins required to make apps function as expected, and the fact that operating systems may be updated by the user at any time. When operating systems or development tools are upgraded it can take some time for related plugins to be updated by their respective developers. Thus, at the moment, it may not be possible to deploy the app to all smartphones without considerable extra effort. However, in initial use of the apps, users have found the questionnaires easy to understand and quick to answer.

3   Discussion

One goal of the AART-BC Project is to develop an understanding of the lived experience of mobility AT users, to further our understanding of their use and abandonment of their ATs. A further goal is to provide better information to clinicians such as occupational therapists and physiotherapists about their patients' use of their mobility ATs in their daily lives "beyond the clinic", to enable them to support their patients more effectively. But the problems of AT use and abandonment are multifaceted and complex. To address these problems both real-time and retrospective data are required. To facilitate the collection of real-time data, we have now developed two apps, ESMMobilityAT and ProbMobilityAT. The first prompts mobility AT users to answer a short questionnaire about their current activities, mobility AT use, any problems with the AT, their mood and fatigue. This questionnaire is delivered seven times a day, to sample across their lived experiences. The second app allows them to report problems with their mobility AT when they occur, meaning that immediate detail about the problems will be recorded.

Deployment of the apps has not been as simple as we anticipated and much attention needs to be paid to how different versions of the Android and IOS operating systems handle a range of issues. Initial reaction from users on the other hand has been very positive, with the questionnaires easy to understand and quick to answer. The smartphone deployed ESM method is not too intrusive for users who have found the whole experience interesting. We are now ready to use the apps in an extensive field study with mobility AT users. We are also planning to extend this approach to the other AT domains such as the use of hearing aids.

Acknowledgements. This research was partially funded by an Engineering and Physical Science Research Council (EPSRC) Grant, Adaptive Assistive Rehabilitative Technology: Beyond the Clinic (AART-BC), No EP/M025543/1 (see http://aartbc.org/). We are very grateful to all our partners in the project: University of Warwick, University College London, Cardiff University, University of Kent, University of Salford, and Oxford Brookes University. We are also grateful to Xujia "Karlie" Luo and Flo Somerfield for helping to pilot the ESMMobilityAT app.

References

1. Cobolt Systems Ltd. Talking Colour Detector (2018). https://www.cobolt.co.uk/products/index/talking-colour-detector1502118659. Accessed 24 Mar 2018
2. Drive Smart Technologies SL. aidColors (2018). Available at the Apple Store: https://itunes.apple.com/us/app/aidcolors/id365495704?mt=8. Accessed 24 Mar 2018
3. Galvin, J.C., Donnell, C.M.: Educating the consumer and caretaker on assistive technology. In: Scherer, M.J. (ed.) Assistive Technology: Matching Device and Consumer for Successful Rehabilitation, pp. 153–167. American Psychological Association, Washington, DC (2002)
4. Goodman, G., Tiene, D., Luft, P.: Adoption of assistive technology for computer access among college students with disabilities. Disabil. Rehabil. **24**(1–3), 80–92 (2002)
5. GreenGar Studio: Color ID Free (2018). Available at the Apple Store: https://itunes.apple.com/bw/app/color-id-free/id402233600?mt=8. Accessed 24 Mar 2018
6. Kintsch, A., Depaula, R.: A framework for the adoption of assistive technology. In: Bodine, C., (ed.) Supporting Learning Through Assistive Technology. Assistive Technology Partners (SWAAAC 2002), Winter Park, CO, pp. E3 1–10 (2002)
7. Laplante, M.E., Hendershot, G.E., Moss, A.J.: The prevalence of need for assistive technology devices and home accessibility features. Technol. Disabil. **6**, 17–28 (1997)
8. Larson, R., Csikszentmihalyi, M.: The experience sampling method. New Dir. Methodol. Soc. Behav. Sci. **15**, 41–56 (1983)
9. Loomatix: Color Grab (color detection) (2018). https://play.google.com/store/apps/details?id=com.loomatix.colorgrab&hl=en. Accessed 24 Mar 2018
10. Martin, B., Mccormack, L.: Issues surrounding assistive technology use and abandonment in an emerging technological culture. In: Bühler, C., Knops, H. (eds.) 5th European Conference for the Advancement of Assistive Technology (AAATE 1999). IOS Press, Düsseldorf, Germany, p. 852 (1999)
11. Phillips, B., Zhao, H.: Predictors of assistive technology abandonment. Assistive Technol. **5**(1), 36–45 (1993)
12. Rehabilitation Research Design & Disability (R2d2) Center (2006) Assistive Technology Outcomes Measurement System Project (ATOMS Project). http://www.uwm.edu/CHS/r2d2/atoms/. Accessed 24 Mar 2018
13. Reimer-Reiss, M.: Factors associated with assistive technology discontinuance. In: Technology and Persons with Disabilities Conference (CSUN), Northridge, CA (2000)
14. Riemer-Reiss, M.L., Wacker, R.R.: Assistive technology use and abandonment among college students with disabilities. IEJLL. Int. Electron. J. Leadersh. Learn. **3**, 23 (1999)
15. Royal National Institute for Blind People. Colorino talking colour identifier and light detector (2018). http://shop.rnib.org.uk/colorino-talking-colour-detector.html. Accessed 24 Mar 2018
16. Scherer, M.J.: Living in the State of Stuck: How Technology Impacts the Lives of People with Disabilities, 2nd edn. Brookline Books, Cambridge (1996)
17. Scherer, M.J., Galvin, J.C.: Evaluating, Selecting, and Using Appropriate Assistive Technology. Aspen Publishers, Gaithersburg (1996)
18. Scherer, M.J., Galvin, J.C.: An outcomes perspective of quality pathways to the most appropriate technology. In: Scherer, M.J., Galvin, J.C. (eds.) Evaluating, Selecting and Using Appropriate Assistive Technology. Aspen Publishers, Inc., Gaithersburg, pp. 1–26 (1996)
19. Scherer, M.J., Sax, C., Vanbiervliet, A., et al.: Predictors of assistive technology use: the importance of personal and psychosocial factors. Disabil. Rehabil. **27**(21), 1321–1331 (2005)

20. Thai, S., Page-Gould, E: Experience sampler: an open-source scaffold for building smartphone apps for experience sampling. Psychol. Methods. Advance online publication (2017). http://psycnet.apa.org/record/2017-26156-001 Accessed 24 Mar 2018

21. Thompson, E.R.: Development and validation of an internationally reliable short-form of the positive and negative affect schedule (PANAS). J. Cross Cult. Psychol. **38**(2), 227–242 (2007)

22. UK Department of Health: Research and development work relating to assistive technology 2012–13 Presented to Parliament pursuant to Section 22 of the Chronically Sick and Disabled Persons Act 1970 (2013). http://www.dh.gov.uk/publications Accessed 24 Mar 2018

23. Verza, R., Carvalho, M.L.L., Battaglia, M.A., et al.: An interdisciplinary approach to evaluating the need for assistive technology reduces equipment abandonment. Multiple Sclerosis (Houndmills, Basingstoke, England) **12**, 88–93 (2006)

24. Watson, D., Clark, L.A., Tellegen, A.: Development and validation of brief measures of positive and negative affect: the PANAS scales. J. Pers. Soc. Psychol. **54**(6), 1063–1070 (1988)

From Assistive Technology to Industry and Back – Experiences with an Applied Domain Transfer

Thomas Neumayr[1], Mirjam Augstein[1(✉)], Sebastian Pimminger[1],
Stefan Schürz[2], Michael Gstöttenbauer[2], Werner Kurschl[1], and Josef Altmann[1]

[1] University of Applied Sciences Upper Austria, Hagenberg, Austria
`mirjam.augstein@fh-hagenberg.at`
[2] LIFEtool gemeinnützige GmbH, Linz, Austria

Abstract. Conceptualization and development of assistive technology often differs greatly from industrial design and development. While assistive technology solutions are required to be highly individualizable to fit the needs of their diverse target group, industrial solutions need to be suitable for mass markets, which is also reflected by sales numbers and prices. While assistive technology often starts at human's very basic needs such as the need for communication, industrial solutions are often intended to increase productivity and thus also financial gain. Nevertheless, development of assistive technology and of industrial components share several common grounds, especially in the area of Human-Computer Interaction (e.g., industrial workers have to deal with functional impairments). Although both domains could greatly benefit from a liaison, a transfer usually either does not take place at all or takes place at a late stage of development. This paper describes an applied domain transfer between assistive technology and industry during all phases of design and development of novel interaction solutions.

Keywords: User-Centered Design · Contextual Design
Domain transfer · Assistive technology · Industrial research

1 Introduction

The conceptualization and development process of Assistive Technology (AT) often differs greatly from conceptualization and development of industrial solutions although many of the underlying requirements and methods are similar. One reason for this discrepancy might lie in the different target groups, another in the different expectations a newly developed solution has to satisfy. Yet, although the target groups and requirements seem to vary greatly at first glance there are a number of inherent parallels. Seemingly obvious differences regarding the target group can be described as follows. AT is usually targeted towards people with impairments. This target group is (i) exceptionally diverse and (ii) often wrongly perceived as relatively small. As the target group varies greatly, its needs vary

© Springer International Publishing AG, part of Springer Nature 2018
K. Miesenberger and G. Kouroupetroglou (Eds.): ICCHP 2018, LNCS 10897, pp. 541–551, 2018.
https://doi.org/10.1007/978-3-319-94274-2_78

also. This makes it difficult to design solutions that (can be configured to) fit the needs of all, which is one of the principles behind Design4All approaches, see Sect. 2. Sales numbers of AT solutions are often relatively small which again makes the products more expensive for users. Approaches to overcome this rely on off-the-shelf hardware as a basis for AT (see Sect. 2). The main requirements for AT solutions are usually related to personalizability (which could be implemented through configurability or system-initiated adaptivity, see [4,5,9,10]). Further, if categorized as medical product there are numerous additional requirements through legal provisions (e.g., related to hygiene or safety).

In industrial development, prerequisites seem to be inherently different. AT solutions are often needed to allow for activities that would not be possible otherwise (e.g., tools for computer-aided communication or special input devices might enable people to communicate with others or interact with a computer). Industrial solutions often aim at increasing productivity or quality of the outcome. While AT often helps to satisfy human's very basic needs which makes it invaluable for the persons concerned and their environment, industrial solutions are usually only introduced if financially worthwhile. As sales numbers are usually high, the price per component decreases which is also crucial regarding the decision to invest in a new solution – new products or components should not be significantly more expensive to what customers (often long-term customers) are used to. Additional requirements are often related to safety, weight, sensitivity to inference factors (e.g., electromagnetic inferences, noise, dust, dirt, extreme temperatures or humidity) and driven by external certification authorities.

In spite of these differences (e.g., individualization vs. suitability for mass markets), AT and industrial solutions share several requirements and could strongly benefit from each other. First, the current industrial evolution towards batch size one seems to converge with the traditional AT conditions. Second, especially regarding interaction with industrial machines, functional impairments arise. For instance, industrial welders cannot use their hands for interaction with the touch-based user interface of a welding machine in order to change parameters like welding current on-the-fly. During this phase, their prerequisites are comparable to those of people with tetraplegia. While in AT a lot of research has been done on alternative input methods using, e.g., voice, eyes, mouth or head gestures and many people with impairments benefit from it, this knowledge has only very limitedly been transferred to industry. Industry could greatly benefit from AT knowledge to deal with functional impairments and AT could greatly benefit from industrial sales numbers and the resulting lower prices.

The project *Welding Interaction in Future Industry (WIFI)* is a shared endeavour of Human-Computer Interaction (HCI) researchers, industrial partners and AT experts. It researches novel interaction methods for industrial welding machines and for people with impairments (who cannot use their hands for interaction) and endeavours to establish a domain transfer between AT and industry both sides can benefit from. This paper describes this domain transfer at the example of the conceptualization and development process of alternative interaction methods that fit the needs of both target groups. It is intended to encourage and help other researchers and practitioners to establish a similar methodology. The process described covers all relevant project phases from the first analysis of requirements to the development and evaluation of functional prototypes.

2   Related Work

This section describes earlier work on AT that considers different target groups and relates to findings or technology gained or designed for other domains.

Stephanidis et al. [16] argue for "Universal Accessibility", designing interactive products not for the "average" user but for groups with special needs. They argue that a system designed for these diverse groups is likely to exhibit high usability for a broad spectrum of users and underpin their suggestions through concepts of self-adaptive web-based systems such as their AVANTI browser. Stephanidis later derives "User Interfaces for All" [14] as practical manifestation of Universal Accessibility, which is concerned with designs "for the broadest possible range of human abilities, skills, requirements and preferences".

More recently, Stephanidis [15] defined the term "Design for All" as a synthesis of the three concepts (i) User-Centered Design (UCD), (ii) accessibility and AT, and (iii) Universal Design. Concerning UCD, he argues that while these approaches involve humans in all relevant stages, it is still the "average" user who is in the focus. UCD, therefore, does not tell designers how they can deal with users that differ greatly from these "average" users. By fusing UCD with aspects of accessibility and AT as well as Universal Design ("approaches toward addressing people's diversity first"), this drawback could be avoided. Stephanidis then shows a number of examples taking into account all three aforementioned HCI traditions, mainly with the help of guidelines and standards, user interface adaptation, and accessibility in the cloud. Although system adaptivity is not the focus of the WIFI project, we expected that keeping the requirements of individuals with special needs in mind would lead to increased usability "for all". As Stephanidis [15] states, "[e]xamining the users in context is claimed to produce a richer understanding of the relationships between preference, behavior, problems and values". This was also the reason why we employed Contextual Design (CD) methodology in both domains and could identify a number of intersections.

Concerning the accessibility and AT branch of the "Design for All" concept, modern technology undoubtedly had a massive impact on the lives of people with handicaps. Due to a variety of assistive functionalities like speech assistants, visual optimization, advanced touch settings and more, more people with disabilities can e.g., use tablets out of the box and standard tablets drastically changed the AT market. Still many people with handicaps are excluded from their use when user interfaces do not support assistive functionalities. The project ATLab [7,12] aimed to make mainstream technology (tablets) usable for people with disabilities. The goal of the project was the creation of a software development framework to help programmers in implementing accessibility features and to speed up the development process in terms of quantity and quality. Besides integrating accessibility from scratch a second focus was on exploiting more cost-effective AT using mass-market products. This allows providing more and better adaptable content to different end user groups in shorter release cycles.

Although we conducted a thorough literature research we did not find approaches that rely on a full domain transfer between AT and industry throughout all phases of UCD as described in this paper.

3   Project Life Cycle

The process followed in the WIFI project is rooted in the Human-Centered Design (HCD) process for interactive systems defined by ISO 9241-210 [8] which involves the following phases: *plan the HCD process, understand and specify the context of use, specify the user requirements, produce design solutions to meet user requirements,* and *evaluate the designs against requirements.* Figure 1 describes our project lifecycle and also depicts the interlocking between the two domains. We subsume the first phases defined by [8] under *requirements analysis,* although our procedure could also be seen as two subphases (contextual inquiries and interviews match *understanding and specifying the context of use* while during our consolidation we *specified the user requirements*). Further, we split up the design phase into *conceptualization* and *implementation*. As can be seen in Fig. 1, the phases of *conceptualization* and *implementation* did not clearly distinguish between the two domains while activities during *requirements*

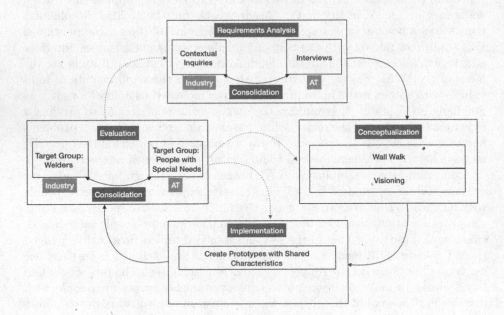

Fig. 1. Project life cycle and domain transfer.

analysis and *evaluation* were conducted for both domains individually in parallel (thus we included a consolidation at the end of these phases).

4   Methods in Different Project Phases

Aiming at the identification, design and implementation of interaction solutions that fit the needs of people with tetraplegia as well as industrial welders who cannot use their hands due to functional impairment, we chose the CD methodology, as described by Beyer and Holtzblatt [2] as a basis for the process introduced in Sect. 3. We decided to employ this time-consuming methodology for the following reasons. First, we hoped to uncover hidden requirements connected to the specific nature of the tasks (i.e., time constraints and demands for high precision when adjusting parameters during welding processes, and requirements in the AT domain). Second, after obtaining a list of requirements for both domains, further design steps could be based upon similarities that have been uncovered in each of the domains. The following sections describe all phases in further detail.

4.1   Requirements Analysis

This section is split up into the domains of AT and industrial welding.

Assistive Technology Setting. The requirements analysis methodology that was followed in the AT domain included the use of personas and qualitative face-to-face interviews based on pre-defined questionnaires. The AT experts in our team already had comprehensive knowledge about their users a-priori, resulting from numerous consultation sessions and incremental user-centered improvements of their most important product, the IntegraMouse[1]. To optimally represent the different user groups in the consortium, six personas [3] were defined. Personas are archetypes of individuals with specific needs and are based on the behaviors and motivations of real people. They can guide decisions about product features, interactions, and visual design and assure an effective user-based end product. Furthermore, qualitative face-to-face interviews with six users (one male), aged between 26 and 57 (M = 40), were conducted. Five participants had a spinal injury, one a muscular disease. The main selection criterion was that they regularly use a computer and control it with alternative input methods. To facilitate the interview, participants with the ability to speak were preferred (we had one non-speaking participant). We visited them in their familiar environment to get a better insight into everyday life and the AT solutions used. Four participants were interviewed at home or at the workplace, one via video call and the interview with the non-speaking participant was conducted by e-mail. The questions covered technological skills, AT devices used, and feature requests. The findings led to a deeper understanding of the users' perspectives. After analyzing the results, ten user requirements were derived that cover configuration software, adaptability of the hardware, ergonomics related to interface elements, input modalities, feedback, interoperability and connectivity.

---

[1] https://www.integramouse.com.

Industrial Research Setting. In the industry branch of our research, the requirements were initially gathered by conducting several Contextual Inquiries (CIs) as a first step of the CD methodology. These CIs consisted of comprehensive interviews and observations of industrial welders in typical work places doing their usual work tasks. Overall, eight CI sessions yielded twelve hours of audio recordings, 16 h of video material, 370 photographs, and 35 pages of written notes. This information we gathered and discussed with the participants was then translated to so-called affinity notes that represent the basic building blocks of CD. The notes can be described as simple observational instances, e.g., "Participant used a component he randomly stumbled across to brace against the working surface" or meaningful quotes, e.g., a participant stated that he wished his welding torch was as light as a pen. In total, more than 400 affinity notes were generated. Next, we created three personas for similar purposes as mentioned for the AT domain. Yet, the method for the creation of the personas differed slightly, as CD offers the possibility to base them on the contextual data (e.g., affinity notes). To achieve an organized overview of the observed instances and learn from the emerging categories, the affinity notes were assembled in a so-called affinity diagram. This was done by interpreting the affinity notes and grouping them according to their actual underlying meaning. E.g., a participant's wish for a light-as-a-pen torch arguably is not about a pen per se, but could mean that the torch should be as small as possible (but well graspable), as light as possible, and as freely movable as possible. Each group consisting of a couple of affinity notes then received a label subsuming the shared theme. The labels served as a basis for a formulation of requirements. E.g., the affinity notes "Hearing is very important to me, seeing not so much" and "A good welder tunes his machinery with his sense of hearing" were labeled "The sound of the welding process is an important feedback to me". Together with another label "Visual feedback of the welding process" this led to the requirements "Feedback of the welding operation must be available for the welders." and "The system must show currently relevant feedback to the welders.". A more exhaustive description of the CI procedure can be found in [1].

Consolidation. As the individual affinity notes were gathered solely in the domain of industrial welding, it was necessary to do a consolidation of the domain transfer by bringing in experts of the AT field and discuss the diagram's contents in the light of their respective findings. Up to this point, it was important not to think in solutions, but concentrate on the functional or permanent impairments that inhibit our users when they want to fulfill their tasks. By keeping this in mind, the next steps could greatly benefit from the requirements analyses in both domains because no design decisions were made prematurely. This means that the requirements of both domains, which are similar concerning users' functional impairments during the interaction, could be considered for both usage contexts. Many of the requirements also had implications for the respective other domain. E.g., the requirement describing the need for timely feedback during welding was also examined in the AT context. Another example concerns a requirement which stated that welders must always be able to focus on the welding process (and not be distracted by interaction activities). This also held true in the AT domain, where users also should always be able to concentrate on their tasks. A requirement from AT stated that users with tetraplegia must always be able to interact even if they can not change their body posture. Interestingly, even here a connection was found as we observed that many welders are used to maintain a fixed posture while welding. Through transfer of the requirements in both directions, a more holistic understanding of the usage contexts was achieved.

4.2 Conceptualization

This phase comprised three major subphases that were conducted in close collaboration of the two domains, thus we describe it based on the subphases here.

Research of Interaction Methods. We conducted an exhaustive research of possible interaction methods, starting at human's physical capabilities (not yet considering impairments) that could theoretically be utilized for interaction purposes. This led to the definition of five input modalities (gesture-based, voice, eye gaze, mouth and brain input) and three output modalities (visual, haptic and acoustic output). These modalities were then split up into concrete methods, technologies and products. During the following research phase we divided the tasks among the researchers of both domains but integrated the findings in one joint detailed catalog describing input methods (on about 160 pages) and one joint catalog describing output methods (about 110 pages). Thus, it was possible to share the knowledge about existing hardware (and software) components, also of those that are only common in their respective field. For interaction methods and related technologies we then defined objective (e.g., sensitivity to extreme temperatures) and subjective assessment criteria (e.g., applicability for people with impairments and applicability for industrial welders). All methods and technologies were then assessed on a six-point scale by 10 team members (involving AT experts, industrial researchers but also industry partners). This step led to a first prioritization of interaction approaches and also to a first exclusion of methods, e.g., when no reliable hardware solution could be found.

Wall Walk. In this subphase, the reduced list of interaction methods and the consolidated affinity diagram (as described in Sect. 4.1) was used to create design ideas (i.e., potential solutions for existing issues) taking into consideration the personas and specific requirements of *both* domains. Experts of both fields together with industry partners performed a so-called wall walk, a process that started with an individual, introspective immersion into the diagram. Next, comments, thoughts and envisioned design ideas were placed near the affinity notes the solutions tried to address using sticky notes. This procedure of first individually obtaining a good and balanced overview and next coming up with concrete ideas to concrete issues guaranteed that the (functional) requirements of the target group are considered in the respective solutions. Eventually, the design ideas were discussed in their particular context among the different experts. Finally, a list of the most capable ideas (about 30) was compiled in plenary.

Visioning. To bridge the gap between the first ideas and more sophisticated concepts, a visioning workshop (again part of the CD methodology) was held where experts of AT and the inquiry team of the industrial domain participated. On this one-day event, the list of the most capable ideas created before was used to combine different compatible solutions to three "visions" of how users could be supported through our prototypes in future scenarios. Thereby, the emerging visions were sketched in a group storytelling process. After that, the different pros and cons of each vision were evaluated and documented. On a separate date, two researchers created a consolidated vision by adopting the positively evaluated parts of each vision and combining them (as long as they were compatible). This consolidated vision containing the thoughts and considerations of both domain expert groups was then used to inform the later design and implementation steps. E.g., in the discussion of the visions, AT experts stated that a specific multi-modal input method (focusing through eye gaze and selecting through voice) did not perform well from a technical perspective in their experience and it was discarded thereafter - although it held high potential from the interaction side.

4.3 Implementation

After preparing the consolidated vision, the first parts of the initial prototype's components were planned. For that purpose, we first relied on the comprehensive review of existing hardware (and software) components created during the conceptualization phase that could be used as a basis for our prototypes. To create a working system with the purpose of proofing the concept of the technology chosen as soon as possible, the teams in both domains followed the rapid prototyping model. In this process early versions were developed to clarify the requirements of the system and to reveal critical design considerations. Rapid prototyping gave the software engineers the chance to "test drive" the hardware together with software to ensure that it is in fact a feasible and promising solution for the envisioned use case. Rapid prototyping was conducted as an iterative process, following a cyclic multi-stage design/modify/review procedure. Development was done in close collaboration of AT and industry domain.

4.4 Evaluation

This section is split into two domains because the evaluation was done separately (with both target groups and different methods) before consolidation of findings.

Assistive Technology Setting. Heuristic evaluation [13] with in-house AT experts as well as scenario-based user tests with AT power users will be executed as soon as a first stable prototype is reached[2]. The main goal of the heuristic

---

[2] At the moment, the prototype is finalized while the evaluation is prepared in parallel.

evaluation developed by Jakob Nielsen is to identify problems associated with the design of the user interface. The researchers' observations during the power user tests will help to further adapt the system to the specific AT requirements gathered in the previous phases. The User Experience (UX) will be assessed after each session using the standardized User Experience Questionnaire (UEQ) [11], which allows a quick assessment of the UX of interactive products.

Industrial Research Setting. To obtain an initial impression of how well our first prototypes work in a realistic usage context, two different stages of a Wizard of Oz test were conducted with five welders. On the first occasion, one welder acted as the intelligent wizard while another welder performed a given welding task using the unaltered welding equipment. This step helped us to create a baseline we could later compare our prototypes to. We measured time, UX (using UEQ) and task load (using NASA TLX [6]). On the second occasion, one welder was trained to act as a wizard not anymore intelligently but rather according to a predefined set of responses to user interactions based on the concept we developed during the conceptualization and implementation phase. This step was useful to further clarify our concepts and details for the prototypes. The third iteration of evaluation will include an identical test setting fully replacing the wizard by our prototype. Afterwards, we will repeat phases as necessary (e.g., revisions of the prototype will lead to another evaluation step).

Consolidation. After the individual evaluation steps in each of the domains, the findings were and will be discussed and categorized in the full consortium. Issues that apply for both domains (even if identified in the evaluation of only one) lead to a joint revision of the prototypes. Issues that apply to one of the domains only are considered in the branch of the respective domain.

5   Conclusions

In this paper we described a domain transfer between AT and industry during the full process of conceptualization and development of interaction solutions. The focus of the paper is not on the concrete solutions themselves but on the methodology used to facilitate a project in which both domains can benefit from each other. In the run-up to the WIFI project we exhaustively researched similar approaches but did not find a comparable transfer that is effective through all HCD phases. There are ideas with similar background in the area of context-aware assistance systems where people with and without impairments should be supported during industrial work tasks (see e.g., the MotionEAP[3] or the HCW4i[4] project). However, there the approach is rather connected to the idea of Design for All (see Sect. 2); most assistance system solutions are not mainly focused on a thorough domain transfer. Conceptualization and development of solutions

---

[3] http://www.motioneap.de.
[4] http://workplace4industry.fh-ooe.at/.

that satisfy the needs of two (seemingly divergent) target groups is challenging without question. Yet, such endeavors bear the potential to not only result in adequate technological solutions (which is probably a shorter-term effect) but also novel cooperations and wider-scale inclusion of people with impairments through the intensified dialogue. This paper is intended to encourage other researchers to apply similar approaches. Further, the description of which methodology was used when, which phases required parallel tasks and consolidation and which allowed for close interlocking, should guide others through similar endeavors.

Acknowledgements. The work described in this paper has been conducted within the scope of the project *Welding Interaction in Future Industry (WIFI)*, funded through the BRIDGE 1 program, managed by the Austrian Research Promotion Agency (FFG). Project partners are the University of Applied Sciences Upper Austria, LIFEtool gemeinnützige GmbH and Fronius International GmbH.

References

1. Augstein, M., Neumayr, T., Pimminger, S., Ebner, C., Altmann, J., Kurschl, W.: Contextual design in industrial settings: experiences and recommendations. In: Proceedings of the 20th International Conference on Enterprise Information Systems, Funchal, Madeira, Portugal (2018)
2. Beyer, H., Holtzblatt, K.: Contextual Design: Defining Customer-Centered Systems, 1st edn. Morgan Kaufmann, Burlington (1997)
3. Cooper, A.: The Inmates Are Running The Asylum. Why High-Tech Products Drive Us Crazy and How to Restore The Sanity. Sams Indianapolis (1999)
4. Gajos, K., Weld, D.S., Wobbrock, J.O.: Automatically generating personalized user interfaces with supple. Artif. Intell. **174**(12–13), 910–950 (2010)
5. Gajos, K.Z., Wobbrock, J.O., Weld, D.S.: Automatically generating user interfaces adapted to users' motor and vision capabilities. In: Proceedings of UIST 2007, pp. 231–240. ACM Press (2007)
6. Hart, S.G., Staveland, L.E.: Development of NASA-TLX (task load index): results of empirical and theoretical research. Adv. Psychol. **52**, 139–183 (1988)
7. Heumader, P., Augstein, M., Burger, T., Hofer, D., Koutny, R., Kurschl, W., Miesenberger, K., Stitz, H., Vieghofer, M.: ATLAB: an accessible cross platform gaming framework for people with disabilities. In: Proceedings of the 2013 AAATE Conference (2013)
8. International Organization for Standardization: ISO924-210: Human-Centered Design for Interactive Systems (2010). https://www.iso.org/standard/52075.html
9. Kurschl, W., Augstein, M., Burger, T., Pointner, C.: User modelling for people with special needs. Int. J. Pervasive Comput. Commun. **10**(3), 313–336 (2014)
10. Kurschl, W., Augstein, M., Stitz, H., Heumader, P., Pointner, C.: A user modelling wizard for people with motor impairments. In: Proceedings of the 11th International Conference on Advances in Mobile Computing & Multimedia, Vienna, Austria (2013)
11. Laugwitz, B., Held, T., Schrepp, M.: Construction and evaluation of a user experience questionnaire. In: Holzinger, A. (ed.) USAB 2008. LNCS, vol. 5298, pp. 63–76. Springer, Heidelberg (2008). https://doi.org/10.1007/978-3-540-89350-9_6

12. Miesenberger, K., Heumader, P., Koutny, R., Kurschl, W., Stitz, H., Augstein, M., Vieghofer, M., Hofer, D., Pointner, C.: ATLab: an app-framework for physical disabilities. J. Technol. Pers. Disabil. **1**(13), 46–56 (2014)
13. Nielsen, J., Molich, R.: Heuristic evaluation of user interfaces. In: Proceedings of the SIGCHI Conference on Human Factors in Computing Systems, pp. 249–256 (1990)
14. Stephanidis, C.: User interfaces for all: new perspectives into human-computer interaction. User Interfaces All-Concepts Methods Tools **1**, 3–17 (2001)
15. Stephanidis, C.: Design 4 all. In: The Encyclopedia of Human-Computer Interaction, 2nd edn. (2013)
16. Stephanidis, C., Paramythis, A., Akoumianakis, D., Sfyrakis, M.: Self-adapting web-based systems: towards universal accessibility. In: Proceedings of the 4th Workshop on User Interface For All, Stockholm, Sweden (1998)

HELP? Attitudes Towards Care and Assistive Technologies from the Perspective of People with Disabilities

Julia Offermann-van Heek[✉] and Martina Ziefle

Human-Computer Interaction Center, RWTH Aachen University,
Campus-Boulevard 57, 52074 Aachen, Germany
vanheek@comm.rwth-aachen.de

Abstract. Increasing care needs represent major challenges for today's care sectors. Developing assistive technologies such as Ambient Assisted Living (AAL) systems pose a potential approach to face these challenges by relieving care staff or facilitating everyday life, e.g., for people with disabilities. Thereby, acceptance is essential for a sustainable adoption of assistive technologies in real life. So far, research has focused on technology-related as well as demographic factors and persons' attitudes (e.g., technical self-efficacy) impacting technology acceptance. In contrast, individual attitudes towards the own situation - in particular individual attitudes towards care – have not been considered as potential influencing factors on the acceptance of assistive technologies. In order to create an appropriate measuring instrument for attitudes towards care, two empirical studies were carried out: In an online survey study (n = 34) persons' attitudes towards the own care situation and their relationships to attitudes towards usage of assistive technologies were studied out of the perspective of people with disabilities. The exploratory confirmed instrument "attitudes towards care" was related with acceptance and perception of assistive technologies focusing on people of different ages with physical disabilities. Results of the second study (n = 64) verified these relationships focusing on elderly people in need of care. This suggests that attitudes towards care are acceptance-relevant for diverse groups of people. The results can be used to investigate relationships between individual perceptions of care and (assistive) technology acceptance in detail and to refine and adapt the attitude towards care instrument for diverse user groups.

Keywords: Assistive technologies · Technology acceptance
Attitude towards care · People with disabilities

1 Introduction

Rising needs of care are omnipresent but also divergent challenges for today's society. On the one hand, in the context of demographic change, a steadily increasing number of older people in need of care pose strains for the care sectors [1, 2]. On the other hand, age-independent disabilities of people cause huge needs of care and assistance as well [3].

© Springer International Publishing AG, part of Springer Nature 2018
K. Miesenberger and G. Kouroupetroglou (Eds.): ICCHP 2018, LNCS 10897, pp. 552–558, 2018.
https://doi.org/10.1007/978-3-319-94274-2_79

Independent from age, most people in need of care desire to live at their own home as long and as autonomously as possible [4, 5]. Assistive technologies such as Ambient Assisted Living (AAL) technologies and systems have the potential to enable and support a more autonomous and independent life within the own home environment for diverse user groups, e.g., by monitoring of vital parameters, detecting falls, or facilitating life using smart home elements [6–8]. To realize assistive technologies that satisfy the requirements of diverse user groups, it is necessary to analyze whether and to which extent such technologies or systems are accepted and if those evaluations depend on the diversity of potential users. So far, there have been several studies investigating the acceptance of AAL and smart home technologies focusing on influencing demographic factors such as age (e.g., [9, 10]) or gender [11]. In current studies, the perspectives of people with disabilities, especially their wishes and needs, are increasingly involved [5, 12]. In contrast, individual care-related attitudes have not been considered as influencing factors for the acceptance of assistive technologies - in particular not from the perspective of people with disabilities.

2   State of the Art

Numerous studies explored the technical development of assistive technologies and systems, their efficiency, functionalities, and reliability [e.g., 6, 7]. Considering professional care contexts, previous research activities were predominantly reduced on efficiency in care [13], patient satisfaction with care [14], and reduction of costs [15] and focused not on perceptions of diverse groups of people referring to their own care situation.

In recent years, the acceptance of diverse assistive technologies was increasingly investigated focusing on influencing user diversity factors such as age or gender [10, 11]. In this regard, current research also considered experience with care as user diversity factor [5] revealing that people with diverse care experiences (care professionals, people with disabilities, relatives of people in need of care, not-experienced people) differ with regard to their perception and acceptance of assistive technologies. These results indicate that in particular individual attitudes towards the own situation referring to disabilities and care needs are decisive for technology acceptance. Referring to people with disabilities, some studies focus on attitudes of people towards people with disabilities [e.g., 16] as well as on the subjective perception of the own disability or rather coping with disabilities [17, 18]. In contrast, feelings and perceptions of people during care, their wishes and needs – in sum their subjective perception of care situations and their attitudes towards their care – have been neglected so far in particular with regard to their potential impact on technology acceptance.

Therefore, the current study aimed for an investigation of people with disabilities' individual perception of their care situation and possible relationships to the perception of assistive technologies.

3 Methodology

Based on preceding qualitative studies, the current study focused on people with disabilities (n = 34) of different ages aiming for an investigation of their attitude towards their disability, in particular their attitude towards care, and their acceptance of assistive technologies. The expoloratory study was directed to the development of an instrument that is able to reliably measure "attitude towards care" as potential influencing factor for the acceptance of assistive technologies. In a first step, this instrument is analyzed focusing on the perspective of people with disabilities. In a second step, it has to be examined if this instrument is basically adaptable to evaluating attitudes towards care of other groups of people in need of care.

As an example for assistive technologies, a holistic AAL system equipped with diverse technologies (e.g., camera, motion detectors, ultrasonic whistles) was evaluated in a scenario-based online questionnaire. All items and constructs based on the findings of preceding qualitative studies.

3.1 Sample

The mean age of the participants was 41.3 years (SD = 13.8, min = 21, max = 81) with 58.8% females and 41.2% males. All participants indicated to be physically disabled and in need of care, while paralysis, spasticity, and muscular disorders were the most frequently mentioned disabilities. More than half of the participants (55.9%) stated to be disabled by birth, while the other participants (44.1%) stated to live with their disability for more than ten years. The majority of participants indicated to be assisted by their families or partners in combination with professional care staff (n = 15) or solely by their families or partners (n = 12), whereas few participants were assisted only by professional care staff (n = 3). Most of the participants (n = 23) reported to need assistance in the areas body care, mobility, housekeeping, and nutrition, while only two participants indicated to need assistance in two of these areas (n = 9 in three of these areas). On average, the participants reported a high daily duration of care (M = 8.8 h, SD = 8.3, min = 1, max = 24).

4 Results

The participants had on average a rather positive attitude towards their disability indicated by rejecting the most negative statements (e.g., helpless, restricting, annoying) and approving most of the positive statements (Fig. 1). Merely, the positive statements "I am very independent with my disability" (M = 3.1; SD = 1.5) and "... I can certain things better than people without disabilities" (M = 2.9; SD = 1.5) were slightly rejected.

Figure 2 shows the participants' ratings referring to their attitude towards care: the participants agreed with the statements that they are glad to have "... someone who helps me" (M = 5.3; SD = 1.1) and that the relationship to their care staff is important to them (M = 5.0; SD = 1.5). Further, the agreement of statements dealing with independency and the approval of the statement "I often feel dependent during my

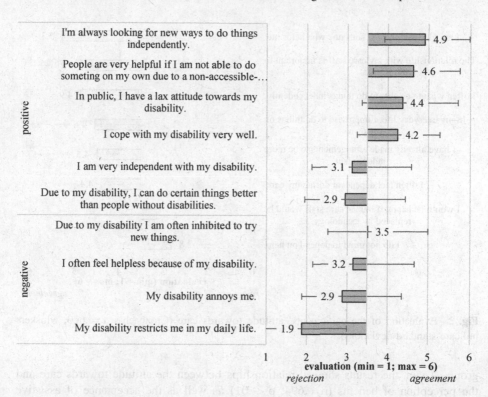

Fig. 1. Evaluation of the participants' attitude towards their disability (Cronbach's α = .720; whiskers indicate standard deviations)

care" (M = 4.4; SD = 1.2) showed that this aspect was of major importance within the attitude towards care.

Using correlation analyses, potential relationships between attitudes towards disabilities and care and acceptance of assistive technologies were investigated in an explorative way. Interestingly, none of the demographic user factors (age, gender, education) was related with the acceptance of assistive technologies.

In addition, the attitude towards disabilities was also not related with acceptance of AAL technologies. Apparently, the positive or negative evaluation of assistive technologies at home is not depending on the disability status of persons. Instead, the attitude towards care correlated with the perception of benefits (r = .420; p < .05) as well as the acceptance of assistive technologies (r = .401; p < .05). Thus people with a more positive attitude towards care including high needs for independency perceived potential benefits of assistive technologies more positive and showed a higher acceptance of those technologies.

Based on these results, the developed construct attitude towards care was also evaluated in a second quantitative study focusing on older people in need of care (n = 64) and their acceptance of assistive medical technologies. The results corroborated (Cronbach's α = .710) that the measurement instrument and the developed construct was able to assess the attitude towards care also for a different user

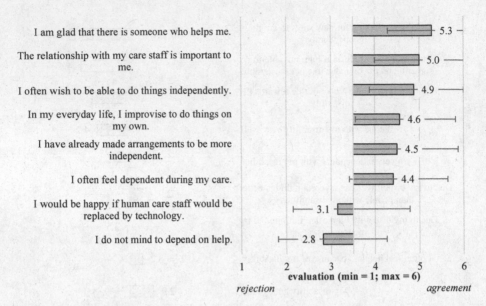

Fig. 2. Evaluation of the participants' attitude towards care (Cronbach's α = .620; whiskers indicate standard deviations).

group. Again, the results showed relationships between the attitude towards care and the perception of benefits (r = .694; p < .01) as well as the acceptance of assistive technologies (r = .309; p < .05).

5 Discussion

In contrast to previous studies in the field [e.g., 5, 11], the presented study focused on individual attitudes towards own disabilities and care situations as potential influencing factors on assistive technologies' acceptance instead of considering demographic factors (e.g., age, gender, education, or "health" status).

The analyses revealed that both applied instruments (attitude towards disability and attitude towards care) could be reasonably used to measure attitudes of people with disabilities. In a first step, the results showed no significant relationships between the attitude towards disability and acceptance of assistive technologies. In contrast, the perception of the own care situation and associated feelings play a decisive role for the acceptance of innovative assistive technologies. These results indicate that the perception and the personal coping with the own situation needing care and support are more decisive for the acceptance of assistive technologies than the general attitude towards the own disability.

In the absence of scales or instruments for assessing the individual attitude towards care, the current study provides a first version of a measuring instrument - in this case - the attitude towards care from the perspective of people with disabilities including aspects such as independency, autonomy, and the relationship to care staff. Further, the results showed that people with a positive attitude towards care (including high needs and efforts for independency) have a more positive attitude towards assistive technologies. The vivid feedback of our participants showed that they desire technologies that help them to help themselves aiming not for a substitution of human caregivers but enabling themselves to have a more autonomous and self-determined life. Comparative results in a second study implicate, on the one hand, that the instrument assessing attitudes towards care is reasonably usable for diverse user groups and that, on the other hand, attitude towards care is an influencing factor on the acceptance of assistive technologies independent of the type of "users". As the current study was a first explorative study in this specific regard, future studies will have to investigate the relationship between attitude towards care and acceptance of assistive technologies in more detail as well as focus on potential influences of other user factors (e.g., knowledge about assistive technologies).

6   Conclusion and Future Work

The study represented a first approach to assess people's attitudes towards care serving as a basis for an extension of the applied instrument and deeper investigations in the future. The relationship between attitudes towards care and the acceptance of different assistive technologies should also be analyzed in more detail focusing on diverse technologies and user groups applying inference statistical analyses to examine group differences and cause-effect relationships.

The first explorative results of the presented study could be used to extend and refine the developed attitude towards care-instrument and to adapt it to different user groups. As the mentioned results of a second study showed, the instrument could be reasonably used for people with disabilities but also for older people in need of care. Thus, in future studies we will investigate to what extent the instrument and its adaptions could also be used to assess hypothetical attitudes towards care (e.g., needs, wishes, concepts of aging and care) for participants who are not (yet) in need of care.

References

1. Bloom, D.E., Canning, D.: Global Demographic Change: Dimensions and Economic Significance. National Bureau of Economic Research. Working Paper No. 10817 (2004)
2. Walker, A., Maltby, T.: Active ageing: a strategic policy solution to demographic ageing in the European Union. Int. J. Soc. Welf. **21**, 117–130 (2012)
3. Geenen, S.J., Powers, L.E., Sells, W.: Understanding the role of health care providers during the transition of adolescents with disabilities and special health care needs. J. Adolesc. Health **32**(3), 225–233 (2003)
4. Wiles, J.L., Leibing, A., Guberman, N., Reeve, J., Allen, R.E.S.: The Meaning of "Ageing in Place" to Older People. The Gerontologist, gnr098 (2011)
5. van Heek, J., Himmel, S., Ziefle, M.: Helpful but Spooky? Acceptance of AAL-systems contrasting user groups with focus on disabilities and care needs. In: Proceedings of the International Conference on ICT for Aging well (ICT4AWE 2017). SCITEPRESS – Science and Technology Publications (2017)

6. Cheng, J., Chen, X., Shen, M.: A framework for daily activity monitoring and fall detection based on surface electromyography and accelerometer signals. IEEE J. Biomed. Health Inform. **17**(1), 38–45 (2013)

7. Baig, M.M., Gholamhosseini, H.: Smart health monitoring systems: an overview of design and modeling. J. Med. Syst. **37**(2), 1–14 (2013)

8. Rashidi, P., Mihailidis, A.: A survey on ambient-assisted living tools for older adults. IEEE J. Biomed. Health Inform. **17**(3), 579–590 (2013)

9. Fuchsberger, V.: Ambient assisted living: elderly people's needs and how to face them. In: Proceedings of the 1st ACM International Workshop on Semantic Ambient Media Experiences, pp. 21–24. ACM (2008)

10. Demiris, G., Hensel, B.K., Skubic, M., Rantz, M.: Senior residents' perceived need of and preferences for "smart home" sensor technologies. Int. J. Technol. Assess. Health Care **24**(1), 120–124 (2008)

11. Wilkowska, W., Gaul, S., Ziefle, M.: A small but significant difference – the role of gender on acceptance of medical assistive technologies. In: Leitner, G., Hitz, M., Holzinger, A. (eds.) USAB 2010. LNCS, vol. 6389, pp. 82–100. Springer, Heidelberg (2010). https://doi. org/10.1007/978-3-642-16607-5_6

12. Kadijevich, D.M., Odovic, G., Maslikovic, D.: Using ICT and quality of life: comparing persons with and without disabilities. In: Miesenberger, K., Bühler, C., Penaz, P. (eds.) ICCHP 2016. LNCS, vol. 9758, pp. 129–133. Springer, Cham (2016). https://doi.org/10. 1007/978-3-319-41264-1_18

13. Holman, H., Lorig, K.: Patient self-management: a key to effectiveness and efficiency in care of chronic disease. Publ. Health Rep. **119**(3), 239–243 (2004)

14. Bleustein, C., Rothschild, D.B., Valen, A., Valatis, E., Schweitzer, L., Jones, R.: Wait times, patient satisfaction scores, and the perception of care. Am. J. Manag. Care **20**(5), 393–400 (2014)

15. Tsai, T.C., Orav, E.J., Jha, A.K.: Patient satisfaction and quality of surgical care in US hospitals. Ann. Surg. **261**(1), 2 (2015)

16. Findler, L., Vilchinsky, N., Werner, S.: The multidimensional attitudes scale toward persons with disabilities (MAS) construction and validation. Rehabil. Couns. Bull. **50**(3), 166–176 (2007)

17. Terrill, A.L., Molton, I.R., Ehde, D.M., Amtmann, D., Bombardier, C.H., Smith, A.E., Jensen, M.P.: Resilience, age, and perceived symptoms in persons with long-term physical disabilities. J. Health Psychol. **21**(5), 640–649 (2016)

18. Power, M.J., Green, A.M.: The attitudes to disability scale (ADS): development and psychometric properties. J. Intellect. Disabil. Res. **54**, 860–874 (2010)

China's Efforts to Information Service for Visual-Impaired People

Chunbin Gu[1], Jiajun Bu[1(✉)], Shuyi Song[1], Zhi Yu[1], Liangcheng Li[1],
Meng Han[2], and Lizhen Tang[2]

[1] Alibaba-Zhejiang University Joint Institute of Frontier Technologies,
Zhejiang Provincial Key Laboratory of Service Robot, College of Computer
Science, Zhejiang University, Hangzhou 310027, China
{guchunbin, bjj, brendasoung, yuzhirenzhe,
liangcheng_li}@zju.edu.cn
[2] China Braille Press, Beijing 100050, China
hanm03@163.com, eicatang_1@163.com

Abstract. In China, there are more than 13 million visual-impaired people,
which obtain information by touching and hearing rather than vision. To help
them access to information more conveniently, many efforts have been made in
China: Firstly, it provides digital resources by building China Digital Library for
Visual Impairment; Secondly, it develops a software called Sunshine Screen
Reader to help visual-impaired people search through the computer; Also, it
promotes SunshineReader, a portable device, to enable visual-impaired people
obtain information from electronic documents and printed text. All these efforts
achieve demonstrable results in narrowing down the gap between visual-
impaired people and information. Generally speaking, most information can be
accessed by CDLVI, Sunshine Screen Reader and SunshineReader.

Keywords: Visual-impaired people · Information service
Assistive technology

1 Introduction

According to the latest data, there are approximate 253 million people with vision
impairment worldwide, 36 million of whom are completely visionless and the
remaining are living with moderate to severe vision impairment [1]. China has a visual-
impaired population of about 13 million [2], which contains 5.5 million blind people
and 7.5 million people with low vision. Compared to healthy people, visual-impaired
people obtain information by touching and hearing rather than vision, which brings
about restriction on information sources. In order to offer adequate digital resources
required by this group of people and overcome the limits of space and time in traditional library, China Digital Library for Visual Impairment (CDLVI) has been built in
2008 by China Braille Press (CBP) to provide comprehensive information and cultural
service for visual-impaired people. Considering that amounts of resources in CDLVI
are limited, CBP develops a software called Sunshine Screen Reader, which can read
all the information displayed on the screen, to assist visual-impaired users in searching

© Springer International Publishing AG, part of Springer Nature 2018
K. Miesenberger and G. Kouroupetroglou (Eds.): ICCHP 2018, LNCS 10897, pp. 559–562, 2018.
https://doi.org/10.1007/978-3-319-94274-2_80

information through the computer. More than that, to help visual-impaired people get information from electronic documents and printed text in daily life, CBP prompts a portal device named SunshineReader, which is ready to transcribe texts into speech format.

The remaining of this paper is structured as follows: Section 2 provides related work to contributions made by different governments. Section 3 introduces the China Braille Press. Section 3.1 presents three main contributions made by Chinese government. Section 4 concludes this paper.

2 Related Work

In addition to domestic work, many efforts also have been exerted by other countries and international organizations to assist visual-impaired people in accessing various information. International Federation of Library Association and Institutions (IFLA) established its Section of libraries for the blind in 1986 [3]. Canadian National Institute for the Blind (CNIB) began to digitalize all its resources in 1998 and set up Integrated Digital Library Systems with the cooperation with Microsoft, which is the first portal for visually impaired people, in 2002. The Bibliothèque nationale de France (BnF) developed Gallica digital library and related accessibility webs in 2005, which could convert the text format into speech. National Federation of the Blind (NFB) prompts NFB-NEWSLINE [4], a reading service that conveys the information from newspapers, magazines and TV listings to visual-impaired people through telephone. American Printing House for the Blind (APH) promoted some assistive technologies such as VisioBook [5], a portable electronic magnifier and distance viewer, and Book Wizard Producer [6], which can create a digital audio book in DAISY format.

3 China's Efforts

3.1 China Braille Press

In China, CBP has spent 65 years ensuring that visual-impaired individuals have access to the information independently. To achieve this goal, great efforts have been exerted to: Firstly, it provides digital resources by building CDLVI; Also, it develops assistive technologies such as SunshineReader and Sunshine Screen Reader, to help visual-impaired people obtain more information.

3.2 China Digital Library for Visual Impairment

To meet the demands of most visual-impaired people and overcome the difficulties of getting information due to the lack of searching platform, CDLVI provides various resources including electronic braille, audio transcription, large print transcription and information about cultural activities such as training, exhibition and lectures. So visual-impaired people can obtain their interested information on this platform without accessibility barriers. Considering that the storage of electronic resources usually needs massive manpower and brings about many problems such as page number error and index error, CDLVI supports the function of smart storage, which includes format error checking and new correct index generation by analyzing the content of the existing index. Additionally, personalized bookmark service is available in this library to help visual-impaired users find resources more quickly and more conveniently. This bookmark system involves three types of bookmarks that can be set in different situations including the most recent page read, highlight and sharing, which used to share resources with others by inserting notes. Moreover, if users want to find any information that is unavailable in this library, they will be notified when the information is accessible. Also, to help users discover new resources, recommendation algorithms are applied to CDLVI. When a user log into this platform, the smart recommendation system will analyze the profile and historical behaviors of the user, and then it provides the related resources that the user may be interested in.

Up to now, more than 110,000 visual-impaired people have been benefited from this platform and more than 50,000 users have registered. In fact, CDLVI has become the main digital information sources for visual-impaired people in China.

3.3 Sunshine Screen Reader

Considering that the CDLVI's capacity of digital resources is limited, visual-impaired people may need to search information from other sources. The software named as Sunshine Screen Reader, which can convert all contents on PC screen into speech format [8], enables its users to get information from most applications installed in the computer. When visual-impaired users are utilizing these applications, Sunshine Screen Reader provides real-time operation instructions and reads search results. More than that, in order to provide visual-impaired people with the concept of orientation, this software apply a new browse mode, in which information on the screen is read word-by-word and line-by-line. So far, this software has supported commercial word processors and standard applications. Also, Sunshine Screen Reader offers some distinctive functions such as adjusting reading speeds according to different contents and altering hot key scheme to adapt to most kinds of keyboard layouts. These hotkeys enable visual-impaired people to select elements needed more quickly. Because of the remarkable practicability of Sunshine Screen Reader, it is supported strongly and promoted by China Disabled Person's Federation (CDPF).

3.4 SunshineReader

Besides the information mentioned above, which is from CDLVI and applications installed on in the computer, the brief but important information in daily life, which comes from electronic documents and printed text, also plays a crucial role in our daily life. In order to make this type of information accessible to visual-impaired people, SunshineReader, a portable device, is developed by CBP to obtain the brief and important information in daily life by text-to-speech(TTS) technology and Optical Character Recognition (OCR). For electronic documents, this device converts text format such as TXT, DOC, HTML, RTF to speech via TTS technology.

Considering information in the printed text such as pill bottle, recipes, magazines and newspaper, SunshineReader gets its contents through Optical Character Recognition (OCR) and obtain the speech by employing TTS. Due to the complexity and particularity of Chinese, SunshineReader applies TTS service developed by IFLYTEK (a famous Chinese company dedicating to Interactive Voice Response, especially in Chinese context) to guarantee the smoothness of sounds and developer-friendliness. Considering the fact that the users may come from different regions, SunshineReader offers various reading modes in diverse accents including Mandarin and Cantonese.

Up to now, more than 50,000 visual-impaired people have used SunshineReader with positive feedback to prove its practicability.

4   Conclusions

All these efforts achieve demonstrable results in narrowing down the gap between visual-impaired people and information, which cannot be obtained by touching and hearing. In order to search information more efficiently, visual-impaired people can choose a suitable product from CDLVI, Sunshine Screen Reader and SunshineReader, according to different scenarios.

Until now, not only government organizations but also many commercial corporations have joint the group that devotes to making efforts to information service for visual-impaired people.

Acknowledgments. This work is supported by Alibaba-Zhejiang University Joint Institute of Frontier Technologies, Zhejiang Provincial Natural Science Foundation of China (No. LZ13F02 0001), the National Natural Science Foundation of China (Nos. 61173185 and 61173186), the National Key Technology R&D Program of China (No. 2012BAI34B01 and 2014BAK15B02), and the Hangzhou S&T Development Plan (No. 20150834M22).

References

1. Bourne, R.R.A., Flaxman, S.R., Braithwaite, T., Cicinelli, M.V., Das, A., Jonas, J.B., et al.: Vision Loss Expert Group: Magnitude, temporal trends, and projections of the global prevalence of blindness and distance and near vision impairment: a systematic review and meta-analysis. Lancet Glob. Health **5**(9), e888–e897 (2017)
2. CBP. China Braille Press. http://www.cdpf.org.cn/sjzx/cjrgk/201206/t20120626_387581.shtml
3. IFIA. International Federation of Inspection Agencies. www.ifia-federation.org
4. NFB-NEWSLINE. National Federation of the Blind. https://nfb.org/
5. VisioBook. American Printing House for the Blind. http://www.aph.org/
6. Book Wizard Reader. American Printing House for the Blind. http://www.aph.org/
7. Klatt, D.H.: Review of text-to-speech conversion for english. J. Acoust. Soc. Am. **82**(3), 737 (1987)
8. Evans, G., Blenkhorn, P.: Architectures of assistive software applications for windows-based computers. J. Netw. Comput. Appl. **26**(2), 213–228 (2003)

Author Index